American Airpower Comes of Age
General Henry H. "Hap" Arnold's World War II Diaries

Edited by

MAJOR GENERAL JOHN W. HUSTON
USAF Retired

Volume 1

Air University Press
Maxwell Air Force Base, Alabama

January 2002

Library of Congress Cataloging-in-Publication Data

Arnold, Henry Harley, 1886-1950.
  American airpower comes of age : General Henry H. "Hap" Arnold's World War II diaries; Vol. 1 / edited by John W. Huston.
    p. cm.
  Includes bibliographical references and index.

  1. Arnold, Henry Harley, 1886-1950--Diaries. 2. World War, 1939-1945--Personal narratives, American. 3. United States. Army Air Forces--Biography. 4. Generals--United States--Diaries. 5. United States. Army Air Forces--History. 6. World War, 1939-1945--Aerial operations, American. 7. Air power--United States--History--20th century. I. Huston, John W. II. Title.

D811.A7318 A3 2001
940.54'4973'092--dc21   2001041259

Disclaimer

Opinions, conclusions, and recommendations expressed or implied within are solely those of the editor and do not necessarily represent the views of Air University, the United States Air Force, the Department of Defense, or any other US government agency. Cleared for public release: distribution unlimited.

This volume is dedicated to my wife Dorothy Bampton Huston and my children Ann Huston Faris and John B. Huston. All of them lovingly tolerated my preoccupation and ill humor while this was being completed.

Contents

Chapter		Page
	DISCLAIMER	ii
	DEDICATION	iii
	FOREWORD	vii
	ABOUT THE EDITOR	ix
	PREFACE	xi
	ACKNOWLEDGMENTS	xiii
	EDITORIAL NOTES	xv
	Notes	xviii
	BIOGRAPHY	1
	Notes	108
1	ENGLAND	
	9 APRIL–1 MAY 1941	125
	Introduction	125
	The Diary	135
	Postscript	174
	Notes	183
2	ARGENTIA, NEWFOUNDLAND	
	31 JULY–14 AUGUST 1941	207
	Introduction	207
	The Diary	216
	Postscript	236
	Notes	252
3	ENGLAND	
	22 MAY–3 JUNE 1942	265
	Introduction	265
	The Diary	292
	Postscript	308
	Notes	316

Chapter		Page
	PHOTO SECTION.	329
4	SOUTH PACIFIC	
	16 SEPTEMBER–2 OCTOBER 1942	345
	Introduction	345
	The Diary	379
	Postscript	403
	Notes	412
5	NORTH AFRICA, MIDDLE EAST, INDIA, CHINA	
	9 JANUARY–17 FEBRUARY 1943	431
	Introduction	431
	The Diary	457
	Postscript	510
	Notes	518
	BIBLIOGRAPHY.	547
	INDEX	561

Foreword

This volume has richly enhanced General Henry H. "Hap" Arnold's reputation as the father of today's United States Air Force. Major General John W. Huston, himself an Army Air Forces combat veteran of the war, has edited each of Arnold's World War II diaries and placed them in their historical context while explaining the problems Hap faced and evaluating the results of his travels. General Huston, a professional historian, has taught at both the US Air Force Academy and the US Naval Academy. A former Chief of the Office of Air Force History and an experienced researcher both here and abroad in the personal and official papers of the war's leaders, he has been careful to let Hap speak for himself.

The result is an account of the four-year odyssey that took Arnold to every continent but one as he took part in deliberations that involved Allied leaders in major diplomacy/strategy meetings with Franklin D. Roosevelt, Harry S Truman, Winston Churchill, Josef Stalin, Charles de Gaulle, and Chiang Kai-shek. At those meetings, Hap recorded the comments of the various participants. His 12 diaries contain his own thoughts, which range from being lost over the Himalayas to comforting the wounded as they were airlifted from the Normandy beaches. He experienced an air raid in London and viewed the carnage in recently liberated Manila. Arnold recorded his honest impressions, from private meetings with King George VI in Buckingham Palace to eating from mess kits with his combat crews in the North African desert—all while perceptively commenting on the many issues involved and assessing the people, the culture, and the surroundings.

This volume offers the best assessment we have of Hap as he survived four wartime heart attacks and continued to work tirelessly for proper recognition of airpower. It will also continue my emphasis while Chief of Staff of the US Air Force on encouraging professional reading through making historical accounts available to personnel of the finest air force in the world, a success achieved in large part because of Hap Arnold.

RONALD R. FOGLEMAN
General, United States Air Force, Retired

About the Editor

Major General John W. Huston was born on 6 March 1925 in Pittsburgh, Pennsylvania. He began his military career as an aviation cadet and was commissioned at age 18 following completion of navigator training. After flying a combat tour in B-17s with the 379th Bombardment Group of England in 1944 and teaching navigation in Liberal, Kansas, he left the Army Air Forces in 1945 and returned to college. He earned the BA degree from Monmouth College (Illinois) and the MA and PhD degrees from the University of Pittsburgh. He began a teaching career at the University of Pittsburgh and continued it at the US Naval Academy, where he became Chair of the History Department. His teaching career also took him to the University of Maryland, the University of Rochester, and Ball State University. He has published in a number of professional journals.

General Huston also served in the US Air Force Reserve, flying in C-46, C-119, C-124, and C-130 aircraft. He served in the Office of the Secretary of the Air Force, as the Mobilization Assignee to the Commander of the 20th Air Division, and as a

Major General Mobilization Assignee to the Deputy Chief of Staff/Personnel at Headquarters USAF. General Huston was recalled to active duty in 1976 as Chief of the Office of Air Force History. He served in that capacity until his retirement from the US Air Force in 1981, when he returned to the faculty of the US Naval Academy. When he retired from the Naval Academy, General Huston was Distinguished Visiting Professor at the US Air Force Academy.

Preface

Although the need for a comprehensive biography of Gen Henry H. "Hap" Arnold exists, this volume does not constitute such a biography. Nor is this work intended as a history of the Army Air Forces in World War II. The aim of the editor has been to place in historical context the thoughts and immediate impressions of Arnold as he recorded them in the diaries he kept through each of his 12 trips abroad during the war. The diaries provide centerpieces for the 12 chapters of this work, each of which is devoted to the trip covered therein.

To promote a better understanding of the man and his journals, a brief biography introduces the diaries. Additionally, a brief description of the political and military background, some explanatory notes, and a postscript analysis are provided in each chapter for a clearer understanding of the setting for Hap's travels covered in that chapter. These rely wherever possible on Arnold's papers and other manuscript sources both in the United States and abroad. In all cases, the aim has been to let Arnold's notes speak for themselves as he recorded them in his diaries.

These journals represent his immediate thoughts and spontaneous reactions rather than the reflective ruminations of a professional American military officer. Arnold had worn an Army uniform for almost 38 years when he began these volumes. His travels over the 51-month span included six major wartime diplomacy/strategy conferences that took him to all but one continent, into most war zones, and through four heart attacks. No matter where he traveled or what topics were discussed, his freshly recorded impressions made at the end of a busy day were not revised or supplemented by second thoughts or considerations of propriety. To this editor, they appear honest, illuminating, and reflective of the character, strengths, and shortcomings of General Arnold. No other American senior officer has left such an extensive, revealing, and contemporary account of World War II from such a vantage point.

Arthur Bryant's assessment of Lord Alanbrooke's journals seems equally applicable to Arnold's diaries: "This book is not a biography, nor is it a history of the war. It rests on a diary compiled in the heat of pressing events. It reveals how the diarist saw himself and those around him, but not how they saw him." Bryant continued, cautioning that a diary "has limitations too, as history . . . written amid the passions and anxieties" of the time.* Arnold probably would have agreed.

---

*Arthur Bryant, *Triumph in the West: A History of the War Years Based on the Diaries of Field Marshal Lord Alanbrooke, Chief of the Imperial General Staff* (Garden City, N.Y.: Doubleday, 1959), 4–5.

Acknowledgments

As all researchers quickly discover, they incur immense debts to dedicated scholars, archivists, librarians, and others who have aided in many ways, from answering numerous obscure questions to listening *ad nauseam* about the diaries. These helpful people are too numerous to be mentioned individually, but the staff of the reference section, United States Naval Academy Library, always went far beyond the dedicated professional service librarians seem to have been born with. Barbara Parker was particularly helpful. The same excellence was always provided by Susan J. Keller, now of the Culpeper County, Virginia, Library System. The staff of the Air Force Historical Research Agency at Maxwell Air Force Base has been a tower of research strength. During academic year 1994–95, a delightful intellectual climate was provided by the United States Air Force Academy as I enjoyed a pleasant yet challenging year as Distinguished Visiting Professor in the History Department. The academy library's special collections proved invaluable, as did the assistance of archivist Duane Reed.

The contributions of knowledgeable historians who read portions of the manuscript resulted in a considerably improved final product. Among those readers were Professors James C. Bradford and Roger Beaumont of Texas A & M University and Tony Arthur of California State University at Northridge. My brother, Robert S. Huston, an emeritus history professor of Ball State University, provided excellent analysis and endured with good humor more of the manuscript than family ties required. Roger A. Freeman of Dedham, England, a careful student of the operational aspects of Eighth Air Force, made helpful suggestions. General Sir Anthony Farrar-Hockley, British Army, retired, provided warm hospitality and excellent suggestions in Moulsford, England, while hearing with exceedingly good grace more about this project than friendship should have tolerated. Long before this project was seriously considered, I enjoyed many luncheons with the late William Bruce Arnold, Hap's second son, who freely discussed his father and allowed me to copy those Arnold papers that have remained in the possession of the family. Gen Jacob Smart, USAF retired, a gentleman airman of the old school, painstakingly annotated, on the basis of his travels with him, portions of Arnold's journal. Lt Gen Devol H. Brett, USAF retired, kindly allowed me to use the papers of his father, Lt Gen George H. Brett, for the years 1940–41. Despite this expert assistance, the errors that remain are my responsibility.

Editorial Notes

Several years ago, when Chief of the Office of Air Force History, I was invited to deliver a paper assessing the contributions of Gen Henry H. "Hap" Arnold. In researching the topic, I consulted the diaries that form the basis of this volume. They represent General Arnold's thoughts during each of the twelve trips he took abroad during World War II.[1]

For reasons that are not clear, scholars have used these diaries unevenly. Forrest C. Pogue, for example, does not cite them in his biography of George C. Marshall, with whom Arnold worked very closely. Similarly, the seven-volume official history of the Army Air Forces (AAF) in World War II was written without access to these journals. They were, however, used by General Arnold in writing *Global Mission*, which appeared in 1949.

Maintenance of a diary was not a new experience for General Arnold. He had kept a journal, however briefly, during his earliest years as an officer, and he maintained a detailed account from 30 September to 21 December 1918, during his 67-day trip to England and France in the closing days of World War I. Fresh encouragement for maintaining a record on his initial World War II trip to England was provided by Lt Gen Delos C. Emmons, an old friend from their cadet days at West Point. After suggesting a list of people to see, installations to visit, and matters to investigate, Emmons advised Arnold to "keep a diary and complete it at the end of each day." He confessed that his own tendency during his 1940 trip to England was to "postpone entries with the result that I forgot some important things."[2]

During these trips, Arnold recorded his impressions of each day's activities in notebooks small enough to fit in his shirt breast pocket. The entries were normally not complete sentences but clauses separated by dashes. Written in private at the end of a generally long and demanding day, Arnold did not seem to have given any thought to the earliest of these being used other than as a reminder of things to be done upon his return. There is some evidence in the later ones that he was considering writing memoirs for which these notes could prove to be valuable resource material.[3]

When Arnold returned to Washington, his handwritten notes for that trip were given to a secretary who provided typed copies. In very rare instances, minor editorial changes were made in his own hand by Arnold to promote clarity. However, no revisions were made to any judgments or observations. The few changes noted were those of spelling or for clearer identification of people or places. For consistency and to avoid confusion, Arnold's notes on the trip covered in each chapter are presented as "The Diary." Hap's own title for that trip's diary then introduces his entries for that journey as found in the typed version located in the Manuscripts Division of the Library of Congress.

At the diplomatic/military wartime conferences, official secretariats were responsible for preparing, distributing, and maintaining files. They organized and printed classified records of the deliberations. Additionally, AAF staff officers who accompanied Arnold at the later conferences maintained official notes of the issues involved in those conferences. As a result, he often confined his diary comments to nonofficial matters. Given the demanding schedule faced by Hap and the other conferees, it is remarkable that he found the time to write as fully as he did in these accounts. Not even Chief of Staff George Marshall, his superior and closest companion on many of these trips, was aware that a diary was being kept. No other American participant seemed able or interested in maintaining such an extensive commentary on a regular basis at these gatherings.

In preparing this manuscript, my aim was to retain Arnold's phrasing, thoughts, and expressions. Even in the typed versions, his jottings were usually clauses separated by dashes. I have combined these clauses into complete sentences and paragraphs without adding to, deleting from, or rearranging in any way the phrasing of the original typed manuscripts. Similarly, Arnold frequently added a period after each letter in acronyms (A.A.F., R.A.F., U.S.) and he usually did not insert a comma in numbers of one thousand or greater (1000). In keeping with current style and to avoid reader confusion, the periods have been removed and the commas have been inserted. Where General Arnold was inconsistent in denoting lists designated by numerals or by letters, I imposed an internal consistency within each list. Since neither Arnold nor his secretary transcribers were consistent in their use of capitalization and hyphenation, I have made limited changes in those areas, however again without adding to, deleting, or changing any words other than indicated here. Brackets indicate the few additions I made, but where misspellings of proper names or places occurred, the few items involved have been corrected without brackets.

Dates: Arnold's generally consistent practice of using the civilian style for dates (April 30, 1956) rather than the military style (30 April 1956) has been retained within the diaries. Wherever Hap did not include the day of the week in the heading to each day's entry, it has been provided without brackets.

Time: When flying, Arnold utilized the 24-hour system for denoting time (1400 hours); when on the ground, he most often used the civilian method (2:00 or 2 P.M.). Whichever method he used has been retained here.

Place Names: Arnold was not consistent in listing the names of the cities or countries relevant to that day's journal entries; names of the major locations visited on that day have been added in brackets.

People: Most of the individuals cited in the diaries were United States Army Air Forces military personnel. They have been identified at first mention by rank, full name, and assigned position at the time the notation was made. If not otherwise noted, they were USAAF personnel. Although the Army Air Forces was officially termed the Army Air Corps prior to July 1942, the terms "Army Air Forces" and "AAF" have been used throughout the annotations unless clarity required use of the term "Army Air Corps." The traditional abbreviations of USA, USMC, and USN refer to the United States Army, Marine Corps, and Navy, respectively. No attempt was made to identify the specific corps or branch (other than AAF) in which someone served; nor was any distinction made between officers holding regular commissions and those who were reservists serving on extended active duty.

Foreign military personnel are identified at first mention by rank, full name, nationality, branch of service, and assigned position at the time of the diary entry. Civilians are identified by full name, title, nationality if other than American, and position held at that time.

Given the many changes in rank and assignment during the four-year span of these diaries, there was no attempt to re-identify individuals who had been mentioned earlier or to list their new rank or assignment unless re-identification was necessary for understanding.

Cables: Arnold often referred to cables, both received and sent. Where located and relevant, the contents of the cables are cited; where they were not found, there is no indication of that fact.

Parentheses and Drawings: Parentheses of this nature ( ) are where they appear in the original. The few drawings in the text, all made in Arnold's hand, have been reproduced as they were in the typescripts.

Identification of Units: Although Arnold and his transcribers were not always consistent, USAAF units are identified in the notes provided in the style of *Air Force Combat Units of World War II.* Squadrons, Groups, Wings, and Divisions are designated by cardinal numbers (525th Bombardment Squadron, 379th Bombardment Group, 41st Bombardment Wing, 1st Air Division). Commands are designated by Roman numerals (VIII Bomber Command), numbered Air Forces by ordinal numbers (Eighth Air Force). Arnold's original designations, although not always consistent with what became standard practice, remain in the text as he recorded them.

Deletions: The single deletion from the original journals was the name of an officer who was summarily dismissed from an operational command by Arnold because of excessive alcohol use. In view of the officer's relatively recent death, and the survival of his descendants, his specific identification did not seem appropriate. The fact that a deletion has been made, however, is noted in the relevant chapter.

Notes

1. The handwritten diary is in the Gen Henry H. Arnold Papers, Manuscripts Division, Library of Congress, Washington, D.C. (hereinafter cited as AP).

2. Delos C. Emmons to Arnold, 7 April 1941, AP.

3. It is difficult to be specific as to when Arnold appeared to be thinking of using the diaries in preparation of a postwar memoir, but those of chapter 8 and after hint of later usage. By the time of chapter 10, kept in the final weeks before the German surrender in the spring of 1945, the suggestion of their importance as a later reference is strong. The nature and content of the diaries, regardless of the time period, do not seem to change significantly over their 51-month period.

Biography

Mr. A [Arnold] ... seem[s] to me really dumb ... But the fact remains that, by being what he is, Mr. A [Arnold] has performed the impossible in building the air force.
—James Gould Cozzens

I couldn't help thinking as his airplane pushed off into the night, that General Arnold had done as much as any man to win this war.
—Adolph A. Berle Jr.

Gen Henry H. "Hap" Arnold's background, schooling, and early career provide little hint of his later dominant role in American aviation. Born in 1886, the second son of five children to a gracious, caring mother and a stern and humorless physician father, his early life was spent in Gladwyn, Pennsylvania, just west of Philadelphia, on what is still called the Main Line. Both parents' ancestors were participants in the American Revolution and Hap's father, Herbert Arnold, had served more recently as a doctor in that "splendid little war" with Spain in 1898. Seeking to continue his military career vicariously through a West Point appointment for one of his sons, Dr. Arnold was disappointed when the oldest, Tom, enrolled instead at Pennsylvania State College to study engineering. His second son, Henry Harley, (called Harley throughout his life by his family) received an appointment when the primary candidate opted for the joys of marriage instead of the rigors of West Point. Arnold was appointed to take his place in the "long gray line" with the class of 1907.[1]

His month-late arrival on 27 July 1903, five months before the Wright Brothers' historic flight from the sands at Kitty Hawk, was one of his few distinctions during the four-year regimen at the Military Academy. Content to remain entrenched in the middle of his class, "Pewt" or "Benny," as his classmates called him, never achieved rank above that of private in the Corps of Cadets. *The Howitzer* yearbook of 1907 referred to him as a "clean sleeve." He was probably bored by the required daily rote recitation in an institution that had changed little since the Civil War.²

Arnold's prowess in other areas was no more spectacular—he achieved some success on the track team as a shot-putter and played as a reserve end and halfback on the football team in his final year. He accumulated his share and more of demerits, earning the title "area bird," accorded those who walked punishment tours under the watchful eye of Lt Col Robert L. Howze, Medal of Honor recipient, commandant of cadets, and nemesis of all the students. Two decades later, Arnold would encounter Major General Howze in another difficult relationship, this time when the latter presided at the Billy Mitchell court-martial trial and presumably voted to convict the outspoken advocate of a separate Air Corps.³

Graduating in June of 1907, Arnold ranked 66 in a class of 111. This was proof of his classmates' assessment that "by diligent efforts, he has overcome any hankering for work that he may have once had and now doesn't do any more than anyone else." Arnold agreed with their evaluation when he recalled in his autobiography that he had "skated along without too much effort in a spot just below the middle of the Class."⁴

Arnold apparently had the normal cadet's interest in young ladies even though he does not comment on this in his memoirs. His classmates must have felt that he enjoyed harmonious relations with females when they inserted a humorous sketch in their yearbook in which a fellow cadet lamented to Arnold that he (the colleague) couldn't "find a girl I like well enough to marry." "Pewt" Arnold's imaginary reply: "Well, my trouble is in keeping away from girls that like me."⁵

His interest in horseback riding during his last years at West Point raised his hopes of being commissioned in the Cavalry, then a coveted assignment. He was commissioned in the Infantry, however, and ordered to the Philippines even though the main thrust of the native insurrection in that Pacific outpost had been quelled by 1907.⁶

The future aviator conceded that, at the time of his graduation in 1907, he did not know "what two brothers named Wilbur and Orville Wright had done at a place called Kitty

Hawk" a few years earlier.[7] Writing home to his mother, Arnold described the balloon flight of Charles Levée in February 1906 but showed little enthusiasm for the novel ascension he witnessed from the frozen grounds above the Hudson River.

> The fellow that sailed around the Eifel [sic] Tower in an airship went up in a baloon [sic] today and there was a pretty big crowd to see him off. I don't know why he selected this place for his ascension, but he did. The balloon was about 25 foot in diameter almost a sphere. He inflated it with illuminating gas. After going up he went due north and was still going north the last I saw of him.[8]

In the peacetime Army of 1907, there was no need for 2d Lt "Hap" Arnold to hurry in joining the 29th Regiment in Manila. A gentlemanly two-week train trip to the west coast after leave with his family in Pennsylvania was followed by seven weeks of visiting friends and awaiting a ship in San Francisco.[9] After a month's journey across the Pacific, Arnold landed on the islands in early December 1907, six months after his graduation from West Point.[10]

The oppressive heat that dictated a short working day, the availability of servants on a lieutenant's modest pay, and the pleasant life on a peacetime Army post with little to do but train and socialize did not prove very challenging to the new officer. Arnold, however, quickly found more arduous work when he volunteered for duty with the Engineers who were mapping uncharted areas of Luzon. A similar assignment on Corregidor then completed his tour in the Philippines. In June 1909 he set sail for home, choosing a pleasant, unhurried route across the Indian Ocean through the Suez Canal and into the Mediterranean before joining old friends in Lucerne, Switzerland. Arnold had developed a romantic interest in Eleanor Pool ("Bee" to her friends; she would become his bride in 1913), who was vacationing in Europe with her family and Arnold spent his remaining free time with them.[11]

During a very short stay in Paris en route back to the United States, Arnold viewed the craft in which Louis Blériot had recently flown across the English Channel. He was unimpressed: "I was not very greatly inspired by its appearance for it seemed to be too fragile looking to have any real value as a means of transportation."[12]

Arnold returned to the routine of garrison life at Governor's Island, New York, reporting in October 1909. A variety of early aviation activities took place that winter. Among other events, Arnold witnessed the Wright Brothers' flight from the island and saw "the first international air meet ever held in America."[13] He later recalled, however, that his primary interest was in getting promoted. Discovering that the Ordnance Department's lowest rank was first lieutenant, he took the examination in April 1911 for admission into that specialty. Upon failing that test, Arnold immediately applied for training in aviation, then under the aegis of the Signal Corps. In the amazing time of two weeks, his application was accepted and he was ordered to proceed to Dayton, Ohio, where he would be taught to fly under the Wright Brothers. He apparently was not discouraged by the response of the 29th Division commander, who replied to Arnold's request for advice as to whether he should pursue a career in aviation with: "If you want to commit suicide, go ahead."[14]

All evidence points to Arnold's enjoying this brief but important interlude in his life as he learned to fly. Favorable weather prevailed in the spring of 1911 in Dayton and on 3 May Arnold flew for the first time. He later wrote directly to the Chief of the Signal Corps indicating that he had flown 27 more times, the flights averaging about eight minutes each. Modern aviators will be amazed to learn that the difference between top speed and stalling speed in the Wright Flyer was eight miles per hour. He soloed after two and one-half hours in the air and was awarded his wings after a total of 3 hours and 48 minutes of flying. He was then one of two aviators in the United States Army Signal Corps.[15]

Following the establishment of the first military airfield at College Park, Maryland, not far from the nation's capital, Arnold arrived there in midsummer 1911. Here he became immersed in a variety of tasks that enhanced his knowledge of the new art of flying and presented many challenges to the young aviator. Arnold worked closely with the mechanics to help them learn the fundamentals as well as the nuances of maintaining aircraft. He taught others to fly and established world altitude records, first at 3,260 and later at 4,167, 4,764, and 6,450 feet. He was the first to fly over the Capitol building in Washington, causing the legislators, in Arnold's words "to adjourn." He was the first to take a congressman for an airplane ride and there is evidence that he flew the first air mail.[16]

In order to gain publicity for this new means of transportation, he and his colleagues were permitted to "moonlight" as stunt fliers in motion pictures. It was while he was flying for these early movies that his coworkers, impressed by his generally genial nature, provided the nickname "Happy," later shortened to "Hap," that would remain with him throughout his life. In 1912 he won the first Mackay Trophy, awarded by the Aero Club of America for "a successful forty-one minute reconnaissance flight from College Park, Maryland, to Washington Barracks, District of Columbia, to Fort Myer, Virginia, returning to College Park." At the same time, the Club awarded him "expert aviator certificate number 4." In a letter to his wife after the arrival of the trophy, Hap described it as "a handsome affair [that] will hold about four gallons so I cannot see how I can fill it with anything but beer."[17]

In the summer of 1912, Hap was visibly shaken by the death of two military aviators whom he had known. One of them, Al Welsh, had helped teach him to fly. A near crash of his own near Fort Riley, Kansas, on 5 November shook his confidence in himself and in flying, as indicated in a letter he wrote to his commanding officer (whom he had taught to fly).

> At the present time, my nervous system is in such a condition that I will not get in any machine.... From the way I feel now, I do not see how I can get in a machine with safety for the next month or two. I personally do not care to get in any machine either as passenger or pilot for some time to come.[18]

He confirmed his feelings the next day: "If I had not been as high as I was, I would have never gotten out alive. I cannot even look at a machine in the air, without feeling that some accident is going to happen to it." He concluded, "for the past year and a half I have been flying in almost any kind of weather at almost any time. That being the case, it would take some awful strain to put me out of commission the way this has."[19]

A fellow officer at Fort Riley confirmed Hap's feelings: "Lieut Arnold has become so nervous as a result that he has not flown since, and perhaps never will again."[20] Arnold's thinking remained the same throughout the next year as he confessed to his mother that "everybody seems to be taking a flight but strange as it may seem, I did not have the slightest inclination to go up." He wondered in a letter to his fiancée whether there was "an unseen hand that reaches out and turns the machines over in the air for there have been so many accidents that have never been explained."[21] Considering the serious nature of fear of flying within the aviation community then and now, it is interesting to note that Arnold mentioned this only indirectly in his autobiography—in a paragraph concerning his testimony before Congress in 1913. "I verified that I was about to be relieved from aviation duty, at my own request. Eleanor Pool and I intended to be married in September; and in those days, you didn't plan to continue flying after you were married—unless you were an optimist."[22]

Arnold was well aware of the high attrition rate among the early Army aviators, most of whom he knew personally. According to one source, 18 of the 24 officers qualified as pilots were killed in crashes during the four years following the Army's purchase of its first airplane in 1909. By the summer of 1913, the US Army had six active aviators and 15 aircraft.[23] Yet Arnold would not fly again as an Army aviator for three years. His assignment to the office of the Chief of the Signal Corps, and his responsibilities for closing down the College Park airport, consumed much of the year 1913.

Publicized complaints by Army aviators in Texas led to the first of many congressional studies and investigations over more than 30 years as to the control, role, and placement of aviation within the US military. With so few Army aviators having his flying background available in Washington, it was not surprising that Lieutenant Arnold was called as one of the witnesses before the House Military Affairs Committee, headed by Rep. James Hay of West Virginia, chairman of the House Military Affairs Committee. When asked whether aviation should remain under the control of the Signal Corps, Arnold replied that until the aviation community became large enough to take care of its own problems it should remain as currently placed. Hap would reiterate this belief, although not consistently, until World War II. During this testimony, he volunteered the information that France had 400 officers assigned to aviation, contrasted with 33 US officers, and that the French had appropriated $7.4 million for aviation while the US Congress had provided only $125,000.

Not surprisingly, the chief officer of the Signal Corps testified against the separation of aviation from his span of control. Others however, such as Riley Scott, an early aviator who had recently resigned from the Army, were not so cautious. Anticipating arguments that would become the mainstay of Billy Mitchell's later preaching and be embraced in part by Arnold, Scott advocated separation of Army aviation from the Signal Corps. He upset many in the hearing room by claiming that aircraft could destroy the almost completed Panama Canal and make a devastating attack on the battleship, which was considered the backbone of national defense of most major nations. It was during these hearings before the Hay Committee that Arnold first met Capt William D. "Billy" Mitchell, who was not yet qualified as a military aviator but was assigned to the War Department General Staff representing the Signal Corps.[24]

Other matters, however, appeared more important to Arnold. On 10 September of that year, he and Eleanor Pool were married. The newlyweds honeymooned on a 12-day Army transport voyage to the Canal Zone before returning to a brief assignment with the infantry at Fort Thomas, Kentucky, after which they spent two years in the Philippines. The young couple arrived during the first week of January 1914. Adapting to married life and peacetime infantry duty in a distant land did not prove difficult for the young couple since lieutenant's pay afforded four servants. While there he first met and was favorably impressed with Lt George C. Marshall, later to become Army Chief of Staff, Arnold's superior and very close friend. Arnold evaluated the young officer in 1914.

> [Marshall is the] main guy for this detachment . . . [who] tells the Colonels where to take their regiments and what to do with them. However everyone agrees that he has the ability to handle the situation so that there is no hard feeling.[25]

In this period, one of his superiors evaluated Hap as "active, zealous and efficient," having "exerted uncommon energy and resourcefulness."[26] Two years and one month after their arrival in the Philippines, the Arnold family, now numbering three (their first child, Lois, had been born the previous year), returned to Philadelphia for a brief reunion with their families. Arnold's new assignment was to join the 3d Infantry Regiment at Madison Barracks in upstate New York.[27]

The continuation of World War I sparked US interest in preparedness in 1916. Soon after arriving at his new post, Arnold was "offered" through the auspices of Billy Mitchell the opportunity to return to flying. The lure of immediate promotion to the rank of captain, an additional 50 percent hazardous duty pay, and a threat by Mitchell that Arnold would be assigned to aviation duty as a first lieutenant if he did not volunteer were strong motivating factors in Arnold's quick acceptance. Not to be discounted, however, was Hap's realization that his heart was not really set on pursuing a career as an Infantry officer. He has left no hint that his earlier fear of flying had been overcome or played any role in his decision to return to aviation. Logic would dictate that Arnold was confident that he could handle any flying assignment.[28]

Captain Arnold reported for duty in June 1916 at Rockwell Field, North Island, San Diego, California, and soon returned to the cockpit. His tour in California was cut short as the prospects of American involvement in the war intensified. In December of that year, he assumed command of the 7th Aero Squadron, then being formed to protect the newly opened Panama Canal.[29]

Before leaving California, however, Arnold became involved in a controversy over the search for two airmen who had crash-landed near the head of the Gulf of California in Mexico. Arnold and other junior officers wanted an immediate search to be implemented and were frustrated at what they perceived to be delay and excessive caution on the part of the more senior officers. Against orders, Arnold and others began to look for the downed aviators who were found nine days later. Although an investigating board agreed with the need for an early search, Arnold's perceived disobedience earned him a fitness report that promised less than a brilliant military future. As his commander (who would be retired summarily just after the United States entered World War I) evaluated him, Arnold "never seemed loyal and willing to cooperate. He is not suited for an independent command." Further, he was "an able young officer of good habits but a trouble maker."[30]

The Arnolds' second child, Henry H. Jr., called Hank by his family, was born in January 1917, just before Captain Arnold departed alone for Washington, D.C., en route to Panama. On the last day of February, Arnold sailed out of New York harbor with his unit. When they disembarked in the Canal Zone 11 days later, they discovered that no suitable place had been selected for an aviation field. After choosing a site, Arnold was ordered to present the information to authorities in New York. As a result, he found himself at sea when the United States declared war on Germany. Arnold had a brief reunion with his family in Philadelphia, where they had just arrived from California, before he traveled to Washington, D.C. When he arrived in the nation's capital, he received orders to remain there.[31] He was now a major, having been promoted just before leaving Panama despite the fitness report he had received in California. Major Arnold settled down to duties in Washington where, to his dismay, he would remain through most of the war. His initial assignment was a three-week tour with two other officers over much of the South and Midwest, choosing sites and signing leases for new training facilities. Soon after his return, he was promoted to colonel without ever having served as a lieutenant colonel. He was, at age 32, the youngest colonel in the United States Army. As assistant director of military aeronautics, he saw and experienced firsthand many of the problems that he would encounter 20 years later when the nation was preparing for World War II. Among the problems first faced by Arnold in 1917-18 were bureaucratic infighting, chaos created by the strain of cooperation between government and industry, rapid and uncoordinated expansion, difficulties in matching available trained personnel with aircraft resources, lack of instructors, safety considerations, and political interference with procurement.[32]

The emphasis by newspapers of the day on the excessive American reliance on French and British aircraft and engines, and the failure of Signal Corps to live up to expectations trumpeted by both Signal Corps and Congress, led to organizational change. Legislation of May 1918 created the Air Service and removed control of Army aviation from the Signal Corps.[33] Prior to the change, Arnold had served as executive assistant to Maj Gen George O. Squier who lost his job as the officer responsible for Army aviation in the new arrangement. Blaming others for his lack of success, Squier disparaged Arnold. In Hap's fitness report, he labeled Arnold as "inferior in judgement and common sense" and "inclined to be disloyal to his superiors and prone to intrigue for his own advantage."[34] Although Squier's assessment was hardly a career-enhancing product for a professional officer, the chief of the newly created Air Service, Maj Gen William L. Kenly, found Arnold's work sufficiently impressive to recommend him for the Distinguished Service Medal. Arnold was praised as one who performed with "promptness of decision, and a soundness of judgement so conspicuous and effective as to bear the fruit of true distinction." The wheels of Army bureaucracy did not respond quickly or favorably, however, and the recommendation of the medal for Arnold was turned down in December 1919.[35]

Added to Arnold's frustrations was his disappointment in not getting to France and into combat. As the summer of 1918 drew to a close, however, Arnold's desire to serve on the Western Front appeared achievable. His new commander authorized him to sail for France by mid-October with orders to become familiar with "aviation organization, methods of training in France, and operation[s] on the front."[36] Awaiting embarkation in New York, Arnold received two diaries in the mail from his wife, one "from each of his two children" with the request that he "write down each night the happenings of the day and bring the books back to us to keep."[37] Thus began Arnold's practice of maintaining a wartime diary that was reinstituted during World War II and is the basis of this volume.

The ubiquitous influenza then gripping the nation did not bypass the Arnold family. Before sailing, Hap was alarmed to learn by letters from his wife that his children appeared to have symptoms of the malady and that his physician father was making as many as 35 house calls a day.[38] Arnold himself was not immune from the infection; he brought on board the USS *Olympic* on 16 October not only his baggage but a serious case of the flu. His cabin mate was Maj Reuben Fleet, later to become president of Consolidated Aircraft Company. Hap spent most of the week's crossing to Southampton in his bunk and, to his dismay, was carried from the vessel in a stretcher.[39] His subsequent eight-day confinement in a nearby American hospital delayed his reaching the fighting, exasperating Colonel Arnold to whom patience was at best an abstract virtue possessed by others. His diary entries of the time were scarcely complimentary to his British hosts. One such observation was that "English women do not know how to wear clothes, have no style and have ankles like fence posts." He also disliked other aspects of what he observed.

> I do not like the conditions in England with relation to our men. They are being used to build everything for the English and nothing for us. Our men who are so much better individually and collectively than the English [are] doing unskilled labor while the English are over in France with their undersize puny afterthoughts. The conditions should be changed.[40]

His Anglophobia was clearer than his diary.

Within 24 hours after his release from the hospital in Hampshire, he was headed across the Channel and hoped-for combat. A variety of circumstances, including bad weather, added to his frustrations and prevented him from engaging the enemy before the war ended. The day before the armistice, he appeared resigned to his fate as he lamented, "Want to go over the lines but it looks as if I will go down in history as a desk soldier." The day the fighting ended, he recorded that he and another officer "had it fixed to go over lines before hostilities ceased on voluntary patrol. Weather was so thick that we couldn't."[41]

He spent the next three weeks observing the results of the fighting, much of the time from the air. While in France he had a "wonderful opportunity to see storehouses, machine shops, ordnance storehouses and hangars and repair shops. [The US forces] have a very good outlay with material and tools to fix almost anything."[42] He submitted a report of his observations upon arrival in Paris, then spent part of his six days there visiting such sites as Versailles and Napoléon's tomb. Arnold's diary entries reflect an opinion of the French that was little, if any, better than his assessment of the English.

> I am beginning to understand why the people over here do not like the "frogs"—we pay rent for the trenches we occupy—pay for the transportation which brings our troops up to the front and must pay before they can fight; pay for the aviation troops that work with our troops—when we are saving France from destruction and a loss in dollars and cents that no amount of charges as above can cover.[43]

Hap would continue to have a low opinion of the French and their leadership during World War II.

He met and dined with such notables as Gen Mason Patrick, who would command the Air Service in the near future, and Billy Mitchell. Before leaving for England, he learned that he was no longer the assistant director of the Bureau of Aeronautics in Washington and assumed correctly that he would be reassigned. It was six days before he could book passage home traveling on the USS *Baltic*. His traveling companions were mostly returning service personnel, but also on board was an "English lady of noble birth and upturned nose."[44]

Arnold was not at all displeased to be reassigned in January 1919 to California, where he remained for the next five years. Performing in a variety of jobs, he also served in several different ranks. Arnold and most other regular officers were reduced after the war from their higher temporary wartime grades to their regular ranks. Arnold was a captain again for one day in 1920 before being promoted to permanent major. He would serve in that rank for the next 11 years.[45] During this period, Arnold and his family developed a fondness for California that would continue throughout his lifetime. He purchased a ranch there during World War II where he lived after retiring in 1946.

His assignments on the west coast varied from air officer of the Western Department at the Presidio in San Francisco to command of Rockwell Field in San Diego, where he experienced difficulties with the Navy. Both military services sought complete control of that flying field. He had a very brief tour with the fledgling Reserve Officer Training Corps unit at the University of California in Berkeley until his commander, a lifelong Cavalry officer, was able to get rid of aviator Arnold. While in the west, he helped publicize the first aerial refueling exploits of the Air Service and the Douglas World Cruiser Flight of 1924. In addition, he originated the use of Army aircraft to spot forest fires.[46]

It was with regret that the Arnold family now numbering five, second son William Bruce having been born in 1919, received orders in 1924 signed by Maj Gen Mason Patrick, now Chief of the Air Service, for them to return east to Washington. There, Hap attended the Army Industrial College's five-month course before becoming information officer for the Air Service. His role in this assignment during the Mitchell court-martial trial and its aftermath threatened to end his military career.[47]

There is little doubt that Arnold and Mitchell, having first met in 1913 when testifying before the Hay Committee, shared common ideas. Mitchell, it is recalled, was responsible for getting Arnold back into flying in 1916. During his visit to France in November 1918, Arnold recorded that he "convinced Mitchell that he and others ought to return to the U. S. to help with the reorganization work."[48] As a result of Billy's rank, success, and publicity in France during World War I, Arnold and many of his fellow aviators looked to the young general as the leader of postwar Army aviation. Arnold may well have expressed the sentiments of many aviators when he wrote Mitchell in September 1921 hoping that Billy would get the job as chief of the Air Service when its incumbent was expected to retire at the end of the year. Their contact continued through correspondence after they returned to the United States and Arnold was stationed in California during Mitchell's highly publicized battleship bombing tests.[49]

Many aviators believed, as did Arnold and Mitchell, in varying degrees of sovereignty for the Air Service. Their ideal was the independence they felt had been accorded the Royal Air Force in 1918. Mitchell's other ideas, articulated stridently in the press of the day, included other changes that most aviators held as necessary, including increased representation of flyers on the War Department General Staff, restriction of naval aviation, and a separate budget/promotion system for Army aviators. Mitchell's position as assistant chief of the Air Service and his penchant for headlines, individual as well as institutional, put him on a collision course with the economy-minded Coolidge administration and the conservative Army General Staff.

Mitchell and many of his followers remained convinced that the highly publicized bombing tests against the battleships had been decisive. They believed these tests should have converted even the most skeptical to the potential of this new weapon they felt would revolutionize future warfare. Mitchell went so far as to insist that because of airpower, armies "will never come into contact on the field of battle." The general continued his attacks on the two sacred cows of the military, the battleship and the infantry, both proven weapons in the minds of their supporters. They were to be replaced by airpower if Mitchell had his way, but many critics insisted that airpower was an unproven weapon that seemed to have its most promise in the minds of its zealous supporters.[50]

Arnold's views at this time were expressed in a paper he wrote upon completion of the Army Industrial College in February 1925 titled "What's The Matter with the Air Service?" In it, Arnold posed questions that he proceeded to answer. The core of Arnold's queries centered on why the War Department General Staff, which lacked aviation expertise, should continue to dictate the equipment, procurement, and utilization of Army aircraft as well as the qualifications, training, and promotion criteria of its personnel. Hap also called for other changes, including an improved training program and stricter enforcement of standards for aircraft materiel.[51]

Arnold's essay was furnished to his new boss, Maj Gen Mason Patrick, who had handpicked Arnold to be chief of information for the Air Service. In his new job, Arnold was charged with articulating the Air Service position on Army aviation issues of the day for the press and the public, an increasingly delicate and difficult task as Billy Mitchell's rhetoric stood in contrast with the more moderate position of General Patrick.

Born six months after the Battle of Gettysburg, Mason M. Patrick graduated from West Point as number two in the class of 1886, the year Arnold was born. He was commissioned in the engineers and spent most of his early career with that Corps. He was a brigadier general when he joined his classmate John J. Pershing in France in 1917. He served there in engineering assignments until tapped by the American Expeditionary Forces (AEF) commander in May 1918 to assume command of the Air Service even though he had never been in an airplane. Pershing explained it this way:

> In all of this Army there is but one thing which is causing me real anxiety. And that is the Air Service. In it there are a lot of good men, but they are running around in circles. Someone has got to make them go straight. I want you to do the job.[52]

Patrick returned to engineering duty on his return to the United States in July 1919 but Pershing, now chief of staff of the Army, reassigned him to serve as chief of the Air Service beginning in October 1921, a position he held until his retirement six years later. Patrick attempted to gain credibility among the aviators by learning to fly in June 1922, instructed by a close friend of Arnold's, Maj Herbert Dargue. However, humorous and not altogether apocryphal tales of the 58-year-old general's efforts to retain his elusive toupee in an open-air cockpit while piloting an airplane did little to enhance his standing. By 1925, he was convinced that change was needed and he made valiant efforts within the system to obtain what he felt were necessary modifications to the existing structure. His differences with Mitchell, Arnold, and most airmen concerning the role, placement, and employment of the Army air arm were primarily related to the methods required to achieve change rather than the substantive issues involved. As a contemporary observer explained it, Patrick and Mitchell were separated by "evolution versus revolution." In recent years, Patrick has been characterized as one who "symbolized the progressive, yet moderate spirit of the Air Service."[53]

In December 1924, Patrick recommended placing "all the component air units and possibly all aeronautical development under one responsible and directing head" and that the "Air commander should sit in the councils of war on an equal footing" with land and sea forces. Patrick's fairness in this period extended to ensuring that Billy Mitchell during his court-martial trial, had access to all Air Service documents he desired. He also cautioned against the "time-worn, threadbare reactionary pleas of those who resisted change" such as assistant chief of staff Maj Gen Fox Connor, who testified that creation of an Air Corps in the War Department "would create an impossible situation."[54]

A summary of Patrick's thinking was embodied in a bill put before Congress in 1926. It would have provided for a single promotion list and budget for an Air Corps that would have reported to the Secretary of War rather than the General Staff. Although never enacted, it showed a realistic appreciation of the distinction between the desires of the airmen and the politically possible, something neither Mitchell nor Arnold fully appreciated.[55] Although the well-known phrase, "Why not just buy one airplane and let the aviators take turns flying it?," cannot be specifically identified as ever having been uttered by the president, many of Arnold's contemporaries felt that Calvin Coolidge and the Army General Staff could have prescribed it. Patrick's generally moderate stand put him in the middle of two extreme positions: Mitchell and his followers on one hand, the Coolidge administration and the remainder of the Army on the other. Mitchell, Arnold, and their supporters failed to realize as clearly as Patrick did that the opposition to their midtwenties demands was based essentially on doctrine and economics. There is also the hint that Mitchell's brashness and penchant for hyperbole were anathema to the "Yankee outlook and reserve" of the occupant of the White House.[56]

Many who had spent their lives in the more traditional corps of infantry, artillery, and cavalry felt that aviation was a fad inundated with young, overly ambitious, undisciplined officers who failed to appreciate that their airplanes were just another weapon in the panoply of those available to the Army. They pointed out that the huge supply of wartime aircraft and aircraft engines, most of them of foreign manufacture that remained in the inventory, were no different from the obsolete equipment Congress was forcing other branches to use before appropriating funds for new weapons. They insisted with some logic that aviation had been utilized in only limited observation and pursuit roles in the recent war and that victory had been gained through the more traditional battle-tested branches. They knew the public perceived aviation as more glamorous than the other elements and that if the unproven claims of the aviators were true, airpower in the future would be a quicker, more economical, and more humane way to victory than was the protracted slaughter of the recently completed war. And in a decade devoid of international strife, as President Coolidge asked, "Who's gonna fight us?," Congress was less than overly generous in appropriating funds for the military. Lacking requested congressional appropriations, every dollar provided for the unproven air arm was one that would not be available for the other branches of the 134,000-man Army. From their viewpoint, the General Staff was composed of senior career officers whose broad views transcended any parochial attachment to specific corps. The Air Service, they felt, had, did, and would receive the same professional, unbiased consideration accorded any other Army component.

By the end of June 1925, after only five months on the job, Arnold appeared to have been successful in maintaining his views and his friendship with Billy Mitchell, yet at the same time to have satisfied the chief. In evaluating his new information officer, Patrick wrote that Major Arnold "has ability. I class him as above average. Not always sufficiently thorough in his work, but has shown improvement in this respect."[57]

Mitchell's failure to secure reappointment as assistant to the chief of the Air Service in March 1925, just as Arnold was learning his new job, would lead to major problems for both of the aviators. Two days after Coolidge's inauguration for a full term of his own, Mitchell was reassigned in his permanent rank of colonel to San Antonio, Texas, hardly an outpost for military advancement or access to the national media. Arnold had arranged Mitchell's farewell luncheon, at which the departing firebrand told his faithful they had not heard the last of him. He promised to take his beliefs on the aviation issues to the American people and to Congress. If Mitchell was eager and willing to speak his mind in official Washington, where some institutional restraints existed, he became even more outspoken in distant Texas.[58]

When the Navy dirigible *Shenandoah* crashed in an Ohio storm in September 1925, Mitchell charged the War and Navy Departments with "incompetency, criminal negligence, and almost treasonable negligence of our national defense." Additionally, he renewed his call for a separate Air Service. Mitchell had to be aware that the national publicity associated with his claims would combine with his extreme language to result in a court-martial.[59]

He got his wish, and Arnold wired his support. Mitchell responded with a relatively noncommittal "Keep your powder dry!" Arnold was, however, established by Mitchell as his "liaison man" and asked to assist by renting an apartment for him in the capital. Hap and other supporters greeted the Mitchells at Union Station and escorted their hero and his wife through the press and an admiring crowd to the Willard Hotel.[60]

President Coolidge, before the court-martial could be convened, attempted to defuse some of the argument and control the situation. He appointed a board headed by Dwight Morrow, a respected diplomat and Coolidge's Amherst College classmate, to "bring out the good qualities of the Air Service and [suggest] what action can be taken for their improvement."[61] As expected, Mitchell was called as a witness. To the dismay of the committee as well as many of Mitchell's supporters, the aviator proceeded to read ad infinitum (and to many it was ad nauseam as well) from his recently published volume, *Winged Defense*. As Arnold later wrote, he and other aviators wanted to yell, "Come on, Billy, put down that damned book! Answer their questions." When Mitchell finally did depart from his tome, he unequivocally advocated a separate air force "with its own separate budget, personnel and mission."[62]

Arnold joined a chorus of witnesses before the Morrow Board calling for a separate air organization, a stand not at serious variance with that urged by either Mitchell or General Patrick. Arnold's most telling moment occurred during his second appearance, when his testimony coincided with the sound of aircraft. Arnold explained that the planes, 35 in number, were "everything we could gather together from all over the US for the Air Force maneuvers."[63]

Hap probably was not surprised at the findings of the Morrow Board, which were released on 2 December, 15 days before the Mitchell court-martial verdict was announced. Neither its timing nor its findings caused much of a stir. Nevertheless, in a pointed reference to the ongoing trial, the Morrow Board disavowed any interest in Army discipline. Reflecting the mood of the decade, the Board insisted that "armaments beget armaments" and wrote that although the next war "may well start in the air, in all probability [it] will wind up in . . . the mud." The Board dismissed the possibility of any nation being able to attack the United States from the air and specifically recommended against both uniting the Army and Navy in a Department of National Defense and establishing a separate Air Department. The report included a comment that "air power has not yet demonstrated its value for independent operation."

The Board concluded that the present US Air Service was as powerful as other air services and that our successes in military and technical development were satisfactory if not superior to the accomplishments of other powers. The Board recommended that the name of the Air Service should be changed to Air Corps and that additional assistant secretaries of War, Navy, and Commerce be created to specifically deal with aviation problems. Many of these recommendations were implemented in the Air Corps Act of 1926.[64]

Despite the Morrow Board report, the primary focus of those interested in military aviation remained fixed on Mitchell's fate. The Court-martial Board handed down its expected verdict of guilty on two counts during the week before Christmas and Mitchell, to the surprise of very few, resigned from the Army effective 1 February 1926. Hap's connection with the episode was not finished, however. He, along with Maj Herbert Dargue, surreptitiously forwarded information to certain congressmen, hoping they would support a restructuring of the current organization. They also sent letters to Air Service Reservists, urging them to lobby their congressmen to support legislation for a stronger air organization that would have greater sovereignty.[65]

An investigation identified Arnold and Dargue as the culprits who had surreptitiously solicited support. Patrick offered Arnold a "Hobson's choice": resign from the service or have a court-martial of his own. To Patrick's surprise, Arnold opted for the military trial, something the Air Service chief did not welcome so soon after the Mitchell trial.[66] Patrick chose instead to reassign Arnold, who, according to the general's press release, had undertaken action "to influence legislation in an improper manner," a violation of Army General Order No. 20. As a result, Arnold, who according to General Patrick "was no longer wanted in my office," was "severely reprimanded" and reassigned. His new post would be "the most insignificant one Patrick could find for him." Consequently, Arnold became commander of the 16th Observation Squadron at Fort Riley, Kansas, home of the cavalry.[67] Ironically, Fort Riley was the site of Hap's serious airplane crash in 1913 that had led him to leave flying temporarily. His departing fitness report, written by the general, was as discouraging as his forthcoming assignment.

> This officer displays above average intelligence. In my opinion, during the period covered by this report, in judgment and common sense he fell below average. In an emergency I think he is liable to lose his head. My confidence in him was greatly shaken. I should now hesitate to entrust to him any important mission. . . . Recently it was necessary to reprimand this officer, to relieve him from duty in my office and to assign him to a field station.[68]

This was hardly a career-enhancing assessment even though Arnold was and would be viewed as a martyr by many of Mitchell's supporters. Arnold understandably remained bitter towards General Patrick and the treatment accorded him for at least the next decade, failing to appreciate that once an investigation had begun with its attendant publicity, the general had no alternative other than to discipline the identified miscreants. Dargue was not banished because, Patrick explained, he had not been as heavily involved as Arnold. Later that year, Dargue was chosen to command the Pan American Goodwill flight, an honor that had to have had the general's approval.[69]

Arnold's feelings as he and his family made their way to an uncertain future in central Kansas are expressed only briefly in his memoirs.[70] The 30 months spent at Fort Riley were critical ones for Hap as he contemplated his actions in the recent national furor over military aviation and his current role of working with the cavalry. He had ample reason to speculate about his future, but the symbolism of his exile from Washington because of his support for the new weapon of aviation and his assignment to the soon-to-be outmoded horse cavalry probably did not occur to him.

In contemplating his actions two decades later and from the vantage point of five-star rank, Hap assessed his actions in 1925 as rash, writing, "We didn't think these things out."[71] His new commanding officer, Brig Gen Ewing E. Booth, had been a judge at the court-martial trial. Ewing's reception of Arnold as he and his wife made their obligatory courtesy call on the general at their new post was clear acknowledgment of Arnold's tenuous position in this assignment. As Hap remembered it, Booth was in the midst of entertaining guests when the Arnolds arrived. He greeted them with "I know why you're here my boy. And as long as you're here you can write and say any damned thing you want. All I ask is that you let me see it first!"[72]

Arnold easily could have become a timeserver at Fort Riley, looking forward to the next 16 months when, in June 1927, he would be eligible for retirement and a half-pay pension for the rest of his life. He chose, however, to throw himself energetically into his new responsibilities. He worked hard to train future cavalry officers, and to educate them about the potential of aviation. Arnold began orientation flights for them, wisely including General Booth and the instructional staff along with students at the school. Problems were devised to show how aviation could broaden the perspective of students beyond the rears of other horses. Stories were retold of how the general, riding in the rear seat, used his riding crop to indicate (to pilot Arnold) where he wished the aircraft to go.[73]

In addition to his work with the cavalry, Arnold's squadron was assigned a variety of other tasks. In the bitterly cold winter of 1927–28, his aircraft were dispatched for a week to

Omaha, Nebraska, to break up ice that was threatening a bridge over the Platte River. Their bombs were successful; the ice was broken and the bridge was saved. Arnold spent May of 1927 serving as chief of staff for Air Corps maneuvers in Texas. This assignment indicated that, even in exile, his talents and potential were still recognized since the assignment had to have been made with the knowledge, if not the consent, of General Patrick.[74]

During the summer of 1927, Major Arnold and his unit were assigned the delicate job of delivering the mail for President Coolidge to his summer White House at Rapid City, South Dakota. Arnold and his pilots obtained the material in North Platte, Nebraska, where it arrived via regular service from Washington, D.C., and then flew it to the president. When Coolidge made his startling pronouncement that he did "not choose to run," Arnold speculated that Mrs. Coolidge "had become tired of public life." His success in 1927 earned Arnold and his aviators the same duties for the president in the summer of 1928, this time flying the mail from Chicago to the new summer White House near Superior, Wisconsin. The presidential commendation for the work of Hap and his unit cited that the "mail was late only one day, and only three [of 175 flights] were cancelled."[75]

The 30-month exile at Fort Riley had many benefits. Living on a peacetime Army post with its relatively relaxed lifestyle permitted Arnold to become reacquainted with his family who quickly adapted to the pleasures of living on Fort Riley. His three children, ages 13, nine, and seven on their arrival in Kansas, were joined by a baby brother in 1927. Motivated in part by the financial demands of a growing family, Arnold achieved some limited success in writing. In addition to authoring six books in what became known as the Billy Bruce series, named for his second son and including considerable biographical material from Arnold's career, Hap supplemented this additional income by writing an occasional piece for periodicals of the day.[76]

Before leaving Washington, Arnold and others had become involved in planning for what later became Pan American Airways. Hap's investment was not to be monetary but he was seriously considered by investors to head the operational segment of the embryonic organization, which would have necessitated his leaving the service. Over the three-year period 1926–29, several such offers came his way and Arnold gave some thought to leaving the Air Corps. He has not left a clear statement of his reasons for remaining in the military, but his love of flying together with the relative success he felt he was achieving at Fort Riley were probably important factors influencing his decision.[77]

Hap was not alone in feeling satisfaction at his accomplishments in Kansas. Arnold had only been under General Booth's command for three months in 1926 when the end of the fiscal year necessitated an evaluation of the aviator. Dated 30 June, Booth chose his words carefully in assessing the major as one whose "services have been exceptionally good. My impression is that he is an able officer. He is a tireless worker, enthusiastic, has a fine spirit of cooperation, is cheerful, and a manner that inspires all other persons to do their best." In response to how well he knew the officer, Booth wrote "Quite well" and remarked gratuitously "Apparently a very pleasing man, with a charming family." Arnold might still be in General Patrick's doghouse in Washington, but his exile at Fort Riley had proven successful thus far.[78]

In his next evaluation of Arnold, covering the 10 months before General Booth was reassigned, the cavalry general was even more positive as he wrote, "An exceptionally able air officer. He has an excellent observation squadron, and it is in excellent state of preparedness for any duty." Commenting that he knew Arnold "intimately," Booth added, "A delightful man with whom to serve."[79] Brig Gen Charles J. Symmonds, Booth's successor at Fort Riley, was equally impressed with Arnold. He evaluated Hap in June 1928 as: "An exceptionally high-grade officer. Pleasing manner, magnetic and natural leader. Takes active part in social affairs. Cooperates to fullest extent. Bright and quick in decision." "Good mixer with civilians. Possesses lots of good hard common sense." In his estimate of the highest command for which Arnold was qualified, Symmonds wrote, "General officer, Air Corps, in peace or war." Arnold continued to be triumphant in Kansas.[80]

As Arnold contemplated what lay ahead, his future must have appeared uncertain. Daughter Lois, now nearing 14, would soon be considering college, an expensive but not impossible aim for the daughter of a professional officer. His Army career would not be harmed by Patrick's retirement in 1927 or by the appointment of Maj Gen James E. Fechet as chief of the Air Corps. Patrick's damning fitness report of 1926 would be balanced by the laudatory ones earned at Fort Riley.

He had not yet been selected to attend the sine qua non for senior leadership, the Army Command and General Staff course at nearby Fort Leavenworth, Kansas. As an Air Corps flyer who had been disciplined for his zeal in support of Army aviation, Arnold did not relish such an assignment but he realized that failure to attend would probably be harmful to his career. In the summer of 1928, Arnold was selected to attend the class commencing that fall and the Arnold family prepared to move 110 miles east to their new home. Attending this course involved an admission, not clearly articulated at the time, that Arnold had at least temporarily abandoned any idea of leaving the Army in the near future.[81]

The commandant at Fort Leavenworth, Brig Gen Edward King, was familiar with Arnold since he too had served as a judge at the Mitchell trial. The general speculated that Arnold's well-publicized activities in support of Mitchell would result in Hap's being "crucified" by non-Air Corps students during the year course of instruction. Arnold commented rather naively that he had not realized "that my friendship for Mitchell probably had gotten me into such a position." He nevertheless resolved "to go to the school and make the best of it."[82] In spite of the fact that the curriculum was rooted in the experience of World War I and seemed to minimize the role and potential of airpower, Arnold found in retrospect that the school was of value since the course "taught the officers to think . . . to make decisions after proper sequence of thought." The director of the school apparently agreed that the instruction had been valuable for Arnold. In his evaluation of the aviator, he wrote somewhat perfunctorily that Hap had been "adaptable, resourceful, and self reliant. Pleasing personality." That Arnold was not universally loved by all in the Air Corps was indicated when the assistant chief informed him that the plan had been to send him to San Antonio following Leavenworth, but that the commanding general of the training center there was "strongly opposed to your assignment."[83]

After Command and Staff School, Arnold served as commander of Fairfield Air Depot in Ohio for two years, the latter part including duty as executive officer of the Materiel Division at nearby Wright Field, then the center of Air Corps procurement, research, and development. He witnessed the contrast between the "no expense spared" wartime pace of procurement and development he had been a part of during 1917–18 with the more deliberate, parsimonious routine of 1929–31. His knowledge of the Materiel Center and its operation would prove to be of considerable value during World War II. This assignment, away from direct flying, would not have been Arnold's first choice and he was not always patient enough to appreciate fully the ongoing advances being made there. He seemed at the time to evaluate research only in terms of clearly defined, immediate operational results. His attitude would be altered considerably during World War II. Important developments taking place there would prove valuable in affecting the types and performance levels of World War II aircraft. He was promoted to lieutenant colonel in February 1931, now having served more than 11 years in the rank of major, not an unusually slow progression in the peacetime American military.[84]

An agreement signed in early 1931 between Army Chief of Staff Gen Douglas MacArthur and Chief of Naval Operations Adm William V. Pratt stipulated that the Navy's air role would be offshore while the land-based Air Corps would assist the US Army in defending the nation's coastlines. This understanding, later repudiated by Pratt's successor Adm William Standley, became the basis for the Air Corps to establish a combat force on each coast. Arnold, given his minimal satisfaction with the Materiel Division assignment, his own and his family's predilection for California, and the opportunity for active command of flying units, sought and obtained an assignment to command March Field, California, where the new west coast wing would operate. His departing fitness report evaluated him as a "superior officer. Qualified for any duty in the Air Corps."[85]

In a letter about this time to an officer who had asked Arnold about his future plans, Hap provided a brief insight into his thinking: [After my tour at March Field, I will be] "in a position to either retire or perhaps the Fates may have something kinder in store for me. I assure you that I am not modest when it comes to getting things for myself. . . . I have a background . . . that few Air Corps officers have. I also believe that I am well qualified to be a Brigadier General." By the end of his current assignment, he thought, "things will be different and I will be not only willing but would like to have such a position, and intend to throw my hat in the ring."[86]

By all measures, the years spent at March Field were among the most demanding, yet in many ways among the most satisfying, for Arnold and his family. Among the many advantages of this assignment was that it not only provided many challenges for Hap but it allowed him to return to the cockpit. March Field's pleasant climate was enhanced by the fact that it was 3,000 miles from Washington, thus permitted some latitude and discretion to its commander. Also there were many activities to be enjoyed on base for all of the Arnolds. Although not realized then, this was the last time the Arnold family would be together as a unit.

The Air Corps suffered a credibility setback when nine bombers led by Arnold's friend and coconspirator in the post-Mitchell days, Maj Harold Dargue, failed to locate immediately and "sink" a targeted merchant vessel, the *Mount Shasta*, positioned 60 miles at sea. On 30 August 1931, the *New York Times* military editor, Hanson Baldwin, a Naval Academy graduate, declared the failure "illustrative of the inefficiency of land-based pilots over water." Arnold felt that the editorial would "have a very detrimental effect." He was "worried as to what will come out of the affair," since "the newspapers all over the country have lambasted us."[87] Arnold's main task was to train his units to assist the Army in repelling any hostile forces; at the same time, he worked to reverse the negative image that had been created by the *Mount Shasta* failure. Arnold's problems were complicated by the depression-mandated austerity that had come to dominate the military as well as all other elements of American society in the 1930s.

Fortunate to have proven leaders and close friends as his key staff, Arnold moved quickly to demonstrate Air Corps competence. An early opportunity to show that progress had been made in training was offered when March Field was tasked to drop foodstuffs to Hopi and Navaho Indians who had been isolated by severe snowstorms in January 1932. The aviators dropped more than 15 tons of food and other supplies in one week, an achievement that gained favorable national news coverage for the Air Corps.[88]

Aware of the gains to be had by educating civic and political leaders about Army aviation, Arnold instructed his key staff to join local community service organizations such as the Rotary Club, American Legion, and Chamber of Commerce.[89] Additionally, Arnold deliberately set out to cultivate the press, the politicians, and the important motion picture industry. Charles Lindbergh's transatlantic flight had encouraged a public love affair with aviation that Arnold understood and sought to exploit. Saturday morning aerial reviews with as many planes overhead as he could muster became routine at March Field. California Governor James Rolph joined Arnold on the reviewing stand for the first demonstration, which was held in March 1932. Arnold had personally piloted a plane to Sacramento, California, and flown the governor to March Field for the review. Newsmen were courted and regular "Open House" days at the base brought the public in for a close-up look at the Air Corps, its men, and its planes. Arnold invited other famous guests who served as magnets for favorable press coverage and public attendance. A succession of famous personalities enjoyed luncheons at the Officer's Club or in Arnold's quarters following the reviews, serving both Arnold's purposes and those of the guests' publicists. Among those attending were Amelia Earhart, Eddie Rickenbacker, Wallace Beery, Bebe Daniels, Clark Gable, and Will Rogers.[90]

Arnold used the Tenth Olympiad, held in Los Angeles, to gain publicity as his airmen participated in both opening and closing ceremonies. Mary Pickford, "America's Sweetheart," honored Air Corps personnel during the games with a reception at Pickfair. Later, she was flown in a bomber escorted by six fighters to Los Angeles. All these events garnered generally favorable notice. On the first Saturday of November 1932, more than 70,000 people attempted to reach March Field to help the wing celebrate its birthday. At the same time, scenes of March Field were being used by movie producers, as were the men and airplanes of March Field. Arnold planned a series of air-to-ground demonstrations, with pilots aloft talking directly to interviewers on the ground. Their conversations would be broadcast over commercial radio stations.[91]

While at March Field, Arnold renewed his acquaintance with Dr. Robert Millikan, Nobel laureate at California Institute of Technology, whom Arnold had first met in Washington during World War I. Arnold's fliers assisted Millikan in the scientist's cosmic ray experiments. Arnold invited Auguste Piccard, the famous French balloonist, to lecture at March Field. Through his work in support of Millikan, Arnold was introduced to Dr. Theodore von Kármán, who had recently arrived from Germany to continue his research in the United States. Arnold's respect for von Kármán grew and they became friends. At Hap's request, von Kármán would later contribute significantly to the AAF in World War II. Despite his friendships with von Kármán and Millikan, however, Arnold's ambivalence towards researchers and the scientific community remained. He frequently spoke of scientists as "long-hair boys"; yet he became increasingly aware that the key to improved aircraft design and performance was often found in the laboratory. Fresh in his memory was the excessive US reliance during World War I on British and French aircraft and engines. Also prominent in his thinking was the insistence of the economy-minded Republican administrations in the twenties that the backlog of obsolete Liberty engines be used before new ones were authorized. He was also aware, however, of the revolutionary changes that were occurring in aircraft design and performance; for example, metal fuselages, retractable landing gears and flaps, variable pitch propellers, higher compression engines, lighter-weight engines, flush rivets, significant advances in cockpit instrumentation and radio navigation, and precision bombsights. Though Arnold's ambivalence remained, there is evidence that his appreciation of the need for research and development as essential ingredients for progress in military aviation increased during his tour at March Field. That increased interest was no doubt spurred on, at least in part, by news of significant advances being made by other nations.[92]

Conscious of the location of March Field in an increasingly populated area 60 miles east of Los Angeles, Arnold became aware of the need to obtain bombing, gunnery, and experimental ranges far from cities. Within nine months of his assuming command at March, Arnold and some of his trusted subordinates began to oversee acquisition of the acreage that today constitutes Edwards Air Force Base. Although only partly successful because of the limited funds available in the thirties (the final section of land was not acquired until 1939), the early acquisition was a reflection of Arnold's vision.[93]

When an earthquake struck the greater Long Beach, California, area on 10 March 1933, Arnold quickly mobilized the resources of March Field to provide humanitarian aid to the victims. That he should seek official approval probably did not occur to him. In any event, he did not do so, and his relief efforts incurred the hostility of the Coast Artillery commander at nearby Fort MacArthur who complained about Arnold's intrusion into his jurisdiction. Maj Gen Malin Craig, Ninth Corps Area commander and the superior of both officers, summoned Arnold to appear and explain his actions. The incident was quickly forgotten, however, amidst glowing press reports of prompt and successful Air Corps assistance.[94] As a result of this incident, Craig and Arnold began a close military as well as personal relationship which would prove to be critical in Hap's later career. Typical of the general's estimate of Arnold and his work during the latter's March Field tenure was an assessment written in July 1934: "Loyal, generous, intensely interested in his work. Takes responsibility easily, and does everything well. Of tremendous energy. Well-informed."[95]

Superimposed on Hap's duties as commander of March Field was responsibility for the Civilian Conservation Corps (CCC). An early New Deal measure aimed at employing the young men of the nation in conservation work, the CCC was implemented by the US Army. In 1933, Arnold found himself faced with the problem of receiving, housing, feeding, and utilizing them while hosting the annual Air Corps maneuvers. Some of the young men worked at March Field but many were utilized in the vicinity as Hap became responsible for more than 7,000 CCC workers at 30 locations in the area. General Craig expressed some reservations at first, writing that the aviator did "excellent work" in this endeavor "but requires supervision." He later upgraded his evaluation of Arnold in this role to "superior."[96]

The Air Mail crisis of 1934 provided another test for Arnold and his units. A noncompetitive bidding scandal in awarding airmail contracts in the closing days of the Hoover administration had resulted in congressional inquiries. Congress discovered that 24 of 27 contracts to fly the mail had gone to only three companies. FDR, hoping to capitalize on the perceived sins of the previous administration, canceled agreements with the existing companies.[97] Maj Gen Benjamin Foulois, now Chief of Air Corps, stated to his regret that Army aviators could begin carrying the mail successfully within 10 days. The task was then given to the Air Corps and, on 9 February 1934, trumpeted to the press in typical Roosevelt fashion. The undertaking would require untrained pilots, many in open cockpit aircraft not equipped for adequate instrument flying, to commence delivering their cargo over unfamiliar routes in the middle of winter.[98]

Chosen to head mail delivery for the western zone headquartered in Salt Lake City, Utah, Arnold quickly established makeshift quarters in the fourth floor of a downtown hotel. The day before the service was to begin, the chief of the Air Corps insisted from Washington that the operation was "organized down to the last detail." Hap, preparing his pilots for their difficult assignment, was less confident as he wrote to his wife: "We most certainly will not get the mail through uninterrupted, but we will get it through when we can. I have preached and ordered that, in case of doubt, the planes will stay on the ground. I told them I didn't care if no mail moved in bad weather. I hope everyone will follow that policy."[99]

Three crashes with loss of pilots took place in Arnold's western zone before the formal starting date. The day after the Air Corps began flying the mail, hair-raising incidents experienced by his young pilots convinced Arnold, not demonstrably a religious man, to write his wife that he had "decided to take an hour or so and went up to the [Mormon] tabernacle to hear the organ."[100] The publicity associated with these and subsequent crashes prompted the Republicans in Congress, not unmindful of the midyear elections barely seven months away, to castigate the Roosevelt administration. As they debated the bill to fund the operation, Cong. Edith Nourse Rogers (R-Mass.) insisted that "the story of the Air Mail will be written in blood across the record of the Roosevelt administration."[101] Three weeks after the first airmail flight, Arnold accurately assessed the situation: "The Air Mail at present is a political football. No one seems to be making any plans to get us home."[102] Continuing crashes and adverse publicity caused the administration to halt the operation temporarily on 10 March 1934. It was continued only after Roosevelt issued stern warnings against future failures. Arnold, who had used the press to his benefit on other occasions, now criticized it as having a "sensation-hunting" attitude that "makes our task an almost impossible one."[103] The administration, for a variety of reasons, halted the Air Corps mail delivery program permanently on 1 June. President Roosevelt, salvaging as much face as possible, announced that it had been only "an experiment." Arnold appraised the program immediately after it was terminated: "We didn't have enough experienced pilots to carry on and had to use inexperienced flyers who lacked the mature judgment, who were afraid to turn back, who did not know when they were getting into trouble, and had too high an opinion of their own capabilities."[104]

Arnold had termed the operation "the greatest peacetime training in history" just before it ended. From the vantage point of his memoirs, written in 1948, he wrote that the episode "gave us wonderful experience for combat flying, bad weather flying, night flying; but, best of all, it made possible for us to get the latest navigational and night-flying instruments in our planes."[105] Interestingly enough, volume one of the seven-volume official history of the Army Air Forces in World War II mentions the Air Mail operation in only one sentence, labeling it an "ill-fated venture," and does not index it at all. Other recent students have labeled the effort a "fiasco."[106]

The results were devastating to the Air Corps. The Speaker of the US House of Representatives articulated to his colleagues and the *Congressional Record* an assessment that was or would be on many American minds: "If we are unfortunate enough to be drawn into another war, the Air Corps wouldn't amount to much. If it is not equal to carrying the mail, I would like to know what it would do in carrying bombs."[107]

During the temporary lull after 10 March, Secretary of War George Dern appointed a board headed by former Secretary of War Newton D. Baker to assess the Air Corps. In early February, three weeks before the Army began carrying the mail, a longtime advocate of Air Corps independence, Rep. John McSwain (R-S.C., called "McSwine" behind his back by Army Chief of Staff Gen Douglas MacArthur) introduced two bills into the House.[108] One, representing the desires of the General Staff to head off any new Air Corps independence movement, provided for creation of the General Headquarters Air Force (GHQAF). This new structure had been called for as early as the decade of the twenties and most recently by the Drum Board report of the previous October. This new organization, if and when implemented, would become the combat arm of the Air Corps and possess aircraft not assigned to the Army Corps areas. Its most significant provision would have the GHQAF report to the General Staff, not the chief of the Air Corps. Most probably reflecting the thinking of Chief of Staff Douglas MacArthur, it represented a politically sound "divide and conquer" strategy. As one recent author explained the purpose, "it would go a long way, they [the General Staff] believed, in quieting what congressional support there was for a separate Air Force and would either pacify or cut the ground out from under Air officers continuing to press for autonomy."[109]

The next day, McSwain introduced legislation that would have given the Air Corps almost everything it desired. It called for virtual independence, its own promotion list and budget, and generally what had been advocated a decade earlier by Mitchell and many of his supporters including Arnold. Witnesses were to be called to testify before the Baker Board and it was clear that McSwain intended to hold hearings on any bill brought before his House Armed Services Committee. These deliberations were to be held in public, but at an inopportune time from the Air Corps standpoint.[110]

FDR's assessment of the Air Corps' efforts at carrying the mail has not been clearly recorded. Given the negative publicity associated with the failed mail delivery mission and his return of the mission to the private sector after only 90 days, the results could not have endeared the Army Air Corps to the administration. The convening of the Baker Board, although announced at the direction of the Secretary of War, could not have been done without White House knowledge and consent. Roosevelt's personal admiration for the Navy and his clearly articulated opposition to Air Service sovereignty during his assistant secretary of the Navy days probably remained unaltered. His willingness to leave the position of assistant secretary of War for Air, which had been occupied effectively since its creation in 1926, unfilled until 1941 is revealing.[111]

Despite the negative publicity associated with the failed airmail mission, the results to Arnold personally had to have been gratifying. Brig Gen Oscar M. Westover, assistant to the chief of the Air Corps and commander of the entire Air Mail operation, submitted a glowing fitness report on Arnold. "An energetic, capable, experienced and exceptionally valuable Air Corps officer; outstanding in his ability to plan and solve emergency problems. An excellent organizer."[112] Westover's impressions would soon influence important decisions about Hap. General Foulois was blamed for the Air Corps' poor performance due to a lack of preparation and training. This result, along with other problems, led him to retire before the end of the next year, an action that would impact on Arnold's future.

The most important result of Arnold's performance in the airmail effort developed just 20 days after the end of the Air Corps' experience. While en route to a long-earned fishing vacation with his wife, Arnold was asked to accept command of a flight of Martin B-10 bombers that would fly to Alaska and return. The clear purpose of the mission was to reclaim the reputation of the Air Corps after the damage inflicted by the airmail episode. Possibly feeling that no professional aviator of his experience and background could decline such an opportunity, Arnold wired his immediate acceptance.[113]

His arrival at Patterson Field, Ohio, where the bombers and crews were being assembled, coincided with Arnold's 48th birthday, 25 June 1934. Pressured to commence the flight as soon as possible, Arnold insisted on choosing his own pilots and staff. He complained that "they are trying to rush me to set a date for starting." However, Arnold understood the critical importance of proper maintenance and preparation, particularly when proposing to fly over unfamiliar terrain that lacked emergency landing fields; he held out for the necessary time.[114] Additional delay was caused by the need to reconvert some B-10s that had been modified for airmail service. There was little doubt in Arnold's mind that this exercise was aimed at countering the unsuccessful performance of the Air Corps in carrying the mail. And he knew that he would be held responsible for the flight's success or failure: "I received . . . letters telling me I was holding the sack with regards to safety, hazard, success and risk."[115] His concerns were both institutional and personal as he speculated that none of the leaders "seemed to think that there was much wrong with the Air Corps. They cannot see the handwriting on the wall. I'm afraid that it is not long before the C of S [chief of staff] will say: 'Allright, you cannot run your own show, we will take it over.' Perhaps it will be a good thing."[116]

Hoping that the bulk of his preparation problems had been solved, Arnold left Dayton, Ohio, for Washington, D.C., where maximum publicity was to be gained as the bombers departed for the long flight. The July 19 takeoff from Bolling Field in the nation's capital saw Arnold sharing the newsreels with the dignitaries on hand to witness the departure. Traveling with overnight stops in Minneapolis, Minnesota, Winnipeg, Canada, and Edmonton, Canada, Arnold complained to his wife that he was "getting good-willed to death."[117] The aviators, having experienced few delays, arrived in Fairbanks on 24 July with only minor maintenance problems. While there, they completed an aerial mapping mission that provided valuable data for studying the geography of Alaska. On the return journey, they enjoyed a stop in Juneau, Alaska. The next leg chosen by Arnold was from Juneau to Seattle, Washington, over almost 1,000 miles of open ocean, then the longest flight of combat aircraft. This prompted the ever-ungracious Rear Adm Ernest King, head of the Navy's Bureau of Aeronautics, to comment that "Army aviation should end at the shoreline." They reached Washington, D.C., on 20 August, after stops in Omaha, Nebraska, and Dayton, Ohio. On returning to March Field five days later, Arnold and his aviators were welcomed home by Governor Rolph of California, Amelia Earhart, and Clark Gable, among others.[118]

The success of the Alaska flight and the favorable publicity it earned for the Air Corps would be important in Arnold's career. On 13 November three months after the flight, Arnold had a congratulatory 10-minute interview with President Roosevelt, who "asked many questions about Alaska."[119] Arnold was awarded his second Mackay Trophy in 1935, but he was disappointed that the War Department did not approve his recommendations for Distinguished Flying Crosses (DFC) for the other participants in the Alaska flight. Not until 1937, when he was serving in Washington, was Arnold himself belatedly awarded the DFC for the Alaska flight; his fellow aviators were never so recognized.[120] The absence of both the Army chief of staff and the secretary of war at the ceremonies associated with the flight, along with the delay in awarding Arnold's medal and the denial of decorations for the other aviators reflected the traditional War Department and General Staff lack of faith in long-range US Army aviation. General MacArthur's denial of the request to take a reserve officer who was also a newspaperman on the flight seemed further evidence of the War Department's desire to minimize the significance of the long-range bombers.[121]

Not all that happened was auspicious for Arnold in this period. During the airmail operation, Arnold wrote to his wife that Chief of the Air Corps Major General Foulois had promised that he would receive the next brigadier general promotion for aviators. When the rank went instead to another, Arnold called on Chief of Staff Douglas MacArthur to inquire why he had not been selected. MacArthur produced the list submitted to him for his approval; Arnold's name was not among those recommended by General Foulois.[122]

Busily engaged in the airmail operations, Arnold responded to the Baker Board's request of Air Corps officers to submit "constructive suggestions" for their consideration. Some of Arnold's staff members and airmail route commanders added their signatures to his written response. It carried 11 signatures when it arrived. Included in Arnold's response were the usual desiderata, such as the need for separate promotion lists and budgets for the Air Corps.

There was a change, however, at least in Arnold's thinking: the report supported creation of the GHQAF that had been recommended as recently as the previous year by the Drum Board. Support for this halfway measure represented a change in his thinking from the previous decade when complete independence seemed at the core of Arnold's, Mitchell's, and other aviators' thinking.

Hap's change in viewpoint may well have been prompted by several factors, among them the operational and administrative inadequacies highlighted by the airmail experience. Many felt these shortcomings might be overcome by separating the combat/flying segments from the planning/administrative functions. Another factor may have been the feeling that the GHQAF, while only half a loaf in terms of independence, was at least tacit recognition of a new role for an Army air arm that would be separated from the Army area ground commanders.

Although the proposed GHQAF would be responsible to the General Staff, hardly an air friendly group, its operation as a semiautonomous agency would offer needed staff experience to Air Corps Officers. Another reason that Arnold supported GHQAF may have been his realization that this proposal, emanating as it did from the Army hierarchy, had an excellent chance of achievement and could be viewed as a first step along the path of eventual Air Corps sovereignty. Some aviators, and this may well have included Arnold, probably supported the proposal because a brigadier would command each of the new wings, thus providing additional promotion opportunities to the rank of general. In his autobiography, Arnold called the GHQAF "the first real step ever taken toward an independent United States Air Force."[123]

The GHQAF came into existence in March of 1935 with headquarters at Langley Field, Virginia. Its commander, longtime Arnold colleague and fellow West Pointer, Frank M. Andrews, elevated to the temporary rank of brigadier general, no doubt strongly influenced Hap's appointment as commander of 1st Wing, which would be headquartered at March Field, Arnold's current location. Arnold's promotion to brigadier general from lieutenant colonel in this new assignment, which became effective in March 1935, had to have been personally gratifying. It represented recognition as a professional aviator, a far cry from his exile from Washington a decade earlier. This new assignment would continue for almost a year.[124]

No commander's job would be easy in the GHQAF. The new organization would be under the War Department General Staff while its procurement and training would be under the guidance of the chief of the Air Corps in Washington. The administrative concerns were handled by each of the nine Army Corps areas scattered throughout the nation. Satisfying these separate masters would not be simple. Some suspected that the jurisdictional guidelines had been established by the General Staff in order to create such confusing and overlapping lines of control that GHQAF would surely fail. General MacArthur's biographer has written that the chief of staff's inspiration for the creation of the GHQAF was that it would obviate "the creation of a separate air department, an idea that was still alive and well in certain media and among some Congressmen."[125] Certainly there could be difficulties between the commanding general GHQAF in his day-to-day command of the units and the chief of the Air Corps in Washington, who would be responsible for working with the Congress and War Department to secure and allocate the personnel and equipment to be used in the field.

General Arnold's responsibilities at 1st Wing remained similar to those he had exercised as commander at March Field except that his span of control, still from March Field, would extend to more units spread over a larger geographical area. Hap had barely settled into his new responsibilities when he was summoned to testify before the McSwain Committee in Washington. The maturity he had acquired in the decade since the Mitchell trial was apparent in his letter to his wife on the eve of testifying, as he wrote: "Is it any wonder that my heart beat has jumped up? I look forward with considerable dread as to . . . what I can say and still maintain my self-respect."[126]

Once back in California, training remained his primary responsibility. His units participated in the Ninth Army Corps maneuvers held in Seattle in September of 1935, during which those attending the maneuvers saw Boeing's new four-engine XB-299 bomber. Prototype of what became the B-17, the XB-299 took off from Seattle and flew nonstop to Dayton, Ohio, at the astounding speed of 232 miles per hour. Although presumably impressed with this aerial feat, the new brigadier was not overawed with the folderol and protocol he found associated with being a general: "Lord, how one gets tired of saying pleasant things and shaking hands." "We Generals all dress up for dinner [in our] glad rags."[127]

Arnold accompanied his units to participate in the first GHQAF maneuvers held in late 1935 in Florida. Flying from their temporary Vero Beach headquarters, their aircraft successfully "bombed" Miami Beach before "destroying" a simulated aircraft carrier more than 100 miles offshore.[128] In the midst of the operation, Hap was summoned to Washington where apparently he met with the newly appointed Army chief of staff, Gen Malin Craig, Douglas MacArthur's successor and Arnold's former commander and occasional golfing partner. Craig was to nominate both a new chief as well as an assistant to the chief of the Air Corps to replace the outgoing Benny Foulois and Oscar Westover. One observer, recalling that Arnold appeared pleased on his return from the capital, deduced that Hap had been told of a new assignment. There is contrary evidence, however, that Arnold would not have greeted any change with any degree of enthusiasm.[129] In any event, Westover's nomination to succeed the outgoing Foulois and Arnold's nomination to replace Westover as assistant to the chief in Washington was announced. This was a major career opportunity for Arnold, since the normal procedure had been that the assistant succeed the chief.[130]

The new Washington appointees appeared a judicious melding of the diverse talents and backgrounds of the new Air Corps leadership. Westover, who had been a year ahead of Arnold at West Point, had acquired the nickname of "Tubby" because of his impressive torso, which he had used to considerable advantage as a wrestler. He had served 10 years in the infantry before joining the Air Service on the eve of US participation in World War I. Qualifying in 1921 as a balloonist (derisively called balloonatics by most aviators), Westover was in many ways the opposite of Arnold. His most adventurous moment came in 1922 when his balloon, competing in the Gordon Bennett Balloon race, strayed into Hungarian air space where peasants, fearing he was in trouble, hauled him out of the sky. Strongman Hungarian ruler Adm Nicholas Horthy briefly interned Westover until the wheels of diplomacy could secure his release shortly thereafter.[131] Serious and essentially without a sense of humor, Westover was a detail man whose service had been much more in headquarters assignments than in the field. Tubby's reputation among long-time aviators was not enhanced by the fact that he had not learned to fly until the age of 40. Nor did his seeming strict adherence to the policies of the General Staff and the chain of command endear him to those who still hoped for Air Corps independence. Westover, who had served as General Patrick's executive assistant during Billy Mitchell's assault on the battleships as well as the reputation of the Navy, disapproved of Mitchell's pronouncements and eagerness to work outside the chain of command. He stated his philosophy this way: "As an individual, I, of course, have my own ideas about what is best for the future, and I am willing to work for the accomplishment of my ideas provided I know definitely that they are not in contravention of the plans of my military superiors."[132]

Shortly after becoming chief of the Air Corps in 1936, Westover issued a statement affirming his policies:

> It should be clearly understood . . . as a basic policy from now on, that all steps looking toward improvement and development of the Air Corps . . . will be properly represented and considered through the normal military channels . . . to the point where decision of higher authority results . . . In the event of disapproval, such decision must be carried out loyally and cheerfully by all persons concerned who in so doing, are charged with refraining [from] discussing such matters with outsiders not in the military service, or in public.[133]

Tubby Westover had been no rebel in the twenties, and he was not going to be one as chief of the Air Corps. Neither would others now under his command be permitted to follow the dissenting paths taken previously by Mitchell, Arnold, and others.

In other areas, however, the new Air Corps leaders appeared to complement one another. The Westovers were reluctant social participants in the Washington whirl and Tubby, explaining that his wife was not in good health, fully expected that his gregarious new assistant and his wife would shoulder the bulk of the onerous handshaking and protocol responsibilities in the nation's capital. More importantly, most aviators saw Hap as an operational type with a background dating to his 1911 Wright Brothers' instruction. This contrasted sharply with Westover's extensive headquarters assignments in Washington and his much later post–World War I training as a pilot. Westover's reputation as a reserved, methodological, detail man was offset by Arnold's reputation as an outgoing, impetuous flier who was often concerned more with the overall dimensions of a problem than with its details. Arnold's earlier support of Mitchell, still praised by most aviators, was now mostly forgiven by other Army officers, which apparently allowed Hap to work harmoniously with the General Staff and to testify credibly before Congress in search of funds, personnel, and new equipment. In many ways, Arnold's background, experience, and credibility among many of the rank and file of Air Corps aviators was an excellent counterbalance to Westover's limited flying experience, caution, and commitment to working within the system. An aviator who was familiar with both men commented, "I believe we have a very fine combination in Tubby Westover and Happy Arnold. Westover can do all the detail work and Arnold can sell our ideas to the General Staff, Bureau of the Budget and Congress."[134]

The Arnold family's return to Washington was less than an enthusiastic one. As Hap remembered in his memoirs, they "said goodby, in tears, to March Field, and moved—back to that hectic town, Washington. I was a gloomy man."[135] Arnold remembered being so willing to remain on the coast in his operational command that he offered to be reduced in rank from brigadier general to lieutenant colonel to remain there.[136] The Arnolds had been on the West coast for much of the past 15 years and it was not going to be an easy transition from the pleasant climate and Hap's relative sovereignty as a base and wing commander. As Hap lamented in his memoirs, "the pure exuberance of that command on the Coast was never to come back."[137] There, the results of training, flying, and hard work were often visible while tasks at the headquarters in Washington were usually viewed as an endless mass of policy discussions and paperwork, the results of which were rarely discernible, tangible, or appreciated in the field. Also involved was the end of living on an air base with its cohesion, esprit de corps, and many family activities. In contrast was Hap's unenviable, solitary commuting from their home in the suburbs to that relic of World War I, the Munitions Building. The transition to living in the much more impersonal civilian community, where he had not lived for the past decade, would not be an overly pleasant one for the general.

The move would be more than a geographical change for the family. While in California, daughter Lois had already enrolled in the relatively nearby University of Arizona. Oldest son Hank would continue in prep school during their first year in Washington and second son Bruce was less than two years away from applying to college. Arnold cautioned his wife that their stay in the nation's capital would be a short one. "I don't want you to sign any leases . . . I won't last in that city three months. Don't get tied up in anything. I will have no official social life . . . I don't like life there."[138] No more than others could he have anticipated that his tenure, which he probably would have termed a sentence with no time off for good behavior, would last until his retirement in 1946.

Another major challenge for Brig Gen Arnold would be that of perspective. For most of the previous decade, Hap had been in an operational environment with planes, personnel, and equipment that had been determined in the nation's capital. Now he would be an important part of the headquarters staff, charged with obtaining funds from a parsimonious Congress and the War Department. He would be involved in determining the types and allocations of planes for use in the field and in establishing Air Corps policies covering everything from the doctrine of employment of aircraft to educational and physical standards for pilots. Although few possessed his breadth and length of experience in the air, Hap would wrestle with the difficulties of equipping, manning, and supporting an institution that was beset with problems rarely appreciated by those outside of Washington. As he recalled his new job, the major challenges involved the "War Department, Congress, appropriations, public opinion, the definition of our program when nobody—not even the G.H.Q. AF—had any real program at all; the headaches of 'defending' our accident rate . . . all became my problems as Assistant Chief."[139]

Foremost among these problems, although not mentioned above by Arnold, was the perception of most Americans that the United States must remain aloof from future wars, a national concept represented in part by a series of Neutrality Acts. This perception, along with the fiscal limitations imposed by the Great Depression, seemed to justify not only limiting the resources provided but restricting the function of the few aircraft available and on order to defensive missions. At the same time, the aircraft industry was developing revolutionary technological advances that would vastly enhance the range, speed, complexity, and destructive potential of planes. With these developments came an almost exponential increase in the cost of each new model. Similar improvements were proceeding apace in other nations that might prove hostile to the United States. From the Air Corps point of view, these changes required a reassessment of employment doctrine, which determined the numbers and types of aircraft to be procured. The increasingly successful offensive use of aircraft in Ethiopia, Spain, and China, together with Hitler's threatened use of this weapon, appeared to justify the need for an expanded and conceivably different role for airplanes in US war planning.

There is little doubt that most Americans had a love affair with the airplanes that appeared overhead in the thirties. This romance, fed by the exploits of Lindbergh and by movies that glamorized aviation, was brought closer to home by the "barnstormers," who thrilled many hamlets. Additionally, the growth of civilian airlines seemed to hold the promise of scheduled airplane travel to most reasonably sized US cities. It was a far cry in the minds of most Americans, however, from marveling at the new sights and sounds in the sky to visualizing the use of American military aircraft against cities such as their own.

Arnold's arrival in Washington coincided with stirrings in his own mind, as well as the minds of many in the Air Corps, of modern aircraft used as offensive weapons, particularly in the strategic sense. These ideas became more clearly developed during Arnold's early years in the headquarters as assistant to the Air Corps chief. The Army's General Staff continued to be dominated by officers who represented the more traditional branches. Most of them continued to view with skepticism any different role for aircraft other than the limited observation and pursuit missions they had performed in 1917–18. Arnold would have to work with them on a daily basis. These and other problems, not the least of which were the increasing threat to world peace and the potential role of US military forces in response to these dangers, made Arnold's duties in Washington most challenging. This was a vastly different headquarters from the one he had been banished from 10 years earlier.

A significant problem faced by Westover and Arnold was the necessity of making the relationship between the Office of the Chief of the Air Corps and the GHQAF, the latter now just a year old, a manageable one. Their assets were acquired and allocated by the chief of the Air Corps in Washington, yet responsibility for their use remained primarily with the GHQAF. Arnold might have had considerable understanding of GHQAF's problems, having very recently been one of its three wing commanders, but his primary loyalty in the chain of command now belonged to the chief of the Air Corps and then to the Army chief of staff. Additionally, all three of the other senior officers involved—Craig, Westover, and Andrews—were Hap's personal friends of long standing. Arnold also was to work closely with the Army General Staff, a body with few aviators and little sympathy for the Air Corps. Complicating matters was the fact that Andrews, as CG, GHQAF, did not report in the chain of command to Westover but to the Army chief of staff. Westover's clear pronouncement on assuming Air Corps leadership, as well as Arnold's own concept of loyalty to his superiors, did not encourage Hap to deviate from articulated policies. Although not a "yes man," Arnold did not carve out any program distinct from the policies of Westover and the War Department during his 31-month tenure as assistant to the Air Corps chief. Any second thoughts Arnold may have had about any conflicting loyalties have not been recorded.

There is little doubt that many in GHQAF considered their new organization as a precursor to the separate air force advocated by Mitchell, Arnold, and others a decade earlier. As a result, GHQAF personnel were discouraged when Hap's testimony before Congress in July 1936, shortly after he became assistant to the chief, was in opposition to separation from the War Department. The appearance of the B-17 in 1935, destined in GHQAF plans to be its main weapon, stirred mixed emotions in Arnold. From the vantage point of 1948, he judged this airplane as "a turning point in the course of air power." He did not hold this view consistently, however, in his role as assistant to the chief. Given its cost and operational complexity, Arnold was concerned that concentrating on the Flying Fortress might be putting "too many eggs in one basket."[140]

A contract for Boeing to build 13 developmental B-17s for the Air Corps had been awarded while Arnold was en route from California to his new assignment in Washington, but the first Fortress did not reach Andrews' GHQAF until March of 1937.[141] Arnold had a voice in the request of 28 May 1936, that the budget then being prepared for fiscal 1938 include Air Corps procurement of 50 more B-17s as well as 11 "ultra-long-range" bombers. There seems no recorded objection by Arnold when the General Staff eliminated the B-17 and substituted two-engine bombers six weeks later. Nor did he object to the General Staff study 10 days later, which included this statement: "Until the international situation indicates the need for long-range types of bombardment . . . no more of that type should be procured except for experimental purposes. That a medium range bombardment [two-engine] . . . type such as the B-18 . . . will fulfill all reasonable military requirements."[142] Arnold had to have been discouraged by this response since he was aware in 1937 that the average time lag between the design of a military aircraft and its being operationally deployed was five years.

Arnold's thinking about the numerous publicity-garnering flights of the B-17s is not reflected in his correspondence. However, as an effective user of the press and media in the past, Arnold had to have quietly admired Andrews' use of the new Fortresses to arouse public consciousness of the new aircraft. Despite difficulties encountered in locating it, three Fortresses found and "bombed" the battleship *Utah* in August 1937. Most Army aviators were convinced that the position reports were deliberately erroneous as furnished by US naval forces.[143]

Speed records were established during the first week of 1938 when a B-17 flew from Virginia to California in 13 hours and returned in only 11 hours. The 11-day "good will" flight around South America with a B-17 reaching Lima, Peru, in one day and Buenos Aires a day later clearly was aimed at demonstrating the long-range potential of the plane, particularly in hemisphere defense.[144] In an exercise that was particularly upsetting to the US Navy, three B-17s, flying in exceedingly bad weather, were able to locate the Italian passenger liner *Rex* more than 600 miles off the Atlantic Coast. The attendant publicity, carefully planned by the Air Corps, dramatized a potentially new role for Army aviation in locating and destroying a hostile fleet as it approached American shores. To what extent this resulted in the Navy demanding that Army aviation be limited to within 100 miles of the shore and Gen Malin Craig acceding to the demand cannot be determined. No contemporary official documents are extant on the issue, although there seems little doubt that such an order was issued.[145] Its appearance prompted Naval Academy graduate Hanson Baldwin, military correspondent of the *New York Times* to write about it.

> The order, which is the outgrowth of the long-smoldering army-navy dispute about their respective responsibilities for over-water flying operations and development, has aroused considerable resentment among those relatively few army officers who know that it has been promulgated. It was asserted that the order handicapped the training activities of the army and made it difficult to develop completely trained crews for such big ships as the "flying fortresses."[146]

There does not appear to be any recorded response by Arnold over this issue. However, Hap's increasing belief in the future of offensive heavy bombardment might not have differed significantly from that of GHQAF. In May 1938, he resubmitted a request for the acquisition and development of an experimental bomber with a pressurized cabin.

Arnold was disappointed but not surprised by the War Department response three months later that "No military requirement exists for the procurement of an experimental Pressure Cabin Bomber in Fiscal Year 1939 or Fiscal 1940 . . . Experimentation and development . . . will be restricted to that class of aviation designed for the close support of ground troops."[147] Less than 18 months later and more than two years before the United States was drawn into World War II, Arnold, now Air Corps chief, took probably the biggest gamble of his career when he authorized what became the B-29 Superfortress.

Arnold's chief, Major General Westover, often could be found at his desk far beyond the normal dinner hour tending to details best left to junior officers. In spite of Westover's seemingly excessive attention to minutiae and heavy reliance on the Arnolds to perform many of the onerous social chores of official Washington, neither Arnold nor Westover has left any hint of discordant relations between them. During Hap's tenure as assistant, a detailed office log of telephone calls, visitors, and correspondence was maintained for the benefit of either general who was absent. Westover's frequent visits to units outside the capital reflected his confidence in Arnold's ability to carry on in his absence. Although vastly different personalities, their relations remained warm, cordial, and effective even though they were not fast friends.[148]

In September 1938, General Westover departed on a routine trip to the west coast. While there, he awarded the annual Daedelian flying safety trophy to Arnold's old wing at March Field. The A-37A Northrop aircraft Westover flew had a reputation among aviators of stalling. Only a month before, Arnold's classmate at West Point, Col William McChord, had been killed in an A-37A crash. Westover and his crew chief were killed when their A-37A went into a high-speed stall and crashed while attempting a landing at the Lockheed plant in Glendale, California. Arnold had just arrived home from his office when he received a telephone call from Maj K. B. Wolfe, the Air Corps plant representative at Lockheed. Wolfe could see the still-burning aircraft and informed Hap there was no chance that the chief could survive the crash and blaze. According to his wife's recollection, Arnold put his head down in grief on the kitchen table, unable to speak. The Arnolds drove immediately to the Westover apartment, hoping to break the terrible news and provide comfort to Mrs. Westover before she learned of the tragedy from other sources.[149]

Succession was expected to be routine since there appeared to be no major impediment to Arnold becoming chief. The procedure that had been followed since Mitchell was denied elevation in 1924 was for the assistant to become chief. Among the factors favoring Hap's selection was that he had developed a reputation as a team player with the Army General Staff. His work as assistant to the chief had helped to offset recollections of his strong support of Billy Mitchell a decade earlier. It appeared that Hap's crusading spirit had been tempered by exile and experience, now replaced by maturity and a more realistic appreciation of the ways of politics and bureaucracies. He had been successful in not becoming a casualty in the ongoing "holy show" between Secretary of War Harry H. Woodring and Assistant Secretary Louis A. Johnson. Hap's Alaska flight four years earlier had gained him a modest degree of favorable public recognition as well as a brief interview with President Roosevelt. The fact that he was one of the few active duty Army aviators who had been taught to fly by the Wright brothers was an additional asset. His aviation experience ranged from many hours in the cockpit to command and staff positions. He also had experience in the development and procurement phases of the Air Corps. He had attended the staff school thought necessary for senior rank in the peacetime Army. His appointment seemed more logical than bringing in a new chief from outside the headquarters. Arnold's succession might provide a smoother, easier transition in policy and leadership for the grieving Air Corps.

In spite of these qualifications, there was opposition to his selection. Those urging an appointment other than Arnold appeared to center on the choice of Maj Gen Frank M. Andrews, commanding general of the GHQAF at Langley Field. A year ahead of Arnold at West Point, Andrews had learned to fly in 1917, six years after Hap. Much more articulate and polished than Arnold, Andrews was firmly convinced that the Army Air Corps' primary emphasis should be on procurement of the B-17 Flying Fortress and on training and preparation for its implementation. Andrews' GHQAF would be the primary user of Air Corps combat aircraft, and he was unrelenting in preferring the B-17 over its more economical but technically inferior competitor, the B-18. Particularly during the 1937 and 1938 procurement and funding cycles, Andrews had bombarded Washington via the Army chief of staff and the Air Corps chief with visits, correspondence, and studies insisting on the Flying Fortress B-17.[150] Andrews' son-in-law, then serving as an aide to the general, had left an otherwise unsubstantiated account that the chief of staff offered to support Andrews for appointment to Westover's position if Andrews would support a more balanced Army and Army Air Corps.[151] Andrews was more prescient in his thinking than Arnold, even though Hap later embraced the B-17 as the premier strategic bomber of the prewar period. However, Hap was considered to have articulated a much more balanced view of Air Corps and Army needs. Andrews' staff had followed their leader in advocating the B-17 and had campaigned for him to succeed Westover. Their advocacy had begun almost from the creation of GHQAF in March 1935 and Westover's selection as chief nine months later.

Although Andrews' remaining papers are circumspect on the issue of succeeding Westover, it is difficult to believe that he was unaware of his staff's zeal in promoting him to succeed Westover when the latter's term was scheduled to expire in 1940. Their goal was to be accomplished in part by denigrating Arnold and his work. In their zeal to have the GHQAF equipped with the most modern aircraft available, Andrews' staff felt that Arnold's less than complete support of GHQAF's aims was little more than treason and that it reflected his unwillingness to jeopardize his own chance of becoming chief. They reasoned that Arnold's recent experience as a wing commander in the GHQAF should have made him more sympathetic to and understanding of the expressed needs of his former command and its leader.[152]

In addition to the support of his staff, Andrews received support from two influential members of the White House staff, Press Secretary Steve Early and Military Assistant to the President Brig Gen Edwin M. "Pa" Watson. Early had been the Associated Press correspondent in Washington during Major Arnold's ill-advised efforts in 1926 to solicit congressional and reservist support for Mitchell and a separate air force. According to one observer, Early remembered that "Arnold had run a propaganda machine" from his office.[153] General Watson, another advocate for Andrews, had entered West Point in 1902 as a classmate of Andrews but did not graduate until 1908 because of academic deficiencies. The three knew each other during their cadet days and had maintained desultory contact.

Arnold had shared a house with Watson in the Philippines for a short time during his 1907–09 tour there. One observer has recalled, however, that Watson didn't like Arnold. Their paths had crossed several times in the past 30 years; Arnold recorded having cocktails with Watson during Hap's brief World War I visit to France in 1918. Col Walter Weaver, a Watson roommate from West Point days who was stationed at Maxwell Field, also recommended Andrews to the White House military aide.[154] Since Pa Watson's extant correspondence shows that FDR often consulted his senior White House military advisor on matters dealing with the armed forces, it seems logical that FDR solicited Watson's advice about Westover's successor. No clear evidence remains that Watson's recommendation was solicited, but two contemporary sources have recorded that both Early and Watson recommended the appointment of Andrews.[155]

Counterbalancing any animus towards Arnold by the GHQAF and two of Roosevelt's staff was the recommendation from Army Chief of Staff Gen Malin Craig. Arnold's and Craig's relationship dated from the early thirties when the latter had been Hap's commander in California. There is little doubt that Craig had recommended if not selected Arnold for his current position as Westover's assistant when Westover was chosen to head the Air Corps in December 1935. In the succeeding three years, Craig as Army chief of staff and Arnold as assistant to the Air Corps chief had frequent if not daily contact. During this period, Washington leadership had been subjected to Andrews' insistence on the B-17. In contrast to Andrews, Arnold supported, as did his superiors, a more balanced procurement program. Arnold's position was dictated mainly by budgetary and personnel matters, strategic considerations, loyalty to his superiors, and the overall perspective he had gained from Washington.

Concerning the final selection of Arnold as the new chief, Col John O'Loughlin, editor of the influential *Army Navy Journal* and a very close friend of generals Malin Craig and John J. Pershing, wrote to the retired World War I hero after Arnold's appointment was announced that Craig had gone to Roosevelt and threatened to resign as Army chief of staff if Arnold was not appointed as Air Corps chief.[156] Not unusual in personnel decisions made by FDR, the factors influencing the president's decision to appoint Arnold have not survived in the records.

If O'Loughlin's account is correct, the president would not have welcomed the resignation of the Army chief of staff over an appointment that appeared to be a relatively minor one among the many made by the White House. Roosevelt was concerned at the moment with several difficulties, among them the serious downturn in the nation's economy and political problems with the legislative branch. FDR's Supreme

Court Reorganization Bill had died at the hands of a Democratic Congress and Roosevelt's efforts to defeat for reelection those members of his party who had failed to support him were not going well. The political pundits were predicting correctly that very few legislators earmarked for defeat by the White House would lose their November bids to return to Washington.[157] Additionally, there was uncertainty tinged with guarded but mounting concern over the implications of Hitler's increasingly strident speeches and the ongoing discussions that led to the 30 September Munich settlement.

In the days following Westover's crash and before a new chief was announced, Hap began to hear about rumors circulating in Washington that he was, in his own term, a drunkard.[158] Arnold later recalled that he enlisted the support of presidential confidant Harry Hopkins to dispel these unfounded slanders. Hopkins was known to have considerable influence with the president and many people used him in a variety of ways to get their views into the Oval Office. Viewed from more than half a century after the events, it appears curious that Hap, admittedly not having known Hopkins well before this incident, was able to enlist his crucial support with the president. There is little doubt, however, that Arnold later developed rapport and strong friendship with Hopkins and, like others, was willing to exploit this access.[159]

Arnold's use of alcohol is subject to several interpretations after 60 years. His statement in his memoirs that he "hadn't had a drink of hard liquor since 1920" is disingenuous. As the diary reflects, Arnold consumed liquor during the many trips covered in this volume, all after 1938. Earlier, during Prohibition, Arnold seemed to have been a user of liquor as he wrote to his wife in 1927 that maneuvers at Brooks Field, Texas, were "a frost since the bootlegger didn't show up."[160] After his daughter Lois' marriage in 1937, Arnold carried on a humorous relationship with her husband, naval aviator Lt Ernie Snowden. Hap referred to it as much in the same vein that had been the custom in American Indians' relationships between fathers and braves who married their daughters. In this ongoing bantering, their correspondence shows that on numerous occasions Arnold received bottles of Scotch representing the 100 horses that the brave would have presented as payment due the father of the bride. A popular brand of Scotch whiskey then and now is "White Horse." Around the neck of every White Horse bottle was (and still is) a small, detachable token of a white horse. When delivery slowed, Arnold humorously lamented to his son-in-law that he had not received any horses "for quite some time. I want to know whether the girl is worth any more horses. I want to know whether a bargain is a bargain or is it a Versailles Treaty. I want some horses." The story became a joke among military colleagues and friends, some of whom helped Lieutenant Snowden pay the "debt" for his bride. When three cases totaling 36 "horses" arrived, Hap acknowledged that one had a "broken leg and had to be shot" but acknowledged the debt was now "paid in full." Another insight is offered by Hap's daughter, Lois Arnold Snowden: Writing to her Mother, she said she had heard that Hap had suffered another hangover. She added, "I wonder how many he has had?"[161] To what extent Hap consumed the Scotch excessively or in public when he served as assistant to the chief cannot be determined with any certainty, but it seems unlikely that his interest in corresponding with his son-in-law was confined to accumulating unopened bottles of Scotch whiskey.

Although the Roosevelt administrations had their share of peccadilloes that were tolerated but not publicly known outside of official circles and Washington gossip, FDR would probably have been reluctant to appoint a known toper as chief of the Army Air Corps in September 1938. Particularly would this have been true at this time of uncertain but increasing international tensions and when some of FDR's trusted White House aides were urging him to appoint Andrews. FDR, ever the consummate political animal, would not have welcomed either the potentially embarrassing appointment of a "drunkard" or the resignation of the Army chief of staff at this time.

In any event, the White House announcement of Arnold's nomination as chief of the Air Corps and his temporary elevation to the rank of major general was made on 29 September, the day before the final Munich settlement was signed.[162]

If Hap had any blueprint for the future at that time, it has not survived. However, there are hints of his thinking in his message to the Air Corps that appeared immediately in the *Air Corps Newsletter*. His initial greeting began by paying obligatory but sincere tribute to the life, work, and contributions of the late General Westover. Continuing, he specifically praised and seemed to offer the olive branch to the GHQAF where the bulk of opposition to his appointment had centered. He highlighted conciliation by citing the "urgent need" for more crews while praising the high level of training already being provided by the GHQAF and stressing that "results can be obtained only if we have complete accord through coordination." Other parts of the short message revealed an awareness of the recent difficulties associated with the campaign to procure only B-17 bombers while Arnold resolved to "build up our tactical units and supply them equipment"; he said the buildup would be "in accordance with the War Department program." While conceding that recent American superiority in planes and equipment was now "definitely challenged abroad," Arnold called for speeding up development programs, a reference to recent cuts in that area by the General Staff. Other elements of the Air Corps, such as the training schools, were called on for "accelerated efficiency" without lowering existing high standards.[163]

In a further move towards harmonious relations with GHQAF, Arnold chose Walter G. "Mike" Kilner to be assistant to the chief and presumably the officer to succeed Arnold after completion of a normal four-year tour. Kilner had been five years behind Arnold at West Point, and flew after learning to fly on the Mexican border. He had commanded the US training school at Issoudun, France, for 14 months during World War I. He and Arnold had served together in Washington on the staff of Major General Patrick. Kilner had been assigned to GHQAF almost since its inception and most recently was Andrews' chief of staff. Hap's selection of Kilner appeared to indicate that GHQAF influence would be present in Washington in the foreseeable future. Unfortunately, Kilner's illness and suicide just after a year as assistant to the chief precluded the long-term effective relationship Arnold had anticipated.[164]

In spite of these actions on Arnold's part, a hard core of officers who served in the GHQAF had continued as Andrews supporters. They chafed under Arnold's leadership and engaged in internecine warfare against Hap until Andrews' tragic death in 1943. Even after US entry into the war, the most extreme of these officers continued to work for an independent Air Force and attempted to have Arnold dispatched from Washington to a field command.[165]

What was the measure of the 52-year-old Hap Arnold as he assumed leadership of the Army Air Corps in 1938? Among his strengths as he began what became more than a seven-year challenge was his extensive experience in military aviation, only World War I combat having escaped his reach during his 27 years of flying since earning his wings. His widespread assignments in operations as well as his having a background in procurement, research, and development may well have been unmatched by any active Army aviator. He had worked in Washington in both war and peacetime, in varying ranks and degrees of responsibility and with varying success, under four different chiefs. Although Arnold's earlier support of Mitchell was still viewed as an asset by many fliers, nonaviator General Staff officers who continued to wield the bulk of power in the Army did not consider his accession a serious threat. He had worked effectively with them during the previous two and one-half years, and his testimony before several congressional committees had mirrored the many changes that had transformed the Air Corps and military aviation over a quarter of a century. He knew and was known by many of the Air Corps pilots serving on active duty and had worked closely with most of those now serving alongside him in senior policy and leadership positions. Given Hap's clear preference to be among airplanes and aviators in an operational environment, his having been on this tour in Washington since March 1936 probably helped him to feel as comfortable as possible there.

Arnold's dedication to hard work and long hours did not change as the approaching war and rapid expansion of the force put increased strain on him and the Air Corps staff. During his long tenure as chief, he continued to demonstrate characteristics of what later generations would term a "workaholic." The staff he inherited in 1938 had been devised essentially over the past decade although no segment of the American military was or could have been structured to anticipate the demands that the war or its prospects brought. Arnold's belief that results were more important than rigid, clear-cut lines of authority led to criticism after the war by Gen Laurence S. Kuter, one of his most respected senior officers, that Hap had failed to use his staff in an orderly, manageable fashion.[166] Arnold's official papers, however, show knowledge of the proper role of a staff. He had relied heavily on an orderly allocation of responsibilities as both a contributing junior officer and a commander. As the demands of Air Corps expansion increased during 1938–41, Hap became cognizant of the need for restructuring the aviation staff within the War Department. In all of this, however, he continued to be acutely aware that he and the Air Corps were integral parts of the US Army and were subordinate to the Army chief of staff. Prior to 1941, many Air Corps functions were performed by Army staff subsections, including plans, intelligence, and procurement. Aviators felt not only underrepresented but that they had to vie with officers of other corps for the desiderata best suited to their particular branches. However, in large part because of Arnold's enhanced credibility, the fliers gained greater control over their assets, plans, and doctrine, particularly in the reorganization of 1942.

Arnold's increased stature in the Washington bureaucracy was not easily acquired, given the problems extant in the political arena. President Roosevelt's continuing penchant for unclear bureaucratic and administrative channels allowed him to act as his own cabinet head, and military matters were no exception. Henry L. Stimson, who became secretary of war in 1940, observed that FDR was "the poorest administrator I have ever worked under. . . . He is not a good chooser of men and does not know how to use them in coordination."[167] In the early thirties, when the economy and its problems were paramount and there appeared no viable international threat on the horizon, FDR's military secretaries were at best ciphers, appointed for a host of political reasons not related to military effectiveness. Even after new leadership was installed in the War Department following Secretary of War George Dern's death, competition in that department brought little comfort to the professional military officer. The new secretary of war was former Kansas governor Harry Woodring, the assistant secretary Louis A. Johnson. The major contributions to the New Deal of the new civilian leaders had been their political support of FDR and their association with veterans' organizations where both had held national office. The main ideological difference between the two was Johnson's more internationalist outlook. The assistant secretary's main ambition, however, was to embarrass, dislodge, and succeed Woodring as secretary of war. Hap found it necessary to remain effective yet neutral in the "holy show" that raged between them. Gen George C. Marshall, who operated as chief of staff for almost a year in this feuding environment, recalled that negotiating between Woodring and Johnson was "the most miserable experience of my life."[168] There is no reason to believe that Arnold viewed his own tenure any differently, although Hap has circumspectly left no comment on the antics of his two civilian superiors during their three-year struggle. He ignored their feuding in his memoirs, a partial explanation for which may be that Louis Johnson was serving as secretary of defense and Harry Woodring was still alive when Hap wrote *Global Mission* in 1948. Another possible explanation is that Arnold generally refrained from disparaging anyone in print. Through it all, however, both Arnold and Marshall appear to have emerged essentially unscathed from working with these two civilians whose knowledge rarely matched their egos or ambitions. Hap's survival of the stormy three-year relationship of his civilian superiors reflected tact and discretion acquired since his more rash actions of a decade earlier. Like the bulk of his professional contemporaries, Arnold remained apolitical. No record exists of his having voted in any national election during his active military career.

His 1926 banishment to Kansas following the Mitchell trial appears to have convinced Arnold to work within the existing system, however imperfect. His critics, particularly those airmen assigned to the GHQAF at Langley Field during the two years Hap served as assistant, were convinced that his balanced advocacies were motivated by his ambition to succeed Westover. Hap conceded, however, that his experience and maturity since the earlier exile had made him more judicious.[169]

Although he remained diligent in cultivating congressional support, Hap operated essentially within War Department guidelines this time. If there was any gloating, smugness, or articulated awareness that the junior officers who had supported Mitchell were now in charge of the Army air arm, there is no hint of it in Arnold's papers. It is clear that he had changed along with the times over the past dozen years.

It is not surprising that Hap and the few Air Corps officers on the General Staff were not producing any significant geopolitical or doctrinal studies of military power employment. Intelligence summaries, Arnold complained, did not regularly come across his desk until he modified the system in 1940.[170] Hap and his senior colleagues had received their undergraduate education just after the turn of the century, the majority having attended service academies. There was little exposure to further formal education except in the various service staff schools, which stressed military matters and paid only peripheral attention to diplomacy, history, or world affairs. What personal reading they accomplished in their careers probably dealt primarily with their particular military subspecialty or was for recreation.

The local newspapers, which relied on brief wire service reports, were often the daily source of information, particularly on isolated bases. Arnold, like many Americans of the day, relied heavily on local movie theaters for entertainment. The social regimens that centered on officer, NCO, and other clubs on military installations were important to all military families. Although professional military writing was not prohibited, few active career Army aviators, perhaps enlightened by Billy Mitchell's court-martial results, sought an audience for their views in national journals. General Westover's insistence that Air Corps officers operate within the chain of command and not publicly disagree with the announced policies of the Air Corps and the War Department had to have been an inhibiting influence on latent crusaders.

Gen Malin Craig and many of the General Staff viewed Arnold in 1938, before he became chief, as holding a relatively balanced position on the issues of new weapons and their usage. After succeeding Westover, however, Hap began to embrace more fully the theory of strategic bombardment. Although the concept eventually became the virtual raison d'être of Arnold and Air Corps, it is difficult to determine whether Arnold shaped institutional goals or was shaped by them.

Although his views were not consistent throughout his career, Arnold hinted at the role of the bomber in his testimony at Mitchell's court-martial: "Distance is annihilated by a few hours." However, there is little other evidence of any strong advocacy of strategic bombing by Arnold in the decades of the twenties. One author has written, without documentation, that Hap was "gaining a reputation as a bombing man" by 1931 and the beginning of his successful tour as commander at March Field. In 1933, Arnold wrote that "the bombers will reach their objective with the pursuit having made but one attack." He concluded that "pursuit tactics must be revamped or the pursuit passes out of the picture." The strategic implications of the B-10 bomber, which Hap had flown to Alaska in 1934, seems to have been minimized by him at the time. He wrote to his wife that the operation was "just a job."[171]

As assistant to the chief, Arnold was aware of Capt Claire L. Chennault's retirement from the Air Corps in 1937, officially for medical reasons. A major factor in prompting Chennault's leaving the service, however, was his advocacy while an instructor at the Air Corps Tactical School (ACTS) that the bomber would not get through to the target if opposed by fighter forces. Arnold was never a student at ACTS and his relationships with that organization cannot be clearly established, but Hap was well aware of its emphasis on strategic bombardment. With both Norden and Sperry bombsights available and a fast four-engine bomber in production, Chennault's advocacy of defending fighters was viewed as heresy at the Tactical School. There, Chennault grew weary of being a lonely voice in the wilderness of strategic bombing enthusiasts. No contemporary comment by Arnold on Chennault's departure from the service in 1937 has been located but the nature of their later World War II relationship does not reflect regret at Chennault's retirement.[172]

By 1938, however, only seven weeks before Westover's crash, the War Department decreed that "experimentation and development for . . . 1939-40 will be restricted to . . . aviation designed for close-in support of ground troops." Arnold, still assistant to the chief, noted that "It is thought that the Chief of the Air Corps should fight this decision."[173] If Arnold was not then as committed to strategic bombardment as he would become later, he increasingly embraced the doctrine. His failure to appreciate the need for fighter escort was a mistake on his part that was to have important consequences on the conduct of the aerial war. It was no coincidence that the main Air Corps war planners in the nine months before Pearl Harbor were recent graduates of or instructors at the Air Corps Tactical School. Strong advocates of strategic bombardment, they were chosen by Arnold and they worked specifically under his instructions.

Arnold's personal characteristics reflected an impatient aviator who was correctly perceived as a man of action rather than one committed to deliberative thought. It is apparent that this impetuosity increased as war approached. Hap, well aware of his own limitations, wrote during the war that he would probably be urging the caisson to go faster as it carried his casket through the gates of Arlington National Cemetery. His impatience was used as a ploy by him after he became chief and it was not unusual for Hap to convene a group (civilian or military did not seem to matter) and harangue them that they were not being sufficiently productive in whatever areas Arnold felt needed improvement. At least one close observer has labeled these antics an "act," but they reflected his intensity and concentration on the tasks at hand. His family recognized his volatility. When daughter Lois wrote that she was planning to marry outside the Army "faith," to a naval aviator, she asked her mother to "Please break the news gently to Papa and don't let him get mad and raise hell."[174] Hap was not excessively cautious. He sometimes took considerable risk in attempting to achieve institutional goals or acting on what he considered to be matters of principle, such as engaging in serious and open disagreement with the president or pushing development of the B-29 before the United States entered the war.

His extant correspondence reveals a man of simple and direct speech and prose. A famous novelist, Ivy league-educated, who wrote a good many speeches as a reserve officer for Arnold during the war, has labeled Hap as "dumb" and "illiterate," an overly harsh criticism by a professional writer. The critic, then Maj James Gould Cozzens, had published his first novel at age 19 and had published 10 more by the time he joined the military in 1942. *Guard of Honor*, the World War II novel that earned Cozzens the Pulitzer Prize for fiction in 1949, included much that he had experienced during his AAF service in Arnold's office. Cozzens, in his own diary, has left an interesting assessment of Arnold's impact on the progress of the war.

> I have a pet theory that one of the reasons that we are winning the war is that . . . the generals who oppose us have a high proportion of intellectuals . . . [who] waste their time weighing complex factors and . . . while they ponder, their simple and single minded opponents take them for all they have. . . . Mr. A[rnold], like his Chief of Staff, seems to me really dumb. . . . But the fact remains that, by being what he is Mr. A[rnold] has performed the impossible in building the air force.[175]

Cozzens' disparagement seems contradictory to Arnold's limited success in the 1920s when he wrote journal articles, fiction aimed at juvenile audiences, and a volume on aviation. Prior to Pearl Harbor, he coauthored three books with Ira Eaker and, although Eaker did much of the writing, Arnold's contributions to the volumes were clearly not the mark of an "illiterate." Further, there is too much correspondence, personal and official, in Hap's own hand in the Manuscripts Division of the Library of Congress and elsewhere to justify Cozzens' evaluation of the AAF chief.[176]

Any assessment of Arnold seems to confirm the impressions of those who have characterized him as "transparently honest" and "able to put his finger on the big issues." During the war at Joint Chiefs of Staff (JCS) and Combined Chiefs of Staff

(CCS) meetings, his recorded remarks were normally confined to land-based aviation issues, an appreciation of both his lack of pretension in other areas and his realization that he remained subordinate to the Army chief of staff. Hap probably would have agreed with the label of "unsophisticated."[177] In fact, he probably would have considered it a compliment. In any event, it is a judgment that is reflected in these diaries.

Arnold was rarely disingenuous, either in personal dealings or in his diary entries. In many ways outside of military air matters, he was naive, reflecting his middle-class origins and mainstream American values. Although he had moved freely among the military and political elite of Washington for five years, Hap said he had been overawed by his abrupt introduction in 1941 into the various levels of stratified British society. His experiences there ranged from extended meetings with Prime Minister Winston Churchill to private sessions in Buckingham Palace with King George VI. As the war progressed, he adjusted comfortably and seemed to enjoy interacting with his British Allies, assessing and commenting on them as well as an array of world leaders that included Josef Stalin, Charles de Gaulle, and Chiang Kai-shek. He seemed genuinely surprised at the facts of life in wartime London during his first visit of World War II in 1941, from the rationing of food to the perils of the blackout. Hap's naiveté was little changed by his membership on the JCS and CCS where worldwide issues of strategy were routine, his testimony before Congress in the last quarter century, or repeated close interaction with Allied leaders of the world.

Not surprisingly, Arnold's beliefs mirrored those of the American military officer corps. His values had been shaped, as had the values of most of his contemporaries, in positions of leadership just after the turn of the century. They had been developed in a relatively narrow hierarchical society that was isolated and in some ways different from segments of mainstream America but in other ways mirrored the thinking of many Americans. There were few Negro troops in the US military, reflecting a civilian society where segregation, either de facto or de jure, was accepted; Hap recorded being shocked to see Negro and white males and females caressing and dancing together in a Canadian Army show in September 1944. It is more difficult to understand or explain his 1945 comment of "too many Jews" among the physicians he found in an American-staffed hospital in Europe. If he is judged as prejudiced or bigoted by the standards of the 1990s, it is worth noting that he had many opportunities to expunge these candid statements from his diaries. His sentiments concerning Negroes do not appear different from his military contemporaries. Although, like Arnold, none of his fellow JCS members were southerners, Admiral King was known to use the pejorative "nigger," Marshall wrote of the "unreliability of negro troops . . . unless supported by white officers," and Spaatz "evinced the paternalistic attitude of his rank and station toward blacks." Their biographers have assessed Spaatz and King in terms of both heritage and their environment, Davis writing of Spaatz as "simply a man of his time" and Thomas B. Buell assessing King as "not a racist in the pejorative sense" but reflecting "the prevailing racial prejudices of his generation." Arnold deserves assessment in the same terms.[178]

Arnold's strong nationalistic feelings are honestly reflected in these writings. His dislike of both the British and French had emerged during his two-month visit to those nations as World War I drew to a close. His Anglophobic sentiments were intensified in the three years before Pearl Harbor, when he struggled to prevent the bulk of increased US aircraft production from being sent to Great Britain at the expense of what he considered the necessary AAF buildup. This issue had, in fact, put him in the White House doghouse and threatened to end his military career even if Arnold remained unaware of the degree to which he had lost the president's confidence. During the military/diplomatic conferences of the war, Hap retained a suspicion of British concentration on Mediterranean and Balkan operations, as did General Marshall and Admiral King. Arnold believed such concentration would lessen the efficacy of American airpower operating strategically from English bases. He was vexed because the British insisted that the AAF join the RAF in nighttime bombing operations, a concept in conflict with Arnold's belief in the effectiveness of daylight attack. Some of his later diary entries and actions reflected

White House thinking as well as his own in countering what was perceived as competing British postwar ambitions in the civil aviation realm of using American-produced aircraft furnished without cost to them under Lend-Lease. On the other hand, Arnold strongly admired the RAF's success in the Battle of Britain and was genuinely moved by the courage of the British people as he observed them stoically continuing their routine amid the debris left by the German blitz. A blind spot in his thinking was the failure to appreciate that the British determination and ability to withstand Luftwaffe bombing might also characterize the German citizenry's reaction to AAF and RAF attacks on their country. His anti-British feelings did not prevent him from enjoying a warm friendship with Churchill, however, and an uneven but essentially pleasant relationship with Sir Charles F. A. Portal, his counterpart as head of the RAF.

Arnold's attitude towards the French was in part explained by what he viewed as that nation's limited contributions in fighting the Axis powers and what he and his fellow members of the JCS felt were Gen Charles de Gaulle's unwarranted pretensions. Italy and Italians earned an equal if not larger share of scorn that was clearly recorded in the diaries. He recorded very few comments about the people or military of the two major enemy nations, Germany and Japan. He had very little contact with them except for his visits to the Pacific theater and Germany in the closing days of the war. However, his having witnessed Japanese destruction in 1945 and hearing reports of Japanese atrocities in the Philippines, where he had enjoyed two pleasant tours as a young officer, may well have influenced his attitude toward bombing Japan's home islands.

His friendship and correspondence show a man of breadth beyond flying and beyond the military. He maintained a close relationship with such diverse individuals as Gutzon Borglum of Mount Rushmore fame, Jack Warner and others of the motion picture industry, and Lowell Thomas of radio as well as Theodore von Kármán and other scientists.

There was little vulgarity about the man, either in these diaries or in his extant correspondence, although his use of profanity in small groups was well known. His swearing, although extremely rare in mixed company, was often used either to vent his own frustrations or to urge greater effort from those whose performance was less than desired. There were no women in his life aside from his wife and daughter.

On the first Monday after becoming chief, Arnold found the time to write briefly to his daughter. Without mentioning his new assignment and promotion, which by now were known to her in California, he outlined some of his frustrations about working in the Washington environment. In a semihumorous vein, he indicated that he was glad he did not have "any more troubles than I have" and, in a clear reference to the Woodring-Johnson feuding, was thankful that he didn't "have to associate with politicians after working hours." He explained that his routine was to drive to the office through congested traffic, "may or may not have lunch," and return home after seeing an "endless number of visitors." "It seems that one thing is barely started and then another comes into being."[179] If Arnold seemed discouraged about the demands on his time and energies as assistant to the chief, little could he have appreciated the magnitude of problems he would face in the next seven years as leader of the AAF.

The Air Corps that Arnold assumed command of in September 1938 consisted of approximately 21,000 personnel and 1,792 aircraft, far below the congressionally authorized strength of 2,320 planes. Many of the planes were obsolete, and congressional appropriations were far below what Arnold and others felt was necessary to reach the authorized strength and, more important, procure modern planes.

Among the many challenges faced by Arnold before Pearl Harbor, three appeared more significant and demanding than others. The first of these, emerging within two weeks after he was sworn into his new position, was Arnold's response to Roosevelt's call for increasing the productive capacity of the American aircraft industry. The second and third problems, closely intertwined with the first, involved the allocation of aircraft among a variety of constituencies while building up and expanding the Air Corps to meet the seemingly inevitable prospect of American involvement in the war. Attempts to resolve these three problems continued to be Arnold's main concerns.

Even before Arnold became chief, the international situation was spurring efforts towards military preparedness and expansion in the United States as well as in Great Britain and France. Among the major challenges facing General Arnold during the first six of the 12 overseas visits chronicled in his diaries were to increase American military aircraft production, determine the types and numbers to be produced, and allocate them among the various competing constituencies. Inextricably bound up with these problems was the impetus towards expansion of the Army Air Corps. Arnold welcomed this impetus, but it conflicted with the desire of President Roosevelt, who was influenced by some of his most trusted advisors, to furnish the bulk of the increased American production to Britain and France. In grappling with these difficulties, Arnold found his leadership position threatened and his military future jeopardized. In the final analysis, however, this early impetus was essential in preparing the nation's aircraft industry and the Army's air arm to meet the challenges of war. As the official AAF history has expressed it, "the success of the American aircraft production program during World War II was to a large extent the result of bold prewar action."[180] Arnold, who had narrowly avoided being relieved of his position during this three-year expansion period, had by July 1941 become recognized as the primary military spokesman for American land-based aviation. He had also regained the confidence of FDR, largely as a result of his trip to England in April 1941.

In January 1938, Baron Amaury de La Grange, a French senator, paid a weekend visit to Roosevelt in Washington. De La Grange had crossed the Atlantic in anticipation of purchasing 1,000 American-built aircraft to improve the "lamentable" condition of the French Air Force.[181] He found his old friend in the White House sympathetic to French aims and fearful of German expansion but unable to offer a great deal of assistance. The French senator was discouraged to learn that the US aircraft industry was almost as deficient as the French, saying, "We cannot immediately obtain from the United States planes needed to re-enforce our weak aviation."[182] In spite of his discovery that "American industry . . . was almost nonexistent for war planes," France in May 1938 placed an order for 100 Curtiss-Wright P-36s, the most advanced pursuit aircraft then available. The Air Corps possessed only three of them at the time. That same month, the British ordered 200 Lockheed Hudson transports and 200 North American Harvard trainers to be built in US factories. Both nations were motivated by their admitted deficiencies in military preparedness, which was made more pronounced by Hitler's annexation of Austria that had taken place just two months earlier.[183]

Arnold, protective of the secrets built into the P-36, opposed a French request to fly and evaluate the fighter they had ordered, but the White House overruled him—a harbinger of future difficulties between Roosevelt and Arnold.[184] At the same time, Arnold had to have been pleased that the French government financed, at a cost of $940,000, a new production line for Curtiss-Wright to build the anticipated P-36s. These orders aroused mixed feelings in Arnold, who was well aware that the increase in productive capacity could begin to transform the American military aircraft industry but was also anxious to bring about the much-needed expansion of the AAF.[185]

Arnold's ideological beliefs in the spring of 1938 probably coincided with the uncertain thinking of many Americans caught between the aggressiveness of the totalitarian states abroad and the strains of isolationism at home. Many did not yet view the dictator states with the disdain that would follow the 1938 Munich settlement and later acts of aggression by the totalitarian states. However, many shared Arnold's uncertainty concerning America's proper role in a world increasingly affected by the totalitarian powers. Hap wondered about aiding the British as requested by their purchasing commission that had arrived in May 1938.

> Are we going to show favoritism to Gr. Britain over other countries? Are we going to assume that Gr. Britain is an ally of ours now and will always be an ally? Should we upset existing policies relative to export of our latest aircraft?
>
> Can we, should we, must we show Gr. Britain our latest airplanes such as the B-17, B-15 or the Bell Fighter [P-39]? It (assisting the British) is liable to put us in the position as an aid to certain nations in war by virtue of furnishing munitions and thereby endanger our neutrality.[186]

Secretary of the Treasury Henry Morgenthau, who would later become an ardent proponent of providing the bulk of America's production to the British and the French, expressed similar sentiments when he asked, "How long do we know that Canada and England are going to be our allies?"[187] These sentiments, expressed only four months before the Munich settlement, would undergo considerable revision in the near future.

As these British and French orders for aircraft were being processed, Arnold was well aware of a policy disagreement within the War Department. In the view of many, US military forces were to be used only in a defensive role and the primary agency for protecting the coastline would remain the United States Navy. According to this view, Air Corps planes were to be used primarily in support of Army ground forces. This concept, combined with US geographical isolation, led many in the military hierarchy to prescribe light and medium bombers along with pursuit planes (note the connotation) for the American Army rather than long-range bombers such as the recently procured B-17. Maj Gen Stanley Embick, a nonaviator and the senior officer responsible for Army procurement, expressed the desideratum in a May 1938 memo: "Our national policy contemplates preparation for defense, not aggression. The Military superiority of . . . a B-17 over two or three smaller planes that could be procured with the same funds remains to be established."[188]

Policy guidance from Secretary of War Harry H. Woodring to the chief of the Air Corps on 29 July 1938 was similar. He instructed that "estimates for bombers in Fiscal Year 1940 [must] be restricted to light, medium and attack types." Arnold's belief in strategic bombardment doctrine, although not yet fully developed in his thinking, cautioned him to recommend that the chief of the Air Corps "fight this decision" by the secretary of war.[189] Woodring's interest was in securing funds to build up all elements, not just the air component, of an American Army that many felt had been fiscally starved over the previous two decades by isolationism and the Great Depression. With less than $37 million to spend for aircraft procurement in 1937, the secretary of war opted for more B-18 twin-engine bombers. The shorter-range B-18 was much less expensive than the B-17, each costing $65,000 rather than the $280,000 for a B-17. One officer assigned to the office recalled that Woodring was "interested in numbers only." Arnold, penning his memoirs 11 years later, remembered that the B-17's superiority was a "mystery" that Secretary Woodring never understood.[190]

Feuding between Woodring and Assistant Secretary of War Louis A. Johnson further complicated Arnold's problems. Johnson, more of an internationalist than the secretary, generally was in favor of larger, longer-range aircraft. However, his views were as much determined by his ambition to oppose, dislodge, and succeed Woodring as they were by ideology. Army Chief of Staff Gen Malin Craig, a friend and golfing partner of Arnold, normally supported the secretary's philosophy of smaller aircraft and balanced funding for all Army elements. Throughout these years, Arnold faced the continuing difficulty of advocating and supervising the buildup of airpower while working harmoniously with his superiors, both military and civilian, many of whom did not share his views.[191]

As indicated earlier, the month of September in 1938 marked a significant turning point in Arnold's career. He was sworn in as chief of the Air Corps on the day the historic "peace in our time" Munich pact was signed. Equally important to the Air Corps was the impact the lack of airpower played in compelling Britain and France to concede to Hitler's demands at Munich, particularly as US President Franklin D. Roosevelt interpreted this lack of British and French airpower.

Considerable information had arrived in Washington from various sources on evaluating the strength of the German Luftwaffe, specifically as contrasted with the deficiencies of British and French airpower. Charles Lindbergh, still a credible observer to the White House, had decried to American military attachés in Britain as early as April 1938, that "present conditions and trends" in England seemed "hopelessly behind in military strength in comparison to Germany."[192] This confirmed his prescient assessment earlier that month that the "contrast between an English factory and an American or German factory is ununderstandable. The English simply do not seem to have an equivalent ability along those lines. God!

How they will have to pay for it in the next war."[193] He reported to US Ambassador William C. Bullitt in Paris that "France seems to be in worse shape from an aviation standpoint than I believed." In his view, the French did not possess "enough modern military planes in this country to even put up a show in case of war."[194] A week prior to Munich, just having returned from a three-week trip to several European countries, including Russia, Lindbergh traveled from his home in coastal France to London at the urgent request of Joseph P. Kennedy, the American ambassador in Great Britain. There he lunched with the American diplomat and agreed to put in writing his impressions of the aviation potential of the major European powers. Kennedy emphasized the urgency of the famous aviator's evaluation by cabling this "confidential expression of his [Lindbergh's] personal opinion" to Washington the same day. In the flier's view, "Germany now has the means of destroying London, Paris, and Praha [Prague] if she wishes to do so. England and France together have not enough modern warplanes for effective defense or counterattack. France is in as pitiful condition." There is evidence that Arnold was furnished a copy of Lindbergh's gloomy assessment.[195]

During this same visit to London, the American flier expressed similar views to Squadron Leader John Slessor, then a senior RAF plans officer, and Air Marshal Sir Wilfrid Freeman, who was responsible for RAF development and production. Lindbergh doubted that Britain and France "could win a war now," labeling the German Air Force "the strongest in the world in both quality and quantity, more powerful than the combined air forces of Britain, France, and the United States."[196] In the week before the final Munich settlement, Lindbergh cautioned Slessor that "our only sound policy is to avoid war now at almost any cost." Three days later, the Air Ministry in London urgently cabled the British attaché in Washington for an estimate of the aircraft that could be bought in the United States for delivery to Great Britain within a month.[197]

American Ambassador to France Bullitt expressed similar discouragement. Eleven days before the Munich agreement,

Bullitt reported that, if war broke out, the "superiority of the German and Italian Air Forces was so absolute over the French Air Force that every city in France and every military objective could be destroyed at will."[198] In the midst of the negotiations, Bullitt wrote Roosevelt: "If you have enough airplanes you don't have to go to Berchtesgaden."[199] Only three days after the signing of the pact, Bullitt lunched with French Premier Daladier, who confided that the "single thing which counted today was . . . strengthening the military forces of France especially in the field of air armament." Lacking improvement in the future, "France would be confronted with ultimatums." Bullitt sailed for the United States two days later to report his findings in person. With the wisdom that hindsight always brings, Daladier conceded three days after the agreement that if he'd had "3,000 or 4,000 planes, there would have been no Munich." At least one source claims that at the time of the forced settlement with Hitler, France had "no more than seventeen modern planes."[200]

Lindbergh provided the gloomiest numerical estimate of all when he confided to his diary two days after the Munich settlement, "France did not have a single modern pursuit plane ready for the defense of Paris!"[201] Immediately following the Munich pact, the British Air attaché in Washington cabled home, saying Roosevelt was convinced that their deficiencies in the air had forced the capitulation of Britain and France.[202]

Even before Munich, word from other capitals had brought disheartening news. The president had learned as early as 11 July from Hugh R. Wilson, US Ambassador in Berlin, that "Germany has produced an air arm second to none in numbers and quality of first-line airplanes." Roosevelt, feeling that the report was credible, shared it with Secretary of War Woodring during a 2 September visit to the White House.[203]

FDR had received reports confirming British and French weakness in the air in the summer of 1938 from leading American aircraft manufacturers when they visited factories in Britain, France, and Germany in the summer of 1938. Coming from executives of Glenn L. Martin, Curtiss-Wright, North American Aviation, Bell Aircraft, and Consolidated, all close friends of Arnold, their not altogether disinterested observations could hardly be ignored.[204] Roosevelt's concern over American capabilities increased after hearing Hitler's strident Nuremberg speech on 12 September, more than two weeks before the Munich agreement. As a result, he sent his trusted advisor, Works Progress Administration (WPA) Director Harry Hopkins, to the West Coast to "take a look at the aircraft industry with a view to its expansion for war production." According to Hopkins, "the President was sure we were going to get into war and he believed that air power would win it."[205]

The next week at the regular cabinet meeting, the president shared his thinking about the nature of the next war. According to Secretary of the Interior Harold Ickes, who was present, Roosevelt developed his "theory of tactics if Europe goes to war." Ickes recalled that FDR would "make the war principally one of the air," justifying this on the basis of less money, fewer casualties, and a greater chance of success as contrasted with a "traditional war by land and sea." In the final week before the Munich pact, FDR discussed with his cabinet the "overwhelming preponderance of Germany and Italy in the air."[206]

On 12 October, the respected unofficial advisor Bernard Baruch, having just returned from a European visit where he had met with Pierre Laval and Winston Churchill, stayed overnight in the White House. To FDR he painted a gloomy contrast between American capabilities and what he had observed and been told about conditions in Europe. He insisted that the United States needed to build "at least 50,000 long-range bombers," a figure proposed by FDR later, in May 1940. In October 1938, however, Roosevelt cautioned Baruch that "the nation is not ready yet."[207] The next day, Ambassador Bullitt, having just arrived from France, provided a firsthand account of his discussions with French leaders during and after the Munich crisis. FDR revealed at his press conference on 14 October that he had "sat up last night hearing the European side of things" from Bullitt.[208]

During the first 15 days following the Munich agreement, the president began moving towards preparedness. He called for an increase in the productive capacity of the American military aircraft industry, a response that represented for him at least a changing view of airpower as a military force. FDR's thinking was partially unveiled on 14 October during his regular press conference when he said "new developments" necessitated a "complete restudy of American national defense." Promising to unveil a plan after the first of the year, Roosevelt bantered in his usual friendly terms with the newsmen. Speaking in generalities, he indicated that although a defense study had been in progress "for about a year," it had been "forced to a head" by recent events, clearly suggesting the Munich crisis. Three other actions he took that day reflected the extent of the chief executive's concern; all impacted on Arnold.[209]

Acknowledging the importance that lack of aircraft had played in the recent Munich settlements, the president agreed to Bullitt's recommendation that the French government dispatch Jean Monnet to the United States "to study how the American aircraft industry could best serve France's need." In addition, FDR asked the State Department to study the means by which the arms embargo provisions of the Neutrality Act could be lifted. In instructions that would most closely involve Arnold, the president directed that the War Department begin planning for extensive expansion of the Air Corps.[210] In view of the strong isolationist sentiment in the nation, congressional elections less than a month away, the recent defeat of his Supreme Court reorganization plan in Congress, and the downturn in the nation's economy, these were bold steps by the American leader. Only the national defense assessment, however, was made public.

As no extant documents have been found to support the presidential instructions, it seems logical that the 14 October request to plan for expansion of the Air Corps was made verbally to Assistant Secretary Johnson. In any event, Johnson lost no time in forwarding Roosevelt's desires to the Army chief of staff. That same day, in response to White House direction, Arnold wrote a letter to the leading American aircraft manufacturers, inviting them to recommend ways to increase aircraft production.[211]

As the various agencies began to draw up their responses, FDR departed for an eight-day vacation in Hyde Park. There he met with Ambassador Bullitt, Jean Monnet who had just arrived from France, Harry Hopkins, and Secretary of the Treasury Henry Morgenthau Jr. In these discussions, Roosevelt suggested 15,000 airplanes per year as a goal for the nation, with 12,000 to be produced in government plants, the remaining 3,000 by the aircraft manufacturers. Morgenthau's long association and close relationship with Roosevelt dated from the latter's days as governor of New York. Their close relationship enabled him to urge that the president take the necessary steps "to stop aggression by peaceful means" and "develop an effective program" that would cause other democratic nations to "take heart." His later actions reflect that Morgenthau shared FDR's newfound belief that aircraft were an essential ingredient in American defense preparedness and would be part of any program emanating from the White House.[212]

This proposed request by the American president with its emphasis on airpower was significant in that it became thus far the largest peacetime appeal in two decades by a strong executive for increased military funding. This was in sharp contrast to the institutionally restrained, timid pleas of the military over the previous years. Many who criticized the testimony of the military chiefs before Congress since the end of World War I felt that the services had been content to ask Congress for what they thought the legislators were willing to appropriate rather than what they felt was needed to accomplish their strategic objectives.[213] In defense of their requests for appropriations since the passage of the Air Corps Act of 1926, however, the aviators had requested for the five fiscal years 1928–32 a total of $260.6 million but had received from Congress only $147.2, or 56.5 percent of their expressed needs.[214] FDR's 14 October public press announcement, together with his other, unpublicized, actions on that same day reflected an appreciation by the nation's chief executive that a lack of air assets had played a major role in the Munich capitulation. Not only did he seem to realize, as had the French and British earlier in the year, the inadequacies of the American aircraft industry, but his concept of military force seemed to have been broadened beyond the role of the United

States Navy as the first line of American defense. This concept differed significantly from his recent actions. Only eight months earlier, he had requested a modest $45 million from Congress, $28 million or 62 percent of which was to be spent on the United States Navy. Only $17 million or 38 percent was intended for the Army, and none of the $45 million was planned for the purchase of aircraft.[215] From this point until passage of the military appropriations bill in April 1939, Arnold's primary task was to make preparations for expansion of the Army Air Corps.

As Arnold and his staff began to respond to the president's instructions, Hap worried about the depth of the chief executive's commitment. Circumspect in commenting on his commander in chief, Arnold has left little specific criticism of Roosevelt's changed thinking. However, the aviator was concerned that, like Woodring, FDR's interest was primarily with numbers of aircraft, reflecting his penchant for seeking simple solutions to complex problems, and the publicity attendant to the announcement of any increase in aircraft production. In later months, as the numbers of aircraft continued to increase, Arnold remained concerned that the president failed to appreciate the need for an infrastructure to support the additional planes. Such a buildup would require aircrews, training bases, instructors, maintenance crews, and ground support personnel, along with many other components of a viable military aviation force. As the AAF chief saw it, "The Army Air Forces had to teach the nation [this appeared to include the president and the secretary of war] that large numbers of planes did not in themselves constitute airpower; we had to show the folly of the 'numbers racket.'"[216] This numbers racket phrase was commonly used pejoratively by airmen in this period as they worked to respond to the constantly changing formulae emanating from the civilian leadership. The aviators felt that insufficient attention was being paid to the need for supporting personnel and equipment, stability of their programs, proper allocation of the aircraft among the various claimants, balance among types to be procured, and potential utilization of the aircraft produced. Nevertheless,

Arnold and War Department officials worked quickly following the 14 October direction from the White House.[217]

Five days later, on 19 October, Arnold submitted to the secretary of war a plan for achieving an increase in the number of Air Corps planes to 6,360 by 1944. This was to be done by purchasing 1,000 aircraft each year, an impressive increase given the fact that the Air Corps then possessed only 1,797 of their congressionally authorized fleet of 2,360 aircraft. Clearly, neither Arnold nor Roosevelt could have envisioned the drastically changed circumstances that saw the nation manufacture 294,436 planes from 1941 to 1945.[218]

If Arnold's 19 October proposal appeared modest, the Army chief of staff's reaction illustrated the thinking of many nonaviator Army leaders that would disturb Roosevelt and present problems for Arnold. According to Morgenthau, when Roosevelt's suggested number of 15,000 planes was relayed to Chief of Staff Malin Craig, the chief responded with "What are we going to do with 15,000 planes?" He questioned whom we were going to fight across "three thousand miles of ocean."[219] General Craig's opposition to any large Air Corps increase and his concern for balance within all segments of the underfunded Army was confirmed by his statement to the Bureau of the Budget 10 days after FDR's 14 October call for aircraft expansion. Craig wrote on 24 October that the "defense of the country . . . rests with ground troops" and that other army elements demanded "more immediate attention" than the needs of the Air Corps, given the more costly maintenance and rapid obsolescence of aircraft.[220] Nor was the chief of staff's position an isolated one within the War Department. The new deputy chief of staff, Brig Gen George Marshall, who would later become a strong supporter of the Army air arm and a very close friend of Arnold, felt that an Air Corps expansion to 10,000 combat aircraft was "seriously out of proportion to what was needed."[221] Although many aviators felt these attitudes were a confirmation of the antiaviation bias that had marked Army leaders since World War I, these senior officers were not necessarily anti–Air Corps. They were advocating programs to achieve a balanced Army to be used in a defensive posture, relying more heavily than the aviators desired on the traditional battle-tested branches, which had been equally underfunded and minimally staffed. At the same time, these other Army components, taking advantage of the administration's recently discovered willingness to seek increased Army appropriations, were submitting their estimates of the funding necessary to meet the world's new conditions.[222]

The president's directions levied changing demands on Arnold and other senior Army officers. Only three days after submitting his 19 October plan for a gradual increase to 6,360 planes, Hap responded to a new request from the secretary of war who now proposed an increase in purchases for fiscal year 1941 from the planned 178 planes to 1,178.[223] The day following this 22 October submission, General Craig proposed to the assistant secretary, with Arnold's concurrence, that instead of the 1,000 planes per year outlined by Arnold on 19 October that would bring the inventory up to 6,000 planes by 1944, the increase should be 2,500 planes per year. The next day, 24 October, in response to "verbal orders," Arnold submitted yet another plan, this time suggesting that the aircraft industry could produce 10,000 planes in two years. This rapid changing of requirements, necessitating four different Air Corps submissions within five days, was a harbinger of the demands that would be levied on Arnold and his air planners until 1945.[224]

On 25 October, Arnold attended a meeting at the Treasury Department where WPA director Harry Hopkins reported his findings concerning aircraft manufacturing. He outlined an achievable goal of 35,000 to 40,000 airplanes to be produced per year, with the Air Corps receiving 31,000-36,000 of them once provision was made for the US Navy. Hopkins estimated that a total of 20,000 of these aircraft could be produced by the existing American industry with the remainder to be built in eight to 10 plants that would be constructed by the government and "operated by the War Department." These proposed numbers were staggering to an Air Corps having a current total inventory of 1,797 planes of which 351 were or shortly would be obsolete. Further, these planes on hand had been obtained painstakingly over the past two decades through an average acquisition of 300 per year.[225]

On receipt of this information, Roosevelt appointed a committee to recommend ways to increase aircraft production. This would be the first of many different groups appointed by the president in the next several years, all with the aim of giving Roosevelt close control of production and allocation. This group consisted of Assistant Secretary of War Louis Johnson, Assistant Secretary of the Navy Charles Edison, and Deputy Administrator of WPA Aubrey Williams. It seems logical that Arnold's recommendations to Johnson on the day before the committee was named, estimating that the aircraft industry "could produce 10,000 planes in approximately 2 years," had been provided to the new group.[226] Moving quickly, they reported to the White House three days later on 28 October with estimates not far from those made by Arnold on 24 October. The committee suggested that the current aircraft industry could raise its current output fourfold from 2,600 to 11,000 airplanes per year. When supplemented with the 20,000 aircraft that could be produced in the proposed government-built plants, the total could reach 30,000 within three years. This would necessitate temporarily freezing aircraft designs and increasing the number of aircraft workers from the current single shift to three.[227]

The frenetic activity associated with determining aircraft production goals and submitting funding proposals for various components of the Army seemed to have lessened temporarily during the next several weeks, at least as far as any direction from the White House or the War Department's civilian leaders. Part of the explanation may have been their preoccupation with political concerns dominated by the congressional midterm elections held on 8 November and the resulting diminution of the Democratic majorities in the Congress. This hiatus did nothing to deter speculation in the press over the administration's intentions for increased aircraft production and funds for the Army. Newspapers reported that the president was preparing to ask Congress for a program involving "a vast air fleet" that would triple the current 1935 Air Corps Baker Board ceiling and, along with other equipment to be requested for the Army, cost more than $300 million.[228]

Two days after the congressional elections of 8 November, probably in response to a request from the assistant secretary of war, Arnold submitted two memos containing new estimates of the numbers of aircraft necessary for the Air Corps and suggesting means of acquiring them. In the first, he proposed that a two-year objective be established to reach a total of 7,000 aircraft, including the almost 2,000 already on hand. Showing concern with the lack of a supporting infrastructure along with the "numbers racket" of airplanes that seemed to have dominated administration thinking in the previous month, Hap recommended that one-half of the 7,000 planes be training aircraft and the remaining 3,500 combat types. Cognizant of the limited number of available trained personnel to fly and maintain 7,000 airplanes, as well as the cost of operating them, Hap suggested that one-third of them be placed in reserve. Relying on the responses from the aircraft manufacturers to whom he had written on 14 October seeking suggestions to increase aircraft production, Arnold's memo estimated that the desired 5,000 aircraft could be obtained realistically within a two-year time frame, given maximum use of existing plants, many of which currently were underutilized or dormant.[229] In a separate memo of his "personal ideas" submitted to Johnson the same day, Hap suggested that the White House convene a "special council" of the military, State Department, and industry to "determine the size of each force." He offered estimates of the size of the major European air forces, indicating that Germany possessed "2,000 bombers with a range of 3,300 miles" and the potential of crossing the Atlantic from West African bases.[230]

Two days after Hap's 10 November memos to Johnson, Roosevelt met with Morgenthau, Hopkins, and Johnson, a newly empowered group becoming an important source of advice on aircraft production. In this meeting, FDR approved Harry Hopkins' suggestion of erecting eight to 10 factories with WPA funds. Two of these factories were to immediately begin production of 2,000 combat planes annually, the other plants to be held in reserve. To Morgenthau's distress, Roosevelt now established 10,000 planes per year as the goal. The secretary lamented, "Every time I have talked to the

President the number he has in mind has become less." In confirmation that Hap's 10 November memo to Johnson had made its way to the White House, the group discussed how "in the shortest space of time" Arnold's goal of 5,000 new planes for the Air Corps could be obtained.[231]

While the Army and the Air Corps were engaged in responding to White House and assistant secretary of war initiatives for planning an increase in their forces, events around the world continued to provide disturbing news. The Japanese had occupied Hangchou in late October, gaining control of China's last major port and forcing the Chiang Kai-shek government upriver to distant Chungking. A week later, Japan announced its "new order" for Asia by economically uniting Manchukuo and China with Japan. The following day, they announced that the Nine Power Treaty guaranteeing Chinese territory integrity was now obsolete. At the same time in Europe, Hitler oversaw the further dismemberment of Czechoslovakia by ceding 12,000 square miles of territory containing more than a million pre-Munich Czech citizens to Hungary. In retaliation for the killing of a German diplomat in Paris, the Nazis unleashed their most blatant anti-Semitic action thus far during the *Kristallnacht*, or Crystal Night, of 9-10 November, smashing and looting Jewish establishments in Germany. Roosevelt reacted to this latest travesty by recalling the US Ambassador on 14 November.

With midterm congressional elections behind him and faced with the deteriorating international situation, Roosevelt held the White House meeting that Arnold has labeled the "Magna Charta" of the Air Corps, and an official historian has termed "momentous," on the day that he suspended US diplomatic representation in Germany. Another author has written that the convening of this group "marked a turning point in the history of national defense."[232] Hap was among the dozen or so officials present, including Hopkins, Johnson, Morgenthau and others from the Treasury Department, as well as Army Chief of Staff Malin Craig who brought along his new deputy, George Marshall. It seems revealing that no representative of the US Navy had been invited. Not unusual in such gatherings, the president did most of the talking. Morgenthau's diary and Arnold's fragmentary account of the discussion jotted on the back of an envelope are the only extant accounts of this important gathering. It appeared clear from what transpired that much of the substance of what had been furnished to Assistant Secretary of War Johnson by Arnold and his staff in the past several days had reached the oval office. The suggestion by Arnold on 10 November for a "special council," along with FDR's increasing concern over international events, probably contributed to the calling of the meeting.[233]

In directing that the War Department prepare a plan for providing 10,000 planes per year over a two-year period, of which 2,500 would be trainers, 3,750 would be combat aircraft, and another 3,750 would be in reserve, the president was using figures similar to those submitted earlier by Arnold. Roosevelt further specified that 8,000 should come from the current aircraft manufacturers and the remaining 2,000 from plants erected with government funds, an allocation very similar to that recommended by Arnold in his memos to Johnson four days earlier. FDR emphasized the problems of the Air Corps, insisting that this branch was "weakest of all the United States armed forces" and contrasted the strength of other nations' air forces using estimates very close to those furnished by Hap. Conceding political realities, the president told the group that although there was a need for an Air Corps of 20,000 planes and an annual productive capability of 24,000 aircraft, he felt that Congress would appropriate funds for only half of those numbers. Consequently, he directed that the Air Corps provide an "acceptable" program for him to submit to the legislature.[234]

Other instructions from FDR included plans for aircraft manufacturers to meet in Washington where they were to learn that the proposed enhanced program would not be based on competition among them but instead rely on fixed fees providing an 8–10 percent return over costs, a welcome practice that essentially was continued throughout the war.[235] The president expressed dissatisfaction with the War Department's emphasis on a "balanced" force, insisting that we needed a "huge air force so that we do not need to have a huge army to follow that air force." Sending a large army abroad, the president said, was "undesirable and politically out of the question." FDR further announced that "long-range bombing is now the duty of the Army," since it has the responsibility of keeping "anyone from landing in North or South America," which he insisted was now a "possibility."[236]

One scholar has written that during the meeting the "president's whole emphasis was upon airplanes. There was none whatever on an air force, a much larger thing." Roosevelt left no doubt as to the importance he had placed on airplanes when he told reporters at the next day's press conference that the discussion "was confined almost entirely to the problem of aircraft."[237]

In spite of FDR's emphasis, Johnson's directive the next day to the Army chief of staff contained instructions far broader than airplanes. The budget the assistant secretary requested for the next two years was to include 10,000 aircraft for the Air Corps with one-half of them remaining in storage. Additionally, seven government-constructed factories capable of annually producing 14,000 airplanes were to be provided along with supporting army services and supplies. Johnson further expanded the presidential directive to include equipping government arsenals, stockpiling critical raw materials, and other activities considerably beyond that of aircraft procurement and maintenance.[238] These actions by Johnson and the Army chief of staff, designed to achieve funding for a "balanced" Army, conflicted with both the White House's more narrow emphasis on increasing the numbers of aircraft and contrasted with Arnold's desire for increased numbers of planes with sufficient personnel and logistical support. These differences were to test Arnold's skill and tact as well as threaten his future.

The day following the 14 November meeting with the president, Hap provided drafts of letters for Johnson's signature to 14 of the major aircraft and engine manufacturers, inviting them to a "secret" conference to be held in Washington six days later.[239] Hap's specific instructions from the War Department in response to the 14 November White House meeting reached him on 17 November with the caveat that there was "no time for normal General Staff procedure. Speed is essential and your efforts should be informal." Other Army staff agencies were ordered to assist Arnold since the estimates had to be processed through the Bureau of the Budget in time for inclusion in the president's message to Congress in early 1939. Permitted to bring in six additional Air Corps executive officers to assist in devising the estimates, Arnold chose trusted aviators, all of whom became general officers during the war.[240] On 17 November, the same day Arnold received his implementing instructions from the chief of staff, he provided guidance for Lt Col Carl A. "Tooey" Spaatz, one of his new executive assistants. In what he termed his "Fundamental Principles of Aircraft Procurement," Hap ordered plans for obtaining 10,000 airplanes in two years, three-fourths of them to be produced by existing manufacturers. Additionally, Arnold advised Spaatz that the desired Air Corps plan should reflect "drastic economies" so as "not to inflate [the] budget." These were to affect everything from cutting flying hours "to the bone" to curtailing cross-country flights and economizing on building construction. All of this was to be done "quietly, no publicity for any phase of this."[241]

Army's response to Roosevelt's 14 November instructions was sent to the White House on 1 December. Submitted by Chief of Staff Malin Craig, it proposed expenditures of $2 billion above the already submitted budget for fiscal 1940. More than one-half of the money would be required to increase and support an Air Corps of 10,000 planes while actively operating only one-half that number. However, the other $815 million would be used for equipping and supporting other elements of an Army that was to be increased by more than 90,000 men.[242]

The president reacted testily to the Army memo in a White House meeting on 10 December, resulting in a second Army response to the White House on 17 December. In a revealing "justification" called the Two-Year Augmentation Plan, the Army planners insisted that their earlier 1 December proposals constituted an "indivisible whole" that defied logical separation since air forces required ground protection for their bases. Seeming almost defiant of Roosevelt's 14 November instructions and his negative reaction to their 1 December proposals, the memo further argued that their program "looked forward toward a balanced Army." It concluded boldly that "Airplanes will not impress foreign leaders and their General Staffs" and that "the ultimate defense of our own territory rests with the ground forces." No real concessions were made to Roosevelt's criticism of their 1 December submission or his concern expressed on 10 December. Instead, the Army, in attempting to head off any possible White House changes, insisted that "Weakness in any major part of this structure may cause the whole to collapse."[243]

Arnold's and the Air Corps' role in this justification does not seem able to be precisely determined. Three days earlier, however, Arnold had submitted drafts of five bills providing for 10,000 planes and other Air Corps improvements.[244] He would have been involved in the portion of the War Department justification calling for 10,000 planes, including 5,600 combat aircraft and 3,750 trainers. Convinced that personnel must be obtained to fly and maintain the craft, Arnold recommended increasing the Corps' strength to 73,000 enlisted men and almost 10,000 officers and flying cadets, a nearly fourfold increase in personnel since he became chief 60 days earlier.[245]

Not surprisingly, the president was displeased with the Army's justification. On the day of its submission, FDR placed eager Treasury Secretary Morgenthau in charge of all munitions purchases, including aircraft. That same day, he authorized the Treasury Department to negotiate with Jean Monnet, who had just arrived from France with the hope of purchasing 1,000 American aircraft for delivery within the next seven months.[246] By these two actions, the Treasury Department became the major, and at times the only, empowered voice outside the White House in determining aircraft production and allocation. To what extent the Army's seeming lack of cooperation and near defiance of FDR's 14 November instructions, particularly as explained in their justification of 17 December, contributed to the War Department, the Air Corps, and Arnold being relegated to spectator roles in this vital area cannot be determined. It would be almost three years before the Army gained a major voice in aircraft production and allocation, earned in many ways because of Arnold's later success at the White House. None of the Army contributors to the 17 December justification, including Arnold if he had been involved, should have been surprised when the White House turned to what was viewed as the more agreeable and willing Treasury Department to implement presidential policies.

After receiving the Army's justification, the president articulated his continuing dissatisfaction with the Army's proposals in a gathering of War Department officials convened in the White House on 21 December. He was no more pleased with the 17 December justification than he had been with the original 1 December submission. He impatiently insisted that, although he had planned to seek congressional funding of $500 million for aircraft, "he was being offered everything except planes." Reflecting his thinking that aircraft were to play primarily a symbolic role, he told those present that he could not "influence Hitler with barracks, runways, and schools for mechanics." The Army chief of staff and others recalled that the dialogue became emphatic and "came close to table pounding," but resulted in a "thorough and careful discussion."[247] Whether Arnold was present is not certain, but he had to have been somewhat satisfied that FDR agreed to request $300 million from Congress for Air Corps expansion. Allocation of $120 million of this for personnel, air bases, and items of support, with the remaining $180 million for procurement of planes, appeared to validate Arnold's insistence on a balanced Air Corps consisting of more than aircraft. The $180 million for procurement was to purchase 1,593 combat planes and 1,424 trainers, which would provide 5,500 aircraft by the end of 1940.[248] This figure of 3,000 new aircraft for the Air Corps remained the number FDR requested in his special message on national defense submitted to Congress on 12 January 1939.

The next day, Arnold reported satisfaction with the number of planes requested and praised the $300 million allocation as "sound and economical." He said it would provide for a "well-rounded air defense," which he felt would not have been possible had the entire amount been committed to aircraft procurement as FDR had originally desired.[249]

In the midst of the frenzy of submitting the numerous plans and legislative bills, Hap found time to think beyond the near term to the future, a characteristic increasingly found in the otherwise frenetic airman. As the Air Corps began to respond to Roosevelt's 14 November instructions, Hap showed considerable foresight as well as knowledge of past problems, which he expressed in a memo four days later. He conceded the urgency of responding to the president and directed Colonel Spaatz to do some "deep thinking" about the problem. Hap wanted to know how productive capacity could be expanded to meet immediate mobilization needs yet retain sufficient orders to maintain a viable aircraft industry after the two-year mobilization program had been completed. "Somehow we must find a way to lick that problem."[250] Unfortunately, the advent of World War II resolved the issue.

Long-term difficulties were created for Arnold and the Air Corps by FDR's 17 December directive that allowed responsibility for purchasing aircraft and munitions to accrue to the Treasury Department. Rear Adm Christian Peoples headed Treasury's Procurement Division, the section primarily involved in these matters. Admiral Peoples was assisted by Capt Harry E. Collins who, like Peoples, was a retired naval officer. These men maintained close contact with the Navy Department and its needs. Since the bulk of the airplanes to be produced were types generally not in significant demand by the US Navy, Peoples and Collins were more than eager to assist Monnet and others in their search for American aircraft. As indicated earlier, Arnold had recommended in March 1938 that France's leading test pilot not be allowed to test fly the P-36 but had been overruled by FDR. During the week that the Munich deliberations were proceeding, the president readily secured Navy cooperation to allow visiting French representatives to test fly Navy planes. Monnet met with Collins, who would replace Admiral Peoples as chief of the Procurement Division immediately following Munich. Collins arranged for Monnet to meet with Captains John H. Towers and Sydney M. Kraus, senior officers in the Navy's Bureau of Aeronautics, who provided estimates of costs and quantities of planes that would be available to France. This close relationship between the Procurement Division's retired naval officers and the active duty captains worked to the benefit of Britain and France. It also served to enhance the Treasury Department's ambition to retain bureaucratic control. Morgenthau not only denigrated other cabinet officials and agencies, but pointed out to the White House the seeming disparity between the immediate cooperation given by the Treasury and Navy Departments on the one hand and the ponderous reluctance of the Army on the other. Perhaps not surprising, very few naval officers hesitated to enhance their standing with the White House at the expense of Army aviation.[251]

In the week that the Army submitted its justification for a balanced force and saw Roosevelt turn to the Treasury Department for overseeing the problems of aircraft allocation, the French purchasing commission arrived back in Washington. Led again by Jean Monnet, the commission sensed that the determining voice in aircraft production and distribution was the Treasury Department's Procurement Division and immediately began to negotiate there, even though most of the aircraft sought by the French remained those developed for the US Army. Arnold was legitimately incensed when, without any communication with him, the retired naval officers in the Procurement Division arranged meetings between the French commission, active duty US naval officers, and aircraft manufacturers. All again offered considerable data and assistance about the types, specifications, and availability of aircraft that might be purchased by the French. Included were details about three Army aircraft in the experimental stage and not yet in production or releasable for foreign assessment or sale.[252] Army regulations prevented the release of any military combat aircraft to a foreign nation until the military had taken delivery of the second production model and forbade demonstration flights by foreign observers. Since any aircraft were destined to be used in combat if necessary, the French wanted to be certain that those considered were the most recent models and included the latest technology and performance capabilities. On the other hand, some of these improvements were not widely known and Arnold was anxious to protect them as much as possible, hence Hap and the War Department's reluctance to grant permission to examine and fly the planes. Arnold had suspicions that the French, who had been permitted against his recommendations to test fly American planes in the spring of 1938 but then failed to purchase the craft, might be on a "fishing expedition" to learn the latest improvements.[253]

Knowing it would take presidential action to get permission for the French to fully assess the craft, Morgenthau went immediately to the White House. His diary recorded him disingenuously telling the president that, although the issue of the French examining the aircraft was entirely out of his line, he was doing this "because you want me to do it."[254] He secured FDR's assent and written direction, drafted by Captain Kraus of the US Navy's Bureau of Aeronautics, that "every consistent facility for inspecting and flying the planes involved" be provided. The aircraft to be assessed were the Curtiss P-40, the Martin 167, and the Douglas DB-7, the latter destined to become the A-20.[255] On the advice of his staff, Arnold was willing to release the P-40 and Martin 167 for evaluation but was reluctant to release the DB-7 since it contained "still valuable military secrets." Additionally, any large French order would delay the fulfillment of the planned 5,500-plane Air Corps expansion program. The fact that he felt the French had negotiated with Navy and Treasury officials without his knowledge did not endear the French mission to Arnold.[256]

Although Arnold protested in his memoirs that the White House accused him of at least "dragging his feet," this was an accurate description of Hap's attitude and actions regarding the French purchasing mission. The Air Corps first delayed action on the French request until they evaluated the impact of potential French orders on production schedules and then Hap, possibly in a moment of pique, ordered all contact ceased with the French mission.[257] The French complained to the White House about the delay through Ambassador Bullitt and, in a White House meeting on 16 January where Arnold was present, FDR strongly reiterated his desire that the French be permitted to fly the DB-7. Morgenthau went so far as to draft memos that Roosevelt signed to the secretaries of the Army, Navy, and Treasury, employing the clear language of "you are directed" to release the aircraft for assessment. The same day the signed directive reached him, Arnold obediently wired Maj K. B. Wolfe, the Air Corps plant representative at the Douglas factory in Santa Monica, California, to allow the French mission to examine and fly the DB-7 "less its secret accessories."[258]

Four days later, during a test flight with French Air Force captain Paul Chemidlin in the rear, the DB-7 crashed. Douglas' civilian test pilot, who had been miffed by French criticism of the airplane after an earlier performance, wanted to "make the Frenchman eat his words, or in other words, to give the Frenchman a ride."[259] At low altitude and with one of its two engines feathered, the pilot snap-rolled the DB-7, went into a spin, and crashed. The pilot ejected at 200 feet but his chute did not open. The Douglas company clumsily tried to identify Chemidlin, who survived the crash, as a mechanic. This effort failed, however, and it was later revealed that a French Air Force officer was flying in "the country's most modern light bomber."[260]

The timing of the crash could not have been worse for the administration, occurring as it did during the Senate Military Affairs Committee hearings on FDR's rearmament program that the White House had announced three weeks earlier. In his 12 January message to Congress, FDR had called for a revision of the Neutrality Act that currently forbade the sale of arms and munitions, including airplanes, to any nation at war. The next day, his submitted budget called for the unheard-of peacetime sum of $1.3 billion for defense. This budget request was followed the next week by a request for a $500 million supplemental appropriation to improve the "utterly inadequate" deficiencies of the nation's military. These submissions included the procurement of 565 airplanes.[261] The isolationists in the Senate saw in these requests not only an America being armed for war but a suspicion that the administration was willing, in violation of the spirit of the Neutrality Acts, to furnish some of the aircraft being requested by European nations should war develop. They seemed partly mollified when General Craig assured them in testimony three days before the crash that the War Department would have the final say on disposition of American aircraft to other nations. On the day of the accident, Arnold testified before the Senate Armed Services Committee that he was satisfied with the presidential request for a 5,500-airplane Air Corps program that would provide planes and supporting personnel. Hap assured the committee that he could not "see any need at this time for anything more."[262]

In the hearings that followed the crash, the isolationist senators sought to embarrass the administration by asking for an explanation of why foreign military officers were flying in the latest American aircraft. They wanted to know who had authorized this foreign pilot's flight in a US aircraft.[263] Arnold responded that he had allowed the flight at the behest of the "Secretary of the Treasury and by direction of the Secretary of War." As Arnold recalled, this elicited the question of "Who is running your Air Force, the Secretary of the Treasury or the Secretary of War?"[264] Led by Roosevelt, administration responses over the next week sought to defuse the situation. They explained that the DB-7 was not an Air Corps aircraft, but one that belonged to the manufacturer who could attempt to sell it where possible. Additionally, FDR and others stressed that orders resulting from the testing of American products could result in employing US workers in plants that were underused, citing Pratt and Whitney's recent layoff of 1,500 men. The handling of any possible purchase by the Treasury Department's Procurement Division was touted as "normal." The announcement at the end of the week that France had purchased 555 American airplanes and that US production capacity had expanded to 1,500 aircraft per year was welcome news in the nation and in the White House.[265]

To Arnold, however, the results were not encouraging. Although the record is not clear, Hap's recollection in his autobiography that he was chastised by FDR and threatened with exile to Guam over his testimony and actions in this incident appears to be incorrect. The chastisement and threat of exile appears to have occurred in association with problems that arose the next year. Nevertheless, Arnold's bitterness over the increased role of the Treasury Department appeared in his memoirs a decade later as he recalled events following the DB-

7 crash. There, he wrote that the "responsibility for building up an Army Air Force was not that of the Secretary of the Treasury. He might give away, sell or what-have-you, every plane produced . . . and would lose nothing by it." The responsibility was Arnold's, he felt, based on obligations he had "to Congress, the President, to the people of the United States." It required planning that could not be done "with a hit-and-miss policy that permitted the Secretary of the Treasury to give away to the French and English whatever he desired."[266]

Dominance by the Treasury Department to the detriment of the War Department appeared logical to the administration, particularly in view of what was perceived in the White House as the reluctance of Arnold and the War Department to accede to presidential wishes. Also, administration officials viewed the Secretary of the Treasury and his department as concerned with broader matters than Arnold and his professional military colleagues. Secretary Morgenthau, considerably influenced by the anti-Semitic and other ideological excesses of the potential enemy nations, was also influenced by American public opinion. Unemployment in the United States was still disappointingly high, and the financial benefit of foreign aircraft orders was welcomed enthusiastically. Among these and other considerations was the isolationist opposition to any large-scale American armament. It is difficult to escape the conclusion, however, that Morgenthau's major concern was the desire for bureaucratic dominance coupled with currying presidential favor. Most revealing are Morgenthau's "triple confidential" comments to his staff a year later on the return of Harry Hopkins, in many ways viewed then as a major competitor for presidential favor. Hopkins had just returned in February 1941 from a six-week trip to England, bringing with him a list of Britain's most needed material that had been devised in conjunction with Churchill. Morgenthau lamented to his staff, "You know this thing of going direct from Churchill to Hopkins to the President isn't so hot. I don't like it. I'm just not going to let anybody spoil the excellent organization and relationship we have here. I just won't let them do it. We've worked together for a long time and nobody is going to come in and spoil it." The Treasury Secretary's Hamiltonian view of himself and his agency as the *primus inter pares* among cabinet departments explains many of his actions. He was often found conveying to the White House with some satisfaction, if not glee, his agency's seemingly national, international, political, and humanitarian concerns while denigrating the War Department leadership, civilian and military, as parochial, jealous, and unresponsive.[267]

Arnold, although not oblivious to politics or bureaucratic infighting, attempted to concentrate on his primary responsibility for achieving and maintaining Air Corps readiness for combat, leaving national politics external to the War Department to others. Maintaining this attitude remained difficult for Arnold since the Treasury Department operated with White House approval as the major controlling authority about how many and even what types of aircraft eventually accrued to the Air Corps for the next two years. Arnold recalled later that he was "taboo" in the White House, where he was "not wanted . . . during the conferences that determined foreign policies, the future of our Army and Navy, and what to me was far [more] important, of the Air Force."[268] Unlike Morgenthau, Hap had no direct access to the White House during this period. His ideas were filtered through his superiors, the Army chief of staff and the secretary of war, who were concerned with achieving a balance between the expensive Air Corps and the other branches of the Army. Neither the continual bickering in the "holy show" between Woodring and Johnson nor the seeming reluctance of Arnold and Army Chief of Staff Craig to cooperate inspired any significant presidential confidence in either the War Department or Arnold in this period.

If Morgenthau confided his gloating and concerns to what was then the privacy of his diary, Arnold was still peeved over the situation when he penned his memoirs eight years later. Circumspect in recalling the period, particularly concerning those individuals who caused him problems and were still living at the time of his writing, Arnold clearly had Morgenthau in mind when he wrote about events of 1940: "It was the rosy dream of some Americans that we could save the world and ourselves by sending all our weapons abroad for other men to fight with. If this priority thus deprived our own air power of even its foundation stones, certain people seemed to take the view that it was just too bad."[269]

Arnold also was faced with ensuring an orderly and coordinated growth of the Air Corps consistent with the strategic thinking of the period, which dictated the primary use of American military power in a defensive posture to protect the nation, the Western Hemisphere, and, if possible, our few outlying possessions. It is difficult to fathom whether Arnold and the other leaders really believed their own rhetoric as they articulated in public the need for an expanded military for defensive purposes. Although unpredictable at the time, it is paradoxical that the Air Corps emerging in this period, which was continually trumpeted to Congress, the press, and the public as a defensive force, would be used almost completely in a strategic, offensive mode in World War II. The tasks charged to Arnold would have been daunting even if he had enjoyed more sovereignty and the confidence of his commander in chief.

Arnold's exile from the White House did not deter him from attempting to prepare the Air Corps, in the seven months before World War II broke out in Europe, for whatever might be in the offing. A fortunate event for Hap and the Air Corps saw Brig Gen George Marshall assigned to the War Department within the month that Arnold became chief in 1938. Almost immediately, Marshall began an eight-day tour of Air Corps installations under the tutelage of Maj Gen Frank Andrews, CG GHQAF. The trip had to have been done with the knowledge if not the consent of Arnold and Westover, as was Marshall's invitation to address the graduating class at the Air Corps Tactical School. There, he stressed the need for expansion of all branches of the Army, told the students that no single branch could win a modern war, and appeared to dissent from the school's emphasis on strategic bombardment. Nevertheless, many aviators including Arnold viewed Marshall's willingness to visit Air Corps bases and become familiar with their problems as a welcome contrast to the attitudes of many senior General Staff officers over the past decade. Marshall's choice of Frank Andrews as the Army G-3, a position never previously held by an aviator, was viewed as another positive sign among airmen.[270] Arnold and Army aviators were further encouraged by FDR's announcement that Marshall would succeed Malin Craig as the Army chief of staff on the latter's formal 1 September 1939 retirement. Although Hap retained gratitude for the support and friendship of departing Gen Malin Craig, Marshall would prove to be a strong but not uncritical friend and supporter of Arnold and the growing air arm of the United States Army.

The issue of expanding the Air Corps was not readily solved, although the president requested and Congress authorized appropriation of funds in April 1939 for 5,500 airplanes. Nor would it have been readily solved even if there had not been other claimants for the still limited productive capacity of the American aircraft industry. Unfortunately, Arnold's earlier experiences with similar problems from his World War I days appeared to be of little help at the moment. Hap's efforts were made somewhat easier, however, by the long, friendly relationship he enjoyed with most of the leaders of the major aircraft corporations, many dating from World War I. Reuben Fleet, now the chief executive of Consolidated Aircraft, had shared a stateroom with Arnold en route to and returning from Europe in 1918. Burdette Wright of Curtiss-Wright had served in uniform with Arnold during the war and most of the decade of the 1920s, and Arnold's second son Bruce would marry Donald Douglas' daughter on the former's graduation from West Point. Arnold had known and been friendly with Douglas, Larry Bell, and Glenn Martin for many years. These personal relationships and resulting mutual trust and understanding were important in Arnold's dealings with these leaders in the following six years.

Another problem for Arnold included reorganizing the structure of the Air Corps consistent with its projected expansion and use while appreciating and controlling demands by some of his close friends, a few in Congress, and some of the press to strike now for complete independence for the Air Corps. The GHQAF, which had been created in 1935, had not worked satisfactorily in the view of many of those involved. Now, given the need to expand the Air Corps and with the increasing possibility of dangerous deployments on the horizon, Hap effected a change that made the CG and the GHQAF responsible to the Air Corps chief beginning in March 1939. Some aviators who had viewed the creation of GHQAF in 1935 as a step forward saw the new alignment as a step backwards. Some even criticized it as a power grab on Arnold's part. Yet if the administration's proposed expansion was to be implemented and if preliminary planning was underway for wartime deployment of the Air Corps, reuniting the planning and operating segments of the Corps had merit. The move had been studied, recommended, and approved in the summer of 1938, months before Westover's fatal crash. The new structure did not last long, however, as rapid changes in the next two years revealed the inadequacies of even this arrangement.[271]

Arnold, increasingly concerned with the need for planning, understood that facts and reasonable assumptions were necessary ingredients for increased aircraft production. Consequently, in July 1939, he convened a conference of the leading aircraft manufacturers in Washington in the name of Assistant Secretary Johnson. If increasing demands were to be made on US manufacturers by the Air Corps as well as foreign orders, it seemed logical to Arnold that the specific productive capacities of the companies be identified. This would seem particularly important in view of the assessment by Assistant Secretary of War Johnson's planning staff in November 1938 that the productive capacity of the American aircraft industry was unknown.[272] Although no precise figures were released at this July conference, Arnold asked the manufacturers to submit specific data as to their capabilities, including such important planning factors as floor space, numbers of workers, machine tool inventories, and cost estimates for operating the facilities. Arnold sought to allay the manufacturers' fears about excessive government control, particularly concerning reports in the press about government-owned aircraft plants. He told them they were going to "write . . . [their] own ticket."[273] Other relevant topics included the problems of multiple shifts of workers, subcontracting, and how to allocate educational orders. Another result of the meeting was the beginning of a search for a meaningful standard measurement of productivity, an important planning tool that would be achieved later.[274]

Although acquiring raw materials and machine tools, hiring engineers and workers, expanding or creating floor space, and conducting research and development, were being undertaken by the aircraft companies, there remained in their minds the nagging question of how long the expansion would last. Although most observers, including Arnold, agreed that much of the world appeared headed for war (which broke out in Europe within 60 days), the manufacturers were concerned about expanding their capacity. They were being asked to meet European orders, provide for peacetime US needs, and planning for possible expansion to support American involvement in any conflict. Since the average lead time from beginning development of a new aircraft to its successful flight-testing and acceptance by the user had been five years in the decade of the thirties, Arnold, foreign buyers, and the aircraft companies were also concerned about how quickly new products could be delivered. Other important considerations included the US constitutional limitation on appropriating funds for the military to no more than two years. The manufacturers wondered how long any European or US Air Corps purchasers would remain viable customers, given the vicissitudes of changing political leadership and/or the fortunes of war. Many of the aircraft executives had vivid memories of vacant factories, and a trade magazine cautioned against their being stampeded into providing unneeded capacity. Arnold pretended no comprehensive answers to these dilemmas, but he increasingly showed they were being considered. He had enjoined his plans section, following the White House 14 November meeting, to do some "deep thinking" about many of them.[275] Very few would have dared predict the overwhelming demand for American-manufactured aircraft that would continue for more than six years after the congressionally authorized expansion to 5,500 Air Corps airplanes in May 1939.

When production began, Arnold and the aircraft manufacturers had difficulty in sorting out the changing priorities for delivery, generally determined by FDR and Morgenthau without significant input from Arnold or the War Department. As large numbers of a model were produced, the unit cost was lowered proportionally and the Air Corps, in receiving delivery later than European nations, was able to take advantage of this saving as well as the financing that had been provided by Britain and France for plant expansion. The later delivery, whose benefits Arnold came to appreciate, was formalized in a more liberalized release policy to Britain of most Air Corps aircraft in March 1940.[276] This permitted the United States to be the beneficiary of refinements and the increased performance of aircraft provided by foreign orders, particularly after the European war began in September 1939. Early but limited combat experience there demonstrated the need for improvements such as heavier armor, better superchargers, more effective offensive armament, and self-sealing gasoline tanks, most of which were incorporated into the production lines to the advantage of later Air Corps models. Other questions that should have been resolved primarily between the manufacturers and the Air Corps were made difficult by the Treasury Department's continuing proprietary interest in controlling the process, which included a general insistence on releasing otherwise secret devices developed by US sources. This procedure was an issue as late as Pearl Harbor, when some of the most important of these devices—such as the Norden bombsight—were not made available to foreign purchasers but were being installed on American models of certain aircraft.

Even though seemingly denied a major voice in aircraft allocation, Arnold and his staff wasted little time in placing orders for aircraft once the April 1939 authorization and appropriation for an Air Corps of 5,550 planes was approved by Congress. The result was that on the outbreak of war in Europe on 1 September, 11 months after Arnold had been elevated to chief, the Air Corps had on hand approximately 2,400 planes, probably none of them resulting from the April appropriation. However, the April legislation had resulted in 1,178 planes ordered but not yet delivered, "1,291 on contracts currently under consideration, 1,143 in competitions still being evaluated, and 186 on options that could be exercised."[277] In the unlikely event that all resulted in flyable planes, they would total 6,198 aircraft, a far cry from the 1,792 on hand when Arnold became chief. One disappointing aspect of these figures was that the Air Corps still possessed only the 12 B-17s that had been acquired for testing in 1937. Also, far too many of those 2,400 aircraft on flight lines and in Air Corps hangars were B-18, P-35, P-36, and A-17 aircraft whose obsolescence would invalidate their use in the war that developed. Some, however, remained valuable training aircraft. An important challenge in Arnold's mind, and one that had concerned him since the White House began announcing goals for aircraft production and procurement in what he termed the "numbers racket," was a lack of trained personnel to fly and maintain the planes. When war broke out in Europe, the GHQAF had only 48 percent of its authorized officers, 39 percent of its enlisted men, and 53 percent of its peacetime authorization of airplanes. Yet it would be charged with operating and maintaining the operating Air Corps arm. Enlightening as well as discouraging was the fact that two-thirds of its officers were second lieutenants whose flying experience generally included only the hours required to become pilots. As events were to demonstrate in the first month of the European war, the Army Air Corps appeared to be no immediate match for the Luftwaffe.[278]

The outbreak of war in Europe in September 1939 did not immediately change Arnold's role vis-à-vis the White House or the Treasury Department. However, after the United States declared neutrality in the war, the Anglo-French cause was aided by Congress' repeal of the Neutrality Act on 4 November. A special session of Congress had been called when the war began. Arms sales to belligerent nations, including aircraft, were now permitted on the basis of their paying cash and shipping the goods out of the United States in other than American vessels.

These changes did not enhance Arnold's chances of retaining what he felt was sufficient US aircraft production for the expansion of the Air Corps. If anything, the advent of war in Europe appeared to increase the influence of the Procurement Division and Secretary Morgenthau with the White House. Much of this unhappy state was caused by the continuing feuding beween Woodring and Johnson within the War

Department, a problem that would continue to vex the military until FDR reluctantly forced a change in June 1940, a change that was welcomed by Arnold and Marshall among many others.

Roosevelt's desire to retain control over production resulted in the White House creating several agencies over the next several years, generally reporting directly to FDR and responsible for production and allocation of military materials. War Department membership and influence, and this included Arnold, was often minimal, as FDR desired, leaving the decisions in the Oval Office.

One problem that had been inhibiting planning for materiel allocation was the lack of coordination between the French and British missions in the United States. This problem appeared to be resolved in late 1939 with the emergence of a combined Anglo-French Purchasing Mission. To work with this newly organized group, the president announced on 6 December, at Morgenthau's suggestion, the creation of what became known as the Liaison Committee.[279] The membership, notably lacking any Army aviator, consisted of the Paymaster General of the Navy and the Quartermaster of the Army. They were to operate under the chairmanship of Capt Harry E. Collins, the retired naval officer serving as chief of Morgenthau's Procurement Division. As the group was being formed, Morgenthau immodestly explained his modus operandi in his diary, writing, "without anybody knowing it," I took the data furnished by the British and French and "walk[ed] it over to the President. Did you know what I did on the searchlights for them? I got them every other one. It was that kind of thing I was able to do, with the President's backing." He would enjoy similar success in getting every other aircraft produced sent to the British, beginning in 1940.[280] There seems little doubt that Morgenthau planned on continuing control through the mechanism of the Liaison Committee and, although a major concern of the group would be aircraft and engine procurement, none of its members except Captain Collins had any significant knowledge of aviation. Arnold may have suggested to the secretary of war that he protest its creation to the president, which Woodring did but to no avail.

As the British and French prepared to order 5,000 aircraft and 10,000 engines, which could not be produced until 1941, they asked for access to and incorporation of recent improvements such as a newly developed supercharger and other items considered secret by Arnold and the War Department. Morgenthau took the case to the oval office where, not unexpectedly, the decision was made to release the materiel. In March 1940, Arnold had angered the White House by testifying forthrightly that the amounts of materiel destined for Britain and France were at the expense of Air Corps expansion. Morgenthau could hardly contain his joy as he reported to his staff, "Oh boy, did General Arnold get it," in a lengthy White House meeting on 12 March. Morgenthau recorded that Arnold was not only threatened with being sent to Guam but was ordered to provide no further resistance to the work of the Liaison Committee. Morgenthau's account implied that both Johnson and Hap were thought guilty of leaking data to the "Republican and isolationist press." Reflecting his normal self-serving role, the treasury secretary told his staff he had informed FDR that if the president "wanted me to do this job, that my effectiveness was just being ruined by Johnson and Arnold." According to Morgenthau, the president said, "if Arnold won't conform, maybe we will have to move him out of town," possibly to Guam. This threat may well have led to Arnold's confusion in his memoirs with the earlier one of January 1939 following the crash of the DB-7 aircraft in California.[281]

It was agreed now that Johnson would publicly announce his support for the Liaison Committee, that he "likes to have . . . Morgenthau in charge of it," and that Arnold "has to keep his mouth shut" and "can't see the press anymore." Hap described the meeting this way: "It was a party at which apparently the Secretary of War and the Chief of the Air Corps were to be spanked and were spanked." He probably would not have been pleased to hear Roosevelt's announcement in that session: "These foreign orders mean prosperity in this country and we can't elect a Democratic Party unless we get prosperity." Arnold would have been dismayed but may well have agreed with Morgenthau that the secretary of the treasury and the

Liaison Committee had, for the time being, won the "battle of Washington."[282]

The result was the continued dominance of Morgenthau and the Treasury Department throughout the remainder of 1940 on the important issue of allocation of American-produced aircraft. Nevertheless, Arnold was able to make significant gains during the period. Prompted by a 14 March 1940 request by the British and French for the release of the latest American aircraft, Hap realized that many current in-production and on-hand airplanes did not have the necessary combat refinements of sufficient armament, self-sealing gas tanks, and armor protection for pilots. When the White House announced on 19 March that all types of American planes would be released for foreign sale, Arnold, lacking the funds to modify either on-hand aircraft or those destined for AAF use, advocated providing these planes to the British and French for their immediate use. The AAF could then defer delivery of existing Army orders of similar aircraft and obtain better-equipped models later. Additionally, Hap felt that, given the urgency of their needs, the British and French might be convinced to assume a part of the cost for research and development of the aircraft.

During a White House meeting on 21 March, Arnold confirmed White House approval of releasing for export to the British and French five types of aircraft, three of medium bombers along with B-17s and B-24s. This meant Britain and France, now engaged in war, would take delivery of 1,500 US-manufactured planes that had been ordered in 1939. At the same time, this would defer acceptance for the AAF, aircraft "approaching obsolescence at the time of delivery."[283] In addition to stipulating that "no military secret will be divulged or released," Arnold was able to obtain for the first time a seat for an Army aviator on the important Presidential Liaison Committee. Further, he secured agreement that the foreign governments would furnish to the United States "complete information . . . on combat performance of American made planes," and would pay some of the research and development costs in the contracts signed with American manufacturers.

The British and French then placed orders for an additional 4,500 planes.[284]

These actions represented a marked change by Arnold from his strong opposition to aiding Britain and France in January 1939 that had caused him such difficulty in the White House when he had vigorously opposed allowing a French officer to fly the DB-7, then under development. Although he was now in 1940 motivated in part by FDR's new and stronger threat to move him "out of town" if he continued to oppose the administration, he also had to have appreciated the political realities of Roosevelt's determination to aid the British and the French to the fullest extent. Consequently, Hap seized this opportunity to secure some benefits for the struggling AAF. One scholar assessed the results of Arnold's actions:

> Indeed the Air Corps had benefited the most. It had "off-loaded" obsolete planes and would replace them with modified models. What better answer could Arnold have found to that problem of obsolescence? The Allied development contribution of $7 million meant that Arnold was spared having to approach Congress for appropriations. . . . Then too, an Air Corps representative now sat with the President's Liaison Committee. . . . American flyers could visit the European combat theaters and . . . American planes would be battle-tested.[285]

Arnold immediately took advantage of the agreement to send observers abroad. Within a month, two Army aviators who were experts in bombardment operations and ordnance arrived in England. After some initial British reluctance to share knowledge, a number of later AAF observers were able to examine the RAF's conduct of the ongoing air war in Europe. At various times they included two of Arnold's closest friends and trusted officers, Tooey Spaatz and Ira Eaker. Among others who were dispatched were Maj George Kenney and Maj Gens Delos Emmons and James Chaney. Spaatz, labeling himself a "high-class spy," returned with valuable information, but he also failed to appreciate some problems that were to plague him and harm later AAF operations over the continent. At the same time, the rapport and friendship he forged with some of the RAF leadership proved invaluable once the United States entered the war.[286]

Hitler suddenly ended the "phony war" by his attack on Norway on 8 April 1940. In the ensuing 75 days of combat,

Norway and five other northern European countries fell to the Nazi onslaught. France surrendered on 22 June. These actions impacted significantly on the United States, the AAF, and Arnold. While the battle for France still raged, and coincidentally on the day Rotterdam was bombed, Arnold and Marshall were authorized during a 14 May White House meeting to increase US pilot production to 12,000 pilots per year, giving the same sense of urgency to producing pilots that Arnold had accorded to acquiring increased numbers of aircraft for the AAF. In contrast to this authorization, during the prewar decade the Army had rarely produced more than 200 pilots in any given year. By April 1939, however, the goal had been established at 1,200 per annum and this had been advanced to 7,000 less than a year later. The 12,000 program established during Hap's May 1940 White House visit would be increased to 30,000 per year by the beginning of 1941.[287]

Equally startling was Roosevelt's request of Congress two days later that the aircraft production capacity of the nation be increased to 50,000 per year and that more than $900 million be appropriated to accomplish this goal. There appears to have been little input from Arnold or the War Department to the White House in determining these figures.[288] In spite of Hap's belief that "The strength of an Air Force cannot be measured in terms of airplanes only," he had to have been encouraged by this pronouncement.[289] Any hope by Arnold or the AAF for an increased role in production of these planes was dashed however, by Roosevelt's memo to the secretary of war 12 days later directing that all "aircraft contracts be cleared through" Morgenthau.[290] After the military agreed that 36,500 of the proposed 50,000 be allocated to the AAF, Arnold recommended that of these 26,500 be tactical and 10,000 training aircraft.[291] The dominance of the Treasury Department in controlling aircraft production and allocation would continue throughout the remainder of 1940. Arnold and the military had but a limited role in determining the kinds of aircraft to be produced, the numbers of each type, their equipment, or their allocation.

Compounding this was the fact that there was little coherent doctrine as to how the AAF might use any tactical planes allocated. Political considerations resulted in the administration insisting to Congress and the American people that the armaments being produced were to be used defensively in the Western Hemisphere. Although there is little remaining documentation to support their dissent, there appears little doubt that the bulk of the military leadership, including Arnold, considered throughout 1940 that these pronouncements were little more than political rhetoric, essentially divorced from what they considered as the reality of a war that would involve the United States. However, the development and dissemination of alternative doctrine was inhibited by the administration's insistence on the defensive role of the aircraft and other armaments being produced.

Other White House actions had to have been pleasing to Arnold and welcomed by him. Much of Roosevelt's dissatisfaction with the War Department's and Arnold's reluctance to support administration policy regarding aid to Britain and France appeared to focus on Secretary of War Woodring. As indicated elsewhere, "foot-dragging" by the Army had caused Roosevelt to turn to the eager secretary of treasury, Morgenthau. Woodring's lack of support for FDR's policies stemmed not only from his isolationist beliefs, but from his backing of Craig (and later Marshall) as well as Arnold who were increasingly concerned about retaining sufficient numbers of American-produced aircraft. Roosevelt was reluctant, however, to dismiss high-ranking administration officials, particularly in an election year. As one scholar has explained, the result was that FDR "followed his unfortunate habit of sweeping embarrassing administration problems under the rug."[292] The president's dissatisfaction was no secret in Washington and FDR frequently discussed the matter with Morgenthau, who urged Roosevelt to "do something about your War Department."[293] Influenced by the now pressing need for a more effective secretary of war in whom he had confidence as well as the rapid German successes in northern Europe, Roosevelt took action. Domestic political considerations, including fall election prospects and recent internationalist speeches by respected elder Republican statesman Henry L.

Stimson, moved Roosevelt to invite Stimson to replace Woodring.[294]

Neither Arnold nor Marshall has recorded any contemporary comment over what had to have been to them a most welcome change. Morgenthau, after showing "surprising but . . . gratifying cordiality" toward Stimson, lost little time in urging that the new secretary of war "get rid of Arnold."[295] From the advent of Stimson's tenure, Arnold found an important ally who, although firmly believing in the necessity of American aid to Britain, became a strong and credible supporter of Arnold, Marshall, the War Department, and Air Corps needs. Hap would have been pleased by Stimson's diary entry three months after taking office that in promoting certain aviators to high rank it showed "that we are attempting to give real independence to the Air Corps and to keep it from domination by other branches of the Army."[296]

If Stimson was interested in ensuring that the Air Corps was not dominated by other elements of the Army, there were those who had not lost their interest in seeking complete independence of the Air Corps. The rapid German military conquests in the spring of 1940 created the perception in the United States that an independent Luftwaffe had contributed significantly to the lightning-like success of the Wehrmacht, which caused renewed interest by the media and some in Congress in a separate Air Corps. Although the evolution in Arnold's changed thinking from the Mitchell court-martial era when he supported independence cannot be traced, the passage of time appeared to have made him more cautious as well as realistic on this issue. In the decade of the thirties, probably influenced by the thinking of Gen Frank Andrews, then his commander in the GHQAF, Hap had testified before Congressman McSwain against a separate defense department. As Andrews explained to his officers in 1935, "a separate Air Force is a dead issue for many years to come."[297]

Arnold later recalled telling "boards and committees . . . that we didn't want an independent Air Force until we could sustain it properly." As he admitted to a congressional committee in July 1936, "we can't at this stage stand on our two feet."[298] George Marshall, the new chief of staff after 1939, agreed with

Hap when he recalled that the Air Corps "didn't have the trained people for it at all."[299] Now working with leaders, both civilian and military, that he respected and trusted and who were giving increased latitude and responsibility to the Air Corps, Arnold appeared convinced that efforts in support of a separate air force would only detract from the important task of creating a viable air arm. Arnold's caution was expressed in his 1940 volume where he conceded that many felt the "defensive air component" (note his use of the word defensive) should be made "coordinate" with the Army and Navy. Hap and his coauthor Eaker, however, proceeded to argue that we "shall be fortunate" if such a change comes "in the calm of peace or at worst, in the preparatory" for war. However the step "should be taken, if taken at all, only after careful planning and mature thought and not with a zest for radical reform." Rather, it should be the result of "gradual evolution."[300]

Hap now seemed to appreciate the nature and extent of the still lingering opposition to a separate Air Corps within much of the General Staff, the weaknesses of the Air Corps and the potentially divisive if not futile struggle that could detract from his primary goal of expanding, equipping, and preparing the Army air arm. Quite simply, Arnold was not only content himself to work within the existing system that was providing increasing sovereignty within the War Department to the growing Air Corps, but he cautioned friends in the media to downplay any talk of a separate air arm. As he explained at this time, "I learned my lesson about crusading a long time ago."[301]

Even though Morgenthau and the Treasury Department continued to dominate the allocation of US-manufactured planes, the Air Corps continued to expand. While the battle for France raged, the proposed expansion of the spring of 1939 that called for 24 Air Corps tactical groups to be ready by June 1941 was increased to 41 groups. Two months later, on 8 August 1940, this goal was expanded to 54 groups comprising 4,000 tactical aircraft, 187,000 enlisted men, 15,000 aviation cadets, and more than 16,000 officers.[302]

Within several weeks after funds were authorized for the productive capacity to be expanded to 50,000 planes per year, the office of the secretary of war signed contracts for 11,000 airplanes. By fall of that year, procurement officers at Wright Field were signing as many as 1,000 contracts a day.[303] Facilities were also expanded as Arnold created three new flying training centers to be located throughout the country.[304] Yet grandiose plans and pronouncements, as Arnold was well aware, did not produce aircraft. During a week in November of 1940, for example, the Air Corps "received only 2 tactical aircraft from the entire" aircraft industry.[305] As late as his return from his first trip to England in May the next year, Hap could write that the "striking force" of the AAF was at "zero strength."[306]

During the summer of 1940, Hap shared the dilemma of many Americans who, although seriously concerned over the recent dominance of the Axis powers in Europe, were influenced by the heritage of isolationism that had impacted much of the nation over the past two decades. For example, Hap and the Air Corps were not significantly involved in the debate over the draft or Selective Service that prevailed in late summer. Arnold realized that the proposed, and finally enacted, provision for a one-year term of service for draftees would not prove productive for the aviation community. In the Air Corps, for the most part, even the required technical training itself normally involved more than a 12-month span. Additionally, the allocation of most US-produced aircraft to the British left little training surplus for the increasing numbers of volunteers who, for the moment, were sufficient for the projected goals, planes, and facilities.

Hitler's abandonment of his planned naval invasion of England resulted in his turning to the air weapon as a means of subduing the British. London became the focal point of the German aerial blitz for 67 consecutive nights before the Nazis began attacking British industrial centers. Arnold, while remaining in close contact with US observers there, shared the uncertainty of Stimson, Marshall, and others as to whether the British could withstand the German onslaught. Arnold quickly learned, however, that the White House and Morgenthau were now even more intent on furnishing aircraft to the British. Although Hap was not present, Stimson and Marshall, in a September White House meeting with

Morgenthau, heard Roosevelt urge that additional B-17s be furnished to the British. When Marshall explained that the Air Corps possessed only 49 available for operations in the United States, "the President's head went back as if someone had hit him in the chest."[307] FDR had hinted in this September session at dividing the B-17s being produced on an even-Stephen basis with the British; by early November, he had directed this equal division.[308]

Throughout the latter part of 1940, as Morgenthau and the Treasury Department continued to control aircraft allocation, it appears that the case for increased numbers of aircraft for the Air Corps was presented in the White House by Stimson and Marshall without Arnold being present. Although the extant documents clearly reflect Arnold being fully consulted by the War Department leadership while furnishing them the rationale and statistics for their arguments, it does not seem unreasonable to conclude that Stimson and Marshall wisely limited the airman to rare White House appearances. They appreciated that with Woodring gone, Arnold remained the most visible reminder (most probably fed by Morgenthau's animus) of what had been perceived as War Department opposition to administration proposals for aircraft allocation.

Yet, although cognizant of his White House isolation, Arnold continued to be importantly involved in the problems of the Army air arm's assuming responsibilities that had to have White House knowledge and assent. One example was the formation in September 1940 of the Army-Navy-British Purchasing Commission Joint Aircraft Committee with Arnold to serve as its chairman. The changed structure in the War Department, which made Arnold one of three deputy chiefs of staff providing the major voice on air matters, had to be viewed as a vote of confidence by Marshall and Stimson.[309]

The September 1940 Destroyer-Bases agreement with the British was consistent with the administration's announced rationale that American armaments and troops were to be used for hemisphere defense. By the deal, the British leased some of their possessions in the Western Hemisphere as American bases in return for US Navy destroyers and a handful of B-17s. Arnold, aware of the additional responsibilities brought on by the use of these bases, lost no time in dispatching personnel to assess the potential of operating airbases in the Caribbean and North Atlantic. The speed of his response is reflected in the survey made of Newfoundland that was completed less than two months after the September agreement was concluded.[310] Not unexpectedly, neither Arnold nor Marshall seems to have made any recorded comment on the important and well-publicized "third term" election campaign that consumed the nation during the summer and fall of 1940.

As 1940 ended, Arnold remained the primary focal point for expanding the Air Corps, controlling all aspects except aircraft allocation. He appeared at least cognizant, if not pleased, with isolation from the White House and the allocation process but seemed undeterred from providing leadership for the other multitude of his responsibilities associated with recruitment, training, organization, and logistics.

The year 1941, however, was to be among the most significant in Arnold's tenure as chief of the Air Corps for he gained the confidence and respect of the president while becoming virtually sovereign in developing the Army air arm. His successes, which continued throughout the war, had essentially commenced with the events chronicled in the diaries that follow.

Notes

1. Arnold's account of his early life prior to entering West Point is in H. H. Arnold, General of the Air Force, *Global Mission* (New York: Harper & Brothers, 1949), 5-6. The Henry H. Arnold Collection, Library of Congress, Manuscript Division, Washington, D.C., box 1, contains correspondence dealing with this early period and is cited as Arnold Papers, hereinafter cited as AP. While the editor was serving as Chief of the Office of United States Air Force History, Arnold's son, the late Col William Bruce Arnold, USAF, retired, while granting permission and encouraging me to edit these diaries, allowed me to copy some of his father's papers. This was personal material not in the Library of Congress collection but located at the "ranch," the Arnold property outside of Sonoma, California, occupied by General and Mrs. Arnold after his retirement in 1946. These were returned to him and are cited as Arnold Papers, Ranch, hereinafter cited as APR.

2. *The Howitzer*, 1907, vol. 8, *Being a Record of the Year at the United States Military Academy* (New York: Hoskins Press, 1907), 42. Arnold is charitable in his autobiography, commenting that the educational experience in his days as a cadet was "simpler," Arnold, *Global Mission*, 7.

3. *The Howitzer*, 1907, 42, 147, 185, 187, 211; *The Howitzer*, 1908, vol. 9, *Being a Record of the Year at the United States Military Academy* (New York: Hoskins Press, 1908), 149.

4. *The Howitzer*, vol. 8, 1907, 42; and Arnold, *Global Mission*, 7.

5. *The Howitzer*, vol. 8, 1907, 322.

6. Arnold, *Global Mission*, 7-9.

7. Ibid., 8.

8. Arnold to his Mother, February 1906, "108 Days Till June," AP.

9. See box 1, AP.

10. Arnold, *Global Mission*, 9-10.

11. Ibid., 1-5.

12. Ibid; and Henry H. Arnold, "Pioneers of the Aerial Trails," unpublished manuscript, AP, 22. Not unusual in autobiographical accounts written long after the event and influenced by a coauthor, literary agent, editor, and publisher, Hap occasionally wrote of events somewhat differently from what the extant documents suggest. For example, on page 2 of *Global Mission*, written in 1948, Arnold records having thought in 1909 of Blériot's exploits in geopolitical terms, a reaction not confirmed elsewhere in the contemporary correspondence. See Arnold getting "all riled up" over the difficulties with his publisher and the writing of *Global Mission* in Henry H. Arnold to George C. Marshall, 2 July 1949, Marshall Papers, George C. Marshall Research Library, Lexington, Va., hereinafter cited as MPMS.

13. Arnold, *Global Mission*, 12-14.

14. Arnold does not mention the results of the examination in *Global Mission* but offers a slightly different wording of his commander's discouraging advice on page 15. The "commit suicide" quote is from Arnold, "Pioneers," AP. Hap's letter of 30 January 1911 to the adjutant general dealing with taking the Ordnance examination is in Old Records Division, Arnold 201 File, Records Group 94, National Archives. His request of 11 April 1911 to be assigned to aeronautical work is in APR.

15. Arnold to Chief Signal Officer, 13, 20, 27 May and 10 June 1911, AP. Confirmation of Arnold's progress is in an undated document on the letterhead of the Wright Company. This indicates that his primary instructor was A. L. Welsh and that in his 10 days as a student he had 28 lessons with flights averaging eight minutes each; see Memo of Lt H. Arnold's Training, 3-11 May 1911, AP; Arnold, *Global Mission*, 16-20, 25-28. See also box 227 for Hap's pleasant reminiscing about the days under the Wrights' tutelage.

16. An unsigned and undated account titled "Flying Done by Officers" lists Arnold as having flown 125 hours 30 minutes in 638 flights averaging 21.1 minutes [sic], AP. The average flight would appear to have actually been 11.8 minutes in duration. This document appears to be an official record of his progress up to 30 November 1912. The adjournment quotation is in Arnold's letter to his Mother, 20 July 1912, APR; and Arnold, *Global Mission*, 17, 30-34. For first Air Mail, see *Washington Post*, 11 July 1912; for altitude records, see *New York Times*, 2 June 1912 and Benjamin D. Foulois, *From the Wright Brothers to the Astronauts: The Memoirs of Major General Benjamin*

D. Foulois with Colonel C. V. Glines, USAF (New York: McGraw-Hill Book Co., 1968), 107.

17. For the origin of the nickname Hap, see Mrs. Henry H. Arnold to Corey Ford, 28 February 1954, AP. Arnold received notice of having won the Mackay Trophy in a letter from Winthrop M. Southworth, 8 October 1912, AP. Hap commented on the liquid capacity of the trophy in his letter to his fiancée Eleanor Pool, who became his wife on 10 September 1913. Thereafter, she was normally referred to as Bee in their correspondence. See Hap to Bee Pool, 20 June 1913, AP.

18. Arnold, Fort Riley, Kansas, to Commanding Officer, Signal Corps Aviation School, Washington, D.C., 6 November 1912, AP; and Arnold, *Global Mission*, 41.

19. Arnold, Fort Riley, Kansas, to Capt Charles P. F. Chandler, Washington, D.C., 7 November 1912, AP.

20. Lt Joseph O. Marborgne to Chief Signal Officer, 10 November 1912, Benjamin D. Foulois Papers, Manuscript Division, Library of Congress, Washington, D.C.

21. Arnold to Mother, 11 July 1913; and Arnold to Eleanor Pool, 20 June 1913, AP.

22. Arnold, *Global Mission*, 43.

23. The statistics are from DeWitt S. Copp, *A Few Great Captains: The Men and Events That Shaped the Development of U. S. Air Power* (Garden City, N.Y.: Doubleday & Co., 1980), 441. In the original manuscript of his autobiography, Arnold provided a less grim account of the numbers killed. According to this account, only 10 of 30 aviators rated as pilots had been killed in crashes. Twelve had "stopped flying within a few months after achieving competence," four had died of natural causes, and two "flew themselves out after two years or more"; original manuscript, 18, disc 5, AP. Force of six aviators and 15 planes comes from John H. Morrow, *The Great War in the Air: Military Aviation from 1909 to 1921* (Washington, D.C.: Smithsonian Institution Press, 1983), 50.

24. House Report 132, *To Increase Efficiency of Aviation Service of Army*. 63d Cong., 2d sess., H.R. 5464, 12 December 1913, serial set 6558.

25. Hap to Bee Arnold, 31 January 1914, APR; and Arnold, *Global Mission*, 44.

26. Efficiency Report, H. H. Arnold, by Col George W. McIver, 9 June 1915, APR.

27. Arnold, *Global Mission*, 44-45.

28. Ibid., 45.

29. Ibid.

30. Efficiency Report, Colonel Gorrell on Capt H. H. Arnold, n. d., labeled by Hap as "awful," "rotten," and "made me stink." See Hap to Bee Arnold, 15, 20 March 1917, APR. A brief account of the missing airmen and search is in Maurer Maurer, *Aviation in the U. S. Army, 1919-1939* (Washington, D.C.: Office of Air Force History, 1987), 105-8. See also Thomas M. Coffey, *Hap: The Story of the U. S. Air Force and the Man Who Built It: General Henry H. "Hap" Arnold* (New York: Viking Press, 1982), 187-89.

31. Coffey, 46–47. Arnold left a typewritten account of his activities from 1 February 1917 to 24 May 1918. This is different from the handwritten diary he maintained from 30 September to 21 December 1918 during his trip overseas in the closing days of World War I. The former is cited hereinafter as AP, World War I account; the latter as AP, World War I Diary. Both are in AP.

32. World War I account, particularly entries for 1 and 5 August 1917, AP; Arnold, *Global Mission*, 58–59, 62–72. See also Jerold E. Brown, *Where Eagles Land: Planning and Development of U. S. Army Airfields, 1910–1941* (Westport, Conn.: Greenwood Press, 1990). Hap's role is covered on 39–44.

33. See Maurer's "Reorganization" chapter, 39–52. See also Arnold, *Global Mission*, 79.

34. Efficiency Report, Col H. H. Arnold, by Maj Gen George O. Squier, 27 December 1919, APR.

35. William S. Biddle of the Adjutant General's Office signed the DSM denial on 23 December 1919, AP.

36. Arnold to Maj Clifford H. Arnold, 8 October 1918, APR.

37. Bee Arnold to Hap, 8 October 1918, AP.

38. Ibid.

39. World War I Diary, 16 and 24 October 1918, AP; and Arnold, *Global Mission*, 83–84.

40. World War I Diary, 31 October 1918, AP. For Maj Gen Patrick's comments on the use of American troops by the British on their airfields in England, see Mason M. Patrick, *The United States in the Air* (Garden City, N.Y.: Doubleday, Doran & Co., 1928), 19.

41. World War I Diary, 10 and 11 November 1918, AP.

42. Ibid.

43. Ibid., 20 November 1918.

44. Arnold met with Mitchell on 16 and 17 November, Patrick on 23 November and 4 December; "no longer Assistant Director" is in entry of 11 December; "lady of . . . upturned nose" is in entry for 12 December, World War I Diary, AP.

45. Arnold, *Global Mission*, 99.

46. Ibid., 88–89, 92. For early animosity between Arnold and the Navy arising from their joint occupancy and use of North Island, Calif., see Maj W. H. Frank to Arnold, 23 September 1920, AP; and Arnold, *Global Mission*, 107–8. For forest fires, see Patrick, 135; for refueling, see Patrick to Arnold, 8 November 1923, AP.

47. Maj Gen Mason Patrick to Arnold, 10 June 1924, AP.

48. World War I Diary, 17 November 1918, AP.

49. See the considerable correspondence between Arnold and Mitchell, 3, 11, 18, 26 January, 26 March, 10, 22 August, 19, 21, 29 September 1921, AP; and the papers of Gen William Mitchell, Manuscript Division, Library of Congress, Washington, D.C. Hap's letter expressing the hope that Mitchell would get the chief's position when Menoher departed is in Arnold to Mitchell, 19 September 1921, AP. See also Copp, 33.

50. For Mitchell's views, see Alfred F. Hurley, *Billy Mitchell: Crusader for Air Power* (Bloomington, Ind.: University of Indiana Press, 1964).
51. A copy of the paper is in AP.
52. Patrick, 6. A slightly different wording appeared in Patrick's obituary in *New York Times*, 30 January 1942; and in Harold B. Hinton, *Air Victory: The Men and the Machines* (New York: Harper & Brothers, 1948), 29.
53. Patrick passed an exam to be a pilot at age 59. The exam was administered by a board of officers, with the result that the "fifty-nine year old general received his wings during a luncheon at the Army Navy Club in Washington on June 26, 1923," Maurer, 59. Rank and file Air Corps pilots would not have viewed this as a legitimate way of earning pilot wings. One account of Patrick's elusive toupee is in Copp, 360. The evolution quote is from Ira C. Eaker, Oral History Interview, 1959–60, Air Force Historical Research Agency (AFHRA), Maxwell Air Force Base (AFB), Ala. See the assessment of Patrick and his leadership, termed "progressive and moderate," in Thomas H. Greer, *The Development of Air Doctrine in the Army Air Arm, 1917-1941*, USAF Historical Study 89 (Montgomery, Ala.: Research Studies Institute, Air University, 1955), 19–28.
54. Copp, 44.
55. Patrick's views as chief are clearly laid out in his autobiography. See also Maurer, 195–96.
56. Copp, 39.
57. Efficiency Report, Maj Henry H. Arnold, by Maj Gen Mason M. Patrick, 30 June 1925, APR.
58. Arnold, *Global Mission*, 116–17; and Copp, 49.
59. Arnold, *Global Mission*, 118. Hap's quote of Mitchell differs slightly from other sources.
60. For an excellent account of the antecedents as well as the court-martial itself, see Michael L. Grumelli, *Trial of Faith: The Dissent and Court-Martial of Billy Mitchell* (Ann Arbor, Mich.: University Microfilms, 1991); Arnold, *Global Mission*, 119; and Copp, 43.
61. Grumelli, 104–5.
62. Arnold, *Global Mission*, 119–20.
63. Copp, 44; and Coffey, 124.
64. Coverage of the Morrow Board appears in *New York Times*, 3 December 1925. See also Maurer, 73–74, 195–96; Copp 40–48; and Grumelli, 126–27.
65. Arnold euphemistically recalls his activities as "writing letters to keep up the fight," indicating that he and Dargue were "called on the carpet to answer for our 'irregular' correspondence relative to changes in the Air Service status." Arnold, *Global Mission*, 122; Copp, 48–49, prints excerpts from Arnold's letters.
66. *New York Times*, 8 February 1926; and Copp, 50, is the source for Hap opting for a court-martial. See also Coffey, 126.
67. Patrick's 2 March 1926 letter of reprimand citing Arnold as the "prime mover in a project for influencing legislation in a manner forbidden by regulations" is in AP. The official investigation of Arnold, Dargue, and two

other officers is in Inspector General, TAG file AG 333.9, National Archives, Washington, D.C. See also *New York Times*, 8 February 1926; and Copp, 50–51.

68. Efficiency Report, Maj Henry H. Arnold, 8 April 1926, by Maj Gen Mason M. Patrick, APR.

69. Copp, 49; and Arnold, *Global Mission*, 122. Arnold's second son, William Bruce, although only nine years of age at the time of his father's exile from Washington, probably reflected the family's lingering hostile feelings more than 40 years later, recalling Patrick as a "pompous s. o. b." See Oral History Interview, William Bruce Arnold, October 1969, United States Air Force Academy (USAFA), Colorado Springs, Colo. The contemporary attitudes of Patrick and Arnold towards each other are reflected during their meeting the next year at the annual 1927 Air Corps maneuvers in Texas. Arnold wrote his wife that Patrick "didn't say much and I didn't either," Hap to Bee Arnold, 27 May 1927, AP. For Patrick's belief that he had prevented Arnold's being court-martialed and that if he had not disciplined Hap then, Arnold "would have done something more severe," see Ira C. Eaker, Oral History Interview, 1959–1960, AFHRA, Maxwell AFB, Ala. Dargue's few personal papers in AFHRA do not mention the issue.

70. Arnold, *Global Mission*, 122.

71. Ibid.

72. Ibid., 123.

73. Ibid., 123–25. For riding crop, see Mrs. Henry H. Arnold, Oral History Interview, AFHRA.

74. Although Arnold's role is not mentioned, there is coverage of these maneuvers in Maurer, 239–42.

75. Arnold, *Global Mission*, 125–26; and Mrs. Henry H. Arnold, Oral History Interview, AFHRA.

76. There is considerable correspondence between Arnold and various publishers in AP, box 2. Arnold's earliest relationships with Lowell Thomas dealt with efforts to secure the latter's assistance. See Lowell Thomas to Arnold, 2 December 1927, AP.

77. See John Montgomery, vice president, Pan American Airways, to Arnold, 27 July 1927, offering Hap a salary of $8,000 per annum (contrasted with Hap's taxable pay as a major of $4,500) and 300 shares of stock along with a promise of 1,500 additional shares. Other offers also came, including a 1 August 1928 offer from Canadian Colonial Airways and a 9 February 1929 solicitation from Boston–New York–Washington Airways for Hap to become vice president and operations manager, AP. See also Hap's comment that he "couldn't very well quit the Service under fire," Arnold, *Global Mission*, 122.

78. Efficiency Report, Maj Henry H. Arnold, 30 June 1926, by Brig Gen E. E. Booth, APR.

79. Ibid., 30 April 1927.

80. Efficiency Report, Maj Henry H. Arnold, 30 June 1928, by Brig Gen Charles J. Symmonds, APR.

81. Arnold, *Global Mission*, 127–28.

82. Ibid., 128; and Mrs. Henry H. Arnold, Oral History Interview, AFHRA.

83. Arnold, *Global Mission*, 127-28; Efficiency Report, Maj Henry H. Arnold, 29 June 1930, by Col Henry A. Byroade, APR; for San Antonio assignment, see Brig Gen James Fechet to Arnold, 24 April 1929, AP.

84. Arnold, *Global Mission*, 128.

85. Efficiency Report, Lt Col Henry H. Arnold, 4 November 1931, by Brig Gen H. C. Pratt, APR.

86. Arnold to Capt E. E. Adler, 28 April 1932, AP.

87. Arnold to Spaatz, 26 August 1931, AP; *New York Times*, 30 August 1931.

88. *Air Corps Newsletter* (ACNL) 16 (25 January 1932): 9; Arnold, *Global Mission*, 134; and Coffey, 154. See also John F. Shiner, *Foulois and the U. S. Army Air Corps, 1931-1935* (Washington, D.C.: Office of Air Force History, United States Air Force, 1983), 112.

89. Coffey, 146.

90. Arnold to Will Rogers and Maj John Park of Riverside, Calif., 19 February 1932, AP.

91. Arnold, *Global Mission*, 133-43, covers these years; see also Mary Pickford, *Sunshine and Shadow* (Garden City, N.Y.: Doubleday, 1955), 320-22.

92. Arnold, *Global Mission*, 139. See Dik Daso, Maj, USAF, *Architects of American Air Supremacy: General Hap Arnold and Dr. Theodore von Kármán* (Maxwell AFB, Ala.: Air University Press, 1997); and Maurer, 422-23.

93. Arnold, *Global Mission*, 136-38. Arnold called Edwards AFB Mohave at the time. Later named Muroc, it was renamed for Glen W. Edwards in 1949. Arnold described it in 1932 as "level as a billiard table." Arnold to Chief of the Air Corps, 26 July 1932, AP.

94. Coffey, 150-52.

95. Efficiency Report, Lt Col Henry H. Arnold, 2 July 1934, by Maj Gen Malin Craig, APR.

96. Ibid., 30 June 1933 and 21 February 1934; Maurer, 349. See Arnold's complaint about the impact of the CCC work on his pilot's training in Arnold to Spaatz, 27 July, 3 August 1933, AP. See also Arnold, *Global Mission*, 141-42.

97. Copp, 106. A dated but excellent monograph on the Air Mail is Paul Tillett, *The Army Flies the Mail* (Tuscaloosa, Ala.: University of Alabama Press, 1955). See also the account in the report of the Baker Board in Newton D. Baker, *Final Report of the War Department Special Committee on Army Air Corps, 18 July 1934* (Washington, D.C: Government Printing Office [GPO], 1934), 893. The best succinct modern account is in Shiner, 125-49. Foulois' memoirs cover the operation on 235-61.

98. Maurer devotes a chapter to the Air Mail operations, 299-317; Arnold, *Global Mission*, 142-45; and Copp, 170-221, is an excellent assessment, emphasizing the human as well as the operational aspects.

99. Arnold, *Global Mission*, 143-44; Arnold to Bee Arnold, 18 February 1934, APR. "Organized to last detail" is cited in *New York Times*, 18 February 1934.

100. Arnold to Bee Arnold, 20 February 1934, APR. Details of the three crashes in Arnold's zone are in Shiner, 135.

101. Congresswoman Edith Rogers is quoted in *New York Times*, 25 February 1934, and in Copp, 194. See also *Congressional Record*, 73d Cong., 2d sess., vol. 78, pt. 3, 3144-55.

102. Arnold to Bee Arnold, 7 March 1934, APR.

103. Arnold to Bee Arnold, 20 April 1934, APR. FDR's letter of 10 March 1934 to Secretary Dern is printed in Copp, 210-11; see also Shiner, 144, 147.

104. Arnold to Bee Arnold, 12 March 1934, APR.

105. Ibid.; and Arnold, *Global Mission*, 144.

106. Arnold, *Global Mission*, 106, 144. The official seven-volume AAF history, *The Army Air Forces in World War II*, written in the immediate post-World War II period, was the work of many authors. Edited by Wesley Frank Craven and James Lea Cate, the seven subtitles of *The Army Air Forces in World War II* were vol. 1, *Plans and Early Operations, January 1939 to August 1942*; vol. 2, *Europe: Torch to Pointblank, August 1942 to December 1943*; vol. 3, *Europe: Argument to V-E Day, January 1944 to May 1945*; vol. 4, *The Pacific: Guadalcanal to Saipan, August 1942 to July 1944*; vol. 5, *The Pacific: Matterhorn to Nagasaki, June 1944 to August 1945*; vol. 6, *Men and Planes*; and vol. 7, *Services Around the World* (Chicago: University of Chicago Press, 1948-1958) (new imprint; Washington, D.C.: Office of Air Force History, 1983). Copp, 220, for fiasco. Shiner titles his chapter "The Air Mail Fiasco," 125-49; and Foulois calls his "The Truth about the Air Mail Fiasco,'" 235-61.

107. *Congressional Record*, 73d Cong., 2d sess., vol. 78, pt. 3, 3144-55.

108. Copp, 222-28, and "McSwine" is on 141.

109. Ibid., 176.

110. Ibid., 222-28.

111. For FDR's attitude in 1919 towards Army aviation, see Greer, 24.

112. Efficiency Report, Lt Col H. H. Arnold, 1 June 1934, by Brig Gen O. Westover, APR.

113. Arnold, *Global Mission*, 145-48.

114. Hap to Bee Arnold, 29 June 1934, AP.

115. Ibid.

116. Ibid., 28 June 1934, AP.

117. Hap to Lois Arnold, 19 July 1934, APR; Hap to Bee Arnold, 22 July 1934, AP; and Arnold, *Global Mission*, 146.

118. The criticism was apparently made at the Seattle Athletic Club on 7 August 1934; see "Hap" Arnold, The Murray Green Collection, USAFA Library, Special Collections, Colorado Springs, Colo.

119. *New York Times*, 14 November 1934; Maurer, 352; and Copp, 253.

120. Murray Green, "Hugh J. Knerr: The Pen and the Sword," in *Makers of the United States Air Force*, ed John L. Frisbee (Washington, D.C.: Office of Air Force History, 1987), 99-126. See also Coffey, 160-61.

121. Telephone conversation transcript, Arnold and Westover, 16 July 1934, AP.

122. Copp, 238, 241–42. The promotion went instead to Lt Col James Chaney. Hap's later occasionally strained relations with Chaney are outlined in Arnold's Diary, presented in chapter 1 of this volume.

123. Arnold, *Global Mission*, 145; and Copp, 129.

124. Arnold, *Global Mission*, 148.

125. D. Clayton James, *The Years of MacArthur*, vol. 1, *1880–1941* (Boston: Houghton Mifflin, 1970), 460. James continued that "MacArthur must have found secret glee in the fact that the effectiveness of the new force stifled the proponents of an independent air arm, at least for the present."

126. Hap to Bee Arnold, 4, 5 August 1935, APR.

127. Ibid., 18, 27 September 1935, APR.

128. Ibid., 10 November 1935; and Coffey, 168–69.

129. Copp, 346; Eugene Beebe, Oral History Interview, AFHRA, Maxwell AFB, Ala.

130. A copy of General Craig's announcement of Arnold's appointment as assistant to the Chief of the Air Corps for a period of four years, dated 30 December 1935, is in AP.

131. An extensive biographical account of Westover appeared in *ACNL*, vol. 21, no. 19, 1 October 1938. Other accounts are in Col Flint O. DuPre, USAFR, *U. S. Air Force Biographical Dictionary* (New York: Franklin Watts, 1965), 253; and in Copp, 147–48.

132. Copp, 148.

133. Ibid., 335–36.

134. For hosting official functions see Copp, 351; Jerry Brant is Copp's source for the "the fine combination," 345.

135. Arnold, *Global Mission*, 153.

136. Ibid.

137. Ibid.

138. Arnold's dislike of duty in Washington was expressed on other occasions. See Hap to Bee Arnold, 9 September 1924, APR, when he wrote that Washington "is at best a nightmare" and the following day to her that "this D___ town will make me forget I am human if I stay here long enough." "Don't sign any leases" is cited in Copp, 351.

139. Arnold, *Global Mission*, 153.

140. "Turning point" is from Arnold, *Global Mission*, 155; "too many eggs" is from Coffey, 176. Coffey mentions Arnold's 1936 testimony against a separate Air Corps on 175. Hap's thinking had been stated the year earlier in April 1935. See US House of Representatives, Hearings on H. R. 7041, 6810, 4348, 4336, 4351, 4911: "To Promote National Defense by Increasing the Efficiency of the Air Corps," 74th Cong., 1st sess., 1936, 1–5, 59–61, 101–3, 183–85.

141. Copp, 381; and Coffey, 174.

142. Hap's seeming acquiescence, as recorded by a bitter critic, Hugh Knerr, is in Coffey, 175.

143. An account by one of the participants is in Curtis E. LeMay with MacKinlay Kantor, *Mission with LeMay: My Story* (Garden City, N.Y: Doubleday & Co. 1965), 140–52. See also Copp, 393–98; Maurer, 403–6.

144. LeMay, 152-56; Copp, 407-8; and Arnold, *Global Mission*, 176.

145. The successful navigator of the B-17s, then Lieutenant LeMay, offers his account in LeMay, 184-93. Copp, 418-27; Arnold, *Global Mission*, 176-77; and Hinton, 83.

146. Quoted in Hinton, 83.

147. Mark Skinner Watson, *United States Army in World War II, The War Department, Chief of Staff: Pre-war Plans and Preparations* (Washington, D.C: Office of the Chief of Military History, GPO, 1950) 45. Coffey, 178, offers different wording.

148. See detailed telephone logs in Arnold Papers, which also lists correspondence for any period either officer was out of Washington.

149. Arnold, *Global Mission*, 169; and Copp, 438-40. See the "eyewitness account" of the crash, apparently by Maj K. B. Wolfe, printed in *ACNL*, vol. 21, no. 19, 1 October 1938.

150. Copp, 399-440, gives an excellent account of the disagreements between GHQAF, Andrews, Chief of the Air Corps Westover, and Arnold.

151. Telephone conversation between DeWitt S. Copp and Maj Gen John W. Huston, 12 March 1995.

152. The most consistent and in many ways most bitter critic and opponent of Arnold from GHQAF was Col Hugh J. Knerr, long-time Andrews confidante and GHQAF chief of staff. His intense dislike of Arnold, unabashed advocacy of an independent Air Corps, and efforts to have Arnold replaced with Andrews, were continued even after Knerr's retirement from the military in 1939. Copp covers much of Knerr's opposition, particularly 290-96, 374-78, 384-88, including his account of Knerr's successful 1939 efforts to get his anti-Arnold views into the White House, 477-79. Knerr's unrelenting opposition to Hap and his crusade for a separate Air Force are confirmed in his personal papers at USAFA. There appears little doubt that both Hap and Andrews were aware of Knerr's activities. Andrews continued after Pearl Harbor to pressure the AAF to get Knerr returned to active duty. Knerr was returned to active service in 1942, but for reasons other than Andrews' efforts. His performance in the Eighth Air Force led to his promotion to major general. He retired as USAF Inspector General in October 1949. Murray Green's biographical account, "Hugh J. Knerr: The Pen and the Sword," in Frisbee, 99-126, is curiously sympathetic.

153. The Diaries of Henry Morgenthau Jr., 12 March 1940, microfilm of originals in Franklin D. Roosevelt Library, Hyde Park, New York, copies in United States Naval Academy Library (USNAL), Annapolis, Md.

154. Coffey, 183; and World War I Diary, 5 December 1918, AP. Weaver's recommendation of Andrews to Watson is in Copp, 442-43.

155. Maj Gen Edwin "Pa" Watson Papers, University of Virginia, Charlottesville, Va., provide many references to his relationship with FDR on military matters but no documentation was located that showed Roosevelt consulting with Watson on the issue of Westover's successor. One of the sources that confirms Early and Watson's recommendation of Andrews is Morgenthau Diary, 12 March 1940. Another is Keith D. McFarland, *Harry H.*

Woodring: A Political Biography of FDR's Controversial Secretary of War (Lawrence, Kans.: University Press of Kansas, 1975), 163-64.

156. See Col John C. O'Loughlin to Gen John J. Pershing, 1 October 1938, box 58, John C. O'Loughlin Papers, Manuscript Division, Library of Congress, Washington, D.C.

157. The Administration's fears were not without basis as the Democratic majority in the Senate was reduced from 58 to 46 and in the House from 244 to 93; *New York Times*, 1-12 November 1938.

158. Arnold, *Global Mission*, 170.

159. Copp, 444-45.

160. Arnold, *Global Mission*, 170; and Hap to Bee Arnold, 16 May 1927, AP.

161. Lois Arnold Snowden to Bee Arnold, 10 August 1938, APR. Copp, 451-52, offers a good account of this relationship, most of which is based on Arnold's correspondence with his son-in-law, box 2, AP.

162. ACNL 21, no. 19 (1 October 1938), printed the special orders of 30 September, appointing Hap as chief with rank from 22 September 1938.

163. Ibid.

164. Ibid.

165. As indicated elsewhere, the ringleader continued to be Col Hugh J. Knerr, although much of the anti-Arnold rhetoric was moderated after Knerr's return to active service in 1 October 1942 and Andrews' May 1943 death. Andrews' death left Knerr without a viable replacement for Arnold.

166. Gen Laurence S. Kuter, USAF, retired, "The General vs. the Establishment: General H. H. Arnold and the Air Staff," *Aerospace Historian* 22, Winter (December 1974): 185-89.

167. The Diary of Henry L. Stimson, 28 May 1943, based on microfilm record in the Sterling Library, Yale University, New Haven, Conn., copy in USNAL, Annapolis, Md., hereinafter cited as Stimson Diary.

168. Copp, 402-8, provides an account of their differences. The term "Holy Show" is from Harold L. Ickes, *The Secret Diary of Harold L. Ickes*, vol. 2, *The Inside Struggle, 1938-1939* (New York: Simon & Schuster, 1953-54), 716 (9 September 1939). The Marshall quote is in McFarland, 149.

169. Although unsigned, there appears little doubt that the letter of 5 December 1939 to the editor of *Liberty Magazine*, stating that "I learned my lesson about crusading a long time ago," was written by Hap, AP.

170. Arnold, *Global Mission*, 169.

171. "Distance annihilated" is cited in Copp, 43; "reputation" is in DuPre, 9; bombers vs pursuit is in Untitled Paper, 1933, AP; "just a job" is in Hap to Bee Arnold, 29 June 1934, AP.

172. See the account of Chennault in Martha Byrd, *Chennault: Giving Wings to the Tiger* (Tuscaloosa, Ala.: University of Alabama Press, 1987), 36-64. Byrd's treatment provides a necessary balance to Major General US Army, retired, Claire L. Chennault, *Way of a Fighter: The Memoirs of Claire Lee Chennault*, ed. Robert Holtz (New York: G. P. Putnam's Sons, 1949).

173. Watson, 35-36; Copp, 433; and Coffey, 178.

174. Arnold to Spaatz, 31 August 1931, AP; and Donald Douglas, Oral History Interview, Columbia University, N.Y., for Hap's "act"; Lois Arnold to Bee Arnold, 22 November 1937, AP.

175. James Gould Cozzens, *A Time of War: Air Force Diaries and Pentagon Memos, 1943-1945*, ed. Matthew J. Bruccoli (Columbia, S.C.: Bruccoli Clark, 1984), vii.

176. Hap was submitting articles for publication as early as 1922. See Hap to his father, 23 August 1922, AP.

177. Slessor's judgment of Hap is in Sir John Slessor, G.C.B., D.S.O., M.C., *The Central Blue: The Autobiography of Sir John Slessor, Marshal of the Royal Air Force* (New York: Frederick A. Praeger, 1957), 326.

178. See Arnold Diary for 15 September 1944, presented in chapter 9, for negroes dancing; for Jewish doctors, 14 April 1945, presented in chapter 10. For King's pejorative usage and an assessment of King on race relations, see Thomas B. Buell, *Master of Sea Power: A Biography of Fleet Admiral Ernest J. King* (Boston: Little Brown & Co., 1980), 341. Marshall's quote on unreliability appears in Stimson Diary, 21 February 1945. Spaatz's excellent biographical treatment mentioning the use of the word "paternalistic" on this issue is in Richard G. Davis, *Carl A. Spaatz and the Air War in Europe* (Washington, D.C.: Center for Air Force History, 1993), 5.

179. Hap to Lois Arnold Snowden, 3 October 1938, AP.

180. Craven and Cate, vol. 6, *Men and Planes*, 299.

181. John McVickar Haight Jr., *American Aid to France, 1938-1940* (New York: Atheneum, 1970), 3-4.

182. Ibid., 8.

183. Ibid., 9-12.

184. Arnold to Chief of Staff, 9 March 1938, AP.

185. Haight, 12.

186. Copp, 414.

187. Haight, 29.

188. Watson, 36.

189. Ibid.; and Copp, 433, has different wording.

190. McFarland, 161-62; and Arnold, *Global Mission*, 167.

191. Copp, 402-4, has a brief account of the Woodring-Johnson feuding. A more extensive treatment is in McFarland, 143-54.

192. Charles A. Lindbergh, *The Wartime Journals of Charles A. Lindbergh* (New York: Harcourt Brace Jovanovich, 1970), 22 (27 April 1938).

193. Ibid., 11 (2 April 1938).

194. Ibid., 35 (23 June 1938).

195. Lindbergh's account of this meeting and its preliminaries are in his journal, 71-73 (19-22 September). Kennedy's cabled report is in *Department of State, Foreign Relations of the United States, Diplomatic Papers, The Ambassador in Great Britain to the Secretary of State, 20 September 1938*, 2 vols. (Washington, D.C.: GPO, 1970), 1, 625, hereinafter referred to as FRUS; and Eaker to General Arnold, memo, no date given, AP.

196. Slessor, 218-20. His "Notes on Conversation with Colonel Lindbergh" appears on 218-22.

197. Ibid., 219; and Haight, 18.

198. The Ambassador in France (Bullitt) to the Secretary of State, 19 September 1938, in Franklin D. Roosevelt, *For the President: Personal and Secret Correspondence Between Franklin D. Roosevelt and William C. Bullitt*, Orville H. Bullitt, editor. With an Introduction by George F. Kennan (Boston: Houghton Mifflin, 1972), 288.

199. Ibid.

200. "Ultimatums" is from Ambassador in France (Bullitt) to the Secretary of State, 3 October 1938, FRUS, 1938, 1, 711–12. Daladier statement cited in Haight, 25; "seventeen planes" in Haight, 13.

201. Lindbergh, 85 (1 October 1938).

202. Haight, 18.

203. McFarland, 164–65.

204. Haight, 14–15.

205. Copp, 445; Robert E. Sherwood, *Roosevelt and Hopkins: An Intimate History* (New York: Harper & Brothers, 1948), 100.

206. Ickes, "principally one of the air" is from 18 September 1938, 469, "overwhelming preponderance" from 28 September 1938, 474.

207. Margaret L. Coit, *Mr. Baruch, Illustrated with Photos* (Boston: Houghton Mifflin, 1957), 467–68; *New York Times*, 15 October 1938.

208. The Four Hundred and Ninety-First Press Conference (Excerpts), 14 October 1938, in Franklin D. Roosevelt, *The Public Papers and Addresses of Franklin D. Roosevelt with Special Introduction and Explanatory Notes by President Roosevelt, 1938 Volume: The Continuing Struggle for Liberalism* (New York: MacMillan, 1941), vol. 7, 546.

209. Ibid.

210. Assistant Secretary of War (ASW) Louis Johnson to Chief of Staff (C/S) Malin Craig, 14 October 1938, AP; and Haight, 27.

211. Arnold's circular letters are dated 14 October 1943, AP.

212. Morgenthau Diary, 17 October 1938.

213. Watson, 29, 144.

214. Maurer, 200–2.

215. Roosevelt, *Public Papers*, 1938, 68–77.

216. Henry H. Arnold, *Report of the Commanding General of the Army Air Forces* (Washington, D.C.: GPO, 1944); and Hinton, 81, 217. Some confusion has been generated over the dates of these initial efforts by the president, a problem for which Arnold may in part have been responsible. In *Global Mission*, 177–80, Hap wrote that on 28 September he was present at a White House meeting where FDR announced his intention of asking Congress for additional funds, much of it to purchase airplanes and increase the productive capacity of the manufacturers. Arnold termed Roosevelt's pronouncement the "Magna Charta" of the Army Air Corps. His recollection of the date appears in error and there is no extant documentation for a meeting on this date, this having been the day prior to Hap's swearing in as Air Corps chief and two days before the Munich settlement was completed. Arnold confused this with a later meeting held on 14 November. Of this later gathering, Hap kept brief notes on the back of a manila envelope, AP.

However, his 28 September insertion of the 14 November memo, in different pencil markings from the body of the notes, suggests that the erroneous dating was done at a later time. As a result of Arnold's dating error and lack of documentation for the 14 October meeting, many writers have concentrated on the 14 November "Magna Charta" conference and ignored the 14 October directions of the president. To this writer, the earlier October instructions were extremely important, representing the initial significant movement by FDR towards air rearmament motivated clearly by the Munich negotiations. At least one result of the 14 October meeting was reflected in the instructions from ASW Louis Johnson to C/S Gen Malin Craig, 14 October 1938, copy in AP; Haight, 27, gives a brief account of the session; and Coffey, 185-87, erroneously agrees with Arnold's confusion of dates.

217. Arnold to secretary of war, 19 October 1938, AP.
218. Morgenthau Diary, 20 October 1938.
219. Quoted in Haight, 49.
220. Gen Malin Craig, chief of staff, to director of the budget, 24 October 1938, AP.
221. Forrest C. Pogue, *George C. Marshall: Education of a General, 1890-1939* (New York: Viking Press, 1963), 334; and Watson, 134-35.
222. Watson, 134-36, cites, for example, Ordnance Branch budget submissions at the time.
223. Chief of Air Corps to secretary of war, 22 October 1938, AP.
224. Chief of Air Corps to assistant secretary of war, 24 October 1938; and chief of staff for assistant secretary of war, 25 October 1938, AP.
225. Haight, 52-53. Numbers and production figures are from Irving Brinton Holley Jr., *United States Army in World War II, Special Studies, Buying Aircraft: Materiel Procurement for the Army Air Forces* (Washington, D.C.: GPO, Office of the Chief of Military History, 1964), 174-78.
226. Chief of Air Corps to assistant secretary of war, 24 October 1938, AP.
227. Haight, 53.
228. See the various accounts in *New York Times*, 16, 18 October and 6 November 1938.
229. Chief of Air Corps to assistant secretary of war, 10 November 1938, AP.
230. Ibid.
231. Morgenthau Diary, 13 November 1938; and Haight, 54-55.
232. Holley, 170, is the source of "turning point." Both Watson, 136, and John Morton Blum, *From the Morgenthau Diaries*, vol. 2, *Years of Urgency, 1938-1941* (Boston: Houghton Mifflin Co., 1965), 48, use "momentous" presumably from the Oliphant/Morgenthau account; Magna Charta comes from Arnold, *Global Mission*, 179.
233. See Arnold's brief account on the reverse of a manila envelope in AP, mentioned in note 216. See also Arnold, *Global Mission*, 177-80; Blum, 48-49; Haight, 55-59; Watson, 136-37; and Holley, 169-70.
234. Watson, 136-38, remains a good, brief account.
235. Arnold, *Global Mission*, 178.
236. Haight, 58; and Blum, 48-49.

237. Watson, 138. Five Hundredth Press Conference, 15 November 1938, in Roosevelt, *Public Papers*, vol. 7, 599.
238. Assistant secretary of war to chief of staff, 15 November 1938, AP.
239. Drafts for assistant secretary of war, 15 November 1938, AP.
240. Watson, 140.
241. Arnold to Spaatz, 17 November 1938, AP.
242. Assistant secretary of war, Memo for the President, 1 December 1938, AP.
243. For 10 December meeting, see assistant secretary of war to chief of staff, 10 December 1938; and chief of staff to assistant secretary of war, 17 December 1938, AP. Haight covers this on 60-61.
244. Watson, 142-43.
245. Assistant secretary of war for president, 1 December 1938, AP; Watson, 142; and Haight, 61.
246. Haight, 71.
247. Ibid., 63-64.
248. Ibid., 65.
249. *New York Times*, 13 January 1939; and Chief of Air Corps to Chief of Staff, 13 January 1939, AP.
250. Chief of Air Corps to Spaatz, 18 November 1938, AP.
251. Haight, 11, 17, for the 1938 flight. See his coverage of the Procurement Division, 37-38, 77-78.
252. Ibid., 78.
253. Ibid., 93. Col James H. Burns of the Office of the Secretary of War also used the phrase "fishing expedition."
254. Morgenthau Diary, 21 December 1938.
255. Haight, 75-76.
256. Ibid., 77.
257. Ibid., 88-89; and Arnold, *Global Mission*, 186.
258. Haight, 91-92.
259. Ibid., 94-95; and Arnold, *Global Mission*, 185.
260. Curiously, Capt Paul Chemidlin was described in *New York Times* of 24 January 1939 as "a representative of the French Air Ministry" and three days later as an "engineering observer" but not as a French Air Force officer. The "most modern" quote is from the 24 January 1939 issue and Arnold, *Global Mission*, 185; see also *New York Times*, 27 January 1939.
261. Haight, 89-90.
262. Ibid., 93-94.
263. Arnold to Maj Gen H. J. Malony, 31 March 1949, quoted in Watson, 133; Arnold, *Global Mission*, 185-87; and Haight, 95. .
264. The Arnold quote is from his letter to Malony cited in Watson, 133.
265. Roosevelt, *The Public Papers*, 27 January 1939, vol. 132, 90-91.
266. Arnold, *Global Mission*, 186.
267. Morgenthau Diary, 1 March 1941.
268. Arnold, *Global Mission*, 186-87.
269. Ibid., 196.

270. Forrest C. Pogue, *George C. Marshall: Ordeal and Hope, 1939-1942* (New York: Viking Press, 1965], 85. Copp, 473-74, covers Marshall's letter to Andrews in 1939 referencing the 1938 travels.
271. Copp, 474, 479; and Watson, 284-85.
272. Holley, 181-86, covers the meeting. "Unknown" is from 168.
273. Ibid., 182.
274. Ibid., 186-93.
275. Arnold to Spaatz, 18 November 1938, AP; and Holley, 184.
276. Craven and Cate, vol. 1, *Plans and Early Operations*, 129.
277. Holley, 194.
278. Maurer, 374.
279. Blum, 111-15; and McFarland 210-12.
280. Blum, 117.
281. Ibid., 118-19; Arnold, *Global Mission*, barely disguises his frustrations from this period; see 193, 196-98. "Move him out of town" and so forth, is from Morgenthau Diary, 12 March 1940; and Arnold, *Global Mission*, 186, confuses 1940 with 1939.
282. Morgenthau Diary, 13 March 1940; and "spanked" comes from Arnold to Assistant Secretary of War Johnson, 14 March 1940, AP.
283. Haight, 207-13; Arnold "Memo for Record," 19 March 1940, AP.
284. Haight, 215-17.
285. Ibid., 230.
286. See among many of Spaatz's reports from London to Arnold: 4 June; 31 July; 5, 9, 24, 27, and 28 August; 4, 8, and 9 September 1940, Carl A. Spaatz Papers, Manuscript Division, Library of Congress, Washington, D.C.; Davis, 42-56, emphasizes Spaatz's role as well as covering the other early AAF observers. Slessor, 315-16, covers his relations with Spaatz in England in this period.
287. See Rebecca Hancock Cameron, *Training to Fly: Military Flight Training 1907-1945* (Washington, D.C.: Air Force History and Museums Program, 1999), 308-11; and Watson, 278-79.
288. A scholar who has examined the question of aircraft production has concluded that "the 50,000 figure finally used was neither an Army nor a Navy figure—it was a Presidential figure concocted by the President and his political associates." Holley, 228.
289. Arnold, *Global Mission*, 178.
290. A copy of FDR's memo is in AP; and Holley, 253.
291. Craven and Cate, vol. 5, *Men and Planes*, 265.
292. Pogue, *George C. Marshall, Ordeal and Hope*, 20-21.
293. Morgenthau Diary, 29 April 1940.
294. Henry L. Stimson and McGeorge Bundy, *On Active Service in Peace and War* (New York: Harper & Brothers, 1947), 318-24.
295. Stimson Diary, 12 May 1943.
296. Ibid., 25 October 1940.
297. Copp, 292; and Arnold to Bee Arnold, 4-5 April 1935, AP.
298. Arnold, *Global Mission*, 161.
299. Pogue, *George C. Marshall, Ordeal and Hope*, 290.

300. H. H. Arnold and Ira C. Eaker, *Winged Warfare* (New York: Harper & Brothers, 1941), 244-45.

301. "Crusading" is in letter to the editor, *Liberty Magazine*, 5 December 1939, AP.

302. Craven and Cate, vol. 1, *Plans and Early Operations*, 105.

303. Holley, 243.

304. Craven and Cate, vol. 1, *Plans and Early Operations*, 112.

305. Marshall to William Knudsen, 11 December 1940, Marshall Papers; Holley, 244; and Slessor, 325.

306. Quoted in Holley, 245.

307. Stimson Diary, 27 September 1940.

308. Pogue, *George C. Marshall, Ordeal and Hope*, 65.

309. Holley, 264-68; for reorganization see Craven and Cate, vol. 1, *Plans and Early Operations*, 114-15.

310. See "Survey of Air Base Units in Newfoundland, 18 October-1 November 1940," copy in AP.

Chapter 1

England
9 April–1 May 1941

Introduction

As 1941 began, many Americans (probably including Arnold and many other military leaders) feared that the United States would be drawn into the European war. The military chiefs, ever circumspect about committing their personal beliefs to their correspondence, were probably convinced that their labors were aimed at preparing the nation for conflict even though the political leadership continued to insist that the ongoing increases in manpower and weapons of war were being made for defensive purposes.

There is no record of Hap's reaction to FDR's 12 October 1940 public statement that the United States was arming only to defend the Western Hemisphere, but more than 16 million American men had registered for the draft by that time. The chiefs probably considered the president's 30 October pre-election "promise" to American mothers, "your boys are not going to be sent into foreign wars," as political rhetoric. Roosevelt's call in the last week of December for a direct arms program to Britain did not appear to have any significant impact on Arnold or the Army Air Forces (AAF) since the majority of American warplanes were already going to the British. If the nation's military chiefs were preparing the nation for war beyond the defense of the Western Hemisphere, there had been little strategic planning. Political factors precluded this, particularly since it would of necessity be carried out in conjunction with the British. Early in 1941, however, three months before Arnold set out on the first journey covered in his World War II diaries, US and British representatives began military staff conversations that Harry Hopkins' biographer has assessed as providing "the highest degree of *strategic preparedness* that the United States or probably any other non-aggressor nation has ever had before entry into war."[1] Suggested by the naval chiefs of the two nations a week after Roosevelt's November 1940 reelection, their talks resulted in agreements called ABC-1 and an air annex, ABC-2, ABC standing for American–British conversations. These agreements, negotiated in Washington, D.C., in the first two months of 1941, provided "the general strategic concept" that would govern "throughout the war."[2]

Curiously, Arnold's autobiography contains no reference to the plan or the AAF representative in the discussions, although it is clear that he approved the selection of Col Joseph McNarney. A West Point graduate, McNarney learned to fly just before the United States entered World War I. Following combat duty in France, he had a variety of assignments. One of those included leading a bomb group under Hap's command at March Field, California, in the 1930s. A member of the new General Headquarters Air Forces (GHQAF) at Langley Field, Virginia, in 1935, McNarney was in the War Plans Division in Washington four years later. He remained there until tapped for duty with the ABC conference. McNarney's promotion within a month after the ABC discussions had been completed and his later progress in reaching four-star rank during the war confirms approval of his work by both Arnold and Army Chief of Staff George C. Marshall.

The eight primary US Army and Navy representatives met "in secret" with their four British counterparts from 29 January to 27 March, although Air Vice Marshal John C. Slessor seriously doubted "whether the fact that we called ourselves 'Mr.' . . . really deceived anybody."[3] Carefully avoiding commitments, the strategists provided a course of action "should the US be compelled to resort to war." They assumed that Germany, Italy, and Japan would be the enemy nations in the event of war. Predicting that Germany would be the strongest of these, they determined that the Atlantic–European area would be the "decisive theater" while the US Pacific Fleet would weaken and "hold" Japan.

Among the measures to be implemented against Germany was a "sustained air offensive," which would be feasible after Allied forces had attained "superiority of air strength . . . particularly in long-range striking forces." Arnold welcomed the premise that US Army air bombardment units "would operate offensively, in collaboration with the Royal Air Force, primarily against Germany's Military Power at its source." Hap also had no difficulty in agreeing with two other basic principles emerging from the discussions: Unity of command within any operational theater and integrity of national forces; that is, American airmen would fly in American units commanded by American officers. Most of their conclusions were incorporated the next month into Rainbow 5, the course of action for war against Germany and Italy. The strategic plans were approved by both service secretaries and sent to the White House in early June. The president "familiarized himself with the two papers" and "suggested that they be returned for his approval in 'case of war.'"[4] The adoption of a general strategy plan, however, did not resolve Arnold's main problem: Allocating airplanes to Britain, the Soviet Union, and China while retaining enough of them to train the 54-group US Air Corps provided for in Air War Plans Division (AWPD)-1.

The explanation Arnold offered in his autobiography for making his first World War II trip to England did not include all the factors: "So many different problems were cropping up with the British that it became apparent I must make a trip to England. I wanted to get personally acquainted with Sir Charles Portal, Air Chief Marshal of the Royal Air Force, and talk many things over with him across the table where it could be done so much better than by cable or through even the best of emissaries."[5] Other factors also motivated this journey, however. Under new leadership since July 1940, the Army had been gaining credibility in the White House. The March 1941 appointment of Robert A. Lovett, a World War I naval aviator, as assistant secretary of war for air added momentum to Army's call for a larger voice in determining the production and allocation of aircraft. However, President Roosevelt's impromptu promises to give US-produced planes to foreign governments still played havoc with those schedules. During Christmas week of 1940, for example, FDR offhandedly promised the visiting Greek Prime Minister 30 additional planes and directed Treasury Secretary Henry Morgenthau to resolve the problem of procuring them.[6]

Roosevelt, disenchanted with the views of defeatist Ambassador to Great Britain Joseph P. Kennedy and with the increasingly strident opposition of isolationists in both Congress and the media, turned to personal advisors whom he sent overseas to become his eyes and ears. Among those who went in the early weeks of 1941 were Harry L. Hopkins, Averell Harriman, William Donovan, and the recently defeated Republican presidential candidate Wendell L. Willkie. The president relied heavily on these emissaries since they did not require Senate confirmation, were not subject to normal congressional scrutiny, and could report privately to him in the White House rather than publicly to Congress, the bureaucracies, and the press.

One of the most influential and important of them, particularly in terms of Arnold's first World War II trip abroad, was Harry Hopkins. Dispatched to England in January 1941, Hopkins established close and important rapport with Churchill on behalf of Roosevelt. Hopkins' success and increasing War Department credibility appeared to diminish the role of Morgenthau and the Treasury Department in determining aircraft production and allocation. This change did not sit well with the treasury secretary, who was resentful of his declining ideological and bureaucratic sway with the president. He complained churlishly to his staff in a "triple confidential" meeting following Hopkins' return in early March 1941: "You know this thing of going direct from Churchill to Hopkins to the President isn't so hot. I don't like it. I'm just not going to let anybody spoil the excellent organization and relationship we have here. I just won't let them do it. We've worked together for a long time and nobody is going to come in and spoil it."[7] Morgenthau had no problem encouraging and accepting Treasury Department control over matters that diminished the roles of other executive departments, but he had difficulty accepting the bypassing of channels by others—particularly if it appeared to threaten the Treasury Department's close relationship with Roosevelt. Eight months after the United States entered the war, Harry Dexter White asked Morgenthau what Morgenthau had meant when he indicated that he wanted to "continue to sit to the left of the President." Morgenthau replied, "I want to retain my rank as second in command in the cabinet because that would give me prestige over the Army and Navy."[8]

Concern continued to mount within the War Department regarding how to meet the domestic needs of the 54-group AAF while foreign commitments were being filled. As early as January 1941, Arnold was expressing his fear that the United States was "leaning over backwards to give everything to the British." This fear, coupled with production delays and the continuing high British priority for engines, added to his feeling that getting airplanes for US units "is more or less a mess."[9] Arnold's clear discouragement was further articulated in War Department meetings. In one such meeting, he stated that the US government was "not motivated by reason and logic but by sentiment and hysteria." He argued that continuing to dispatch large numbers of aircraft to Britain would make it impossible to achieve an American Air Force in being.[10] Secretary of War Henry L. Stimson shared Arnold's concern when the secretary found that the Senate Foreign Relations Committee, following his testimony to them in closed session in late January 1941, was "rather horrified by the airplane situation." The secretary of war entertained the idea of becoming involved in production matters himself during the temporary illness of Lovett.[11]

In laying the foundation for Arnold's first trip abroad, Hopkins' mission to England in early January 1941 was crucial. Arriving in London on 9 January, he was received warmly as a confidant of the President. Hopkins was given the red carpet treatment, which was increasingly provided for any Americans who might be useful to the British cause. He spent weekends with Prime Minister Churchill, accompanied him on visits to bases, and quickly convinced his host of the American president's desire to assist the British in any way possible. On his return to Washington six weeks later, Hopkins brought with him a 14-point list "of the most urgent requirements of the British as approved by Winston Churchill." Any symbolic similarity to Wilson's Fourteen Points of 1918 was not emphasized. General Marshall learned of the list and informed Arnold on 27 February, "We are going to be forced to some very radical thing or departure." He sent a memo to Arnold, requesting "a solution before an unfortunate one is forced on us."[12] Averell Harriman, who was a strong advocate of massive aid to Britain and became Lend-Lease coordinator, found considerable skepticism among American military officers concerning the enumerated British needs. One officer expressed it this way: "We can't take seriously requests that come late in the evening over a bottle of port."[13] The Hopkins list included the "maximum number" of B-17s with spare parts, bombs, ammunition, and crews; 200 training aircraft; five additional "completely equipped" civilian flying training schools; ferrying US-made bombers to England by US pilots; engines for Lockheed aircraft and necessary propellers, guns, and ammunition for P-40 fighters. A final request was for 80 trained observers to "acquaint Britain with the use of our planes."[14]

Arnold responded on 6 March to Marshall's 27 February request. In what was probably a familiar analysis, Hap opined that filling the British list would "eliminate the present objective of building up the Air Corps" and reduce "to the vanishing point the low combat strength." Supported by his Air Corps Plans section and the War Plans Division (WPD), Arnold argued that this approach would result in the Air Corps being stripped of effective aviation. Insisting that unless a viable program for the Air Force was established and maintained "against pressure," Hap suggested that General Marshall not "accept responsibilities for defense . . . in the western hemisphere." Labeling the effort to arm the Air Corps as "piecemeal reinforcement," Arnold joined WPD in recommending that a "joint military mission should determine how many planes we should be sending to the United Kingdom while considering our interests."[15] Without realizing it, Arnold may well have suggested his first trip to England.

Hap's response to the chief of staff found its way to the White House, which caused Arnold to prepare a memo for the record on 10 March. In it, he conceded that he "was informed this day that the President of the United States objected very strenuously to the attitude taken by me in connection with aid to Britain as shown by my memo" of 6 March. Arnold insisted in defense of his views that the chief of the Air Corps has to "make recommendations to the Chief of Staff as he sees them." Conceding that it was not his job to outline objectives for the Air Corps, he complained in a seeming criticism of the White House, "so far no one has given us a real decision as to what our objective is." Insisting that it was necessary for him to make recommendations before any decision was reached, Arnold underscored the point understood by military personnel that once the decision was made, "then it is up to the officers involved to carry on without any further argument." In a reference that is not completely clear, Arnold wrote, "the President gave this [Arnold's 6 March memo] to Hopkins who expressed himself in no uncertain terms about me regarding these recommendations." It seems logical in view of later developments that Hopkins supported Arnold to FDR and may well have suggested that Hap be sent abroad to observe firsthand the same conditions Hopkins had seen in Britain.[16]

The timing of Arnold's demurrer could not have been worse, coming as it did when the debate over Lend-Lease was reaching a climax. A reluctant Congress was now considering all-out aid to Britain while the president feared that too many American military personnel, as exemplified by Arnold's memo, opposed what the White House would interpret as the will of the American people. Passage of this legislation promised to resolve the major problem of payment for the supplies while providing the president wide discretion in allocating them. Opposition by the professional military, particularly Arnold, whom the president had by implication threatened earlier to send to Guam, was not what Roosevelt desired as the bill passed on 11 March.

Perhaps because of Arnold's expressed opposition, Hopkins became concerned that his British hosts had asked for "too much"; he was "fearful," in Marshall's words, "that we might not fully understand their requests." On the day before final congressional approval of Lend-Lease, Marshall went to the White House to discuss the list. In a luncheon meeting with Marshall, Hopkins suggested that a contingent of American military leaders, specifically including Arnold, travel to England for a "two or three days conference" to validate the list with their British counterparts.[17]

Unknown to Marshall, Hopkins had already discussed the matter with Averell Harriman and planned to recommend that Arnold be sent abroad to "get the treatment."[18] Arnold would receive the same open and warm reception accorded other Americans whom the British felt could be useful to their cause. He would meet many leaders in the British hierarchy, probably experience an air raid, and see the Royal Air Force (RAF) in action. He would appreciate the extent and nature of British needs for American aircraft and gain sufficient credibility in the White House to avoid forced retirement.

This latter prospect was much more likely than Arnold could have imagined despite Secretary of War Stimson's submission of Arnold's name along with two others for promotion to permanent major general. President Roosevelt did not forward the names to the Senate for confirmation because of "his objection to Arnold." In discussions with Stimson about Hap being forced to retire, Marshall appeared resigned to the possibility of losing his senior airman. The record is not clear as to whether the chief of staff fought to retain his AAF chief.[19]

Secretary Stimson discussed the matter of Arnold going abroad with Assistant Secretary of War John J. McCloy on 20 March and with both McCloy and Lovett on 21 March. He concluded that it would probably be a good idea to "send General Arnold to England" so the airman could "get a bird's eye view of the situation and a firsthand feeling of the atmosphere."[20] To what degree the secretary viewed the journey as an effort to save Arnold's career is not clear. Stimson, who was clearly committed to doing all possible to assist the British, was aware that the military leaders of the Army, including both Arnold and Marshall, were less committed to all-out aid. Their lessened sympathy resulted from their continuing concern, as expressed in Arnold's 6 March memo, about how American military needs could be met at the same time that British and other requirements could be supplied from the still limited American production.

Stimson, by now an admirer and supporter of Arnold, was cognizant of the fact that FDR was seriously considering replacing Hap and forcing his retirement. It appears that Arnold was not aware of his low standing and his potential forced retirement; in late 1939 or early 1940, he recalled having a drink with the president prior to a small dinner in the White House and realizing that I was "out of the 'dog house.'"[21]

It is not clear when the aviator first learned that he was to make this journey. Certainly he had known by 25 March, when Stimson informed the British air attaché and others of Arnold's proposed travel. The next day, the attaché cabled the Air Ministry in London that, if convenient to his prospective hosts, Arnold could "pay a long-deferred visit to England for four or five weeks."[22]

This news spawned a transatlantic exchange of telegrams for the next two weeks covering British preparations for Hap's travel. Appreciative of the benefits to be gained from Arnold's visit, British diplomats in Washington reported to London that the proposed trip was "more than a gesture and is of real importance to future British-American cooperation."[23] The gracious and rapid response from London offered to facilitate all details of the venture. News of the trip was relayed quickly to appropriate British officials. Air Chief Marshal Charles Portal was "delighted" over the prospects while Churchill noted a laconic "good."[24] The air attaché relayed to Portal that Arnold had expressed the purpose of his visit as "firstly to see Europe through your eyes and those of the Senior members of your staff and of CinC Bomber, Fighter and Coastal Commands. Secondly to discuss training and thirdly to see from long range point of view how the US Air Corps could best help RAF in an active manner."[25]

Coordination within the air staff in London was begun and RAF personnel in Washington recommended data to be provided for Arnold in London. British leaders proposed that the American general be flown to England in one of the new B-17s being delivered to the RAF but the US State Department cautiously vetoed this idea as a possible violation of American neutrality. Arnold then planned to use the regular Pan-American

Clipper service into Lisbon, leaving on 9 April. On his arrival, Arnold was to be met by Portal and flown to London.²⁶

Lord Beaverbrook, minister of aircraft production, suggested that the American general visit the huge modification center at Burtonwood in Lancashire where all US and British planes would be displayed or flown for his observation. In the most generous gesture of all, Beaverbrook proposed that Arnold be permitted to see their most secret advanced project: the revolutionary Whittle jet engine then under development. "We would even allow him to see the Whittle engine, which has made its first jumps [9 April]. We have not shown it to a soul yet. Indeed we have even flown it on cloudy days so that the angels could not see it. But what is forbidden to the angels shall be permitted to the General."²⁷ Clearly, Arnold's visit was viewed as an important one to the British leadership.

The British drew up a very detailed visitation schedule, including suggestions that Arnold be shown the considerable amount of work necessary to modify American aircraft for combat. This was aimed at countering criticism in the United States that American-produced aircraft were sitting idly on British airfields.²⁸

As the British preparations progressed, Harriman and Hopkins continued their efforts to ensure that Arnold would get the "treatment" while in England. Hopkins wrote to Churchill, suggesting people and places the aviator should visit. Harriman, now on the scene in London, recommended that Arnold have an audience with King George VI and a meeting with Foreign Secretary Anthony Eden.²⁹

Five days before Hap's departure, Hopkins sent a letter introducing Arnold to Churchill. In it, he suggested that the Prime Minister "see that he [Arnold] has the appropriate contacts with the people whom he should see." He added that Arnold was "one of our ablest military men" as well as "one of two or three very high ranking officers in the US Army whom the president is anxious to be exposed to the actual warfare." The letter was accurate in pinpointing Arnold's differences with the White House, observing that Hap's "point of view is that our army should be built up at all costs" and that the airman "has a tendency to resist efforts to give adequate aid to England."[30]

Arnold's agenda was to be a full one. The main objective was to determine the numbers and types of US aircraft to be produced and allocate them among the various claimants, the two major ones being the expanding AAF and the fighting RAF. Other points to be covered were the potential for the United States to train British pilots and for US crews to ferry aircraft across the Atlantic. A host of other items would also require examination by Arnold during this trip.

If either the myriad and complex problems to be considered or the precarious nature of his position as AAF chief daunted Arnold, he left no indication of it as he departed Washington with his family and his aide, AAF Maj Elwood R. Quesada. It would be Arnold's first visit to England in 22 years.

Maintaining the fiction that the United States was a neutral nation, Arnold and Quesada traveled in civilian clothes as they boarded the Pan-American Clipper bound for Lisbon. Whether he realized it then or indeed ever, this first of four wartime visits to England was a major milestone in Arnold's career. The diary he kept during this important journey covers in detail his activities, impressions, and thoughts.

The Diary

TRIP TO ENGLAND APRIL 1941
MAJOR GENERAL H. H. ARNOLD

<u>Wednesday, April 9, 1941</u> [Washington, D.C., to New York City]

Drove to New York with Bee, Lo and Ernie.[31] Pete Quesada to meet me there.[32] Dinner with Guy Vaughan, the Birdie Wrights,[33] then to the theatre. Family all petered out so no night club.

<u>Thursday, April 10, 1941</u> [New York to Bermuda, en route to the Azores]

On to LaGuardia Field[34] to take off on Pan Am at 11:00, no it is 12:00, no again it is 1:00 P.M. The preflight test delayed our departure. Lunch as guest of Elmer Hazlett[35] at Administration building restaurant after a tour of the airport. Plenty of press men and photographers but gave out no interview, just answered a few meaningless questions.[36] Practically the entire Curtiss-Wright organization there to see us off: Vaughan, Gordon, Wright and wife.[37]

Off at 1:15, twenty-five second [takeoff] run on water. Yankee Clipper, Boeing four-engine boat; eighteen passengers, crew of eleven.[38] Cruised at 8,000 feet to Bermuda, 670 miles away, 135 knots [speed]. Broken clouds at 5,000 feet. Two US cruisers headed NW about 150 miles out of Bermuda.

Bermuda low, horseshoe-shaped island, coral atoll, highest point 380 feet. No springs or wells, all water comes from rain that is collected from roofs and rocks on side hills skinned of dirt. Roofs treated with white cement to insure clean water. Landed at 6:10 P.M., EST [Eastern Standard Time] or 7:10 Bermuda time.[39] Governor's aide met me;[40] landed on island in bay. Consul Beck also met us.[41] Only one dredge working on our airport development, too slow, should have at least three. Talked to Maj [Major] White on phone, he is in charge of our construction. Expects to have project completed in six months. Hard coral may delay completion. Will see him on my return.[42]

Dropped off ten passengers and took on 12, among others joining us, Mrs. [John G.] Winant, wife of [US] Ambassador to England. Sent my respects to Governor by aide. Also took on two Boeing mechanics headed for England. Took off at 9:10 EST; next stop Horta, Azores.

Friday, April 11, 1941 [Horta, Azores to Lisbon, Portugal]

Went to bed, fine bed.[43] Weather good all night. We lose three hours between New York and Horta, Azores. Awakened at 7:00 A.M. but it happened to be 10:00 A.M. Horta time. Breakfast aboard ship; good chow, fed in relays. Skipper says there is good land plane site on island east of Horta [on] Terceira, 40 miles east of Horta. Perhaps I can get a sight of it.[44] Overcast to broken clouds below us at 5,000 feet.

Landed Horta 9:50 A.M. EST, distance about 1,700 miles. Good Friday. German steamer *Louise Bordenhofer* [sic] here for 18 months, needs paint badly. Another ship with her but it steamed out several months ago and was sunk by British destroyers.[45] Terraced green hills on island, windmills on hills pumping water. People all dressed in black. Spanish type of houses and forts, reminds me of Manila. An old fort almost in ruins, still used by troops as barracks. General listlessness among all people. New fort on hills with two 6-inch guns. Soldiers in all kinds of uniforms. Equipment does not look very modern. Women in modern dress styles and hair dressing; 3 horse wagon hitched abreast, saddles on near horse pulling a military wagon, horses scrawny like Mexican. Everywhere there is German machinery.

Took off at 11:35 A.M., EST. Island of Terceira; Skipper flew over it for me; plenty of sites for airports, small fields but long level stretches; NE side of island best; 7,000 foot runway possible. Island about 45 miles long, road runs around island with villages and houses almost continuous. Seaport on s [south] side with small airport. Highest point on island about 2,500 feet, plenty of good water. Overcast sky and clouds below until we reached Lisbon at 7:59 EST. Could see lights for miles. Skipper made good landing in dark. Distance about 800 miles, Lisbon time 12:59 A.M.

Saturday, April 12, 1941 [Lisbon, Portugal, to England]

Circled town and harbor for 30 minutes. Dixie Clipper, not Yankee pulled into dock stern first. Met by Mr. Hibbard of [American] Embassy no Ministry; also Maj Caum, Military Attaché; Jack Kelly of Pan Am; Wing CO Jack Schrieber, British Air Attaché.[46] Took 45 minutes to clear customs.

Went to Hotel Avis,[47] arrangements completed to leave this A.M. at 8:00. Air Vice Marshal Slessor did a good job in fixing up an early departure;[48] most people wait here for days. Arrived at hotel at 3:00 A.M. City very clean, does not look like semi-tropical city in that respect. Talked with Hibbard, Slessor and Schrieber until 4:45, then to room for bath and shave.

[According to] Hibbard:

Spain in very bad condition, no crops and morale is very low. We must support Franco or another period of chaos and desolation.

Portugal: in a period of prosperity but does not know what to do with it.

Hibbard recently came from Belgrade. Would rather have Germany than Russia.

Greece: even with British aid cannot hold Germans, another Dunquerque in sight.

Yugoslavia: has shot her bolt, will accept German terms.

Italy: thru [sic], no one need expect anything from her.

Turkey: shows no inclination to do anything but wait for what happens; calling men to colors but will not fight.

Russia: does not have any intention to fight, fears Germany so much that she will run at slightest provocation.

Germany: still getting stronger, has not yet reached her peak.

Now for that shave. Avis is a fine hotel, sorry that I cannot stay and enjoy its bed. Breakfast: coffee and toast. Auto to airport, about 20 miles out; no one there but passengers of all nationalities. Arrived at 6:30: German, Spanish, Portuguese, British planes lined up side by side.

Our plane is a dirty-looking camouflaged DC-3 from the KLM line.[49] British officials of Imperial Air Lines showed up at 7 A.M.[50] We were weighed in with all other passengers but as we had overweight baggage were allowed to carry two bags in our hands which did not count. Slessor, Quesada with his courier pack, and I all alike. The plane is crewed with old KLM men: the pilot is Parmentier, the pilot who finished 2nd in London-Australia race.[51]

Took off at 8:00 A.M. and landed at Oporto at 9:00.[52] Country looks very much like coastline of southern California between Los Angeles and San Diego. In air again at 9:15, headed out to sea, broken clouds below us, altitude 6,000 feet. Passengers more quiet, a feeling of restraint. Two bunches of flowers being taken by Dutch pilots to London for their families; marigolds and another kind I don't know. Lunch aboard plane: sandwiches, fruit, coffee. Slessor, talking at 4:30 A.M. last night in Avis Bar: "Bah Jove lemons: I think that I will take them with me. There are none in London." The first time I realized that there was a shortage of fruit or food in London.

Arrived in Bristol at 3:15 P.M.[53] Figuring from the position of sun, the plane must have traveled NW to a point about 300 miles W of Bristol. There, blinders were put in all windows and we picked up a fighter escort.[54]

Bristol bombed last night, mostly in area around waterfront and among warehouses. Airdrome potted with craters but no damage to buildings. Houses built very close to each other and many damaged; roofs taken off, windows and doors smashed, can be seen from the airport.[55]

Arrived ahead of time, no one to meet us. While waiting, Chief of Civil Aviation called and waited with us.[56] Air Chief Marshal Portal called on phone and expressed regrets at not being here to meet me but did not know of my time of arrival, told him everything OK.[57]

Departed for London in Handley Page 99 with Slessor, Quesada and a British Naval Captain.[58] One airport after another until we reached London, all camouflaged with planes dispersed even to outlying fields. Far more hard-surfaced landing strips than I expected.

Met at Hendon by Portal and Scanlon.[59] Air defense and ground defense weapons of all kinds on the field; armored cars, made up on old second-hand chassis by the Air Force. Sandbags around machine gun nests, and AA [antiaircraft] guns. Barbed wire protection around all gun emplacements.

A drink of sherry with Portal and then on to the Dorchester.[60] Shorty Cummings, Miff Harmon[61] and two young British bomber pilots in their room. Bomber pilots say that after being over Germany for twenty-four times, no way possible to use a [bomb] sight that requires more than 30 second straight approach. I cannot go with them 100 per cent but believe that we will have to develop a new sight.[62]

Dinner with Portal and Scanlon. Dead tired and to bed right after dinner, slept thru to morning. All curtains in room closed so that no light escapes. Card on dressing table re ration cards for everyone.

Sunday, April 13, 1941 [England]

Easter. A grand hotel, have a suite with Quesada. Portal a very savvy man. Gave him an outline of my mission last night: "to find a practical way in which the Army Air Corps can be of maximum aid to British."

Awake at 9:00 A.M., breakfast in room: chocolate, rolls, 2 pieces of sugar only in bowl, very small ones; 2 pieces, very small ones of butter. At [American] Embassy at 9:45; conference with Slessor, Harmon, Scanlon, Lee[63] as to schedule and best way to accomplish tasks with "musts" first and other things later. The [British-prepared] pre-arrival schedule was thrown in wastebasket.[64] Interview with twenty newspaper men and women, photographers by the score.

Lunch with Slessor and Medhurst, Assistant in charge of plans.[65] Their plans section works quite similar to our Air Corps Plans Section and WD [War Department] General Staff (Air matters only).

RAF story of destruction of Italian fleet. Two cruisers damaged by air attack, others came to aid with British fleet waiting. Fleet opened fire and Italian fleet no more.[66]

Conference with AVM Garrod[67] re:

1. Plan for British using 1/3 of our training facilities and establishments.[68]
2. Furnishing ferry pilots.[69]
3. Air route across North Atlantic, via Greenland and Iceland.[70]
4. British using Navigation School at Miami.[71]

Requested some kind of reply prior to my departure. All training in RAF even in Operational Training Units is under Garrod.[72]

Called on AVM Freeman, Assistant to Portal,[73] outlined to him

1. Troubles now existing in Ferry Service from US to England.
2. Necessity for establishing a priority by types for production.[74]
3. Gave him my personal approval on additional [US] heavy bomber production.[75]

4. Establishment of and necessity for a Ferry Service for Army Air Corps [flying planes] across Atlantic. B-15, Curtiss transport and DC-4 all discussed.[76]

Tea in Freeman's office. Tour through London, saw where 24 or more blocks were leveled by bombs; house after house destroyed and burned, docks destroyed with their stores and supplies. Sherry with Scanlons.

Beaverbrook called and asked me for dinner;[77] regretted and made it Tuesday. Told him that I would call formally tomorrow, Monday; told him "no formalities." He insisted upon calling formally so I guess that he will. No air raid thus far, only blackout and I'll say that it is really black. On to bed at 11:00.

Monday, April 14, 1941 [England]

Slept till 7:45, breakfast in room: canned fruit, rolls, chocolate. Embassy at 9:00, worked on schedule until 10:00. Long talk with Ambassador Winant.[78] [According to Winant] Weygand and Petain both old men.[79] [He] Fears for France if break occurs with Germany. Both want Britain to win but will not help. England on clothing ration. Bread made of potato and wheat flour. Situation in East Mediterranean very serious.[80] Harmon can go home when Royce comes to take his place.[81] He [Winant] agrees that Reserve Officers can fill out in Embassy and thus save Regular Officers; agrees that there should be an Air Officer on all boards and committees that meet with British so that lineup will be balanced with theirs: Army, Navy, Air.

Left for Beaverbrook's office. Met the Beaver, Dawson, Westbrook;[82] talked over Ferry Service situation. He agreed to our plans, plans adopted for submission prior to leaving Washington. Everything subject to approval by Washington. Asked for and was told that I could get for Army Air Corps 2 Spitfires, 2 Hurricanes, 2 Wellingtons, 2 night fighters.[83] Arranged for program to see British planes and factories. Was assured I could see everything that they had. Will meet B's [Beaverbrook's] men tomorrow and work out details of production and ferry problems.

Lunch with Harriman, Scanlon, Courtney, Quesada.[84] Discussed all topics taken up with British. Gave Harriman complete picture. Harriman told me to hold Saturday for Churchill. Had already promised Beaverbrook the week-end but told Harriman that I would cancel the Beaver's invitation. Called on Harris, AVM, deputy to Portal, discussed general topics.[85] Stayed until 5:45; tea.

Am amazed at calm and peaceful attitude of office personnel, no hurry or excitement anywhere. Sandbags on all streets, bomb holes and craters almost everywhere but business goes on just the same. [Barrage] Balloons so far have brought down 114 British and 17 German planes. Talked over present and future pursuit and bomber planes with Harris.

Called on Balfour, Assistant Secretary for Air.[86] Had sherry with Freeman, Balfour and Courtney. Special pass needed for all buildings but arrangements always made so that I do not have to wait. Home via Buckingham Palace, string of 12 bombs with one hitting the palace, others close enough to break windows; several across street in park, wing of palace damaged. The Beaver went home sick and did not call on me.

Went out to go to dinner with Balfour. Blackout: streets all dark, no lights anywhere except a single small beam from taxis, beam thrown downward, not a light from any window. Remarkable that anyone can find their way about. Slessor home with flu. Dinner with Balfour, Harris, Courtney and Street.[87] They say that this restaurant is famous for something but I haven't found out what.

If it weren't for the soldiers carrying gas masks, tin hats and the general wreckage from bombs, there would be little indication of war. Sinking of ships causing extreme shortage of supplies. Beaver's figures show that loss in production amounts in some months to as much as $33\frac{1}{3}$ percent. Last month production — 1,800 planes, 1,200 [of them] combat.

Tuesday, April 15, 1941 [England]

Breakfast 8:00. Dawson's office at 9:30. Talked over:
1. Experts from factories in US to England.
2. Experts from RAF to Wright Field.[88]
3. Standardization of equipment and shipment of planes for England complete and ready to fly even if US equipment must be installed [once they reach England].

4. Engines and carburetors.
5. Visit to Napier Works.[89]

Then visited Westbrook and discussed: 1. Ferry Service. 2. Priorities for production, transportation. 3. New 12,000-plane [production] program.[90]

Car waiting at 12:30 for Quesada and me to go to Fighter Command. Arrived at AVM Douglas' headquarters at 1:15, had lunch.[91] Met Sweeney coordinator for Eagle Squadron.[92] Squadron now moving up to front for combat duty: a good thing, either it fights or is disbanded, in my opinion. Douglas a very charming and highly intelligent man. Talked over day fighters, night fighters, pounds per sq. ft.,[93] runways, new types of planes.

Went through Air Defense Headquarters, saw plotting boards, all very similar to our set-up under Chaney.[94] No Germans in sight anywhere; British squadron flying towards Calais. Four German squadrons took off and it looked like a scrap but no soap. Went down to sector headquarters,[95] still no Germans. Then down to wing and still no Germans in air.[96]

Coldstream Guards turned out in my honor.[97] Inspected two Polish squadrons, one took off on alert. Couldn't find Czermack. Gave them a salute and they all cheered in Polish.[98] Airdromes prepared for attack, planes all dispersed in positions sheltered by embankments. Polish have both Spitfires and Hurricanes. Low hangars sunk almost to level of ground. Barbed wire everywhere, infantry guards, armored cars (home-made). All men looked alert, eager, keen.

From Douglas:

1. Maximum performance of pursuit, day, desired, at both 23,000 and 37,000 feet. Two planes if necessary.
2. DB-7 a good night fighter with modifications.[99]
3. Enlisted pilots are unquestionably an asset. Should be about $33\frac{1}{3}$ per cent [of the total pilot force].
4. Junior Automatic pilots not needed in pursuit. These planes are only in clouds a very few minutes and auto control not needed.[100]
5. British have gone 100% for hard surface runways.
6. One hangar only on all new fields.[101]

Returned to London, dinner by Australian Premier Menzies, all brass hats: General Dill, CG British Army; Admiral Pound, Chief Naval Operations; several members of cabinet such as Bevin, Minister of Labor; Secretary of State for Air Sinclair; Assistant Balfour; ACM Portal, CO RAF; his assistant Freeman; Semple, MP [Member of Parliament]; Arthur Greenwood;[102] Ambassador Winant. Grand dinner.

After sitting about a bit and waiting for others to go home, I started. Then the sirens started, searchlights flashing everywhere, AA guns crackling, AA shells bursting. Still far away, for the guns across the street have not started firing.[103] Several br-umps some distance away, fires, the lights cross closer, the AA guns firing is closer and their shells bursting. They seem to be all around London, bursting bombs on all sides with their br-ump. The AA guns across the street start firing, the planes are overhead, the noise is deafening. It recedes, all is silent again. Another at 12:00; the searchlights, the starlike shells bursting, the incessant cracking of the guns, always getting closer and louder. A fire here, another there, they seem to cover as much as a city block, closer and closer, br-r-rump. Flames high in the sky, two, three city blocks on fire. The noise again recedes, the night becomes silent, but the fires burn on. The raid is over; I leave the window and go to bed.

Wednesday, April 16, 1941 [England]

Clear sky, balloons still hanging in the sky, visible in every direction. Smoke from fires here and there but London goes on just the same. One AA shell hit in street last night and skidded two blocks before exploding. Four enemy aircraft shot down.

Went to Napier works to see Saber engine, just starting production. Coming out at rate of five a week, only 120 produced so far. New factory being built at Liverpool, full information sent to Washington in cable. Looks good as a liquid-cooled 2,000 hp [horsepower] job for production in US.[104] Lunch with Sir Henry Tizard, talked over scientific developments.[105]

[Visited] Bomber Command in P.M., AVM Peirse in command. Discussed technique, materiel, planes, etc. Light bomber has no place in RAF; nothing that LB can do that medium or heavy cannot do better. Entire headquarters and plotting establishment built underground.[106] Starting out 200 planes for Berlin tonight; plans changed to Bremen, 24,000 lbs. of bombs will be taken.[107] All very enthusiastic over 4,000 lb. bomb; it carries 3,000 lbs. pounds of explosive. Made of thin plate shell, riveted together, a steamfitter or sheet metal job rather than a forging or welding. Explodes above ground so that results are obtained by blast rather than fragments. Spoiler checks speed, results: Germans [dropped one] at Hendon where 36 houses were completely destroyed and over 100 others made uninhabitable; Emden, where same results obtained [by the RAF].[108] We must have some at once. Only 140 bombers available for mission.[109]

Flew from Bomber Command to Wing Station near the Wash; [they fly] Wellingtons, about the same as our B-18s.[110] Each plane loaded with six cases of incendiaries, five 500 pound bombs.

[They] took off singly at two minute intervals, two 4,000 pound bombs taken along; target Bremen shipyards. Heard Squadron CO [Commanding Officer] give instructions to crews, very much the same as our technique. Awaited [their] return to hear of results from crews. Each crew interviewed by Intelligence Officer. Must be a sort of psychologist, as he knows just what questions to ask to get complete and accurate answers.[111] Six hundred mile trip each way. All planes from this station returned safely, all but one dropped bombs on target, one shot down a JU-88.[112] It came down out of clouds directly in rear and was shot down almost immediately.

Airdrome dark for returning planes; red light in center of field with small line of markers, all electric. Each plane fires identification signal on approaching field. Beacon on nearby field guides planes to vicinity. As plane circles, tee is lighted, turned off as plane straightens out for glide. Glide path may be secured from instrument which shows red for too steep, amber for too shallow and green for correct angle of glide.[113] Floodlights turned on until wheels hit ground, turned off then. Small truck with dimmed lights guides plane to parking place. Each member of crew interviewed as to weather, route, altitude, searchlights, flak (AA guns),[114] target, where bombs struck, enemy aircraft, etc. Planes took off at 8 [P.M.] and first one returned at 2:30 [A.M.]. Heavy bombing [by the Germans] to the south, probably London.

Call on General Dill, CG of Army. Talked about Russia, Turkey, Spain, Portugal, Balkans, England and Greece; the shore line from the Wash to Lands End.[115] He hopes for a return of 1918 conditions when the German morale broke for apparently no good reason. [Met with] General Venning, General Nye, discussed Army-Aviation cooperation.[116] Spitfire, Hurricane or DB-7 the proper plane although the Artillery prefer puddle jumpers.[117] No place for [auto]gyros or balloons.[118] Speed necessary for accomplishment of missions even though the observer cannot get details. The slow plane will not survive.

Call on Gen Ismay, C of S (Chief of Staff) for Churchill.[119] He is more optimistic. Went through War Room where Army, Navy and Air operations are coordinated, all given special treatment on their own maps; all maps kept up to date. Returned to hotel at 8:00 P.M.

It was thought that the mountains might stop the German Panzer Divisions, but nothing in the Grecian–Jugoslav campaign has indicated that such is the case. The Panzer Division gets through apparently because no way has been found to stop them when the armored cars come in large numbers. They may fall into tank traps or ditches but the others keep right on going. One means of defense heretofore successful was to let the fighting wave go through and then stop the supply column. Thus the fighting wave slows down and stops for petrol. This may have happened to the British armored column whose disappearance seems to have been more or less of a mystery. British consistently estimate German first-line aviation strength at about 2,000 under our estimates. Perhaps they are right, their line of reasoning seems to be OK.[120]

Thursday, April 17, 1941 [England]

Up at 8:00, breakfast at 8:30. Batman took my clothes away and almost dressed me.[121] Took off for London at 9:10; Simmons (Portal's aide), Scanlon, Quesada and AVM____[Peirse, C of S (chief of staff)].[122]

Flew over Cambridge, an unusually beautiful city, has finely shaped steeples and spires. Bomb craters all along the way, [bombs] seem to be dropped on all industrial centers with mostly misses. Some very close to fine old houses.

British bombers from ser [sergeant] pilots and bombers [bombardiers] to AVM insistent that precision [bomb]sight that requires more than 20 sec [seconds] of straight flying on approach to the target can never be used on account of AA guns and enemy aircraft, except at extremely high altitude. We should therefore start design of one that requires but a 20 sec run in case we may be wrong. Personally, I don't believe we are. I think that British have much to learn about bombing, but who am I to question two years of bombing in real war. Hence, the study as soon as I get back. British are not using Sperry sight.[123]

Saw the devastation from German 4,000 lb. bomb; it was terrible. Landed at Hendon, veil of smoke over London. Wing CO at Hendon said that London had been very hard hit last night, the worst raid yet.[124] RAF car with chauffeur waiting for me. Said "good bye" to AVM [Peirse] and pilots.

Signs of bombing everywhere as we drove to the Dorchester. People salvaging what they could from wrecked stores, glass all over streets, buildings flattened, fire departments working everywhere, traffic rerouted where streets were impassable. Such a disturbance in Washington would have caused almost unbreakable traffic jams; here traffic moves in orderly manner in spite of wrecks and diversions. Report that Selfridges destroyed.[125] Four bombs dropped within 150 feet of hotel, two houses flattened. Glass everywhere but hotel unscathed. Bombs made craters and broke water and gas mains. Five hundred German planes took part with six shot down. Raid started at 10:00 P.M. and continued until 5:00 A.M. Harmon and Cummings stayed at window all night and watched, each one hoping that the other would suggest going down into the bombproof shelter, neither did.

Britain back at work [after the raids] in a determined sort of way. Fires still burning this P.M. Wrote 10 cables,[126] lunch at Claridges; [cost] one pound six shillings for three of us, lunch only mediocre.[127] Conference with Winant, Harriman, Lee, Scanlon, all about cables.

RAF optimistic over outcome of war. Carrying on missions from Iceland to Singapore; works with Navy in Atlantic, Mediterranean against sub bases, surface raider bases, Focke-Wulf landing fields;[128] for Army in Greece, Egypt, Iraq; against all kinds of installations in Germany. Navy not too optimistic; natural, as they have had some hard bumps and are spread from hell to breakfast on oceans all over the world. Army almost pessimistic; they have been awaiting equipment while other parts were withdrawing and getting beaten; [suffering from] inaction and lack of equipment.

Friday, April 18, 1941 [England]

Glass, glass everywhere, shops with crockery, glass and beautiful nicknacks and glass on shelves but windows and doors blown out. Bakery shop with no front, women selling delicious hot bread and rolls. Antique shop with furniture, almost priceless, spread all over street and sidewalk, some uninjured. Large holes in streets, bomb craters with unknown results on water and gas lines. Workmen making temporary repairs in mains, bomb shelters being made in cellars and old bomb craters.

Debris-moving details starting work at once so that quite often the debris is gone within 24 hours after the bombing. Pathetic sights of people trying to gather such of their belongings from wrecked homes as were not destroyed. Very few small children still in Blitz area.[129]

An air combat over London at 20,000 feet or more. Ribbons of condensed vapor twisting and intertwining over the city. Real sky writing but who wins?[130] We can't tell down here below. The sun is shining and London is smiling, only a little, in a grim sort of way. Hundreds of people killed and injured but the papers give a small official notice of the name and simply killed in action; no details, just a small notice. Occasional bright flowers in window box. The fire at Selfridge's is still burning but steps are already being taken to open on the ground floor with no third or second. People still groping in the wreckage of their homes for salvage; brick and sandbag barricades up in front of many buildings. Scars on buildings from bomb fragments and more bomb holes, fires still burning in ruins. Vacant spots in house rows where houses used to be. Six thousand bombs dropped last night, 600 people killed, 4,000 injured. Hospitals filled, hospitals evacuated to the country and small towns. Clean up the city and then wait for another one. Back of it all a determination not to be wiped off the map. Sent 12 cables back to Washington.

Luncheon given by Sinclair, Secretary of State for Air; all brass hats, see menu for list.[131] Lunch at Savoy where land mine had hit between hotel and river. Gaping hole over underground [subway] which had both ends filled. All windows and doors in front of Savoy blown out,[132] the hotel a bit drafty.

Went to Air Raid Protection [Headquarters] and met Mr. Sinclair in charge.[133] Map of London showing where all bombs dropped have hit, spread all over London; in most cases close to RR stations, switching points, power stations or transformers, bridges, arsenals, docks, warehouses, factories, but a lot that are not. This organization built up to take care of everything connected with destructive efforts of raids: killed, wounded, fires, gas mains, water mains, etc.

Packed for trip to Ditchley, built in 1700s.[134] Now owned by Mr. Tree; Mrs. Tree was Miss Nancy Langhorne of Virginia.[135] Harriman and I are going together. Lost en route, chauffeur cannot find way when signs are all gone. Instead of arriving at 7:30 we arrived at 8:30; never know where you are going with signs down.[136] Raining. Castle with large grounds, high ceilings, beautiful colored paintings of Chas. II and wife, son, other paintings by masters.[137] Living room and library beautifully furnished in original furniture. Eight for dinner: Churchill, Harriman, Mrs. Tree, CO of Guards, Brendan Bracken,[138] Hap and two women, ladies so and so.

Talked with Churchill until 2:00 A.M., then to bed in wing overlooking fine old garden, old prints all over the walls. Valet an excellent one, took all clothes and laid out Scanlon's dinner coat.[139] Bed shaped like a sleigh with curved, huge ends. Still blackout as no light must escape from windows, this necessary as Germans drop bombs on houses where lights show. Churchill said: "Russia like an immoral crocodile waiting in the depths for whatever prey may come his way." Sentinels all around house to protect Prime Minister. Our discussions covered a multitude of subjects from the pleasure of sleep to the horrors of war.

[According to Churchill] In 1941 few gains can be expected. The German Army can roam at will over Continental Europe. North Africa: this battle of North Africa can and must be won with American aid. 1942 is a year of increasing strength for our Army but we must plan for 1943. There must be bases in Greenland for our aircraft.[140] Long-range bombers must be furnished to the British as fast as we can get them over. In the Azores there should be squadrons of our Navy ready to operate if and when Germany takes Portugal. Armor equipment in the British Army seems to be ahead of trained personnel to handle it. Once again we hear the statement: "England never wins battles but always wins wars." We must plan new equipment out for 1943: pressure [pressurized] cabins, long-range bombers, larger bombers.[141]

At the present time, submarines seem to be licked by convoys. Focke-Wulfs must be licked by pursuit planes, pursuit planes operating from vessels in convoys, pursuit planes operating from these ships will land where fuel permits. Pilots will save themselves if they can.[142] Few British and Allied ships were sunk in April but many German ships were sunk by the new method the British Coastal Command is now using. In this, the light bomber flying low over water releases bomb just as the bomber reaches the target. The bomb is still dropping at an angle when it hits the water. If it hits the ship it usually hits just about the water line. If it hits the water it bounces and penetrates the sides of the ship. The British have had wonderful success by this method.[143] Planes start out flying where a ship is thought to be. If they make contact with one, OK; if not, they return to their home base and start out again.

Saturday, April 19, 1941 [England]

Still raining. This place has tremendous lawn with big trees and a lake. Tea furnished in bed, curtains opened by valet, wonderful view of garden. Garden outlined by shrubs rather than flowers. No signs of war but the tramp of sentinels on the flagstones, the footsteps of the guards with sentinels changing post.[144] Harriman said to meet him at breakfast at 8:30 but I came down at 9:00 and no one was in sight. Around the room there are hung some of the oldest deer heads known. They were shot back in the 1600s by various people. Under each is a nameplate, following are two examples:

> 1608 From Fox Hole driven what could I do, being lame I fell.
>
> Before the King and Prince near Rosamund her well.
>
> 1608 August 26 Monday. King James made me to run for life from Dead Man's riding.
>
> I ran to Goreil Gate where Death for me was biding.[145]

Original owner of this house was Sir Henry Lee who married the bastard daughter of Charles the Second.[146] Five hundred acres surround the house, original house built in 1600, rebuilt in 1720. Architect Gibbs also painted many of the pictures and designed and made the furniture. Also many Chesterfield pictures around the walls;[147] furniture coverings, wall coverings, gilt. Trimmings are all original, colors are greens and blues which have faded out, yellows and red still retain colors. Original upholstery on chairs.

British plan base in Basra [Iraq] and an air depot 1,000 miles from Cairo [Egypt]; 2,500 men will be sent there at once.[148] Our talks today included Norway, Azores, Morocco, Dakar, Suez, Greenland, Iceland. We also talked about publicity in America, including the proper propaganda by someone who understands the psychology of the American people and what information would do the most good.[149]

Lunch with Prime Minster Churchill and Mrs. Churchill, President Benes of Czecho Slovakia, Prime Minister of Czecho Slovakia, Chief of Staff of Czcho Slovakian Army and Harriman. Czecho Slovakians wanted to know why the United States had failed to recognize their government [in exile]. I did not know the answer so could say nothing.[150] Reviewed Czecho Slovakian troops about 30 miles away;[151] 2,000, all that is left of an army of 1,500,000. They gave a wonderful demonstration for the appearance of Churchill; all fine looking, keen and alert, equipped by the British and wear British uniforms. Rode around the country with Churchill during which time the topics of discussions were Spain, Portugal, Persia, Tripoli, Sicily and Italy.

Churchill has a wonderful knowledge of all phases of operations and a remarkably retentive mind; is well liked by all people and is met with enthusiastic demonstrations everywhere he appears. Portal present at castle upon return. Pope's "Rape of the Lock" was written at Ditchley Castle.[152] After talking with Portal more convinced than ever [United States] must take up with Sperry a new type of bombsight requiring 20 second straight bomb run, two targets only. Portal also talked about 6,000 pound bomb; he was advised that we are experimenting on glide bombs.[153]

Some of the Czecho Slovakian stories I heard today were very sad. One Czecho Slovakian Major General had not heard from his family at Prague since May a year ago and must not write, as it would bring hardships to his family.

Surprised to see Portal at Ditchley Castle. Portal only 47, yet commands the whole Royal Air Force.[154] Churchill and Portal both say we must come into the fight. Dinner for 14. After dinner gathered around table. General talk with Churchill and Portal as to who was brains in Germany. Portal is a brilliant man who does things, is capable and knows his job. Prime Minister a huge personality and has a most wonderful mind. On to bed at 2 A.M.

Sunday, April 20, 1941 [England]

Send hams [upon return to the US] to Dill, Beaverbrook, Portal and Mrs. Tree and _____. Up at 8:30; breakfast at 9:00, Lady Portal and ACM Portal. Showed valet how to pack my bag. Twenty minutes with Churchill while he was working in bed dictating; tell the President that with you we win.

Guard of honor waiting for me as I stepped out the front door, inspected guard, platoon from guard stationed at Ditchley. Rode with Portal to Hartford[155] where Beaverbrook had display of all types of planes, some very impressive, some not so hot: Typhoon, Mosquito, outstanding; DB-7 with 12 guns, another with four cannons. All brass hats there:

Forrestal,[156] Harriman, Winant, Beaverbrook, Lee and many RAF high rankers.

The Beaver, Pete and I rode through London to the Beaver's place.[157] Talked all afternoon re: ferry service, interchange of planes, necessity of experts in England from our factories, necessity for British experts in USA, British production, effect of bombing on production, Saber engine development programs.

Dinner with Lord of the Admiralty, Alexander; General Dill; General Pyle, Chief of AA Arty [artillery]; one member of Parliament, name not known.[158] Only one AA man from USA has visited Pyle's outfit; we should have more. Efficiency of AA getting better all the time since they have hitched [radar] detectors to guns. At start, [shot down] one plane for every 40,000 rounds fired, then

    1 for 20,000 [rounds]
    1 for 9,000 [rounds]
    1 for 4,000 [rounds]
  March 1 for 2,500 [rounds]
  April so far 1 for 4,000 [rounds]

They have about 500 guns scattered about England. Before and during dinner we talked of Egypt, Greece, air warfare, Turkey, shortage of tanks and AA guns. Toothpicks at dinner, good dinner with roast turkey, etc.

Who was it told me that I would not need a dinner coat in England? [Needed one at] Ditchley, yes; tonight also; I hope that Mike's looks well. Beaverbrook's place a magnificent home.

Monday, April 21, 1941 [England]

Up early, sun shining, blackouts even in the country. The Beaverbrook estate stands a couple of miles across from one hill to another with a fine valley and stream between. Large lawns with roses, yew trees, tulip trees, hyacinths, well-trimmed hedges 20 feet high, etc.

The thought prevalent in last night's conversation was through it all a fear of losing but a calm determination to carry on in spite of everything. I was greatly surprised when Beaverbrook turned to me and said: "What would you do if

Churchill were hung and the rest of us in hiding in Scotland or being run over by the Germans, what would the people in America do? We are against the mightiest Army the world has ever seen."[159]

A modern Army should have one Armored Division out of every three Divisions but it is apparently impossible on account of production. Alexander, First Lord of the Admiralty, said last night he had only one ship in the whole fleet which could really withstand a determined bomb attack and that was their latest battleship. He further said that we had two new battleships but so have the Germans and they could really put up a battle line with nine good ships against us.[160]

In talking over possibilities of invasion of England everyone agreed that Germany could establish a bridgehead on England anytime she was willing to make the sacrifice. They were of the opinion that the attack would be made in the vicinity of Dover. It would be done by establishing a line of mines at each end of the Channel, protect the minefield by smoke and make a landing after a devastating bomb attack. It was not a question of whether they could make the attack but whether the British could keep them from extending the bridgeheads after they were established.

Back to battle-scarred London, bombed and re-bombed; Saturday night bombed again. Waterloo Bridge[161] reported to be hit and closed, Thames reported to be blocked. Two railroad tunnels closed up. Beaverbrook's house in town was demolished by a bomb which hit the kitchen, the force of the explosion then went through the underground passage to the house and literally tore its way through from the cellar to the roof. Bric-a-brac and glass was [sic] found in the cellar unbroken and things which were normally on the third floor were found on the first floor, everything was all mixed up together. Rooms, including his famous wine cellar, disappeared completely.[162]

I noticed that people don't smile as they walk along. They have a solemn expression. A pile of debris, made up of what used to be houses and other buildings, covers a large section of a park, a beautiful park. Here they are sorting out the debris, salvaging what they can. Everywhere there is grim reminder of what happened yesterday, last week, last month, what may happen tomorrow, what may happen any day.

Unpacked my duds back at the Dorchester. Mike's black tie is gone but in place of it I have a jar of shaving cream which does not belong to me. I will give it to Mike in place of his black tie. I don't know which valet did that on me.

Worked on cables all morning. Ambassador Biddle called, talked with him for an hour about Polish situation, the Pole command in England.[163] Lunch with Top Sopwith and wife, had a fine time. Haven't seen Sopwith since I flew against him in aviation competition in 1911, would have known him anywhere. He now is head of the Hurricane series of airplanes.[164] Had Miff Harmon with me for lunch.

Saw Forrestal and Admiral Ghormley. Admiral Ghormley would not change his mind as to necessity for an Air Officer on the [US-British] Military Commission being set up in London.[165] He is all wet because the British have a strong combination, Air-Army-Navy, against which we have Army-Navy. War is an Air war today. The Air alone can bring Germany to its knees if anything can. The Navy can only insure the existence of England, the Air can bring the war home to central Germany and break down morale. The Air today is helping the Navy in cooperating with convoying of merchant ships. It is destroying bases for submarines, bases for the surface raiders and Focke-Wulfs. In addition to that it is working with the Army in Greece and Egypt, in Iraq, in Singapore, and on top of it all, everybody expects the Air to raid factories and military installations in interior Germany. The land phases will not and cannot be in the picture except in a minor role for some time to come, as a matter of fact until the whole picture is changed.

Several people came to see me and asked about my fishing trip and I expressed my regret to all of them that I was not able to go fishing. Cocktail party in the afternoon given by the Scanlons. Met Trenchard for the first time since 1918. He is the fellow who started Mitchell on an independent Air Force. He still has the same fire he had back in those days.[166]

Only two ports in all England now receiving cargoes, 90% of all supplies being received come in through Liverpool and

Glasgow. Dinner with the Scanlons, Miff Harmon and Miss Helen Kirkpatrick. She is one of Colonel Knox's (Secretary of the Navy) reporters in London. Two large unexploded bombs still imbedded within one block of the hotel.

Miss Helen Kirkpatrick, upon asking her what conditions in Europe would be with regard to certain areas, gave the following reply:

(1) By September Germany will have completed the conquest of Greece.[167]
(2) The movement through Greece will continue until it meets the column coming to the east across North Africa and both will take Suez.
(3) Turkey will be driven east of Bosporus.
(4) Spain and Portugal will have been invaded and conquered.
(5) Germany will be at Tripoli, Morocco and Dakar.
(6) Fewer ships will reach London.
(7) Air raids will have broken morale of civilians in large cities.
(8) England will be tottering.

Tuesday, April 22, 1941 [England]

Met British Military and Air Attaché last night. He had with him three British aviators who had just escaped from the Germans. They claim the following to be conditions in occupied Belgium: there is very little if any meat; every man gets one piece of bread the size of an orange each day; there are plenty of vegetables. The question of heating is a problem, only those living near the mines can get coal readily, others have to find means of securing it. Clothing is very difficult to secure. They escaped through France to Spain and Portugal.[168]

Milk is rationed in London now to three pints a week, three very small lumps of sugar a meal, saccarine [sic] is in sight everywhere. Ice cream is synthetic and has no taste to it. There are scarcely any sweets, no fresh fruits, a small dried-up apple looks good to everybody and is eaten with relish. There is very little variety in meats and very small portions.

We must modify all our exhaust stacks on engines in order that the glare will not be visible at night; this is urgent. At the

American Embassy Forrestal gave me instructions to be sure to see [Secretary] Knox [in Washington] after I had seen Admiral Pound and the First Lord of the Admiralty with regard to North Atlantic operations.

Tizard didn't think so much of our development planes on our development program. He thought that many of the planes and some of the engines might be thrown into the scrap pile. Admiral Osburn wants two [aircraft] turrets developed in the US instead of one. I told him to prepare a study and see if he can convince me. If he could, I would send the cable. If he didn't, I wouldn't. As it developed, he didn't convince me and I didn't send the cable.[169]

Sir Arthur Street came to see me relative to payment for gasoline and oil in civilian and military schools in our training program. This had been covered in a cablegram that I sent to the United States, so no further action was taken.

Spent the rest of the day with Admiral Pound in the Admiralty. The Admiralty has been hit in its interior by two bombs with very destructive results. It knocked out the communication overhead between the two buildings, knocked out most of the windows and doors so that everywhere in the courtyard the windows and doors are covered over by canvas and black tarpaper.

Here is the condition in North Atlantic area. When the escort for the convoys went out 300 miles, the submarines were always waiting just beyond. When the convoy action was extended, the submarines were at the 17th meridian.[170] When the destroyers went out beyond that, the submarines were waiting at the 22nd.[171] When they operated from Iceland, and further extended their zone of action with the convoys, the submarines were waiting at the 30th meridian and finally at the 35th meridian.[172] The destroyers first operated out of Scotland and then out of Ireland. Now they can go no further. It is, therefore, important that the US establish airplane patrol bases to Greenland, Newfoundland, and Nova Scotia so that the whole sea-lane will be covered as the British already have patrol bases operating out of Scotland and Northern Ireland. This is essential in view of the operations of not only the submarines but also of the Focke-Wulfs.[173]

The surface raiders have caused tremendous losses in shipments.[174] They have been operating in the South Atlantic and the Indian Ocean very effectively. Normally they have supply boats meet them in that portion of the Atlantic southeast of Bermuda where there is little or no shipment. This puts them in a strategic position to meet the stream of ships crossing the Atlantic. At the present time ships move as follows: all merchant ships south of Natal [Brazil], cross the Atlantic at Natal and join up with convoys off Freetown [Sierra Leone]. All ships moving around South Africa steam close to shore during their entire trip around South Africa until they reach Freetown where those with speeds less than 13 knots are formed into convoys. The convoy system, however, is not entirely satisfactory.

The submarines being faster can take a potshot at the convoy, then move forward and wait for it and then take another potshot. Those ships moving in the West Atlantic all follow a general path close into the West Indies inside of Bermuda until they reach Nova Scotia where they follow their regular convoy route across the North Atlantic. The method of attack by submarines [at] present is to stand pretty well off in the distance and discharge torpedoes in a fan-shaped figure so that it is very difficult when the merchant ships are hit to tell from which direction the torpedo has come. The Focke-Wulf's method is to drop them right over the ship, drop a bomb and go about its business. The British expect to stop this by putting Hurricanes on merchant ships, shoot them off by catapult after which the Hurricane will have to drop in the sea close to the merchant ship or get to the nearest shore. What the British need more than anything else in connection with their shipping in the North Atlantic is 50 PBYs and more destroyers.[175] Anything they can get will be greatly appreciated.

Saw the [US] Ambassador for a few minutes. Called on Lord Beresford; tell Lovett.[176] Had dinner with General Dill; talked about everything, war and business. The gist of his talk, however, was that when the war broke out his army had no rifles, no tanks, and very few supplies.

Dill said that he never realized what poor soldiers the Italians were until 5,000 of his soldiers captured over 120,000

Italians.[177] In the present campaign in Egypt, it was his opinion that the Germans made the Italians attack because the Italians used too much water when there was a shortage of water. In this way the Italians were taken prisoners and the Germans didn't have to bother with them anymore.

Air raid sirens off and on all day today, no bombing ships came over. Drove home in the blackout, like driving through a tunnel. Another air raid warning when we went home. Went to sleep and don't know whether any airplanes came or not.

Wednesday, April 23, 1941 [England]

Returned Mike's dinner coat. Prepared cable for Lovett and Marshall. Went to Air Ministry: discussed air transport with Portal, saw message from Morris Wilson. Assured Portal and Freeman that we were only trying to help and that we had no wish or desire to upset any apple carts.[178] Suggested that Wilson get in touch with Lovett. Discussed with Air Ministry strength of German Air Force, their method of determining strength, possible flaws in method. [According to the British estimates the German Air Force consists of the following]

Active combat	3,400
Transports	1,700
Total	5,100
Bombers - about	1,400
Fighters - about	1,500
Miscellaneous - about	500
In addition to above - reserve	1,500

Went through balance of War Plans set-up with Medhurst. Had lunch in my room: soup, tea, toast, one small, very small block of butter, two small lumps of sugar.

Twenty-eight Wellingtons on mission to Brest, had to return to alternate airdromes, 6 crashes, 4 total wrecks with fire and loss of entire crews. Two Stirlings did not return from Germany and there is no information as to why, somewhat of a mystery to the British. B-17 went up to 37,000 feet with full load; surprise?[179] One hundred forty barrage balloons can be seen from my window on a clear day.

Conference with Portal, Freeman, Courtney, Tizard, Medhurst covering: revision of procurement programs, priorities for production, development program. Told Beaverbrook that what I was trying to do was to help, not to hinder. We would do what we could along all lines but we did not want to create the feeling that we were trying in any way to interfere with their organization. Beaverbrook replied that he was fully aware of that and was fully appreciative of our offers. He did not want us to slow up at all in what we were doing for them. He would take care of the troubles in his organization.

Thursday, April 24, 1941 [England]

Breakfast at 8:00. No bombing here last night, Plymouth got Hell though.[180] Writing cables again in office at 9:00; 10:00 called on Balfour, Street and Barrett.[181] Discussed final arrangements covering training British pilots in US. Stopped into office and said adios to Secretary of State for Air Sinclair, Portal, Freeman, Medhurst and Harris; 11:00 adios to Beaverbrook (officially). The Beaver gave as his priority list of British requirements: 1. Ships, 2. Anti-tank guns, 3. tanks, 4. bombers, 5. AA guns.

Arrangements completed to go to Bristo tomorrow and then on to Bristol. Will see the Beaver at Poole tomorrow night.[182] We take off for Lisbon from Poole in a flying boat.

Twelve o'clock called on the King [George VI] solo. Buckingham Palace is a wonderful sight in spite of the fact that it has lost most of its windows from bombings, fine old paintings in every room. Arrived too early and sat in waiting room for a few minutes. A Major General came in and took me to the King's secretary;[183] talked with him for a few minutes. Then came the messenger that the King would see me. A long walk down seemingly endless corridors, pictures of royalty all along the walls, here and there horses, famous horses of former kings. Suddenly entered a room, the King. We shook hands, sat down by the open fire and talked. We talked of everything from Hitler to Washington, from war to peace, from conditions in England now to those of two years ago, of our help to England, our Air Corps. He is a fine gentleman with charming personality, the kind of man that I always imagined the British King would be.

People always tell one how to enter and greet a king but why is it that none ever tell a fellow how to leave a king? What do you say? What do you do? Who starts this leaving business anyhow? After being there for somewhat over a half-hour, it seemed the proper thing to do to get out, but how? Well, I did my darndest and left after a most interesting visit. Returned to Embassy, conference with the Ambassador, decided that there would be no newspaper conference.[184]

The King sent following to Secretary of War and President: "Please express my appreciation to everyone for their assistance and aid. Was so glad that world conditions were bringing our two countries so close together."

Called on General Dill. [According to Dill] British tanks are ng [no good]; having unusual troubles in Egypt; whole outfits stalled and put out of action. British and Germans are about even in fighters now, Germans have 2 to 1 advantage in strength of bombers. If we take into consideration the distances involved, it makes the difference about 4 to 1 in German favor. Beaverbrook gave as tank production total of 500 last month. [Charles] Lee says no soap, he says the maximum that have been produced in any month 235. I credit Lee. British strength in [Army] Divisions: total 45; in England 36 (these are new figures). British well on way to establish air assembly depot at Basra. This essential for future operations and to eliminate possible losses by subs in Atlantic.

Take-off time for Poole postponed as flying boat late, may not take off for another day. The three Boeing clippers should be used between London and Takoradi rather than on a trans-Atlantic line; British need air transportation between London and Takoradi badly and no other plane can do it. Many others can do trans-Atlantic, B-24 for instance.[185] Talked over cables sent with Harriman.

Went to # 10 Downing Street, met Brendan Bracken, one of the few men who sided [with] and supported Churchill through his ups and downs. Number Ten is a beautiful old building. It was hit by a bomb that demolished the kitchen and knocked out some windows. The whole wing of the Treasury next door is gone. The Grenadier Guards are guarding # 10. Inspected their barracks, an unpainted wooden barracks like our CCC ones.[186] They have no bunks, no recreation room, kitchen is the end of the barracks. Eat and sleep in same room, one table in center, dirty mattresses folded back to form passage down along wall, no trunk lockers or wall lockers.

Called on Anthony Eden.[187] He stated that the US should give economic help to Morocco; this is essential to get Americans into that country to see what the Germans are doing there; they have been moving in for some time. Ships in ports would help a lot. We should also have ships going into Casablanca to find out what is going on there. One of the most vital points, the Azores; we should have ships there, warships. That would or might dissuade the Germans from taking over. Egypt needs help badly: tanks, bombers, anti-tank guns and AA guns. Basra, very important to eliminate the long haul across Africa. The aviators don't like the flight as it is a long, hard flight across desolate, desert, jungle country.[188]

Message from Winant and Harriman: be sure and point out the real need for the Boeing Clippers between London and Takoradi; also expedite the Ferry Service.[189]

Gave dinner for all the brass hats; this and the lunch and a small dinner all that I have done. Dinner seemed to go off well. No air raid tonight. At dinner discussed invasion of England. Dill, Beaverbrook, Freeman and Sinclair all believe that it can be done and will be tried. All, however, believe that the Germans will have an impossible task in extending the bridgehead.

Friday, April 25, 1941 [England]

Took off at 8:30 for Hawker works.[190] Saw new 2 engine, 2,000 horsepower each, 450 miles an hour, three man [crew] mock-up.[191] Also saw Typhoon with Brewster radial 2,000 horsepower engine;[192] Hurricane with auxiliary gas tanks to permit long-range ferrying. Went to Langley, noted smoke pots all around aviation factory. Smoke pots placed at 50-foot intervals, same general type as used in orange groves [in the US], the idea being that in case of air alarm, the smoke pots are lighted, completely obliterating the plant. Balloons locked in area completely surrounding Langley factory.[193]

Hurricane or Typhoons never have ground looped; asked the reason why. Was told it was a definite relationship with weight on the three wheels and distances between the three wheels.[194] Requested that they give me this information in writing. It is coming over in the [diplomatic] pouch.

Went to Martin plant near Langley.[195] Saw tube and wire bracing plane, streamlined with metal panels. Had all kinds of gadgets. Asked Dr. Ed Warner to go and take a look at it.[196] Went to Vickers works, saw the Wellingtons being constructed [with] geodetic construction; looks to me as if it will require a great many more man-hours than our present monocoque.[197] British do not consider this as they say the geodetic segments are put together by women outside of factory. Saw a big press put out of action by bomb which killed 90 workmen, press completely out of line, probably never be able to be used again.

Hangars completely camouflaged, all parts of factory camouflaged by screens draped over roof and walls. Screens at Wellington works made by utilizing shavings of metal from lathes. These shavings have been painted. Most factories have air raid shelters in the side of the hill.

Talked with test pilot who has been taking his airplane up above 35,000 feet consistently (according to his story) without any ill effects. Told Armstrong to get in touch with him to determine why they could and we couldn't.[198] Received telephone call to return to Embassy at once. Noted pressurized eggs which British are inserting in upper front portion of Wellington fuselage to get high altitude tests. Looks like a good experimental procedure but does not look very practical as it is very blind insofar as the pilot is concerned.[199]

Returned to Embassy and got a lot of cables which were bothering people. Prepared replies and told Beaverbrook of the answers. Gave small dinner party at Dorchester. Ambassador called at the room to say adios, so did Portal.

Saturday, April 26, 1941 [England]

Breakfast with Harmon, Cummings and Pete [Quesada]; Simmons, Portal's aide, joined us. Said adios to the bunch in the hotel and took off for Bristol in an RAF car with Pete and Simmons, 8:50 A.M. Beautiful ride through Reading, Bath to Bristol, arrived at Bristol one hour late. Westbrook all in a stew as were the officials of the Bristol Company. The chauffeur did not know too much about the roads and all of the signboards were gone, the only ones up said east, west, north or south.

Had a grand lunch at the Bristol works, all of the officers and engineers were there. Went through the Bristol airplane and engine works: it was hit by over 40 bombs; one building was completely demolished, the engineering laboratory; other bombs did more or less damage; some did not explode; others detonated upon hitting the roof; one took out an engine test stand.

Bristol making nightfighters. Has engine mounts which permit change of engines in 45 minutes, done by standardizing attachment fittings at firewall.[200] Furthermore they have engine mounts so that on two planes either liquid or air-cooled engines can be installed. When engine leaves the factory it is complete with all accessories, pumps and cowling. The engine is placed upon a truck and rolled into a crate which has ramp tracks included as part of crate. Tracks fold up over door.

Bristol Engine Works going after sleeve valves in a big way, 80 per cent of all Bristol engines now have sleeve valves. Rolls Royce engine practically the only one now being used by British which does not have sleeve valves.[201] Climbed all over night fighter, a very compact plane, the Beaufighter, has a trick seat arrangement which, upon pulling a lever, forms an inclined plane that drops the pilot head-first backward down through a hatch.[202] After tea, was given data re a new Bristol development for a two-engine fighter. Principal feature was two engines, air-cooled, facing each other, driving a shaft with clutch to transmission in each wing to two propellers. They claim great performance. Am sending data back with pouch.[203]

Visited the town of Bristol, block after block destroyed by bombs, entire retail shopping district destroyed, they had to build up a new one. Fire gutted great numbers of houses, churches and warehouses; hundreds of tons of supplies destroyed, docks made unusable. Quaint old city, has a church built atop the old Roman wall. Saturday afternoon and people are going about their business just the same as usual.

Have been billeted with Mr. F. O. Wills' manor house [in] Abbot Leigh, [he is] one of England's largest tobacco merchants. Manufactures one of England's best-selling cigarettes.[204] House about one mile from center of Bristol; original house built in 17__. Foundation on solid rock, cellar cut out of the rock. Bomb shelter in cellar; beds, couches, chairs for those who may not be able to sleep. Family: Mrs. Wills, son, daughter-in-law and daughter. Chatting in living room after dinner when air raid siren sounded. Excellent dinner, salmon from Scotland. House has been hit twice by incendiary bombs. Large bombs have hit in adjacent field. AA guns started firing at 11:00 P.M. Bombs dropped on city. Refused invitation to sleep in bomb shelter; went to bed and slept like a rock.

Sunday, April 27, 1941 [England to Lisbon, Portugal]

My host tells me that the raid last night was quite intensive; I think he is disgusted because I slept through it. Thinking over last night's dinner: sherry, thick soup, fresh salmon, cauliflower, toast, champagne, blanc mange, port and coffee: shortages are about the same as in London.[205] Sugar, fresh vegetables, fresh fruits, tea and selection of meats. Pet dogs are being killed [in London] due to lack of dog food. All meats are rationed and that leaves little for Fido.

Maid awakened me this A.M. by bringing in tea; she opened curtains and let in the sunlight. There are blackouts in the country just the same as in the city. The room I occupied had window protection of heavy boards mounted on rubbers to protect against bomb fragments. Breakfast at 7:20: canned tongue, one egg, didn't know technique of cooking egg on side table so caused some commotion when I assumed that it was already cooked. As in all British houses everyone helps themselves from side tables: toast, rolls, tea, breakfast food and sausage.[206] Place has 40 acres; Wills family have lived there for many generations. Packed car and rather regretfully said adios to a beautiful place.

Took off in car at 8:00 A.M. Met Scanlon and Simmons as Pete and I only stayed at Wills' house. Beaverbrook had us billeted [there] as he did not want us to take any unnecessary risks by sleeping at hotel in town. The RAF driver started for airport and much to Simmons' disgust, got lost; Simmons takes lead and he gets lost. It is a good thing that we left in plenty of time or we would have missed the plane. Mr. Wills finally catches up to us in his car. He leads and then he gets lost; we stop. After asking a few questions we again take off and finally reach airport in plenty of time. We were very cordially received; weighed in but given a very large allowance. Quite a few people there to see us off: the President of the Bristol works;[207] Shelmerdine, Director of General Civil Air Transport; Wills. Took off at 8:30, landed at 9:00 near Lands End; that is airport of two-engine fighter squadron, it brought down the first Focke-Wulf plane a couple of nights ago.[208]

Off again at 9:30 for Lisbon. American by name of Campbell on board. He is wheat expert, land reclamation expert and has been talking with British about tanks.[209] His data same as I have already received. Out of 600 tanks that started from Cairo only 42 reached Italian positions, only 7 knocked out by enemy action. Balance out of action due to poor construction of tracks.[210]

Blinders over windows until we were about 300 miles out. We are flying in a KLM DC-3. My guess of course [flown] is 260 degrees for about two hours, then 185 and finally 120. The only way I could guess was from sunbeams entering through holes in blinders for first part of trip and position of sun thereafter. Ran into storm along Spanish coast, ceiling about 600 feet, cliffs about 300 high. Beautiful villages, finished in blues, yellows and reds. Rain and fog; Lisbon comes into view through the fog; the lighthouse, the harbor, the Columbus monument, a replica of the Santa Maria standing some 100 or more feet high, just the prow with the crew crowding forward.[211] More fog and rain and I knew that we could not reach the regular airport. We flew south, past the town and came to a military airport. It was a welcome sight. Within 15 minutes after we landed the fog and rain were right down on the ground. Portuguese of all kinds crowded around the plane; we wait for the officials to clear us. Landed at 5:20 P.M. after a trip of about 1,000 miles. The customs inspection was a long, drawn-out affair.

Colonel Caum, the US military attaché, took us to town in his auto. His chauffeur had an accident, bent the door of the car. No spares in Lisbon, it is still bent. The hotel, a wonderful place for ex-kings, princes, dukes, duchesses, intriguers, diplomats and ladies willing to buy or sell anything. The Avis, that's the hotel name; there are no keys for the doors.[212]

Dinner with Pete, Mike, Caum and Hohenthal,[213] Assistant military attaché from Berlin. Clipper sailing tomorrow with full passenger list.

From Hohenthal: Germany has 270 divisions, 18 motorized Panzer divisions, and 22,000 first-line airplanes. Upon being told of British estimates of German air strength, stated that he could make no other estimates. Believed that his was just about as good estimate as that of the British. German objectives: to disarm all continental Europe; to eliminate all British naval bases from continental Europe such as Gibraltar, Malta, Alexandria, etc; to build up Navy (Japan included); to insure foreign trade; to build up economic system covering all Europe. Invasion of England not probable unless absolutely necessary to accomplish above. All Germans in full support of war and out 100% to win. The younger people enthusiastically support the war, the older ones as a necessity. Only about 7,000,000 Nazis in Germany. Germans can take any or all of Europe any time they want to. Can go into Asia or Africa at will, have ample reserves to fill all gaps. No shortage of strategic items except heavy oil. Make cloth out of straw and potatoes. Has about the same texture as any cloth and apparently just as warm. Is used by Army as well as civilians. No shortages of rubber as synthetic supply ample. Plenty of light alloys, magnesium. Food limited but ample to keep body and soul together. Everybody gets bread, small ration of meat, vegetables but no fats, and rationed sugar. No chickens available. [Invasion] Boats are now being taken away from the [English] Channel. Russia will not fight the Germans. Germans want 100 subs that the Russians now have. Will probably go into Ukraine this year. Already have permission to send two divisions into Spain. Spain impoverished, no food. Probably will take Gibraltar from Morocco. Hundreds of German officers in Morocco, Casablanca. German consulate already established in Tunisia. Unrest now in Denmark and Belgium but cannot amount to anything. Will send in report on Morocco and effect of British 4,000 pound bombs. There is no general devastation from bombing in Berlin as in London. German General Staff not in Berlin now, spread out in many places. Think some are in Potsdam.[214] All German generals, whom he questioned, convinced that they could invade England with 90% certainty of operation being successful. Plans are all completed. Hitler uses General Staff continuously, he is guided by their recommendations for all of his operations. His ideas, their plans. People in Germany want peace, but want their peace.

Lisbon is a peaceful place, no sirens, no AA guns, no bombs and no blackouts but perhaps tomorrow no freedom, for if Germany comes, Portugal will probably surrender after a telephone defense.[215]

<u>Monday, April 28, 1941</u> [Lisbon, Portugal, to Bolama, Portuguese Guinea]

Up at 7:30, took a walk through town. Lisbon has clean, wide streets, some have 3 lanes, some have 2 with parkways between. Trees growing in the parkways. Automobiles, but most people walking. Donkeys pulling carts, donkeys with side packs carrying milk and vegetables. Small donkeys with legs slender as match stems, big donkeys with heavy feet; men, women and children driving or leading them. Plenty of vegetables and milk, things that England needs so badly. Houses of all colors; reds, yellows and blues for primary colors, other colors used as trimmings. Wrought iron gates all with different designs. Patios filled with trees and flowers, "Bell of Portugal" roses,[216] mosaics on walls of houses made into designs and pictures, one showing a battle scene. People walking everywhere, all well dressed. Only one beggar that I saw and he was not persistent. Only saw one group of urchins, three youngsters going through trash cans. Young men wearing overcoats over their shoulders, not because they were cold but because they have them and want to show them off. The bull ring with Moslem towers, dome-shaped on top of the towers.[217]

Milk cans of weird shapes and all sizes, vegetables and more vegetables. Such is the Lisbon that I saw. There may be a squalid side, but I did not see it. The women carry everything on their heads: vegetables, milk, dry goods.

Lunch at the hotel, given by Leslie, manager of the Atlantic Division, PAA; Winslow, Captain of the group along; PAA representative, Jack Kelly;[218] Mike Scanlon, Pete Quesada, all present. In the afternoon took a trip out to the Casino, which is surrounded by beautiful palm trees and flowers. The Casino was not working. The local resident said that the habitues of the Casino were like bugs that buried themselves in the woods during the day and came out at night.

Returned to the hotel to pack. The Avis Hotel got its name for a family of kings. The house was built to commemorate the family, was built about 100 years ago and changed into a hotel quite recently.

Took a cab to the airport; all other passengers were there when we arrived. Campbell, a Montana wheat man was present; Carnegie, representative of the RAF, going to the US for training; Phenix back from Germany; Mrs. Craine, wife of one of the [US] attachés at the Embassy in Madrid; the Allison representative returning to the US to get more maintenance men for England.[219] The balance a queer assortment of people; looked very much as if they were getting out of Lisbon before the storm broke.

There is a storm center southwest out of Lisbon with rain and high wind. We took off in rain and light fog with strong swells for Bolama,[220] 1,830 miles away. Climbed up through clouds to 11,000 feet and cruised above the overcast; 28 passengers aboard.

Phenix saw Berlin; he wants to come home. His story about food in Berlin not the same as that given by Hohenthal. Phenix says there is a distinct shortage in meat, bread and butter, but not a serious one. He also stated that Germany must not be underestimated, either in staying power or in power of armed forces. The people are apathetic as to the course of the war but determined to win.

Tuesday, April 29, 1941 [En route to Bolama, Portuguese Guinea, via Dakar, Senegal]

Awoke in time to go on deck with the Skipper to take a look at Dakar.[221] Approached Dakar at about 25,000 feet, four or five miles away from the city.[222] The harbor appeared to be well-filled with boats; about 14 merchant ships riding anchor, one of which appeared to be airplane carrier at first, probably uncompleted French battleship;[223] 3 other warships, 2 of which appeared to be submarines; 3 seaplanes in harbor; about 14 two-engine bombers, 2 wing, [twin] engine pursuit planes. Two runways, each about 5,000 feet long, at right angles to one another.

Good breakwater for the harbor facilities along the docks. Additional airports can be located without difficulty. No signs of any AA guns, land defense guns on ridge.

A camera would have been a Godsend but Portuguese check cameras when the planes leave Lisbon and inspect them when the planes land at Bolama. By the time we went over the cape near Dakar,[224] we were down to 1,600 feet. Over Dakar about 9:15 A.M., Lisbon time. Ran into a 60-mile headwind last night that slowed us up so three hours late to Dakar.

This is the next to the last regular passenger trip Pan American takes over the Dakar-Lisbon route and in view of that fact will probably be unable to straighten out the camera situation. It is very doubtful if any pictures will ever be taken of Dakar.

Return to Bolama at 11:15 A.M., Lisbon time; 8 degrees north of the equator[225] and very hot, no ventilation in the plane. African coast looks quite uninhabited. Black natives, blacker than any I have ever seen. We anchor off shore and go to the dock in a boat. Natives wear little or no clothing. Apparently no rhyme or reason to the kind of clothing they wear. Sun boiling down like a furnace. A short walk, about 100 yards from the end of the pier to the Pan American building. A tremendous tree being cut down and cut into pieces with hand axes. They chop out a section of about 4 feet in order to cut the tree into pieces, the tree about 8 feet in diameter.

Went to Pan American lunchroom for breakfast. Natives of all kinds, shapes and description. Had breakfast of ham, scrambled eggs, rolls, lemonade to drink. Heat so bad I returned to Pan American office where the Governor had his aide waiting for me and offered me his car to inspect the island.[226]

Portuguese Air Corps Major and local Flight Sergeant Major, pilot since 1917, went for a ride. We inspected 4 radio stations, one long wave goniometric, one short wave goniometric.[227]

Both completely equipped and ready to operate but closed down due to no operating personnel being available. One long wave commercial station operating part time. An airdrome control set not operating. All of this equipment is German manufactured.

The airport consists of a cleared space about 3,000 feet square, two runways, administration building uncompleted. Lights for runways being installed. Hangar made of bamboo sides and grass top, houses a Puss Moth.[228]

Left airport and inspected native villages. Huts made of adobe with grass roofs; roofs have to be replaced once a year. No partitions in the buildings. They have bedsteads but no mattresses. Houses very clean, only equipment being a bedstead. Small boxes piled up, arranged in sizes like a pyramid which they apparently use for all their belongings. Kitchen is in outer shed attached to the house. The houses have no floors but clay, very clean but very smelly. All the children have big potbellies, probably as a result of eating mostly bananas.

Returned to the city and had lunch with the Governor, VAZ Montiero, and his wife. Lunch very heavy for the tropics: four kinds of wine, all made in Portugal. First course, omelet; second course, peas, meat; 3rd course, French fried potatoes; 4th course, canned apricots and native oranges. Talked of conditions in Bolama and his former station at Santa Tomas[229] until about 2:55 when I bid the Governor and his wife adieu. The house very comfortable, furnished by the Portuguese government. Wonderful glass and silverware which looked to be of the older period but the furniture in some cases was quite modernistic. The drawing room furniture was exceptionally fine and very old. The Governor does not like Bolama very much, much preferred his old job at Santa Tomas. A new palace is being erected for him in the next town.

Went aboard the plane at 4:00, took off for Belem [Brazil] at 4:25 local time. The soil at Bolama very poor, yellow clay. They say it is better back in the jungle. Most of the items exported come from the jungle and are sent out to the town of Bolama. Portuguese Sergeant Major[230] offered me a ride in his airplane in the afternoon which I refused.

<u>Wednesday, April 30, 1941</u> [Bolama, Portuguese Guinea, to Trinidad, British West Indies, via Belem, Brazil]

Crossed the equator during the night. Landed at Para, Brazil, at 7:15 A.M., Bolama time, (4:15 Para time). Para is now called Belem.[231] Ran through 2 storms during the night. Still dark when we approached and landed. Para looks like a fairly large town.

Plane landed by using a row of lights extending down the harbor. Was given green flares and green lights as we approached the town. Pilot made an excellent landing.

Although it is still dark, it is quite hot. So many passengers it takes quite a time to get them aboard the boat for transfer to the barge where we will have breakfast. The barge, run by Pan American, has staterooms where baths, shaving, etc., are possible. We do not go ashore. Delightful breakfast on the barge under a canvas shelter. Cool breeze coming across the water. Breakfast: papaya, pineapples, bananas, eggs (scrambled), Brazil nuts, orange juice, coffee, rolls, toast.

Back to Clipper after about a two hour delay; still hot. Took off at 7:15 A.M., Belem time. Had a brief but meaningless interview with reporters. Sent a message of greetings to General Montiero, CS [Chief of Staff] of the Brazilian Army; Montieth, PAA resident manager, sent message for me.[232] Crossed equator second time at 8:15 A.M., altitude 5,000 feet, not even a bump. Country below a vast jungle extending from the mouth of the Amazon to Pernambuco.[233] That city looks quite attractive after so much endless jungle; over city at 1:00 P.M., soon back over known terrain.

Landed at Trinidad at 3:00 P.M., met by Major Bump, AC [Air Corps] and Asst. Engr. in charge of construction. Went over construction projects at Trinidad, Antigua, Santa Lucia, British Guiana. Major Odgen in charge was out looking over coast defense gun sites.[234] Tent camp coming along fine. Air Corps facilities show progress; clearing well along, runways started with grading. Squadron here from Panama with B-18. They live in tents at commercial airport. Lack of shipping space prevents construction from moving along faster. Impression gained that British merchants and realtors are getting while the getting is good at the expense of our troops.

Aide from Governor extended greetings from Governor Young; sent him mine and regretted not enough time to pay respects in person.[235]

Took off at 6:00 P.M., flew over Antigua[236] and was able to see new airport construction, field well cleared and runway started. Not enough beds for sleeping so everyone sat up all night. In addition to 27 passengers, we had 11 new crew and 11 old crew.

<u>Thursday, May 1, 1941</u> [Trinidad, British West Indies, to Washington, D.C., via Bermuda and New York, New York]

Arrived Bermuda at 3:05 A.M. Had a long talk with Capt. Searles, [US] Navy and Maj. White, US Engr. Corps, in charge of construction for Navy and Army.[237] Seems to be moving more slowly than at other places. Only one dredge pumping at flying field, 2 more coming some time. Received special consideration by revenue and censors, ran me through at once.

Took off at 5:50 A.M. with 8 additional passengers, total aboard 57. Perfect weather, landed at LaGuardia at 11:35 A.M., scads of cameramen and reporters. Gave a limited interview in which I did not discuss war.[238]

Beebe and Hill waiting with C-41.[239] Brought Scanlon and Carnegie with me to Washington. Landed at Bolling [Field],[240] 1:30 P.M., Washington time.

Covered mileage as follows:

London to Lisbon (route out over Atlantic)	1,000 miles
Lisbon to Bolama	1,830
Bolama to Belem	2,000
Belem to Trinidad	1,065
Trinidad to Bermuda	1,309
Bermuda to New York	670
New York to Washington	220
[Total]	8,094

Actual distance, Lisbon to New York 3,000 [miles].

Monday in Lisbon, Europe; Tuesday in Bolama, Africa; Wednesday in Belem, S America; Thursday in Washington, N America.

Postscript

Although its implications may not have been completely clear to Arnold at the time, one of the most important results of his travel occurred five days after his return to Washington. On Tuesday morning, 6 May, he was summoned to a meeting in the White House where those present along with the military service secretaries included Secretary of State Cordell Hull, Secretary of the Treasury Morgenthau, General Marshall, and Adm Harold R. Stark, chief of Naval Operations. The first item of business was Arnold's report on his trip, during which he covered not only aviation matters but also strategic areas of concern that had been discussed.[241] Stimson labeled the airman's presentation "quick, clear, and very observing" while FDR commented, this was the best account he had yet received from anyone "of the situation in Great Britain."[242] The *New York Times* printed that Arnold, as an "expert observer," had reported optimistically that Britain could succeed against the German attack and maintain "mastery of the air."[243] Stimson hoped that the president's reaction would "remove" the animus that the secretary of war found against Arnold in both FDR and Morgenthau.[244]

President Roosevelt was not quick to resolve the issue of Arnold's retention/retirement despite the fact that Hap's public pronouncements now appeared encouraging and closer to presidential desiderata. In a 12 May speech before the Women's National Democratic Club, Hap praised the utilization and performance by Britain of American-produced aircraft. In his remarks, although conceding the "hard task" of acquiring the airplanes necessary for both nations, Arnold was optimistic about our ability "to surmount either the quantity or quality problem." He described in some detail how the British were using the major American-produced aircraft, insisting that this "should give an answer to our critics who claim our planes cannot be used and are not being used in combat overseas." Arnold was reported as predicting that, when called on to fight, the Air Corps would be the "equal of that of any foreign power." These remarks were reflective of the message the White House was trying to get to the public and Congress about the role and use of American aircraft by the

British. Who more credible to make this favorable assessment than the Air Corps chief?[245]

As late as 16 May, two weeks after Hap's return, Marshall remained pessimistic about Arnold's retention. Marshall reported, in a secret memo for the secretary of war, "a serious complication has developed" with regard to the nomination of the three generals for promotion. According to Marshall, FDR still declined to "accept the nominations because of his objection to Arnold." The criticism of Hap in the White House, so the Army chief of staff surmised, stemmed from two problems. The first was the ghost of Arnold's participation in the attempt to get congressmen and aviators to support creation of a separate "Air Service" in the 1926 aftermath of the Billy Mitchell court-martial. Steve Early, now very influential as FDR's press secretary, had been a Washington correspondent at the time and still remembered Arnold's actions with some disdain. Additionally, Marshall speculated, "hostility" remained with Morgenthau because of their earlier differences over furnishing airplanes to Britain. The matter of FDR's objections to Arnold appeared sufficiently serious to Marshall that he advised the secretary of war not to raise the issue of promotions with FDR since "it will increase his [FDR's] resistance to the Arnold matter."[246] There is no evidence that Marshall suggested to Secretary Stimson any efforts by the War Department or himself as chief of staff in behalf of Arnold's retention.

Whether or not Stimson followed Marshall's recommendation, FDR sent Arnold's name to the Senate for confirmation as a permanent major general a week later, 23 May.[247] Since Arnold's permanent rank was that of colonel, this nomination skipped over the rank of brigadier general and granted him two promotions, an advancement not accorded the other two generals on the same list, reflecting a newly found confidence in Hap by the president. As usual in such cases with Roosevelt, the reasons or persons prompting such a change have not been recorded. Clearly, however, the excellent impression the aviator had made in the White House together with his optimistic public statements concerning AAF progress and cooperation with the British were factors in his favor.

From this point, Arnold's position in the White House was secure; he was invited to attend all the major wartime diplomatic and military strategy conferences, beginning with the August 1941 meeting with Churchill in Argentia, Newfoundland. Several results other than the important one of Arnold's retention as Air Corps chief stemmed from this 23-day trip, though it is difficult to assign precise credit to Hap for the other changes that ensued. Some of the resulting initiatives had been discussed earlier at various levels on both sides of the Atlantic, but Arnold's visit added clearer perspective for their implementation.

Even on arrival in New York, Arnold's remarks reflected positively on the journey. In the brief interview during the 30 minutes he was on the ground there before flying to the nation's capital, Arnold told reporters he had been impressed with the morale of the British people. He said he found King George VI a "charming and delightful gentleman" and added that the British were "very fortunate" in having Churchill as their leader in this crisis period. Further details that appeared in the press presumably were based on data carefully crafted and provided by Arnold and/or the AAF. In at least one instance, accompanying Group Captain David V. Carnegie, then deputy director of Training for the RAF, was described only as a "British subject and former officer of the Royal Flying Corps" (which had ceased to exist in 1918). According to these press reports, Carnegie had arrived with Arnold to "observe aviation training courses."[248]

Although Hap's diary reflected no personal fear as he made his way through the blacked out streets of London during a Luftwaffe raid, this and other experiences with bombardment had a significant influence on him. If the wailing air raid sirens were not alarming enough, Arnold had a constant reminder of the potential threat from the air as he viewed the array of anti-aircraft guns and barrage balloons gracing Hyde Park outside his hotel window. An eager observer as he visited RAF Bomber Command headquarters and operational squadrons, he noted and filed away many details of their operations. He met with experienced crews and discussed their problems, which ranged from the efficacy of bombsights to the weight and lethality of bombs. On his return to Washington, he directed research into the most effective bombsights for American usage and incorporated into AAF practices many of the procedures he observed in use by RAF aviators.

Some of the procedures and equipment Arnold had seen on this trip were in use when the editor of these diaries flew a combat tour from England in 1944. Although not mentioned in the diary, Hap may have met with a *London Times* columnist (Peter Masefield) and discussed bombing techniques the columnist had learned from combat experiences. According to Masefield's recollections of their conversation, Arnold asserted that the United Kingdom was now an "outpost of America."[249] Having been informed in various discussions that the British preferred heavy over medium bombers, Arnold cabled this information to Washington.

Three days after Hap's arrival back in the United States, the president directed the secretary of war to seek an increase in production of heavies to 500 a month. This was to be done by increasing heavy bomber production at the expense of mediums at two plants—one in Omaha, Nebraska, the other in Kansas City, Kansas.[250] That same day, the Sunday following his arrival in Washington, Arnold telephoned Philip Johnson, the president of Boeing and the leading manufacturer of the B-17, to discuss means of reaching the increased production goal. Johnson responded four days later with specific suggestions, one of which was standardized production.[251]

Hap admired the British people as they bravely continued their everyday tasks, working stoically around the debris and dislocation caused by the German aerial assault. Informed by some of his pessimistic hosts that Britain was on the verge of collapse, and having personally seen the destruction in London and elsewhere brought about by German bombs, Arnold's belief in the power of strategic bombing was strengthened. He believed that airpower could destroy civilian morale, bring about economic collapse, and secure victory. Arnold and many other airmen retained this conviction through much of the war; however, neither then nor later did they acknowledge that bombing might strengthen the enemy's resolve and determination as it had done for the British. If a free people continued their daily routine under such attacks, why would not an enemy population, living under a strong totalitarian regime, endure similar or even greater devastation? Arnold's belief in the efficacy and potential of airpower, his conversations with many British leaders, and the bombing results he saw on this trip explained his diary entry of 21 April: "War is an air war today. The air alone can bring Germany to its knees if anything can."

Not unexpectedly, Arnold set in motion other activity on his return. He had been greatly impressed during the weekend of 18–19 April, when discussions with Churchill continued until 2 A.M. on both nights. This was followed the next day by further conversations with Britain's minister of Aircraft Production Lord Beaverbrook. On the following Monday morning, in a cable to Washington, Arnold recommended that the Air Corps assume responsibility for ferrying newly manufactured aircraft to Montreal. British pilots could then be utilized to fly them overseas. This plan would give American pilots some experience in flying the latest aircraft models and it would save a great deal of time for British airmen who would not have to ferry them across the Atlantic Ocean. The president directed that US airmen fly the new aircraft to Montreal, Canada.[252]

The president's directive implemented a proposal that had been discussed on several occasions in England and had been one of the recommendations Hopkins brought back from his January–February visit.[253] Twenty-eight days after Hap's return to Washington, the Air Corps Ferrying Command was established. In directing this action to "help the British get this job done with dispatch," Roosevelt had to have been influenced by the assessment of British needs as recounted by Arnold, the subsequent Air Corps study, and Hap's recommendation.[254] Col Robert Olds, a longtime Arnold friend and a pilot since World War I, was named its commander. This organization became the forerunner of the Air Transport Command (ATC), which came into existence 13 months later. ATC, according to AAF official history, added "a new dimension to air warfare" and resulted in "an air transportation system such as had never before been envisaged."[255]

The British, for several months before Arnold's arrival, had been seeking assistance in training their personnel in the United States. Discussions on the subject had taken place as early as September 1940, during the Battle of Britain.[256] The RAF was attracted by the obvious advantages of flying in a peaceful environment in considerably less congested airspace and predictably better weather. This need was among other items brought back in February by Hopkins.[257] FDR directed Arnold to examine the possibility and Hap had convened the operators of six civilian flying schools in the month before his departure.[258]

Arnold's specific proposal while abroad was that one-third of total US training capacity be made available to the British. The proposal was readily accepted by them, prompting General Marshall to seek White House authority to use Lend-Lease funds for the purpose.[259] Once funding was authorized, Arnold lost little time in reconvening the civilian school operators to discuss use of their facilities for training RAF pilots with the assistance of RAF observers.[260] When legal difficulties threatened quick implementation of the program, Churchill cabled Roosevelt and Hopkins was brought into the picture. By 21 May, the legal questions had been resolved and the program appeared headed towards early implementation.[261] At the same time, Arnold arranged for Pan American to make room in its Miami Navigation School to train RAF navigators.[262]

Among the most significant results of Arnold's first trip to England since World War I was his being given the plans and specifications of the Whittle jet engine. That Arnold did not record any information about this generous gesture in his diary is not surprising in view of its secret status in Britain. By Arnold's account in his memoirs, he immediately brought in Larry Bell of Bell Aircraft to produce an aircraft and Dr. R. Schoultz of General Electric to provide an engine, sharing with them the materials he had been given by the British.[263] Arnold encouraged the AAF Materiel Division in Dayton, Ohio, "to do everything possible to expedite this project."[264] Under a cloak of tight secrecy, the first US jet aircraft (the Bell XP59-A) made its first test-flight 17 months to the day from Arnold's arrival back in Washington. Only 50 of the aircraft, however, were produced in the United States before 1945.[265]

As Beaverbrook had promised, Arnold's visit resulted in an exchange of current aircraft, spare parts, mechanics, and test pilots sent to research facilities of each nation. Less than a month after Arnold's return, the British were preparing two Spitfires, two Hurricanes, one Defiant, and two Wellingtons for shipment. These aircraft reached New York, en route to Dayton, on 25 June 1941.[266] The United States was to furnish four P-39s, three P-38s, a B-25, and a B-26. The British already possessed and were using a number of B-17 and B-24 heavy bombers. The first of the other airplanes left for England during the first week of June.[267]

There were other results that were not reflected in Arnold's diary. He wrote in *Global Mission* that the British furnished "samples of British and German" incendiary bombs. Discussions about the incendiaries within the War Department and with Dr. Vannevar Bush gave Arnold his first acquaintance with napalm, which he concluded "was the start of a new era in incendiary bomb construction."[268]

This trip had to have influenced further the change that Roosevelt gradually made in control over the production and allocation of aircraft. Since December 1938, Arnold's role in the process had been seriously limited in favor of Morgenthau and the Treasury Department. Hap's optimistic view that the problems of building up the AAF and supplying the RAF were being resolved, laudatory accounts of the trip's successes, and Roosevelt's assumption that the military was now committed to extensive aid to England affected the president's decisions. The role of Morgenthau in AAF production and allocation matters declined further, but did not completely disappear. After Arnold's return, FDR announced that Lend-Lease matters were being consolidated under Maj Gen James Burns, a West Point classmate of "Pa" Watson, who had been serving as military assistant to the assistant secretary of war.[269]

It is difficult to evaluate any change in Arnold's thinking as a result of this trip. He left no record regarding the extent to which any of his Anglophobic feelings, which arose during the World War I period, had been reduced or intensified by the aircraft allocation difficulties he had experienced before going abroad. However, his attitude was surely influenced by the 30 months during which Morgenthau's eager domination of aircraft allocation to the British resulted in Arnold's being in the White House "doghouse." And Arnold might have known that many AAF officers held resentments against Britain. Most probably agreed with Slessor's assessment of Morgenthau: "He is completely ignorant about anything to do with defense and his position . . . as a protagonist of aid to Britain has . . . probably done more harm than good . . . since it has been intensely resented by the service people."[270]

Group Captain Carnegie, who had traveled to the United States with Arnold, found similar resentment within the AAF staff because of US aircraft being given to Britain "coupled with the feeling that we are not putting them to proper use." That AAF officers held these sentiments is understandable since the British possessed 16 B-17s while the AAF had only 14 of them.[271]

Arnold's presence in England, his sharing their peril from the air and viewing their devastation while meeting and working closely with their leaders, caused him to comment sympathetically in the diary on the people, their leaders, and their determination. On the other hand, it is not clear to what extent his optimistic public utterances were tempered politically to mollify the president and others. Although naive in many ways, Arnold did not fail to understand that he had been given "marching orders" and that he had been sent abroad "to soften his opposition to sending our best planes abroad." However, when he wrote his memoirs seven years later, Arnold concluded that the British had been desperate and sincere, and had not overstated the difficulty of their military situation and their needs.[272] Additionally, as he committed to the privacy of his diary, he greatly admired Churchill, Beaverbrook, Portal, King George VI, and the other British leaders with whom he had established effective rapport.

If Arnold himself had ambivalence about the results of his trip, the visit had to have been a success from the British viewpoint. Churchill, in communicating with FDR, predictably termed Arnold's offer of training facilities "splendid" and "very welcome."[273] Portal wrote to Hap of his "deep appreciation for your keenness to help us," adding that he was deeply impressed by Arnold's "sympathy and understanding" and his "readiness to bear sacrifices in the equipment of your own service."[274]

There is little doubt that both Harriman and Hopkins believed that Arnold had responded well to the "treatment." The former concluded that Arnold had a "real grasp" of the situation and had gained the respect of the British. After describing Hap's weekend at Ditchley, Harriman wrote that Beaverbook "took him on," which resulted in Arnold's "prompt acceptance" of the need for a reassessment of the aircraft production program. These sentiments most probably made their way through Hopkins into the oval office.[275] Other assessors of the mission, however, later concluded that Hap had been subjected to "intense propaganda" by the British while being "lionized far beyond his expectations."[276]

As his diary entries reflect, Arnold made numerous notations about intelligence matters—a practice more prevalent on this trip than on any subsequent ones. On later trips, as he was generally accompanied by a larger staff and often was billeted at and visited secure Allied military facilities, the need and value of his personal intelligence observations were diminished. It seems logical to assume that Arnold made written reports to the War Department and AAF Intelligence staffs on his return, but there are no records of this in his personal papers.

Rarely did Arnold record any extensive reflection or rumination on this or other trips, most logically due to a lack of time for such luxury. He realized the significance of this journey, however, and reconsidered the problems posed by his journey. He wrote to Assistant Secretary Robert Lovett: "I agree with them, [the British] that an increased flow of heavy bombers to the United Kingdom is very desirable and may perhaps be a deciding factor in the battle for England. However, I am also of the opinion that we must build up an air force in the United States."[277] The dilemma posed by these two competing problems was to remain a dominant and difficult one for Arnold during the next two years.

Notes

1. Robert E. Sherwood, *Roosevelt and Hopkins: An Intimate History* (New York: Harper & Brothers, 1948), 273, emphasis in original.
2. Sir John Slessor, G. C. B., D. S. O., M. C., *The Central Blue: The Autobiography of Sir John Slessor, Marshal of the Royal Air Force* (New York: Frederick A. Praeger, 1957), 341.
3. See Slessor, 343-58, for the most complete account by a participant. See also Mark Skinner Watson, *United States Army in World War II, The War Department, Chief of Staff: Prewar Plans and Preparations* (Washington, D.C.: Office of the Chief of Military History, Government Printing Office, 1950), 367-82.
4. Watson, 384.
5. H. H. Arnold, General of the Air Force, *Global Mission* (New York: Harper & Brothers, 1949), 215.
6. Diary of Henry Morgenthau Jr., 1 January 1941, Franklin D. Roosevelt Library, Hyde Park, N.Y.
7. Ibid., 1 March 1941.
8. Ibid., 25 August 1942.
9. Arnold to Andrews, 22 January 1941, Gen Henry Harley Arnold Papers, Library of Congress, Manuscript Division, Washington, D.C., hereinafter cited as AP.
10. Diary of Col Paul McD. Robinett, 6 February and 3 March 1941, George C. Marshall Research Library, Lexington, Va.
11. Diary of Henry L. Stimson, 30 January 1941, Sterling Library, Yale University, New Haven, Conn, hereinafter Stimson Diary.
12. Marshall to Arnold, 27 February 1941. An account of Hopkins' trip is in Sherwood, 257-58.
13. W. Averell Harriman and Elie Abel, *Special Envoy to Churchill and Stalin, 1941-1946* (New York: Random House, 1975), 15.
14. The entire "Memorandum for the President, Strictly Confidential" is printed in Dewitt S. Copp, *Forged in Fire: Strategy and Decisions in the Air War over Europe, 1940-1945* (Garden City, N.Y.: Doubleday & Co., 1982), 490-91; and Sherwood, 257-58.
15. Robinett Diary, 3 March 1941; WPD for Chief of Staff, 3 March 1941, Marshall Library; Arnold undated memo, c. 3 March 1941, AP; Spaatz to Arnold, 4 March 1941, Gen Carl Andrew Spaatz Papers, Library of Congress, Manuscript Division, Washington, D.C., hereinafter SP; Arnold to Chief of Staff, 6 March 1941, AP.
16. Memo for Record by Arnold, 10 March 1941, AP.
17. Marshall to Secretary of War, 10 March 1941, George C. Marshall Papers, George C. Marshall Research Library, Lexington, Va., hereinafter cited as MPMS.
18. Hopkins' trip and its aftermath are in Sherwood, 230-63.
19. Marshall to Secretary of War, secret memorandum, 16 May 1941, MPMS.
20. Stimson Diary, 20-21 March 1941.

21. Arnold, *Global Mission*, 194.
22. Public Record Office (PRO), Air Ministry Record (Air) 8/487, Air Attaché Washington to Air Ministry, 26 March 1941.
23. Ibid.; Morris Wilson to Minister of Aircraft Production, 28 March 1941.
24. PRO, Air 8/487, DAFL [sic] to Portal, 28 March 1941; PRO, Air 8/487, E. A. Seal to R. H. Melville, 31 March 1941.
25. PRO, Air 8/487, Air Attaché Washington to Air Ministry, 26 March 1941.
26. Ibid., 28 March 1941; and PRO, Air 8/847, Squadron Leader Simmons to Pilot Officer Riger, RAF, Hendon, 3 April 1941.
27. PRO, Air 4/487, Beaverbrook to Portal, 11 April 1941.
28. The problem continued throughout the next year. See Arnold's observation in chapter 3 of the diary when he landed in Prestwick, Scotland, on 25 May 1942. For British perspective concerning the work necessary to be done on American aircraft after arrival in England and before they became operational see PRO, Air, 8/294, Air Ministry to Air Attaché, Washington, 23 March 1941 and Note by Chief of the Air Staff "Faults in American Aircraft," 24 March 1941.
29. Harriman to Hopkins, 24 April 1941, Harry L. Hopkins Papers, Franklin D. Roosevelt Library, Hyde Park, N.Y.
30. Ibid.; and Hopkins to Churchill, 4 April 1941.
31. Arnold and Eleanor A. Pool, known to her husband and close friends as Bee, were married in 1913. Lois (Lo) E. Arnold, their first child, born in 1915, was married in 1937 to then Lt (j.g.) Ernest (Ernie) M. Snowden, a US naval aviator.
32. Maj Elwood R. "Pete" Quesada, chief Foreign Liaison Section, Intelligence Division, Office of the Chief of the AAF, accompanied Arnold on this trip.
33. Guy Vaughan, president and chairman of the board, and Burdette S. Wright, vice president, Curtiss-Wright Corporation. During his Army service 1918–1928, Wright had served with and become a close friend of Arnold.
34. Located in Flushing Bay, Queens, and named for the mayor of New York City, LaGuardia became the commercial airport serving that area following its opening in October 1939.
35. Director of the Bureau of Aviation, Department of Docks, City of New York.
36. The next day, the *New York Times* carried an account on page 15 under the heading: "General Arnold Flying to London. Mission: Air Corps Chief Will Serve as Observer of War There for Three or Four Weeks." "Refusing to answer any questions except on such subjects as the coming baseball season, General Arnold would not discuss his mission other than to confirm a War Department report that he would be an official observer in London. 'I am sorry,' he said, 'but there is nothing I can tell you.'" *New York Times*, 11 April 1941.
37. Myron B. Gordon, vice president and general manager, Curtiss-Wright Corporation, which had headquarters in New York City.

38. Pan American Airways had at least four Boeing 314 four-engine flying boats providing thrice weekly service between New York and Lisbon. They were normally designated with names preceding the word Clipper and Arnold's was called the *Dixie Clipper*. He corrects this naming error in his entry for 12 April above. Coincidentally, Arnold had been present in Washington in 1939 when Mrs. Franklin D. Roosevelt christened this airplane, the first of the genre.

39. Arnold, as most aviators and airlines still do, normally referred to local time at his location.

40. Lt Gen Sir Denis J. C. K. Bernard was governor of Bermuda; his aide is not otherwise identified.

41. US Consul General William H. Beck.

42. Maj Donald G. White's six-month estimate was not far in error. Kindley Army Air Base, Bermuda, was officially opened 29 November 1941, and the first aircraft landed there 15 December. The United States had been given the right to use Bermuda as well as other Western Hemisphere locations for 99 years in a lease from the British by the Destroyer-Bases agreement of September 1940. Arnold discussed the progress of construction with Major White on his return through Bermuda on 1 May as well as the ongoing work at other Caribbean islands when he landed at Trinidad on 30 April and Bermuda again on 1 May. See entries for those dates above.

43. The aircraft was described as equipped with "standard passenger compartments convertible into sleeping compartments for forty." Arnold made several recommendations to Pan American on his return, among them redesign of the berth. He also commented on the desirability of a bulletin board to inform passengers of the position and altitude of the plane. He even suggested that a "betting pool" be established with the passenger most accurately predicting the landing time being given a token prize. On later overseas trips, Arnold often established a "betting pool" among the passengers and crew. See Jane's *All the World's Aircraft* (London: Bridgman, 1940), 163c. Arnold's letter and Pan American's response are in AP.

44. Arnold, alert to the future, was assessing the possibility of constructing airfields on the islands. Great Britain had secured from Portugal the right to use Lajens airfield on the east coast of the island of Terceira in October 1943, after which a joint British-American agreement of December 1943 extended landing rights for "ferried aircraft" to the United States. The United States moved its operations to an American-built and operated base on the island of Santa Maria in August 1944. In September 1946 the United States abandoned the Santa Maria base and moved air operations to Lagens, now called Lajes, on Terceira. This site is still used by the USAF.

45. The local legends Arnold recorded in his diary were not always completely accurate. The *Luise Bornhofen* and her sister ship the *Klaus Schoke*, both of German registry, were caught in the Azores on the outbreak of war in 1939. The latter was intercepted by the British armed merchant cruiser *California* when she attempted to escape from the Azores in December 1940 but her crew scuttled the ship rather than permit its capture. The *Luise*

Bornhofen was sold in 1943 to Portuguese owners and sailed at least until 1950 when she disappeared from Lloyd's registry.

46. First Secretary Frederick B. Hibbard and Maj Norman C. Caum, assistant US Military Attaché, US Embassy, Madrid; Wing Cmdr Jack Schrieber, RAF, British Air Attaché, Madrid.

47. Named for the royal family that ruled Portugal from 1383 until 1580, the hotel is no longer in existence. At the time of Arnold's visit, it was one of the luxury hotels of Lisbon.

48. Air Commodore John C. Slessor of the RAF was returning with Arnold to Britain from the United States on the clipper after months of deliberations in Washington as the British representative in the ABC-1 discussions.

49. KLM or Koninklijke Luchtvaart Maatschappij, Royal Dutch Airlines. It continued to operate from other countries after the fall of the Netherlands in the spring of 1940.

50. Imperial Airways and British Airways were combined on 1 April 1940 to form the British Overseas Airways Corporation, currently British Airways.

51. K. D. Parmentier, Dutch aviator who arrived in Melbourne on 23 October 1934.

52. Oporto is the second largest city in Portugal, located approximately 200 miles north of Lisbon. Given the limited range of the DC-3, this stop was made primarily to refuel before the over-water flight to England.

53. Bristol is a port city in Gloucestershire, southwestern England.

54. The blinders were curtains placed on the windows to darken the aircraft from the outside, reducing the danger of interception at night and preventing passengers from observing defenses when the aircraft neared and traversed British territory.

55. Sir John Rupert Colville, *The Fringes of Power: 10 Downing Street, 1939-1955* (New York: W. W. Norton Co., 1985), 373. Churchill has provided an additional description of the devastation of the city with the "large building next to the University . . . still burning," making the scene "moving." Winston S. Churchill, *The Second World War*, vol. 3, *The Grand Alliance* (Boston: Houghton Mifflin, 1950), 44.

56. Lt Col Francis C. Shelmerdine, Director General of British Civil Aviation.

57. Air Chief Marshal Sir Charles F. Portal, RAF, chief of the Air Staff.

58. Arnold was in error; no model 99 existed at the time. Handley Page numbered their models consecutively and the Halifax bomber in production since 1939 was Handley Page 57. A Handley Page 99 mock-up four-engine bomber was eventually built, but not until 1953. There seems to be no clear record of what type of aircraft was used. The British originally planned to fly Arnold from Bristol, departing RAF Whitchurch, six miles south of the city, in a DeHavilland Flamingo, a twin-engine transport used for VIP flights. It is hard to imagine Arnold confusing the type of aircraft in which he was flown. The British naval captain is not otherwise identified. PRO, Air, 4/487, Squadron Leader Simmons to Pilot Officer Ridger, 3 April 1941.

59. Site of RAF airfield in northwest London; Brig Gen Martin F. "Mike" Scanlon, US Military Attaché for Air, London.

60. Well-known London hotel on Park Lane, facing Hyde Park, where Arnold stayed during this visit. The park was the site of a large number of barrage balloons and antiaircraft guns.

61. Lt Col Charles M. "Shorty" Cummings, assistant US Military Attaché for Air, London; Brig Gen Millard Fillmore "Miff" Harmon, then on duty as a military observer in London.

62. Arnold's interest in bombsights was motivated by the difficulties in obtaining sufficient number of Norden sights to meet Army needs, given the critical nature of that instrument for pinpoint high-altitude bombing. Even though by now the US Navy, in control of the manufacture and distribution of the device, had rejected "high altitude horizontal bombing in favor of dive bombing" against ships, the AAF faced a "bleak situation" in obtaining sufficient number of them to "fight a war." The most recent student of this problem concludes this was because of the "obstructionism and covetousness" of the Navy and Norden. Hap probably would have agreed with the author's wondering about the Navy in this matter if "both services were serving the same country." See Stephen L. McFarland, *America's Pursuit of Precision Bombing, 1910-1945* (Washington, D.C.: Smithsonian Institution Press, 1995). The quotations come from pages 71, 135–48.

63. Col Raymond E. Lee, assistant US Military Attaché for Air, London.

64. The prearrival schedule had been devised by the British. An undated copy of it entitled "Program for Visit of General Arnold . . . for the period 14 April to Friday 18 April" is in PRO, Air 8/487. See also Elwood R. Quesada, Oral History Interview (OHI), Columbia University, New York.

65. Air Vice Marshal C. E. H. Medhurst, RAF, Air Staff Member for Plans.

66. The reference was to the recent battle of Cape Matapan, Greece, 28–29 March 1941, where the British suffered slight damage to one cruiser and lost one pilot and plane while the Italians lost three cruisers and two destroyers.

67. Air Vice Marshal Sir A. G. R. Garrod, RAF, Air Staff Member for Training.

68. Arnold underestimated the impact of this offer. According to Colonel Lee, this proposal took away the breath of the British so that they were "completely staggered by this offer which so far exceeded all their expectations." Gen Raymond E. Lee, *The London Journal of General Raymond E. Lee*, ed. James Leutze (Boston: Little Brown & Co., 1971), 240. In writing to FDR, Churchill termed the proposal "splendid, unexpected and a very welcome addition." Churchill to FDR, 10 May 1941, in Warren F. Kimball, ed., *Churchill & Roosevelt: The Complete Correspondence*, vol. 1, *Alliance Emerging October 1933–November 1941* (Princeton, N.J.: Princeton University Press, 1984), 183.

69. As subsequent entries indicate the question of ferrying aircraft manufactured in the United States was a problem discussed on several occasions by various officials with Arnold on this trip as well as later. Eight days after this first meeting and following several more conversations on the

topic, Arnold cabled to Washington that the AAF consider assuming responsibility for ferrying American-built aircraft from the factories to Montreal where Canadians would take over and assume responsibility for their delivery from nearby Dorval airport to an eastern terminus in Prestwick, Ayrshire, Scotland. See the discussion in Wesley Frank Craven and James Lea Cate, eds., *The Army Air Forces in World War II*, vol. 1, *Plans and Early Operations, January 1939 to August 1942* (1948; new imprint, Washington, D.C.: Office of Air Force History, 1983), 314–28; and Postscript to this chapter.

70. An agreement between the United States and the Danish Minister in Washington assuring protection for Greenland against an attack by a "non-American nation" was signed the day Arnold left Washington on this journey. Since air force personnel had already been dispatched to Greenland three weeks earlier Arnold was aware of the provisions of the agreement granting the Untied States the "right to construct, maintain and operate . . . landing fields" there. The result was the establishment of a shorter but weather-sensitive route for aircraft bound for England, which Hap discussed in this and other meetings with British officials. See the discussion in Craven and Cate, 122, 342–49.

71. At the request of the AAF, Pan American Airways opened a school to train navigators, the first class commencing instruction in Coral Gables, Fla., in August 1940. After the AAF opened its own school, RAF students were admitted to the Pan American course in 1941.

72. Aviators were sent to Operational Training Units (OTU) after their initial flying qualification where they received more specialized training in a particular aircraft after which they were normally sent to combat units, optimally flying the type of aircraft flown in the OTU.

73. Air Chief Marshal Sir Wilfrid R. Freeman, RAF, vice chief of the Air Staff. Arnold erred in his rank; Freeman served as Air Chief Marshal.

74. This data was important in establishing production as well as allocation schedules. The United States continued for the next year to urge the British to list priorities for their needs.

75. See discussion in Postscript to this chapter.

76. Arnold's reference to the B-15 is not clear since that experimental aircraft, a forerunner of the B-17 was never produced beyond the prototype. He probably meant the B-17. The transport was the Curtiss-Wright CW 20, twin-engine monoplane, later designated the C-46; DC-4 was the Douglas Aircraft Company's four-engine, low-wing, monoplane transport designated C-54 by the AAF. Ferrying of aircraft remained a problem until after Pearl Harbor. See the discussion in the Postscript to this chapter.

77. Born Max Aitken, the Canadian-born newspaper tycoon was then minister of Aircraft Production, briefly in May 1941 minister of State and in late June 1941 became minister of Supply. A blunt speaker, disdainful of inhibiting procedures and bureaucracies, he shared Arnold's primary concern with results. Generally strongly supported by Churchill, Beaverbrook often clashed with the RAF leadership whom he unaffectionately termed "the bloody air marshals."

78. John G. Winant had replaced Joseph P. Kennedy who had resigned as ambassador to Britain in November 1940.

79. Gen Maxime Weygand, minister of Defense and commander of French forces in North Africa, was 74 years of age; Marshal Henry Petain, Premier of Vichy France, was 85.

80. Although the reference is not specific, events in the eastern Mediterranean were hardly favorable to the British at this time. Only a week earlier the Germans had invaded Greece and Yugoslavia and their success would force a surrender in Greece only 10 days later followed by the British withdrawal from that country. At the same time German Gen Erwin Rommel's advance in the Libyan-Egyptian desert forced the evacuation of Benghazi, Libya, on 4 April and there was considerable doubt over the British ability to hold Tobruk in northeast Libya.

81. Brig Gen Ralph Royce arrived in May 1941 to serve as assistant US Military attaché for Air with Harmon returning to become, as a major general, CG of Interceptor Command, Fourth AF.

82. George G. Dawson, editor of the *Times* (London); Trevor L. Westbrook, director of Aircraft Repairs and American Aircraft Production, British Ministry of Aircraft Production (MAP).

83. Beaverbrook was as good as his word and seven aircraft reached New York on 25 June en route to the AAF experimental testing center in Dayton, Ohio, where the bulk of AAF aircraft assessments took place. The shipment consisted of two Spitfires, two Hurricanes, two Wellingtons, and one Boulton Paul Defiant. The other night fighter was a Bristol Beaufighter that was to be dispatched later. Not only were the aircraft sent but equipment such as engines, turrets, radios, and other spare parts along with trained maintenance personnel. The agreement was reciprocal and Arnold agreed and sent to the British for test and evaluation P-38, P-39, B-25, and B-26 aircraft. Their correspondence is in Arnold Papers. See mention in Postscript to this chapter.

84. W. Averell Harriman, now US Lend-Lease coordinator with the rank of minister; Air Marshal Christopher L. Courtney, RAF, Air Staff member for Supply and Organization.

85. Air Vice Marshal A. T. Harris, RAF, deputy chief of the Air Staff. Arnold met often with the British airman beginning when the latter served with the RAF purchasing commission in Washington in 1938 continuing after Harris came to the United States in June 1941 to represent the RAF and later following Harris' assignment as AOC Bomber Command in May of 1942. There are several mentions of their relations in Marshal of the R. A. F. Sir Arthur Harris, G.C.B., O.B.E., A.F.C., *Bomber Offensive* (New York: Macmillan, 1947).

86. Capt H. O. Balfour, British Parliamentary undersecretary of State for Air.

87. Sir Arthur W. Street, British Permanent undersecretary for Air.

88. See note 83.

89. D. Napier & Son Ltd., works were in Acton Vale, a western suburb of London, where they produced aircraft engines.

90. The number of aircraft to be produced in the United States for use by American and Allied forces fluctuated during the war. In this period goals were normally announced by President Roosevelt amid considerable publicity. The first such startling announcement, mentioned in the introduction to this chapter, was made on 14 November 1938 and called for a minimum of 20,000 planes to be produced in the United States augmented by expansion of the annual productive capacity to 24,000 per year. This resulted, however, in congressional authorization in April 1939 for only 5,500 units. Following the fall of France in May 1940 Roosevelt went before Congress and requested production of not less than 50,000 per year. After Pearl Harbor, Roosevelt established goals of 60,000 for 1942 and 125,000 for 1943. The actual production of military aircraft by the United States in the years 1941–1945 was: 1941 - 19,433; 1942 - 47,836; 1943 - 85,898; 1944 - 96,318; 1945 (through August) - 46,001. See Wesley Frank Craven and James Lea Cate, eds., *The Army Air Forces in World War II*, vol. 6, *Men and Planes* (1955; new imprint, Washington, D.C.: Office of Air Force History, 1983), 350.

91. Given their success in the Battle of Britain, Arnold obviously was anxious to visit this organization, at the time one of nine home commands of the RAF, now commanded by Air Marshal W. Sholto Douglas who had succeeded Air Marshal Hugh C. T. Dowding, the hero of the Battle of Britain. Headquarters were located at Northolt airfield in Middlesex just outside London.

92. Col Charles Sweeney and his namesake nephew were both closely associated with the Americans who flew in RAF Eagle Squadrons from 1940 to September 1942 when most were integrated into the AAF. Arnold had met with the elder Sweeney in Washington as early as 1940. See Philip D. Caine, *Eagles of the RAF: The World War II Eagle Squadrons* (Washington, D.C.: Brasseys, 1993).

93. The reference is to the weight of aircraft that can be supported on runways and taxiways, normally expressed in pounds per square foot.

94. Large horizontal tables with maps affixed on which attacking and intercepting aircraft were tracked with information furnished by radar and ground observers. Maj Gen James E. Chaney would arrive in May 1941 as head of the nucleus mission proposed by the ABC conversations and head the Special Army Observer Group (SPOBS). The reference was to the system then in use under Chaney as CG, Air Defense Command with headquarters at Mitchel Field, Hempstead, Long Island, New York.

95. Sectors were defined geographical areas within the four groups into which Great Britain had been divided for fighter defense. A sector contained numerous airfields and from the operations block in one of these, a sector controller directed British fighters in the air battle.

96. As Douglas recalled in his memoirs, the scramble of British fighters from Northolt which Arnold witnessed, was not "stage managed" but the "real thing." In a later demonstration that afternoon by No. 601 Squadron, Arnold "shook everybody" by speaking to the airborne British fighter pilots over the radio thanking them and wishing them well. Douglas wondered

what the Germans, who monitored the RAF communications network, would make of the strange non-British voice. Sholto Douglas, Baron Douglas of Kirtleside, *Combat and Command: The Story of an Airman in Two World Wars by Lord Douglas of Kirtleside with Robert Wright* (New York: Simon & Schuster, 1966), 474.

97. One of the foot guards regiments of the Household Division traditionally charged with guarding the residences of the British royal family and other officials.

98. Many fliers who escaped to Britain after their native countries were occupied continued to fly against the Axis. They normally operated as national squadrons of Free Poles, French, Dutch, Czechoslovakian, Norwegian, Belgian, Greek, or Yugoslavian under the operational control of the appropriate RAF command. At their zenith the Poles had 14 squadrons of some 15,000 men and according to an RAF assessment, "their fighting record was . . . unsurpassed." Arnold no doubt visited Northolt where Nos. 303 and 306 Squadrons were operating as Polish units. Czermack, otherwise unidentified, was apparently a Polish leader but an extensive work on the Polish Air Force fails to identify him. See M. Lisiewicz, ed., *Destiny Can Wait: The Polish Air Force in the Second World War; Foreword by Viscount Portal of Hungerford* (London: Heinemann, 1949).

99. Douglas Aircraft Company's Boston attack bomber which was manufactured in the United States for the British, similar to the United States designated A-20.

100. Although the RAF utilized enlisted pilots and the AAF had a small number prior to Pearl Harbor, the bulk of the pilots produced by the AAF were officers. Automatic pilots are control mechanisms incorporating a gyroscope which initiated corrections on the control surfaces of aircraft to maintain a steady and preset course and altitude without assistance from the human pilot. At this time they were utilized in heavy bombardment and transport aircraft. A simplified or "junior" system was under consideration for fighter aircraft but due to space and weight limitations and the fact that the pilot desired the aircraft under his positive control in combat, they were generally not installed in US fighters in World War II. The General Headquarters AF headquarters at Langley Army Air Field, Virginia, was then, according to Arnold, "making a strong bid to get automatic pilots in all [US] fighters." Arnold, *Global Mission*, 220. They were seriously considered for possible installation in 1945 in long-range fighters escorting B-29s against Japan. For enlisted pilots see Lee Arbon, *They Also Flew: The Enlisted Pilot Legacy, 1912-1942* (Washington, D.C.; London: Smithsonian Institution Press, 1992).

101. This practice was generally adhered to in constructing airfields in Britain for AAF use after Pearl Harbor. See Roger A. Freeman, *Airfields of the Eighth: Then and Now* (London: After the Battle Magazine, 1978).

102. Robert G. Menzies was prime minister of Australia; Field Marshal Sir John Dill, chief of the British Imperial General Staff; Admiral Sir Dudley Pound, first sea lord; Ernest Bevin, deputy leader, Labor Party, and minister without portfolio, British War Cabinet; and Sir Archibald Sinclair, British

secretary of state for Air. Arnold presumably meant Lord Forbes-Sempill, a Scottish peer serving in the House of Lords; Arthur Greenwood, minister without portfolio, British War Cabinet.

103. A large concentration of antiaircraft guns was located in Hyde Park just across the street from Arnold's hotel.

104. Napier's "Sabre" was a 24-cylinder liquid cooled sleeve-valve engine powering the Hawker Typhoon fighter; the engine was not produced in the United States.

105. Sir Henry T. Tizard, British Permanent Secretary of the Department of Scientific and Technical Research.

106. Air Marshal Richard E. C. Peirse, RAF, Air Officer in Command (AOC in C), RAF Bomber Command, whose headquarters were located at Walter's Ash in Buckinghamshire, just west of London. With an extensive underground operations center, it was situated in wooded country and known throughout the war by its codename of Southdown. The attempt at secrecy of its location was extended to using as its post office address High Wycombe, five miles distant.

107. The figure of 24,000 pounds of bomb as it appears in the typescript is confusing. If correct, this meant that each of the 200 aircraft carried only 240 pounds of bombs, obviously an error. If he meant 24,000 tons this is also erroneous since the Wellington aircraft from No. 37 Squadron had a maximum capacity of 4,500 pounds each per mission.

108. The enthusiasm for this bomb first dropped on Emden the night of 31 March–1 April 1941 was apparently short-lived since the RAF unleashed only 217 of them during the entire war. The AAF did not use them. See Sir Charles Webster and Noble Frankland, *The Strategic Air Offensive Against Germany, 1939–1945*, vol. 4, *Annexes and Appendices* (London: Her Majesty's Stationery Office, 1961), 31. Spoilers are attached to an aerodynamically designed body to break down the airflow around the body so as to slow its movement or decrease its lift. Hendon is a residential area and the site of an RAF station in the northwest section of London near Hounslow. Emden is a city in Lower Saxony, northwest Germany.

109. Arnold, according to his companion, was "very unfavorably impressed by their Bomber Command. It was pathetic . . . in that their idea of what was big to us was little." Quesada, Oral History Interview.

110. Most probably one of the squadrons of RAF Group 3. The closest one to the Wash was No. 57 Squadron at Feltwell, Suffolk, which flew on the mission described. The Wash is a 15 to 20 mile wide shallow, marshy inlet of the North Sea between Lincolnshire and Norfolk in east England. The AAF B-18 was the standard metal, twin-engine midwing bomber of the late 1930s, built by Douglas and still in use at the time in training and areas such as Panama.

111. This debriefing of combat crews after each mission by intelligence and other officers was adopted for American crews after Pearl Harbor.

112. Junkers 88 was a twin-engine, all-metal, low-wing aircraft; probably Germany's most versatile airplane, it was used as a long-range day and night fighter as well as a dive and torpedo bomber.

113. This was a movable marker normally made of wood and visible from the air indicating to the pilot the landing direction being used on the airfield at the time. The radar used in landing was a very early version of an instrument landing system (ILS).

114. Flak became the common acronym for antiaircraft missile and shrapnel. The term was taken from the German words Flieger (fly or flight), Abwehr (defense), Kanone (cannon). Explosion of the shells in the air near targeted airplanes produced a black puff of smoke as well as the potentially lethal shrapnel, all becoming an uncomfortable threat to airmen in World War II and since.

115. Lands End, Cornwall, is in the southwesternmost part of England whereas the Wash is in eastern England. This is a figure of speech, the equivalent of saying from one extreme to the other.

116. The typed copy of the diary in the Library of Congress erroneously identifies the officer as General Hemming. Arnold's handwritten original shows Gen Walter K. Venning, British Army, later quartermaster of the Army; Gen Archibald E. Nye, British Army, vice chief British Imperial General Staff.

117. Puddle jumpers were small, single-engine aircraft, such as Piper Cubs, normally used in observation or liaison work.

118. The autogyro was an early forerunner of the helicopter with lift provided by a large horizontal blade and stubby wing with short takeoff and landing ability. It was powered by an engine mounted in the front.

119. Gen Sir Hasting Lionel Ismay, British Army, chief of staff to Churchill.

120. The British unit that disappeared is not otherwise identified. Some British used radio intercepts of aircraft communications as their primary basis of estimating Luftwaffe strength. Others, among them Beaverbrook's Ministry of Aircraft Production, estimated German aircraft output at this time "by the advertisements appearing in the German papers for technical staff." See PRO, Air 8/294, Beaverbrook to Morris Wilson, 4 January 1941. United States estimates of enemy potential utilized data gathered by the military attachés that was integrated with other sources and assessed by the few intelligence officers then in the AAF.

121. A batman is a soldier servant to a British Army officer.

122. Squadron Leader D. G. Simmons, RAF; Air Vice Marshal R. H. M. S. Saundby, RAF, senior air staff officer (SASO) to Air Marshal Peirse of Bomber Command.

123. The Norden bombsight, normally requiring more than 20 seconds of a bomb run to properly align the target and insert the necessary calculations, was used almost exclusively by American heavy bombers in England after 1942.

124. Confirmed by Colville, 16 April 1941, 374.

125. Well-known London department store on Oxford Street, just north of Grosvenor Square and the American Embassy. The store was heavily damaged but not destroyed.

126. Sent through the American Embassy to Washington dealing with a variety of topics among them British gratitude for Arnold's offer to provide for one-third of American training capacity for British airmen as well as changes in aircraft production to heavy bombers rather than fighters.

127. Famous hotel on North Brook Street, just a block east of the American Embassy. Although the rate of exchange for the British pound fluctuated slightly during the war, at this time it was worth just over $4.00, placing the total cost of the luncheon at $5.25 for three persons.

128. Focke-Wulf Flugzeugbau had manufactured military aircraft since its founding in 1924. During World War II its most famous product was the Focke-Wulf 190, single-engine, single-seat fighter. At this time, however, Arnold referred to the FW 200 Condor, four-engine, low-wing, cantilever monoplane, used by the Germans against British shipping from bases in France and Norway.

129. Short for blitzkreig from the German blitz (lightning) and kreig (war). In its shortened form it was used to denote the German bomber offensive against the British from July 1940 to May 1941. Many British children had been evacuated from urban to rural Britain, to Canada and other safer countries.

130. Although Arnold had established a world altitude record of 6,540 feet in 1912, this was his first experience with contrails which became commonplace as high altitude aircraft were developed. They are visible trails of water droplets or ice crystals formed in supercooled air when disturbed by the passing of an airplane. He compared these naturally produced contrails with the skywriting advertisements produced by pilots in the United States in the prewar period who released a vapor to spell out their commercial messages to those below.

131. Neither menu nor list of attendees found in AP.

132. Savoy Hotel in the Strand in London, famed as hostelry and restaurant.

133. Not otherwise identified.

134. Called Ditchley Park, now the site of an Anglo-American conference center, located in Oxfordshire approximately 12 miles northwest of Oxford. It had long been the home of the Lee family from whom the American Civil War Confederate General, Robert E. Lee, was descended. When fears arose that the Germans on moonlit nights might be able to locate and bomb Chequers, the official country home of Prime Minister Churchill, located just north of Butler's Cross in Hertfordshire, he, his staff, and guests used Ditchley Park as an alternative, optimistically safer weekend retreat.

135. Robert Lambert Tree, conservative member of Parliament, was married to Nancy Moncure Perkins of Richmond, Virginia, widow of Henry Field of Chicago.

136. With an attempt at invasion by the Germans thought to be imminent in the summer of 1940, the British removed many road signs leaving only those indicating cardinal directions.

137. Charles II, Stuart King of England, 1660–1685. The paintings are not otherwise identified.

138. Parliamentary Secretary to Churchill.

139. Arnold decided on the advice of British officers then serving in Washington that he would not need a dinner jacket on this visit. He borrowed Gen "Mike" Scanlon's for this and other occasions on this trip. Arnold, *Global Mission,* 229.

140. Arnold was informed while in London that the day he left Washington on this journey the United States and Danish Minister in Washington had agreed to permit use of Greenland for US bases. Two air bases, Bluie West 1 and Bluie West 8 were built in Greenland in the next year. See chapter 2 of this diary for their role in transatlantic flying.

141. There is little doubt that Arnold was thinking of the long-range B-29, then in the development stage, which became operational in 1944.

142. During 1941 the British decided to place catapult equipment on 50 merchantmen, the ships being designated "catapult aircraft merchantmen" or C.A.M.s with the first engagement between a Hurricane launched from these ships and a German Focke-Wulf taking place 1 November 1941. See early British thinking about this method in PRO, Air 8/294, Beaverbrook to Morris Wilson, 4 January 1941.

143. This is the technique of skip-bombing which Arnold had tested on his return at the AAF Proving Ground at Eglin Field, Florida and later used with success by the AAF, primarily in the Pacific.

144. The American poet John Ciardi, a B-29 gunner who flew from Saipan, as well as some others have captured the paradoxes of the peace and tranquility of wartime events with more martial ones. See John Ciardi, *Saipan: The War Diary of John Ciardi* (Fayetteville, Ark.: University of Arkansas Press, 1988).

145. This reference is not clear. James I, 1603-1625, was on the throne at the time indicated. There are many references in British literature to Rosamond, daughter of Walter de Clifford, reputed mistress of Henry II in 1174.

146. King Charles II, 1660-1685, sired a number of illegitimate children. One of them, Sir Henry Lee, was ennobled after his marriage to an illegitimate daughter of Charles II. Her mother, Barbara Villiers, Duchess of Cleveland, later Lady Castlemaine, was the monarch's mistress from his restoration in 1660 until at least 1671.

147. Although the original manor house dated from the thirteenth century the house in which Arnold stayed was designed by James Gibbs, noted British architect strongly influenced by Sir Christopher Wren. Ditchley House was built from 1720 to 1726. Arnold probably saw many of the portraits of Philip Dormer Stanhope, 4th Earl of Chesterfield (1694-1773) done by Thomas Gainsborough and others.

148. The British had established a major supply base in 1940, at Basra, Iraq, at the head of the Persian Gulf and used it for a variety of purposes in support of their Middle East operations. It became a major reception point for American-built Lend-Lease aircraft and supplies destined for the Soviet Union. At the Argentia conference covered in chapter 2, the British urged that the base be operated by American personnel which was later adopted.

After the United States entrance into the war it became an important stopping point for American aircraft destined for China and India.

149. Bracken who was present at this discussion was appointed shortly afterwards as minister of Information and arrived in New York in June 1941 to supervise the British program. There was considerable communication between the British officials in Washington and RAF headquarters in this period concerning the "bad" press being generated in the United States because of the impression that US-produced aircraft were not being fully utilized and that when they flew combat against the Luftwaffe, the newspaper accounts did not reflect as creditably as desired in British or American papers. Various PRO files contain these communications. See the particularly critical assessment of British information efforts in the United States by Air Vice Marshal Harris from Washington using such terms as their "incredible fatuity" by a "moribund outfit" in whom it is "utterly impossible" to "awaken to some sense of . . . vital importance" to fully inform the American public. PRO, Air 8/294, Harris to the Air Ministry, 25 July 1941.

150. Eduard Benes, president of Czechoslovakia from 1935 until his resignation after the Munich agreement of September 1938, organized and became president of the Provisional Czech government in exile in London in 1940. Arnold meant Maj Gen Sergie Ingr, CinC of the Czech Army and later Minister of War. The United States, citing "legal difficulties," did not recognize this government until 31 July 1941.

151. Their camp was near Leamington, Warwickshire.

152. Students of Alexander Pope do not confirm that *Rape of the Lock* was written there.

153. Glide bombs were those fitted with airfoils to provide lift and allow the launching aircraft to remain further from the target than a plane launching conventional bombs. Those eventually used by the United States were designated "GB" followed by a number such as GB-1 or GB-4, both of which were first used in 1944. There is an exchange of letters in the Spaatz Papers in the Library of Congress discussing proposed use of GBs in the European theater as early as September 1942. Also discussed was a pilotless projectile that would furnish its own motive power and fly independently of aircraft. Interest in a self-propelled aerial vehicle for use by the American military had existed as early as 1917 when Charles F. Kettering developed a 300 pound self-propelled, pilotless plane capable of carrying 300 pounds of explosives. Arnold was optimistic as to the potential of this weapon, which he termed the "bug" and part of the purpose of his journey to Europe in October 1918 was to demonstrate this weapon to Gen John J. Pershing. Later calling it a "cousin" to the German V-1 and V-2 rockets launched against Britain in 1944, Arnold maintained in this later period an interest in the development of the 1917 weapon. An AAF redesigned and improved weapon was flight tested in the United States in 1941. At the time Arnold was considering whether to abandon the existing four-engine bombardment program "in favor of something else" such as a modified "bug." Radio-controlled, the expendable 1941 model could be produced, in Arnold's opinion, for between $800 and $1,000 each as contrasted with the $400,000 materiel

cost plus the nonexpendable 10 man crew of a heavy bomber. In spite of its successful flight in December 1941, Arnold along with Kettering and William Knudsen, director of National Production, concluded that the limited range of the "bug" could not be improved sufficiently for use other than from Britain to Paris, thus sparing interior Germany. On this basis the project was temporarily shelved in August 1943. After the Germans unleashed their V-1 rockets in June 1944, Arnold and the Air Staff pushed for mass production and use of the US equivalent, then designated JB-2. Technical problems, Spaatz' lukewarm enthusiasm for the weapon, competing priorities for productive capacity and shipping space limited production to fewer than 1,400 by the end of the war. However as late as January 1945 Arnold directed the production of 100 "buzz bombs" a day, increasing to 500 a day; Arnold to Spaatz, 13 January 1945, Arnold Papers. There is coverage of glide bombs as well as unmanned aircraft in Conrad Crane, *Bombs, Cities and Civilians: American Airpower Strategy in World War II* (Lawrence, Kans.: University of Kansas Press, 1993), particularly chapter 6, "The Lure of Technological Innovation-Better Bombs," 78–92. There is brief coverage in Dik Daso, Maj, USAF, *Architects of American Air Supremacy: General Hap Arnold and Dr. Theodore von Kármán* (Maxwell Air Force Base, Ala.: Air University Press, 1997), 80–82. See also Spaatz Papers; Lewis H. Brereton, *The Brereton Diaries: The War in the Pacific, Middle East and Europe* (New York: William Morrow & Co., 1946), 373; Arnold, *Global Mission*, 74–76, 260–61; and Craven and Cate, vol. 6, 253–62.

154. Arnold was born in 1886 and was just about to reach 55 years of age, eight years older than Portal.

155. City, Hertfordshire, just north of London. Most probably they visited the DeHavilland airfield at Hatfield, not far from the town of Hertford which the British would pronounce Hartford. Arnold correctly identifies the town in Arnold, *Global Mission*, 233.

156. James F. Forrestal, undersecretary of the US Navy, in London at this time to confer on Lend-Lease matters.

157. Beaverbrook bought Cherkley, near Leatherhead, Surrey, about 30 miles south, southwest of London in 1911. According to his biographer, it had "no architectural merit." See A. J. P. Taylor, *Beaverbrook* (New York: Simon & Schuster, 1972), 72.

158. Albert V. Alexander, first lord of the Admiralty; General Frederick Alford Pile, British Army, commanding, Anti-Aircraft Command.

159. This was probably adapted from a conversational scenario that Churchill was fond of posing to visitors at this time with a "world in which Hitler dominated all Europe, Asia and Africa and left the US and ourselves no option but an unwilling peace." See Colville, 2 May 1941, 362.

160. HMS *Prince of Wales*, just being completed at the Commell-Laird shipyard and its sister ship, HMS *King George V* were the newest British battleships. When the war began in 1939, the German fleet consisted of two completed battleships, *Scharnhorst* and *Gneisenau*; two others nearing completion, *Bismarck* and *Tirpitz*; three pocket battleships, *Deutschland*, *Admiral Scheer*, and *Graf Spee*, scuttled in Montevideo harbor in December

1939, and three heavy cruisers, *Hipper, Prinz Eugen* and *Blucher,* lost in the invasion of Norway, April 1940. Those remaining and the heavy cruiser *Seydlitz,* nearing completion, were probably included in the British calculation of nine.

161. Waterloo Bridge spanned the Thames River in London between Westminster and Blackfriars bridges.

162. Stornaway House was bought by Beaverbrook "to reconcile my wife to country life." It was in the borough of Mayfair in London overlooking the gardens of St. James Palace and Green Park. When Beaverbrook went to retrieve an item from his bombed house he was surrounded by a group of angry Londoners who mistook him for a looter. See Taylor, 240, 454-55; and Arnold, *Global Mission,* 226.

163. Ambassador A. J. Drexel Biddle, Ambassador Extraordinaire and Plenipotentiary to the governments of Czechoslovakia, Poland, Netherlands, Belgium, Norway and, later in 1941, Greece and Yugoslavia. All of these governments established "in exile" headquarters in London following their defeat and/or surrender to the Germans in 1939-1941.

164. Early aviation pioneer who designed the famed Sopwith Camel and in 1941 was Chairman, Hawker-Siddeley Aircraft Company. Sopwith's flying exploits in the United States when Arnold first competed with him are chronicled in the *New York Times* during September 1911.

165. Rear Adm Robert L. Ghormley, USN, assistant chief of US Naval Operations was in London with the Special Naval Observer Group called for in the ABC planning. Ghormley, along with other US Navy senior officers, was no admirer of Arnold, the AAF or land-based air. His later strained relations with Arnold are covered in chapter 4.

166. Now 68, Marshal of the RAF Hugh M. Trenchard headed the Royal Flying Corps in World War I where he met Brig Gen William Mitchell, then commander of the American Expeditionary Air Force. There is no mention in Arnold's diary kept on his trip to Europe in October-December 1918 that he met with Trenchard, AP.

167. Miss Helen P. Kirkpatrick, London correspondent of the *Chicago Daily News,* which Col Frank Knox published prior to becoming secretary of the Navy in 1940. The day she was making her predictions the British decided to evacuate Greece, which surrendered to the Germans three days later, 24 April.

168. Not otherwise identified. The arranged meeting illustrated the desire of the British to furnish as much information as possible to Arnold including recent firsthand observations of conditions in German-occupied territory.

169. Adm E. O. B. S. Osburn, president, Air Gunnery Technical Board, British Ministry of Aircraft Production.

170. Longitude of the middle of Iceland.

171. Longitude of Reykjavik, Iceland.

172. Thirtieth meridian is the longitude of the eastern quarter of Greenland and western Azores; thirty-fifth meridian is the longitude of eastern third of Greenland.

173. As the Germans used the Focke-Wulf 200 Condor, it would leave Brest or Bordeaux, France, conduct raids against naval targets in and around the British Isles and fly to Norway where it was refueled and sent against British shipping the next day en route to its home base in France.

174. As in World I, German surface raiders were either cruiser class vessels or former merchantmen converted to prey on Allied shipping.

175. The PBY was Consolidated Aircraft Corporation's Catalina, twin-engine, high-wing patrol bomber, its major production model being the PBY-5.

176. Lord Beresford is not otherwise identified.

177. This occurred during the campaign in Cyrenaica, Libya, with the surrender of Italian general Berganzoli near Beda Fomm to British Gen A. P. Wavell on 17 February 1941.

178. Morris Wilson, president, Royal Bank of Canada, was appointed by Beaverbrook as his personal buying agent to purchase American aircraft and arrange for their shipment to Britain. Portal was no doubt circumspect in hinting at the continuing competition and difficulties between the RAF and Beaverbrook's ministry of Aircraft Production. Beaverbrook had little love for the "bloody Air Marshals" who in turn considered him "a merciless critic and even enemy." To what extent Arnold in his own mind viewed this bureaucratic competition as similar to that between the AAF and Morgenthau's Treasury Department is not recorded. Arnold respected Beavebrook's openness, disdain of red tape and ability to get things done. A brief but still diplomatic glimpse into the problems from Beaverbrook's perspective is provided in Arnold's entry in the final paragraph to this day's entry below. The quotes are from Taylor, 414-19; and Churchill to Beaverbrook 15 December 1940 printed in Winston S. Churchill, *The Second World War*, vol. 2, *Their Finest Hour* (Boston: Houghton Mifflin Co., 1948), appendix 699.

179. This aircraft was RAF operated. The British were having problems with the B-17 while Arnold and the AAF maintained faith in the capabilities of the aircraft. There is an account of British difficulties in Roger A. Freeman, *B-17: Fortress at War* (New York: Charles Scribner's Sons, 1977), 12-29.

180. The city of Plymouth in Devonshire had been bombed for three successive nights, 21-23 April.

181. Edward W. Barrett, coordinator of Information in the London office of the US Office of War Information.

182. Bristo is not otherwise identified; Poole is a channel port in Dorestshire, southwest England.

183. Neither is otherwise identified.

184. Even though no departure press conference was held the British press, motivated no doubt by security considerations, withheld information concerning Arnold's departure until after he had reached Washington. The *Times* (London), 2 May 1941.

185. Takoradi is a port, Gold Coast, now Sekondi-Takoradi, Ghana. With the threat posed to both air and sea traffic in the Mediterranean and into the Middle East after the fall of France in 1940, the British began in

September to establish an air route into Cairo across central Africa from Takoradi. A contingent of AAF personnel, of which Arnold would have had knowledge, had reached there to "aid in the operation" as early as March 1941 the month before Arnold's departure. Wesley Frank Craven and James Lea Cate, eds., *The Army Air Forces in World War II*, vol. 2, *Europe: Torch to Pointblank, August 1942 to December 1943* (1949; new imprint, Washington, D.C.: Office of Air Force History, 1983), 3-5; Churchill, *Their Finest Hour*, 453-54. Pan American turned over to the British several Boeing Clippers that Pan American had ordered prior to the war.

186. One of the regiments of foot guards traditionally charged with guarding #10 Downing Street, which in modern times had become the London residence of the British prime minister. The Civilian Conservation Corps (CCC) was a New Deal program which existed from 1933 to 1942 providing work and vocational training for unemployed, single, young men through conserving and developing the natural resources of the United States with logistical support and training furnished by the regular Army 1933-1935, later by reserve officers and noncommissioned officers. Arnold's experiences with the CCC at March Field, Calif., mentioned in the biographical sketch of this volume are outlined in Arnold, *Global Mission*, 140-42.

187. British Secretary of State for Foreign Affairs.

188. Arnold's reference here is not clear. No doubt pilots disliked flying the width of the African continent from Dakar to Freetown in Sierra Leone and then on to Lagos, Nigeria. From there the route led to Fort Lamy in French Equatorial Africa (now Njamena, capital of Chad) and thence to Khartoum in the Sudan. An American B-24 had surveyed this route as early as the autumn of 1941. After the entrance of the United States into the war, Basra, Iraq, and Tehran, Iran, continued as major American bases for aircraft destined for the Soviet Union, China and India. See Craven and Cate, vol. 1, 326-29.

189. The United States contracted in August 1941 to purchase one of Pan American's four-engine Clippers (on which Arnold traveled on this trip), leasing the plane back to Pan American which then operated it for the AAF. Only one trip, that a survey flight, was completed over the US-West African route prior to Pearl Harbor but the fleet was increased after December 1941 and regular service established. Craven and Cate, vol. 1, 324.

190. Hawker-Siddeley Aircraft Company works were in Kingston-on-Thames, Surrey, just southwest of London.

191. Mock-up aircraft were preproduction models. This aircraft was apparently never put into production.

192. Arnold meant the Bristol rather than the Brewster engine, an experiment never put into full-scale production.

193. Langley is located in Essex, approximately 15 miles south of Cambridge.

194. This is a curious entry since Arnold would have been very familiar with ground-looping, the violent turn of an airplane while taxiing, landing or take-off, resulting in its wing(s) striking the ground.

195. The Martin-Baker Aircraft Co., Ltd., works were in Higher Denham, Buckinghamshire.

196. The aircraft and gadgets are not otherwise identified. Dr. Edward Warner was a member of the US Civil Aeronautics Authority, serving in England on the Lend-Lease staff.

197. Vickers-Armstrong Ltd., factory was located in Weybridge, Surrey, just southeast of London. In monocoque aircraft construction the outer skin carries all or a major part of the stress; in geodetic, strips of veneer are wrapped around formers with the veneer depended upon to carry the major stress.

198. Maj Frank A. Armstrong, US combat observer in London.

199. Pressurized eggs were test compartments which led to pressurized cabins in Mark V and VI models of the Wellington bombers and, later, the AAF B-29s.

200. Designed as a long-range interceptor, the Beaufighter was used as an antishipping and night fighter in Europe and the Mediterranean and for close air support in Burma. In aircraft a firewall is a partition built between the cockpit and engines to contain the spread of engine-originated fire.

201. The Bristol Aeroplane Company had been experimenting since 1926 with single-sleeve valve engines to replace push-rod operated overhead valves.

202. This was an early ejection seat.

203. This airplane was apparently never manufactured in quantity.

204. Abbot-Leigh parish is in Somerset on the river Avon, just west of Bristol. The cigarette was Wills' Gold Flake.

205. Blanc mange is a sweetened, flavored dessert made from gelatinous or starch substances and shaped in a mold. Arnold is writing facetiously here.

206. For another American view of this custom, see Charles A. Lindbergh, *The Wartime Journals of Charles A. Lindbergh* (New York: Harcourt Brace Jovanovich, 1970), 157.

207. G. Stanley White was president of the Bristol works.

208. Arnold probably landed at RAF St. Eval, Cornwall, where No. 262 Squadron was equipped with Westland Aircraft Company Whirlwinds, twin-engine, single-seat fighters. The reference to shooting down the first Focke-Wulf is not clear. The first FW 200 was shot down over Britain July 1940 and the first FW 190 in November 1941. Arnold may have been told that this was the first FW 200 shot down by No. 262 Squadron.

209. Thomas D. Campbell, identified in the *New York Times*, 2 May 1941, as the "world's greatest individual wheat grower," was president of Campbell Farming Corporation, Hardin, Mont. Arnold and Campbell became acquainted during this trip and corresponded for several years. See Arnold Papers.

210. This problem is not otherwise identified.

211. Arnold meant the Monument to Discoveries on the shore at Belem, a suburb of Lisbon. Erected in 1936 the tall statue honors the work of the Portuguese Prince, Henry the Navigator. It is an impressionistic depiction of three sailing vessels, one superimposed over the other, showing the outline of the prows of the ships facing to the sea.

212. Arnold did not commit to this diary the information that while he took his walk through the city his bags in the Hotel Avis were rifled and two photos given him by the RAF showing German success in camouflaging Hamburg harbor were stolen. Arnold, *Global Mission*, 239.

213. Lt Col William D. Hohenthal, USA, had served as assistant US Military Attaché, Vienna, Austria.

214. Potsdam is a German city on the Havel, adjacent to the southwest boundary of Berlin, formerly East Germany. The Halder Diaries make no mention of such a removal at this time. Franz Halder, *The Private War Journal of Generaloberst Franz Halder, Chief of the General Staff of the German Army, 14 August 1939 to 24 September 1942* (Arlington, Va.: University Publications of America, 1975).

215. This was a token defense.

216. A rose common to Portugal with pink buds which turn to pale pink and white when open.

217. Built of red brick in 1892 the Campo Pequena ring was located in the Lumiar section of the city.

218. None are otherwise identified.

219. Group Captain David Carnegie, RAF; State and War Department directories fail to show anyone named Phenix serving in Germany at this time; Mrs. Earl T. Craine, wife of Third Secretary, US Embassy, Madrid, Spain; maintenance men not otherwise identified. Allison Engineering Corporation had contracts at the time for maintenance of British aircraft in Britain.

220. Bolama is a city in Portuguese Guinea, now Guinea-Bissau.

221. The pilot was reluctant to fly over Dakar, Senegal, saying it was against regulations but Arnold prevailed insisting that it was "far more important for me to get the information I needed than it was to worry about getting into trouble." No doubt Arnold intended to gain as much knowledge as possible concerning the French fleet in the harbor. As would be expected there is no report of this in the Arnold papers. The quotation and account of the incident are in Arnold, *Global Mission*, 239.

222. The typed copy in the Arnold papers reflects 25,000 feet but there is little doubt that Arnold meant 2,500 feet since the service ceiling of the aircraft was only 16,000 feet and fuel and other considerations would have precluded an approach this close to his landing destination at such high altitude. Also at 25,000 feet Arnold's powers of observation of the details in the harbor would not have permitted him making the comprehensive notes he did.

223. With the fall of France the French battleship *Richelieu* remained uncompleted in Dakar harbor where the British attacked her in June 1940 with carrier-based aircraft to prevent her use by the Germans. She was later fitted for action by the French but the Darlan surrender in November 1942 precluded her participation in preventing the US invasion of North Africa. She was later repaired in the Brooklyn, New York, Navy Yard and saw wartime service with British fleet units in both the Atlantic and Pacific.

224. The reference is to the Cape Verde peninsula.

225. Bolama is at 12 degrees north latitude.

226. VAZ Montiero was the governor.

227. Neither is otherwise identified. Goniometric refers to direction finding.

228. DeHavilland Aircraft Company's two/three seat long-range monoplane, wooden construction with fabric covering, this airplane came into the RAF inventory in 1930.

229. Probably a reference to Sao Tomo and Principe, Portuguese possessions off the west coast of Africa.

230. Not otherwise identified.

231. Belem is the capital of Para state in northern Brazil and the chief port of the Amazon basin.

232. Neither is otherwise identified.

233. Pernambuco is a state in northeastern Brazil of which Recife is the capital.

234. Maj Arthur L. Bump was supervising construction of US facilities on Trinidad and other British Caribbean possessions obtained by the United States under the Destroyer-Bases agreement of the previous September. Major Ogden is not otherwise identified.

235. Maj Sir H. W. Young was the British governor.

236. Antigua in the Leeward islands was another British possession where the United States gained the right to establish a military presence in the Destroyer Bases deal of 1940. An AAF contingent arrived there in September 1941.

237. Capt Paul J. Searles, USN.

238. *New York Times* account of Arnold's return, 2 May 1941, reported that he was "silent on the war situation" and "declined to discuss the military situation there," saying only that he had "a very broad view of England's war machine and steps being taken to build up that war machine," *New York Times*, 2 May 1941. See Postscript to this chapter.

239. Capt R. E. "Gene" Beebe served as Arnold's pilot at the time; the copilot on this flight was Col Edmund W. Hill, Air Inspector, AAF Headquarters, Washington, D.C. After General Westover's crash in 1938, Arnold was directed never to fly except in a two-place aircraft with a copilot. He seems to have followed that order throughout his remaining career. The C-41 was a modified DC-2, Douglas Aircraft Company's low-wing, twin-engine transport.

240. On the east bank of the Potomac River in the District of Columbia, Bolling Field was the main operating base for nonnaval military aviation in the nation's capital from its opening in July 1918 until the termination of flying activities there in July 1962. Most of Arnold's wartime departures and arrivals by air were from Bolling or Gravelly Point, present Reagan National Airport, located on the west shore of the Potomac in Virginia. Andrews Air Force Base, the main operating base for military aircraft in the Washington area today, did not commence operations until December 1944.

241. Arnold, *Global Mission*, 241.

242. Stimson Diary, 6 May 1941.

243. *New York Times*, 7 May 1941.

244. Stimson Diary, 6 May 1941.

245. *New York Times*, 13 May 1941.

246. Marshall to Stimson, 16 May 1941. It appears clear that Maj (Lt Col as of 4 May 1941) Walter Bedell Smith was Marshall's conduit with the White House where Smith met almost daily with the president's military aide General Watson on War Department matters. See Marshall's illuminating secret memo for Stimson, writing, "Smith tells me" and "please do not allow Smith's connection with these matters . . . to go further." Marshall to Stimson, 16 May 1941. Note also Robinette's comment that Smith "goes over to the White House nearly every day to pull the Chief's chestnuts out of the fire or to push some cause"; Robinett Diary, 22 April 1941.

247. War Department Press Release, 23 May 1941, copy in Arnold Papers; also in *New York Times*, 24 May 1941. The press release emphasized that of "the list of officers advanced in rank, that General Arnold is given two [permanent rank] promotion." The other two officers recommended at the same time were Brig Gen Courtney H. Hodges to be chief of Infantry and Col William N. Porter to be chief of the Chemical Warfare Service.

248. *New York Times*, 2 May 1941.

249. Peter Masefield, Oral History Interview, 10 July 1971, Special Collections, US Air Force Academy Library, Colorado Springs, Colo.

250. Arnold to Hopkins, 18 April 1941, box 302, Hopkins Papers, FDR Library, Hyde Park; Harriman to Hopkins, 24 April 1941, box 302, Hopkins Papers, FDR Library, Hyde Park; and FDR to Stimson, 4 May 1941, copy in AP.

251. Philip Johnson to Arnold, 8 May 1941, AP.

252. Craven and Cate, vol. 1, 314.

253. Spaatz to Arnold, 26 May 1941; Arnold to Spaatz, 27 May 1941; and FDR to Stimson, 28 May 1941, copies in AP.

254. FDR to Stimson, 28 May 1941, AP.

255. Wesley Frank Craven and James Lea Cate, eds., *The Army Air Forces in World War II*, vol. 7, *Services Around the World* (1958; new imprint, Washington, D.C.: Office of Air Force History, 1983), 3.

256. Lt Col Carl A. Spaatz, Memo of Conference, 3 January 1941, Spaatz Papers; and PRO, Air 8/378, Air Attaché, Washington to Air Ministry, 7 March 1941.

257. PRO, Air 8/378, Air Chief Marshal Sir Charles F. Portal to Air Vice Marshal Sir A. G. R. Garrod, RAF, 7 March 1941.

258. PRO, Air 8/378, Air Attaché, Washington to Air Ministry, 7 March 1941.

259. PRO, Air 8/378, Garrod to Arnold, 17 April 1941; PRO, Air 8/378, Air Attaché, Washington to Air Ministry, 18 May 1941; PRO, Air 8/378, Air Ministry to Air Attaché, Washington, 23 April 1941; PRO, Air 8/378, Chief of the Air Staff RAF, to Air Attaché, Washington, 23 April 1941; and Marshall to FDR, 23 April 1941, Marshall Library.

260. PRO, Air 8/378, Group Captain David V. Carnegie to Air Commodore D. A. Cochrane, RAF, 4 May 1941.

261. PRO, Air 8/378, Lord Halifax to Churchill, 5 May 1941; PRO, Air 8/378, Roosevelt to Churchill, 21 May 1941; and PRO, Air 8/378, Air Attaché, Washington to Air Ministry, London, 22 May 1941.

262. PRO, Air 8/378, Air Attaché, Washington to Air Ministry, 9 May 1941.
263. Arnold, *Global Mission*, 242-43.
264. Arnold to Brig Gen Oliver Echols, 28 May 1941, AP.
265. Ibid.; Daniel Ford, "Gentlemen, I Give You the Whittle Engine," *Air and Space*, no. 2 (October/November 1992): 88-98.
266. Director General of Aircraft Equipment, RAF to Echols, 26 May 1941, AP.
267. PRO, Air 8/294, Air Attaché, Washington to Air Ministry, London, 28 and 31 May 1941 and 4 June 1941.
268. Arnold, *Global Mission*, 243.
269. *New York Times*, 7 May 1941.
270. Air Commodore John Slessor, RAF, April 1941, "Personal Impressions of the American Defense System as a Result of Five Months in this Country," John Slessor Papers, Air Historical Branch, RAF, London.
271. PRO, Air 8/378, Carnegie to Cochrane, 8 May 1941; Marshall to Lt Gen Daniel Vanvoorhis, 17 May 1941, Marshall Papers; and Estimated Strength of American Aircraft in RAF, 29 July 1941, AP.
272. Arnold, *Global Mission*, 235; Quesada Oral History Interview; and Masefield Oral History Interview.
273. PRO, Air 8/378, Churchill to FDR, 10 May 1941.
274. PRO, Air 4/487, Portal to Arnold, 23 April 1941.
275. Harriman to Hopkins, 24 April 1941, Hopkins Papers.
276. Allen Andrews, *Air Marshals: The Air War in Western Europe* (New York: Morrow, 1970), 191.
277. Arnold to Lovett, 8 May 1941, AP.

Chapter 2

Argentia, Newfoundland
31 July–14 August 1941

Introduction

The Atlantic conference, with Roosevelt, Churchill, and their staffs, was the second occasion for Arnold to maintain a World War II diary. Although the meetings with the British consumed only four days in the bleak surroundings of Argentia Bay, Newfoundland, Arnold recorded his thoughts and movements there, as well as to and from the conference, over a span of 15 days.

The "long and complicated" genesis of this meeting is beyond the scope of this introduction,[1] but Roosevelt had entertained the idea of meeting with the British Prime Minister at least as early as December 1940, after his successful reelection campaign.[2] In January 1941, following his penchant for using trusted emissaries rather than representatives of the established bureaucracy, the president dispatched his favorite confidant, Harry Hopkins, to England to test the waters for a face-to-face exchange.[3] Since both leaders had great faith in the power of their own personalities in negotiations, Hopkins' assessment that he was to be the "catalytic agent between two prima donnas" was not far off the mark.[4] In his six-week visit, Hopkins was so captivated by the prime minister that he spent 12 of his first 14 evenings with Churchill. Hopkins returned not only as a leading advocate of all-out aid to the beleaguered British but a strong proponent of a face-to-face Churchill-Roosevelt meeting.[5]

A series of events intervened to delay the immediate meeting that Hopkins had urged on his return. Roosevelt was consumed with the congressional debate over the Lend-Lease Act and seemed pleased with if not encouraged by the assessment of conditions Arnold brought back from England. Additionally, FDR felt tied to Washington until the Appropriations Bill was approved. Churchill was occupied with many problems, not the least of which were losses in the Balkans, the forced British evacuation of Greece, and Erwin Rommel's successes in North Africa. Both leaders became reluctant to leave their respective capitals in the uncertain days following Hitler's 22 June invasion of the Soviet Union.

The early dramatic successes of the German advance into the Soviet Union prompted a second trip by Hopkins to London in July, during which the Argentia meeting was planned. As the prime minister expanded his entourage to include military advisers, Hopkins wrote to Roosevelt from London to "bring Marshall and Arnold with you."[6] The suggestion to include Arnold reflected both Hopkins' appreciation of the role of air in the war he was witnessing in the skies over England and his strategy discussions with Churchill. It also was consistent with Hopkins' support of Hap just prior to Arnold's trip to England in April 1941 and when the aviator was being labeled an alcoholic in September 1938.

The Argentia meeting marked Arnold's inclusion in what eventually became the Joint and the Combined Chiefs of Staff although not all the later members of either group were present in Newfoundland. Membership in these elites was significant to Hap for several reasons. First of all, his invitation by Roosevelt into this coterie of advisors together with FDR's promotion of him to permanent major general 10 weeks earlier signified that Arnold was no longer out of presidential favor. As a consequence, this meeting became the first of seven Allied wartime conferences to which Hap was invited. Equally important, Arnold's attendance represented a continuing appreciation by the president of the importance of airpower as a military force coequal with the more traditional roles of ground and naval forces. Although FDR's thinking at this time was not clearly spelled out, his concept of the strategy necessary to defeat Hitler had, since the Munich conference of 1938, increasingly stressed the significance of air forces and strategic bombardment. More recently, he was influenced by the role of the RAF in the Battle of Britain as well as the growing stridency of American isolationist sentiment, which railed against the specter of sending another American Expeditionary

Force (AEF) abroad. Although the Air Corps did not, at the time of this meeting, enjoy the sovereignty that many Army aviators had desired for several decades, Arnold and many others were pleased with the enhanced recognition now accorded the Army air arm. In these and subsequent negotiations, the US Air Corps enjoyed parity with the RAF, which had been an independent service since 1918. Not clearly articulated by him at the time, the fact that he was emerging as a more prominent spokesman for production and allocation had to have been satisfying to Arnold. That Secretary of the Treasury Morgenthau, who had previously coveted and enjoyed a dominant role in these areas, was not among the invitees must have been particularly satisfying.

Hap discovered while at this conference that both delegations contained members who gratuitously offered recommendations about aircraft production and distribution. Arnold agreed with his British counterpart's suggestion that in the future the chief of the British air staff should deal solely with Roosevelt or Arnold about these topics, further evidence of Hap's enhanced role on both sides of the Atlantic.[7] Arnold as well as others had noted before the Argentia meeting that the various British agencies and personalities that were involved in soliciting American military assistance lacked a central point of control. One of the tangible results of this conference was the British agreement to create a central clearinghouse in Washington to coordinate and present their diverse needs.[8]

As became typical of too many Allied wartime meetings, the British staff officers were much better prepared than their American counterparts. Part of the explanation for this was FDR's penchant, if not obsession, for secrecy, which, in the words of one scholar, was achieved "at high cost in preparation for the United States military."[9] No doubt partially motivated by concern for Churchill's safety on the high seas, Roosevelt's secretiveness also reflected his often playful relationship with the American press. As a result, Army Chief of Staff Marshall was informed of the conference less than 72 hours before having to depart the nation's capital.[10] And since Marshall was enjoined from telling his civilian superiors of the proposed meeting and Arnold was on an inspection trip with

Lovett, no planning or strategy sessions were held before they left Washington. Assigning Arnold and Marshall to different cruisers during the sea voyage also precluded Hap's discussing conference strategy with his chief of staff while en route. This evoked Marshall's assessment that we were "going into this one cold"[11] and a biographer concluding that "murky was the word for the American position."[12] The conferences with the president on the USS *Augusta* en route to Argentia were "few in number and brief in duration," resulting in an assessment of United States preparations as "slipshod."[13]

In stark contrast, the British had planned for this conference both in London and during their five-day sea voyage. Thus they enjoyed an advantage over the Americans, who arrived without any serious consultation or staff work among themselves or, more important, any idea of what the president desired or hoped to accomplish. The British preparation resulted in the British Chiefs of Staff submitting to the American delegation at Argentia a 22-page document on 10 August, the second day of the conference. Entitled "General Strategy Review," this proposal had been fully staffed, had received Churchill's approval, and had been completed four days before they left London.[14] Such preparation for conferences on the part of the British was to prevail during other Allied wartime meetings. It seems clear, however, that Hap had some appreciation of the high-level nature of the conference and its potential topics. Before leaving Washington, he held discussions with two of his closest aides and gathered as much statistical backup as possible in his "black book" in preparation "for anything."[15]

The leisurely four days at sea allowed Arnold to record some thoughts about strategy, aircraft production, and aircraft allocation, issues he felt would be important at the conference from the AAF viewpoint and ones he had struggled with for almost three years.[16] Hap's major problems continued to be the difficult proposition of building up the AAF to meet any impending emergency, most probably now considered by Arnold and the other American military leaders as war involving the United States, while at the same time responding to the direction of the president. To many US military leaders, their commander in chief was willing to furnish aircraft and munitions to those fighting the Axis powers without a plan and without a significant understanding of the impact of this largesse on the viability of the American military. Hap felt, overoptimistically, that the problem of future aircraft aid to the British had now become more manageable, in part because of what he had learned during his April visit there. Hitler's 22 June invasion of the Soviet Union drastically altered the equation.

Two days after the German attack, Roosevelt announced that the United States was prepared to aid the Soviets but that a list of their materiel needs would first be necessary.[17] Within the week, the Soviet Ambassador to Washington, in a gesture that foretold Soviet demands throughout the war, presented a series of unrealistic requirements of nearly $2 billion worth of materiel including 3,000 bombers and 3,000 fighters.[18] The request made its way to the War Department where both Marshall and Arnold viewed it with considerable uneasiness. Arnold was pleased that General Marshall was "unalterably opposed to the release of any US pursuit planes" to the Soviet Union until sufficient numbers had been placed in the Philippines. Another concern was the lack of pursuit and light bombers available for maneuvers with the US Army, which had resulted in a "complete deficiency in army-ground training" that must not be continued further. Unfortunately, it did continue.[19]

German success on the eastern front in the five weeks before Arnold and Marshall set out for Argentia had resulted in the Wehrmacht conquering 750,000 square miles of territory in their nearly 400-mile drive eastward. Finland's entrance into the war against the Soviets on 25 June, combined with the rapid German advance, prompted Josef Stalin's "scorched earth" policy. On 17 July, in the first of many pleas, Stalin called on the West for a second front. These events convinced the White House that immediate aid to the Soviet Union was necessary. On the day Arnold learned that he was to return immediately to Washington for the Argentia meeting, FDR met the Soviet Ambassador and two Soviet generals in the White House. Soon afterward, Roosevelt issued specific instructions for assistance to be furnished the Soviets.

The next day, in a 45-minute stern lecture to his cabinet, FDR expressed his dissatisfaction with the limited American aid being furnished to the hard-pressed Soviets. Insisting that the Soviets had been given the "runaround," he demanded that instead of promises "whatever we are going to give them, it has to be over there by the first of October, and the only answer I want to hear is that it is under way." His further instructions included a "token" number of planes, including 10 four-engine bombers and Garrand rifles "to help their morale." According to his diary, Stimson responded to the president that his statements were unfair since neither he nor the War Department had ever seen any list of "Russian wants." The secretary complained that it was "the uncorrelated organization which the President had set up that was responsible." Treasury Secretary Morgenthau could hardly contain his glee at the discomfort of Secretary of War Stimson at this meeting.[20]

That same day, Roosevelt gave specific directions to Col Philip R. Faymonville, the US military attaché who had just returned from Moscow. The AAF was ordered to ship 200 P-40 airplanes to the Soviet Union, 40 of them to come from the undelivered British allocation. In Arnold's absence, Marshall was disturbed that FDR had ordered that, if necessary, the remaining 160 were to be taken from US pilots currently training with the aircraft.[21] Marshall's statistics showed that there were only 90 P-40s then "in active commission" and to comply with the president's orders to furnish the 160 would reduce the US pursuit plane inventory to six squadrons, all of different types and less modern than the P-40. The number of other planes available to the AAF was even less encouraging. The AAF then possessed only 40 B-17s while another 30 were being modernized. Nine of those 40 were earmarked for Hawaiian defense, leaving only 31 remaining for use by the 150 crews ready to train in that airplane and an additional 170 crews anticipated for training in the next three months. The AAF was in the process of taking possession of its first B-24 but it had not yet been delivered. The United States had 50 B-25 medium bombers on hand in addition to 50 B-26s, of which only 12 were in commission.[22] Marshall and Arnold took these discouraging statistics to Argentia and were well aware of the contrast between the relatively few aircraft in the AAF inventory and the 982 US-manufactured airplanes estimated to be in RAF hands by 1 November.[23] Marshall's and Arnold's concerns over aid to the belligerents at the expense of US Army air and ground requirements were shared by Secretary of War Stimson. On 1 August, the day FDR directed immediate assistance to the Soviet Union, Stimson expressed his agreement with Arnold and Marshall while venting some of his frustrations.

> I am the only man in the whole government that is responsible for the difficult decision of whether we can give up planes or other munitions with safety to our own defense. All of these other people are just hell-bent to satisfy a passing impulse or emotion to help out some other nation that is fighting on our side and they have no responsibility over whether or not our own army and our own forces are going to be left unarmed or not.[24]

From Arnold's comments in his diary while at sea, as well as earlier writings, he was well aware of the important connection between strategy, production of arms, and a viable American military force. He realized, however, as did Marshall and others, that no effective mechanism existed within the US government for coordinating and determining responsibilities and priorities. Given Roosevelt's well-known predilection for layering over various agencies rather than setting forth clear lines of responsibility and authority, there did not appear much hope for change. Never challenging the American concept of ultimate civilian control, Arnold and his colleagues were puzzled by the vast difference in operating methods between themselves and the civilian political leadership.

As taught in the staff colleges and practiced in maneuvers, the military normally first set forth a plan outlining their strategic objectives, which they then contrasted with an assessment of the strength of the opposition. Next came an evaluation of the means or tactics to achieve the established aims, all carefully determined by the assets available in troops, aircraft, tanks, and logistical support. This approach contrasted sharply with what they felt had been the lack of any plan or clear strategic objectives, any direction on the means to be used to achieve whatever aims were anticipated, or any consistent estimate of assets to be available, from the political leadership. These political estimates seemed to vary almost from week to week as American materiel was promised in a seemingly offhanded manner to Axis opponents. Yet the military leaders faced the risk of being immediately responsive to any emergency and felt that the public would hold those in uniform rather than the political leaders accountable for any shortcomings. To many in uniform, much of the hue and cry in the aftermath of Pearl Harbor was ample proof of their dilemmas.

Prospects at Argentia were not encouraging. Arnold and Marshall had to have remembered with some discomfort the list of 14 military items desired by the British that Hopkins and Churchill had generated "over a bottle of port," or so the critics complained. Hopkins had submitted these items to the president when he returned from England in February and had become an important factor in threatening Arnold's tenure and in the decision to send Hap abroad.[25]

If Arnold and Marshall worried about the president's determination to continue allocating extremely scarce American-manufactured aircraft to the British on an ad hoc basis, their concern was heightened at the prospects of a face-to-face meeting between Roosevelt and Churchill. Arnold, remembering how impressed he had been by Churchill, assumed that the prime minister's eloquence in outlining Britain's peril might well influence Roosevelt to continue delivery of US aid regardless of its impact on American strength and preparedness. And, as persuasive as Churchill himself might be, the added presence of Hopkins, by now the closest and most trusted advisor to FDR on matters of assistance to the belligerents and a vocal partisan of maximum aid to both Britain and the Soviet Union, could prove even more detrimental to the desired American military buildup. Hopkins, returning from his second trip to England along with Churchill and his advisors on His Majesty's Ship (HMS) *Prince of Wales*, had just completed a hectic five-day visit to the Soviet Union where he met with Stalin and was provided a dire picture of Russia's difficulties.[26] Even Hopkins, however, was aware of Roosevelt's tendency to be swayed by the "first person who came into his office with an idea" and of what Marshall disparaged as his commander in chief's "cigarette-holder gesture" in directing action.[27] The military leaders' concern about the potential undue influence of Churchill and Hopkins continued as a major factor throughout the war. Arnold and other American leaders often found the British suggesting, if not threatening, that their case would be appealed either to Hopkins or through Churchill directly to the president if the solutions they sought were not achieved at the military leadership level. Meeting with his colleagues upon returning to England, the RAF vice chief of staff, the only British airman present at Argentia, reported on the discussions there.

> [The American military leaders] were evidently extremely concerned that the influence over the president exercised by certain civilian advisors notably Mr. Harriman and Mr. Hopkins. They clearly wanted the British chiefs of staff to deal as much as possible with their military counterparts in the US. We could not of course fall in with this suggestion clearly on the matter of aircraft allocation. Mr. Harriman and Mr. Hopkins were our basic friends.[28]

He could have articulated further the implication of his statement that getting materiel assistance through these civilians would continue to be the conduits of choice for the British. Harriman and Hopkins, of course, had no responsibility for, and limited knowledge of, the potential employment and readiness of the American military.

Arnold's carefree four days on the USS *Tuscaloosa* permitted him to consider the potential of the meetings that lay ahead. Always circumspect in commenting in writing about the commander in chief, Hap was clear but careful in his diary comments of 6 and 7 August concerning conference prospects. In many ways, his brief entries on those two days reflected his frustrations since the American buildup had begun almost three years earlier. In his seven-line entry on this topic on 6 August, Hap continued his call for "adoption of a plan" in order for the military to "meet the present international situation." He advocated limiting materiel aid to Britain and others to "only such items as they can use effectively" and only after meeting American needs under the "adopted plan." His final point emphasized the necessity for the "experts," clearly meaning military professionals as opposed to political operatives, to study the proposals and their ramifications before commitments were made.[29] Much of what was contained here had been expressed in his 6 March memo that assessed Hopkins' 14 items and jeopardized Arnold's promotion and retention potential.

Once they reached Argentia and Arnold had a chance to discuss his thinking and the prospects for the meeting with Marshall, Hap continued to expand his thinking. As he commented in his journal, he told the Army chief of staff there were three requirements governing decisions to be made there. These requirements reflected a strong belief that the United States would shortly enter or be drawn into the war. Foremost among these was the need for "an accounting" to the American people as to what the Army and the AAF had been doing with the time and considerable money already provided towards preparedness. The public, according to Arnold's estimates, would demand "action and not excuses," and would hold the military rather than the politicians responsible for any lack thereof. "We will be holding the sack." Additionally, reiterating the theme of the previous day's entries, Hap insisted that Britain, thus far the major recipient of American aircraft, aircraft engines, and aircraft parts, be given aid only sufficient to "maintain her existence."[30]

Arnold's feelings as the conference prepared to open, had to have been mixed. He must have been filled with apprehension about the ability of the AAF to meet potential challenges, yet in many ways he was encouraged by the limited but important progress that had been made in the previous three years. No doubt his American military counterparts shared his concern about the strength of their own components along with an uncertainty about what was to be expected, promised, or developed from this first meeting of Roosevelt and Churchill.

The Diary

NOTES ON ROOSEVELT-CHURCHILL CONFERENCE

Thursday, July 31, 1941 [Baton Rouge, Louisiana, to Ellington Field, Texas]

Radio received en route Baton Rouge [Louisiana] to Ellington:[31] "Return to Washington, arriving not later than 10:00 P.M., Saturday, August 2nd. [Gen George C.] Marshall." Answered: "Message received and will comply. Arnold."

Friday, August 1, 1941 [San Antonio, Texas, to Washington, D.C.]

Spent day inspecting Brooks, Duncan, Kelly, Randolph, all in excellent shape. Duncan doing excellent work in shop, turning out two modernized B-17s a day.[32] Randolph: an exceptionally well-performed ground review of cadets, demonstrated excellent training and control of cadets, instructors' review with 252 planes.[33] Saturday took off at 7:25 A.M., flew non-stop to Washington, arrived at 4:30 P.M. EST. Called Marshall, told to be ready for trip leaving Sunday at 12:00 noon from Gravelly Point, Washington [Reagan National] Airport, take an O. D. [olive drab] uniform and be prepared to be away for 10 days.

Sunday, August 3, 1941 [Washington, D.C., to New York City to Smithstown Cove, Long Island, New York]

Spent A.M. with "Tuey" [Tooey] and Bill Street, brought black book up to date, collected additional data so as to be prepared for anything.[34] Returned home, called Marshall and confirmed instructions, will take Sam Browne belt.[35] Arrived airport 11:55, took off in my C-41, Parker as pilot, Marshall, Burns, Bundy, and Arnold.[36]

Arrived LaGuardia at 1:15, lunch at airport restaurant.[37] Cross city in cars to 125th Street, met by Sherman (Navy).[38] By barge to a Destroyer Leader, caught up with Stark and Turner.[39] Down North River through Hell Gate, out East River to College Point[40] where [USS] *Augusta*, King's flagship, and [USS] *Tuscaloosa* were anchored.[41] Transferred to *Tuscaloosa*, Marshall and Stark to *Augusta*.

Cruised out to east with 4 destroyer leaders in advance, anchored and spent night at Smithstown Cove.[42] I ranked the Admiral's cabin, special orderly, and cabin boy, but don't know what to do with them. Marshall's bag on *Tuscaloosa* by mistake, delivered when we anchored.

Monday, August 4, 1941 [At sea, Smithstown Cove, Long Island, New York, to near Nantucket Island, Massachusetts]

Awake at 7:00 A.M. to find ship in motion. Dressed by 7:30, cabin boy put out clothes for me. See now that I will run out of clothes before I return; thank God there is a laundry aboard. Where are we going? And why? Certainly the crew and ship's officers do not know. Twice I was about to be informed and twice someone came up and I heard nothing.

Tour of ship: light cruiser, 8 5" guns, 4 turrets (12 8" guns).[43] Paravane drill[44] (cut-off lobster pots), gun drill, magazines, fire control, three planes catapulted. Destroyers out in van, zig-zag course. Pick up planes without stopping ship. (Captain [L. P.] Johnson, commanding). King giving instructions from *Augusta*. Maneuvers took us out beyond Montauk Point, outside of Block Island, anchored about 4:00 P.M. at Martha's Vineyard, a very attractive island.[45]

Turner, Burns, Bundy, and I called on Admiral King. Asked for and received instructions as to who, which, or what to salute first. As I was senior, I had to do the trick first, did not make too many mistakes.[46] King quite mad because we came aboard his ship and he knew nothing about it. He gave us a look, got mad and went out to cool off prior to our getting in his office; cooled off rapidly.[47] Marshall and Stark came in.

Marshall told us of our "Brenner Pass" conference ahead.[48] Returned to the *Tuscaloosa*, dinner, walk on deck, movie. Understand we take off at 6:00 tomorrow morning. S W [Sumner Welles][49] and A H [Averell Harriman] will meet us at "Brenner Pass."

Tuesday, August 5, 1941 [At sea, off coast of New England]

Joined by [USS] *Potomac* during night.[50] Underway at 6:30 A.M., headed toward Nantucket Light.[51] *Potomac* not with us, five Destroyer Leaders, *Tuscaloosa* and *Augusta*. Following message received by all concerned:

TO BE DELIVERED SIMULTANEOUSLY TO ALL THREE PRESENT BY OFFICER OF PUBLIC RELATIONS: "AFTER A NIGHT OF RESTFUL SLEEP, PRESIDENT CONTINUING CRUISE IN NORTHERN WATERS TO UNDISCLOSED DESTINATION. ATTIRED IN SPORT SHIRT AND SLACKS, PRESIDENT ENJOYING SEA AIR FROM FAN-

TAIL. IN RESPONSE TO QUESTIONS FROM MEMBERS OF PARTY AS TO SCOPE OF CRUISE, PRESIDENT ANNOUNCED NO DEFINITE SCHEDULE OR LOCALITIES AND THAT WEATHER AND ANGLING PROSPECTS WOULD DETERMINE EACH DAY'S MOVEMENTS. PRESIDENT SPENT SOME TIME DISCUSSING AFFAIR[S] WITH COMMANDER IN CHIEF ATLANTIC FLEET. ALL ON BOARD WELL."[52]

Weather clear. Two planes from *Tuscaloosa* in air flying over flotilla, picked up plane while cruising at 10 knots. Had to turn out of formation (into wind to do it), fell back from formation about 10 miles and had to step up speed to regain position. Destroyer fell back with us, caught up shortly before reaching Nantucket Light. Dropped our paravanes and changed course to northeast. Inspected mess; sailors eat much more than soldiers.

Admirals are wonderful fellows: they travel (as I am now) deluxe; a bath (with Roman bathtub), portholes that sailors look thru while one performs such acts as he must, a large bedroom with a double bed, and a sitting room, an orderly and a room steward, push buttons and bells everywhere. I am enjoying the luxury while I can.

Three times an orderly came up to me and repeated a lot of words. The first time I asked for a repeat and even then could not make out what was said; after that I always said, "all right." At last I have found out what it was: "The officer of the deck requests authority to make it 8 bells." In the Army to say the same thing: "The Officer of the Day wants to know if the commanding officer desires to change the time or shall we go ahead and have the clocks strike 8 o'clock." What a tradition to have handed down through the years. All day we have been zig-zagging in our course, paravanes out to pick up any mines that may have been planted. Tonight we are running with our lights darkened. All the same war zone.

News announcement: from London, Atwell, M P [Member of Parliament], states that Churchill will be out of London on affairs of state for next few days;[53] from Gabriel Heatter: "Is it possible that Roosevelt and Churchill will meet somewhere in Labrador, Newfoundland?"[54]

Wednesday, August 6, 1941 [At sea, New England waters, headed for Newfoundland]

Light fog, steaming at about 15 knots, still headed NE. Fog broke, sun out, speed 20 knots, sea calm, sky clear.

Newspaper indicates that Churchill landed by plane at St. John's. How? They have no airport at St. John's. Nothing much new; getting much colder. Off Nova Scotia at noon, off Cape Sable about 4:00 P.M.[55] Not a boat, not a ship, plenty of cold, blue water, quite a contrast to the heat of Savannah, Tampa, Tallahassee, New Orleans, Houston, San Antonio last week. We should reach Placentia Bay tomorrow morning. I would like very much for three things to happen:

(a) Adoption of a plan for developing our Army and Navy to meet the present international situation.
(b) Acceptance of the policy of giving Britain, China, etc., [only] such items as they can use effectively after meeting our requirements under our adopted plan.
(c) No commitments being made until experts have had a chance to study over the propositions and all ramifications.

Thursday, August 7, 1941 [At sea, en route to Argentia, Newfoundland]

Paravanes went out at 4:00 A.M.; God, what a noise, vibrations and clattering and hammering; how can one sleep? Land in sight when I got up at 6:45 A.M., entering Placentia Bay.[56] Picked up [USS] *Arizona*[57] and two destroyers during night. Two Navy boats (PBYs)[58] unreported since last night, later discovered safely at anchor in a bay at Nova Scotia. Argentia in sight and close abeam after breakfast.[59] Low clouds, cold, chilly, penetrating air. Land appears to be not unlike Alaska, geologically speaking; deep ravines, low trees and undergrowth, occasional cleared area, small towns all around bay. Two minesweepers working away ahead of us as we steamed into harbor. Can see construction on Naval Base. Argentia coming along nicely, one pursuit group from Army to be stationed here.[60]

Called over to *Augusta* by Marshall at 10:00: Burns, Bundy and I. Talked over aid to Russia, token gifts only, (planes for one pursuit group during September, October, November, P-40s) (5 B-25s a month during September, October, November). Build up Philippines to 1 group P-40s and 1 group B-17s.[61]

Called for by President, he was catching toad fish, dog fish and halibut. Carried out instructions to have Elliott [Roosevelt] here tomorrow; Harms here also.[62] Finished message for President's signature. After much saluting and clicking of heels to Admirals, captains and flags on stern of ship, returned to *Tuscaloosa* in time for lunch.

Give England only such material as she can effectively use and then only such that we will always have at least 50% of our total production. If we can get away with that, we will be doing something.

Told Marshall there were three major considerations governing our decisions:

(a) An accounting to the people of the US as to what we have been doing with regard to building up an Army and Air Force. We have had money and time and they, the people, will demand results.
(b) Such aid as we can give to Britain to maintain her existence.
(c) We must be prepared to put a force into the war if and when we enter. The people will want action and not excuses. We will be holding the sack. Time then will be just as important to us as it is to the British now.[63]

Went aboard *Augusta* at 4:30. Sort of heavy seas, almost fell into sea when little boat went down and gangway to big ship went up. Conference with Marshall over principles we would like to have accepted for control of production. Marshall OK'd.

Conference with President Roosevelt, King, Stark, Turner, Beardall, Marshall, Arnold, Burns, Bundy, "Pa" Watson.[64] Discussed: convoys; defense of convoys; US responsibility for getting cargoes safely delivered, too late to start shooting after attack is made, responsibility for safety applies to whole convoy and not only to a part, line of [US] responsibility extends east of Azores and east of Iceland; duties and responsibilities of Navy; what British may want from [US] Navy, ships from US Maritime Commission;[65] tanks from Army, airplanes; troops in Iceland, Marines, relief by soldiers; airplanes to Russia; aid to

Philippines, B-17s, P-40s, tanks, AA guns; turn deaf ear if Japan goes into Thailand but not if it goes into Dutch East Indies.[66]

Admiral King gave a most delightful dinner for President, [I] said good night and back to *Tuscaloosa* for movie and to bed.

Friday, August 8, 1941 [Argentia, Newfoundland]

Dark day, but not raining. The water on the *Tuscaloosa* picks up something that affects it queerly. One starts to wash one's face or hands in clear, crystal water but when one uses soap, bingo, the water turns blue. Investigation reveals that there are two ships in the Navy that have that particular peculiarity.[67]

After a rather late rising, 7:15 A.M. breakfast and then to my room to help write a proposed outline of policy covering aid to Russia, Britain, China, etc.[68] A haircut in my room, not so hot.

In came Harms and Elliott Roosevelt. Harms' first statement was that he had only been here two weeks, hadn't been able to take hold of details; we shouldn't have come when we did, we all arrived 300 years too late to do anything for the country anyhow; he had never in his life seen a place that had less excuse for being. With that introduction, we got down to business. He needs:

(1) A staff.
(2) A clearer conception of his mission, probably it must be redefined.
(3) To get around to his various activities more.
(4) Someone to take care of details while he is away.
(5) To probably move his headquarters to Argentia.[69]

About the time we were getting well squared away on Harms and his troubles, Marshall came in and said: "Come on in the amphibian with me, the C in C [commander in chief] has given us permission to fly to Gander Lake[70] and St. John's." Captain L. P. Johnson, a fellow who always thinks of his Army uninvited guests, insisted we wait for a pick-up lunch; we did. We then took off in the boat to the USS *Dolphin*, thence in a whale boat to our OA-9.[71] We flew for 2½ hours from Argentia to

Gander Lake to St. John's and returned to a mooring by the *Dolphin*.

Newfoundland's predominating natural features are: small lakes and large lakes, outcropping of rocks, large rocks, solid rock hills, small clumps of pine none over 20 feet high, many deep bays, narrow railroad and it is narrow gauge, less than a dozen good roads, remarkably few trails, cattle and horses conspicuous by their absence and one of the finest surfaced flying fields with the facilities being developed but still a long way to go to catch up. Gander Lake Airport had 24 Hudsons awaiting the trans-Atlantic hop. Construction going along slowly, too slowly. The proof of the accuracy of the above characteristics re Newfoundland is that Belle Island is so entirely different with its cultivated areas and large iron mining activities that it is the exception proving the rule.[72]

Returned to Argentia about 4:00. Navy station there is moving right along; Gander Lake needs a push. Heavy seas arolling. Several new ships in harbor. We now have corvettes, destroyers, destroyer leaders, cruisers, one battleship, two tankers, one aircraft tender, about 18 PBYs and PBYMs.[73]

As we started for our ships, we saw a large 4-engine flying boat arrive. Where from? The US? What for? Carrying two distinguished passengers? Who? Well, S W [Sumner Welles] and A H [Averell Harriman]. Returned to *Tuscaloosa* to find nothing much of interest with probably everyone taking a nap. Elliott Roosevelt indicated that perhaps the President would like to have the AAF take over the trans-Atlantic ferry service. Then what?[74]

Saturday, August 9, 1941 [Argentia, Newfoundland]

Up late, couldn't find my trousers, they were there where the cabin boy hid them all the time. Dark ship, dark cabin, long hours of sleeping, late at breakfast. Conference relative to change in route of ferry service to Montreal, Holsternborg, Glasgow, with alternate fields at Baffin Land, Fort Chimo and Northwest River.[75]

[HMS] *Prince of Wales*,[76] battle-scarred from *Bismarck* action, steamed into port, flags flying, sailors paraded, sideboys up, band playing, Marines at present arms, 2 destroyers.

A shot from *Bismarck* hit her bridge and killed everyone there but Captain and one other, another put her after-turret out of action. Several more hit and did minor damage but one "15" hit her under the water line, made a circuitous path around, causing all kinds of damage and then came to rest in the bowels of the ship without exploding.

Ordered to *Augusta* at 9:30, received on deck by President, Stark, Marshall, King, Watson, Elliott Roosevelt, and F. Roosevelt, Jr., others.[77] First to appear from below Sumner Welles then A. Harriman, soon a boat from the *Prince of Wales*, Harry Hopkins came aboard.[78]

[According to Hopkins] The Russians are confident, claim 2,500 plane output a month without counting 15 training planes a day; 2 ac [aircraft] factories destroyed by German bombs. Stalin claims the Russians have 24,000 tanks, claims that Germans have had to change organization of Panzer Divisions on account of fact that Russians seep in "between advanced elements and attack German lines of communications. Now Germans attach tanks and armored cars to all motorized elements."

Finally band plays *God Save The King*, side-boys, sailors paraded, Winston Churchill comes up ladder and salutes President. Churchill wears a Navy cap and a uniform, then follows Admiral Pound, General Dill, Air Vice Marshal Freeman, then the others.

General talking, all seemed glad to see me, breaking up into groups with opposite, Freeman and I. Buffet lunch in King's suite. After lunch Marshall, Dill, Burns, Harriman, Freeman and other Army and RAF came to my suite on *Tuscaloosa*.

Long conference lasting all afternoon. Discussed:

1. British program.
2. Change in ferry route.
3. Necessity for more H. B. [heavy bombers]. British want 6,000 more than we are producing.
4. More fuel tanks in DB-7 and Martin 187 to permit of flying across S Atlantic.[79]
5. Change in M. B. [medium bomber] production at Omaha and K C [Kansas City] to H. B. [heavy bomber].[80]

Marshall and Dill and their staffs left at 3:30; Freeman, Harriman, Burns and I left at 4:30 for *Prince of Wales* for a sherry or scotch. Did all the chores on boarding. Went to Admiral's lounge and had sherry, joined by Lord Cherwell, Martin, Commander Thompson.[81] Later as we were leaving PM [prime minister] came in, had quite a chat with him. Then went to War Room where they keep for PM a complete record on map of all ships, convoys, bombings, sinkings, all other items of interest. Back to *Tuscaloosa* for dinner at 6:00, papers from Harry Hopkins re Russia at 6:15, dinner 6:30. No clean pajamas, borrowed the Skipper's.

Was sitting at dinner on *Tuscaloosa* when a bomb shell exploded.[82] Twice during P.M. a messenger came in and tried to deliver a message to me: "If General Marshall is aboard notify him that he is expected aboard the *Augusta* at 18:45 for dinner." Twice I said that Marshall was already aboard the *Augusta* as far as I knew. At 6:55 P.M. at dinner an orderly came in with message from *Augusta*: "Re my 2149 Arnold should be substituted for Marshall." What a position for a guy to be in, ten minutes late for a dinner at which the President, PM, a 5 star admiral, 4 four-star generals and admirals and air chief marshals. I took off from the *Tuscaloosa* and walked into dinner just five minutes later. Everybody seated with a vacant chair; made my apologies and took my seat between Harry Hopkins and A C M [Air Chief Marshal] Freeman. Embarrassed, I'll tell the world. That Captain's gig never traveled so fast in its life.[83] Fine dinner.

Speeches by President and PM; Pound, Dill, Freeman also spoke. British want to free 50 destroyers and corvettes from Halifax for duty in South Atlantic where German subs are now concentrating. British state shipping losses dropped from 500,000 [tons] in April to 180,000 in July due to ability to lick two types magnetic mines and an acoustic mine and better means of combating subs and planes. British long-range plan is to keep giving as little as possible in remote areas where they can meet Germans on even terms, always hoping for a break, a miracle, an internal breakdown of morale.[84]

An invitation to go to church aboard the *Prince of Wales* tomorrow by command of the President. Home to bed at 12:00, missed the official pictures by being late. Awakened at 1:00 [A.M.] to be given a written invitation to church:

USS *Augusta*, August 9, 1941

MEMORANDUM FOR THE STAFF:

The President will embark in the destroyer *McDougal*[85] and go on board the *Prince of Wales* for Divine Services tomorrow, Sunday, at eleven o'clock. He will remain on board for luncheon with the Prime Minister. After luncheon the President will return to the *Augusta* by the same means. The Prime Minister has invited the following persons to luncheon on board *Prince of Wales* tomorrow:

The President	Major General James H.
The Honorable Sumner Welles	Burns, USA
Admiral Harold R. Stark, USN	Rear Admiral Richmond K.
General George C. Marshall, USA	Turner, USN
Admiral Ernest J. King, USN	Captain John R. Beardall,
Admiral Ross T. McIntire (MC)	USN
USN[86]	Captain Oscar C. Badger, USN
Major General Edwin M. Watson,	Captain Carleton H. Wright,
USA	USN[87]
Major General Henry H. Arnold,	Captain Elliott Roosevelt, USA
USA	(ACR)
	Ensign Franklin D. Roosevelt,
	Jr., USNR

The Honorable Harry Hopkins
The Honorable Averill Harriman

J. R. Beardall
Captain, U. S. Navy
Naval Aide to the President

<u>Sunday, August 10, 1941</u> [Argentia, Newfoundland]

Afterthoughts of dinner, highlights of Churchill's speech:

(1) Aid to Britain in Near East: too many men, too much equipment there to even think of withdrawal; need aid in ships, planes, civilian mechanics.

(2) Attack Germans' extended line in Persia, Iraq, Russia, N Africa; anywhere they can be met on even terms.

(3) Give Britain aid in convoys, so that she can use her 50 corvettes and destroyers now in Halifax at other places in other areas where German subs are now concentrating against convoys.

(4) Far East: make up an ultimatum signed by England, Russia and US: if Japan moves south into the Malay Peninsula, we will by force throw her out.

Sunday, August 10, 1941 [Argentia, Newfoundland]

Tried to copy Freeman's British program for a fighting air strength of 10,000, [planes including] 4,000 H. B. [heavy bombers]; the thing scares me, it is so big and I know that they cannot meet it. British prod. [production of] H. B. [heavy bombers] 500 a month, US prod. H. B. 500 a month. We can't do it as easily as that: 2,000 pilots a month. Where will they come from? Wishful thinking.

Time for boat to *Prince of Wales*, waited 30 minutes. US Destroyer came alongside. President came aboard, band playing *Star Spangled Banner*, sailors all paraded on afterdeck. Each Chief of Staff with his opposite: Pound, Stark; Dill, Marshall; Freeman, Arnold; Roosevelt, Churchill sitting out in front, in center of hollow square. Church services very impressive.[88]

After church, conference with Freeman. His program is now clear: Britain has built it around our entire production; 100% of all planes produced in US go to Britain; US Army, Navy, Dutch, Chinese, get none; Britain gets all. [US] O P M [Office of Production Management] figures have at last confused almost everyone; believe it wrong to send them out so indiscriminately. Freeman told of misapplication of figures and deliveries and very much disappointed.[89] Told him I could not change policies, all I could do was to make recommendations re change of policies.

Lunch call came while talking. Officers, US Navy, British Navy, Air Forces, Armies, all assembled in Ward Room, sherry; President and Prime Minister went in to lunch and the rest of us. Table seating attached.[90]

Prince of Wales withdrew from action with *Bismarck*. Had *Bismarck* followed with attack perhaps *Prince of Wales*, being more or less out of action, would not have come off so light. However, *Bismarck* missed that bus.

After lunch, PM toasted President; President toasted King [George VI]. Good lunch: caviar, vodka, mock turtle soup, grouse, champagne, potatoes, peas, rolls, ice cream with cherry sauce, port, coffee, brandy. PM and President both spoke for a few minutes, President withdrew.

Destroyer told by Admiral Pound we would have a meeting of Chiefs of Staff. Waiting with Freeman then Stark and Marshall went aboard destroyer with President. Destroyer pulled away amid cheers from British sailors. No staff meeting until 9:00 A.M. Monday. Stopped and chatted with the PM awhile. Captain of ship told me that my boat was ready. Said goodbye to PM. Much to my surprise saw marines, band and sailors lined up at gangplank. They gave me a send-off as a Chief of Staff, I did my best to receive it as one. Back to *Tuscaloosa* with Burns, 4:50 P.M.

This has been a most interesting day. The church service out on deck in Placentia Bay with British warships, Canadian corvettes and destroyers and US warships was most inspiring. I can't make up mind as yet whether most of us are window dressing for the main actors or whether we are playing minor roles in the show. Freeman will not talk training nor has he as yet been willing to take up civilian aid in the Near East. Looked over [British] Chiefs of Staff memo re the strategic situation. It is a sound paper in some respects from my point of view but needs study, much study before we accept it.[91]

Back to *Augusta* at 5:50: Marshall, Dill, Freeman, Arnold, Burns, Watson in with President; PM Churchill joined later. Talked over production of tanks, big bombers, increase of production, Liberia airfields, Dakar, Azores, Cape Verdes, Canaries, Azores. Still talking priorities and their all-around effect when 7:00 came up and we had to get out.[92]

Fog and high rain as we took off in barge and went aboard the *Prince of Wales*; that is the weather I had heard was normal in Newfoundland. We have been very fortunate so far. Sat around for a while in the Admiral's cabin waiting for the dinner guests of General Dill: Dill, Marshall, Freeman, Welles, Cadogan, Burns, Hollis,[93] Bundy, Leach and Arnold.

Leach, captain of *Prince of Wales*: it was in Scapa Flow with men from yards still in turrets when it received word to take off in pursuit of *Bismarck*. Captain was away fishing; he returned posthaste and arrived before steam was fully up to pressure. Ship must have been hit badly as Captain said the carnage, wounded and dead on bridge was so bad that he withdrew from action. He was only man not wounded or killed. They had a hard time intercepting the *Bismarck*, their courses approached at 90°, but due to snow and sleet missed. Then he changed course and paralleled *Bismarck* until they made contact. Home to *Tuscaloosa* in rain at 11:00 P.M.

Monday, August 11, 1941 [Argentia, Newfoundland]

While preparing for Chiefs of Staff conference it became very evident that the RAF must be having a terrific time trying to gear their organization and activities to our organization. The sole representative of air for Britain is ACM Freeman. With the US Admiral Stark, General Marshall, Admiral Turner, General Burns, Comdr. Sherman, General Arnold and to a small extent Col. Bundy all give ideas and opinions re aircraft and their use. No wonder that Freeman said: "When Portal comes over, I am going to insist that he sees just two people, the President and you."

Left at 9:50 with Turner, Bundy and Sherman for the *Augusta*. Conference in Admiral Stark's office where we went over the British C of S [chiefs of staff] estimate of the situation. All American brass hats left at 10:50 for the *Prince of Wales*. PM came aboard Augusta for chat with President. Conference with British in Admiral's cabin aboard the *Prince of Wales*: Pound, Dill, Freeman, Stark, Arnold, Turner, Sherman, Bundy, General _____ [Dykes][94] British General Staff; adjourned at 1:00.[95]

We return by plane, we leave *Tuscaloosa* at 6:00 P.M. tonight; we do not leave *Tuscaloosa* at 6:00 P.M. Late lunch after return, late for lunch; Sp [Spanish] or cheese omelet.

Beaverbrook rained in and grounded at Gander Lake, will be down tomorrow.[96] Conference in my stateroom suite: Freeman, Yool,[97] Burns, Harriman, Sherman and Arnold. What the British want: my God what a list and what things:

[we made] no promises, just see what can be done.[98] Conference broke up at 6:45, buffet supper in wardroom.

Movie, *Northwest Passage*.[99] Didn't see the end as we had to darken ship with ¼ of a reel to go, bed at 11:00 P.M. What a day.

Tuesday, August 12, 1941 [Argentia, Newfoundland]

The end of an epoch-making series of events and a day filled with interesting and inspiring meetings. Up at 6:45, walked deck in rain until 7:30; breakfast. Quite innocently and for want of something to do, nothing was scheduled, I asked Bundy if he wanted to go over to the *Augusta* to see if General Marshall had any last minute instructions. Bundy said "yes"; Sherman wanted to go also; off we went at 9:00. Discussed with Marshall British requests for aviation aid and he agreed with my recommendations. In came Stark and Sherman and then Hopkins, then we all discussed the propositions. Hopkins very bitter as to attitude of American public with regard to all out industrial production. Calls attention to [manufacture of] 600,000 autos last month when we need airplanes, engines and tanks so badly.

When all matters were decided, Stark said: "I have to be aboard *Prince of Wales* at 11:30 to continue discussion re Far East." Marshall: "I will go over with you and say goodbye to Dill." I asked Bundy if he didn't want to go over ahead of time and say adios to Freeman and Dykes. We took off at 10:30 and were aboard at 10:45. Ran into the PM, who insisted upon my going in his cabin and having a glass of port. Then he asked if I was going to be present at Chief of Staffs meeting. I had to admit that I had never heard of it; he said I was expected; to be held at 11:30. He then took me into Admiral's cabin and left me with H. Hopkins, Harriman and Beaverbrook.[100]

Beaverbrook just arrived from Gander Lake. A B-24 crashed ten minutes after take-off and killed 17 of our American pilots. That is third big plane they have lost on take-off. They do not use check lists and I am afraid that they accordingly do not make proper checks on instruments and gadgets.[101]

Met Admiral Pound and he told me of C of S meeting. I told him that I did not think that General Marshall knew of it. Heard bugles blowing, met Freeman and went on deck, Stark and Turner coming aboard; Marshall came later, Stark went off and left him. Pictures taken of Chiefs of Staff together and each with opposite.

C of Staff meeting: brought out the necessity of British establishing a clearinghouse of requirements to cover all needs: Britain, Canada, New Zealand, Australia. Also to go into priorities for Army, Navy, Air so as to cover each theatre of operations; reorganization of missions in Washington so they have a head;[102] what will US do if they enter war; ABC plan. Sherry served during meeting; Admiral Pound presiding; Stark, Dill, Marshall, Freeman, Arnold, Turner, Dykes, Sherman.[103]

Meanwhile instructions came to be aboard the *Augusta* at 2:15; took off from *Prince of Wales* after bidding adieu to skipper and ship's officers. Dropped *Augusta* passengers and were told that we would pack and take our baggage aboard Captain's gig and go to Navy four-engine flying boat immediately after leaving *Augusta*. Returned to *Augusta*, had lunch, paid bills, packed bag, said goodbye and thanked officer personnel. Arrived on *Augusta* amid usual piping, saluting, side boys, officers of the deck, Marines, etc. Met Elliott Roosevelt and signed order re photographs that were taken during session here, letter to Mint Kaye re printing.[104]

Called into King's cabin with other brass hats. All there assembled on quarterdeck in front of airplane hangar: Stark, Marshall, King, Arnold, Turner, Burns, Bundy, Sherman; ship's officers and personnel in rear; Elliott Roosevelt and Franklin Roosevelt, Jr., acting as aides. President came down and took position facing us; Sumner Welles, Hopkins, Harriman standing together. Then Pound, Dill, Freeman in turn said goodbye to the President and went down our line saying goodbye. Finally the Prime Minister came down and did the same thing. One after another went down the ship's ladder to their boat, band playing *God Save the King*.

After the President had retired we said goodbye to King and his ship's officers and took off in gig for the *Dolphin*. Weather was getting bad so that by the time we arrived it was decided we would not take off. Went to *Arizona*; Welles and Harriman still aboard; Welles heading for the *Tuscaloosa* and my old cabin, Harriman taking the Beaver to Gander Lake. Assigned cabins. There at 5:00 P.M., flags and pennants flying from *Prince of Wales*, low hanging clouds cutting off view of shore, fog forming, the *Prince of Wales* with decks lined with sailors pulls up anchor, band playing *Star Spangled Banner*, Winston Churchill, Pound, Dill and Freeman standing on afterdeck. The *Prince of Wales* steams out of the harbor. 1st the *Augusta* plays *God Save the King*; the Marines and sailors aboard the [USS] *Arkansas*[105] at attention with band playing *God Save the King*. The *Tuscaloosa* follows suit, the destroyer and escort pick up speed rapidly and follow the battleship (camouflaged). Signals being sent by lights and flags. The *Augusta* picks up anchor and is followed by the *Tuscaloosa*. We can see Marshall, Stark, Watson, yes and the President on the bridge. The destroyers follow the two heavy cruisers; all merge into and disappear in the fog. The harbor is deserted except for a couple of destroyers, a tanker and the *Arkansas*. The meeting in the harbor of Placentia is at an end. No publicity of any kind to be given prior to 9:00 A.M. Thursday.

Wednesday, August 13, 1941 [Argentia, Newfoundland, and environs, to Quonset Point, Rhode Island]

Left *Arkansas* in a rain storm for Aircraft Tender *Dolphin* at 6:30 A.M. Arrived at tender to find that weather would not permit taking off today and probably tomorrow. Turner, Burns, Bundy returned to *Arkansas*, Sherman and I inspected Naval Air Station at Argentia.[106] Runways will be ready for landing Dec. 1, barracks will be ready Dec. 15. Inspected Army site; no plans, no materials and man in charge states that it will require one full year after materials and plans are received before men can come in.

Took a ride to Placentia country; very much like Alaska, green vegetation, tundra, low trees, but mostly spruce and fir. Roads fair only, ran out of road at the light at Placentia. Went across in a dinghy, five cents per passenger. Town of Placentia only 500, not town of Argentia. Soldiers and officers will have to make their own pleasures. Intermittent rain and fog all the way.

Hired a taxi and drove out towards St. John's for ten miles. Gave taxi driver a bottle of ale and he started talking: Newfoundlanders, (name pronounced to rhyme with understand), don't like English or Canadians and would like to become part of US. Placentia used to be a fishing town, had been for 200 years. Now everyone wants to work and is working at US bases for more money than they ever had. Women wearing silk stockings for first time in life, everyone accuses [US] Marines of paying for them. [US] Navy command [consists of] about 5 officers and 150 men, mostly Marines.

Returned to Argentia to find message: "Return to *Dolphin* at once"; signaled for a boat. Called on Governor of Newfoundland and aide in private car before making contact at Argentia.[107] Took boat in rain, met gig from *Arkansas*; Turner, Burns and Bundy. Went aboard 4-engine flying boat, took off at 1:15, flew blind for 200 miles, came out into blue sky.[108] Passed *Augusta, Tuscaloosa* and five destroyers at 4:20; we signaled, they signaled. Heavy headwinds, landed at Naval Air Base near Newport, Quonset, at 7:15 P.M. Tried to call Wis 3329, no one home, no answer.[109]

Thursday, August 14, 1941 [Quonset Point, Rhode Island, to Washington, D.C.]

Quonset. The Providence [Rhode Island] papers say that [Clement] Attlee will broadcast important meeting of Roosevelt and Churchill at 9:30-10:00 or at some other hour.

The Conference in Retrospect

From my point of view, realizing that there were many talks and conferences at which I was not present, hence there may have been many things happen of which I have no knowledge:

General: the British prepared, hurriedly, a strategic estimate of the situation, agreed to by all, as a guide during the conference. It was drawn up with a view of covering operations, British and ours, in various theatres, also to obtain maximum aid and assistance from the US. It did not include Army or Air Force playing more than a very secondary role, hence it did not mention nor did the British representatives bring up point of our building up our Army or Navy for active participation in the war.

The British representatives did not realize the almost impossible load being placed upon us by Army, Navy, Air Force, all asking for what each wanted, 100%, with no funnel or central sieve to coordinate the various demands. They did not appreciate that on top of this load we had to take care of the needs of China, Russia, British colonies, Dutch East Indies. Then we also had to make such military dispositions as to insure that Japan would think before acting in Far East.

The British as usual asked for everything they wanted regardless of whether we have or ever will have an Air Force. They never blinked an eye when they asked for 100% of our production. They would have taken all the Army, Navy, British, Chinese, Dutch planes and engines. At the same they asked that we establish depots from Iceland to Singapore to repair and maintain all of their American planes. They wanted us to train their combat crews and be responsible for the ferrying of their two and four-engine planes across the Atlantic by these trained crews. Furthermore we were to ferry all bombers possible across with our pilots, [via] P A A [Pan American Airways].[110] There was no thought given by the British as to coordinating their Army, Navy, Air requirements or balancing them against production. They never gave a moment's thought as to what we might be called upon to do: Philippines, Hawaii, Panama, Iceland, Newfoundland, Azores, Natal and then perhaps operations in Europe. With what? After we gave them everything? Then they said, we will give you planes to operate there when you arrive. They wanted us to send bomber and pursuit squadrons complete with all their equipment to become acquainted with the British communications and command systems.

Fortunately we were able to get away without promising or giving away everything we had. As a matter of fact, we might have lost everything we owned, including our pants, but we didn't.

I think, however, that the conference was invaluable as it gave the British a much better understanding of our problems and certainly gave us a better understanding of not only their problems but also their urgent desire to get everything they can regardless of effect on the other fellow. I must admit that Freeman accepted our refusals gracefully. The conference certainly brought home to Stark, Marshall, Turner and I believe to Hopkins and Harriman the necessity for setting up a board to determine up [sic] and lay down policies re allocation of war supplies to not only British but also Russia, China and all other nations.

The meeting will probably be called epoch-making, historical, etc., etc., perhaps the 8 Points will make it so but in my opinion the estimate prepared by the [British] Chiefs of Staff was hastily prepared and not followed through.[111] That was the only document I saw outlining the purpose of our meeting but what the President and Prime Minister had to say when together I know not.

Certainly the military minds seemed to follow the same line of thought when all the demands and requests were forgotten. This meeting of the minds certainly becomes manifest with regard to:

(1) Aid to Russia.
(2) The seizure of the Azores.
(3) The reinforcement of the Philippines.
(4) The handling of Japan if that nation moved further southward.
(5) Iceland's defense.
(6) Occupation of Canaries and Cape Verdes.

but not with regard to:

(1) Occupation of Dakar.
(2) Occupation of Morocco.

The conference dragged on for at least two days too long for there was a potential disaster in being just as long as those ships were anchored and assembled in Placentia Bay. Each day that passed increased the risk and hazard. We all breathed a sigh of relief when the *Prince of Wales*, the *Augusta*, the *Tuscaloosa* and their destroyer escorts pulled out of the harbor. The conference was well worthwhile.

Took off Quonset 6:45, arrived Anacostia 9:00.[112]

Postscript

The Argentia meeting, to Arnold and the AAF, reflected many of the problems that had existed and would continue throughout much of the war. Beyond the obvious advantage of the British and the American chiefs becoming personally acquainted, they gained a clearer picture of the expectations as well as the capabilities of each other.

The 10 August delivery of the British General Strategy Review to the American chiefs is revealing. They requested that the Americans' "major points of criticism" be communicated later that same day so the British chiefs would be able to discuss any differences on the following day.[113] To suggest that the Americans could and should digest, seriously consider, and respond to this 22-page document, which contained 39 items, in the remaining few hours of the day presupposed American acceptance of most of the British document and strategy. As one participant lamented, the British were "hoping to treat strategy while the Americans presumably remained under the Prime Minister's oratorical spell."[114] However, the ensuing delay in accepting the principles of the document, as an accompanying British officer complained, resulted in their "having given away the strength of our position" since the British chiefs "present a united front on the strategical questions, while it is clear that theirs [the US] do not."[115]

The next day, as Hap's diary reflected, the US chiefs met for an hour coordinating their response and reviewing their instructions that no commitments were to be made.[116] Unfortunately, no detailed account of their discussion remains. Then, adjourning to the *Prince of Wales*, they met for two hours with their British counterparts in one of the most extensive and important sessions held by the military at Argentia. Arnold, however, no doubt relying for future reference on his annotations on the document, has provided only a minimum of insight into his participation in this two-hour session. He may have been reluctant to commit to the diary his significant disagreements with General Marshall and Admiral Stark over the British reliance on heavy bombardment.

Pound presided and began the meeting by reading each of the 39 proposals. After Admiral Stark, speaking for the American contingent, interjected that the "meeting was for discussion only and that considered comment . . . would be sent later after thorough study," the discussion began. As the conferees proceeded through the items, covering only 15 of them in the session, "methodical analysis soon gave way to intemperate interpretations."[117] As the interchanges continued, it became clear that one of the problems was that the British intended that the thrust of their deliberations would concern strategy. Churchill, having no doubt about the attitude of the American chiefs towards production and allocation for the British, probably intended to discuss these issues in detail with FDR, whom Hopkins had already characterized as much more friendly towards arming Britain at the expense of American expansion. The prime minister having ruled out the British chiefs discussing production, they brought only one piece of paper on that topic to Argentia. The US chiefs, however, according to RAF Vice Chief Freeman, were interested only in discussing the problems of production. No further sessions were scheduled to consider the General Strategy Review, probably reflecting British disappointment about American unwillingness to discuss strategy.[118]

It was logical that the British, now entering their second full year of war, were seeking a commitment and agreement on strategy from their strongest potential ally. The American chiefs on the other hand, although moving increasingly toward belligerency, were still at least nonbelligerent if not strictly neutral. "Argentia demonstrated just how detached the US was" from the war.[119]

The strategic concepts presented by the British represented a considered analysis based on deliberations within their government. The Foreign Office, the War Cabinet, and the military services were adjusted to the thinking and imprimatur of the prime minister. The US military leaders, however, found themselves with a president who "could not or would not provide guidance" on strategy.[120] Lacking any clear strategic vision other than the ABC-1 plan of March 1941, US military planners were inhibited by not knowing if, when, or where America might become involved, who their enemies would be, the degree of participation anticipated, the political and strategic aims of their involvement or, most important to them, the means to be employed to achieve their aims. Additionally, the strength and preparedness of the American military precluded fulfilling any significant strategic commitments at that time.

With their expulsion from the continent at Dunkirk a year earlier, the British had been forced to adopt a strategy of bombardment aimed at crippling German morale. Their bitter memories of World War I trench warfare, the destruction caused by the Nazi aerial "blitz," their limited manpower resources, and their relatively safe launching bases impelled them to resort to the bombardment strategy as the most viable, immediate means of attacking the Third Reich. At the same time, they were attempting to stem Axis advances in the Mediterranean and Middle East while increasing their strength and awaiting the hoped-for intervention of a strong American ally.

The main thrust of the British paper, ignoring the politically real problem of how US civilian leaders were to lead a divided nation into war, called unabashedly for American entrance into the fray. This was to be brought about as soon as possible since, according to the British, "the longer it is delayed the greater will be the leeway to be made up."[121] Affirming the strategy agreed upon earlier in the ABC-1 discussions, the emphasis was to be on destroying "the foundation" of the Nazi "war machine" even if Japan entered the war. Cast in Churchillian rhetoric, the affirmation called for destroying not only the Nazi war machine but "the economy which feeds it, the morale which sustains it, the supplies which nourish it . . . and the hopes of victory which inspire it."[122]

Several areas around the world were covered; for example, Spain, Gibraltar, Morocco, the Middle East, and Singapore. The strategy against Germany and the European continent was proposed to be blockade, bombing, subversive activity, and propaganda.[123] However, there was little doubt as to the British intent that the "bombing offensive must be on the heaviest possible scale." "We [must] give to the heavy bomber first priority in production." Since through Hopkins and

Harriman the British were well aware of FDR's opposition to dispatching another AEF, the report concluded, "we do not foresee vast armies of infantry as in 1914-1918." Those ground forces required would be mobile, armored divisions that would hand over liberated areas to resistance groups. Success in bombardment along with the other strategy would result in such a "radical decline in the fighting value and mobility [of the German army] that a direct attack [on the continent] would once more become possible." Catering to the known US bombardment enthusiasts, which included Roosevelt and Stimson as well as Arnold, the British concluded that the methods proposed "may by themselves be enough to make Germany sue for peace." This methodology, which emphasized strategic bombardment and minimal use of large land armies on the continent, was advocated by the British for the next two years. Victory with American participation would be "not only certain but swift."[124]

Exchanges in the two-hour session on 11 August reflected not only many of the British-American differences but some within the American delegation as well. One observer's notes reflected "little evidence of a hearty cooperation but rather a critical attitude on the part of the Americans" towards the British strategic paper.[125] A major area of disagreement aside from the call for immediate intervention that quickly became evident between Marshall, Stark, and the British was the latter's emphasis on bombardment as the key to victory and their insistence that heavy bombers have first priority in the American production of materiel. Marshall and Stark "argued tenaciously" against this, causing the British to conclude that the Americans' opinions were "so substantial" that first priority for heavy bombers would not be achieved unless Churchill wrote Roosevelt that, without the desired increase, "we are not going to win the war."[126]

The objections of the two American chiefs were based on many factors, among them the escalating demand in the United States for increasingly scarce personnel, machine tools, manufacturing space, raw materials, and engineering and manufacturing skills needed to produce other aircraft, tanks, munitions, and ships. An additional major factor was

Marshall's and Stark's skepticism concerning the ability to achieve victory by bombardment. Another difficulty was the expanding number of American pilots who lacked a sufficient number of aircraft to effect proper training, a situation that would be made worse if the expectations of the RAF representative at Argentia were achieved; that is, 100 percent of the bombers produced would go to Britain. As the discussion continued, the Americans expressed dissatisfaction with British usage and maintenance of US-manufactured aircraft already in the Middle East and added concern about other demands made on American assets such as the critical need for airplanes in the Philippines and the newly announced obligations to the Soviets.[127]

Other portions of the British Strategy Review elicited equally frank exchanges as Arnold discussed the projected allocation of the estimated 4,590 heavy bombers to be produced in the United States by June 1943, promising 25 percent of them to the British. However, following Air Vice Marshal Freeman's claim of "considerable persuasion" on his part, Arnold gave a "tentative promise" of increasing the British share to 50 percent. As the discussion continued, Hap expressed pessimism about the progress and potential success of the B-26. He also was critical of the allocation of P-40s to the Soviet Union in view of their scarcity and their requirement for 100-octane fuel, which was not currently available in the Soviet Union.[128]

There seems little doubt that Arnold had mixed emotions as he silently concurred with the British emphasis on bombardment as currently the most effective way of waging war against the German-held continent. This was balanced, however, by Hap's strong sense of loyalty and his appreciation that he was subordinate to Marshall. This would explain his reluctance here and elsewhere to disagree publicly with his superior. He also was concerned, as were Marshall and Stark, that even though heavy bombers were urged to become the main priority for American production, the British felt little compunction in believing that the majority of them should be sent to Britain. From the American military viewpoint, their distribution currently was being made haphazardly by FDR without what they felt should be proper consideration for the necessary AAF buildup.

The role of the heavy bomber (in Arnold's mind, primarily the B-17) was becoming increasingly important not only to the British in operational use but as a deterrent to Japanese expansion in the Far East. As early as a year prior to the Argentia meeting, studies in the War Plans Division (WPD) had suggested that in the Philippines "the principal reliance would be placed on air power not only to deter an attack on Luzon but to defeat one if made." However, as Arnold and most of the Air Corps officers were aware, the total number of US airplanes of all types in those islands at the time numbered 37, hardly a viable deterrent. Nevertheless, as the official Army history of this period has concluded, this promise was a "belated but significant recognition of the airplane's role in strategic planning."[129] With the White House and the War Department, including Hap and the AAF, concentrating on Europe and having an inadequate number of aircraft available to meet British combat needs and American expansion, little was done in the next year towards increasing air strength in the Philippines. Those in the islands had to make do with the second-rate equipment on hand. Only P-40Bs could be considered reasonably modern aircraft among the B-18s and P-35s that arrived there in any quantity in the next year.[130] Japanese actions in July 1941, particularly in occupying Indochina, prompted renewed interest in bombers as a deterrent in the Philippines. In the week before departing for Argentia, the AAF was planning to dispatch 165 heavy bombers to Luzon, a significant increase in view of the fact that plans called for only 220 B-17s to be produced in the next six months. Preparations for sending the first group were briefed to and approved by FDR at the US chiefs' 7 August meeting in Argentia.[131] As Arnold commented in his memoirs, this was "a distinct change in policy" and represented a new role and importance for land-based air. Securing agreement by the president for the Philippine reinforcement was also a maneuver that the American chiefs hoped would allow FDR to limit the promises made to the British once Churchill arrived in Newfoundland.[132]

Three weeks after Argentia, the first of the B-17Ds left Hawaii. The airplanes and crews arrived in the Philippines a week later, after a circuitous route involving stops at Midway, Wake, Port Moresby, and Darwin, all destined to become more familiar names to Americans in the next four years.[133]

Other aspects of the heavy bomber issue had to have been on the minds of the American officials at Argentia even though they may not have been articulated fully at the time. Included in these was the fact that the British request for the total US production represented a change in their attitude towards heavy bombers. As Secretary of War Stimson observed the day after Arnold and Marshall returned from Argentia, all the British "want now is great big four-engine bombers" without realizing "how the cupboard was bare." Stimson pointed out that we are now "far behind in [production of] those because they knocked them so hard in the beginning." As he recalled, all they wanted early in the war was pursuit planes but now have "entirely reversed their position" and "are so thoroughly delighted with the Flying Fortresses." Unfortunately, this had resulted in a four-month lag in their production.[134] The early British usage of the B-17 had, in the RAF's opinion, proven highly unsuccessful, a result the Americans blamed on the users rather than the equipment.[135]

Other difficulties, particularly in the minds of Arnold and Marshall, included the persistent belief that British requests in Washington for materiel assistance were not coordinated. Additionally, reports of recently manufactured American aircraft sitting idly on British airfields, along with British confusion as to disposition of spare parts, were on Arnold's mind at Argentia. These reports would be confirmed by his observations during his next visit to England nine months later.[136]

The British conclusion that their General Strategy Review failed to enjoy a favorable acceptance by Marshall and Stark was confirmed as their American cousins moved slowly to provide a written response. On returning to Washington, General Marshall sent it to the Army staff for assessment. It was another month before they made their recommendations and two more weeks elapsed before a coordinated position was agreed upon with the Navy. It was 25 September, seven weeks after receiving the paper at Argentia, that a reply was sent to London. Arnold's role is not clear in the strong rejection of the British emphasis on victory through airpower. Possibly the crux of Marshall's disagreement was summed up in the cover letter: "It should be recognized as an almost invariable rule that wars cannot be finally won without the use of land armies."[137] Faced with the skeptical American attitude and the slow pace of their response, it was an additional two months later, on 21 November, when the British planning staff met to consider the American positions. For whatever reasons, their response did not reach the United States until 10 December, three days after Pearl Harbor.[138]

Other events were consuming so much of the time and energies of both British and American planners that there is little record about the tortured course of this British proposal over the four months between its submission at Argentia and its adjudicated response in Washington. One can speculate that the British, discouraged at the American attitude, were not far from what Churchill, writing in 1949, suggested as the theme of his volume, *Their Finest Hour*: "How the British people held the fort ALONE till those who hitherto had been half blind were half ready."[139]

In the continuing frenetic pace of the US military in this period, it is easy to assign too much credit to the Argentia conference for what happened in Washington in the months immediately following the meeting. Nevertheless, it was clear to Arnold that Marshall and Stark were far from agreement with Roosevelt, Stimson, Lovett, and himself on the primacy of strategic bombardment and the need to emphasize heavy bomber production. It has remained somewhat curious that Arnold continued to enjoy a high degree of confidence by the Army chief of staff during this time, considering their major disagreement over the primary strategy to win the war. Yet Arnold's experience at Argentia strengthened his accord with his fellow military chiefs in opposition to the British request that the bulk of manufactured airplanes as well as other munitions be allocated to them. Hap, while not clearly expressing his beliefs on the need for massive ground forces to ensure victory on the European continent, was hopeful that

Churchill's disparagement of the need for large land armies would prove to be the case.

Several significant events transpired in the United States while Arnold and the other leaders met in Argentia. Just hours before Churchill and his entourage departed gloomy Placentia harbor in the *Prince of Wales*, word was received that the US House of Representatives by the narrow margin of one vote, approved extension of the Selective Service Act. One observer noted that the news "dropped like enemy bombs" on the decks of the two capital ships.[140] If the British had any doubt about the difficulties faced by FDR and his military leaders in leading the nation into war as the British desired, building US forces while negotiating with and supplying a belligerent nation in the face of strong isolationist and congressional reluctance, the news of the closeness of the vote had to have been enlightening.

While Arnold was at the conference, the newly formed War Plans Division of the AAF was at work on what became known as AWPD-1, a plan for employment of air assets should the United States become involved in war. It eventually became a part of the so-called Victory Program, providing an estimate of resources necessary for the US Army other than the AAF. Both blueprints resulted from FDR's 9 July directive to the services that they prepare and submit by 10 September an estimate of "overall production requirements required to defeat our potential enemies." The order was probably inspired by Harry Hopkins and his primary military advisor on Lend-Lease, Maj Gen James H. Burns, both of whom were at Argentia.[141] Completing the assigned task illustrated the difficulty of estimating assets to be needed when theaters of operations, strategy to be employed, and identification of potential enemies could not be clearly determined.

The AAF War Plans Division, which drew up AWPD-1, had only been created three weeks earlier. If normal procedures had been followed, Army aviators would have been assigned to assist those already in the Army War Plans Division in preparing the Army response. The final product probably would have resulted in the AAF being projected for use in much the same manner as it had been since the Army bought its first airplane more than 30 years earlier; that is, primarily supporting Army ground troops. When asked to provide aviators to assist in the planning, Lt Col Harold L. George, chief of the AAF Plans Division and reputed to have dropped more bombs than any other in the AAF, "raised strong personal objections" to the proposed methodology. Arnold then met with Brig Gen Leonard T. Gerow, chief of the overworked WPD. They agreed that the AAF Plans Division could prepare its own annex, exercising care to reflect the guidelines in Rainbow 5 and the ABC-1 discussions of January–March. There is little doubt that Chief of Staff Marshall had approved the proposed method.[142]

Arnold's role in the creation of the estimate is not altogether certain but may be assumed. One of the authors of the resulting plan, which was to be called APWD-1, quoted Lieutenant Colonel George:

> This decision and action of General Arnold has not been given proper recognition. . . . If he had answered General Gerow's request . . . by sending several officers to [WPD] no individual . . . would have been able to determine the effect of such decision on the development and employment of United States aviation during World War II. . . . The basis for development of U. S. Air Power would have been as an auxiliary of surface warfare.[143]

It seems certain that Arnold either chose or approved the four AAF officers selected to draft AWPD-1. Arnold was aware that they all had been very recent students or instructors at the Air Corps Tactical School, which stressed bombardment. The fact that all became general officers early in the war validated Arnold's approval of their work, which they completed in seven days while the Argentia meeting was proceeding.

The plan they submitted operated on the basic premise that the bomber would "get through" and destroy the national economic structure of an enemy nation. It relied extensively but not exclusively on achieving the "break-down of the industrial and economic structure of Germany" by disrupting or destroying their electric power, transportation, and petroleum systems, along with "undermining" German morale. Contemplating that an invasion of Germany might be possible within three years, as it actually was, the planners optimistically wrote that a land offensive "may not be necessary" but that airpower would be there to "support a final offensive" if required. Relying on bombing accuracy, its major innovation was its contradiction of the "prevailing doctrine of the employment of . . . aviation," which essentially had limited aircraft to support ground forces. It agreed with the major British premises in their General Strategy Review even though AWPD-1 had been completed without any knowledge of the British proposals at Argentia.[144]

It is clear that Arnold approved the plan as it was briefed extensively in the first three weeks following Argentia. Those who heard and apparently approved the proposal included General Gerow, the bulk of the general and air staffs, Robert A. Lovett, Averell Harriman, William S. Knudsen, and many officials from the Office of Production Management. General Marshall heard the plan and directed that it be briefed to the secretary of war without exposing it to objections of the joint board; there, the Navy would be in a position to oppose the AAF claim on significant amounts of the nation's industrial assets. Briefed a month after Argentia, Secretary Stimson gave his approval and promised to arrange a date for the plan to be presented to the president.[145] On 25 September, 15 days after Roosevelt's suspense date for a reply to his 9 July directive, the entire "Victory Program" for the US Army, including the AAF's AWPD-1, went to the White House. There appears no evidence that AWPD-1 was ever formally approved at the presidential level. Its framers would have been disappointed to have learned that, a month after its final submission and 10 weeks after their hurried completion of the draft, the president "had not yet looked into the Victory Program," commenting "I don't know just what I want."[146]

In response to another White House request, Arnold and the AAF staff produced on 9 September another plan, known as AWPD-2, that covered allocation of aircraft based on estimates of production from 1 October 1941 through 30 June 1942. AWPD-2 provided for two-thirds or approximately 9,700 of the 14,802 aircraft scheduled to be manufactured in that time frame to be allocated to an anti-Axis pool with the remaining 5,000 planes to be allocated to the AAF.[147] Until production of aircraft in the United States reached significant proportions in 1943, the allocation of aircraft remained a major problem for

Arnold, little encouraged by his experience at the Argentia meeting.

AWPD-1 was the most comprehensive official statement of the AAF's belief in strategic bombardment as the major method to bring about the defeat of Germany. If implemented, it would have created an independent role for Army aviation beyond the circumscribed function heretofore allocated to them by the Army. It was an articulation of what had become an article of faith for Arnold and much of the AAF. However, as Arnold later complained, "We had plans but not planes."[148]

To what degree Arnold influenced the evolution of AAF institutional thinking about the primacy of strategic bombardment or he in turn was influenced by the beliefs of the organization he had headed for three years is impossible to ascertain. Hap, while assistant to the Air Corps chief in the period following 1936, had been reluctant to support Gen Frank M. Andrews and the General Headquarters Air Force (GHQAF) staff in urging that only the B-17 be procured as a heavy bomber. By 1941, he appeared to be not only a convert but also a chief advocate of strategic bombardment. Like all humans, however, his thinking was not always consistent. Less than three months after World War II began in Europe, he was concerned about the vulnerability of bombers. "A doctrine which has been widely propounded in certain Air Corps circles for many years, to the effect that pursuit aircraft and fighter aviation can be minimized on the basis that ftr a/c cannot shoot down large bombardment planes in formation, has not been proven wholly tenable."[149] A year later, in the midst of the German blitz against London, Hap asked the Air Corps Board to study and make recommendations for developing pursuit planes to provide for "the protection of aircraft in flight."[150] Even when AWPD-1 had been approved and submitted to the White House, Arnold told West Point cadets, "fighters have been allowed to drift in the doldrums."[151]

His commitment to strategic bombardment appeared clear only in parts of *Winged Warfare*, the volume he coauthored with Col Ira C. Eaker that was published in 1941. Promising to discuss "the principal phases of air power and air defense" in the book, the authors offered to "suggest the form and shape . . . of air defense" necessary to "stop the present world-marauding air forces." Writing that the "bomber is the essential nucleus of an Air Force" and "is distinctly offensive in character" as contrasted with the defensive fighter, they insisted, "battles and wars are won by a vigorous offensive and seldom, if ever, by the defensive." They conceded, however, that the bomber is "like a snake in the grass, a particularly unpleasant fellow." They argued that the "most economical way of reducing a large city to the point of surrender, of breaking its will . . . is not to drop bombs in its streets, but to destroy the power plants which supply light, the water supply, the sewer lines." Much of this thinking was reflected by AWPD-1, although it appears certain that the AWPD-1 planners did not have access to either Arnold's manuscript or the published volume before writing the plan. The authors further contended that bombing attacks on civil populace are "uneconomical and unwise." Critical of an air force built around defensive fighters, they reasoned that bombers "are winged long-range artillery. They can no more be completely stopped once they have taken the air than the big shell can be stopped once it has left the muzzle." Yet in other parts of the book they appeared less than confident about the ability of the bomber to "get through." In their chapter entitled "Defense Against Air Attack," Arnold and Eaker conceded that in good weather in the daylight, "pursuit aviation . . . can pretty nearly bar the air to the bomber." Citing the recent Battle of Britain, the authors noted that the RAF had "demonstrated that a well-equipped and courageous fighter command, can . . . make the attack of bombing formations expensive and uneconomical."[152]

Although it is hardly surprising that much of Arnold's current thinking was codified in AWPD-1, Army Chief of Staff Marshall's concurrence is surprising indeed. If implemented, the plan would preempt large quantities of materiel, skills, and manpower that otherwise would have been available for the much needed buildup of other segments of the Army. Particularly would the chief of staff's approval appear inconsistent with his and Stark's arguing "tenaciously" at Argentia against the British proposals that American heavy bombardment production receive the highest priority. Additionally, the

Victory Program and its accompanying AWPD-1, both approved by Marshall as sent to the White House, were clearly contradictory. The main thrust of the Victory Program minus AWPD-1 called for a massive ground army of six million men that would require 30 months in training before invading the continent of Europe. The framers of the air plan conceded this possibility but for the most part their proposal implied that any invasion could be negated by the success of strategic bombardment. One author explained Marshall's agreement with these seemingly contradictory plans in terms of practicality. "Pressed from one side by advocates of 'victory through air power' and from another by those prepared to block U. S. military expansion to channel munitions to nations actively opposing the Axis powers, Marshall . . . opted for the rival . . . [he] knew rather than competitors whose ultimate purposes and requirements were beyond the War Department's jurisdiction."[153] An additional facet suggested by this explanation was that Marshall was well aware of Arnold's zeal but that the zeal was balanced by the airman's loyalty to Marshall and the chain of command. In addition, there was an appreciation by both generals that any invasion could proceed only after air superiority had been achieved and that an extensive strategic bombardment campaign would probably best achieve it. Further, as chief of staff and as long as the president's enthusiasm for strategic bombardment could be kept within reasonable bounds, Marshall would have reasonable discretion and direction over how total Army funds and manpower were allocated.

Like Arnold, however, Marshall's thinking was not always consistent. In November 1938, after he had toured Air Corps stations as the new deputy chief of staff and had been "schooled" in airpower and its needs, he urged procurement of the B-17 in maximum quantities, lauding its many potential uses.[154] By the time of Argentia, it seems not unreasonable to assume that both Arnold and his Army superior were agreed on the necessity for successful strategic bombardment, given the limited options possible for the first two years of American participation in the war. They differed, however, on whether strategic bombardment would negate the need for a massive ground invasion of the European continent. Marshall and Arnold would also not always agree on how much of the nation's war assets provided to the US Army would be allocated to the AAF for strategic bombardment. The discussions at Argentia, and the attack on Pearl Harbor less than four months later, may well have clarified to both men the areas of their agreement as well as disagreement.

The AAF had a vital interest in the US-British mission to Moscow that was agreed upon at Argentia. There seems little doubt that FDR's discussions with Churchill, supplemented with Hopkins' fresh assessment of the needs and fighting in the Soviet Union, influenced the decision to dispatch the delegation led by Harriman and Beaverbrook to the beleaguered Soviet Union. Maj Gen James Chaney, who had been serving in London, was the AAF representative in the group that began deliberations in Moscow on 29 September and resulted two days later in the first of four Soviet protocols signed during the war. By its provisions, Britain and the United States would each supply the Soviets with 1,800 aircraft in the period ending 30 June 1942, with a considerable number of the British contribution coming from planes allocated to them by the United States.[155] The bulk of these were to be tactical rather than strategic aircraft, most of them pursuit planes, light bombers, and medium bombers. For example, the United States accepted from the manufacturers in the years 1940 through 1944 a total of almost 23,000 P-39 and P-40 aircraft. Yet at the peak of their inventory in 1944, the AAF had on hand only 4,600 of them. Even allowing for attrition caused by training accidents and their limited US use in combat, the figures reflect that the bulk of them went to Britain and the Soviet Union. The Soviets in particular "valued . . . the P-39 for its effectiveness in low-level support of ground troops."[156] The problem of furnishing them to the Soviets, however, became extremely complicated as the president gave highest priority to the Soviet needs, superseding both American and British requirements. Whereas there was flexibility and some "horse-trading" with the British, as the official history has concluded, the Soviet protocols were regarded as "a contract so binding" that they left "no real choice but faithful . . . execution" for the AAF.[157]

Another result of the conference, probably instituted by Arnold, was the dispatch of Maj Gen George H. Brett to the Middle East. Discussions at Argentia had shown little US interest in British problems in that area except for the use and maintenance of American-manufactured aircraft in that theater. Arnold's instructions to the departing Brett requested that he look into problems of maintenance, equipment, ferrying, training, and establishing a school in the area to train US mechanics. The British demands for American airplanes to support operations there had been discussed during Arnold's April visit to England and would continue through most of the next year as the British relied heavily on American fighters and medium bombers to support them. To the American chiefs, combat in that theater appeared tangential to the main plans in ABC-1, Rainbow 5, and the Victory Program with its accompanying AWPD-1. Brett's September mission resulted in the United States establishing repair facilities in Cairo although the US chiefs retained only minimal interest in operations in that part of the world.[158]

What was to be made of Arnold's first experience, the first of seven, as a bit player at summit diplomacy? One official Army historian has concluded that the military discussions "carried no commitments and led to little in the way of immediate results because of the wide gap" between the British General Strategy Review and the "American responses to those views."[159] On the other hand, Arnold appeared pleased with his personal acceptance as a chief and the enhanced role of the AAF as a major military service virtually on a par with the RAF. At the same time, he was concerned with the seemingly excessive demands made upon AAF resources by the British "regardless of its effect on the other fellow." The problem of aircraft allocation would continue to be of concern to Arnold for the next 18 months and prompt his travel to Britain in May 1942. He appeared satisfied at Argentia that we were able to get away "without promising anything or giving away everything we had." Arnold's conclusions that he and the other military leaders were "window dressing for the main actors" as well as minor role players "in the show" are revealing.[160] As was typical of the man, his optimism prevailed as he reflected on the conference, lauding the "meeting of the minds" and an appreciation by each of the two nations of their areas of agreement, disagreement, limitations and, to some degree, hopes for the future. Unlike most of the other diaries, the schedule of meetings before, during, and after the conference appeared to permit considerable reflection by Hap about the events and significance of this gathering. Neither Arnold nor any of the other American participants in the cold waters of Newfoundland dared speculate that the United States would be attacked at Pearl Harbor within 115 days after they left Argentia.

Notes

1. Theodore A. Wilson, *The First Summit: Roosevelt and Churchill at Placentia Bay, 1941*, ed. rev. (Lawrence, Kans.: University of Kansas Press, 1991), 6.
2. Ibid., 8.
3. Robert E. Sherwood, *Roosevelt and Hopkins: An Intimate History* (New York: Harpers & Brothers, 1948), 231.
4. Ibid., 236.
5. Wilson, 12–14.
6. Hopkins to FDR, 26 July 1941, Henry L. Hopkins Papers, Franklin D. Roosevelt Library, Hyde Park, N.Y., quoted in Wilson, 26; and Sherwood, 317.
7. Diary of Henry H. Arnold, 14 August 1941, Library of Congress, Manuscript Division, Washington, D.C.
8. See Arnold Diary entries for 11 and 12 August, and note 72 for 12 August.
9. Wilson, 30.
10. Ibid., 29.
11. George C. Marshall, transcript of interview by Forrest C. Pogue, 15 January 1957, George C. Marshall Papers, Marshall Library, Lexington, Va. Cited hereinafter as Marshall interview; also quoted in Wilson, 29.
12. Forrest C. Pogue, *George C. Marshall: Ordeal and Hope, 1939–1942* (New York: Viking Press, 1965), 142.
13. Wilson, 68.
14. Arnold's annotated copy of the document, dated London 27 July 1941, is in Gen Henry Harley Arnold Papers, Library of Congress, Manuscript Division, Washington, D.C., hereinafter cited as AP.
15. Arnold Diary, 3 August 1941.
16. Ibid., 6, 7 August 1941.
17. *New York Times*, 25 June 1941.

18. *Department of State, Foreign Relations of the United States, Diplomatic Papers*, 2 vols., *1941* (Washington, D.C.: Government Printing Office [GPO], 1970), 1, 79–81.

19. Marshall to Arnold, Confidential, 16 July 1941, George C. Marshall Papers, George C. Marshall Research Library, Lexington, Va., hereinafter cited as MPMS; also printed in Larry I. Bland, ed., and Sharon R. Ritenour, assoc ed., *Papers of George Catlett Marshall*, vol. 2, *We Cannot Delay, July 1 1939–December 6 1941* (Baltimore: Johns Hopkins University Press, 1981), 567–68, hereinafter cited as MP.

20. Diary of Henry Morgenthau Jr., Franklin D. Roosevelt Library, Hyde Park, N.Y.; Diary of Henry L. Stimson, Sterling Library, Yale University, New Haven, Conn.; and Chief of Staff to Secretary of War, memo, Bland and Ritenour, vol. 2, 582, all dated 1 August 1941.

21. George C. Marshall, memo to the Secretary of War, Secret, 1 August 1941, MP; also printed in Bland and Ritenour, vol. 2, 581.

22. Ibid.

23. Unsigned memo "Estimated First-Line Strength of American Aircraft in RAF as of November 1, 1941" in AP.

24. Stimson Diary, 1 August 1941.

25. Undated copy in Sherwood, 257–58.

26. Sherwood, 323–48.

27. Pogue, 141.

28. Public Record Office (PRO), Air Ministry (Air) 8/891, meeting to receive an account of the [RAF] Vice Chief of Staff's Discussion with the US Chiefs of Staff at Argentia, 20 August 1941, Kew, England. Cited hereinafter as VCAS Meeting.

29. Arnold Diary, 6 August 1941.

30. Ibid., 7 August 1941.

31. Ellington Field, Houston, Texas, was a training site during World War I. Although not used in the interwar period, construction on the World War II installation commenced in August 1940 after which it was utilized for a variety of training activities. It was no longer under USAF control after 1974.

32. All of these bases except Duncan Field, which was incorporated as part of Kelly Field in March 1943, are currently in operation by the USAF in the greater San Antonio, Texas, area. Once assembly line production with its required standardization was established for an aircraft, it became quicker and more economical to send the completed aircraft to modification centers such as Duncan for changes necessary for the use of the plane in a particular mode and/or theater than to make changes on the assembly line. At this time Duncan Field was modifying B-17s sent directly from the manufacturer with armament and other special equipment.

33. Along with Assistant Secretary of War for Air Robert A. Lovett, Arnold attended a review and graduation parade for cadets who were completing their flight training on this day at Randolph Field.

34. Brig Gen Carl. A. "Tooey" Spaatz, chief of staff, AAF Headquarters; Col St. Clair "Bill" Streett, deputy chief of Operations, AAF Division, War Department General Staff. The black book was a compilation of statistics

maintained for Arnold outlining the Air Corps program dealing with personnel, aircraft, air bases, production, finance, and so forth, and carried by him on this trip and others for reference. Although of a later vintage, there is a black book maintained for Arnold in AP, box 242.

35. A leather belt supported by a light strap passing over the right shoulder, originally designed to support the sword worn on the left, introduced in the late nineteenth century into the British Army by Sir Samuel James Browne who was one-armed. It was adopted by officers in the US American Expeditionary Forces and the US Marine Corps in World War I. American and British officers were photographed wearing the belt at this conference.

36. Maj Gen James H. Burns, USA, assistant for Lend-Lease; Lt Col Charles W. Bundy, USA, War Plans Division, who served as recorder during this conference.

37. One author, without clear documentation, has written that Arnold and the others, concerned about possible recognition by a newsman, "fled" through a rear door before completing their lunch. Wilson, 253.

38. Comdr Forrest P. Sherman, USN, War Plans Division, Office of the Chief of Naval Operations, identified by Arnold in his autobiography as an "old friend of mine." H. H. Arnold, General of the Air Force, *Global Mission* (New York: Harper & Brothers, 1949), 247.

39. A Destroyer Leader was normally larger than the average destroyer, oftentimes with accommodations for the commander of the destroyer flotilla. Adm Harold R. "Betty" Stark, USN, chief of Naval Operations; Rear Adm Richmond Kelly Turner, USN, director, War Plans Division, Office of the Chief of Naval Operations.

40. North River also termed Hudson River; Hell Gate is the narrow channel of the East River between Ward's Island on the west and Astoria, Queens, on the east, the Triborough Bridge currently spans this passage; College Point is on the east shore of Flushing Bay, Queens, New York City.

41. Adm Ernest J. King, USN, commander in chief, Atlantic Fleet. The *Augusta* was a heavy cruiser of the *Northampton* class, completed in February 1930 and until recently the flagship of the commander in chief, Asiatic Fleet; *Tuscaloosa* was a heavy cruiser, *Minneapolis* class, completed in August 1934.

42. These destroyers, USS *McDougal*, USS *Moffett*, USS *Sampson*, and USS *Winslow* were from Destroyer Division 17. Actually, five destroyers were involved in the escorting, the four above plus the USS *Madison*; Wilson, 7. Smithstown Bay is just west of Port Jefferson on the north shore of Long Island.

43. The ship carried nine 8-inch guns and eight 5-inch antiaircraft guns.

44. Paravanes are devices towed at an extended angle by vessels to sweep mines.

45. Montauk Point is the eastern tip of Long Island; Block Island is 10 miles south of the Rhode Island coast, at the eastern entrance to Long Island Sound; Martha's Vineyard is an island approximately five miles south of the Massachusetts coast.

46. The reference is to the naval custom of saluting the ensign on the stern and requesting permission to board a naval vessel.

47. In his account in his autobiography, Arnold elaborated: "While we were at anchor on Monday, August 4th, Admiral Turner, Burns and I went over and called on Admiral King. We had not followed protocol—we had not announced our coming and Admiral King was annoyed. However, everything soon cleared up." Arnold, *Global Mission*, 247. As one would expect given his personality, King makes no mention of this visit in his autobiography.

48. The typescript reads Bremer Pass but Arnold's handwritten diary shows Brenner, one of the few examples of differences between the typescripts prepared by the secretaries and Arnold's written account. The term was apparently used at this briefing and then dropped as no other participant refers to the meeting in this manner. The reference is to the several conferences held previously at Brenner Pass in the Alps just south of Innsbruck, Austria, by Hitler and Mussolini, the most recent on 2 June, making this an undesirable comparison.

49. US Undersecretary of State Welles had been acting as Secretary during July while Hull recovered from an illness. His arrival by air on 8 August permitted Welles to limit his absence from Washington.

50. Former US Coast Guard patrol boat USS *Electra* built in 1934 used at the time by Roosevelt as the presidential yacht.

51. About 50 miles southeast of Nantucket Island at 40 degrees 30 minutes N, 69 degrees 28 minutes W.

52. The intention was for the USS *Potomac* to cruise in view of the shore to convince the press and others that the president was on board fishing while in reality he was traveling to Argentia to meet with Churchill. The subterfuge was fully exploited, with the *Potomac* flying the presidential flag. When it passed through the Cape Cod Canal, according to Admiral King, "an individual vaguely resembling Roosevelt, dressed in summer white clothes, sat on the quarterdeck . . . smoking cigarettes and waving genially." See Ernest J. King and Walter Muir Whitehill, *Fleet Admiral King: A Naval Record* (New York: W. W. Norton, 1952), 333.

53. Since neither the House of Commons nor the House of Lords had a member named Atwell, Arnold clearly meant Clement Attlee, Lord Privy Seal and Labor Party leader who announced in Commons on 5 August that Churchill "will not find it convenient . . . to attend an important debate on the progress of the war." *New York Times*, 6 August 1941.

54. Well-known American radio news commentator with Station WOR and the Mutual Broadcasting Company in New York, noted for his nightly opening phrase: "There's good [or bad] news tonight."

55. St. John's is a Newfoundland city approximately 75 miles east-northeast of Argentia on the east coast of the Avalon Peninsula. Cape Sable is an island off southern Nova Scotia.

56. Placentia Bay is the large body of water, approximately 60 miles wide and 90 long, west of St. John's in southeast Newfoundland.

57. Battleship, *Pennsylvania* class, completed in 1917, sunk at Pearl Harbor by the Japanese, 7 December 1941.

58. PBY Catalina was Consolidated Aircraft Corporation's twin-engine, all metal, long-range, patrol-bombing flying boat.

59. Town, east shore of Placentia Bay, Newfoundland.

60. US forces had taken over this base 15 May 1941. On the entrance of the US into the war, plans were changed. Instead of a pursuit group being sent, the 49th Bombardment Squadron, equipped with B-17s, arrived at Argentia 16 January 1942. They were used primarily in antisubmarine patrol work.

61. This meeting was the first opportunity for the American military leaders to coordinate their positions for the upcoming sessions. The aid to the USSR was a follow-up on Roosevelt's directive in the cabinet meeting of 1 August that a "token" gesture of planes be furnished to the Soviet Union. The discussion highlighted the dilemma of providing airplanes to strengthen Philippine defenses while strong demands were made to send them elsewhere. The decision to send the planes to the Philippines, confirmed in the meeting with FDR that afternoon, had been urged by the British and generally rejected by the United States since February. The British logic was that a strong Philippine defense would in effect deter Japan moving south against Singapore in view of the location of the Philippines to threaten the Japanese lines of supply and communications. See the discussion in Mark S. Watson, *United States Army in World War II, The War Department, Chief of Staff: Pre-war Plans and Preparations* (Washington, D.C.: Office of the Chief of Military History, GPO, 1950), 393–400. This was a tentative commitment to furnish aircraft to the USSR. An Anglo-American mission proceeded to the Soviet Union the next month in September and in the protocol signed by all three nations on 1 October, the British and the United States each agreed to furnish the Soviet Air Force 1,800 aircraft during the period ending 30 June 1942.

62. Capt Elliott Roosevelt, AAF Reserve officer, son of the president, stationed at the time at Gander Field, Newfoundland; Brig Gen Henry W. "Swede" Harms, CG, Newfoundland Base Command.

63. There appears no other confirmation of Arnold's statement in his memoirs that these principles were accepted by Marshall, Stark, and "finally by the president"; Arnold, *Global Mission*, 248. There seems little doubt that these "considerations" were part of Marshall's and Stark's thinking as well; see Wilson, 115–20.

64. Capt J. R. Beardall, USN, naval aide to the president.

65. As a result of this meeting, an order was given by Roosevelt on 4 September directing that German surface raiders attacking the shipping routes between the United States and Iceland were subject to sinking. It further stipulated that the US Navy would henceforth be permitted to escort convoys of ships not of American registry and that Canadian ships were permitted to escort American ships. Although not announced until the next month, arbitrarily extending the Western Hemisphere area of United States responsibility eastward to the Azores was among the most significant military actions taken by the United States at Argentia. At this time, the US

Maritime Commission controlled the allocation of US merchant ships to the British.

66. A recent American scholar of the conference has written that FDR "reviewed matters that his subordinates should expect the British to request." Wilson, 66-67. Arnold was no doubt pleased that the aircraft aid to the Philippines was to be used not only to improve their defenses but also as a deterrent to potential Japanese aggression, a role for land-based air newly accepted by the US leadership; Wilson, 66.

67. This problem and the ships are not identified in Navy historical records.

68. Although the outline has not been located in Arnold's papers, there seems little doubt that it expressed Hap's thinking as reflected in his diary entries of 6 and 7 August. There he expressed a need for a distribution plan balanced between the needs of the British and Soviets as perceived in Washington and the requirement to build up the AAF.

69. Headquarters of the Newfoundland Base Command were not moved to Argentia but remained at Newfoundland Airport at Gander Lake. There is a brief account of the early growing pains of this command in Wesley Frank Craven and James Lea Cate, eds., *The Army Air Forces in World War II*, vol. 1, *Plans and Early Operations, January 1929 to August 1942* (1948; new imprint, Washington, D.C.: Office of Air Force History, 1983), 156-57. Arnold showed uncharacteristic restraint in this meeting with the recently assigned American aviator commander in Newfoundland. Very soon after he returned to Washington, however, Arnold acted to relieve him, effective 30 September, at the same time reducing him to the rank of colonel "because he had definitely demonstrated that he does not measure up to the job." His new assignment was as commanding officer (CO) of the Pendleton, Oregon, Army Air Base, a marginally demanding wartime position, resulting in Harms not being promoted again during the war. According to one observer, Arnold was still so incensed with Harms that when the latter reported to Washington en route to Oregon, Arnold "would not shake hands with him." This was an example of Arnold's unwillingness to accept excuses or what he considered as lack of diligence in accomplishing necessary tasks even among friends and long-time associates. Harms had graduated from West Point in 1912, been a pilot since 1915, and Hap had met with him several times during the latter's trip to Paris in 1918. Possibly feeling compassion for the relieved officer, Arnold wrote Harms letters of encouragement when the latter was hospitalized in November 1941. See Arnold to Dryden, 4 September 1941, AP; refusal to shake hands is from Lt Gen Barney M. Giles, Oral History Interview, 12-13 May 1970, Air Force Historical Research Agency, Maxwell Air Force Base (AFB), Ala. For meetings in France, see World War I Diary, 3 November, 7, 9 December 1918.

70. Gander Army Air Base, east central Newfoundland, had been serving the British and Canadian air forces since 1936. The first American troops arrived there in May 1941, after which the base was a joint American-Canadian facility. US interests there were terminated in June 1961.

71. USS *Dolphin*, destroyer-aircraft tender commissioned in 1921 with accommodations as a flagship; OA-9 was Grumman Aircraft Company's twin-engine, high-wing, six-place amphibian.

72. Belle Island is off the northern tip of Newfoundland.

73. Corvettes are armed and highly maneuverable escort ships, smaller than destroyers. PBYMs were Consolidated Aircraft's four-engine, long-range patrol aircraft.

74. At this time, the newly created AAF Ferry Command was restricted to ferrying aircraft to the "point of ultimate take-off" for Britain, which at this time meant a Canadian airdrome. See chapter 1.

75. Arnold meant Holsteinborg, port in southwestern Greenland; Baffin Island is across Davis Strait and Baffin Bay, west of Greenland; Fort Chimo is a small town in northern Quebec on the Koksoak River and North West River is a town on Lake Melville, eastern Labrador. All these locations were important in establishing an aerial route across the North Atlantic.

76. Britain's newest battleship, *King George V* class, which had been engaged in the battle against the German battleship *Bismarck* in May 1941 was itself later sunk by the Japanese in the South China Sea three days after Pearl Harbor.

77. Ens Franklin D. Roosevelt Jr., USN, son of the president, assigned at the time as executive officer of the destroyer, USS *Mayrant*.

78. Harry Hopkins was dispatched to the Soviet Union on 28 July to assess conditions firsthand for the American president. He returned from Russia via Great Britain and traveled to Argentia with Churchill and his advisors on the *Prince of Wales*.

79. Martin Company's model 187, a twin-engine medium bomber called the Baltimore, was produced entirely for the British. The very few delivered to the AAF were designated A-30.

80. Labeled by Wilson as a "bull session," the discussion centered on the problems of getting heavy bombers to England, Wilson, 90. The Glenn L. Martin Nebraska Company, a subsidiary of the Glenn L. Martin Company, operated a US government-constructed bomber assembly plant on the site of what later became Strategic Air Command Headquarters, Offutt AFB, Omaha, Neb. During the period of Arnold's diary, it manufactured B-25 medium bombers for the AAF, PBM-3 Mariner long-range patrol bombers for the US Navy, and Model 187 Baltimore medium bombers for the British. In December 1941, North American Aviation Company opened a new assembly plant adjacent to the Fairfax Airport, Kansas City, Missouri, manufacturing B-26C bombers.

81. Lord Cherwell, born Frederick A. Lindemann, principal scientific advisor to Churchill; John M. Martin, principal private secretary; Comdr Charles R. Thompson, RN, Churchill's naval aide.

82. Arnold is writing figuratively here, not literally.

83. The captain's gig is a small boat used at the discretion of the ship's captain. Admiral King's comment to Arnold as he took his seat that his absence had not been noticed was consistent with the admiral's relations with Hap. Arnold, *Global Mission*, 251.

84. Termed *one of the most important events of the conference*, Churchill held the stage in a "masterly review" of the world situation and called for "strategic bombing as the means to victory." There seems disagreement as to the extent to which he called for US intervention, the most conservative account recording that he called for it "by inference." Arnold neglected to record that Hopkins enthralled his listeners about conditions he found on his recent trip to the Soviet Union; Wilson, 93-95. In his memoirs, Arnold provided a more complete coverage of the Prime Minister's remarks. As Hap concluded, it "gave us a clear indication of the reports we might expect from the British at the staff conference to follow"; Arnold, *Global Mission*, 252-53.

85. US destroyer, *Porter* class, commissioned in 1936.

86. Admiral McIntire was President Roosevelt's physician.

87. Captain Badger was chief of staff to Admiral King; Wright was captain of the *Augusta*.

88. The service was designed for maximum effect even down to the British "dress rehearsal" held on board the *Prince of Wales* en route to Argentia. The scripture, probably chosen by Churchill and read as custom demanded by Captain Leach of the *Prince of Wales*, was most appropriate. Taken from the first chapter of Joshua, it admonished potential allies: "There shall not any man be able to stand before thee all the days of thy life: as I was with Moses, so will I be with thee; I will not fail thee, nor forsake thee. Be strong and of good courage." The British Prime Minister chose the hymns, including *Eternal Father, Strong to Save, O God Our Help in Ages Past,* and *Onward Christian Soldiers*, with the lines, appropriate from the British standpoint, of "marching as to war. . . . Christ the royal master, Leads against the foe; Forward into battle." Prayers for the service had been printed in advance and were distributed to the worshippers. The loss of the USS *Arizona* and the *Prince of Wales*, noted Churchill in his memoirs, meant that almost half of those naval personnel assembled (including Captain Leach) would have lost their lives before the end of 1941. See Winston S. Churchill, *The Second World War*, vol. 3, *The Grand Alliance* (Boston: Houghton Mifflin, 1950), 431-21; AP has mementos of the service.

89. Arnold clarified the issue in his memoirs, indicating that Freeman had used "very optimistic . . . hastily arrived-at statistics" furnished by the US Office of Production Management. Arnold explained to the British airman that figures to be used had to be based on actual production, not estimates. Although "greatly disappointed," he appeared to accept Arnold's explanation. Arnold, *Global Mission*, 253.

90. Table seating chart not located in AP.

91. Dated 31 July 1941 and prepared by the British Chiefs of Staff, it contained their General Strategy Review. Copies were provided to FDR, Admiral Stark, and General Marshall as well as Arnold. The paper was divided into two parts, the first entitled "The Present Strategical Situation" and the second "Present and Future Strategy." Covering a variety of topics and geographical theaters, it addressed possible US intervention in at least three different instances and stressed the advantages that would accrue to earlier rather than later American involvement in the hostilities. It con-

cluded: "US intervention would not only make victory certain, but might also make it swift." No doubt its emphasis on strategic bombing contributed to Hap's assessment of it being "sound in some respects." His annotated copy is in AP.

92. There appears no fuller account of this informal meeting.

93. Sir Alexander Cadogan, British permanent undersecretary of State for Foreign Affairs; Col Leslie C. Hollis, Royal Marines, assistant secretary, British War Cabinet.

94. Brigadier Vivian Dykes, British Army, secretary, British War Cabinet.

95. This two-hour meeting was as important as any the American military attended. See discussion in Watson, 402–5; Wilson, 128–32.

96. Lord Beaverbrook had only been invited to participate in the conference by Churchill in a cable sent on 7 August, hence his late arrival by air. He continued to Washington after the conference to discuss matters of supply and procurement. There is an excellent picture of him emerging seemingly in a hurry, from the B-24 that had just landed at Gander in Carl A. Christie with Fred Hatch, *Ocean Bridge: The History of the RAF Ferry Command* (Toronto: University of Toronto Press, 1995), 221–22. In the photo, he is shown clutching his hat against the wind with one hand and carrying a considerable sheaf of papers in the other. See A. J. P. Taylor, *Beaverbrook* (New York: Simon & Schuster, 1972), 481.

97. Group Captain W. M. Yool, RAF, staff officer, Office of the Chief of the Air Staff, RAF.

98. In what was and would remain a familiar plea for at least the next year, Freeman insisted on British priority for American-produced aircraft.

99. Starring Spencer Tracy and Robert Young, the movie recounted Robert Rogers' Rangers daring expedition against the Saint Francis Indians in the French and Indian War, providing its viewers with a very timely account of Anglo-American cooperation in a previous world struggle.

100. This was just one of the several communications/arrangements lapses at this conference. Later meetings were marked by much improved efficiency on the part of the British-American secretariat.

101. A step-by-step list of tasks thought necessary for proper and safe operation of an aircraft. It became standard operating procedure in the AAF during World War II and has remained so by the USAF. It also remains commonplace in commercial flying. Probably developed at Langley Field, Va., in 1937 for use with the then complex new B-17 because an earlier experimental model had crashed at Wright Field, Ohio, when a crew member failed to release the control locks.

102. After Pearl Harbor, Churchill named Sir John Dill to head the British mission in Washington. He served in that position until his death in November 1944. During his service there, he and Arnold developed a close relationship. In honor of his accomplishments in that role, special arrangements were made for his burial in Arlington National Cemetery, Va.

103. The ABC plan refers to the British-American staff conversations held in Washington from 29 January to 27 March 1941 that were discussed in chapter 1. In view of the planned sailing of the *Prince of Wales* that after-

noon and the "absolute chaos on board" prior to departure, the meeting was a short but important one. The US chiefs continued to decline to provide specifics of their intentions if they entered the conflict, but all spent considerable time on aircraft allocation. "Absolute chaos" is from Wilson, 134; see Portal to Arnold, 3 September 1941, AP.

104. Col Minton W. Kaye, director, Photographic Map and Chart Section, Headquarters AAF, who became responsible for printing the pictures taken at the meeting by USAAF photographers. They had been flown hurriedly from Gander to record the events after FDR had discovered, contrary to his prior agreement with Churchill, that the British brought along two "writers" to make a "historical record" of the event. The contretemps is recorded in Wilson, 55, 85–86; and H. V. Morton, *Atlantic Meeting* (London: Metheun, 1943), 5.

105. Arnold here and below meant the *Arizona* and not the *Arkansas*. The latter name, however, is in the handwritten account.

106. The US Navy had begun construction of a naval operating base at Argentia on 29 December 1940. Although not formally opened until 15 July 1941, work continued on various parts of the base.

107. Vice Adm Sir H. T. Walwyn was the governor of Newfoundland.

108. Blind flying is total dependence on instruments without reference to the ground or other points of reference outside the cockpit.

109. Naval Air Station, North Kingston, R.I., on the west shore of Narragansett Bay. Wis [Wisconsin] 3329 was Arnold's home telephone number in Washington.

110. In view of US neutrality, some American-built aircraft destined for the British were flown under contract to Pan American Airways. See Craven and Cate, *The Army Air Forces in World War II*, vol. 1, *Plans and Early Actions*, 329–31.

111. The official communiqué issued jointly by the two governments contained eight major points and was printed in the *New York Times*, 14 August 1941, under a banner headline: "Roosevelt, Churchill Draft 8 Peace Aims, Pledging Destruction of Nazi Tyranny; Joint Steps Believed Charted at Parley."

112. US Naval Air Station, east bank of the Anacostia River, Washington, D.C., contiguous to Bolling Army Air Field.

113. Watson, 403.
114. Wilson, 121.
115. Ibid., 121–22.
116. Ibid., 116.
117. Ibid., 121–22, 129.
118. VCAS Meeting.
119. Wilson, 128.
120. Ibid., 118.
121. British General Strategy Review, 31 July 1942, copy in AP.
122. Ibid.
123. Ibid.
124. Ibid.

125. Watson, 404.
126. VCAS Meeting.
127. Watson, 402-4.
128. VCAS Meeting.
129. Watson, 416.
130. Craven and Cate, vol. 1, 177.
131. Quoted in Michael S. Sherry, *The Rise of American Air Power: The Creation of Armageddon* (New Haven, Conn.: Yale University Press, 1987), 105, note 77.
132. Arnold, *Global Mission*, 249; and Wilson, 66.
133. Craven and Cate, vol. 1, 178-79.
134. Stimson Diary, 14 August 1941.
135. See assessment forwarded to Arnold by Gen Brett on 19 September 1941. This discouraging statistical account, dated a week earlier, concluded that it is "open to question whether 2 of an estimated 40 [B-17s operated in combat by the British] actually have hit the assigned objectives." Summary of B-17 . . . in Bombing Operations, 12 September 1941, AP. Roger A. Freeman, *B-17: Fortress at War* (New York: Charles Scribner's Sons, 1977), 10-33, provides a good coverage of the British problems with the airplane.
136. See for example Arnold Diary, 25 May 1942.
137. Cited in Wilson, 217.
138. Watson, 408-9.
139. Winston S. Churchill, *The Second World War*, vol. 2, *Their Finest Hour* (Boston: Houghton Mifflin, 1948), ix.
140. Sherwood, 367.
141. Wilson, 40.
142. Haywood S. Hansell Jr., *The Air Plan that Defeated Hitler* (Atlanta: Higgins-McArthur, Longino & Porter, 1972), 65.
143. Ibid., 66.
144. Ibid., 70-88; and Wilson, 63.
145. Stimson Diary, 12 September 1941; and Wilson, 216-17.
146. Morgenthau Diary, 23 October 1941; Hansell, 93-96.
147. Craven and Cate, vol. 1, 133.
148. Ibid., 150.
149. Arnold to CG GHQAF, 14 November 1939, AP.
150. Arnold to C/S, 25 September 1940, AP.
151. Quoted in Jack Samson, *Chennault* (Garden City, N.Y.: Doubleday, 1987), 9.
152. Henry H. Arnold and Ira C. Eaker, *Winged Warfare* (New York: Harper & Brothers, 1941), xii, 133-34, 144-45, 176.
153. Wilson, 64.
154. DC/S to C/S [Chief of Staff], 29 November 1938, cited in Thomas H. Greer, *The Development of Air Doctrine in the Army Air Arm, 1917-1941*, USAF Historical Study 89 (Maxwell AFB, Ala.: USAF Historical Division, Research Studies Institute, Air University, 1955), 101.
155. Craven and Cate, vol. 1, 133; and Wesley Frank Craven and James Lea Cate, eds., *The Army Air Forces in World War II*, vol. 6, *Men and Planes*

(1955; new imprint, Washington, D.C.: Office of Air Force History, 1983), 401.
 156. Craven and Cate, vol. 6, 214.
 157. Ibid., 401.
 158. See Arnold to Brett, 19 August 1941, AP.
 159. Watson, 401.
 160. Arnold Diary, 4 August 1941.

Chapter 3

England
22 May–3 June 1942

Introduction

The problem of aircraft allocation did not appear any easier of resolution after the August Argentia Conference than previously. Not only did British requirements continue; the Chinese began to lobby Washington more effectively for assistance, further complicating the president's directive that the Soviets should have first priority for allocations. From Arnold's perspective, all these requests had to be evaluated along with the need to fulfill the agreement among the Americans at Argentia to buttress Philippine air defenses by sending P-40s and even more scarce B-17s to the islands. As relations with the Japanese continued to deteriorate in the autumn of 1941, the necessity for building up the AAF to meet what appeared increasingly to be the probability of war became imperative.

When the Japanese attacked Pearl Harbor, the authorized manpower strength of the Air Corps was 348,535, a far cry from the 20,196 on duty three years earlier when Arnold became chief.[1] The total number of aircraft possessed had been increasing from the 1,792 on hand in September 1938, but the power of its combat arm, the GHQAF, the most important operational AAF unit now that the nation was at war, was far from encouraging. Five months before the Japanese attack, Hap reported that the Air Corps possessed only 523 tactical aircraft in nine groups, almost 60 percent of them bombardment planes. The numbers of aircraft delivered to the AAF since that time had not resulted in any significant improvement by 7 December.[2] Further, Hap was all too aware that many of those on hand were obsolete B-18 and P-36 aircraft, lacking speed, self-sealing gas tanks, gun turrets, armament, and other accouterments necessary to survive in combat. Even the more modern planes had structural defects or were lacking spare parts as a result of the unprecedented expansion of the industry. Illustrative of problems in the period was that of propellers for the P-39, which were in short supply for the emerging airplanes. A temporary solution used was to fly the new aircraft to an AAF base, "remove the propeller," and ship it back to the manufacturer for installation on a newly manufactured aircraft.[3] More encouraging was the increase in the yearly productive capacity of the American aircraft industry, which manufactured 19,433 planes in 1941 with 8,723 of them delivered to the AAF. Less encouraging was the fact that two-thirds of these were training airplanes.[4]

US entry into the conflict affected the Air Corps as significantly as it did all other segments of the nation. For Arnold, a major impact was the need to reassess aircraft allocation to the Allies while increasing the effort to achieve a strong AAF. That effort could now be more clearly defined in terms of aims, strategy, and tactics. The major change necessary in aircraft allocation was with the British quotas, a problem that Arnold had faced on several occasions even before he became the Air Corps leader.

The existing Slessor arrangement had resulted from the ABC conversations of January–March 1941. Although never formally approved, it was essentially followed in the first six months after its submission on 29 March 1941. It called for Britain to retain all the output from her own production facilities, all US-produced aircraft from their orders already in process, which included the now-surrendered French orders, and an allocation from the continuing American production as well as the "entire output" from any new US expansion. If America were to be drawn into the war, any new US capacity would be allocated between them on a 50-50 basis. Although it had served as a planning basis, the Slessor arrangement had pretty well lapsed as a serious basis of allocation by the time of the Argentia meeting, at least on the part of Arnold and the United States.[5]

A new agreement was forged between the two English-speaking Allies during the Arcadia Conference, with Churchill and his military staff in Washington for a three-week visit from 22 December to 14 January, immediately following Pearl Harbor.

In spite of outraged American public opinion against the Japanese for their attack, the new Allies reaffirmed their Europe First policy, which had been emphasized as war strategy in the earlier ABC-1 planning conference. Concentration on this theater would allow Arnold's AAF with its growing but still inadequate fleet of heavy bombers to join the RAF in aerial attacks against northern Europe. Hap hoped these day and night attacks would validate much of his and the AAF's belief in strategic bombardment. From Arnold's viewpoint, the other major development as a result of this meeting was a new agreement between Arnold and Air Chief Marshal Portal on aircraft allocation that was approved by Churchill and Roosevelt as the conference ended on 14 January. Arnold's very fragmentary notes kept during these Washington meetings contain little insight into the origins of the new allocations.[6]

While the Arcadia Conference was in session and before the new agreement had been worked out, FDR directed Stimson to establish a total US national production goal of 60,000 aircraft for 1942. Of these, 45,000 were to be tactical aircraft and 15,000 were to be trainers. This represented an increase of 14,000 aircraft from the previous target of 46,000 that had been proposed for 1942. In dividing the proposed 60,000 aircraft, the Arnold–Portal agreement, signed in Washington on 14 January 1942, allocated 34,830 to the AAF, 10,220 to the US Navy, and 10,382 to the British. Medium and light bombers along with pursuits made up more than 82 percent of the proposed British distribution. The British share of total production was approximately 5 percent for heavy bombers, observation planes 4 percent, and transports 8 percent. The allocations were subject to "periodic readjustments" when justified by changed conditions.[7] Considering the devastating losses to American naval and land-based airpower in Hawaii and the Philippines, the distributions agreed upon in these December 1941–January 1942 meetings were extremely generous towards the British. They also reflected an unrealistic American optimism.

These high hopes, which were based on the prospects of vastly increased American productive capabilities and the large reservoir of men and resources now formally committed to the defeat of the Axis powers, were quickly dashed. In the first six months of the war, military disasters struck the Allies in the Pacific and elsewhere. For example, Japanese forces occupied Thailand and attacked Hong Kong in the first week of the war, forcing British evacuation there. Singapore, Midway, and Wake Island were struck by the Japanese, who effected the surrender of Guam while successfully landing on Luzon in the Philippines. Allied land-based air partisans took little comfort in the sinking of a new British battleship and battle cruiser off the Malay coast three days after Pearl Harbor by Japanese aircraft operating from Saigon. The day before the convening of Arcadia, Wake Island fell to the Japanese, who had established air and naval superiority in the Philippines. Douglas MacArthur was forced to evacuate Luzon, a prelude to later last-ditch resistance on Bataan and Corregidor. Fortunately, the Air Corps was able to salvage its few B-17 bombers that remained in the Philippines by flying them to Australia. Further south, little opposition was mounted against Japanese landings in Borneo. The Philippine government abandoned Manila on the opening day of the conference. One day later, the Hong Kong garrison surrendered.

Faced with these losses and anticipating more, it appeared that Hap was having second thoughts about the plan less than a month after the signing of the Arnold–Portal agreement. It would allocate for 1942 almost 11,000 aircraft to Britain and its dominions. This number represented 31 percent of total expected American production of operational planes. At the CCS meeting of 10 February, Hap indicated a need for an immediate "complete study" of aircraft production of all Allied nations. He insisted that only with this information could the overall problem of distribution be properly considered.[8] The documents are not clear as to whether the British realized that this proposed review was a harbinger of significant changes in the Arnold–Portal accord, but it seems logical to assume that Hap would not have introduced the matter unless he anticipated an increase in the numbers of aircraft available for the AAF, which would necessitate a numbers decrease to Britain.

The British leaders who were in Washington soon began to understand that difficulties lay ahead for the Arnold–Portal commitment. On 6 March, they expressed concern to London for "getting our heavy bomber assignments." Their request appeared to conflict with both Arnold's "aim to expand" the AAF and the US Navy's desire for more aircraft to conduct patrol and antisubmarine efforts. As a result of these developments, the RAF delegation in Washington asked the Air Ministry in London for "all relevant information to support your requirements for bomber and coastal command usage."[9]

As Arnold continued to doubt the wisdom of providing so much of the 1942 production to the British, he felt considerable pressure from a variety of sources to begin the planned US bomber offensive from England. Full implementation of such an offensive would require reconsideration of the Arnold–Portal division. On 6 March, Secretary of War Stimson, now strongly committed to the concept of US strategic bombardment from English bases, asked Arnold to provide a timetable for arrival of the bombers in England and a projection of the number of bombers to be deployed there.[10] By 11 March, British observers in Washington were fearful that a "large proportion" of available aircraft would go to the Pacific and the British need for "urgently needed assistance" for aircraft in the Middle East would not be met. They predicted "a more forceful assertion of US claims on aircraft coming off US production lines."[11]

Churchill on 29 March exerted additional pressure for the Americans to begin their aerial offensive when he cabled FDR that the "need to bomb Germany is great" and lamented that the expansion of the bomber forces thus far had been disappointing. The British leader revised a metaphor he had used earlier: "Never was there so much good work to be done and so few to do it." He expressed concern about the projected summer attack by US planes, hoping the plan would not "decline into a second rate affair." He stressed that even a hundred American bombers before the end of May would be valuable, particularly in freeing British aircraft for antisubmarine patrols. The prime minister failed to register any connection between fulfillment of the Arnold–Portal quotas and the ability of the AAF to commence extensive European bombing operations.[12] FDR's relay of Churchill's request to the CCS meeting two days later for their consideration reflected continuing interest by the president in the urgency of strategic bombardment.[13] On the same day the prime minister cabled FDR, a British observer in Washington reported to London that the "Arnold-Slessor ratios are as favourable as we can hope for."[14]

In the discussions that ensued at the CCS meeting on 31 March, General Marshall spoke in support of the "importance of the heavy bomber offensive from the United Kingdom." The Army chief of staff repeated the earlier request made to the British to "provide the US Chiefs of Staff with the fullest information" about their resources in each theater, something the British promised to fulfill. Arnold stated in the meeting that one heavy bomber group was being prepared to deploy to England in May, followed by two more in June. For the second time since Arnold introduced the topic on 10 February, the CCS in their 31 March meeting recognized the need for "an immediate review of the present aircraft resources" of the Allies "together with the proposed expansion programs."

The specific data needed, Arnold explained, included the strength of the current air forces, "the proposed expansion, the present and proposed production programs and the missions to be performed by the aircraft of the United Nations in the various theaters." Hap again emphasized the impossibility of proper allocation without this review.[15] In the continuing discussions at this meeting and elsewhere concerning the allocation of aircraft as well as other assets, a constant thread running through the documents reflected the United States repeatedly asking the British for full information concerning aircraft numbers, their deployment and use, in short, as the senior RAF officer in Washington explained, "the somewhat impatient [US] demands for more information as to what we were doing with all our available aircraft."[16] This reflected an American suspicion that the British were less than forthcoming in providing these important planning figures. As Air Chief Marshal Evill reported from Washington, the Americans continued to be dissatisfied over what they felt were British "undisclosed resources, unnecessarily large reserves" and uneconomical use of aircraft.[17] Consequently, the CCS "invited" Arnold, Rear Adm John Towers, head of the US

Navy's Bureau of Aeronautics, and British Air Marshal Evill of the CCS to furnish the necessary assessment from their respective viewpoints, presenting a "complete picture of all US and British air resources." The "complete picture" should include such factors as operating strength, reserves, production, proposed expansion, and "present distribution by theater, including movements already in progress or arranged."[18]

The British Air Mission in Washington immediately relayed the CCS request for data to London, emphasizing the need for "complete frankness" as a requisite for "satisfactory cooperation." The British in Washington seemed more attuned than the Air Ministry in London to the American concern over less than full information being provided.[19] Six days later, the British Air Mission articulated to London for the first time that it was "clear" that the United States wanted to "get away from the Arnold-Portal agreement," a judgment concurred in by Britain's stalwart friend in the White House, Harry Hopkins.[20] This was confirmed by Hap's presentation to the CCS on 8 April. Using graphs reflecting the agreed-upon Arnold–Portal allocations for the year, "the whole implication," according to the British representatives present, was "that the present distribution is wrong" and that they would from now on face "increasing pressure for allocating a greater portion of US production" to the AAF. The British gloomily concluded that the "tendency," as expressed in their cable that day to London, was "to edge us off the US platform."[21]

On that same day, Arnold briefed Stimson on the data presented to the CCS. Although Hap has left no comprehensive assessment of his sentiments at the time, it appears logical that his views were in agreement with those of the secretary. Stimson termed the situation "frustrating"; that is, "continuing a distribution of the bulk of the weapons to the Allies on the assumption that they are doing all the fighting." The secretary of war recorded that Arnold was "trying to get a reconsideration . . . so that we will get more of the planes." Hap concurred with Stimson's assessment that the American effort to get more planes to the AAF was being defeated by our "giving so many of them away." The figures showed that combining the total of British production with the US allocation of tactical aircraft (as opposed to training planes) meant that the British were scheduled to get approximately 58 percent of total US-British production in 1942.[22] The next afternoon, Stimson presented the same figures to FDR who, according to the secretary, was "very impressed" with the seriousness of the problem. When Roosevelt suggested a possible increase in production as a solution to the problem, Stimson cautioned against taking this risk, a caution that the president "apparently accepted."[23]

As Arnold, Towers, and Evill were attempting the requested assessment, the British began an extensive transatlantic dialogue between RAF headquarters in London and other British agencies, marshaling arguments to be presented in Washington for retaining the existing distribution and forestalling any major change in Arnold-Portal. These arguments were made repeatedly to Hap before and during this trip to London and were continued on both sides of the Atlantic until Roosevelt and Churchill approved, on 22 June 1942, the new accord that was negotiated by Hap during his second World War II trip to Britain.

The British justification for continuation of the Arnold-Portal division appears less self-serving when viewed half a century later through the prism of their difficult situation. In their attempts at retaining what they felt was needed, their main arguments were directed not only towards Arnold but were provided whenever possible to the White House, Hopkins, Stimson, Lovett, Marshall, and as many of the Army Air Forces and War Department staffs as they felt could be influenced. The British acknowledged that those Americans to whom they directed their pleas appeared in favor of revising the existing agreement, which would allocate fewer aircraft to the British. They even took the opportunity while Hap was in England in April to attempt to convince Marshall that the Arnold-Portal allocation should be retained.[24]

In broadest terms, the Air Ministry asked its Washington representatives to emphasize the major issue: that the promised aircraft should continue to be used immediately in combat where there was a demonstrated strategic and tactical need and where trained crews awaited only American planes.

They argued that, since the entire British operational and training programs had been planned around the agreed-upon Arnold–Portal plan, it should continue. In particular, they pointed to what they considered to be potential military "disasters of the first magnitude" or "debacles" facing them in the Middle East and India, where they described their positions as "precarious."[25] In an appreciation of the continuing US military reluctance to become involved in British Mediterranean, Middle Eastern, and Indian operations, London conceded that their American ally was not overly concerned with problems in those areas and was unwilling to commit full-fledged air units there unless commanded and flown by Yank pilots. Acknowledging the military implications of building and training an AAF air armada, which they argued could not be effectively deployed until at least 1943, the British warned that the only diversions desired from Arnold–Portal were those "necessary to prevent . . . losing the war while . . . preparing to win it."[26]

Part of the problem, the British insisted, was that the United States had underestimated the resources required for what the British termed an "overambitious expansion" of the ongoing and planned AAF buildup to 84 groups. Here, they probably meant Arnold, although he normally escaped harsh criticism by name. Reduced to the simplest terms, the British argued that immediate commitment of aircraft to combat transcended American training needs for airplanes and aircrews whose impact was months if not years in the future.[27]

The British also complained that the Soviet allocations, particularly when increased in this period, came from their quotas rather than the American and suggested that all aircraft for the Soviets be furnished from the US share.[28] Their rhetoric in defending Arnold–Portal was not always restrained, insisting at times that any redivision would be "calamitous to the war effort," "a folly and a danger," should be "strongly resisted" and that the agreement "cannot now be altered." Further, the Air Ministry noted what they felt was the AAF tendency to "grab everything they can for themselves and our aircraft are diverted and our supplies frequently raided."[29]

In a departure from their strategic and logistical arguments, they argued that they had a moral right to the continuation of the Arnold–Portal arrangement because of their pre-1939 aircraft orders. They felt that these orders, followed by their assumption of existing French orders when that nation surrendered in June 1940, had made possible the expansion of production in those early years.[30]

The exact role of Arnold in all of this was not clear to the British. At times, the AAF general was characterized as in a dilemma, "well-intentioned," and that he "recognizes the importance" of the British needs. However, they felt Hap was under "considerable" pressure from above and below "to take over more of our supplies" and may well have seen taking the British allocation as the only way out. On the other hand, the British conceded that Arnold was "averse to unfair and unruly action," such as the priority given to the Soviet allocations.[31] Further, the British felt that Arnold was attuned to the political and public opinion ramifications of the problem and that both Roosevelt and Hopkins were "strongly affected" by Arnold's contention that large numbers of US-trained pilots only awaited aircraft to take them into combat. This argument would have an impact in the White House, particularly as the lack of airplanes for American pilots was portrayed in the US media. The shortage of planes for US pilots was caused in large part, according to the media, by British allocations.[32]

FDR's thinking in the matter, as relayed to Britain by Hopkins, did not reflect creditably on the Oval Office. Hopkins reported that FDR claimed, contrary to the facts, that he had "never heard" of the Arnold–Portal agreement of January 1942. Hopkins' habit of reporting to the British the thinking of the White House as well as other senior American officials, particularly from the AAF standpoint in this and later periods, needs fuller assessment than this study will allow. The British often gleefully reported the presidential advisor's "spilling the beans" about the chief executive's thinking. To what extent this undermined the American military's negotiating positions can only be conjectured.[33]

The day before Arnold's departure, the British conceded that the onus was on them to make their case "entirely afresh" for any continuing distribution. As reported by Hopkins, Roosevelt indicated that justification for any future allocations might have to be made airplane by airplane. Now well aware of Churchill's ability to influence Roosevelt, the British took some comfort in the fact that any new agreement would be subject to final acceptance "at the highest level" between the two democratic leaders.[34] Arnold was aware of this and at no time during the discussions about aircraft allocation, either in Washington or in London on Hap's 12-day odyssey, did he fail to appreciate that any agreements were subject to final Roosevelt–Churchill acceptance.

As to fulfillment of the existing Arnold–Portal agreement in the first three months of 1942, British aircraft delivery figures reflected that it had been carried out with what they conceded was "reasonable fidelity" and they anticipated that this would continue if no change were made. By their computations, 1,510 aircraft had been received for the year "against a promise of 1,632," with only slight deficiencies in certain types offset by surplus deliveries in others. None of the few losses appeared to affect British plans or operations.[35]

The idea that Arnold should make this trip to London may well have originated with Hap himself. The first indication of such a possibility was on 12 April, when the British delegation in Washington cabled the Air Ministry: "Arnold now has definitely stated . . . that he and John Towers propose to bring proposals [for revision of Arnold–Portal] to London for final discussion." The visit was tentatively scheduled to take place in early May. Prior to the proposal that Hap go to England, negotiations on reallocating Arnold–Portal quotas had reached an impasse.[36]

Arnold's difficulties with the British were exacerbated by the increasing demands for American aircraft brought about by US deployment to war theaters, particularly to the Pacific. Additional complications arose from the priority given to the Soviet needs, the small but growing AAF training and expansion requirements, and other claimants. On 25 March, two weeks before the first suggestion that Arnold was to go abroad, Roosevelt approved Marshall's plan for invading the European continent in 1942, a proposal that clearly necessitated achievement of air superiority. Although the operation, code-named Sledgehammer, was abandoned (for 1942) in July, planning for the buildup of airpower and for dispatching air and other units to England was already underway. In an operation code-named Bolero, which was encouraged and supported by Roosevelt, Churchill, Stimson, and Lovett, additional aircraft would join the RAF in strategic bombing and in achieving air superiority for eventual invasion of the European continent.[37]

Lashio, Burma, fell to the Japanese on 29 April, resulting in the closing of the Burma Road, the last effective surface route over which China could be supplied by the Allies. FDR sent a memo to Arnold within a week, expressing concern that the air ferry route to China was endangered and directing Hap to "explore every possibility both as to airplanes and routes." He seemed clear in instructing his airman that it was "essential that our route be kept open, no matter how difficult." This created another serious problem over aircraft allocation that would not be resolved until well into 1943.[38]

At the same time, Soviet generals visiting Washington saw American transports and requested 200 of them. Secretary Stimson believed the US planes were "better than anything they have." He strongly advocated denying their request, citing the existing shortage of transport airplanes in the AAF. The White House finally agreed with Stimson, but only after strong pleas that Roosevelt reject what Stimson called "a new raid being made upon my air forces." No agreement was reached in the White House with regard to Churchill's 12 May request for 200 US-made transports. Instead, in a reflection of changing administration thinking following Arnold's recommendations, it was decided that additional transport capability would be sent to England when available but that it would constitute US units with American aircraft and crews.

Arnold later acted, with encouragement from the White House, on the suspicion that the close relationship between Britain's civilian airlines and their government portended possible postwar distribution of the transports acquired under Lend-Lease to the civil British air carriers, which would give them an advantage in postwar competition. The matter was complicated by the denial of scarce transport planes to US civilian airlines during the war. Allocation of transport planes remained a problem for Arnold throughout the bulk of the war.[39]

Another example of the turbulence in the orderly planning, allocation, and movement of aircraft was reflected in a 14 April memo from Arnold to Deputy Chief of the Air Staff Brig Gen Laurence S. Kuter: "As a result of a conference with the President this morning, it is very desirable that every effort be made to expedite movement of all airplanes towards India. Get in touch with all concerned and tell them all to step on the gas consistent with safety of the crews and to insure that the planes will arrive."[40]

The delay between the first indication on 12 April that Arnold was going to Britain and his departure six weeks later on 23 May is not easily explained. Part of the answer lies with the CCS-empowered Arnold-Evill-Towers group, which attempted a solution that would have negated the need for an overseas trip. Although they met at least three times, their efforts failed to produce an agreement. It is not surprising that Evill did not concur with Arnold's recommendation that the British allocation be reduced by 5,000 planes.[41] The Joint Chiefs of Staff (JCS) apparently was not in favor of Arnold going to London but their reasons were not clearly stated. The White House showed little interest during the bulk of the six-week period of delay, Hopkins having "tipped off" the British that the administration was concerned about an "uprising" of public opinion when it was revealed that American pilots had no planes to fly. Hap appeared absolved since the British reported to London that he was under considerable pressure and "being held back" from going to London.[42] On the other hand, as Arnold continued to have trouble in reaching any agreement on reallocation, he reported to Stimson that the British were "just being stubborn."[43]

From the vantage point of 57 years later, the British rationale for an overseas visit to England by Arnold rings somewhat hollow. What they advocated as the aims and anticipated results of the visit appear able to have been achieved in Washington. They stressed that Hap, while in London, would arrive at a "basis of agreement for allocation of aircraft," review the present distribution arrangement and the expected aircraft production, explain the nature of the expansion that he could implement, and provide them a firsthand account of his and their problems. Additionally, they wanted Arnold to see at firsthand the reality of the British air situation, which was not critical in the British Isles where he would be visiting.[44] Hap's US critics may well have concluded that implicit in much of this verbiage was the anticipation that Hap, being feted and exposed to pressure at the highest levels while again visiting the operating commands, would become more sympathetic to the British needs as he had appeared to have been a year earlier. This was to be achieved in an atmosphere far from both his staff and the naysayers in Washington.

With or without an Arnold trip to London, sentiment in Washington, including the White House, the secretary of war, the War Department, Arnold, and the AAF staff, appeared to concur that the Arnold–Portal agreement if not dead had little chance of retention in its post–Pearl Harbor form. For example, a 20 May brief presented to the joint staff planners reported that current commitments would "absorb all aircraft allocated to the Army Air Forces in 1942." Such an event would leave none for the projected US Air Force in Europe, where Hap and many others in Washington had pinned their hopes for early United States effective operations and validation of the concept of strategic bombardment.[45]

A major catalyst in reviving the trip was Churchill's 12 May cable to FDR. The prime minister requested a loan of 200 Martlets (US F4F Grumman Wildcat carrier-based aircraft) and 200 US transports "as early in June as possible" for use by British airborne troops. Knowing of Roosevelt's interest in bombing Germany, he emphasized that aircraft would have to be taken from the bombing offensive if the requested planes were not forthcoming. Making that connection was curious in view of the lack of commonality between the different types of aircraft whose functions were not readily interchangeable. Churchill referred to the existing agreement with Portal as though it was fully operative and would continue in force even though he had been informed by his staff of extensive US efforts to modify it.[46] FDR's reply, sent four days later, was crafted in part by Arnold and his staff along with the Navy's

Bureau of Aeronautics. Roosevelt turned down the request for the Martlets. His carefully drawn response to the request for transports informed Churchill of the American plan to send eight groups of US transports (416 planes) to England. Two of the groups would commence movement in June and would be "made available" to help the British airborne units. By November, the entire move would be completed. This was the first clear indication that FDR had accepted AAF and War Department recommendations that these aircraft should operate as US units flown and supported by Americans.[47] Three days later, on 19 May, FDR sent another message to Churchill, reemphasizing his thinking that American aircraft would be manned by American crews. However, he pointed out, "current schedules of aircraft allocations do not permit us to do this." Alluding to changes in conditions since Lend-Lease in March 1941 and the so-called Arnold–Portal agreement of January 1942, FDR indicated that the CCS would from now on determine the strength of aircraft in the various theaters, subject to his and Churchill's approval. Emphasizing one of Arnold's main difficulties with the British over the percentage of aircraft in reserve, in operational units, and in training squadrons, FDR indicated to Churchill that these would be maintained at "the minimum." This was in reference to the British practice of requiring that their operational units be equipped with a reserve of 100 percent of their airplane strength at all times, in contrast to the AAF standard of a 50 percent in reserve. FDR, in his own hand on the draft that became the message that was sent, added that American crews would be "assigned to man American-made planes far more greatly than at present." He indicated that Arnold and Towers would leave for London "at once" to discuss the details of this "broad policy."[48]

Churchill responded the next day in terms that had been expressed frequently by the Air Staff to Arnold and others in Washington ever since a revision of Arnold–Portal had been suggested. His insistence that the only objective should be the "maximum impact on the enemy" was another way of repeating the British theme that the planes should go immediately to the British on the fighting fronts rather than to the AAF for its buildup and training programs. Agreeing that Arnold and Towers should travel to London, Churchill went on to make sure that FDR was aware of Arnold's proposed reduction of 5,000 airplanes programmed for 1942 under Arnold–Portal. Churchill pointed out that the loss of these would reduce by 100 squadrons the force they hoped to have in action within the year. Then, repeating the latest Air Ministry reasoning, Churchill hoped the president would consider how the loss of these 100 squadrons would be replaced by American units.[49] On the major issue of aircraft allocation, Arnold's task in London would not be easy.

FDR issued "marching orders" to Towers and Arnold at a 20 May White House meeting where Hopkins, Marshall, and King also were present. Arnold's memoirs reported the president stressing to Churchill that his policy of Americans flying US manufactured aircraft should prevail except in the Soviet Union and in North Africa, where the British were using American pursuits and fighter-bombers successfully. Arnold may well have winced at FDR's promise that the United States would be committed to replacing combat losses of American planes in use by any Allied nation "regardless of what the . . . losses might be." Additionally, the United States was to construct and operate maintenance and supply depots for servicing American airplanes in disparate parts of the world, ranging from Australia to West Africa, India, and the Middle East. Hap probably agreed when Admiral Towers expressed serious doubts that their British ally would "agree to accept any modifications [of Arnold–Slessor] of real magnitude."[50]

Arnold's interest in making the trip was not confined to aircraft allocation and revision of the Arnold–Portal agreement. During the first week in February, the advance cadre of what later became Eighth Air Force had departed from the United States to launch preparations for the arrival of American aviation units in England to begin the strategic bombardment campaign.[51] The advance unit was under the command of newly promoted Brig Gen Ira Eaker, Arnold's long-time friend and coauthor. Difficulties soon arose between Eaker and the resident American aviator there, Maj Gen James Chaney. A West Point graduate in the class behind Hap, Chaney had learned to fly during World War I and now was commander of United States Army Forces in the British Isles (USFBI). Operating from headquarters in London, Chaney reported not to Arnold but to Marshall. As one author has characterized him, Chaney had "remained clear of the bitter battles waged over air independence" and was viewed by the General Staff "as the sort of deferential airman with whom it liked to deal."[52] He had served as an air attaché and most recently been responsible for the air defense of the northeastern United States before going to England. Arnold had been impressed with his optimistic reports of British chances of surviving the German blitz. Chaney had arrived in London on this present assignment just after Arnold's return in May 1941, having been informed by Marshall that if American forces were sent to Britain, "he would serve either as commander or chief of staff."[53]

Although Arnold's written instructions to Eaker as he prepared to leave the United States in February directed that he operate "under the supervision" of General Chaney, Eaker quickly found the USAFBI London staff of 35, of whom only four were aviators, antagonistic to Eaker's mission. Arnold had instructed Eaker to establish bomber command headquarters and make provisions for the physical facilities and training programs the American aviation units would need to ensure their early entry into effective combat. This would be done while understudying British Bomber Command and learning from their experience.[54] As Eaker's biogapher has written, Chaney "wanted no part of Arnold's plan to set up a separate air force command . . . with Chaney . . . as theater commander." Chaney intended that Eaker and his aviators would operate closely under his jurisdiction and not as a separate command. He believed the tactical American air units would essentially be token forces committed to defense of the islands while the heavy bombers would operate in conjunction with the RAF, meaning night bombing.[55]

The differences were greater than this, however. They reflected philosophical, jurisdictional, and organizational disagreements that were being resolved in Washington on a larger canvas than the operation of the Eighth Air Force Bomber

Command in England. Curiously enough, Arnold makes no mention of the struggle in his autobiography. He and his publisher might have been concerned that these administrative details and the internecine quarreling could detract from popular reader interest. Also, Hap was rarely disparaging of anyone in his memoirs, and to have discussed the issue would have necessitated discussion of Chaney. These considerations, in addition to the fact that Arnold won this struggle, may have influenced his decision not to include the controversy.

In simplest terms, Arnold visualized three main air components—pursuit, bomber, and service—reporting to an overall air force commander who in turn would be subject to the theater commander. Under this arrangement, Eighth Air Force in England would be organized along lines he felt would be the most efficient way to operate. Such an organizational arrangement not only reflected Hap's strong belief in unity of command of air units and integrity of forces; it anticipated the 9 March 1942 reorganization of the War Department, which recognized quasi-autonomy for the AAF.

This arrangement would also be the most effective way to demonstrate that the growing Army air arm was now capable of its own administration and operations, albeit within War Department guidelines, and was prepared for a sovereign existence if and when the movement for independence succeeded. This dream was now clearly postponed, however, in Arnold's mind until after the war.

This proposed structure would allow the Eighth to operate in conjunction with the RAF but separate from them, given their insurmountable differences over night versus day bombing as the best means for success against Germany. Chaney, who had been in London for more than a year, had the benefit of on-site experience and rapport with the British. He also appreciated a system like that of the prewar period, which would be responsive to his direction as putative theater commander. Arnold's organization, however, would also give air operations relative freedom within the theater, particularly as Carl A. Spaatz, who was named Eighth Air Force commander before Arnold's departure, proposed that the Eighth be authorized to work directly with the RAF to resolve any problems.[56]

Eaker, given his close relationship with Arnold over the years, was not reluctant to relate his early problems to Hap, beginning almost from his arrival in late February. As he recorded after his first meeting with Chaney and staff, he "found a complete inflexibility of mind" in their opposition to an AAF in England.[57] An example of the antagonism of the staff to the air effort was a member of Chaney's staff who returned any paper "which mentions Army Air Forces, requiring them to be rewritten to eliminate the word "Air."[58] Eaker may have outmaneuvered Chaney when, instead of remaining in London and being integrated and conceivably buried as a part of Chaney's staff, he relied on Arnold's instructions that he "understudy" the RAF bomber campaign. He located himself and his small staff of eight to the countryside west of London, setting up headquarters virtually contiguous with RAF Bomber Command. For a time, while settling in, Eaker actually lived with RAF Bomber Command's commander, Air Marshal Harris, and his family.[59]

In the beginning, Marshall and the War Department sided with Chaney in the dispute. By late March, however, when large numbers of AAF units were programmed for the British Isles in support of Bolero, and following the reorganization of the War Department, Marshall was subtly attempting to persuade Chaney to work towards the AAF desideratum. Chaney failed to take the hints from Washington and a harmonious relationship failed to develop between the London staff and the Eighth Air Force nucleus. Nothing had improved the situation there when Arnold departed for England.[60] Arnold, however, having survived and presumably won the bureaucratic "battle of Washington" over aircraft allocation two years earlier, probably had a sense of déjà vu in this important jurisdictional tussle, which revolved around Hap's strong faith in strategic bombardment and the need for an effective organization to achieve this objective. The fact that the controversy involved several of his own leaders (Chaney, Spaatz, Eaker) did not make the matter any easier to resolve.

From the January Arcadia Conference until Hap's departure for London in May, many problems other than division of aircraft concerned Arnold but the question of aircraft allocation remained the most important one to the future of the Army air arm. Arnold had gradually been confirmed as the de facto AAF representative in the councils of the senior military, serving as a sitting member of the JCS and the CCS. The former was the term used for the military service representatives of the United States, its counterpart in Britain being the COS or chiefs of staff. The term CCS referred to the chiefs of the two Allies, the United States and Great Britain, a body that met continually. Arnold's inclusion in these groups had begun with his membership in the delegation at Argentia where he was paired with the senior RAF officer present, Vice Chief of Air Staff Freeman. The placement was continued at Arcadia, where he met on equal terms with Air Chief Marshal Peter Portal. Although never formalized on paper, the arrangement continued throughout the war with Arnold in attendance representing the Army air arm at JCS and CCS sessions. In this travel to England, he went as a full member of both the JCS and CCS. However, as indicated elsewhere, Arnold never lost sight of the fact that he and the AAF were component parts of the US Army and were subordinate to Chief of Staff George Marshall.

Many other problems concerned Arnold in the period between Arcadia and his departure for England on 24 May. Not the least of these was the reorganization of the AAF (as well as other Army elements) within the War Department to meet the complex challenges of global war. The resulting change, in March 1942, was a reflection of Arnold's growing stature with Stimson, Lovett, and Marshall. More important, it represented an evolutionary compromise with various other solutions that had been tried for a satisfactory placement of the Army air arm within the War Department. The main impetus for the change that was made in March, however, even though its primary architect was an aviator, had come from Marshall's frustration with a War Department that retained much of a structure devised just after the turn of the century.

As indicated earlier, Arnold was aware of and had been involved in many of the problems between the GHQAF, the agency responsible for operational deployment and potential combat of the Air Force, and the Office of the Chief of the Air Corps in Washington even before he became chief. The chief was responsible for relations with the War Department, Congress, and the White House, as well as funding, procurement of personnel and airplanes, and a host of other tasks divorced from training and operational activities.

Hap's bringing the GHQAF under the chief of the Air Corps in March 1939 had failed to resolve all the difficulties. Eighteen months later, with the appointment of Arnold as deputy chief of staff in addition to his duties as chief of the Air Corps, the Air Corps appeared to gain greater freedom within the War Department. The most significant prewar step towards greater sovereignty was represented in Army Regulation 95-5, promulgated on 20 June 1941, wherein the Army Air Forces was created with Arnold as its chief. GHQAF, which had existed since 1935, disappeared and was replaced by the Air Force Combat Command. The regulation gave Arnold control over "all aerial operations," responsibility for the air defense of the nation, and an authorized air staff to carry out these and other duties.[61] If this was not the independence Billy Mitchell (and Arnold in the 1920s) had advocated and the most extreme of the airmen had sought since, it seemed the optimum possible with war on the horizon. There is no evidence that Arnold was dissatisfied with this new arrangement. His rapport and effective relationship with Chief of Staff Marshall appeared to guarantee a smooth use of air assets with considerable freedom of action no matter what the structural guidelines or regulations. As Marshall recalled after the war, he tried to give Arnold "all the power" and "his head" as much as he possibly could.[62] Although there were aviators within the newly created AAF who sought complete independence, the Air Staff in early October deferred "for the duration all attempts to secure complete independence."[63]

Spaatz, as Commanding General, AAF Combat Command, probably furnished additional impetus for additional freedom within the War Department when he suggested through Arnold in late October 1941 that a "compact General staff of autonomous air, ground and service forces" be created. Arnold made a similar proposal to Marshall in the next month and the chief of staff directed the War Plans Division to develop a plan "incorporating its principal features." Arnold was attempting to navigate the turbulence caused by those aviators who, supported by some of the press and a few congressmen, advocated complete independence. On the other hand, Marshall and other War Department officials including Arnold himself felt there was sufficient latitude in the current framework to meet the challenges of global war. Hap also believed that any effort expended on advocating or seeking independence would have been better spent on preparing for the inevitable conflict.[64]

The planner of the new structure, modeled closely on the Spaatz and Arnold recommendations, was Joseph McNarney. Now a major general, McNarney had been the Air Corps representative at the ABC conversations of early1941 and had seen service in England with the Special Observer Group. Most recently, he had been the senior Army aviator assigned to the Roberts commission investigating Pearl Harbor responsibility. Although chosen by Marshall, there remains little doubt his selection had been coordinated with, if not suggested by, Arnold. Working quickly and without publicity, he recommended and secured approval of a new organization of the War Department. Three new commands—Army Ground Forces, Army Air Forces, and Army Service Forces—replaced a multiplicity of branches and entities. The former general staff was reduced drastically from 304 to a total of 36 for G-1, G-3, and G-4. However, the 36 now included a higher percentage of air officers. The change, which became effective as of 9 March 1942, specified that the AAF mission was to procure and maintain equipment "peculiar" to the AAF and to "provide air force units properly organized, trained and equipped for combat operations." All of significance that seemed missing was the authority of its chief to command in combat, which in the war that developed remained with the theater commander.[65]

Many other tasks had consumed Arnold's energies in the nine months since he traveled to Argentia in August 1941. As important to Arnold as the acquisition of aircraft were the equipment, facilities, and trained personnel to operate and maintain them. The Air Corps, like most American institutions, did not expand in an orderly fashion with the advent of war. The desires of the commander in chief, deployment of units into combat, appropriations by Congress, and availability of airplanes, among other factors, determined expansion. With an increase in the numbers of tactical groups came a need for personnel to man and support the units. The goal was 24 groups in April 1939, 54 in June 1940, and 84 in March 1941. One month after Pearl Harbor, on 7 January 1942, the goal was increased to 115 groups. Six months later, it was increased again to 224 groups. Within another 90 days, the aim became 273 groups. Providing trained personnel to man this 11-fold expansion within 30 months was in many ways among the most difficult challenges facing Arnold and the staff. Congress authorized increases in manpower strength to match the additional groups, but securing and training the necessary manpower could not be accomplished in the same way that an aircraft could be built.[66]

One AAF response to public demand and the administration's demand for action to counter Japanese successes was the Doolittle raid on Tokyo. It provided an unusual opportunity for Arnold to display cooperation by the Navy and the AAF to demonstrate the long-range effectiveness of airpower using both land and sea resources. It seems surprising, in view of the raid's limited tactical but important psychological success, that there have not been more claimants for having fathered the idea. Arnold has conceded that he did not know who originated it. It appears that the idea was born when the Arcadia meetings were being held in the December 1941–January 1942 time period although there was no discussion of it with the visiting British. A week before Christmas, Amon G. Carter, a Fort Worth, Texas, newspaper publisher, suggested the possibility of bombing the Japanese home islands to Maj Gen Edwin M. "Pa" Watson, FDR's military aide, who then forwarded the idea to Hap. In notes written during a 4 January meeting at the White House, Arnold wrote: "We will have to try bomber take-offs from carriers." Arnold's response to Watson's memo on 7 January suggested that the Air Corps would "have a solution" to the problem "in the near future."[67] Ten days later, naval officers on Admiral King's staff called on Arnold and presented data suggesting that an Army B-25 medium bomber could take off from an aircraft carrier, thus confirming studies that were already under way separately in the Air Corps.[68] The credit for choosing James H. Doolittle to lead the raid is not clear from the documents. Doolittle has written that he volunteered for the command and had some difficulty convincing Arnold to accept him. It is clear, however, that Arnold provided unstinting support for the effort. Having learned to fly in World War I, Doolittle served on active duty until 1930. While on active duty, he earned a rare doctorate in aeronautics. Then, while working with private industry, he was a frequent participant on boards and commissions and in experimental flying. Doolittle was recalled to active duty in 1940 and was one of the observers Arnold sent to England to assess conditions there. Although the physical damage done by Doolittle's 18 April 1942 raid on Tokyo was negligible, psychological and strategic results were extremely important. The threat posed by aircraft to the Japanese home islands had been confirmed. At the same time, the raid demonstrated the potential of AAF aircraft if allocations to other Allied nations could be kept within bounds.[69]

The passenger list of Arnold's airplane as they departed for London on 24 May was, as Hap recalled, a "notable group of high-ranking officers." Foremost among the passengers was Maj Gen Dwight D. Eisenhower, chief of the newly named Operations Division (OPD) that had replaced the old War Plans Division. Ike's tasks were multiple, among them discussing with the British planning for the Bolero buildup and the proposed Sledgehammer invasion of the continent. A narrower but very important assignment from Marshall was for Ike to assess the organizational difficulties between Chaney, Arnold, and the Eighth Air Force and to evaluate Chaney's suitability as the senior Army officer in Britain. He could conceivably become the commander or at least the senior air officer of the forces deployed against the continent in Sledgehammer and Bolero. The newly created Army Ground Forces structure, which would have a major role in these operations, was represented by Brig Gen Mark Clark. Rear Adm John Towers could speak for the Navy air arm in any revision of Arnold–Portal.[70]

As they departed Washington in the TWA-operated aircraft, they flew the route that would be utilized later by thousands of aircraft headed for combat in the European theater. Arnold's experiences on this trip served to acquaint him with the bases that had been recently acquired and were equipped to support the mission of getting aircraft to England. He also became educated to the perils of North Atlantic flying, the most significant of which was weather. His plane, even with high-ranking passengers guaranteeing priority treatment for servicing the plane, an expertly maintained aircraft, and a professional crew, did not reach London until the morning of their fourth day. Arnold could not have appreciated fully the events that were to transpire, among them the thousands of crews that would follow him. Most of them flew in newly manufactured airplanes piloted and navigated by American aviators who were in the vast majority of cases less than a year away from their civilian pursuits. These young airmen set an amazing safety record in traveling the route taken by Arnold or slight variations of that route. By the end of August 1942, 386 AAF aircraft had flown the North Atlantic to England, using the same route Arnold had flown. The number attempting that crossing increased to a total of 920 by the end of 1942. Only 38 planes failed to reach Prestwick, Scotland, representing an accident/loss rate of 4.1 percent, less than one-half of the estimated 10 percent. Hap's emphasis on building up AAF forces for the strategic bombing effort was reflected in the fact that approximately 700 of these 920 planes belonged to the Eighth Air Force.[71]

In recording the conditions he saw en route, Hap displayed his normal impatience with what he viewed as less than maximum effort towards winning the war. The leisure time furnished by the weather delays permitted Arnold to concern himself with everything on the bases, from the quality and temperature of the food served in the messes to the physical surroundings and neatness of the airfields. As was his wont, he attempted to resolve some of the problems he encountered. In Prestwick, he observed "airplanes all around the field," strengthening the suspicion among Hap and many of the AAF staff that inefficient use was being made of US-produced planes that were in critical demand by US forces.

The need for arriving at an aircraft allocation agreement, the main purpose of the trip, appeared sufficiently urgent that the British scheduled negotiations over the issue on the morning of their arrival. Churchill, presiding at the opening session, used a briefing paper furnished by Portal to outline objections to any change. These were the same arguments that had been coordinated and voiced in Washington to Arnold and other Americans ever since it became clear that the United States desired a revision of Arnold–Slessor. The Prime Minister questioned why, with an estimated US annual production of 60,000, it was found necessary to question the 5,000 planes programmed for the British. This refrain, sounding almost petulant half a century later, would appear often in Churchill's rhetoric as he contrasted what he portrayed as the relatively miniscule assistance requested from the United States with the perceived vast, if not unlimited, resources of America. For example, Arnold quoted Churchill at the second Quebec conference in September 1944 as saying, "With all your wealth of airdromes would you deny me a mere pittance of a few?"[72] The remainder of Churchill's arguments had been raised to Arnold and others in Washington. Hap voiced equally familiar objections, including arguments from his White House instructions just before leaving the United States, in his response. Arnold not only lauded the talents of US airmen; he outlined the many demands levied on American production facilities. Churchill responded with an assessment of the military situation in various theaters where the British were engaged. Following this opening session, Arnold appeared optimistic after a private garden walk with the prime minister and later talks with Portal. Another long meeting was held that afternoon and then assistants from both nations attempted to work out the details. The next day, as discussions continued in London, Arnold journeyed to the suburbs to visit Eaker at his new headquarters as well as the nearby RAF Bomber Command.

By the third day in England, Hap's normal optimism seemed to wane. He was discouraged in part by what he felt was an unwillingness by Admiral Towers and the US Navy to cooperate towards solving the problem. Apparently, as his diary entries indicate, an afternoon session alone with Portal and Freeman provided the basis of a tentative agreement. Arnold committed the agreement in detail to his diary for Thursday, 28 May. In general terms, it reduced the number of aircraft to be furnished to the British while emphasizing medium bombers, light bombers, and pursuit aircraft for their use. All agreed on the importance of retaining or increasing air strength in existing theaters by dispatching American units to North Africa and the Near East. Some consideration was given to the problem of coastal command and the need for aircraft in antisubmarine patrols, although Arnold remained ambivalent about the importance of this use of airplanes as contrasted with the need to bomb German targets. Conferences in London with a variety of people consumed most of Friday. On Saturday morning, after four days of negotiation, Arnold and Portal signed a "proposed agreement on the allocation of planes."

Late on Saturday afternoon, Hap departed for Chequers where he and Towers among others stayed the weekend with the prime minister. Although he has furnished no details in his diary, Arnold's two hours alone with Churchill on Sunday morning probably dealt essentially with the issue of aircraft distribution as reflected in the tentative Arnold–Towers–Portal agreement signed the previous day. The other American weekend guests included Harriman, Eisenhower, and Somervell. Churchill telephoned Harry Hopkins in the White House Saturday night, apparently "in good spirits" as he impressed his guests with the RAF strategic bombardment effort by sending more than 1,000 planes against Cologne that night and said he was going to "stay up all night and await results." Arnold talked with Hopkins via phone from Chequers and the latter reported to Roosevelt that Hap's mission had been "very successful."[73]

Monday was spent saying good-byes, and the bad weather that prevented their departure allowed Arnold to visit and study the operations of a nearby RAF Fighter Group. Flying out the next afternoon from Prestwick, after having spent just a week in England, Arnold got another taste of the bad weather that could plague the North Atlantic air route almost any time of year. He did not arrive in Washington until the next day, after a brief stop in Labrador.

As would be the case for most all of his overseas diaries, the demands on him on his arrival in England and after his return to Washington left little time for rumination or assessment of the trip. The negotiating sessions were lengthy and difficult, given the importance of the issues involved. Dinner out every night with a host of other leaders, often until late, left little time for contemplation or exhaustive diary entries. Possibly as close as he came to an overall evaluation was this reaction on his last full day in London: "England is the place to win the war; get planes and troops over as soon as possible." This assessment was jeopardized when he landed in the New World and news of both the Battle of Midway and the Japanese invasion of the Aleutians reached him. He became alarmed at reports of delays and diversions of combat aircraft and crews originally headed for the European theater. As Arnold confided to the diary, this "nullifies practically everything I have done." Little could he have appreciated that the events of the next 60 days would have an even greater impact on the buildup of the AAF and the strategic bombardment offensive than the difficulties with Britain over aircraft allocation. Those events included the invasion of Guadalcanal and the decision to attack North Africa instead of the European continent.

The Dairy

TRIP TO ENGLAND
May 22, 1942–June 3, 1942
LIEUTENANT GENERAL H. H. ARNOLD

<u>Saturday, May 23, 1942</u> [Washington, D.C.; Montreal, Canada; Goose Bay, Labrador; Gander, Newfoundland]

Took off	Bolling Field	7:15 A.M.
Arrived	Montreal, Canada	0:05 A.M. (406)[74]
Took off	Montreal	1:35 A.M.
Arrived	Goose[75]	4:15 P.M. (809)
Took off	Goose	6:05 P.M.

Headed to sea, 540 miles, run into ice; fog [forecast] at Prestwick;[76] returned to Gander,[77] arriving at 12:30 P.M. Passenger list as follows:

Lieutenant Commander G. W. Anderson, USN
Lieutenant General H. H. Arnold, USA
Colonel E. H. Beebe, USA
Major General M. W. Clark, USA
Brigadier V. Dykes, BA
Major General D. D. Eisenhower, USA
Air Marshal D. C. S. Evill, RAF
Group Captain H. P. Fraser, RSAAF
Commander E. R. Jackson, RN
Rear Admiral J. H. Towers, USN
Colonel H. S. Vandenberg, USA[78]

Crew list as follows:

Captain Bryan[79]
First Officer Trimble
Second Officer Wagner
Flight Officer Gwartney
Flight Engineer Proctor
Radio Operator Master Sergeant Walsh
Second Officer Shook
Extra Second Officer - name not known
Extra Navigator - name not known

Goose Bay airdrome well advanced, one runway finished with gravel. Lack of accord with RCAF; RCAF commanding officer is not fired with any enthusiasm.[80] Mess with RCAF (by order of their commanding officer), awful; changed that. Field can accommodate 400 men soon and 700 within a couple of months. Sent wire to Washington to get supplies and personnel to start [USAAF] mess.[81]

No control tower operating although tower is built and we have qualified personnel to operate. Told Spaatz to send up operating officer and G-4.[82] Montreal made arrangements with Bowhill to continue Stratoliner to London.[83] Rain and cold at Goose, blind flying for two hours from Goose. Ice at 10,000 feet and fog predicted at Prestwick hence we turned back. General Brant[84] awaited us at Gander. Had cup of coffee, then to bed.

Sunday, May 24, 1942 [Gander, Newfoundland, en route to Prestwick, Scotland]

Up at 10:00 A.M. local time, 7:30 Washington time. Sent telegrams to:

> Lovett to straighten out control at Goose, preferably USA, second choice RAF.[85]
>
> Harmon - to make plans for replacing personnel, supplying, changing location, adding new facilities at Crystal, Bluies and Goose.[86]
>
> Ferry command - to put in Commanding officer and staff to handle North American ferry system at once.

Rained all night and up to 1:00 P.M., expect to take off at 6:00 P.M. All Labrador and Newfoundland barren with rock outcrops, patches of snow on ground, ice on lakes. Weather cleared up at 2:00 P.M. Took trip over Gander: debris, junk, trash forms from old buildings everywhere, no one even tries to clean up. Officers Club a fine building. Went through RAF Ferry Command hangar. Blue sky with clouds on horizon.

Took off Gander at 5:44 P.M., distance to Prestwick 2,000 miles; 6:30 crossed coastline, overcast areas broken and clear. Good weather all the way across, one front hit but not bad, only thirty minutes.

Monday, May 25, 1942 [En route to Prestwick, Scotland]

Sighted two convoys both escorting destroyers. Asked us for identification; we flashed return signals and proceeded OK.[87] Sighted very rough, rugged, green, serrated coast of Scotland at 8:00 A.M., passed into bay, narrowest part of Scotland at 9:15 A.M. Biggest bay I have ever seen: islands, peninsulas, capes, ships, finally a flock of landing craft, speedy, hold 50 to 100 men, maneuvering around the bay, 6 of them.[88]

The town of Prestwick: military facilities and equipment everywhere, camouflaged trucks, tents, Blister hangars.[89] The airport [with a] long concrete runway, 700 feet. Heavy rain just passed, low clouds. Liberators, Hudsons, British Beauforts and Blenheims all around field.[90]

Met by A. W. Durston from Coast Defense Command on northeast coast;[91] 15 minutes by air, indicates how deep the bay is. Good breakfast. Cows in all fields: plenty of milk, cream, butter, meat and only 300 miles from London. A good room in the hotel, a shave and bath. Weather bad in London, we take off around 6:00 P.M. Visited facilities at Prestwick; control station has a fine set-up, coordinates movement of all incoming planes by intersection, voice and by identification.[92] Planes all around the airport, mostly Liberators; turrets fitted, extra gas tanks, take about 1½ days each; changes for navigators take about two weeks. Civilian firm has hangars dispersed at intervals for this purpose, employs 8,000 men.[93]

Checked weather and it looks OK for tomorrow but not for tonight. Towers, Eisenhower, Clark, Evill and Anderson all expect to go to London by train tonight; Vandenberg, Beebe and I will go with plane tomorrow A.M. Oh yes Evill just said that the Prime Minister is having a conference in the morning and wants us all to go down by train tonight. We left Beebe and Vandenberg and drove to Glasgow, no signs of bombing raid of last year except boarded-up glass windows.[94] [We travel on the] Scottish Chief: three sections, each one with about 24 cars.[95] The station a mess, hundreds of men, women, and children just milling around. Fields green and cultivated. Cattle and sheep by the hundreds. Countryside looks very prosperous but the cities very poorly, empty stores, no goods in windows. Hundreds of people lined up on street waiting to get into bakeries. Barrage balloons over shipyards at Glasgow. We had a special car, each one had a stateroom with unique attachments, assorted for various purposes.

Tuesday, May 26, 1942 [En route from Glasgow, Scotland to London, England]

Went to bed on train last night at 9:45 P.M., awoke this A.M. ten minutes out of London. Air Marshal Freeman came in while I was shaving; Chaney and Ambassador Winant met the train. Went to Claridge['s] Hotel with Winant. Breakfast with Winant, Chaney and military attache.[96] Had a few minutes talk with Eaker then McClelland came in.[97] Winant gave me information re Molotov: wants treaty with US guaranteeing integrity of certain countries.[98] Long discussion with Chaney and Winant re efficiency of US pursuit, P-39 especially. Chaney doubts efficiency of both P-38 and P-39, thinks we are doing wrong by using either. I told them both that we had to at least give them a trial in combat.

Portal's office at 10:00 A.M. Long talk about everything but why I came over then short talk on the main issue. That was first indication that the task was not going to be an impossible one. At the Prime Minister's at 11:00; general discussion among Prime Minister, Portal, Lyster,[99] Courtney, Harriman, Towers, Ismay, Evill, Slessor, Anderson and Arnold. Prime Minister could not understand why, with [US] 60,000-plane production [per year], we raised issue over 5,000 planes to British. [He] wanted to be sure that effective fighting strength in any theatre was not decreased. Was in general in favor of American pilots flying American planes. Reiterated necessity for maximum impact against enemy; must have maximum number in action and greatest possible number of bombs dropped. It was a question of maintaining strength for the next few months, not a year from now. Wanted all of us to talk openly and frankly.

Then asked for me to give any remarks if I cared to. Outlined following:

1. Exceptional men in US—cream of nation.
2. These young men could fly US planes better than any other youngsters.
3. Lend Lease and Defense Aid hearings before Congress, Secretary of War, Chief of Staff, Chief of Air Force all informed Congress that by furnishing planes to other nations we would build up production capacity for ourselves when needed.
4. People of US knew that.
5. People of US wanted a US Air Force.

6. People wanted action in Europe.
7. Present allocation would not permit us to meet our Australian, Indian, Hawaiian coast defense commitments.
8. We wanted above all things to retain strength in defense areas and build up in other areas.
9. Had no intention of allowing any theatre to have smaller number.

Then outlined the many calls [for aircraft] made on us.

Prime Minister then outlined situation in various theatres calling attention to India, Middle East, China, and Bolero[100] in particular. I then outlined our air transport difficulties, China problems, India and Australia programs and our plan for ferrying planes to Bolero.

Prime Minister called on Towers. Towers said his problem was simple and could be ironed out without difficulty. [US] Navy needed only torpedo planes, dive-bombers and fighters for carriers with patrol bombers; that was all. I politely asked, after Prime Minister agreed, if they did not also need heavy land-based bomber support. Towers said: "Why certainly."

Meeting broke up after Prime Minister gave instructions for detailed discussion in afternoon. Walked and talked with Prime Minister for 30 minutes in garden. I may be mistaken but believe that we can sell our point. Lunch with Eaker, Beebe and Vandenberg. Meeting 3:00 to 6:00 with Portal's henchmen, Towers, Anderson, Arnold and Vandenberg. Discussed General Principles prepared by Portal's crew.[101] They accepted general idea for reallotment [of aircraft] but fear decrease in strength at some theatres. Agreed to bring General Principles back to hotel and give comments. Left Vandenberg to compare our program with British to see wherein we cannot meet their requirements.[102] Home in time to unpack. Sent ham, candy and oranges to Harris.[103]

Dinner by Portal: Pound, Brooks, Chaney, J. C. H. Lee, Eisenhower, Clark, Courtney, Freeman, Harris, Evill, Towers, Stark, Arnold present. Dropped in a few minutes to see Jackie Cochran[104] with Harris and Towers. Portal, I believe, will agree [with proposed new allocation] if I can find a way to meet Heavy Bomber requirements for Coastal Command and Near East.

London is a far different city. People are not the diffident, harried, listless ones I saw last year, they have pep and show an interest in life. City is cleaned up, bomb marks are rapidly disappearing, iron fences are being torn down very rapidly. Two high-ranking "brass hats" have said that with another week's blitz both London and Liverpool would have folded up.

Wednesday, May 27, 1942 [London, England]

Conference with Freeman and Arnold re weather and radio [facilities] for movement of combat units across the North Atlantic. Conference with Vandenberg re his work with Slessor; they gave him a thorough going-over but he finally came through OK. They finally said that he was bringing over too many planes.

Went to [RAF] Bomber Command, Harris; Pinetree, USABC [Army Bomber Command]; South Down RAF B[omber] C[ommand]; High Wycombe.[105] Bomb rack: British carries three times as much as ours, our bombs carry 2 times as much explosives; 1,000 and 2,000 pound British bombs must have DB-7 universal shackle and rework fins.[106] Can we get ours over? RAF Bomber Command: total planes, 640; in commission, 450; pilots and crews available, 380.

Saw Harris and went over pictures of raids on Rostock, Augsburg; most of towns destroyed; Heinkel works a wreck, fuselages pulled out of buildings and lined up in yards.[107]

Went to Eaker's command, a fine place, Wycombe Abbey, a girl's school, large extensive lawn, gardens, river, buildings old. Visited by Pitt, Gladstone, Breresford. (See attached).[108] Has his staff well-trained and functioning. Inspected a guard of honor, mess, tents, camps, all in good shape. Saw Claude Duncan, Woggie Towle.[109]

RAF estimate of German AF:

Total combat planes	4,000
On Russian front	1,800
In N. Africa	1,000
In W. Africa and balance	900

Lunch with Harris, Mrs. Harris, Portal, Eaker and Evill. Returned to London for meeting with Pound, Portal, Lyster and Towers re Coastal Command planes. RAF wants nine squadrons [totaling] 144; attrition, seven months, 100, [for a total of] 244 B-17s. Desire them between May 31–December 31, 1942; attrition based upon 12-15% per month, need a range of 1,400 miles, carry eight 450-pound depth charges, will accept one that carries four. A. S. V. a necessity. Now using Whitleys, Hampdens, Hudsons, Catalinas.[110] [They] Will receive 150 Catalinas: 10-[in] May; 120-June and July; 20-August.

Have swapped 85 Venturas to Navy for same number of Catalinas.[111] Told them that the number looked excessive and that the whole question had to be decided upon as to which use was the more important, using heavy bombers to carry bombs into Germany or go out hunting for submarines. Told them I would think it over.

Called on Winant and told him of conferences to date, also told Chaney, also told Eisenhower. Sent oranges to Stark, Portal, Prime Minister. Saw Somervell for a few minutes.[112] New armor-piercing bomb (data re this in Office Director of Bombardment),[113] will penetrate 5-inch armor and then a 2-inch armor. Doodle Bug mines come up fifty times in different directions.[114] Dinner with Eisenhower and Chaney's staff. Our plan for using all American planes influences British OTUs [Operational Training Unit] in US. How many will they want? How many will we want? Cubs?[115]

Thursday, May 28, 1942 [London, England]

Conference with Anderson and Vandenberg re progress Working Committee.[116] British apparently in a confused state regarding just what use will be made of American planes. [Their] Overhead far too great for us; B-25, B-26 cases in point.[117] Office 20 Grosvenor, saw Chaney, Lyon, Lay and McClelland.[118] Conference, Freeman presiding, at Air Ministry. Brought out lack of plan from RAF to compare with ours. So far, Towers has not played the game three times:

1. When asked if Navy could send units over to help out on Coastal Command, he replied: "He had too many other activities at home."

2. Volunteered information that he had a solution for more transports: stop manufacturing B-17 planes at Long Beach [California] and build cargo planes. When Freeman asked what the Navy was willing to give up, Towers said: "Nothing, as nothing the Navy could give up would help."
3. After trying to get figures to compare RAF and US, the British finally agreed to have theirs prepared by tomorrow A.M.; ours were finished yesterday. Slessor asked if we couldn't include [US] Navy figures in ours. I asked Towers, Towers asked Anderson, who replied that we could. Tonight, Anderson stated that Towers had told him that he was informed that the Navy would state tomorrow A.M. that they couldn't prepare data in time, and that they requested a delay.

It was apparent at today's conference that we weren't getting anywhere, hence I made two appointments: first, to see Courtney at 4:30 and talk over airports [in Great Britain to station incoming US] Bombers, Pursuit, Transports, and Observation; second, meet Portal and Freeman at 5:30 and see if we could come to some kind of agreement. Our conference talks are getting us nowhere. We have decided upon the fundamentals, now all that remains is to agree upon the details.

Lunch with Eaker, Vandenberg and Mrs. Harris. 3 P.M., conference with Chaney, Eisenhower, Somervell and Chaney's staff re priority of troops coming over between now and September. We agreed to his cable; [at] 4:30 P.M., went over all airports for USA in England. Agreed that:

(1) We would have bare necessities of life rather than all the comforts of home. No city sewers for a base when pits would be OK.[119] Runways, 5,000 feet instead of 6,000 feet.[120]
(2) All units except first ones would stop off in North Ireland.
(3) We would take over air defense of North Ireland.
(4) Our reception centers and rest areas would be [in] North Ireland.[121]

(5) Pursuit squadrons would work with British until they became seasoned and then be formed into American groups.
(6) We would take over [air defense] sectors as soon as airdromes became available and our troops were seasoned.[122]
(7) We would pool our resources for building airdromes.
(8) We would be given airdromes as fast as they could be built, all of them by December.
(9) There were enough airdromes available but only by having some doubling up.[123]
(10) That there were about 500 Observation planes not heretofore included that must be taken care of.
(11) That the local people there would decide where the Observation fields would be, but always near the [US Army] Division with which they worked.

Hurried from that conference and went to see Portal. Told him that I wanted to come to an understanding right now if we could; he agreed. After some discussion, it was finally accepted that I should take home for approval in Washington the following:

(1) In general, the air strength in all theatres would be maintained or increased.
(2) All American crews available would be supplied with American planes.
(3) US would furnish to Bolero about 300 Heavy Bombers complete with crews.
(4) Except for a possible number of Heavy Bombers for Coastal Command, British would get no heavy bombers. In view of duties to be performed, I am of the opinion that these planes should be PBYs and that they should come from the Navy and the Navy should help out Bolero by furnishing crews.
(5) RAF counts on using for coastal work British flying boats: Catalinas; Flying Fortresses 9 [squadrons of] 16 [aircraft per squadron for a total of] 144; attrition, 100. This is to be reached by December 31st. I assured

Portal that I would not agree. Suggested that for my consideration he propose:

Liberators in RAF	50
Additional to December	90
Attrition from then on	--

(6) British take no Medium Bombers except 108 in North Africa to be manned and operated by American personnel. Otherwise we furnish them 108 B-26s for them to operate.

(7) We let the British have all Martin Baltimores. We take under advisement proposition of giving RAF the Hudson production. We give RAF DB-7s for turbinlite squadrons and attrition.[124]

(8) British state that 1,440 [US] Pursuit is more than can possibly be used in England; agreed that 1,000 can be used and will be OK.[125]

(9) Near East: British need a total of 100 Heavy Bombers in Near East; if we do not operate, they must. Hence, we must increase Halverson to 1 group and Brereton by 2 squadrons of Heavy Bombers, or furnish 100 Heavy Bombers and replacements to British. This is dependent on RAF agreeing that those planes in India are under Stilwell and can be pulled out in case of emergency, only after securing permission of Stilwell.[126]

(10) British need and cannot secure from any other source 480 Pursuit, have counted on American Pursuit. Hence we must furnish to British for general support in North Africa and Syria 6 groups of pursuit or we must furnish them 480 planes and replacements.

(11) That Portal will come to America to receive final decision in this case.[127]

Left Portal and Freeman and went to Chaney's cocktail party, everybody and his brother there. Asked Mountbatten to go home with us. Dinner with J. C. H. Lee;[128] back to room at 10:15, now 11:30, after talking over with Eisenhower and writing this up.

Friday, May 29, 1942 [London, England]

Breakfast at 8:00 with Towers and Stark, general conversation almost entirely about Pacific theater and aerial strength. Towers, contradicting himself, stated that he now had a large number of single-engine seaplanes and several squadrons, exact number he couldn't fix on account of their constantly shifting; PBY units operating along East Coast and Gulf [of Mexico]; that the single-engine seaplanes were coming out at the rate of 100 per month. Stark asked about production of PBYs and Towers said 60 per month. Repeated that Joubert, Coastal Command, said he could not get crews to man Flying Boats at a rate greater than 30 per month.[129]

Returned to hotel in time to meet Tizard. Have we Radar 271?[130] [The British version] Can pick up and track low-flying (under 100 feet) aircraft and ships. Should be mounted at about 200 feet elevation, listeners there can locate detectors and can jam them.[131] Have we any? British have and use them against German detectors. 4,000 pound bomb can be used very effectively as a mine, we should look into it, blast effective at distance very damaging.

Jet propulsion, RAF has three engines: 1 ready to fly, 1 improved on test stand, 1 being built for long-range planes. They are very pleased with results and are confident as to future of jet propulsion. Have had surging trouble but think they have licked it.[132]

Conference with Chaney; he was fearful that I was committing the Army Air Forces when such commitment should be decided by Spaatz and Hunter, noticeably method of training pursuit and airdromes for pursuit. I assured him that my only interest was in insuring that our pursuit became acquainted with RAF communications operating technique, procedure, language, etc., in the shortest space of time. How they did it was not my job, the former was. I also assured him that I would fix things so that anything I did could be changed except fundamental principles, after Spaatz and Hunter came. The main thing was to secure the maximum effectiveness of our Air Forces so as to lick our enemies.[133]

Lunch with Secretary of State for Air Sinclair. Better understanding with Portal. I will let him know whether it is essential that he come to the US. If Prime Minister comes Portal will not come; if not we will decide in Washington.

Conference with Douglas for an hour, gave him same talk as above and told him to be sure and tie in with Spaatz and Hunter. Hunter would command US pursuit but he, Douglas, would direct operations.[134] Portal, Freeman reopened Light Bomber and Coastal Command question. Portal wants all deliveries of planes but A-20s, I held out for a total of 700 planes here for operations with ground troops. Both sides agreed to think matter over and try and find a solution. Conference with Eisenhower and Somervell; told Somervell about possible needs for transportation to Middle East and asked if he could meet it. He is looking matter up. Late for Admiral Stark's dinner, all "brass hats"; broke up at 11:00 P.M.

<u>Saturday, May 30, 1942</u> [England]

- 08:30 - dictating proposed agreement with Portal re allocation of planes (See attached).[135]
- 10:00 - with Lord Mountbatten re part air plays in making bridgehead in France. Took Eaker with us.
- 11:45 - signed agreement with Portal and received Beebe's report.[136]
- 12:30 - shopping with Eaker.
- 1:00 - lunch.

London of 1942 is far different from London of 1941; no dogs on streets, very few seen; 1941 they made London sidewalks a mess. Now men, women and children have lost that expression of dreaded expectancy, they have a cheerful look on their faces, they smile and walk with a determined air; that look of almost fearful bewilderment is gone. The shops are open but with very little in stock, everything but jewelry requires coupons. Bread and meat lines form in and near all shopping areas. No glass, debris, broken water mains, gas fires, unexploded bombs; in fact, the Huns have not been here for about a year; last May they were still coming. Pianos are playing, men are whistling, London is changed. Talked with

Ira [Eaker] until 2:30; 2:40 DeGaulle [sic] called and said his engagement for 2:45 was off.

Packed my bag and at 4:00 took off for Chequers, not Checkers, with the Ambassador and Towers; reached Chequers at 5:30. Beautiful big house, built first about 1320. The estate of 1,200 acres was first mentioned in Domesday Book in 1086.[137] In 1173, owner was clerk of the Exchequer, next owner became known as Dechequer. In 1909 it was given to the Crown as a home for the Prime Minister. Large lawns, beautiful terrace, brick walls, chimneys look aged and probably date back to 1480. Barbed wire all around now with soldiers on guard. Beautiful, large, yew pine trees several hundred years old. Inside there are paintings of all kings, queens, owners, and many other subjects, also armor. Great halls, dining rooms, halls, bedrooms, servants' rooms, almost beyond count; house itself is rectangular with three stories. Anne Boleyn's sister was supposed to have been held a prisoner in the tower room.[138]

Guests: Winant, Portal, Ismay, Harriman, Towers and Arnold, Prime Minister and Mrs. Prime Minister; Harris and Eaker in for dinner. Continued talk after movie until 2:00 A.M. The State Bedroom (the Bishop's room, the Archbishop of Canterbury used it), the bedstead with its mouldings, panels and niches is of the 1600 period; chairs, chests and stoves of the 1600 period. Learned today that I brought with me the Arnold guillotine. Once again tonight I was told that the number of planes we contemplated were not needed, that shipping would not be available. My memo to Portal was accepted, apparently almost in full; I get my answer tomorrow.

<u>Sunday, May 31, 1942</u> [England]

Did not wake up until 9:00, tried to get my valet until 9:30, couldn't find my clothes, got clothes, found hot water, shaved and dressed. Had breakfast with Towers in the large dining room, served on a tray: prunes, coffee, one egg boiled (the only one I have seen in England), toast and honey. No one up but "Pug" Ismay, the Prime Minister dictating, Portal has gone. Towers locked in the can [toilet] and could not get out: great consternation, plumbers, carpenters, valets, chambermaids, but Towers had to climb out the window.[139] Conference with Prime Minister alone in gardens from 11:15 to 1:15.

Talked the reallocation out and am ready to report to Washington; my proposal still stands. Very pleasant dinner with Lady Portal, Portal and Mrs. Morris (wife of radio broadcaster here).[140] We talked of everything but present war. Completed conference with Portal and have some, plenty of figures, to take home; hope they will be satisfactory. In bed at 12:30 A.M.

Monday, June 1, 1942 [England]

Up at 8:00 A.M.; 8:00 A.M. Somervell called up; tell Styer that OK for Everhart to go to Maxwell [Army Air Base, Alabama] provided that organization in black book is approved.[141] To Air Ministry at 9:30, final conference with Freeman and Portal. Adios to Sinclair, on to 20 Grosvenor, signed memo to Portal.[142] Saw Chaney, adios to Winant, message to President:[143] England is the place to win the war; get planes and troops over as soon as possible.

Weather bad, can't take off until 6:00 P.M. Off to # 12 Fighter Group [RAF] W. C. Mallory [commanding].[144] Lunch, watched a sweep over Bruges [Belgium], some enemy action but only half-hearted. [Saw RAF] Movies of aerial combat. Weather looks worse. On to Intelligence Centre, here they reproduce, study and evaluate all photos. They also make records of damage resulting from bombs, study photos to locate Radex,[145] antiaircraft, ground defenses, etc., using stereopticons[146] and special instruments, make maps from photos, make relief sections of critical areas and model reproductions of installed facilities.

Won't take off until tomorrow. Stopped by Northolt to get baggage. Back to Claridge['s], went to theatre. Dinner with Ira and Gene Beebe at _____, back to hotel at 10:45 P.M.

Tuesday, June 2, 1942 [England to Prestwick, Scotland, en route to Goose Bay, Labrador]

Breakfast with Ira [Eaker] and Gene [Beebe] at 7:45 A.M. Bernie Lay brought letter to sign at 8:15, Chaney arrived at 8:25. Took off in car with Chaney and Ira for Northolt at 8:30.

All passengers at plane when we arrived. Passenger list the same as when we came over except we left behind: Air Marshal Evill, Group Captain Fraser, Commander Jackson. Took on: Lord Mountbatten, Air Marshal Slessor, Mr. Averell Harriman. Took off at 9:30 A.M., arrived at Prestwick at 12:00. Met by the Station commanding officer.[147] Had a glass of port, fine lunch. Checked weather, we cannot stop at Iceland, straight to Goose, much to Jack Towers' disgust.

Saturday night, Gene Beebe, not having any of his own, slept in the Prime Minister's pajamas. Gene had a very good time on this trip and found it interesting.

Took off from Prestwick at 1:45 P.M. Weather across Atlantic poor to fair to good, wind against us most of way, about 30-40 miles per hour. Didn't see a thing but rain, sea, clouds, and occasionally the sun. Headwind cut down our speed to 135 miles per hour, came into Goose long after dark. Change in time about four hours so we had four extra hours of darkness. Landed at Goose at 5:30 A.M., L[abrador] DST; 3:30 A.M., GMT; 12:30 A.M., Goose Time.

<u>Wednesday, June 3, 1942</u> [Goose Bay, Labrador, to Washington, D.C.]

Met by all local officers, dark and drizzling, cold and penetrating. Rode in jeep to mess hall. Breakfast: roast beef, partially boiled potatoes fried, string beans, bread and coffee; coffee hot, everything else cold. Quite apparent why US troops do not care for Canadian mess, however my telegram to Washington when I went through seems to have stirred things up; we start our own mess this week. Canadians very shortsighted in trying to prevent it. Radio and weather also being coordinated.

4 B-17s have already gone through to Bluies but ordered back to Presque Isle, [Maine];[148] 35 loaded cargo planes ordered unloaded, held on alert. While I realize the motive of this action, it nullifies practically everything that I have done. One of the greatest fears of Churchill is that we will not be able or will not send over the planes we plan. He realizes the necessity for a United States Air Force, he wants the largest that we can get sent over at once; he wants it to fight alongside the

RAF but he fears just what has happened; reasons, and good ones for delaying the movement.[149]

A. D. Smith must go to Goose and straighten things out; Barney Giles to England to take over all repair and maintenance.[150] Took off from Goose in dark at 1:15 A.M. Goose time. Everybody but the crew went to bed, up at 4:30 Washington Daylight Time. Talked with Harriman until 5:30; he has same fears that I have; we are so afraid of a Japanese raid that we are apt to postpone our main objectives; that must not be.[151] Riding through fog and light rain.

Postscript

The results of Hap's journey in terms of securing a revision of Arnold-Portal had to have been labeled at least a partial success by most everyone involved. Since the agreement, signed on 30 May before Hap left London, was not considered by any of the participants to have been the final word on the issue, Arnold, Slessor, and their staffs continued to refine the proposed distributions on their arrival in Washington. As negotiations proceeded, Slessor optimistically reported to London that they were "not going at all badly" and that RAF Chief Portal would probably not have to travel to Washington to participate.[152]

Discordant voices, however, were being heard from the dominions about the proposed distribution. Prime Minister Jan Christian Smuts of South Africa informed Churchill of his opposition to the 30 May proposals. Stressing the dangers posed to the "great sea route" around the Cape, Smuts speculated to Churchill that, even if US units were dispatched to the area in lieu of American-made aircraft, the Yank airmen could not do the job. The situation would be politically "impossible" and would lead to an "explosion of public opinion" in his country. His rhetoric was similar to that used by the British in arguments posed before Arnold's departure for London, suggesting that any change would be lamentable and impractical, and that any alteration should be stoutly resisted.[153]

The Australians, who were in more immediate danger than the South Africans, were able to gain an audience with FDR on

6 June for their Minister of Foreign Affairs, Herbert L. Evatt. At that meeting, Evatt received the impression that Arnold and Adm William D. Leahy would visit Australia "within the next month" in view of the threat posed by the Japanese southward advance. Three days later, Arnold strongly suggested to Marshall that no such trip be undertaken since he could "see no earthly good" emerging from such a journey in view of "so many important things to be done here." With his emphasis on the buildup of AAF forces in Britain, Arnold had no desire to travel to the Pacific and by implication lend credibility to the air needs of that theater over the European buildup.[154]

On 10 June, Arnold confirmed to Portal that he and Slessor had reached an accord that he felt would be sufficiently acceptable to eliminate the need for the RAF chief to cross the Atlantic.[155] Two days later, Arnold met with FDR to report on this agreement. The president approved it and cabled a synopsis of its provisions to Churchill that same day. In the message, which was prepared by Arnold, FDR reaffirmed to the prime minister the principle that US-produced aircraft would be manned by American crews, with the exception of some light bombers in England and pursuit aircraft in the Middle East that would be manned by the RAF. Disappointing to the British was Roosevelt's inability to provide the promised P-39s, which he justified by the need to maintain the American fighter forces necessary for the anticipated European bombardment offensive while fulfilling commitments to the hard-pressed Soviets. Britain's loss would be partially offset by the promise of 55 American groups to be deployed to the British Isles, India, and the Middle East.[156] Although unmentioned in FDR's message, the P-39 was then the backbone of the fighter force in the Pacific.

Churchill's reply of the next day acknowledged his having read "with great interest" the president's cable but added somewhat peevishly that he failed to understand how any agreement could have been crafted since Slessor lacked the power to concur in any arrangement "without previous reference" to London. Churchill indicated he was awaiting the full text of the agreement, which he hoped would "relieve our anxiety." He stressed that any differences could be resolved at the meeting of the two leaders in the United States that was planned to take place within the week.[157]

Prior to Churchill's arrival in the United States on 18 June, Portal had furnished the prime minister a complete account of the agreements reached thus far with Arnold. In tabular form, it showed the evolution and results of the discussions that had taken place in London and Washington on this topic over the previous six months.

Type of aircraft	Arnold-Portal allocation of 14 Jan 1942	Allocation proposed by General Arnold May 8	Allocations tentatively agreed on as of June 12
Heavy bomber	447	26	54
Medium bomber	1,160	140	00
Light bomber	999	490	956
Dive bomber	702	63	625
Pursuit	2,105	248	704
Totals	5,413	967	2,439 (sic)

In summary, the figures reflected that Arnold and Portal had agreed during Arcadia in January to provide 5,500 planes for the British from American production but reconsideration in the spring of 1942 caused Arnold to propose that this number be reduced to just under 1,000. The trip to London and subsequent negotiations now proposed that the British receive a total of almost 2,500.[158]

Going beyond the numbers, Portal explained to Churchill the specifics of the tentative agreement. Some of the British losses would be compensated for by the American promise to provide 40 squadrons of US aircraft with AAF crews by 1 April 1943, and the American chiefs, subject to final CCS approval, would consider meeting Dominion needs in Australia and New Zealand. Portal, however, remained skeptical of the American ability to meet the proposed timetables while questioning whether the agreed-upon US units would be "adequately trained." Other areas of disappointment to the British included the reduction in heavy bombers, the bulk of which had been intended for use in Coastal Command. Some of these losses would be offset, however, by allocation of 500 flying boats of various types to the British. The reduced allocation of transport aircraft led Portal to label the proposed settlement "definitely unsatisfactory" on this issue, but this was in part balanced by the eight American transport groups intended for use in Britain as a common pool for airborne forces. Slessor remembered that the differences over transport aircraft were not resolved until the hour before the agreement was finalized in the White House. If not for the reduction in P-40s, currently in heavy use in North Africa, and the aircraft for antisubmarine warfare, Portal felt the "negotiations had proceeded not unfavorably."[159] Arnold, Towers, and Slessor agreed to the distribution, with minor modifications, on Saturday, 21 June. Roosevelt and Churchill approved the distribution on the following day, and Arnold promised that he would get every P-40 possible into the Middle East. The British, meanwhile, continued to press Admiral King on the need for Catalina flying boats.[160]

As Arnold, Slessor, and others were ushered into the White House to receive Churchill's and FDR's reactions to their proposals, the prime minister had just learned of the significant British defeat the previous day by numerically inferior German forces at Tobruk. This loss, with more than 33,000 taken prisoner, dictated the atmosphere and the emphasis of the meeting. As Slessor recalled the scene, the two political leaders "were in no mood to interest themselves in details, but asked whether we were satisfied, heard what we had to say, initialed our report and dismissed us."[161]

It would be difficult to evaluate the results of the agreement other than as a limited victory for the AAF and Arnold, however temporary it may have been. It enhanced the prospects of providing most of the heavy bomber production to the ongoing buildup of the US strategic forces in England. Additionally, it promised sufficient aircraft to both support crew and maintenance training for the growing AAF and dispatch equipped US air units to various combat areas while attempting to fulfill the demands of other claimants such as the Soviet Union and China.[162] Shortly after returning to Washington, Arnold sent an optimistic "thank you" note to Churchill, even while negotiations with Slessor continued. Hap labeled the journey a "decidedly worthwhile trip" and assured the prime minister that he need have no "great concern" regarding allocation or the numbers of American units promised to arrive in England.[163] The settlement was no panacea, however, and the shortage of aircraft would continue for at least another year, dictating Arnold's next trip abroad three months after approval of Arnold-Towers-Slessor and several other allocation agreements.

While institutionally significant for the AAF, it had to have been personally satisfying to Arnold that he now enjoyed sufficient White House confidence to have become the primary Allied arbiter of American-produced aircraft distribution. This was a decided change from his trip to England a year earlier when his continuance as Air Corps chief was seriously threatened, primarily because of this issue. Hap's problems of the past three years, created in large part by Secretary of the Treasury Morgenthau and his Procurement Division, appeared now to be in his past.

Other results from the trip were important to the AAF if not to Arnold personally. Eisenhower and Arnold reported to Marshall the lack of effectiveness and harmony in the command relationships in England, particularly as concerned General Chaney and the Eighth Air Force. From Arnold's viewpoint, Chaney failed to appreciate the sense of urgency and the need for a different command structure, which Arnold attached to the movement and preparation for combat of the newly arriving Eighth Air Force units. Eisenhower conceded "an uneasy feeling that either we do not understand our own commanding general [Chaney] and staff in England or they don't understand us." On 20 June, Marshall nominated Eisenhower as Commanding General, European Theater of Operations, United States Army (ETOUSA), even though Major General McNarney had been recommended to replace Chaney. Three days later, Ike returned to England as Chaney's replacement.[164] This event triggered a series of challenges that led to Ike's becoming Supreme Commander of the Allied Forces in Europe. Chaney, unfortunately, would not be promoted again. Nor would he be given any position of significant responsibility during the remainder of the war.

This diary, more than any of the others, suggests that the demands being placed on Arnold caused him to provide only brief mention of several other important discussions that took place. For example, RAF officials agreed with Arnold on a total of 127 airfields for the AAF as well as their UK locations during his 28 May meeting with them. In another instance, when he met with Portal and signed the agreement on allocation on 30 May, Arnold presented a detailed list of American units and a specific timetable for their arrival in England to the RAF chief. Neither list nor timetable was cited in the diary.[165]

Hap's Thursday night dinner alone with Maj Gen John C. H. Lee earned only passing mention in the diary but it had to be an important meeting. The major issues discussed there were no doubt the logistical planning and problems associated with the dispatch and arrival of the Eighth Air Force units to England. In Arnold's mind, this movement was second in importance only to reaching an airplane reallocation agreement with the British. Lee, an old friend from cadet days at West Point where he was two years behind Arnold, was now the Services of Supply commander in England and in this assignment was the key Army logistics officer for arranging and distributing the materiel support that would accrue to the AAF. Even more significant to Arnold was Lee's major role in determining shipping priorities into the theater and his control over Army construction battalions.[166] Since the issues with Portal and Lee involved major overseas movements, Hap's regard for safeguarding security information may have been, in addition to time constraints, a factor in their not being covered more extensively in the diary. Additionally, Arnold had furnished written confirmation of these proposals in negotiations with the RAF, negating the need for their detailed inclusion in his diary.

The buildup and operation of the Eighth Air Force in England remained a major concern of Arnold for the next two years. The magnitude of the task was seen in his proposal to Portal during their 30 May meeting that 66 AAF combat groups arrive by March 1943. These were to be 19 heavy bombardment groups, 12 medium bomber groups, 12 light bomber groups, 15 pursuit groups, and eight others to support the bombers. In all, 700 heavy bombers, 800 medium bombers, 342 light bombers, and 960 pursuits would be in England by 1 April 1943. In spite of these ambitious plans, Hap was aware when he left for Washington three days after presenting this to Portal, that the 1,871 Eighth Air Force personnel now in the United Kingdom did not possess a single airplane.[167]

Even though Eaker and Spaatz, the generals in charge of the mission, were two of his most trusted officers, Arnold retained a very keen interest in the details of the movement. He was constantly providing directives and advice, all impatiently aimed at getting the Eighth into combat as quickly as possible. Constant attention from Washington was not always warmly welcomed by Spaatz and Eaker, who continued efforts to educate Arnold, generally without any great success, about the difficulties involved. For the next 18 months, given the diversion of assets from the strategic bombardment effort caused by the Guadalcanal and North African invasions, Arnold was constantly urging greater effort and quicker success. He would make another trip to England 15 months after this journey, and would later be involved in the relief, euphemistically called reassignment, of one of the major commanders of the bombing effort.

An example of Arnold's impatience for results that turned out badly was one of the rare instances that Stimson and Lovett have characterized as Arnold coming up with "half-baked" ideas.[168] Hap's reassuring 10 June letter to Churchill soon after his return to the Pentagon promised "we will be fighting with you on July 4th," a date with significance on both sides of the Atlantic. As a consequence, Arnold directed Spaatz to ensure that a mission be flown on the promised day even though no American unit was ready for such a test. Although Eaker joined Spaatz in protesting the premature nature of such a raid, Arnold persisted.[169] Hap's motivation was probably a combination of the desire to justify the large investment in the European bombardment buildup, a hope to duplicate the favorable publicity that had resulted from the daring Doolittle Tokyo raid six weeks earlier, and an effort to balance the Navy's trumpeted bombardment success at the Battle of

Midway in early June. This motivation was in addition to fulfilling his commitment to Churchill. How better to justify the enormous commitment of resources and demonstrate the AAF's readiness to begin its strategic bombardment campaign against the Germans in northern Europe than an Independence Day attack? Using borrowed RAF airplanes hastily repainted with US markings, a minimally trained flight of six American crews flying A-20s and escorted by RAF Bostons carried out a low-level attack against German airdromes on the Dutch North Sea coast. By any measurement except publicity in the press, the 4 July mission was a failure. Seven American airmen died in the raid. As Spaatz laconically and sarcastically recorded in his diary after he decorated the lead pilot a week later, "The cameramen and newspapermen finally got what they wanted—and everybody [presumably including the impatient Arnold] seemed contented." Hap prudently omitted any reference to the raid in his memoirs.[170]

While Arnold spent the bulk of his time and energies in the four days after arriving in London on the allocation problem, he dispatched his accompanying aide, Col Eugene H. Beebe, to assess the operation of the maintenance facilities in modifying the arriving American-built airplanes for British and US operational use.[171] The evaluation could prove valuable in Hap's understanding the seeming delay between the arrival of US airplanes and their being ready for combat. Additionally, such an assessment would permit Arnold, Spaatz, and Eaker to determine the extent to which existing British maintenance and depot facilities, manned essentially by British civilian workers, would be able to meet the requirements of the numerous AAF units now scheduled for arrival. Beebe's report to Arnold on 1 June was critical of the existing situation and was not well received by Portal. In a letter to Arnold 10 days later, the RAF chief questioned the accuracy of Beebe's report even though General Brett's assessment a year earlier had identified similar deficiencies. Portal wrote that he did not "believe that General Chaney would accept" Beebe's conclusions and recommendations. Given the limited time available for evaluation, Portal's objections that Beebe's report had been rendered "without going fully into all the relevant facts" were probably valid.[172] A result of this journey and Beebe's analysis was that both Eaker on the scene and Spaatz, who arrived in the British Isles on 18 June, considered it a high priority to establish AAF standards and control over maintenance and repair facilities. They immediately set out to establish them for the expected AAF units. As Spaatz' biographer has concluded, "For the next two weeks [following his June 18 arrival in England] Spaatz threw himself into the task of preparing a logistics and base structure . . . capable of sustaining the Eighth over a prolonged campaign."[173]

Arnold's optimism over the trip and its results does not seem unwarranted. It had produced, largely as a result of his negotiations, an essentially favorable allocation of aircraft between the British and the Americans and had influenced the naming of a new US theater commander who appeared more sympathetic to AAF plans and needs. The journey saw the completion of plans for installing a new team of AAF leaders in Britain who shared Arnold's convictions concerning the US strategic air offensive. Hap could reflect on successful negotiations with the British on many of the logistical details essential to the arrival and preparation for combat of the American airmen. Any euphoria on Arnold's part as a result of the journey, however, was neither recorded nor long-lived.

Notes

1. Wesley Frank Craven and James Lea Cate, eds., *The Army Air Forces in World War II*, vol. 1, *Plans and Early Operations, January 1939 to August 1942* (1948; new imprint, Washington, D.C.: Office of Air Force History, 1983), 249.

2. Arnold to War Plans Division, 7 July 1941, Gen Henry Harley Arnold Papers, Library of Congress, Manuscript Division, Washington, D.C., hereinafter cited as AP.

3. Arnold to Lovett, 14 June 1941, AP; and Irving Brinton Holley Jr., *United States Army in World War II, Special Studies, Buying Aircraft: Materiel Procurement for the Army Air Forces* (Washington, D.C.: Office of the Chief of Military History, Government Printing Office [GPO] 1964), 245.

4. The program called for 18,000 airplanes; actual production for the year was 19,433. Holley, 555.

5. H. Duncan Hall, *North American Supply* (London: Her Majesty's Stationery Office, 1955), 309.

6. Arnold's brief and cryptic notes on three small pieces of paper appear to have been written during the actual sessions, precluding any extensive commentary. Copies of his notes are in Henry H. Arnold Papers, Murray Green Collection, US Air Force Academy Library (USAFAL), Colorado Springs, Colo.

7. Craven and Cate, vol. 1, 247–49.

8. Combined Chief of Staff (CCS) Meeting, 10 February 1942.

9. Public Record Office (PRO), Air Ministry Records (Air) 8/634 and also in 8/637, Portal from Evill, 6 March 1942.

10. Diary of Henry L. Stimson, microfilm record in the Sterling Library, Yale University, New Haven, Conn., copy in US Naval Academy Library, Annapolis, 6 March 1942, hereinafter cited as Stimson Diary.

11. PRO, Air 8/891, RAF Delegation, Washington to Air Ministry, 11 March 1942.

12. Churchill to Roosevelt, 29 March 1942, AP; also in Warren F. Kimball, ed., *Churchill & Roosevelt: The Complete Correspondence*, vol. 1, *Alliance Emerging October 1933–November 1941* (Princeton, N.J.: Princeton University Press, 1984), 434–35.

13. CCS Meeting, 31 March 1942.

14. PRO, Air 8/634 and 8/637, RAF Delegation, Washington, to Air Ministry, 29 March 1942.

15. CCS Meeting, 31 March 1942.

16. PRO, Air 8/634, Evill to Portal, 12 April 1942.

17. Ibid.; and PRO, Air 8/647, 19 April 1942.

18. CCS Meeting, 31 March 1942.

19. PRO, Air 8/1050, Joint Staff Mission, Washington to Chief of Staff, London, 2 April 1942.

20. PRO, Air 8/634, Dill to Portal, 8 April 1942.

21. Ibid.

22. Stimson Diary, 8 April 1942; and PRO, Air 8/634, Summary of Arnold-Portal Agreement, 9 April 1942.

23. Stimson Diary, 9 April 1942; and PRO, Air 8/634, Summary of Arnold-Portal Agreement, 9 April 1942.

24. PRO, Air 8/647, Evill to Portal, 19 April 1942; and PRO, Air 8/1050, Portal to Marshall, 16 April 1942.

25. PRO, Air 8/634, Summary of Arnold-Portal Agreement, 9 April 1942; PRO, Air 8/1050, Portal to Marshall, 16 April 1942; and PRO, Air 8/647, Portal to Evill, 17 April 1942.

26. PRO, Air 8/1050, Portal to Marshall, 16 April 1942.

27. Portal to Evill, 17 April 1942; and PRO, Air 8/647, Evill to Portal, 19 April 1942.

28. PRO, Air 8/1050, Portal to Marshall, 16 April 1942.

29. Evill to Portal, 19 April 1942; PRO, Air 8/647, Portal to Evill, 14 May 1942; and PRO, Air 8/634, Summary of Arnold-Portal Agreement, 9 April 1942.

30. PRO, Air 8/647, Sir Henry Self, memo, subject: Regarding Moral Right to Output, 18 May 1942; and PRO, Air 8/647, Portal to Evill, 14 May 1942.

31. PRO, Air 8/647, Evill to Portal, 19 April 1942 and 14 May 1942.
32. PRO, Air 8/647, Evill to Portal, 14 May 1942.
33. Ibid.
34. Ibid.; and PRO, Air 8/647, Joint Staff Mission, Washington to COS, 22 May 1942.
35. PRO, Air 8/634, W. L. Talquin to Vice Chief of the Air Staff, RAF, 30 April 1942.
36. Stimson Diary, 16 May 1942; and PRO, Air 8/647, Dill to COS, n.d., c. 15 May.
37. See the accounts in Forrest C. Pogue, *George C. Marshall: Education of a General, 1880-1939* (New York: Viking Press, 1963), 302-20; and Craven and Cate, vol. 1, 574-76.
38. FDR to Arnold, 5 May 1942, AP.
39. Stimson Diary, 25 April 1942. For denial of transports for British use at this same time see PRO, Air, 8/647, Evill to Portal, 14 May 1942; Churchill to Roosevelt, 12 May 1942; FDR to Churchill, 16 May 1942; and Kimball, 484-86. The issue of American manufactured transports for the British continued as a problem as late as the 12-16 September 1944 Octagon conference in Quebec. See chap. 9.
40. Arnold to Kuter, 14 April 1942, AP.
41. Clark G. Reynolds, *Admiral John H. Towers: The Struggle for Naval Air Supremacy* (Annapolis: Naval Institute Press, 1991), 388.
42. PRO, Air 8/647, Evill to Portal, 14 May 1942.
43. Stimson Diary, 11 May 1942.
44. PRO, Air 8/647, Portal to Evill, 14 May 1942.
45. Quoted in Grace Person Hayes, *The History of the Joint Chiefs of Staff in World War II: The War Against Japan* (Annapolis: Naval Institute Press, 1982), 786.
46. Kimball, 484-85.
47. Ibid., 485-86.
48. Ibid., 486-87.
49. Ibid., 487-88.
50. H. H. Arnold, General of the Air Force, *Global Mission* (New York: Harper & Brothers, 1949), 308; and Reynolds, 389.
51. James Parton, *"Air Force Spoken Here," General Ira Eaker and the Command of the Air* (Bethesda, Md.: Adler & Adler, 1986), 130-40.
52. DeWitt S. Copp, *A Few Great Captains: The Men and Events That Shaped the Development of U.S. Air Power* (Garden City, N.Y.: Doubleday & Co., 1980), 150-51, has a brief biographical sketch of Chaney.
53. Craven and Cate, vol. 1, 577-78; and Pogue, 128.
54. Initial Directive to Bomber Command in England, 31 January 1942, AP.
55. Parton, 134.
56. See Craven and Cate, vol. 1, 578-79.
57. Eaker to Spaatz, 1 March 1942, Gen Carl Andrew Spaatz Papers, Library of Congress, Manuscript Division, Washington, D.C., hereinafter cited as SP.
58. Ibid.

59. Craven and Cate, vol. 1, 585-86; and Parton, 135.
60. Craven and Cate, vol. 1, 587.
61. Ibid., 114-15.
62. Pogue, 290.
63. There are many examples of this in Craven and Cate, vol. 1 and vol. 2, *Europe: Torch to Pointblank, August 1942 to December 1943* (1949; new imprint, Washington, D.C.: Office of Air Force History, 1983).
64. Craven and Cate, vol. 1, 262.
65. Ibid., 262-66; and Pogue, 291-99.
66. Rebecca Hancock Cameron, *Training to Fly: Military Flight Training, 1907-1945*, (Washington, D.C.: Air Force History and Museums Programs, 1999).
67. Memo of White House Meeting, 4 January 1942, AP; Arnold's account is in *Global Mission*, 298-300; and Arnold to Watson, 7 January 1942, AP.
68. James H. Doolittle, *I Could Never Be So Lucky Again: An Autobiography of General James H. "Jimmy" Doolittle with Carroll V. Glines* (New York: Bantam Books, 1991), 233-35.
69. Doolittle's recollections of the preparations prior to loading of the airplanes on the carrier is in Doolittle, 230-55. See also undated and unsigned "Proposal for the Bombing Attack on Tokyo" presumably prepared by Doolittle and submitted to the Commanding General, Army Air Forces printed in Doolittle, 540-44. The account in the official history is in Craven and Cate, vol. 1, 438-44. An earlier popular coverage by Lowell Thomas and Edward Jablonski differs in some details with the previously cited accounts. See Lowell Thomas and Edward Jablonski, *Doolittle: A Biography* (Garden City, N.Y.: Doubleday & Co., 1972), 156-204.
70. Arnold, 208; and Pogue, 302-20.
71. Craven and Cate, vol. 1, 645.
72. See PRO, Air, 8/647, Portal's Briefing Paper for Prime Minister, 22 May 1942. Running single-spaced on three legal-sized sheets, the arguments were phrased in terms that would allow maximum use of Churchillian rhetoric. Arnold Diary, 14 September 1944, presented in chapter 9.
73. See Arnold's congratulatory memo to Harris, 31 May 1942, AP; and Hopkins to FDR, 30 May 1942, Harry L. Hopkins Papers, Franklin D. Roosevelt Library, Hyde Park, N.Y., box 295.
74. The numbers in parentheses were distances Arnold noted in nautical miles to the locations identified.
75. Goose Bay, Labrador, at the southwest corner of Lake Melville, was leased to the United States by Great Britain for 99 years in the Destroyer-Bases agreement of September 1940. Airfield construction commenced in September 1941 and the first aircraft landed two days after Pearl Harbor, the rapid completion a reflection of the perceived need for the base as a link in the air routes across the North Atlantic. The weather conditions in Labrador were generally more favorable than those in Newfoundland and, as a result, the former served during the war and later as the more important

link in pre-jet travel across the Atlantic. The United States returned control and jurisdiction to Canada in June 1973.

76. Prestwick Air Base (AB), Ayrshire, Scotland, on the west coast approximately 30 miles southwest of Glasgow, was a logical location as the eastern terminus of the North Atlantic air route.

77. Gander AB, eastern central Newfoundland, had been serving the British and Canadian air forces since 1936. The first American troops arrived there in May 1941, after which the base was a joint American-Canadian facility. US interests were terminated in June 1961. The British termed the route from Washington to Montreal to Gander to Prestwick the "Arnold line" in reference to Hap's travel. See Craven and Cate, vol. 1, 318.

78. Lt Cmdr George W. Anderson, USN, aide to Admiral Towers; Col Eugene H. Beebe, Arnold's aide and pilot; Maj Gen Mark W. Clark, USA, chief of staff to commander, US Army Ground Forces; Maj Gen Dwight D. Eisenhower, USA, assistant chief of staff, Operations Division [OPD], US War Department General Staff; Air Chief Marshal Douglas C. S. Evill, RAF, RAF representative to the CCS. Neither Fraser of the Royal South African Air Force nor Jackson of the Royal Navy are otherwise identified. Rear Adm John T. Towers, USN, chief, Navy Bureau of Aeronautics; Col Hoyt S. Vandenberg, assistant chief of staff, Operations, AAF Headquarters.

79. The civilian TWA (Transcontinental and Western Air) crew members other than the pilot are not otherwise identified. A military radio operator accompanied them, which enabled them to use classified communications data. On the return trip, Arnold wrote a letter of appreciation to the pilot, Capt Otis Bryan, with whom Arnold was to fly later, praising him for his professionalism. Then Bryan made a particularly difficult landing on 3 June 1942 at Bolling Field in adverse weather with a 200-foot ceiling that Arnold labeled "a superb piece of flying." Slessor called their arrival in Washington a "hair-raising performance" but mistakenly identified the pilot as Otis Steele. Arnold, reflecting his confidence in Bryan, later chose him, by then a major in the AAF, to fly President Roosevelt to the Casablanca Conference. See Craven and Cate, vol. 1, 374; Arnold to Bryan, 3 June 1942, AP; and Sir John Slessor, G.C.B., D.S.O., M.C., *The Central Blue: The Autobiography of Sir John Slessor, Marshall of the Royal Air Force* (New York: Frederick A. Praeger, 1957), 411.

80. Royal Canadian Air Force (RCAF) Commanding Officer is not otherwise identified.

81. The cable dated 24 May is in SP. In it, Arnold requested that 28 kitchen personnel be sent immediately.

82. Now a major general, Spaatz was chief of the AAF Combat Command. With some modifications following the French system since World War I, staff sections in the US Army were designated as G-1 Personnel, G-2 Intelligence, G-3 Training and Operations, and G-4 Supply. The AAF that was created in the reorganization of 20 June 1941 adopted the same functional divisions, labeling them A-1, A-2, and so forth. Arnold, a creature of habit, was still referring to them in the previous manner.

83. Air Chief Marshal Sir Frederick W. Bowhill, RAF, commander, RAF Ferry Command. In view of the relatively few four-engine aircraft with overseas capability available to the US military after Pearl Harbor, the crew and airplane used on this flight were leased from TWA, which had commenced flying this route for the AAF in April 1942. The Stratoliner was the Boeing four-engine, all-metal, low-wing, monoplane, the commercial version of which was designated as the Boeing 307. The AAF purchased only five of these in World War II, calling them C-75s.

84. Maj Gen Gerald C. Brant, CG, Newfoundland Base Command, had replaced Brig Gen Henry W. Harms who had been relieved by Arnold following the Argentia Conference.

85. Two of the three cables Arnold sent this day, describing conditions at Goose as "far from satisfactory," are in AP and SP. In the one to Lovett reflecting his displeasure, Hap informed the assistant secretary of problems concerning the operation of the control tower, the messing facilities, and the lagging construction. Hap insisted that the RCAF "does not have full appreciation of the importance" of the tasks and the need for "elimination of all lost motion." Arnold pointed out that the "corrections must be made at Ottawa" including the "desire for AAF control" and "careful supervision of the communications and meteorology operations." Arnold to Lovett, 24 May 1942, SP.

86. In the cable to Maj Gen Millard F. Harmon, chief of the Air Staff, Arnold indicated the number and skills of the "urgent" messing personnel to be sent. He also discussed changes that were necessary at the locations identified. Crystal was the name given to the three weather stations established in September 1941. Crystal I was located at Fort Chimo, Labrador; Crystal II was at the head of Frobisher Bay, Baffin Island; Crystal III was at Padloping Island, just off the northeast coast of Baffin Island. Bluie West I was the code name for the American airfield at Narsarssuak, Greenland, where work commenced 1 September 1940 and resulted in an airfield with a steel-matted main runway becoming operational by June 1942. Work on Bluie West 8 at Sondre Stromfjord on the west coast above the Arctic Circle commenced in September 1941. Bluie East 2 at Angmagssalik on the east coast was completed in September 1941.

87. In order to distinguish friendly from hostile aircraft, signals were required from aircraft passing over naval vessels. Normally, flares of prearranged colors were fired from the plane.

88. The reference is to the narrow land area approximately 35 miles wide stretching from the Clyde on the west to the Firth of Forth on the east. The bay was the Firth of Clyde.

89. Blister hangars were temporary structures of British design constructed of steel or timber named for their resemblance to a blister in view of their length and shallow appearance.

90. Arnold meant 7,000 feet. These aircraft were used primarily by the British Coastal Command in antisubmarine work.

91. Air Vice Marshal A. W. Durston, RAF, AOC, Coastal Defence Command, Northeast Coast.

92. Prestwick control was able to identify incoming planes and monitor their progress through either voice or radio signals or both transmitted from the aircraft. The planes' signals were plotted from two separate stations and the intersection of them revealed the location of the transmitting aircraft. While pleased with Prestwick's ability to handle the relatively limited air traffic at this time, Arnold was dissatisfied with Prestwick's later operations. See Arnold Diary, particularly entries for 1 and 3 September 1943, presented in chapter 4.

93. The modifications of the American aircraft were necessary to adapt the planes for combat in the European and Middle East theaters. Arnold was very concerned that while the British continued to press their requests for delivery of large numbers of American-produced aircraft, "too many of the planes were just standing there when they were badly needed elsewhere." This attitude influenced his thinking about allocation during the discussions on this trip and later. This resulted in Arnold's dispatching his aide, Colonel Beebe, to assess modification and maintenance operations in England while Arnold was occupied in London with the allocation question. See Arnold Diary entry for 30 May. The quote is from Arnold, 309; see also Slessor's account, 407.

94. Glasgow had been heavily bombed the previous year by the Germans on 19 March 1941, just prior to Arnold's first visit to Britain.

95. The Scottish Chief was a crack British train operating between Glasgow and London.

96. The military attaché is not otherwise identified.

97. Brig Gen Ira C. Eaker, now CG, US Eighth Bomber Command; Brig Gen Harold M. McClelland, assistant chief of staff for Operations and Training, United States Army Forces British Isles (USAFBI).

98. Vyacheslav Molotov, the Foreign Minister of the USSR, had just left London for a conference with President Roosevelt in Washington. He returned to London en route to Moscow. The main topic of his conversations with US and British leaders concerned the opening of a second front. A full account is in Robert E. Sherwood, *Roosevelt and Hopkins: An Intimate History* (New York: Harpers & Brothers, 1948), 554–79; Winston S. Churchill, *The Second World War*, vol. 4, *The Hinge of Fate* (Boston: Houghton Mifflin, 1950), 326–42.

99. Vice Adm Sir Arthur Lyster, RN, commander of Aircraft Carriers, British Home Fleet.

100. This was the code name for the build-up of American forces in the United Kingdom.

101. Copy of General Principles not located.

102. Arnold delegated the detailed negotiating, subject to his own approval, to Col Vandenberg.

103. Air Marshal Arthur T. Harris, RAF, AOC, RAF Bomber Command.

104. Mrs. Floyd B. Odlum, American aviatrix and cosmetic entrepreneur better known in aviation circles as Jackie Cochran, was serving at the time as a flight captain in the British Air Transport Auxiliary. Arnold indicated that it was during this trip "we first talked over the idea of creating an organ-

ization of women pilots in the United States Air Force." He appointed her as director of Women's Air Force Service Pilots (WASPS), an integral part of the AAF, in July 1943. See Arnold, 311, which is the source of the quote.

105. Code-named Pinetree, USAAF Eighth Bomber Command was located in a former girl's school at High Wycombe, approximately 30 miles northwest of London in Buckinghamshire. The aviators were amused by the instructions still posted above the call buttons on their bedroom walls directing "Ring for Mistress." The RAF Bomber Command Headquarters with the code name of Southdown was located five miles away.

106. Bomb shackles were devices on which bombs were hung in the bomb bays of aircraft. Universal shackle refers to a type that could be utilized on any size bomb then being used on the DB-7 airplane. The bomb fins had to be modified to allow their use on AAF planes.

107. Ernest Heinkel Flugzeuwerke factory and main offices were located just northwest of Rostock, a city in northeast Germany. Augsburg is a city just west of Munich in Bavaria; the target in that much-bombed city was the Messerschmitt factory. The RAF had just conducted raids against these two cities.

108. William Pitt and William Gladstone were leading British prime ministers in the eighteenth and nineteenth centuries respectively. Although not clear, Arnold's reference was probably to John Beresford, chief advisor on Irish affairs to William Pitt. At least two other important British officials in the eighteenth and nineteenth centuries were named or titled Beresford. No attachment accompanies the diary in the Library of Congress.

109. Col Claude E. Duncan had been in Britain since January and would become, in June 1942, CG of the Provisional First Bombardment Wing, Eighth Air Force. Col Stewart W. Towle Jr., chief of staff, 8th Fighter Command.

110. These aircraft were being used primarily in antisubmarine work by the RAF Coastal Command.

111. Built by Lockheed in the United States, the twin-engine, low-wing British Ventura had achieved only limited success with the RAF Bomber Command in 1942 in daylight operations and as a consequence was used with Coastal Command after the summer of 1943. Also American-built, Consolidated Aircraft Corporation's PBY Catalina twin-engine, high-wing patrol flying boat was utilized throughout the war by Coastal Command.

112. Lt Gen Brehon B. Somervell, USA, CG, Services of Supply, US Army.

113. Data on this matter not located in his papers but apparently was shown to Arnold in the office indicated.

114. The remotely controlled airplane, General Motors "Bug" (GMA-1), loaded with explosives and designed to crash into its target, had originated in 1917.

115. Twin-place, single-engine, light monoplanes built in the United States by the Piper Aircraft Company and others for observation, training, and liaison duty.

116. Colonel Vandenberg headed the Working Committee, negotiating with the British, that was augmented by AAF officers from Chaney's and Eaker's staffs.

117. Arnold referred to the fact that British planning used the figure of 100 percent reserve of aircraft in units as opposed to the United States factor of 50 percent. This caused allocation problems then and later.

118. Arnold used as his headquarters during this visit the four-story brick-faced building still standing on Grosvenor Street just one and one-half blocks west of the American Embassy in Grosvenor Square. Renovation for American use was necessitated by the heavy damage inflicted when a bomb struck across the street in May 1941. As the number of American visitors and staff in London increased, the building was obtained for additional American office space. Brig Gen Alfred J. Lyon, director of Supply, USAFBI; Capt Bernie Lay, one of the eight AAF officers who had arrived in England with General Eaker in February 1942 to form the nucleus of the Eighth Air Force, served as a member of the Secretariat and Working Committee during Arnold's visit. He later wrote the very successful *Twelve O'Clock High*, a fictionalized account of events in the Eighth.

119. The issues were broader than sewer pits. Eaker on the scene since February had earlier insisted on providing the "normal American standards" to maintain morale. This included American rather than British rations along with other amenities such as showers and heated buildings. See Eaker to Spaatz, 1 March 1942, SP.

120. The bulk of the bomber bases built in England for AAF use were labeled Class A type and built by the British Air Ministry Directorate-General of Works. There was a main runway of 6,000 feet minimum with two intersecting runways of 4,200 feet each. See Roger A. Freeman, *Airfields of the Eighth: Then and Now* (London: After the Battle Magazine, 1978), 8.

121. This did not occur, as reception centers were located in England; nor were any rest centers developed in this period.

122. Given the need for AAF as well as RAF fighters as escorts of US bombers, the sector defense was retained by the RAF. As Spaatz defined the role of AAF fighters, they were to support "our bombers in an effort to secure air *Supremacy* and not for the defense of England." Quoted in Craven and Cate, vol. 1, 623; emphasis in the original.

123. For the early practice of setting two US bomb groups on the same base, see Freeman, 6–10.

124. Turbinlite missions combined radar with airborne searchlights, using high-powered lights fitted into the nose of the DB-7, or Boston, which the British were using as a night fighter. Accompanied by a Hurricane fighter, the Boston would detect an enemy plane with radar and illuminate it with its searchlights in such a way that the Hurricane could then attack. Slow speed and technical difficulties impeded the Turbinlite units, which were replaced with radar-equipped night fighters.

125. Like all estimates in this period, the numbers of AAF airplanes and airdromes were expanded far beyond the discussions held here. For exam-

ple the AAF would eventually occupy and use 127 airdromes in the UK; Craven and Cate, vol. 1, 631.

126. Col Harry A. Halverson commanded a detachment of 23 B-24s that were originally intended to bomb Japan from Chinese bases. The unit was delayed and did not reach the Middle East until June 1942 en route to China. It was retained following Erwin Rommel's success in breaking through the British defenses in Cyrenaica in the summer of 1942 and reassigned to the recently created Middle East Air Force, eventually becoming the nucleus of the Ninth Air Force. Maj Gen Lewis H. Brereton, now CG, Tenth AF, India. Lt Gen Joseph W. Stilwell, USA, CG, US Army Forces, China-Burma-India (CBI) Theater, both of whom had been requesting an increase in their heavy bombers.

127. It was not necessary for Portal to travel to the United States on this issue since Air Vice Marshal John C. Slessor accompanied Arnold back to Washington to continue the negotiations. As Arnold wrote to Portal on 10 June, "We must not consider the trip cancelled—just postponed." AP.

128. Vice Adm Louis Mountbatten, RN, serving as chief of Combined Operations, accepted Arnold's invitation and flew with him to Washington. Arnold no doubt was anxious to discuss during dinner with Lee the difficult logistics problems facing the Eighth Air Force in England as it was planned to expand there.

129. Air Marshal Sir Philip Joubert de la Ferte, RAF, AOC, RAF Coastal Command.

130. Arnold meant SCR 271, long-range fixed aircraft detector radar.

131. Jamming is the act of rendering a radio or radar set ineffective by use of either countertransmissions or a confusion reflector.

132. Surging is an uncontrolled transient and abnormal rush of power in an aircraft engine.

133. Spaatz arrived on 18 June in Britain to command all AAF units in the UK. Brig Gen Frank O'D. "Monk" Hunter, would become CG, 8th Fighter Command. Chaney's concern that Arnold was making too many firm commitments, which would deprive Spaatz and Hunter of the necessary on-site flexibility, proved ill-founded in view of later developments. These remarks and Arnold's continuing impressions of Chaney's performance, his seeming lack of aggressiveness in this assignment, along with serious disagreements with Arnold and Eaker and presumably confirmed by Eisenhower's observations, on the problems of the AAF in England resulted in Chaney being reassigned. There is an account of Arnold-Chaney differences in this period in Craven and Cate, vol. 1, 579–89. See Arnold Diary presented in chapter 11 for Chaney's assignment in the Pacific towards the end of the war.

134. Given the RAF's extensive experience in the British Isles, it was agreed that Douglas would direct the operational use of fighters. This quickly led to an early agreement between the United States and the British that the main use of AAF fighters would be in escorting bombardment aircraft. US planes could be used in defense of the British Isles in an emergency. However, except in a few isolated instances, German bombers did not attack US airfields in Great Britain. See Craven and Cate, vol. 1, 622–23.

135. Dated 30 May 1942, Arnold's memo contained the proposed allocations that became the basis, with some slight changes, of the Arnold-Towers-Slessor agreement approved on 22 June in the United States. Copies of the signed tentative agreement and Portal's 10-page reclama, dated the following day, are in AP.

136. Beebe's original instructions from Arnold and his final report, which was critical of British maintenance and supply operations and the delay in modifying US-produced planes for combat, are in AP.

137. This was the general census of people and land in England that was taken in 1085–1086 by William the Conqueror.

138. Chequers was the Tudor mansion dating from 1566 near Princess Risborough, Buckinghamshire, presented to the British government in 1917 by Lord and Lady Lee (nee Ruth Moore of New York) of Fareham as the country residence of the British Prime Minister. Mary Boleyn was Henry VIII's mistress sometime after 1521 and prior to her sister Anne's marriage to the monarch in early 1533. Mary was later imprisoned at Chequers by her niece Queen Elizabeth.

139. Towers, whose relationship with Arnold dated from 1911 when they were both young aviators, insisted that the impish Hap had locked him the bathroom. See Reynolds, 391.

140. At least 50 persons with the name Morris were associated with the British Broadcasting Company at this time. Most probably the lady was the wife of Dennis Morris, chief of programs, BBC, Birmingham.

141. Maj Gen Wilhelm D. Styer, USA, chief of staff, Services of Supply, US Army; the *Army Register* for that year has no listing for Everhart. The organization proposed is not otherwise identified.

142. The memo to Portal on this date has not been located. Although there is no mention of it in this diary, Arnold held a press conference with British and American reporters at 20 Grosvenor Street on this day. It lasted approximately 15 minutes and the questions elicited guarded responses. Most of the queries dealt with planning for the arrival and use of American aircraft and crews to Britain, allocation of airplanes between the two nations, and the role of airpower in conquering Germany. Hap responded with predictable platitudes such as "having seen quite a lot" and that he was "returning to the US with a much better understanding of this whole thing." A transcript is in AFHRA, Maxwell AFB, Ala.

143. The message to the president has not been located, but it probably contained a summary of the points tentatively agreed upon by Arnold and the British as contained in the memo signed by Portal earlier in the day.

144. Arnold was mistaken here, since headquarters of No. 12 Group was located at Church Fenton, Yorkshire. The time involved would not have permitted him to travel that far. He meant No. 11 Fighter Group, located in Uxbridge, Middlesex, approximately 11 miles due west of London. He was greeted there by Air Vice Marshal Trafford Leigh-Mallory, now AOC of No. 11 Group, with whom the AAF would not enjoy warm relations. Northolt, RAF airfield at Ickenham, Middlesex, where they stopped to pick up their baggage is only a short distance from Uxbridge.

145. Arnold meant DERAX, the US Signal Corps' acronym for early radar, specifically direction-finding equipment.

146. Stereopticons were projectors used with a pair of photographs of the same scene to create a three-dimensional illusion for the use of photo interpreters. Arnold later installed similar equipment in his AAF office so he and visitors could get a clearer picture of the bombing successes of American airmen.

147. This officer is not otherwise identified.

148. Presque Isle is a town, northern Maine, approximately 15 miles south of the Canadian border, identified as one of the "principal terminal bases" of the North Atlantic route. Craven and Cate, vol. 1, 344.

149. The Battle of Midway, 3-5 June, was taking place between American and Japanese forces near the Pacific Island of that name while Arnold was en route back to Washington. Fearful that Japanese success in the battle would presage new threats to Hawaii and the West Coast of the United States, all AAF combat aircraft were placed on a six-hour alert and many of them were shifted from their East Coast staging bases en route to England to the West Coast. See for example the movement of the 91st Bombardment and the 1st Pursuit Groups outlined in Craven and Cate, vol. 1, 641.

150. Col A. D. Smith, commander, Eastern Sector, ATC. Arnold apparently changed his mind regarding this assignment and Brig Gen Barney McKinley Giles continued as CG, 4th Bomber Command at Hamilton Field, California, remaining in that position until he went to Washington as a major general in 1943 to become assistant to Arnold and later chief of the Air Staff.

151. Although the outcome of Midway was still in doubt, Arnold and Harriman speculated on its impact on the war and the prospective build-up of American forces in Europe. Now returning fresh from discussions in London aimed at implementing the "Europe-first" strategy, Arnold was concerned that the demands of the Pacific War and the alarm caused in the United States by the Japanese threat of Midway combined with their successful landings in the Aleutian Islands on 3 June would cause a reassessment of priorities and require reallocation instead of European-bound AAF personnel and equipment to the Pacific. A long-range result of the Battle of Midway was an "enduring debate" over types and numbers of aircraft to be produced and allocated among the various US services, theaters, and Allies. This protracted discussion would be the primary reason for Arnold's next trip abroad in September 1942.

152. PRO, Air 8/648, Slessor to Portal, 7 June 1942.

153. PRO, Air 8/647, Smuts to Churchill, 9 June 1942.

154. Arnold to Marshall, 10 June 1942, AP.

155. Arnold to Portal, 10 June 1942, AP.

156. PRO, Air 8/648, Roosevelt to Churchill, 12 June 1942; also in Kimball, vol. 1, 509.

157. PRO, Air 8/648, Churchill to Roosevelt, 13 June 1942, also in Kimball, vol. 1, 511.

158. PRO, Air 8/648, Portal to Churchill, 16 June 1942.

159. Ibid.; and Slessor, 413.

160. PRO, Air 8/1360, signed copy no. 2, 21 June 1942; and PRO, Air 8/48, Slessor to Portal, 22 June 1942.

161. Slessor, 413.

162. See for example Maj Gen M. F. Harmon, chief of the Air Staff, anticipating that the ongoing negotiations in London would result in additional aircraft for Maj Gen Lewis H. Brereton's Tenth Air Force, then in India; Harmon to Brereton, n.d., c. 25 May 1942, AP.

163. Arnold to Churchill, 10 June 1942, AP.

164. Arnold, 315; and Dwight D. Eisenhower, *The Eisenhower Diaries*, ed. Robert H. Ferrell (New York: W. W. Norton & Co., 1981), 21 May 1942, 58.

165. Craven and Cate, vol. 1, 630-31.

166. For the role of Lee and his relationship with the VIII Service Command see Craven and Cate, vol. 1, 649; and Craven and Cate, vol. 2, 602, 606. There is a copy of the specifics of the proposed 66 AAF groups entitled "Programme of Arrival of U. S. Army Air Forces in the U. K." dated 30 May 1942, in AP. It was given to Portal by Arnold on this date.

167. Arnold to Portal, Accommodations of USAAF, 30 May 1942, AP.

168. Stimson Diary, 20 January 1943.

169. Arnold to Churchill, 10 June 1941, AP; Arnold's directive to Spaatz, 28 June 1941 is in both AP and SP.

170. Quote is from Spaatz Command Diary, 11 June 1942, SP; see accounts in Richard G. Davis, *Carl A. Spaatz and the Air War in Europe* (Washington, D.C.: Center for Air Force History, 1993), 90; Parton, 166-67; and Copp, vol. 2, 259. The official history euphemistically suggests that the mission "had not been an ideal operation with which to inaugurate the American air offensive," Craven and Cate, vol. 1, 658-60. For a glimpse of Arnold's efforts in this period to find another dramatic way to attack the enemy, see his memo to the Advisory Council asking them to use their imagination and recommend additional ways to bomb the Japanese home islands following the Doolittle raid of a month earlier; Arnold to Advisory Council, 18 May 1942 and the suggestions made in their responses of 21, 27 May and 10 June, AP.

171. Beebe had been tasked the day before the group left Washington. See Arnold's Memo for Col Beebe, "Duties While in England," 22 May 1942, AP.

172. Beebe's 1 June Report to CG, AAF is in AP; PRO, Air 8/848, Portal to Arnold, 10 June 1941; and Brett to Arnold, 24 October 1941, AP. Apparently, Eaker felt that Beebe's report had considerable merit when he wrote on 16 June, "all were in agreement as to the soundness of your recommendations." See Hqs AAF in British Isles to Beebe, 16 June 1942, AP.

173. Davis, 83; and Craven and Cate, vol. 1, 632-39.

AMERICAN AIRPOWER COMES OF AGE

VOLUME 1

PHOTO SECTION

USAF photo

Henry Harley Arnold, age 13.

USAF photo

Arnold as West Point cadet, class of 1907.

USAF photo

Arnold learning to fly, 1911.

Lt Col Arnold with Beebe Daniels and Major Spaatz, March Field, 1932.

USAF photo

Lt Col Arnold, circa 1935.

USAF photo

Hap and his second Mackay Trophy.

USAF photo

Hap as the new Air Corps Chief, 1938.

Mrs. Arnold sees her husband off to England, April 1941.

Photo courtesy of National Archives

London, 1941.

Photo courtesy of National Archives

London, 1942.

Arnold receives the Distinguished Service Medal on his return from the Pacific. Adjutant General James A. Ulio reads the citation as Assistant Secretary of War Robert Lovett and Arnold's crew observe.

General H. H. Arnold, General George C. Marshall, Captain Forrest B. Royal, Admiral William D. Leahy, and Admiral Ernest J. King at a December 1943 JCS session of the Cairo Conference.

USAF photo

Arnold flanked by the US Army delegation in the shadow of the pyramids at the 1943 Cairo Conference.

Brig Gen Clayton Bissell greets Hap in Chungking, February 1943.

USAF photo

Arnold with his troops in the North African desert, 1943.

USAF photo

General Arnold with AAF air and ground crews in the western North African desert, late January 1943.

Chapter 4

South Pacific
16 September-2 October 1942

Introduction

Any satisfaction Arnold gained from his moderate success in securing a more favorable allocation of US-produced aircraft as a result of his trip to Britain in May 1942 did not last long. Following his return to Washington in the first week of June, he spent much of the remainder of the year struggling to maintain the strategic and logistical focus of JCS and AAF on the "Europe First" strategy that had been adopted in the early 1941 ABC staff conversations. This had been reaffirmed during the January 1942 Arcadia strategy meetings in Washington following Pearl Harbor and, from Hap's viewpoint, remained the emphasis of most of the political and military leaders of the two major Allied powers. Arnold's actions and impressions gained during his May–June trip to England, and his endeavors on his return, reflected his continuing belief that success in the war would most quickly and efficiently be achieved by the daylight strategic bombing of Germany. Although no American-manned heavy bomber had lifted from British soil in combat thus far, Hap eagerly and impatiently awaited the beginning of this operation to which so much unproven theory and so many resources were now committed. However, Arnold was faced with two serious challenges to this strategy before any significant number of raids by the AAF could be undertaken. The first challenge was the decision to invade North Africa in November 1942. The second was the US Marines' assault on Guadalcanal, which necessitated a reassessment of assets to that theater. These events threatened to delay if not seriously inhibit the strategic daylight bombing campaign. Consequently, it was not until 1943 that the American daylight bombing operation in Europe received a viable allocation of aircraft and support from British and American sources.

American optimism about opening a second front in Northern Europe in 1942, code-named Sledgehammer, was dimmed by Rommel's successes in the desert and a seemingly easy string of Japanese victories as their forces swept southward through and beyond the Philippines to pose a realistic threat to Australia. At the same time the British, never as enthusiastic over the prospects of a cross-Channel invasion as their American cousins, remained convinced, probably correctly in retrospect, that any ground assault in 1942 against German forces in Northern Europe was premature and would fail. The British began an effort to convince the American president that alternatives to the autumn Sledgehammer invasion and the Bolero buildup for 1943 should be considered. It became clear to Arnold as well that, regardless of how American-produced aircraft were allocated between Britain and the United States, any American bombing effort against northern Europe would be limited to a token effort during 1942. However, in view of FDR's clearly expressed desire that American forces be committed to offensive combat somewhere during 1942, Hap was determined that the strategic bombing would begin as quickly and forcefully as possible.

The coincidental arrivals of Major General Spaatz in London and Churchill in Washington on the same day elicited no notice even though their missions were not without a common thread. Spaatz was to command the US bombing effort in England, Churchill was to argue for diverting American aircraft to other endeavors. The American aviator's clear mandate was to receive, support, and lead into combat the US Eighth Air Force, Hap's primary instrument for the daylight bombing effort from English bases. Churchill's announced mission in the United States was to secure the "earliest maximum concentration of Allied war power upon the enemy."[1] In the CCS deliberations on the day after his arrival, one of Churchill's accompanying officers outlined his leader's task as the desire to discuss a "possible reorientation of combined policy."[2] As the official AAF history concluded, "In plainer English, he was not too keen" about Bolero and its Sledgehammer predecessor.[3]

After approval by the British cabinet, the conclusion that they were not willing to undertake a cross-Channel assault in 1942 was transmitted to a disappointed visiting Soviet Foreign Minister, Vyacheslav Mikhailovich Molotov.[4] While with FDR at Hyde Park in June before coming to Washington, Churchill took the opportunity to impress upon the president that an attack against German forces in North Africa should be studied as the best means short of a full second front for relieving pressure on the Soviets.[5] Such an operation, first called Gymnast and later Torch, had been discussed between the two staffs as a possibility during the January Arcadia meetings in the United States. Even though the issue had been explored further in June in Washington by the CCS with their British visitors, no clear decision was confirmed until a month after Churchill's return home. In the meantime, Eisenhower had arrived in England as the European Theater commander and was working with Spaatz towards the Sledgehammer invasion and the Bolero buildup, both of which would require air superiority as a *sine qua non* for success.

Although the decision to proceed with Torch was not confirmed until after late July meetings in London, it had in many ways been preordained by various events after the Arnold–Towers–Slessor agreement of 22 June. The fall of Tobruk to the Germans on 21 June was followed by other Allied reverses. On 27 June, Convoy PQ-17's 34 vessels were dispatched to the Barents Sea port of Murmansk, USSR. Twenty-three of the 34 ships were sunk en route, 14 of them American. These losses, combined with declining British fortunes in the desert, destroyed any slim appetite the British might have had for a cross-Channel operation. The success of Rommel's forces on 1 July near El Alamein, Egypt, only 80 miles west of Cairo, added impetus to the idea of an invasion in North Africa to relieve pressure on the hard-pressed British forces there. The fall of Sevastapol to the Germans on 2 July, hardly encouraging news to the Allies, probably contributed to the thinking that an invasion in North Africa could drain German forces from the Soviet campaign. The next day's vote in the House of Commons on a no-confidence resolution, although resolved decisively in favor of Churchill's continuation, added further political impetus to the need to avoid potentially losing endeavors.

The prime minister's continuing reluctance for the proposed cross-Channel fall invasion was reflected in his 8 July telegram to FDR that no "responsible" British senior officer could recommend the 1942 Sledgehammer operation.[6] Two days later, Marshall and King, having consulted Stimson as well as Arnold, informed the president that if the United States was to "engage in any other operation than forceful, unswerving adherence to Bolero . . . we should turn to the Pacific and strike decisively against Japan."[7] FDR rejected the Pacific idea four days later, calling it "something of a red herring." He then directed Marshall, Hopkins, and King to proceed to London with written instructions to secure agreement on "definite plans for the balance of 1942" and "tentative" ones for 1943.[8]

On their arrival, facing stiff British determination to undertake Torch, the Americans conceded the problems with Sledgehammer. By 22 July, they had generally agreed or been resigned to an invasion in North Africa. Eisenhower labeled the day Torch was decided as "the blackest day in history."[9] From Arnold's and the AAF's perspective, however, the inclusion in the deliberations of the CCS in London that a "readjustment" and "withdrawal" of 15 AAF groups from the current commitment to Bolero be made "for the purpose of furthering offensive operations in the Pacific" was precisely what Hap feared.[10] Admiral King, even before the Guadalcanal operation began on 7 August, was inclined to insist that a firm commitment for the additional air support had been made. It was not illogical that King and those responsible for defense of the Pacific area assumed that, since the Sledgehammer invasion of the European continent in 1942 had been cancelled, assets formerly committed there would be made available to areas involved in actual combat. However, in the week after his return from London, General Marshall explained to General Eisenhower that he regarded the proposed 15-group withdrawal as something "which gave us liberty of action though not necessarily to be carried out in full and no dates were mentioned." Although Admiral King and other advocates of Pacific operations interpreted this as a firm commitment, the

CCS agreement stipulated that the 15 groups were to be "over and above the . . . forces required from Bolero for operations in North and North West Africa." For the remainder of the year, King insisted repeatedly that an obligation to divert the groups to the Pacific had been made and that planning and shipping assignments had been made on that basis. Not surprisingly, Arnold immediately protested the possible diversion and insisted throughout the remainder of the year, generally supported by Marshall, that the 15-group withdrawal was not intended to be at the expense of Torch and the Bolero buildup.[11]

The decision to abandon Sledgehammer was not well received by Stimson, Marshall, Arnold, or very many others in the War Department. If the main thrust of US-British operations was to be in North Africa, it left the embryonic but potentially huge AAF assets that had already arrived, were en route, or had been programmed for England and the strategic bombardment offensive, without a clear raison d'être. Whatever force remained in England after aircraft were diverted to support Torch would lack sufficient numbers to make any meaningful impact on any daylight strategic bombing campaign. Without a clear mission for these units, they would become likely targets for dispersion to other theaters such as the Middle East and the Pacific, as had been discussed by the CCS in London. The thinking that Admiral Towers had expressed to Arnold and Churchill during their May visit to London, that manufacturing capability currently committed to heavy bombers should be converted to transport and patrol planes, would have greater credibility now that the Eighth's bombers were seemingly without a clear mandate. Also, any possible timetable for the buildup and operation of the Eighth would be upset by Torch.

Arnold, a CCS and JCS member, was not unaware of these deliberations. He wrote to Spaatz on the day Marshall and the others departed for London to negotiate with the British, apologizing for not having been able to send more airplanes to the Eighth. But, Hap pointed out, "until this whole question of what our main objective is and when we are going to tackle it [has been resolved], I don't believe it will ever be possible for us to have a definite concrete plan which we can follow."[12] He expressed some of the same sentiments to Eisenhower after the decision for Torch had been rendered, writing, "we must concentrate our air forces to secure maximum power rather than disperse them."[13] For whatever reasons, the JCS seemed uncertain, after Marshall, Hopkins, and King returned, whether a definite commitment to Torch had been made by the president. In this situation, feeling that the final decision still might be influenced, Arnold wrote to Marshall and strongly urged that the "maximum number" of AAF units be committed against Germany from British bases as soon as possible. Additionally, Arnold recommended against both reinforcing the Pacific theater until plans for Bolero/Torch became clear and holding units in mobile reserve in the United States, the implication being that they be sent to England for the strategic bombing campaign. Hap's plea was motivated in part by the 24 July CCS discussion of possible diversion of 15 groups to the Pacific. Even though the issue undoubtedly had been discussed in detail between them, it was not unusual for Arnold to put his beliefs in writing to the chief of staff and to pen Memos for the Record setting forth his thinking.[14]

In an evening session at the White House the next day, 30 July, FDR left no doubt that a decision had been made. Stating that in his role as commander in chief he had settled on Torch, the president directed that it was to be implemented as early as possible even if the "assembling of means" to support it "should take precedence over other operations" such as Bolero.[15]

The resulting gloomy mood of Arnold and other leaders in the War Department was reflected in Stimson's diary entry of 7 August. Expressing discouragement at the decision and its implications, Stimson presciently predicted that if Torch was undertaken, Bolero was "out the window" until at least 1944. Lovett and Arnold shared the secretary's sentiments and were "all very blue" about it since Torch "cut into the air force preparations terrifically." Showing Hap's influence on his thinking, Stimson wrote, "our air force which ought to be handled as a big, powerful mass with all of the flexibility of air power to be ready to be switched from one theater to the other has been split up into fragments and the prospect of a powerful mass is further off than ever." He continued almost bitterly: "The president has a happy faculty of fooling himself and this is one of the most extreme cases of it that I have ever seen because he must know that we are all against him on GYMNAST."[16]

The month of August following FDR's decision to proceed with the North Africa invasion was an important period for affecting the American strategic bombardment campaign from England. The problems included getting the Eighth into the air, establishing a separate identity from the British who continued to promote combined RAF-AAF night operations, proving that daylight bombing was viable, and fending off attempts at diversion of air units destined for Britain to support Torch or to reinforce the Pacific.

Even as preparations for the North Africa invasion proceeded, Arnold seemed determined not to be deterred from the buildup of the Eighth Air Force in England. It is logical to assume that his continued emphasis on a campaign that both FDR and Churchill had encouraged and supported was motivated strongly by the hope that early results from the AAF bombing of continental targets would not only ensure the flow of units earmarked for the Eighth but relieve pressure for assigning them to North African and Pacific operations. Eisenhower, Spaatz, and Eaker became recipients of urgent communications from Arnold suggesting, cajoling, directing, and insisting on the earliest possible maximum performance of the heavies. The tone of the messages was not always restrained but reflected in many ways the importance of the effort as perceived by Arnold as well as those on the scene in England. These exchanges, at times straining the oldest and strongest ties of Arnold with his commanders and associates, were to continue until aerial supremacy was achieved two years later.[17]

The newspapers of both countries, even in a censored environment, did not seem to be helping Arnold in his struggle to ensure the Eighth buildup. The *New York Times'* front-page story on 8 August proclaimed that the aerial attack was "not being carried on because of British-American inability to agree on methods or objectives." Spaatz' printed reply, encouraged by Arnold and given less prominence on an inside page three days later, explained that diversion of assets, bad weather, and the necessity of training inexperienced crews, rather than policy disagreements, were responsible for any delay.[18] Arnold, aware of the influence of this newspaper, later in the war provided its editor with detailed briefings and timely strike photos in hopes of favorable coverage.[19] As the time of the first combat mission loomed closer, Arnold and Spaatz attempted to make their case in the media on both sides of the Atlantic. Two days before the first mission, Arnold held a press conference in Washington labeled by the New York Times as "perhaps the most active military press conference held in Washington since the war began." He provided considerable off-the-record information and identified his major problem as that of getting airplanes to Britain. In all probability forewarned of the criticism that would appear the next day in the British press, Arnold's released text ran for more than 65 column inches in the New York Times. Covering every combat theater where AAF planes were engaged, Hap discussed each US-produced aircraft, citing its performance in contrast to enemy losses. The ratios cited were exceedingly favorable regardless of where used or flown by AAF, RAF, Soviet, or dominion pilots.[20] The following day, Peter Masefield, in the Sunday Times of London, wrote that neither the Flying Fortress nor the B-24 was suitable for daylight bombing. He hinted at failure and the tragedy of squandering American lives unless they were "adapted" for night operations and joined the nightly raids of the RAF. Masefield suggested that the American heavies were best suited for coastal patrol work and recommended that AAF bomber pilots be trained to fly at night in the proven Lancasters, which then could be manufactured in the United States.[21] The next day, Spaatz responded to a cable from Arnold and held a joint press conference with the RAF that served to announce the first mission of the Eighth flown that day and lauded appreciatively and correctly the cooperation received from the British and the RAF.[22] There seems little doubt that Masefield's importance in British journalistic circles provided him access to the thinking of the RAF leadership.

Although circumspect in their public pronouncements about the beginning American effort, there was little doubt in the RAF that the Yanks faced difficulties in their daylight efforts. There was instead a general feeling, expressed frankly among RAF personnel, that the American daylight effort would fail. This pessimism was to prevail among the civilians as well as the military and would threaten continuation of the strategic effort by American bombers until the Combined Bomber Offensive agreement was reached at Casablanca in January 1943.[23] Masefield has recorded his recollection of a meeting with Arnold held at Hap's request in the aviator's London hotel room in which the AAF chief sought to explain the problems faced by the daylight efforts and presumably gain more enlightened British press coverage of the Eighth. Although Masefield does not recall when it occurred, and Arnold failed to note it in his diaries, the meeting most probably happened during Hap's September 1943 visit covered in chapter 6.[24] These efforts were a continuation of Arnold's generally successful use of the press as well as the motion picture industry to advance his and the Army's cause of aviation.

It seemed particularly important at this time as well as later, given the decisions being made to divert strategic bombing assets elsewhere and printed doubts about the viability of daylight bombing, to respond to some of the other more publicized critics of the AAF and its strategy. A condensed version of Alexander de Seversky's widely acclaimed volume *Victory Through Air Power*, had been printed in the July issue of the *Reader's Digest*, bringing its message to a wide national readership. Declaring that the "present state of our military aeronautics is far from comforting," Seversky left no doubt that Arnold was the culprit responsible for the "woeful backwardness of our military aviation." He went on to insist that the "very people who rammed inferior equipment down their throats are still in charge" and that we need to "clean house at the top." Among his prescriptions for victory was bombing mainland Japan with aircraft like the B-19, similar to the B-29 then in the development stage. Not doubting our technological abilities, he lamented that it is "our strategic thought that lags so badly." Even Secretary Stimson attempted to counter the Seversky criticism, using among others Capt Eddie Rickenbacker whose comments on the early "successes" of the heavy bombers from England were highlighted during his appearance at the secretary's news conference of 15 October.[25]

Arnold, in a letter to Spaatz one week before the Eighth flew its first mission, expressed the urgency of beginning operations in the face of potential diversions. Hap explained that he was "gravely concerned" about the time it had taken to prepare the units for combat. Referring to the possible loss by the Eighth of temporarily idled aircraft to other claimants, Arnold wrote that the "strategic necessity for immediate or early initiation of effective, aggressive American Air Force offensive operations becomes more and more apparent here daily." Suggesting that Spaatz not fall into what Hap labeled the "McClellan error" of over caution and excessive preparation, he insisted that his commander adopt the "aggressive and offensive principles" of the Luftwaffe rather than the "apparent lethargy of our British friends."[26] Spaatz, generally candid with Hap, responded quickly that while appreciative of the difficulties Arnold faced in Washington in defending and supporting the Eighth, he wanted his chief to understand the problems involved in beginning aerial combat from nothing and from English bases. As to the McClellan comparison, Spaatz reminded his chief and old friend that there was also a Burnside, a reference to the impetuous Union officer who had been relieved twice during the same Civil War. Additionally, Spaatz and Eaker both expressed optimism to Washington and, as was typical of their communications over the next 16 months, indicated that the strategic bombing campaign would succeed if only enough aircraft and crews were made available. In August 1942, Spaatz estimated that with 200 planes the AAF could be successful in crippling the German economy and ensuring air supremacy by the spring of 1943. He optimistically wrote Arnold that the "war can be won in this Theater . . . but for God's sake keep our Air Force concentrated here."[27] This overoptimism from his commanders, in the European theater in particular, was to mark their communications with Arnold throughout the war. The result was Arnold believed and probably wanted to believe a great deal of their predictions concerning the results that could be achieved by building up the Eighth Air Force and, later, the Fifteenth for the strategic bombardment of Germany.

The first raid finally was flown by Eighth heavies as 12 B-17s were dispatched on 17 August against marshalling yards in the Rouen-Sotteville area of France. It was not an impressive performance except as a beginning since the target area, only 150 miles from London, was 300 miles from the Ruhr and almost 600 miles from Berlin. Thirty-one of the 111 airmen who took part in that first raid were killed or missing in subsequent missions. Arnold immediately forwarded Spaatz' optimistic account of the first B-17 raid to the president and informed Spaatz that news of the operation "came just at the right time" to counteract British pessimism about American aircraft. Hap indicated that Roosevelt was aware of Masefield's critical article in the *Times*.[28]

A variety of problems, foremost among them bad weather and the diversion of resources, severely limited the number of raids throughout the remainder of 1942. Only four more were flown in August, four in September, three in October, eight in November, and four in December—a total of 24 raids in the first four and one-half months of operation. Although these missions reflected the Eighth flying 1,547 sorties while losing only 32 aircraft, a loss rate of less than two percent, far smaller than anticipated, none of them had penetrated German air space and all had been escorted by RAF fighters.[29] If accurately reported by Morgenthau on 9 September, "neither Hopkins nor the President are very confident" about our efforts thus far in the air since none of the targets thus far attacked included any of the "tough cities."[30] On the other hand, Spaatz, reflecting his and Eaker's thinking about the bombardment campaign, continued to express optimism to Arnold. Spaatz' late August letter was a typical encouragement for Arnold to emphasize and defend the Eighth and its operations from England. As he insisted to Hap, the "war must be won against Germany or it is lost. The defeat of Japan, as soul-satisfying as it may be, leaves us no better off than we were on Dec. 7. The war can be lost very easily if there is a continuation of our dispersion. It can be won and very expeditiously if our effort is massed here and combines its strength with the RAF."[31] There seems little doubt that Arnold agreed with Spaatz' analysis.

Two days after the Eighth's first mission, a cross-Channel attack on Dieppe was undertaken. Involving more than 6,000 British and Canadian troops, it suggested that the cancellation of Sledgehammer had been the correct decision since more than 3,600 troops were casualties and more than 106 aircraft were lost. None of the objectives were reached and it seemed little consolation that its major accomplishment was learning the location and type of German defenses to be expected in any invasion of the continent.

As preparations proceeded for the North African invasion, Arnold's actions reflected his ambivalence towards that operation. Once it became established that Torch's air assets would be drawn primarily from those in place or en route to Britain for the Eighth and Bolero, Arnold expressed concern that not enough planes were being provided to ensure the success of Torch. Consequently, he "protested strongly" that unless the number committed to North Africa was expanded beyond the planned 675 AAF aircraft, disaster would result. In his view, an immediate increase of four additional heavy bombardment groups and four pursuit groups was required. Arnold insisted that, in view of Torch being our "first major effort," it was important that everything possible be done for it to succeed. He blamed the limited number of airplanes available for the North African invasion on the concentration of them in the South Pacific and believed that success in that theater "will not win the war." Interestingly enough, support for Arnold's position was provided by Chief of Staff Adm William D. Leahy. His penned addendum two days later to Arnold's memo suggested that all planes possible be saved for Torch and that Hap's analysis was "exactly correct." He insisted that, in the Pacific, Ghormley and MacArthur should be supplied instead with additional ground troops, "partially trained if none better are available."[32]

The air organization tasked to control the North African invasion was the Twelfth Air Force, which was established three days after the Eighth's first raid. The Twelfth was commanded by Maj Gen James H. Doolittle, the leader of the April B-25 raid against Japan. Being supplied initially with planes, crews, staff, and logistics from the assets of the Eighth, the Twelfth was logically code-named Junior. Although opposed to the operation in general and doubtful of its success, Eisenhower, Spaatz, Eaker, and Doolittle worked in harmony to ensure the best possible results. When the Twelfth departed England for North Africa, only two months after its creation, the Eighth had supplied Junior with 3,198 officers, 24,124 enlisted troops, and 1,244 aircraft. Spaatz perceptively commented on the viability of the Eighth, after the departure of the Twelfth for North Africa, "we haven't much left."[33] This in spite of Eisenhower's request to Washington for five additional heavy groups for the Eighth. Even as the Eighth was being denuded, Arnold pessimistically explained to the chief of staff that in his opinion Torch had less than a 50-50 chance of success.[34]

Hap's attitude towards the Torch invasion continued to change, however. By the end of August, he felt that the AAF should consider the North African and European theaters as a complementary, single unit—in contrast to the Pacific. The invasion of North Africa was being extensively planned beyond any prospects of it being cancelled prior to the landings 10 weeks hence. As a consequence, the Eighth and Bolero aircraft and crews being drained for Torch were expected to redeploy to England once that operation was completed. The remaining units, then combat veterans, would join in the ongoing strategic bombardment campaign and Operation Roundup, the full-fledged invasion of France later termed Overlord. Evidence of this thinking were the letters written by the new chief of the air staff, Maj Gen George E. Stratemeyer, clearly operating as a surrogate for Arnold, to senior officers in Europe alarming them about increased diversions of aircraft units to the Pacific. They were asked to "bombard" the War Department with messages to Marshall signed by Eisenhower, Patton, and Spaatz. The thrust of their communications was to be that the "bombing offensive against Germany must be intensified to the limit of our capability" and under no circumstances "should we permit diversion of forces" except for the "most urgent security measures elsewhere." The picture that was painted was that continual pressure was being brought to bear "to send more and more air strength to numerous and indecisive areas," obviously referring to the Pacific, and that these diversions would succeed "only at the expense of . . . the European-African theater." These other requests for AAF assets could best be countered by "specific demands" by those officers in the theater directly responsible for the success of the North Africa invasion. In a thinly veiled reference to the Navy and its pressures, the contrast was made that whereas "we" were inclined to "scale down" our requirements, the needs of others "are not so modestly presented." The situation was presented as one of "urgency" in view of the planned diversion of another heavy group to the Pacific prior to 10 September. The officers responded quickly as Stratemeyer had requested.[35]

If the diversion of assets to Torch was a major problem in establishing the strategic bomber offensive from English bases, the request for increased numbers of aircraft to be furnished in support of the Pacific and other operations was equally challenging. Even though the attack on Pearl Harbor had produced a strong public outcry for action against Japan, the Arcadia meetings in Washington immediately following the US entrance into the war reaffirmed the strategy that had been agreed upon nine months earlier in the ABC conversations. The 31 December 1941 Arcadia statement reaffirmed the thinking that Germany "is still the prime enemy and her defeat is the key to victory." Further, it was agreed that only "the minimum of force necessary for the safeguarding of vital interests in other theaters should be diverted from operations against Germany."[36] Quantifying the subjective phrase "minimum of force" and prescribing how to safeguard "vital interests" remained difficult problems through much of the war.

During the early part of 1942, Japanese successes in the Pacific and the seeming lack of any clear plan of offensive operations against Germany, other than the AAF strategic bombardment campaign, provided compelling arguments for sending a larger portion of the limited US military assets to the Pacific. For most of the year, the distribution of resources between these two main theaters was done on an ad hoc basis, the most serious limitations being the lack of shipping and the lack of airplanes. As a historian of the Joint Chiefs of Staff in the Pacific has observed however, "it was aircraft for which the cries were the loudest."[37] Not only were there insufficient planes being produced to meet worldwide commitments, a problem faced by Arnold before the commencement of these diaries, but it became a serious question of where, when, what types, and in what quantity to position the limited aircraft that were available.

It appeared to Arnold and many Army and AAF leaders that the United States Navy, particularly but not only its leader Adm Ernest J. King, had never really accepted the "Europe first" strategy of the Allies. Combined with this view was Arnold's perception of a hostility exhibited by the Navy, and specifically by the admiral, towards the AAF as an institution and Arnold as an individual. Hap had been well aware of the competition between the two services since his days at Rockwell Field in 1923, where he had shared responsibility for joint operation of the base with the Navy in the aftermath of the Mitchell bombing trials. The arguments were over prestige, roles, and missions, which translated into assets to be allocated by a parsimonious Congress following White House budget submissions.

King had spoken publicly against any increased Air Corps role as early as 1935, although his reputation as an aviator was hardly enviable. He had reluctantly gone to flight school as a captain at the age of 48 and, after soloing at Pensacola, "never again flew alone." His biographer has described his flying as "erratic" and the commander of a squadron King flew with asked him "whether you know enough to be scared."[38] King's personal animus towards Arnold was expressed by his comments that Arnold "didn't know what he was talking about" and that Hap was a "yes man for Marshall."[39] Eisenhower, whose position in OPD required considerable interface with the Navy, observed that King was "an arbitrary stubborn type" and the "antithesis of cooperation, a deliberately rude person, which means he's a mental bully." A British observer of JCS and CCS meetings has commented that King rarely addressed Arnold directly in these gatherings, opting instead to ignore Hap while directing his comments about air matters to Marshall.[40] King reserved the few courtesies in his life for women to whom he was not married.

Other naval officers also exhibited hostility. For example, Rear Adm Ghormley, the senior American officer in Britain and known in Navy circles as a "King man," had been reluctant to allow AAF representation on the US Special Observer Corps he headed. Arnold's plea that such an arrangement would parallel the established British structure, and would acknowledge the critical role air had played in both Hitler's successes on the continent and RAF's success in preventing a German invasion of England, fell on deaf ears. Arnold would encounter Ghormley's hostility again on this trip to the Pacific.

Few commanders struggling with inadequate resources against seemingly relentless foes in the combat areas of 1942 had the luxury of contemplating in any detail the "Europe First" strategy that had been fashioned by their leadership. Fighting to stay alive and achieve their assigned objectives, the officers sought the maximum of men, planes, ships, and logistical support from higher headquarters. In the Pacific, for example, four different requests for airplanes were received in February by the CCS; none could be met in full without taking from other commitments.[41] Bombers, given their range and potential lethality, were the most often requested aircraft. Yet 308 of the 628 bombers produced in the United States that month were given to the British (who were not heavily engaged in the air in the Pacific), 155 went to other nations, and 170, or 37 percent, were provided to US forces.[42] During the first eight months of the year, requests for aircraft and crews from US assets reached Arnold from Roosevelt, the secretary of war, the Army chief of staff, the CCS, the JCS, Churchill, Portal, and individual commanders where Allied forces were engaged in combat. In the first eight months of 1942, requests were made for AAF planes to be dispatched to the Philippines, Middle East, Panama, Galapagos Islands, the Soviet Union, China, Egypt, Alaska, India, New Guinea, New Caledonia, New Hebrides, Hawaii, Fiji, Burma, Australia, South Africa, New Zealand, Ireland, North Africa, and the North Atlantic. The most persistent requests came from the Pacific, where Japanese successes continued to threaten not only the lines of supply and communications between the United States and Australia but Australia itself. Requests were also made for troops, ships, munitions, and logistical support, but aircraft appeared to dominate the list of items requested.

Even after the fall of the Philippines and the Dutch East Indies, and Japanese gains in New Guinea, Arnold and the Army continued to emphasize the Europe First guidelines. Arnold felt they had been clarified again by the president as recently as 6 May when divergent JCS views concerning aircraft to be deployed either to Europe or to the Pacific were presented to him. FDR had responded with the terse "I do not want 'Bolero' slowed down." Roosevelt indicated that the assets to be sent to the Pacific were "a sufficient number of heavy and medium bombers and pursuit planes in order to maintain the present objective there at a maximum."[43] Obviously, the problem would be in translating "sufficient number" and "maximum" into actual airplanes and crews.

While the United States was mobilizing in earnest and preparing to manufacture vast quantities of aircraft, ships, and weapons, and to train tens of thousands of military personnel to operate them, the means most readily available to strike Germany remained, in the eyes of the Army, the heavy bombardment initiative. Many factors favored this strategy, among them a comparatively safe base of operations in an industrialized nation that was also an ally engaged in the same strategy and from whom much was to be learned. Additionally, there were weapons and trained aviators in being, along with ardent theorists who proclaimed that, if successful, the heavy bombardment strategy might invalidate the need for a massive and costly invasion of the heavily defended European continent. Additionally, bombardment's trumpeted pinpoint targeting of military objectives appeared to make it more palatable to an American public that maintained, at least this early in the war, a distaste for the bombing of "undefended" cities. Also, bombardment was presented as a quicker and more humane way to end the conflict than the carnage and stalemate of the previous war's trench fighting. The AAF clearly welcomed this strategy, not only in view of Arnold's belief in the efficacy of strategic bombardment, but as a raison d'être for an Army air arm whose use had been limited to tactical battlefield support of ground forces. Some AAF leaders, although Arnold does not seem to have drunk very deeply of this elixir, felt that a successful strategic bombardment campaign could in and of itself force the collapse of Germany. The appeal of such a panacea had been embraced by many, including FDR and Churchill, at least prior to Pearl Harbor.

Believing that Germany was by far the strongest and most difficult enemy, Marshall and Arnold often pointed out that the defeat of Japan, however desirable, would not result in the destruction of German power. They had doubts that the Russian resistance, which was now being severely tested before Sevastapol and Stalingrad, could continue without immediate relief. They further appreciated that the defeat of the Soviets would present a much more difficult task than Japanese advances for eventual Allied success. In the thinking of many Army and AAF leaders, the alarming movements of the Japanese, as long as the lines of communication between the United States and Australia were maintained, would not be as difficult to reverse or overcome as success of the Germans in the Soviet Union and the Middle East. Even after Sledgehammer had been abandoned for 1942, planning continued for the Bolero buildup and the Roundup invasion of Europe, now anticipated in April 1943. But these would be possible only after the Allies had gained air superiority and destroyed or seriously inhibited Germany's industrial capabilities. While amassing sufficient strength and resources to accomplish these aims, aerial attacks against northern Europe seemed the most efficient use of available assets consistent with the agreed-upon overall strategy.

The Navy, on the other hand, believed it was essential to limit southward Japanese expansion and, if opportunities developed, to attack the enemy's newly acquired possessions, thereby limiting consolidation of the gains made by Japanese forces in the early months of the war. Navy leaders were concerned about further Japanese movement, particularly to the south and west into Australia and India. Given the distances, the terrain, and the need for support facilities that inhibited the deployment of large land forces, the Navy understood that their ships, along with Marine amphibious forces and Navy and AAF air, had to be the main instruments for success. With their power weakened as a result of Pearl Harbor and the corresponding need to husband their remaining resources, the Navy looked to increased AAF support—particularly the mobile heavy bomber. Among the most telling of the Navy arguments was that, except in North Africa and the North Atlantic, there was little immediate threat by the Germans to the British-American cause since the bulk of the Wehrmacht and Luftwaffe were committed to the Soviet front. This reasoning, articulated increasingly in 1942, would be repeated to Arnold by most of the senior naval officers he met during this trip to the Pacific, along with MacArthur. They argued that Allied forces in the Pacific faced fierce Japanese fighting every day and required reinforcement now. This view, voiced by the Navy and echoed by other Allied units in the Pacific, demanded that immediate additional assets be committed to the ongoing fighting in the Pacific instead of being stockpiled for Sledgehammer, Bolero, and Roundup. This line of reasoning was difficult to refute when lives were being lost due to inadequate resources. Another compelling plea that Arnold and Marshall heard with some consistency was that the dynamics of war required a frequent reassessment and reconsideration of priorities. As the official AAF history has explained, the cancellation of Sledgehammer "opened the way for the Navy . . . to ask for a review of priorities heretofore based on the assumption that Western Europe must be invaded at the earliest possible moment."[44] These arguments stimulated Arnold to spur the Eighth's heavy bombers into action from English bases as quickly as possible.

The Army agreed with the Navy that the 4,500-mile line of supply and communications between Hawaii and Australia had to be kept open. The question of whether the cost in troops, airplanes, ships, and supplies was too high in terms of sacrificing the agreed-upon European strategy and the denial of assets to other theaters was occasionally debated. The US Navy, accustomed to a succession of replenishment bases for its fleet, desired sufficient aircraft and support facilities to be stationed in each of the bases along that line, not only as protection while the fleet was absent but also as launching points for attacks on existing Japanese holdings. Their desideratum included both short-range and long-range aircraft. The former, pursuit planes and medium bombers, were to be operated in local defense while the latter consisted of heavy bombers capable of long-range operations. The AAF, given its aim of providing the bulk of its heavy bombers to England for the strategic bombardment campaign against Germany, believed in concentrating its heavies at two bases along the chain—Hawaii and Australia—rather than allocate them piecemeal throughout the string of bases. From these locations, it was argued, the mobile forces would be capable of rapidly responding within one day's flight to any trouble spot and would be the most efficient use of the limited number of planes available. Consistent with this thinking was the dispatch of the B-17-equipped 43d Bomb Group in February 1942 from their base at Bangor, Maine, to Sydney, Australia, traveling via Capetown, South Africa.[45]

The AAF conceded that its disposition of forces would not permit immediate defense of individual islands against raiding parties but argued that it could concentrate Army aircraft when necessary to oppose an enemy landing force. The Navy took serious issue with this strategy: "Exclusive reliance on long-range aircraft from Hawaii and Australia to meet needs for the defense of intervening communications will jeopardize the safety of these communications and of the forces overseas which depend on them."[46] Other differences separated the Navy and the AAF in terms of use. The AAF's concept of strategic bombardment, yet to be tested over European skies, relied on large formations that warranted fighter escort even though this assistance was not considered vitally important at this stage of the war. Their massed numbers offered concentrated firepower against enemy fighters while relying on large bomb patterns to destroy ground targets.

In the Pacific, individual aircraft, Navy or AAF, produced single or very small bomb patterns, required successful individual navigation, and generally lacked fighter support over the long water expanses. This necessitated different crew training, equipment, and operating techniques between the two theaters. As of early May 1942, the AAF counted 2,005 US airplanes in the Pacific and 374 from New Zealand for a total of 2,379. Even considering the vast distances involved, they were deemed sufficient by the Army to provide a "minimum of force necessary for the safeguarding of vital interests."[47]

During the month of March, as Axis successes continued, there was an increase in requests for airplanes from many quarters. Rommel's continuing eastern push in the North African desert resulted in at least three communiqués to the United States from the British for immediate support there. In one, Portal asked for three light bombardment and two pursuit groups.[48] On 6 March, Stimson urged Arnold to increase the speed of the proposed strategic buildup in England and requested a timetable for the transfer of bombers there.[49] Two weeks later, having just returned from an inspection trip to Panama, Stimson strongly suggested that Arnold speed up the arrival of B-24 bombers to that theater. Hap was able to locate 17 of them for deployment but explained that their dispatch would not "leave many reserves" in the United States.[50] MacArthur's arrival in Australia on 17 March added a strident voice for additional military resources to be committed to the Pacific area, particularly after he was appointed commander of the Southwest Pacific area and proposed a strategy to attack Japanese positions rather than defend Australia.[51] Yet Arnold had to have been encouraged by the decision by the Joint Chiefs on 16 March that it was preferable to "begin to build up in the United Kingdom (UK) forces intended for offense at the earliest practicable time" and to "provide forces in the South Pacific area in accordance with current commitments."[52]

However phrased, these words could not mask the considerable dilemma of where critically short airplanes were to be sent. On 29 March, Churchill cabled FDR to ask for "even a hundred American bombers" to be expedited into action over the continent from English bases.[53] That same day, Admiral King wrote Marshall that it would be "impossible to hold our position in the Pacific" without reinforcement of air units. He requested dispatch of an additional heavy bomb group and suggested that units earmarked for that area be speeded up, "even given priority over movements to Europe, the Indian Ocean, and the Middle East." The Army turned down the Navy's request, noting that the invasion plans for Europe were scheduled to "absorb all available forces."[54] The disagreements about the deployment of AAF aircraft to separate theaters could not be illustrated more strikingly than by these two separate requests made on the same day.

In the first week of April, in response to a query from Roosevelt as to the strength of defenses in New Caledonia and Fiji, the Navy asked for two groups of heavy bombers, two of mediums, one of dive bombers, three-plus groups of pursuits, two of observations, and four additional squadrons of patrol and scout observation aircraft. The Army response, coordinated with Arnold, while acknowledging the inadequacies in aircraft in those areas, declared that the demand for aircraft elsewhere justified any risk involved.[55] Arnold continued throughout the period to oppose the dispatch of any additional units to the Pacific beyond those that had already been committed.[56] Nevertheless, the question of proper allocation consistent with the overall strategic emphasis as well as the realities of combat continued to be debated in the JCS, the CCS, and the White House throughout most of this period.

Arnold not only had to seek a more equitable distribution from US production by reducing the British allocation but also to evaluate conflicting demands on where AAF planes were to be located, when, in what numbers, and how used. Army and Navy planners' disagreement on the numbers of aircraft necessary for the South Pacific islands by late April showed these considerable differences in their estimates: JCS 267, AAF 194, Navy 367, War Department Plans Department (OPD) 156.[57] Even after US Navy successes at the battles of Coral Sea in May and Midway in early June, uncertainty as to Japanese intentions prompted increased requests for assets in the Pacific. After the battle of the Coral Sea, plans were underway to reinforce the air units on Fiji and New Caledonia.[58] Oftentimes, these requests were accompanied by Navy estimates that their current positions could not be maintained without reinforcement and that the additional units should be sent even at the expense of any European commitments. On 24 May 1942, the day after Arnold had departed for London on the trip covered in chapter 3, Admiral King recommended to the CCS immediate transfer of some naval units in the Atlantic to the Pacific. Further, he urged that the movement of air forces to the Pacific "should be given priority 'even over Bolero.'"[59] General Marshall, who was also absent from the Pentagon at the time of King's submission to the CCS, replied on his return that dispatch of air units to the Pacific had already been accelerated and other units had been redeployed, but that there were not enough aircraft available to meet the current Navy suggestions.[60]

On 2 July, the JCS authorized the Navy to invade the Solomons. The invasion's aim was to prevent further Japanese expansion but its authorization did not improve the aircraft allocation problem. That same day, the position of Commanding General, Army Forces, South Pacific Area, was established and the JCS directed that two mobile air forces be created, one in Hawaii and one in Australia. Each would contain at least one heavy bomber group and the operation of each would be under the direction of the JCS.[61] The 19th Bombardment Group, although battle-weary from fighting from the Philippines through Java to Australia, became the Mobile Air Force, Southwest Pacific, with headquarters in Australia. The 11th Bombardment Group was the Mobile Air Force, Central Pacific, with headquarters at Espiritu Santo in the New Hebrides. They would be joined by the 43d Bombardment Group, which was then operating from Australia but would move to Port Moresby in mid September. All were equipped with B-17s.

Marshall's continuing appreciation for the role of air, particularly given the extant problems over aircraft allocation and his willingness to use qualified AAF officers in senior positions, led him to name Maj Gen Millard F. "Miff" Harmon as the new Army leader in the Pacific. Five years behind Arnold at West Point, Harmon had learned to fly during World War I, served in combat in France, and commanded units under Hap in the First Wing on the West Coast during the 1930s. His assignment since January had been as chief of the air staff in

Washington, a post that gave him a close overall view of AAF's worldwide problems including the many demands for more aircraft. Leaving immediately for his new responsibilities, Harmon reached his headquarters at Noumea, New Caledonia, on 28 July. His instructions, carefully crafted by Marshall, directed that he was to be subordinate to the navy commander in the area, Vice Adm Robert Ghormley, commander South Pacific (COMSOPAC), whom he was to assist in planning for the use of Army forces. He was also directed to make an assessment of his new command and submit an estimate of the Army forces necessary in the area. Most important from the AAF's and Arnold's viewpoints were his orders that, at least for the moment, "operations in the Pacific were to be restricted to those necessary to support the strategic defensive, and that requirements . . . were to be held to a minimum consistent with that role." These instructions could not have stated the Army/AAF position more clearly.[62]

Given the imminence of the Guadalcanal invasion scheduled for 10 days after his arrival, Harmon moved quickly. He learned that his existing air assets consisted of two heavy bombardment groups, two medium bombardment groups, one light bombardment group, and three fighter groups. In addition, two transport squadrons and one photo squadron were available. These bases were manned by a total of 1,602 officers and 18,116 enlisted men.[63] This was not necessarily an awesome force, given the distances involved, nor did possession of an aircraft necessarily equate to its operational utility or readiness.[64] If Arnold anticipated that Harmon, having been privy while in Washington to the many demands for aircraft and crews from all over the world, would be reluctant to press the case for assets for his new command, Hap was badly mistaken. After assuming command and assessing the needs as well as the responsibilities of his organization, Harmon joined the chorus of those pleading for additional aircraft and crews, clearly to Arnold's annoyance.[65] Only two days after arriving in Noumea, Harmon, presumably impressed by the vast distances involved in his new command, requested a complete C-47 squadron, three B-24 aircraft, and basic trainer airplanes, the last for local travel.[66] His estimate of the additional forces needed, which was forwarded five days later, included two full infantry divisions plus more infantry and artillery units. For his air strength, the new commander indicated that he needed 12 additional squadrons, six of them fighters including three scarce P-38s, along with six bombardment squadrons. Admiral King, clearly pleased by the airman's report, indicated to General Marshall that Harmon's estimates were "approximately what he himself estimated."[67] The new AAF Pacific leader reiterated these needs the next day to the War Department.[68] Commensurate with his responsibilities, Harmon continued throughout the next month to plead for additional assets, air and ground, measuring his requests against what he felt the circumstances demanded rather than what he knew was possible. As the official AAF history observed, "while . . . in Washington, General Harmon had been a member of those councils which determined the direction and flow of the Army's air units; now he was at the other end of the line—and it was by no means the main line."[69]

Two days later, US Marines invaded Guadalcanal. Given the fierce Japanese opposition and the fact that American success was in doubt for the next three months, it was not surprising that during the early weeks "the War Department was bombarded with requests from the Pacific, particularly for more aircraft."[70] Only two days after the operation began, the Navy suffered one of its worst defeats ever when four cruisers (three of them American) were sunk, another was damaged, and two destroyers were damaged in night action at Savo Island. Within a week, the Japanese landed at Buna on New Guinea, took control over the passes on the Kokoda trail, and moved to threaten the Allied base and airfield at Port Moresby, a distant base of support for Guadalcanal. In many ways, these losses influenced American naval strategy through the early months of the operation. Given its early defeats, the Navy was reluctant to commit more of its remaining ships, both combatant and support, and clamored for long-range patrol bombers along with assistance in preventing Japanese reinforcements reaching Guadalcanal or New Guinea. Japanese naval surface superiority at night seriously inhibited the ability of the Navy to resupply the Marines on Guadalcanal. To the AAF, a nonexistent supply system and the lack of a usable all-weather runway limited operations from Henderson Field on Guadalcanal, particularly for bombers for which requests were the most frequent. The AAF fighters operating in the area lacked range and, more important, could not effectively compete in air combat with the Japanese aircraft. Consequently, numerous calls went to Washington for more efficient long-range aircraft such as the scarce P-38.

The first four naval battles in the months following Savo Island were not altogether successful for either side. At one time during the campaign, the Allies had only one operational fleet carrier and one undamaged new battleship in the entire Pacific, a circumstance that increased the call for land-based air reinforcements.[71] Not until the mid-November Naval Battle of Guadalcanal did it appear fairly certain that Allied power would prevail. The Japanese then came to appreciate that they could not resupply Guadalcanal sufficiently and the argument over allocation of aircraft to that theater abated. Complete Japanese withdrawal from the island did not occur until the first week of February 1943.

However, the struggle for more assets to be sent to the Pacific instead of being sent to Europe was being played out in Washington long before the tide of bitter fighting on Guadalcanal turned in favor of the United States. Discussions in the capital between the Army and Navy illustrated the differences between the two services, centering on their seemingly incompatible strategic concepts of assets needed and how, where, what, and how many to commit. Even half a century later, the brief remaining accounts of their discussions and correspondence reflect the strong emotions and personalities involved.

The early permission, given by Marshall two days after the Guadalcanal invasion, for Harmon to divert aircraft units passing through en route to Australia and allowing the naval commander, Vice Adm Ghormley, to move any AAF units necessary within his sphere, failed to prove sufficient to the demands.[72] At the end of the second week of the heavy fighting on Guadalcanal, Admiral King and General Harmon renewed their requests for additional air assets. Five days later, Harmon reported the air situation as critical.[73] Even though Arnold may well have been viewed as dogmatic and unyielding by Harmon and the Navy for not providing more assistance, Admiral King was informed on 20 August that 90 aircraft were en route to Australia that could be diverted as Harmon or Ghormley directed. Additionally, 44 more fighters were being prepared for the Pacific, some just emerging from the modification centers.[74]

Hap continued, however, to recommend against any sizeable movement to the Pacific theater, including the 15 groups that Admiral King insisted had been promised by the CCS on the July cancellation of Sledgehammer. Arnold's arguments were summed up two days before his departure for the Pacific when he explained that there was a "lack of common understanding as to the accepted overall strategic policy of the United Nations," clearly meaning the Europe First strategy.[75] By the time of the Guadalcanal invasion, Arnold was beginning to insist that the European-North African theater was a single entity as far as air assets were concerned and hence one could not be changed without serious impact on the other. Further, supported by Marshall, he argued that the president and the prime minister had agreed on the Torch operation that had been accepted by the CCS and JCS and was now being planned for implementation within the next 10 weeks. In determining the allocation of assets for Torch as well as elsewhere, Marshall indicated that priorities adhered to "conform to those prescribed by higher authority" who in turn have given the "highest" priority to Torch. He suggested that any desire to change these priorities should be submitted to the authorities who had made the determination, clearly meaning FDR and Churchill.[76]

It is curious that Admiral King, generally moderately successful in White House dealings, did not seek to have the issue adjudicated there. In addressing the needs of the Pacific, Arnold articulated that the only available additional aircraft for deployment had to come from "theaters where the war can be won." Reallocation of assets would, he felt, result in their being furnished to areas where success would make no significant contribution to winning the war. On the other hand,

Arnold argued, the war could be lost if Torch and Bolero failed. In fact, Arnold viewed the results of moving more aircraft to the Pacific during the first week of the Guadalcanal invasion as "very, very grave" and suggested to Marshall that we "should be moving planes from the Pacific to the North African and European theaters."[77] As Arnold lamented in a memo at the time, "None seems to think in terms of winning the war. All seem to think in terms of meeting the easier enemy first."[78] Hap confirmed this message to his staff, enjoining them to instruct commanders in "minor" theaters of their need to exist with a minimum of assets so that an "overwhelming number" of aircraft would be available in the major theaters such as Europe and North Africa. As he directed the staff, "we have an education job as well as an allocation job."[79] Further, even if assets were diverted from the planned North African invasion, Arnold felt they could be employed more productively in Europe than on the periphery of the Japanese empire since Germany's vital industries and sinews of war were within reach of Allied bombers whereas those of the Japanese remained beyond the bombers' range. In expressing his concern about the success of Torch, which he gave less than a 50-50 chance of success even with the air assets planned, Hap insisted that the German Air Force not be allowed to divert its strength to North Africa. He recommended that German airpower be kept occupied by Allied aircraft based in the United Kingdom.[80]

In discussing the tactical employment of air, Arnold insisted that there were sufficient planes in the Pacific. Their success, he argued, depended on proper placement, use, and logistical support, the last being the responsibility of the Navy. To demands that the airfields be saturated, Arnold repeatedly asked what the saturation point was. He insisted it was wrong to have aircraft sitting idly on Pacific islands when they could be employed productively elsewhere, an argument that was turned against him concerning the desultory operations of the Eighth in England. Arnold concluded, erroneously in the judgment and experience of those using the airplane, that the existing AAF P-400 pursuits in the Pacific were the equal of their Japanese opposition. Hence there was little need to accede to the requests for the P-38, the scarce, most modern, very successful, long-range, high-altitude plane. Given their shortage, Arnold further resisted sending more of them to the Pacific since it was the only plane capable of being flown from the United States to the European-North African theater and was then judged as the US pursuit aircraft best capable of operating against the Luftwaffe. As Arnold summarized his views at the end of the first month of the Guadalcanal fighting, that operation has "put us in a very tight spot." However Hap felt it was necessary "that we do what we can to insure its success," stressing that he was "doing everything within my power" without weakening the European effort.[81]

Admiral King, who continued to lead the Navy's struggle for more air assets to be sent to the Pacific, argued that the allocation of the 15 groups "promised" to be diverted from Sledgehammer had become an integral part of the planned assets for the Pacific. He emphasized that the Guadalcanal invasion was not only the first step towards halting the Japanese but was the first offensive operation against them. Its failure, he said, would be a significant blow to American prestige. In what was the most difficult argument to be refuted by the Army, he continued to stress that the Bolero buildup had resulted in no combat missions having been flown prior to 17 August. Even after the first mission of the Eighth on 17 August, the few raids that were flown elicited the logic that these aircraft could be used every day in combat in the Pacific. Further, the admiral pointed out that the implementation of Torch was more than 90 days away and support for that operation could be built up. This was, he argued, in direct contrast with the immediate desperate fighting and loss of lives being experienced in the Pacific. He insisted that the Guadalcanal invasion proved the need for reallocation of forces and reassessment of strategy when circumstances changed.[82]

In the early September discussions, King continued to insist that the 24 July CCS agreement to furnish the 15 groups from Bolero to the Pacific represented a definite commitment. He had to have been disappointed that Marshall expressed a contrary viewpoint in unclear language, explaining that the understanding "had been recorded only as an agreement for the transfer of planes from one jurisdiction to another." Given the difficult situation in Guadalcanal by early September, it was of little consolation that Marshall offered, "once commitments to Torch and possibly the Middle East had been fulfilled [allocations] should be made in accordance with strategic necessity as the planes became available." When pressed for what the priorities would then be, the Army chief of staff indicated his continuing belief in the strategic bombardment campaign, insisting that it would cause German losses of aircraft production along with "diverting" aircraft from the Eastern Front. This use "gives the greatest return for the investment of forces."[83] This support of Arnold's position offered scant hope for the hard-pressed forces in the Pacific to persuade the Army leadership in Washington.

The argument was continued when the Navy proposed that the need for fighter aircraft in the Pacific was great enough to justify their being taken from Torch and the Middle East. Arnold then discovered a newfound enthusiasm for the North African invasion, stating that the strategic bombardment offensive and the Middle East campaign were complementary to Torch, which was to be "the beginning of the offensive against Germany."[84]

Neither side in the Washington discussions restricted their arguments to abstract strategic considerations. King's points were buttressed by the pleas of the Pacific admirals supported by the Army leadership serving there, both air and ground generals, including a gloom and doom assessment from MacArthur.[85] Navy undersecretary James R. Forrestal's assessment, based on a recent trip to the Pacific theater, was provided to the White House and brought into the discussions. King also introduced the most recent analysis of Adm Chester Nimitz, Commander in Chief, Pacific Ocean, who had met with King and Forrestal in California on 7, 8, and 9 September.[86] Arnold countered with the letters that Stratemeyer had solicited, almost surely at Arnold's direction, and had been sent to the War Department and Marshall from Eisenhower, Spaatz, Eaker, Patton, and Mark Clark. These were all in agreement concerning the critical nature of the air assets to be retained in England for the strategic bombardment initiative and the necessity for the maximum assignment of planes for the success of Torch. Eisenhower specifically requested 10 bomber groups and five fighter groups be maintained in the UK by 15 October, increasing to 20 heavy bomber groups, 10 medium groups, and 10 fighter groups there by 1 January 1943. Arnold felt Eisenhower's comments were of such importance as to be briefed to the JCS and the president, which apparently was done.[87] Surviving accounts of these deliberations, particularly in the days immediately before Arnold's departure, leave little doubt that traditional service rivalries as well as personal antagonisms entered into the discussions.

Arnold attempted at this time to capitalize on Roosevelt's 24 August 1942 request to the chief of staff that Arnold prepare an estimate of the planes necessary for 1943 "in order to have complete air ascendancy over the enemy."[88] As a result, the AAF produced Air War Plans Division-42 (AWPD-42), another blueprint for fighting the war from the air. Arnold immediately informed General Spaatz of the request and Brig Gen Haywood S. Hansell, one of the authors of the September 1941 AWPD-1, returned from England to prepare the new document, bringing what little data existed from the five raids already flown. Marshall appreciated that the work of the group would be "of such far reaching importance that it will probably determine whether or not we control the air."[89] Completed with little empirical data, hence like its predecessor AWPD-1 based mostly on theoretical calculations, it was completed in two weeks time and submitted on 9 September 1942. There is little doubt that it was devised in close consultation with Arnold. A major premise of AWPD-42 was that a simultaneous air offensive was not possible at the moment against both Germany and Japan. The plan assumed that the Soviet Union would be driven out of the war and that German forces would be released from that front. The numerically inferior Allied ground troops would therefore have to depend on the larger and superior Allied air effort to perform two tasks: destroy Germany's industrial base and defeat the Axis air forces. The study concluded that priority would have to be granted to aircraft production in 1943 and 1944 to support the air offensive against Germany. Thus, AAF planners ran the risk of antagonizing the Navy and the Army since such priority could be at the expense of their ships, tanks, and other armament programs. The plan proposed 2,225 AAF heavy bombers for the European theater and proclaimed that it was "perfectly feasible to conduct accurate, high-level, daylight bombing under combat conditions in the face of enemy antiaircraft and fighter opposition." The AAF would do its job through "systematic destruction of vital elements" in Germany by "precise bombing in daylight," complemented by the RAF's "mass air attacks on industrial areas at night to break down morale." No clearer statement of Arnold's concept of strategic bombardment could have been made.

The proposal went into considerable detail, estimating bomb tonnage, operating altitudes, and numbers of sorties to be flown. It predicted that, with combined RAF/AAF use of almost 4,000 heavies by January 1944, a ground invasion of the continent would be possible by that spring. Some 177 targets in seven strategic areas were identified for destruction, with highest priority given to German aircraft factories. These were followed by submarine building yards, transportation, electric, petroleum, aluminum, and rubber industries. The Navy was not pleased with AWPD-42's emphasis on Europe and the planners' rejection of that service's request for 1,250 heavy bombers for long-range use. The Navy, considerably less than satisfied with the substitution of 8,000 trainers, initially rejected the plan when it was submitted to the JCS.

Total worldwide air commitments would require production in 1943 of 63,018 combat airplanes to operate in 281 groups, 78 of them flying from the United Kingdom. The resulting estimate, including trainers and Navy aircraft, called for a total production necessary for 1943 of 139,000 airplanes, later reduced to 107,000 planes when it was discovered that the higher number could not be attained. Although rejected by Admiral King, the plan was approved by the War Department while Arnold was in the Pacific. By 15 October it had been accepted by the president who then made the production of planes in 1943 a "must" item, stating that the objective "will be given the highest priority and whatever preference is needed to insure its accomplishment." Although some negotiations resulted in dilution of the priority, the official history assessed AWPD-42 as having come "closer than any document . . . produced in AAF Headquarters to being a comprehensive bombardment plan."[90] Although Torch and the demands for supplying the Pacific threatened dispersion of the bombardment effort from England, the production goals established in AWPD-42 validated Arnold's belief in the primacy of the strategic effort over European skies for 1943. The British would agree to AWPD-42 strategy in the Strategic Bombing Offensive agreement made during, and in part because of, Hap's next trip abroad in early 1943.

Arnold's and AAF's problems were not vastly different from those faced by the rest of the Army, the Navy, and most of the civilian society during the first year of the war. The major difficulty was that the demands made on the existing resources were far greater than what was available. For example, as the planning for Torch proceeded, concern in the Army was raised about the potential efficacy of air-ground cooperation in North Africa. Development of these tactics had not been given the highest priority as Arnold and the Air Staff concentrated on the strategic bomber offensive. Although Army Field Manual (AFM) 31-35, *Aviation in Support of Ground Forces*, had been published in April 1942 before the decision was made to invade North Africa, paper promulgation of procedures was not a viable substitute for live exercises, training, and perfecting techniques in a nonlethal environment. The major impediment to exercises was the lack of airplanes, a situation that prompted Army Maj Gen Jacob L. Devers to insist, in a personal letter to Arnold on 5 September, "there is no air-ground support training. We are simply puttering. Cannot something be done?" Arnold's reply, sent to Devers while Hap was in the Pacific, summarized Hap's dilemma: "There is just so much aviation available for cooperative training in this country with the Army Ground Forces." When Stimson raised the same issue with him the day after his return, Arnold stated that the medium and light bombers necessary "were being sent to Russia and the British," leaving none for AAF-Army ground training.[91] Testing in combat, of coordination between the

American air and ground forces, was to begin only six weeks later in North Africa.

Similar to the rest of the American military's grappling with shortages in 1942 as they tried to project limited power overseas at the same time they were raising and training fighting forces, the expanding AAF needed aircraft and personnel. Arnold, having been involved in the problem for more than three years, was well aware that equipping, training, and deploying an AAF group for combat required more than airplanes. Highly trained crews were needed to operate the craft and a miniature city of technicians and support personnel were required for the Groups to function wherever assigned. The AAF was very lucky if it could produce a fighter pilot within his first year of service, and the time required for training other aircrew members and technicians was not appreciably shorter. A major problem facing all the military was projected exponential growth in 1942. The planned strength of 84 AAF Groups at the time of Pearl Harbor was increased on 7 January 1942 during the Arcadia conference, to a new expansion target of 115 Groups and 998,000 personnel—to be reached by the end of the year. This goal was superseded in July 1942 by a new one of 224 Groups and, three months later, to 273 Groups, all in need of airplanes, crews, and support personnel.[92]

The allocation discussions for the Pacific continued along seemingly irreconcilable lines until, following a particularly contentious 15 September JCS meeting, General Marshall determined that Arnold should travel to the Pacific to assess the air situation at first hand. In the meantime, major aircraft allocation changes would await his return.[93] Marshall has left no explanation for his decision to send Arnold, but the recent trip of Undersecretary of the Navy Forrestal to the Pacific and Nimitz' recent travel to California to meet with King, both providing fresh accounts of conditions at Guadalcanal, probably influenced the Chief of Staff's decision.

Arnold has left little personal comment on the prospects of making the journey but his extensive diary entry for 16 September, probably written during the long flight to California two days later, was an accurate, detailed summary of the military problem from his perspective. The preparations, which were made hastily, showed a realistic appreciation of the operational dimensions of the trip. The modified B-24 to be used was then the most suitable long-range aircraft available and its double crew would permit Hap to complete most any travel schedule, subject only to the operational limitations of the plane. He was careful to take along not only Colonel Cabell, a member of his own Advisory Council, but also a senior AAF officer then serving in the War Department's OPD, where allocation schemes would be approved. The itinerary was laid out to meet with most senior officials, many planning staffs, and operational commanders as well as to view combat operations as closely as safety would permit. He intended to visit the major headquarters of both services, but the distances involved and the limitations of the aircraft required stopping at relatively isolated islands where he could evaluate the roles and assets of these bases. As important as any other result would be the opportunity to make his own assessment of the problems and needs for air assets at many levels and locations in the theater. The 15-day journey, traveling more than 21,000 miles, and crossing 15 time zones twice in an unpressurized propeller-driven aircraft with no bunks and a normal cruising speed of 165 knots, would be a challenge for the 56-year-old aviator. But Arnold lost no time in complying with Marshall's direction, leaving Washington less than two days after the order was given.

The Diary

TRIP TO THE SOUTHWEST PACIFIC

<u>Wednesday, September 16, 1942</u> [Washington, D.C.]

Non-agreement in higher circles on two points:
   a. Limitations and capabilities of P-39 in combat.

b. Number of airplanes we should send to Southwest Pacific to help Ghormley. Re a. above, Harmon has sent in at least 2 messages in which he makes the bald statement that the P-39 (P-400) is of no use in operation in his theatre and will be used in case of extreme emergency only; that the Navy F-4-F is of much greater value and can be used; that he needs fighters of the P-38 type. All of the above in spite of the fact that the score of P-39s vs. Jap Zeros to date is 4 to 1 in favor of P-39s for last week in August, 2 to 1 for month of August, and in last combat was about 10 to 1. This in Australia.[94]

Further the performance of the P-39 is at least equal to F-4-F and in most cases superior. P-39 has better firepower, armor and tank protection, and more speed, but is not so maneuverable and can't climb as fast. Harmon was told that: P-39s were the only planes available; he was getting more of them; he could improve them by taking out about 1,500 lbs. of equipment; that MacArthur had been requested to send him some P-38s but said "none to spare." Ghormley and Nimitz both took up Harmon's battle cry and shouted to the high heavens. Every brass hat in Washington has heard the echoes.[95]

Re b. above, [Admiral] King for some time has tried to get more planes in South Pacific; tries subterfuge and cunning. Navy is trying to run a land war, relying upon Army Air and Marines to put it across, but does not want to have its battleships or cruisers meet Jap Navy or get sunk. Navy is departing from true role of operations.

Japs have a total of about 385 planes (except carriers) spread from the Celebes eastward to Solomon Islands inclusive;[96] so far not more than 2 carriers with 150 planes, total 535 planes. We have in Australia, Southwest Pacific islands and Hawaii a total of over 900 planes with 280 more en route.[97] There are only two bases from which land planes can operate against Japs in Solomons. From the Northwest to Bougainville Australia they must operate against Rabaul.[98] Ghormley now has over 200 planes. The two [Allied] bases can only handle 80 planes, balance must sit and wait at rear airdromes.

Navy wants to send in more and more planes apparently with view of making that their main theatre by employing most of our aircraft. Southwest Pacific can never be anything but minor theatre until Germany is beaten. Our policy must be to build up air strength against Germany until we break her morale, defeat her air force, destroy her industrial capacity to produce, and render immobile her transportation. Our day bombing and the British night bombing have demonstrated that we can do those things to Germany if we do not disperse all over the world.

The Air Force is now called upon to perform almost the impossible: fight in 8 different theatres and maintain aerial supremacy in all of them. In addition every theatre commander is yelling his head off for overwhelming [air] superiority. Frederick the Great's thoughts on the subject:

> Never give battle merely to beat the enemy. Your aim should be to carry out plans which would be impossible without victory. Small minds want to defend everything. Intelligent men concentrate on the main issue, parry the heavy blows and tolerate small evils to avoid a greater one. He who wants to defend everything saves nothing.

The Navy is hard-pressed at Guadalcanal. It does need a shot in the arm. It needs it badly but in my opinion the shot can best come by getting new leaders who know and understand modern warfare, men who are aggressive, who are not afraid to fight their ships, who know how to get the best out of their ships, the air, and their land support; men who will meet the Japs' ships at night or day in a way that will get the maximum effectiveness out of our fleet and outsmart the Japs. So far I am afraid that it has been the other way around.[99]

Prior to JCS meeting, Marshall said that he thought it would be a good thing if I went out to South Pacific and had a look around. Forrestal is just back and has a good story that adds to the flames.[100] I said: "O. K., perhaps it may cause me to change my mind and some of my ideas on distribution and employment of aircraft." Quite a flare-up at JCS when King asked for more planes for South Pacific. I said that planes were not what they needed; landing fields were the determining factor, not planes. All they could do with planes, more than 80 or 100, was to have them sit on landing fields and miss training, get stale, while in England they could be used against Germans every day. King said there should be a reconsideration of allocations every time there was a new, critical situation. The Navy was in a bad way now. I told him that Marshall and I had agreed to divert 15 P-38s down there and to send one squadron of heavy bombers from Hawaii. So we were helping the Navy. He, King, replied we must keep the theatre saturated. I replied: "What is the saturation point? Certainly not several hundred sitting on airdromes where they can not be used. That does no one any harm." Then it came out that I was going down there and further action would be withheld until my return.

Thursday, September 17, 1942 [Washington, D.C.]

Made arrangements to get a C-87 (B-24 made into cargo plane) out on West Coast for trip with two complete crews, so that once we start we can keep right on going. I will use my plane from Washington to Hamilton.[101]

Friday, September 18, 1942 [Washington, D.C. to San Diego, California]

Pete, Bill Streett, S. Cousins, E. McCabe[102] and I, with crew, climbed aboard my C-47 at 3:55 [A.M.]. Raining most of night. Bad spark plugs in spite of fact that plane was OK when brought to Gravelly from Bolling. Actually took off at 8:50 [A.M.], 5 hours late.

Saw Marshall yesterday and he gave some hints as to my actions which I appreciate. Here they are: "Listen, don't get mad, let the other fellow tell his story."

After we finally had the plugs changed, we flew overcast, blind and between layers and on top, en route to St. Louis. Steward doing very well.

Arrived St. Louis, [Missouri]	1:00 P.M. EST
Arrived Albuquerque, [New Mexico]	7:25 P.M. EST
Arrived San Diego, [California]	11:30 P.M. EST

Overcast and local storms all the way across the United States.

Saturday, September 19, 1942 [San Diego, Santa Ana, Long Beach, Santa Monica, California]

Met Laddon and US Army representative at Consolidated at 8:15 A.M. Made arrangements for President's visit, gave them information as to what was expected.[103]

Took off for Santa Ana at 9:30, arrived 10:00, inspected depot. Talked to commanding officer, Interceptor Command squadron.[104] Gave talk to 11,000 cadets awaiting flying instruction and getting pre-flight training. It was a most inspiring sight, a wonderful group of men. Looked over Orchestra, every man in it a star, most all get [$]20,000 a year [as pre-war civilians], no wonder it makes such a hit on the radio. Told Cousins to get Surles to come out and see it.[105]

Met Cousins' staff and gave them a short talk. Talked to his office force. All these talks by invitation and apparently well appreciated. Landed at Long Beach 11:30, met Ralph Spake.[106] He has a fine place and well-run. Airplanes come in and going out all the time, uses over 200 pilots just for ferrying; planes all over the place.

Landed at Santa Monica at 12:15, Douglas factory and field well camouflaged; cottages, streets and trees all over the factory. The [air]field looks like a city development and a lumber yard; a dummy factory and airfield where a golf course used to be.[107] Don Douglas sick in bed, went to his house with Branshaw.[108] Told them of President's visit. Made up telegram to send to Harry Hopkins outlining steps that should be taken to secure [production of] 130,000 planes next year.[109]

Lunch with Bill Henry, Rocky, Carl Cover, Branshaw and Lee Raymond re proper publicity to prevent another Seversky rampage.[110] Ice Follies in P.M.[111]

Sunday, September 20, 1942 [Santa Monica, Hamilton Field, California en route to Honolulu, Hawaii]

Took off from Santa Monica 11:20, took John Costello[112] with us to Hamilton, arrived Hamilton 1:30 P.M. Went to Pratt's house: [present] Giles, Kepner and Lotha Smith.[113] Talked over operations, supply, etc.

Trans-Pacific plane C-87 (modified B-24) awaiting us. Made arrangements for C-47 to get back to Bolling, am taking steward with me. Passenger list and double crew, also estimated schedule as follows:

Pilots	Navigators	Radio [Operators]
Major Ping	Lt. Hansman	Sgt. Fulton
Captain Elkins	Capt. Arnoldus	S/Sgt. J. Hemingway
Captain Skanall		
Major Peterson[114]		

Crew Chief	Passengers	Steward
Sgt. Rhodes	Gen. Arnold	Cpl. Canapi
	Gen Streett	
	Col. Cabell[115]	
	Lt. McCabe	

Date	From	To	Dist[ance]	[Flying]Time	Depart[ure]	Arr[ival]
9/20 (Sun)	Hamilton	Hawaii	2.130	14:00	8:30	8:00
		On the ground 3:00				
9/21 (Mon)	Hawaii	Christmas[116]	1.158	6:30	11:00	17:00
		On the ground 3:00				
9/22 (Tues)	Christmas	Fiji[117]	1.915	13:00	20:30	7:00
		On the ground 5:00				
9/22 (Tues)	Fiji	New Cal[edonia][118]	660	4:30	12:00	15:30

Took off 9:00 P.M., estimated arrival Honolulu, 13 hours. Good weather, [distance to be traveled] 2,400 miles.

<u>Monday, September 21, 1942</u> [En route to Honolulu, Hawaii to Christmas, Line Islands en route to Viti Levu, Fiji Islands]

Not bad sleeping sitting up in reclining chair. Intermittent fog and clear weather all night. Clouds at daybreak, 8:00 A.M. PST [Pacific Standard Time], we are about three hours out, one hour off our estimate.

Breakfast: glass milk, two bananas, piece of fried chicken. Passed a convoy: 11 ships, 2 destroyers, about 80 miles out. Arrived Hickam on the dot, 8:20, the Filipino steward won the landing pool.[119]

Emmons, Hale and their staffs met us (after we had been fumigated).[120] Emmons just returned from trip to South Pacific; [he] spent time with Harmon, Ghormley and MacArthur. Emmons is impressed with MacArthur's estimate of situation.

MacArthur's estimate: (according to Emmons)

(a) Japanese are concentrating in South Pacific.
(b) They can overrun Solomons at will and are going to do it.
(c) They can take New Guinea because MacArthur has not the strength to stop them.
(d) They will take Fiji.
(e) They will concentrate for a drive against Hawaii.
(f) They will take South America.
(g) The United States is in far greater danger from invasion from Japs than from Germans. Jap invasion of America is almost a certainty, by Germans almost an impossibility.
(h) Navy cannot stop Japs.
(i) Never before has power of heavy bombers been so impressive and so necessary.

Emmons heard the above and immediately returned to Hawaii. Emmons has done a wonderful job in getting in new air bases, defending them with ground troops and anti-aircraft, deploying his ground troops through islands, and making plans to meet any attack. His dummy planes are such that they fool anyone, even at short range. Most all of damage to Pearl Harbor has been corrected.[121]

Navy's use of heavy bombers at Midway was not 100% effective by any means.[122] Navy has no conception of supplies, installations and facilities required to operate land-based aircraft. Emmons agrees that war cannot be won in Pacific. We should hold Pacific strategic ports at all costs and win war against Germany.

Called on Nimitz, was in midst of meeting with his staff: Halsey, Spruance and his Chief of Staff.[123] Nimitz very optimistic as compared to Emmons. Emmons is convinced that Guadalcanal cannot be held, Nimitz is just as sure that it can.

Nimitz' idea is that:
- Japanese shipping losses are so great that they cannot keep up such operations indefinitely.
- Japs are getting worried. They will probably hold north shore of New Guinea, and try to take [Port] Moresby[124] and move southeast against Guadalcanal.
- Think that they have only about half as many men there as we have, that we can meet their move and defeat it.

- That Guadalcanal airport will be ready for use within a few days.[125]
- That Japs will move through Ellice Islands.[126]
- That the Jap losses in planes last month were terrific [at]

Guadalcanal	150
New Guinea	250
Midway	250
[total]	650 (all planes from two [Japanese] carriers lost)[127]

- That Jap planes and pilots are both of inferior quality.
- That war can be won in Pacific.
- That bombardment of Germany is of no use.
- That targets of first priority for our aviation in Australia is [sic] shipping.
- That there is no need for more aircraft in Alaska.
- That Japs have no idea of moving eastward from Kiska.[128]
- That Japs will not reinforce Kiska in either planes or ships.
- That Japs are moving everything to the southeast, planes, troops, and ships from Sumatra, Philippine Islands, Borneo and Celebes.[129]
- That his (Nimitz) losses have been very heavy in ships.
- That he told Ghormley to keep his ships in harbor at Noumea.
- That we would see the *Saratoga*, 1 battleship (probably the *North Carolina*) and 1 heavy cruiser (*Chicago*) coming into Honolulu for repairs, and we did, heavily protected by about ten destroyers; destroyers and cruisers zig-zagging all over the place.[130]

Nimitz very surprised at [my] schedule and wired ahead to McCain[131] to meet me en route. I asked him (Nimitz) for any suggestions as to my trip and gave him stopovers. He had no suggestions and told him I would see him upon return.

Arrived at Hickam and took off at 11:00 A.M., 1,100 miles to Christmas. Emmons states that MacArthur feels that Marshall has not treated him (MacArthur) as he should when MacArthur brought up Marshall.[132] Emmons also stated that MacArthur was very dramatic in putting on his show but was not in good health. MacArthur blames Brereton and Eubank for failure of air in Philippine Islands.[133] Nimitz has only a hazy idea as to location of the Japs main force but is certain that it is forming somewhere north of New Guinea, northwest of Guadalcanal, south of Truk.[134]

Landed at Christmas Island at 5:45, island about 30 miles in diameter, a coral atoll, level for large trees, 100,000 coconut trees, one shrub of mangrove type, no other trees. British representative and 22 natives there when we came,[135] now the island almost completely protected by barbed wire, machine-gun pits, emplacements for 75s and 155s, observation towers and patrols on beach. Airport with 2 runways excellent, other runways on roads. All tents and shacks camouflaged in cocoa trees, very hard to see. Roads leading to all points, small herd of cows. Only two native women on island, no liquor, but stills just starting. Everything gives one the impression of an efficient and well-regulated post. All troops relieved after six months service, although some stay over. Air unit looked very good. Lost two planes so far, one P-39 and one C-53; P-39 just disappeared on mission, C-53 would not follow radio instructions.[136] Had supper with officers, took off at 9:00 P.M., distance to Fiji 1,900 miles.

Wednesday, September 23, 1942 (should be 22d and Tuesday but is Wednesday)[137] [Viti Levu, Tonga Tabu, Fiji to Noumea, New Caledonia]

[Flying at] 8,000 feet altitude sufficient to clear practically all fronts and above all overcasts. Have passed three fronts, all fairly mild. Normal weather is broken patches of low clouds, water fairly calm. 2 hours [time] difference between Christmas and Fiji.

Crossed equator at 9:40 P.M., 90 miles south of Christmas. We landed on island of Viti Levu, Fiji, at the town of Nandi. Nandi and Narewa airports, stabilized runways,[138] headquarters Western Air Force.[139] [Consists of]

US Command	New Zealand Air Force
85 officers	32 officers
60 pilots	400 enlisted men
1,400 men	
Nandi-Narewa	
11 B-26	8 Hudson

32 P-39	3 Vincent[140]
6 B-17	
49	11

No bomber trainers, no aerial gunnery for bomber gunners, no aerial gunnery for pursuit, no bombing for over a month.

Tongatabu: 1 pursuit squadron, no gunnery, nothing but flying, can't use runway for bombers. Admiral McCain prescribes training and operations, General Beightler is in command and gives orders for operations.[141] Air Command does not have a clear-cut idea as to functions and chain of command. The commanding officer must be taken out right away: Seltzer out, Cook in.[142] Accommodations seem to be very good, small shacks used by officers and men. Inspected both fields and installations, if anything too much dispersion. They need airdrome security forces. Beightler came over and gave Bill Streett his list of requirements.

Took off 10:00 A.M. for New Caledonia, distance 660 miles. This island's population is about 20,000 Fijis and 30,000 Hindus.[143] Sugar, pineapple, almost same vegetation as Hawaii. All the islands delightfully cool.

Tongatabu: 1 pursuit squadron being wasted; no training, no shooting. We should take squadron commanding officer from Christmas. He is a good Group commanding officer.[144]

Should arrive Noumea 2:30; New Caledonia in sight. Looks like a brown, hilly island, looking much the same as Southern California hills (Plaines des Gaiacs).[145] Landing field is 180 miles north of Noumea; B-17s, B-26s and P-39s parked around iron ore run-way. Nate Twining waiting for us.[146] Took a B-17 and flew 120 miles to another airport 30 miles from city, 2 short runways.[147] General Patch waiting for us. Drove 30 miles to city in an hour and quarter.[148] Harmon up at Guadalcanal. Went to Patch's house, changed clothes and then out to Ghormley's ship, his headquarters.[149]

There were McCain, Ghormley and Callaghan[150] all waiting for me with blood in their eye[s]. Ghormley lost no time in telling me that this was his theatre and no one could tell him how to command. I took it and said that all I wanted was information. I was not trying to tell him anything about how to command. Things went smoother after that.

Ghormley is worried about logistics of operations; has 80 ships in harbor here that he can't unload. Gas and supplies at Guadalcanal very short; ships very hard to get in.[151] Fears another big Jap movement to the southeast, his Marines only holding on by a shoestring. McCain is his Air strategist. He has had experience with our pilots and uses that information to clinch his remarks. Navy has built up a theory of operations around long-range patrols from Fiji, Espiritu Santo and Canton to the northwest and west.[152] Can't hold islands if supplies cannot get in, can't get supplies in if Jap bombers come down and raid ships. Must have B-17s to send out on reconnaissance and fighters to stop bombers. However, most of the ships have been sunk by subs (I will try and confirm that).

Patch is very insistent that Navy had no plan of logistics. The Marines and Navy both would be in one hell of a fix if he had not dug into his reserve stock. Twining says that his pilots find the P-39 much superior to the P-400 and are satisfied with it. [The P-400 was a low-altitude export version of the P-39.]

McCain keeps quoting what our pilots say and reluctantly accepted the possibility that the P-39 might be OK, but wants nothing but P-38s. Take United States Army Air experiences out of McCain's talk and there is nothing left. He says little if anything about Navy planes. McCain finally admitted the possibility of using some PBYs for search operations.

Left Ghormley's flagship with everyone back on good terms. Saw Admiral Noyes who was last to leave the *Wasp*. He is sure that Ernie is OK but thinks that he is on way back to San Diego to get new equipment.[153] Back to Patch's. Admiral Darlan, Free French, saying goodbye, heading for the United States, Dakar, Fiji, Tahiti, he will not say, De Gaulle's orders.[154]

My estimate so far is that Navy has taken one hell of a beating and are now hanging on by a shoestring. Have not the logistic set-up to insure success. The Marines are very tired and will grab anything as a possible aid to give them confidence. At this writing it is B-17s and P-38s. McCain leaves tomorrow for Washington.[155]

Reports being circulated about New Guinea are bad: Australians will not fight, give way without even firing a shot;

Port Moresby may soon be taken; Japs will take over all New Guinea, etc. Radio came in from Marshall telling of a conference here between Nimitz, Ghormley, Emmons and MacArthur; by inference I am to attend.[156] That looks to me to be a fine thing but I am apprehensive over what the effects will be when MacArthur and Ghormley get together. From what I hear both have jitters.

<u>Thursday, September 24, 1942</u> [Noumea, New Caledonia]

First Nimitz, then Ghormley, finally McCain: "Your bombers are doing no good over in England; your fighters are being wasted in Europe; here is where they can be of use; here is the only place where they can get results; MacArthur may need them but we need them more than he does." The whole question revolves around: Where is this war to be won? What is our plan for winning the war? Is this not a local affair and should it not be treated as such? In any event, everyone from the Chief of Naval Operations on down should be indoctrinated with one plan for winning the war. So far everything we have seen indicates the necessity of having one theatre extending from Honolulu to Australia; one commander who can dictate an operating policy against one foe; one man who can move his forces to the place where they will be most effective; one plan for using all our forces and rotating them to be used as reinforcements and as replacements.

Two airports for landing at Noumea: (1) Plaines des Graiacs, 150 miles out of town; (2) Ton Tou Ta, much smaller, 40 miles from town.[157] (1) has long 500 [sic] [5,000] foot runways made of iron ore; everything turns red and engine cylinders get badly scored; [make] low approaches and anything can land; most of planes parked here were well-dispersed; men live in tents, no town anywhere in sight. (2) shorter runways only used for fighters and transient planes, 40 miles to town over fair road.

Noumea reminds me of New Orleans insofar as buildings and signs are concerned. Natives are black but not negros, make excellent soldiers, not spoiled. Absence of wild life although deer and wild boar are supposed to be in hills. No citrus fruits, mangoes or coconuts.

[Arnold's findings thus far]

(1) P-38s here but no way to get them from boat to flying field, too big to get over road, no docks near either field. May have to float them to point up beach where improvised airport can be used.

(2) P-39s well received by pilots and Harmon.

(3) General campaign by Navy against high altitude bombing from top to bottom although our high altitude B-17s have made plenty of hits, turned back the main drive of the Japs against Guadalcanal, and have been generally effective. Data against high altitude bombing fed to Harmon, Baldwin, Mel Maas and used by Ghormley and McCain.[158]

(4) Navy supply system on shore a joke. Army had to give Marines and Navy 20,000 pairs of shoes and tons of other items in order for operations to be as effective as they are.

(5) Navy did not give importance to either airports or gasoline, accordingly for quite some time planes had no reserve of gas at all and little for operations.

(6) Harmon and his staff realize limitations of air operations due to facilities and airports. Ghormley does not [want] and resents any questions as to his plans for use of air. McCain wants to go whole-hog for B-17s but finally admitted that half of the search load should be taken over by PBYs.

(7) Marines resentful on account of having to continue fighting; thought Army would take over.

(8) Navy's use of surface craft amateurish compared to Japs.

(9) Every time Navy tried to employ carriers in orthodox manner for covering fleet or for dive bombing support they lost a carrier.

(10) Becomes more and more apparent that until there is one command, one plan, one thinking head, we will continuously misuse and hold idle our Air Force and our Army and always have too many reserves waiting for something to happen. No area in Pacific can operate

against Japs without it having a direct effect upon all other areas. Until we do have one command small numbers of Japs in different areas will immobilize large numbers of troops and airplanes.

(11) Navy cannot handle land operations effectively. They are afraid to run ships into Guadalcanal and hold them there until the things needed for most land operations are unloaded. Heavy equipment was not unloaded at all or held over while priority was given to other less important items.

(12) The Marines' 12 [aircraft] transports doing a grand job. Make 800 miles trip into Guadalcanal and carry enough gas for return and still carry 3,000 pounds cargo. Have brought out 450 wounded.

(13) Army set-up at Caledonia OK, Patch doing an excellent job.

(14) Most bombing missions carried out at extreme range of planes, worst possible conditions for bombing accuracy.

<u>Friday, September 25, 1942</u> [Noumea, New Caledonia to Brisbane, Townsville, Australia]

Up at 3:00, breakfast at Patch['s] house, 4:15. McClain (Army),[159] Cabell, Peterson, McCabe, Streett, Arnold; Twining and Harmon kibitzing. On our way to airport 4:30, arrive airport 5:45; Marine DC-3 with ex-general manager Northwest Airways took us to our plane.[160] Off for Brisbane 7:10, distance 850 miles, arrived 12:00 noon. Kenney awaiting me.[161] Took Lockheed to an airport closer to Brisbane where MacArthur and Sutherland were awaiting.[162] Australian vegetation and cultivation reminds me of California.

Started MacArthur talking about the war, the Japs and plan for winning the war. [According to MacArthur:]

1. Japs are better fighting men than Germans.

2. Pick of Japs are in South Pacific.

3. MacArthur does not have the troops to hold Japs, only two Divisions, and those partially trained.[163] Australians are not even good militia. Navy support is nil.
4. Air has passed from below average under Brett to excellent under Kenney; Walker and Whitehead outstanding; would not exchange Air Force units for any others.[164]
5. Japs can take New Guinea at will, can take Fijis, will then control Pacific for one hundred years.
6. Japs move into Aleutians is part of the general move into Siberia.
7. Need 500 more airplanes to hold Japs. Our planes are fine, excellent. Give him any kind of combat type.
8. England can only be considered as a besieged citadel.
9. No second front can possibly be established from England.
10. Any move into North Africa is waste of effort.
11. Sufficient numbers of Air bases can never be established in England to provide air cover for second front.
12. Japs have much better coordinated team than Germans.
13. Our present cordon defense system across Pacific is as old and out-of-date as a horse and buggy.
14. Our plan should be to give more aid to Russia, put troops in there, work from interior lines against Germany and Japan.
15. We should stop building up an Army that we can't use, building tanks and autos that we can't send overseas.
16. Build up Australia as a reservoir of supplies, troops and planes, use them in any direction against Japs.

Had a wonderful lunch with Kenney and Wilson. Talked over their troubles, have memo from Kenney.[165] Kenney told of knocking down 12 Zeros as they took off, machine-gunning staff conference of Japs on porch and in Lae house,[166] burned house and killed all. Carrying first one company and then one Regiment over to Moresby, and thus making passage over mountains possible toward Buna and eventually cutting off Japs threatening Moresby.[167]

Eichelberger and Kenney.[168] Kenney has destroyed since August 2nd, with loss of only 40 of his planes, the following Jap planes: 150 in air, 175 on ground. He is a real leader and has the finest bunch of pilots I have seen. All those who were worn out and nervous wrecks are now eager to fight and withdrawing their requests to go home.[169]

Off for Townsville at 4:30 P.M.[170] Thinking it over, MacArthur's two hour talk gives me the impression of a brilliant mind, obsessed by a plan he can't carry out; frustrated, dramatic to the extreme, much more nervous than when I formerly knew him, hands twitch and tremble, shell-shocked.[171]

Arrived Townsville after dark, 8:30; moonlight, circled and landed. Met by Whitehead. Plan to take off for Port Moresby, 600 miles away at 2:30 A.M. Conferred with Whitehead staff until 10:30, then to bed.

Saturday, September 26, 1942 [Townsville, Australia to Port Moresby, New Guinea to Townsville, Australia to Espiritu Santo, New Hebrides]

Up at 1:45, breakfast at 2:00, off with several of my officers in a B-17 at 2:30. Stoddard, Hank's classmate, was co-pilot.[172] Everybody hunting a bunk, sleeping on catwalks, around ball turrets and everywhere they can find a place. Awake at 6:00, New Guinea coast at 6:30, supposed to be met by fighters, all guns manned and tested, a fine wide-awake crew. Just heard that Japs raided Darwin last night.[173]

Landed Port Moresby at 7:15, met by General Blamey, Gen. Rowell and Gen. Walker.[174] After greetings, Blamey and Rowell withdrew. We had breakfast, talked over 19th Group: war-weary; pilots experienced but indifferent; been in war since the Philippines but individualists; too many stars; know all the answers. Told Whitehead and Walker that I would find a way to either exchange Group [as a whole] or send in ten combat crews per month as replacements.[175]

Six airdromes at Port Moresby, capable of taking care of 14 squadrons. Dispersion areas and taxi-ways excellent. Most of youngsters highly pleased with planes they have to fly. Called on General Blamey. He seems highly pleased with the way things are going. Everyone else very critical of Australians and their ways of doing things. Talked to General Eichelberger, I believe that he will put some pep in the Aussies. He already has plans to go from defense to offensive. Six B-17s returned from raid on Rabaul, hit one merchant ship. Weather became quite hot by noon. Had lunch at Officer's Mess.

My impression of situation in New Guinea:

(1) If we don't take the offensive, the Japs will.
(2) We have enough troops to do it (4,000 Japs).
(3) By doing it we can secure air bases at Buna, Lae, Salamaua and operate strongly against Rabaul.
(4) If we don't, we will lose Port Moresby and south side of New Guinea and open up north shore of Australia to attack.[176]

General Blamey has no idea of attacking unless he is forced into it. Port Moresby raided by Australians, everything looted, houses torn down.

At airport at 1:00 [P.M.], took off at 1:15, fighter escort for 60 miles. One engine got rough and was feathered at 1:50.[177] Five newspaper men came to see me, I gave them a talk off the record.

An F4 (P-38) on photo mission was jumped and lost one engine, pilot continued on one engine. Took photos and then returned home and made safe landing. Weather good, blue sky, should reach Townsville at 5:15 P.M. Came in on three engines, landed 5:45 P.M. Took off 11:00 P.M. for Espiritu Santo [distance] 1,350 miles. Nineteenth Group must be returned to the States: bombing poor, no trainers, one squadron came into Port Moresby like a bunch of recruits.[178]

Sunday, September 27, 1942 [Espiritu Santo, New Hebrides to Noumea, New Caledonia]

Good trip, [clouds] low broken, scattered and covered. Espiritu Santo a very rough, ragged island almost completely covered with brush and trees, mountains slope down to shore. Landing field on level area south end of island, landed 7:15.

Met by Colonel Saunders and General Rose.[179] Field cut out of coconut palms and jungle, steel mat used for part. 18 B-17s on field, 6 more off on mission in which they hit 2 steamers. Dispersion points cut into jungle. 50 Navy planes; dive bombers, torpedo planes from carriers on field.

Saunders deserves much credit for looking after men and at same time carrying on such successful operations. Losses 12: 2 shot down; 8 lost due to bad weather, and navigation troubles; 2 lost due to running out of gas, most of them night flights. Saunders' idea is to have 4 squadrons operate from 2 runways, 2 squadrons in reserve in rear, 2 squadrons on leave and recreation. He agrees on maintenance and repair [depot] at Townsville. The more I see of these installations the more I am convinced that we must have one commander [in the Pacific theater]. Had long talk with Fitch.[180] He is a solid citizen and not too demanding. Wants more planes but not to extent of ruining other operations; very reasonable. Very necessary that we earmark replacements for definite stations. Must have different set-up for food for operating squadrons; sandwiches for crews on missions.

Took off Espiritu Santo at 11:15, normal trip to Caledonia, arrived 2:15 P.M. Will try Noumea Field.

It's the seniors who are jittery; the juniors have no doubts and are positive of the action that must be taken. Fitch is not worried about Guadalcanal. Saunders is not worried. What about Marines? Arrived at Noumea.

Nineteenth Group [to be moved] out of Australia, 1 squadron change with OTU in the United States, 1 squadron change with Hawaii. Group commanding officer [to be sent] from United States or Ramey from Hawaii.[181] Air depot for repair of aircraft [to be established] at Townsville. [Use] PBYs for search missions, Hawaii, South Pacific isles and Australia. Puddle jumpers: 20 for Australia, 24 to Harmon; Cessna: 20 to Australia.[182]

Monday, September 28, 1942 [Noumea, New Caledonia]

Australian is not a bushman, he is not a field soldier, he is nothing but a city slum dweller. The Massachusetts soldiers knew more about the New Guinea jungle in two days than the Australians in two years.

Carmichael and Connelly both available and one or the other should be available for transfer to United States in replacement for Ramey, Hawaii, or Beebe, OTU. Need two Group commanding officers. Will send Davies home, 43rd Group involved here, 19th Group above.[183]

Continuous experience indicates the effectiveness of high altitude bombing:

1. High altitude bombing permits of continuous day after day effort.
2. Our losses permit this. Navy bombing indicates losses so serious after dive-bombing that further effort is negligible after one attack. Midway: 4 [dive-bombers] back out of 44; Coral Sea, Solomons, 7.
3. In every case in which Navy has tried dive bombing it has lost a carrier.
4. When dive bombers are used in small numbers they do not get hits.
5. Low ceilings do not permit dive bombing.
6. When intercepted by Zeros dive-bombers do not get home; B-17s do get home. 10 Zeros [destroyed] for every B-17 lost. Average in South Pacific operations, 320 bombs, 34 hits on ships.

Samples [of Arnold's findings]

No ball turret. Improvised mount for hole in floor for B-26. In wrestling with gun against Zero, new gunner who took place of wounded man had jam and improvised mount failed. Gun dropped and hit Zero on ring cowl. Cowl went through tail and disintegrated. Kenney gave gunner Purple Heart and bill for gun. Gunner asked if he could return Purple Heart and get credit on cost of gun.

Sent various cables to Marshall and Stratemeyer on many subjects to clear up things here and in Australia.[184] After lunch took trip around bay in Patch's launch. Saw the *Hornet*, two antiaircraft cruisers, two heavy cruisers, destroyers and many tankers and other ships, totaling about 80.[185] Patch told me of Marines going by his headquarters making all kinds of cracks about the Army not aiding the Marines at Guadalcanal. All he needs is Navy boats.

Conference 4:30 P.M., aboard Ghormley's ship: [present] Nimitz, Ghormley, Callaghan, Turner, Arnold, Harmon, Sutherland, Kenney, Streett and Ritchie.[186] Nimitz gave outline as to reason for meeting. Ghormley told of progress of operations, probable Jap movements and Navy's future plans. Sutherland gave MacArthur's ideas. Turner talked about the Navy strategy. I talked on generalities.[187] Out of it all came:

(1) Navy is not going to help MacArthur to get to Rabaul before they do.

(2) What was started as a big offensive now is classed as a limited offensive to stop Japs from further advance.

(3) Navy and MacArthur can see no other operations than those in the Pacific; Germany does not present danger that Japs do.[188]

Returned from conference 8:30,[189] leave tomorrow for day's rest in country.

<u>Tuesday, September 29, 1942</u> [Noumea, and LaFoa, New Caledonia]

Everybody getting ready to go somewhere: Kenney and Sutherland to Brisbane; we have decided, Ping, Ritchie, Streett, Peterson, McCabe and I, to go fishing.[190] Wrote letters of commendation to Kenney and Harmon.[191] Harmon and Patch had to go and meet Nimitz. Took off in cars at 11:00 A.M., dropped baggage at plane, then on to LaFoa. Met by General Sebree.[192]

Lunch, trip through troop concentration area and across Island. Pass 5,000 feet, jungle thick, very few local animals, few orchids, coffee and plenty of cattle, all well-fed. Back to LaFoa by 7:00. Met Patch and Harmon at Hotel, excellent food, French proprietress.[193] Heard instructions to Colonel Fuller [sic] who will command task force to reinforce Marines at Guadalcanal. Gave him my best wishes.[194] On to bed.

Wednesday, September 30, 1942 [New Caledonia to Canton, Phoenix Islands]

Weather here delightfully cool. So different from Caribbean which has same latitude. Major Ashwell in charge of the Caledonia Guada-Espiritu ferry service for the Marines.[195] [They use a] C-47, 32,400 lbs. gross weight; 1,600 gallons [of] gas, crew 5; [runs from] New Caledonia (Talati) to Guadalcanal to Buttons to Roses to Efate to New Caledonia.[196]

Up at 5:00, breakfast; off at 5:40 for fishing, at dock 6:00, stuck on bar 6:20-7:00. Fishing in back of reef (reef goes practically all way around island). Catch: 60 lb. cod, Patch; 40 lb. cod, Sebree; 24 lb. king, Pete; 12 lb. sea salmon, Hap; 10 lb. barracuda, Ping; 10 lb. barracuda, McCabe. Back to dock 12:30, Hotel for lunch 1:15, to airport at 4:00, take off 5:00. Patch and Harmon there to see us off, Cabell returned from Guadalcanal. All Marines wanted to know when Army was going to relieve them. Understood that they were to be there for a few days only, then to be relieved.[197]

Transport arrived at dock while Marine battalion was fighting it out with 1,000 Japs. Sent out a second battalion to relieve the first battalion but because ships will not stay at dock, danger of being sunk, called second battalion back; it stacked arms and unloaded ship. Commanding officer had to make decision, aid to first battalion or get supplies. Gasoline at Cactus determining factor, can't operate B-17s until situation is corrected.[198]

Although Navy expected Army to support their operations with B-17s the landing field was the last thing they fixed up. Guadalcanal now has two radars operating, gives 25 minutes advance warning of approaching aircraft. Two new runways being developed. Raids on Cactus and concentration of ships seems to point toward a determined move on part of Japs. But where?

Wednesday September 30, 1942 Repeat. The same day over. [Canton, Phoenix Islands to Honolulu, Hawaii]

Went through a couple of fronts but otherwise a broken cloud condition almost continuously. Navigator did a good job, hit Canton right on the nose. Landed at 6:45 A.M. Canton time, 1,700 miles from Caledonia.

The personnel at Canton have done a grand job. Camouflage excellent, dispositions as well as can be expected with limited equipment. Guns: 4-4"; 4-75 mm; 2-155 mm. Runways in good condition, bunkers being completed, new men as replacements being received. Have 18 P-39s, 6 of which are set up. Men seemed to be in excellent spirits.

[Conditions at Canton discovered on this trip]
(1) Tour for all personnel should be not more than 6 months.
(2) Need 100 more Air Force men.
(3) Need more infantry.
(4) Time has come for a survey of the mission of these island ports to determine their strength and composition of their garrisons. It would seem to me that fighters are stationed there because it is the easiest thing to do. It has no relationship to the mission required of the garrison. Light Bombers? Medium Bombers? Fighters? Which will do the best job?

[Distances to be traveled en route home to Washington]

Townsville to New Caledonia	1,000 [miles]
New Caledonia to Canton	2,000
Canton to Hawaii	1,900
Hawaii to San Francisco	2,430
San Francisco to Washington	2,500
	9,830

Shall we have fortified posts, cordon defense all along the ferry route or shall we have a mobile Air Force to send where needed? Air Ferry route across Pacific needs one man to run the show with representative at each stop, thus keep up schedule and stop removing supplies from plane prior to reaching destination.

On at least one occasion when a bomber crew had to take to its life rafts:
(1) The [drinking] water had been in the containers so long it stank.
(2) The rations were spoiled.
(3) Other items necessary were in bad shape.

Query:
(1) How often is the water changed?
(2) How often are the rations and equipment inspected?
(3) Who requires these inspections and sees that the equipment is kept up to standard?[199]

Japs and United States use same [radio] wave length. When flying over Buna, United States fighters saw 12 Zeros about to take off. Called down: "Come on up you yellow-bellied sons of bitches; we can't get a medal for knocking you down on the ground." As each one took off he was shot down until a total of ten was reached. The other 2 pilots cut their motors and jumped from the planes and ran. Our boys got both planes and pilots, no losses of P-39s.

Colonel Landon now in the United States. Why did we send him to Bob Olds? (See letter to Emmons).[200]

Arrived Hickam 9:15. Emmons [suggests control of] New Caledonia, New Britain to MacArthur.[201] OK to send either Meehan or Ramey to Australia.[202] Reorganize forces at Canton, take Pursuit away from Christmas. Notify Harmon that Saunders' requisitions are not getting to Hawaii. Where do they go?

Emmons getting along 100% with Nimitz. Thinks Nimitz about the most brilliant naval officer he has met. Trouble in Pacific is Navy doctrine of having and retaining control; will do everything to retain control. Put Naval officers in command and give them higher rank so that they will retain command. Under no circumstances must an Army officer command a Navy unit. Navy does not understand ground or air operations. They have no idea as to planning logistics or supplying troops. Their plan for putting air units along islands is lousy. Think that very soon the whole show in Solomons will break down due to lack of supplies. Emmons thinks that the planes set up for him are ample if he ever gets them and can keep them. But there should be two heavy groups available on Pacific Coast to be sent over in case of emergency.

Dinner at Willis Hale's. Conference: [present] Hale, Emmons, Streett, Arnold. Bed at 11:15. Blackout here fairly complete except for Pearl Harbor, [where] 24 hour work [precludes blackouts].

<u>Thursday, October 1, 1942</u> [Honolulu, Hawaii to San Francisco, California]

Up at 4:15 [A.M.], raining, took off 5:35, 2,400 miles to San Francisco. Memo to George re after war airlines; Cabell has this.[203] Farthing to come home to Fort Worth, then two weeks leave and then Flight Surgeon, then to Henry Miller.[204]

Flying over layer of clouds most of trip. About 200 miles out saw 3 ships in convoy, about 1,200 miles out saw steamer, it started zig-zagging when it saw us. Broken clouds and clear water beneath us about one-third of the time. Signed certificates as Neptunus Rex for all of the Neophytes who crossed the equator.[205] Our weather man in Hawaii gave us a bum steer. His course almost East and then Northeast gave us headwinds all the way. We changed course but too late.

Landed Hamilton 9:50, too many searchlights played on us. They came from all directions and blinded the pilot. Giles, Kepner, Lotha Smith, Kiel[206] and others met us. We all went to Joe DiMaggio's for dinner.[207] Talked to Stratemeyer [via telephone] and tried to talk him out of a medal ceremony upon landing. Received message from Marshall re statement of Commander Thach that no major ship had been sunk by horizontal bombing or by Army.[208]

<u>Friday, October 2, 1942</u> [San Francisco, California to Washington, D.C.]

Twenty-four hundred miles to Washington, took off 11:15 P.M. On take-off one super-charger (# 4) caught fire and it looked for a while as if that would be the end of our trip.[209] Fire went out finally and supercharger started to work properly. Making good speed over Laramie [Wyoming] at 7:00 A.M., PST, 220 miles per hour. Due at Washington at 4:00 P.M. Told to land at Bolling, arrived 4:10 and told to circle while General Stratemeyer came.

Landed and saw band, movie cameras, newsmen, Lovett, Marshall, Stratemeyer, Ulio[210] and all Air Staff. With great ceremony I was given the D[istinguished] S[ervice] M[edal] and all of the others with me the Flying Medal.[211] Lovett pinned it on. It was a complete surprise. I thought that they might give me a palm for my D[istinguished] F[lying] C[ross]. So the actual flight to and from Australia ended, but there is still lots to be done. Total of 127 hours and 35 minutes [flying time logged], average for trip 8½ hours [flying time] per day.

Postscript

This 15-day odyssey was the third of nine trips Hap made to a combat theater during which he kept a World War II diary. Since Arnold's return in May from England three and one-half months earlier, the Allies were hard pressed to claim important victories and the prospects for success in the Pacific, where he was headed, were not encouraging. Hap's attention to the details of the journey crowded out any extensive introspection or anticipation as he left Washington. His first day's entry, however, clearly set out his views on the controversies prompting the trip.

He followed his previous diary practice of recording the thinking of those he encountered. The seniors' moods ranged from the nervous pessimism of MacArthur and the seeming despair and indecisiveness of Ghormley to the more positive outlooks of Nimitz and Kenney. Hap found that the closer he approached the combat zones the more optimism he found. Also, he was impressed with the confidence of the junior officers in contrast to their seniors. On the other hand, some pessimism returned to Washington with Arnold when he reported on the day following his return that he felt the Japanese could take Guadalcanal if they came "with all their strength."[212] His travels along the islands en route to and from the Pacific theater allowed him to assess their potential and he pondered as he returned whether there was sufficient raison d'être to maintain extensive air assets at some of these locations.

Consistent with his practice in other diaries, he carefully noted details ranging from the care and feeding of combat crews through the effectiveness of their life rafts and other equipment to the characteristics and performance of their airplanes. He made judgments about the effectiveness of the leaders he met as well as the morale of the crews. Due to limited time and safe distances from combat operations, these assessments depended entirely on those relayed by the senior commanders. However, he dispatched Col Cabell of his

Advisory Council, who was accompanying him, to fly to Guadalcanal and report about the combat situation there.[213] In later trips, he sought to mingle and talk with the aviators themselves, making his own evaluations of their morale and satisfaction with their aircraft. Some AAF leadership changes at the bombardment group level were implemented as a result of his visit but these were not at variance with the wishes and recommendations of the on-site commanders. Arnold, on this and other trips, normally recognized and respected the prerogatives of the senior AAF leaders charged with fighting the war.

Col Cabell has written, without other corroboration, that one of the "main purposes" of the journey was for Arnold to "take a careful reading on MacArthur" on behalf of the JCS who were concerned about the general's stamina to continue "on the long road to Tokyo." Although the colonel was greatly impressed with MacArthur's four-hour briefing, Cabell informed Arnold that MacArthur "should be relieved by a younger, more vigorous man." Although Hap agreed with the apparent physical frailties they saw, he disagreed with the suggestion that MacArthur be replaced, insisting that the general's spirit "would carry him through." Arnold, according to Cabell, intended to make that recommendation to the JCS on his return.[214]

Unfortunately for the historian, the comments recorded in the diary appeared to have satisfied Arnold as a complete record of his journey since no formal, written report of his findings appears to have been submitted. He apparently reported orally to a host of people, however, including Roosevelt, Marshall, Stimson, King, Forrestal, and Secretary of the Navy Knox. The latter did not welcome Arnold's criticism of the Navy and abruptly terminated that interview.[215] As reflected in his actions and correspondence after his return, there seemed to have been little change in Hap's thinking or, from his critics' viewpoints, his prejudices. The Pacific area commanders Arnold met on this trip were unanimous in their view that they needed additional aircraft. Hap, however, continued to believe and stress to them, as he had and would continue to stress back in Washington, that the European theater was where the strategic and logistical emphases were to be maintained. Arnold retained these views before, during, and after this trip. During the 28 September conference on Ghormley's flagship, he was equally frank but less than encouraging to the leaders there who were responsible for the fighting in that arena. Others recorded him as telling them that their theater "was only a small facet of the world military picture and had less claim to support than several others." As he continued to explain, "everything in the US [is] turned towards . . . Torch," he continued to be critical of what he viewed as the "stacking up of aircraft in reserve" in the Pacific, suggesting that until all these planes were committed to combat, no additional AAF planes would be furnished.[216] His views remained consistent as he informed General Kenney on his return that the emphasis has to be in Europe and that the Pacific theater was a "defensive" one.[217] His comments at the same time to the Eighth Air Force commander in England seemed clear: "Sometimes one theater has first priority, sometimes it's another, all of which detracts from our main effort. I am doing my best to keep in mind the principles . . . about having one main theater and all others being secondary. I assure you that the trip to the South Pacific did not change my viewpoint."[218]

Since much of the debate in Washington over allocation difficulties had been with the Navy and Admiral King's demands for additional assets, it was not surprising that many of Arnold's criticisms during and after his return were reserved for what he saw as that service's shortcomings in the Pacific. This journey appeared to strengthen his thinking that sufficient assets were available to both the Army and the Navy but that they were not properly positioned, correctly used, or logistically supported. This conclusion was confirmed when he viewed the 80-plus unloaded ships riding at anchor in Noumea harbor. He was particularly impressed by this in view of the serious needs of the Marines and the air units on Guadalcanal for reinforcements and supplies that had been emphasized in discussions at recent JCS and CCS meetings in Washington. It had been and would be emphasized that the lack of shipping was a critical factor limiting worldwide operations. A Marshall biographer has written that Hap's account of the "chaotic supply situation left a lasting impression on

Marshall."[219] It is difficult to conclude to what degree if any Arnold's comments were influenced by the unfriendly reception he felt had been given him by several Navy senior officers in the Pacific, particularly Ghormley and McCain, the two "King men." It seems logical that King had informed them as well as Nimitz, who was in no way discourteous to Arnold, of Hap's consistently strong opposition in the JCS to more air assets for the Pacific. Arnold generally concluded, as noted several times in his diary, that a major part of the problem was the failure of leadership, both Army and Navy, not only to use effectively the assets on hand but to operate a viable supply system. This difficulty, which was not resolved completely before the end of the war, would become an important issue discussed during Arnold's visit to the Pacific as late as the spring of 1945.

Arnold's verbal report to Secretary Stimson and Secretary Knox on Admiral Ghormley and his seeming inability to resolve the major operational and logistics problems of the theater probably had little impact on Ghormley's relief within three weeks after Arnold's return. The other "King man" he met on this trip, Rear Adm John McCain, had been reassigned to become the Navy's Chief of the Bureau of Aeronautics in Washington even before Hap made this journey. In this new position, McCain was to have considerable dealings with Arnold and the AAF. His attitude towards Hap, expressed soon after he arrived in Washington, may well have represented the thinking of other naval leaders and is revealing. McCain said the three-star AAF leader should be given four stars and placed in command of all our forces in hell. This animus may well have been reciprocated, even if not articulated, by Arnold.[220] The trip did not lessen Arnold's resolve to retain the bulk of the air assets for Europe although he conceded the difficulty of the task. As he wrote Eisenhower in the two weeks before Torch was to be launched: "as fast as I get units set up to go in one direction, the Navy takes them away from me and makes me send them in another direction."[221]

The student of Arnold can ponder why his attitude appeared unchanged as a result of the trip. Among the explanations would be that Hap was so convinced of the rectitude of his strategic views and the soundness of the existing distribution of assets that he did not make the trip with an open mind. Marshall's comment that Hap should not get mad and should "let the other fellow tell his story" is relevant in assessing Arnold. A more favorable view of him would be that what he saw confirmed his and Marshall's suspicions that improper use of assets, failure to provide an adequate supply system, and deficiencies in leadership were the real problems. None of these could be resolved by furnishing more support. Another point in favor of Arnold's consistent view of the situation was that the arguments he heard from local commanders differed little from those advanced by Admiral King, which Hap felt had been answered in Washington.

On the day following Arnold's return, King informed Marshall and Admiral Leahy of anticipated renewed Japanese activity aimed at either the Solomons or New Guinea. Within the week, the enemy had successfully resupplied Guadalcanal and landed 3,000 more troops on the island.[222] American prospects there remained unclear for the next six weeks. Arnold and Marshall, although aware of increased Japanese advances, found it difficult to furnish significant additional resources, whether sea, ground, or air. The major inhibiting factor was the lack of reserves since the ships sailing directly from the United States for the North African invasion, set for 8 November, were already being loaded and made ready to depart US ports. Another problem was the serious lack of airplanes and crews who, even if they could be taken from their training programs, could not reach the Pacific theater in any reasonable time. Nor could their indispensable ground personnel and equipment be dispatched due to the lack of shipping and the required time en route. Roosevelt was alarmed by potential difficulties in the Pacific as the Torch invasion was about to be launched "little more than a week before the fall election."[223] He requested that Marshall, Arnold, King, and Leahy "make sure that every possible weapon gets into that area to hold Guadalcanal" even though it might mean delay to "other commitments, particularly to England." Additionally, he requested a review of the "number and use of all combat planes" in the United States.[224] Marshall coordinated with

Arnold and reported two days later that the combat airplanes in the United States were the "bare minimum to provide a basis for . . . training and for a minimum of security." He pointed out that the only possible source of heavy bombers were those in England to support Torch and that, although efforts were being made to furnish additional air assets to the Pacific, the problem was lack of shipping.[225] Actually, on the day of FDR's directive, Marshall had informed Admiral King that AAF reinforcements were en route and would bring the number of heavy bombers in the theater up to the 1 January 1943 recommended strength of 70, medium bombers to 52, and 145 of the 150 fighters recommended. Admiral King would not get the anticipated 15 groups, but every effort was being made to prevent disaster in the Pacific while moving forward with the North African landings and retaining aircraft in the United Kingdom. These actions constituted a clear validation of Marshall, the Army leadership, and Arnold's faith in the strategic bomber offensive.[226]

Hap continued to urge that some of the problems he saw could be resolved by the appointment of a single commander for the entire theater, an idea shared by Marshall and advocated unsuccessfully several times to the president as recently as three weeks after Arnold's return.[227] Apparently, several who accompanied him on the trip shared his thinking and on their return they, but not Arnold, floated several specific change proposals, even naming possible overall commanders to the War Department. Arnold would continue to advocate a single Pacific commander throughout most of the war.[228] Concerned that his recent findings make their way to the president, Arnold, within the week after his return, wrote to his White House conduit Harry Hopkins emphasizing, as he had in the days before his departure, the continuing need to prevent diversion of assets, particularly to prevent the Germans from strengthening their air forces.[229]

Changes were made in some areas as a result of his visit. Anticipating increased cooperation with the new commander, Vice Adm William F. Halsey Jr., who replaced Vice Admiral Ghormley, Arnold added an AAF officer to Halsey's staff within a week after the change of command. The AAF officer chosen,

Col Frank Everest, was to assist Halsey's staff in mission planning, airfield location, supply, and other problems. Arnold knew Everest well from his service the previous year in the Plans Division at AAF headquarters. Everest later commanded the 11th Bomb Group in the Pacific and after the war became a four-star general.[230] An AAF officer on Halsey's staff was an improvement but there seems little doubt that Arnold discussed with his senior officers in the Pacific the problems with the existing command arrangement there. As constituted, commander air South Pacific (COMAIRSOPAC), the position occupied by Admiral McCain before he moved to Washington, was responsible for all air units assigned to the South Pacific area, including those of the AAF. Aside from the normal AAF desire to have its operational units under an army aviator, there was a feeling, expressed by Arnold to Admiral King, that the offensive capabilities of the AAF's long-range B-17s were not being used to capitalize on their strike capability. They had been assigned instead to reconnaissance, a mission that could in shorter-range situations have been carried out by Navy patrol craft. Arnold and others felt that, even when enemy ships were detected, the B-17 reconnaissance aircraft and their crews were often at the optimum of their range. Their effectiveness was then severely limited. Both Arnold and Harmon sought greater use of this scarce weapon in strike rather than patrol missions.[231] Additionally, Harmon felt that although he was ultimately responsible for the training, deployment, and supply of AAF units in this command, the new, more sympathetic Navy COMAIRSOPAC, Aubrey Fitch, determined their operational use. Even more complicated was the fact that there was no overall AAF organization to coordinate the air activity west of Hawaii. To what extent Harmon's message to Washington that there was "too little imagination" being applied by Admiral Fitch in the use of AAF assets influenced Arnold and Marshall to act on the problem is not known.[232] Since neither Halsey nor Fitch objected to its creation, a new AAF organization emerged in the Pacific in December 1942. This organization became the Thirteenth Air Force, joining the existing Fifth in Australia and the Seventh in Hawaii. Harmon would not gain complete operational control of AAF units in the South Pacific until later, although the need for such a command arrangement was discussed by Arnold during this trip.[233] Neither this journey nor the new organization changed Hap's thinking that the air units in the Pacific, particularly the heavy bombers, were to be concentrated in mobile units rather than allocated piecemeal on a variety of bases along the chain of islands as desired by the Navy.

If one of Arnold's traits was his ability to look to the future even when current problems appeared difficult, an excellent example was Arnold's memo, written in Hawaii and cited in his diary of 1 October, to Gen Harold George, CG of Air Transport Command (ATC). Having just flown the 5,000 miles from Australia to Hawaii and contemplating the additional 5,000 yet to be covered to Washington, Arnold showed a keen interest in the postwar civilian air activities in this vast area. While specifying that nothing should be done to interfere with the conduct of the war, Arnold noted that other nations were "definitely acting along these lines" and a US failure to act competitively would result in our being "losers."

Arnold directed that a committee or board be established within ATC to identify those policies in place as well as what "policies" and "action" should be taken "to insure that our military air transport routes and facilities are establishing and furthering our postwar position in the air transport field." This board was charged to submit a report within 60 days. Sensitive to the fact that the main US competitor in the postwar period would be our British Ally, Arnold instructed that no publicity be given to the committee and that its work be known "only to those persons" required to work with it. A response from ATC entitled "Preliminary Report on Future Air Transport Possibilities by the Special Committee of the AAF" was submitted to Arnold on 30 November. The report included a finding that present and prospective US air routes "should be calculated to establish and further the postwar position of the US in world air transportation." It continued that, given the unique position of the AAF, it should use ATC to ensure "American dominance in international air transport."[234] Arnold maintained constant interest, supported by the White House, on this issue of postwar air routes. He noted this problem on more than one occasion in subsequent diaries. It remained an item of concern as late as the Second Quebec meeting in September 1944, when the RAF head, Air Chief Marshal Portal, strongly supported by Churchill, asked for a squadron of the latest AAF long-range transport C-54s. Arnold denied the request. Although he based his denial on a shortage of the planes, an important reason was concern over their ultimate use on postwar air routes by British civilian airlines.[235]

Arnold did not record any overall analysis or satisfaction with the results of the trip. He probably was pleased that many of his and Marshall's beliefs were validated by what he saw. Conditions in Guadalcanal improved significantly in the next six weeks, in large part because of the Navy's success against Japanese surface units, thereby preventing their reinforcements from reaching the island. This in turn reduced the urgency of, and the demand for, aircraft to that theater. Primary concern now shifted to the invasion of North Africa, which was scheduled for 8 November.

If Arnold took any comfort from the fact that the 15 groups had not been committed in toto to the Pacific, unappreciated by him was the fact that an even greater assault was being made on the daylight strategic bombardment concept. This challenge would come from the British ally, who had the ear of the White House and wielded considerable influence there. Problems remained in other parts of the world, however, and Arnold would set out on the longest and most demanding trip of his career within three months of his return. It would be long not only in distance but also in time, an extremely taxing journey requiring almost six weeks. In a rare admission about the demands of his travels, Arnold conceded to Kenney six days after he returned from the Pacific that he was "so tired that I felt I had just recovered from a jag."[236*] As to the future, his notation in the diary as he landed back in Washington from this first wartime trip to the Pacific, "there is still lots to be done," would prove to be an understatement.

---

*jag: a state or feeling of intoxication, usually by liquor.

Notes

1. Wesley Frank Craven and James Lea Cate, eds., *The Army Air Forces in World War II*, vol. 1, *Plans and Early Operations, January 1939 to August 1942* (1948; new imprint, Washington, D.C.: Office of Air Force History, 1983), 570.
2. Combined Chief of Staff (CCS) Meeting, 19 June 1942.
3. Craven and Cate, vol. 1, 570.
4. Forrest C. Pogue, *George C. Marshall: Ordeal and Hope, 1939-1942* (New York: Viking Press, 1965), 327-28.
5. Martin Gilbert, *Winston S. Churchill*, vol. 7, *Road to Victory, 1941-1945* (Boston: Houghton Mifflin, 1986), 127-28, citing secret Churchill memo of 20 June 1942.
6. Churchill to FDR, 8 July 1942, cited in Warren F. Kimball, ed., *Churchill & Roosevelt: The Complete Correspondence*, vol. 1, *Alliance Emerging, October 1933-November 1941* (Princeton, N.J.: Princeton University Press, 1984), 520-21.
7. Pogue, 340.
8. Roosevelt to Marshall, 14 July 1942, George C. Marshall Papers, George C. Marshall Research Library, Lexington, Va., hereinafter cited as MPMS.
9. Pogue, 347.
10. CCS, 94th meeting, 24 July 1942.
11. Grace Person Hayes, *The History of the Joint Chiefs of Staff in World War II: The War Against Japan* (Annapolis: Naval Institute Press, 1982), 173-74; Marshall to Eisenhower, 30 July 1942, Henry Harley Arnold Papers, Library of Congress, Manuscript Division, Washington, D.C., hereinafter cited as AP; and Arnold to Eisenhower, 30 July 1942, AP. Nine of those proposed were combat groups, four were transport, two were observation.
12. Arnold to Spaatz, 16 July 1942, AP.
13. Arnold to Eisenhower, 30 July 1942, AP.
14. See for example Craven and Cate, vol. 1, 574; Arnold to Chief of Staff, 29 July 1942, AP; Arnold, Memorandum for Record, 11 August 1942, AP.
15. Memo for the United States JCS, of Conference at White House, 30 July 1942, AP.
16. Diary of Henry L. Stimson, Sterling Library, Yale University, New Haven, Conn., 7 August 1942.
17. See for example Arnold to Spaatz, 9 August 1942, AP. For the viewpoint that Arnold was more demanding of Eaker than Spaatz, see James Parton, *"Air Force Spoken Here," General Ira Eaker and the Command of the Air* (Bethesda, Md.: Adler & Adler, 1986), 169-72.
18. *New York Times*, 8, 11 August 1942.
19. For Spaatz' cultivation at this time of Arthur O. Sulzberger, publisher of the *New York Times*, which had to have been done with the knowledge if not at the urging of Arnold, see Richard G. Davis, *Carl A. Spaatz and the Air War in Europe* (Washington, D.C.: Center for Air Force History, 1993), 103. Cyrus Sulzberger was a "guest participant" at later poker games with Eaker, Spaatz, and Elliott Roosevelt. See Parton, 367-68.

20. *New York Times*, 16 August 1942.
21. *Sunday Times* of London, 16, 23 August 1942; Parton, 170.
22. Davis, 97.
23. See, among many examples, Churchill "Notes on Air Policy," 22 October 1942; Public Record Office (PRO), Air Ministry Record (Air) 8/711, Archie Sinclair, Secretary of State for Air to Churchill, 23 October 1942; and Slessor to Chief of Air Staff, 25 October 1942, Slessor Papers, RAF Historical Branch, London.
24. Peter G. Masefield, Oral History Interview, 10 July 1971, Special Collections, US Air Force Academy, Colorado Springs, Colo.
25. *Reader's Digest*, July 1942, 120-37; and Stimson Diary, 15 October 1942.
26. Arnold to Spaatz, 9 August 1942, Carl Andrew Spaatz Papers, Library of Congress, Manuscript Division, Washington, D.C., hereinafter cited as SP.
27. Spaatz to Arnold, 11, 21 August 1942, AP.
28. Arnold to Roosevelt, subj: Reply to Peter Masefield's Criticism of Flying Fortresses and Liberators, 19 August 1942; and Arnold to Spaatz, 19 August 1942, AP. The loss statistics are cited in Roger A. Freeman, Alan Crouchman, and Vic Maslen, *Mighty Eighth War Diary* (London: Jane's, 1981), 10.
29. Freeman, Crouchman, and Maslen, 11-32.
30. Diary of Henry Morgenthau Jr., 9 September 1942, Franklin D. Roosevelt Library, Hyde Park, N.Y.
31. Spaatz to Arnold, 27 August 1942, AP.
32. Arnold, Memo for Record, 14 August 1942; and Arnold to Chief of Staff, 19 August 1942, AP.
33. Davis, 109.
34. Arnold to Chief of Staff, Subj: North African Operations, 19 August 1942, AP.
35. Stratemeyer to Spaatz, Doolittle to Patton, 25 August 1942; and Spaatz to Arnold, 31 August 1942, AP. See also Arnold's cryptic message to Spaatz the next day, implying that the letters were sent at Arnold's behest and suggesting to Spaatz that the latter should read "between the lines," Arnold to Spaatz, 26 August 1942, AP.
36. "American-British Strategy," 31 December 1941, Arcadia, ABC 4/CS 1 cited in Hayes, 768.
37. Hayes, 106.
38. Thomas B. Buell, *Master of Sea Power: A Biography of Fleet Admiral Ernest J. King* (Boston: Little Brown & Co., 1980), 76.
39. Ibid., 404.
40. Eisenhower's comments are in Dwight D. Eisenhower, *The Eisenhower Diaries*, ed. Robert H. Ferrell (New York: W. W. Norton & Co., 1981), 48, 50.
41. Hayes, 67.
42. Ibid., 769.
43. Roosevelt to Marshall, 6 May 1942, MPMS.

44. Wesley Frank Craven and James Lea Cate, eds., *The Army Air Forces in World War II*, vol. 6, *Men and Planes* (1955; new imprint, Washington, D.C.: Office of Air Force History, 1983), 280.

45. Brief statistics on accomplishments, leadership, aircraft, and stations of this and other AAF units are to be found in Maurer Maurer, ed., *Air Force Combat Units of World War II* (Washington, D.C.: Government Printing Office, 1961), 99–101.

46. JCS, 48th meeting, 2 May 1942.

47. Wesley Frank Craven and James Lea Cate, *The Army Air Forces in World War II*, vol. 4, *The Pacific: Guadalcanal to Saipan, August 1942 to July 1944* (1950; new imprint, Washington, D.C.: Office of Air Force History, 1983), 16.

48. PRO, Air 8/634 and 8/637, Evill to Portal, 6 March 1942; PRO, Air 8/891, Portal to Evill, c. 8 March; RAF DEL[egation] to Air Ministry, 1 March 1942; and PRO, Air 1050, Dill to Portal, 20 March.

49. Stimson Diary, 6 March 1942.

50. Ibid., 19 March 1942.

51. Hayes, 121.

52. Ibid., 114.

53. Churchill to Roosevelt, 29 March 1942; and Kimball, vol. 1, 434–35.

54. Acting Chief of Staff to King, "Strategic Deployment Against Japan," 6 April 1942, AP; Hayes, 117.

55. Hayes, 117.

56. Arnold, Memo to R & R, 21 April 1942, AP.

57. Hayes, 118.

58. Ibid., 129.

59. King to Marshall, 24 May 1942, MPMS.

60. Marshall to King, n.d., MPMS.

61. Hayes, 147–48.

62. Marshall to Harmon, 7 July 1942, AP.

63. Craven and Cate, vol. 4, 7.

64. It is difficult if not impossible to unscramble aircraft figures used by the military in this period with any degree of accuracy, given not only the varying totals reported to various agencies but the fact that then as now the possession of an aircraft was and is not the same as its being operationally ready. For example see Maj Gen George C. Kenney's diary entry for 6 August 1942 and his assessment of the status of the planes reported to be under his command as of 1 August. Although his figures do not add up correctly, of the 517 aircraft reported to be possessed, his analysis showed only 150 (29 percent) ready for combat. Only 70 of his 245 fighters were combat-ready and none of the 53 light bombers were ready for combat. Just over one-half (37) of 70 medium bombers and two-thirds (43) of 62 heavy bombers (B-17s) were combat-ready. Diary of Maj Gen George C. Kenney, Air Force Historical Research Agency, Maxwell Air Force Base, Ala. Arnold's impatience apparently allowed him to forget his problems as a commander of various units during the 1930s when retaining a satisfactory in-commission rate for his airplanes was a major and constant headache. The vicissi-

tudes of war while operating in the tropics in primitive combat conditions at the end of an uncertain supply line controlled by another service did not make the task easier for a commander of any rank.

65. Arnold's language in his 16 September diary was not intended to be complimentary when Hap wrote, "Harmon . . . makes the bald statement" and "Ghormley and Nimitz both took up Harmon's battle cry." During the two days at Harmon's headquarters in Noumea, Hap recorded his name in the diary only along with other participants at a meeting. This was in contrast with Hap's laudatory comments and details of conversations with Maj Gen George Kenney, the other newcomer in the area. Arnold, with MacArthur's support, secured Kenney's promotion immediately whereas another four months passed before Harmon was recommended. Hap's feelings towards Harmon (who was lost in March 1945 on a flight to Hawaii) as recorded in his memoirs in 1948 were that we "weren't helped very much by reports received from . . . Harmon." H. H. Arnold, General of the Air Force, *Global Mission* (New York: Harper & Brothers, 1949), 337.

66. Harmon to Marshall, 30 July 1942, AP.
67. Hayes, 176.
68. Harmon to Maj Gen St. Clair Streett, OPD, 5 August 1942, AP.
69. Craven and Cate, vol. 4, 34.
70. Ibid., 46.
71. The naval battles were Eastern Solomons, 24–25 August; Cape Esperance, 11–12 October; Santa Cruz Islands, 26 October; Naval Battle of Guadalcanal, 12–15 November; Tassafronga, 30 November 1942. The USS *Enterprise* had been damaged on 23 August in the battle of the Eastern Solomons; USS *Saratoga* was torpedoed four days later leaving only the *Wasp* among the carriers until she was torpedoed and sunk 15 September; the battleship was the USS *Washington*. E. B. Potter, *Nimitz* (Annapolis: Naval Institute Press, 1976), 698.
72. Craven and Cate, vol. 4, 46.
73. Ibid., 47.
74. Marshall to King, "Reinforcement for South Pacific and Hawaiian Areas," 20 August 1942, MPMS.
75. Craven and Cate, vol. 4, 48.
76. Draft, Arnold to King, 5 September 1942, AP.
77. Arnold to Hopkins, 13 September 1942; and Arnold to Marshall, 12 August 1942, AP.
78. Arnold, Memo for Record, 11 August, AP.
79. Minutes, Air Staff Meetings, 5, 26 August 1942, AP.
80. Arnold to King, 14 September 1942, AP.
81. Arnold to Spaatz, 3 September 1942, AP.
82. King to Arnold, 5 September 1942, AP.
83. JCS, 32d meeting, 8 September 1942, cited in Hayes, 185.
84. Cited in Hayes, 185.
85. MacArthur to Marshall, 30 August 1942, MP. In addition to the pessimism expressed to Arnold during their 25 September meeting, MacArthur's subsequent estimates of the situation and the prospects for

Allied success continued exceedingly gloomy. See MacArthur to Marshall, 17 October 1942, MPMS.

86. There is a brief account of the meeting in Hayes, 186; Potter, 186–88.

87. Cited in Davis, 113; Eisenhower to Marshall, 5 September 1942, MPMS.

88. Roosevelt to Marshall, 24 August 1942, MPMS. Arnold reproduced part of the letter in *Global Mission*, 335.

89. The Marshall quote is cited in Parton, 181.

90. See the discussion of AWPD-42 in Craven and Cate, vol. 2, *Europe: Torch to Pointblank. August 1942 to December 1943* (1949; new imprint, Washington, D.C.: Office of Air Force History, 1983), 277–79, 288–96, 301, 353.

91. Devers to Arnold, 5 September 1942; Arnold to Devers, 23 September 1942, AP; and Stimson Diary, 3 October 1942.

92. Growth figures are from Craven and Cate, vol. 6, 278–80 and vol. 7, *Services Around the World*, 32.

93. JCS, 33d Meeting, 15 September 1942, cited in Pogue, 388.

94. Vice Adm Robert L. Ghormley, USN, now commander, South Pacific Area. Discussion continued in Washington concerning the allocation of aircraft between the various services and theaters. Maj Gen Millard Fillmore "Miff" Harmon Jr., had just assumed command of US Army Forces in the South Pacific on 26 June with headquarters at Noumea, New Caledonia. His newly created organization served as the single Army agency through which the War Department maintained contact with its scattered elements in the Pacific and with which the US Navy acted in securing Army cooperation. The reference is to two messages, not located, sent on 4 and 6 August just prior to the US invasion of Guadalcanal on 7 August. Mitsubishi Reisen A6M (Japanese Zero) was a low-wing monoplane, single-engine fighter. As Arnold recalled just before he departed on this trip: "There was quite a flare-up at the Joint Chiefs of Staff meeting when Admiral King asked [on 15 September] for more planes for the South Pacific." Arnold, *Global Mission*, 338.

95. The performance of the P-400, an export version of Bell Aircraft Corporation's P-39, proved "painfully inadequate" against the Japanese fighters and bombers which struck Henderson Field on Guadalcanal from altitudes above 20,000 feet. This American fighter lacked proper superchargers, had an inadequate high-pressure oxygen system, and was limited by its rate of climb to combat altitude, a key factor in fighter operations. Defense at high altitude became the responsibility of US Marine Corps pilots flying Grumman F-4-F Wildcats while the P-400 was relegated to low-level strafing and close support of Marine units. The P-38s were not available for combat in this area in any significant numbers until November 1942. Arnold, from his Washington vantage point, appeared unwilling to concede the inadequacies of the P-39/P-400. The quotes are from Craven and Cate, vol. 2, 34, where there is a brief discussion of the problem. Ghormley had requested P-38s from MacArthur as early as 3 September 1942. In view of his relations with Ghormley, Arnold felt that the Admiral was not congenially disposed towards either Arnold or the AAF. Their relations would not improve when Arnold visited him on this trip; see diary entries for 24 and

28 September 1942. Adm Chester W. Nimitz, USN, then CINPCAC, Commander in Chief Pacific Fleet and Pacific Ocean Areas, US Pacific Fleet.

96. Celebes, the largest island of East Indonesia, across Makassar Strait from Borneo, is 2,500 miles west northwest of the Solomon Islands, which are approximately 1,500 miles north of Sydney, Australia.

97. See the discussion in note 64 above relating to evaluating aircraft strength in terms of those assigned as opposed to those that are operationally available.

98. Arnold presumably meant Espiritu Santo Island in the New Hebrides, where B-17s began operating on 30 July, and Port Moresby on New Guinea where that type aircraft had been flying since 19 July. Bougainville is the northwesternmost and largest of the major islands in the Solomons chain. Rabaul is a port, northern tip of New Britain Island, Bismarck Archipelago. Its natural harbor, considered one of the finest in the world, had been taken by the Japanese in January 1942 and was the base from which they expected to launch their anticipated invasion of Australia. It would become a major target of Allied airpower until bypassed by American forces in 1944.

99. Arnold, even from as far away as Washington, was alluding to the Navy losses of 9 August at Savo Island and essentially describing the performance of Admiral Ghormley, who was relieved by Admiral Nimitz one month after this diary entry. Naval officers eventually agreed with Hap's assessment, among them Ghormley's superior, Nimitz, who observed that Ghormley "was not sufficiently bold and aggressive." Nimitz and his staff felt that Ghormley was not "tough enough to meet the approaching challenge" nor "did he have the personality to inspire his subordinates to heroic measures." Arnold generally confirmed Ghormley's shortcomings as timid and vacillating to Secretary Stimson. See Potter, 196-97; Arnold, *Global Mission*, 338; Stimson Diary, 3, 18 October 1942. A fair assessment of Ghormley's problems and leadership is provided in Richard B. Frank, *Guadalcanal* (New York: Random House, 1990), 333-35.

100. Undersecretary of the Navy James V. Forrestal, had just returned from a two-week inspection trip to the South Pacific, traveling as far as New Caledonia while assessing supply problems. The specific story is not otherwise identified but he painted an unrealistically optimistic picture during his press conference on 13 September, having been impressed during the trip with the "complete harmony existing" between the two services. His report, noting "it was so strong that it was difficult to tell what service any man was in," contrasted sharply with Arnold's impressions on this trip. During Forrestal's pessimistic presentation to the president about the tactical conditions he found, Secretary of War Stimson suggested that Forrestal had a bad case of "localitis," to which Forrestal replied that if the Marines were "wiped out" at Guadalcanal public reaction would give Stimson "a bad case of localitis in the seat of your pants." The decision that Arnold would make this trip was made by General Marshall the previous day, 15 September. Potter, 188.

101. Hamilton AAF Field, 40 miles north of San Francisco, California.

102. "Pete," Maj Clair A. Peterson, continued as Arnold's aide and pilot; Maj Gen St. Clair Streett, Operations Division, US War Department General Staff. The only officer named Cousins listed in the *Army Register* for this period is Maj Gen Ralph P. Cousins, CG, AAF West Coast Training Center, Santa Ana, California, where Arnold visited on 19 September. It is possible that Arnold's diary reflected the wrong initial of Cousins. If so, the latter probably accompanied Arnold west on this trip. Lt E. A. McCabe was Arnold's aide, although he is erroneously identified in *Global Mission* (339) as a colonel.

103. I. M. Laddon, vice president and chief, Consolidated Aircraft Corporation, headquartered at Lindbergh Field, San Diego, Calif. The Army plant representative is not otherwise identified. Although it was not public knowledge because of wartime security, Roosevelt had left Washington two days earlier, 17 September, on a two-week rail trip to the West Coast, inspecting plants and military bases. He traveled first to the northwest then visited the Douglas Aircraft plant in Long Beach and the Consolidated assembly line at San Diego on 25 September, that same day dedicating the new Marine Corps training base at Camp Pendleton. He returned to Washington on 1 October, after which the news media were permitted to carry stories of the journey.

104. No repair or supply depot as such existed at Santa Ana at this time. The AAF West Coast Training Center located there was known in the vernacular of the day as a "repo depot" or replacement center for personnel, hence Arnold's calling it a depot. The P-38 equipped 332d Fighter Squadron had just arrived on 10 September for duty at Santa Ana from its previous station at Paine Field, Washington. Its commander is not otherwise identified.

105. Although several AAF bands gained considerable fame, particularly the one formed at Yale University under Capt (later Maj) Glenn Miller, the professional musicians then serving in the military who constituted the 39th and 40th AAF bands at Santa Ana were not identified by name in their unit histories. They were, however, gaining considerable publicity by making radio broadcasts in the greater Los Angeles area. See *History of Santa Ana Army Air Base, Installment 1, 1942*, Maxwell AFB, Ala.: Air Force Historical Research Agency (AFHRA), 1941, 346–48. Maj Gen Alexander Surles, USA, chief of Public Affairs, War Department, Washington, D.C.

106. Col Ralph E. Spake, CO, 6th Ferrying Group, ATC, Long Beach Army Air Field, Calif.

107. Main office and works of the Douglas Aircraft Company, Inc., were located in Santa Monica, a suburb 12 miles west of Los Angeles. The factory and airfield had been camouflaged for fear of Japanese raids. There are pictures of the deception at this field in the *New York Times*, 8 January 1995, 36.

108. Donald Douglas was president, Douglas Aircraft Company, Inc., and a close personal friend of Arnold; Brig Gen Charles E. Branshaw, CG, Western District, Air Materiel Command, Los Angeles.

109. The goal of 130,000 aircraft to be produced by the United States during the year 1943 had originally been suggested on 3 January 1942 during the first month after Pearl Harbor; by the fall of 1942, the president was

pressuring the War Department for an increased goal. Arnold and the Secretary of War as well as many others continued to use Harry Hopkins as a "conduit" to transmit their unofficial estimates of requirements to the White House although the specific telegrams mentioned here are not located. See the discussion in Craven and Cate, vol. 1, 245-51.

110. William H. Henry, CBS news commentator and *Los Angeles Times* writer; Carl A. Cover, vice president and general manager, Douglas Aircraft Company, Inc.; Rocky and Lee Raymond are not otherwise identified. Maj Alexander P. de Seversky was a vocal critic of AAF procurement, overall strategy, and plans for the war. He had founded the Seversky Aircraft Corporation in the mid-1930s, a predecessor of Republic Aviation. At Republic he had been involved in various arguments with Arnold and AAF procurement officers and had been forced out of top management of his company. The specific outburst is not otherwise identified but his book *Victory Through Air Power* had been published in the spring of 1942 and had appeared in a condensed version in the July issue of the *Reader's Digest*, July 1942, 120–37, where it elicited widespread comment and controversy.

111. This was a popular traveling ice-skating revue playing at the time in Los Angeles.

112. John Costello was a California member of the US House of Representatives serving the 15th District, greater Los Angeles area.

113. They were Col Fabian L. Pratt, flight surgeon; Maj Gen Barney McK. Giles, CG, Fourth Bomber Command; Brig Gen William E. Kepner, CG, Fourth Fighter Command, all of Hamilton Field; Col Lotha A. Smith, CO, Hammer Field, Fresno, Calif.

114. The crew members other than his pilot/aide Maj Clair A. Peterson and Maj Robert A. Ping are not further identified.

115. Col Charles Pearre "Pre" Cabell, chief, Advisory Council, AAF Headquarters.

116. Christmas Island is a large atoll in the Pacific, due south of Hawaii.

117. The Fiji Islands are in the Melanesia group in the South Pacific, south-southwest of Christmas Island.

118. New Caledonia is in the Loyalty Islands, approximately 800 miles due east of Australia.

119. Hickam Army Air Field, located in Honolulu, Hawaii.

120. Lt Gen Delos Emmons, now CG, Hawaiian Department; Maj Gen Willis H. Hale, CG, Seventh Air Force. Fumigation of aircraft landing in Hawaii was required then and now to inhibit bringing unwanted insects onto the island.

121. Damage inflicted by the Japanese in the 7 December 1941 attack.

122. It is not clear what Arnold meant here. Although from the AAF viewpoint there were serious extenuating circumstances governing their operation, the use of land-based AAF bombers, albeit under the command of a naval officer, Capt Cyril T. Simard, against Japanese naval vessels at the Battle of Midway, 4–6 June, failed to validate Billy Mitchell's extreme claims of the 1920s following his staged attacks on naval vessels. Arnold conceded six years later in his memoirs that, although Midway "was the reality which

the Army Air Force had simulated for years . . . when the opportunity came, we did not measure up to the high standard we had set for ourselves." Marshall remembered after the war that the AAF, although using pinpoint bombing there, "were not ready to use it successfully." The legacy of the 17 AAF B-17s at Midway, in the words of the AAF official history was "an enduring debate." As late as a year later, Adm Jack Towers was disturbed over AAF claims. See Clark G. Reynolds, *Admiral John H. Towers: The Struggle for Naval Air Supremacy* (Annapolis: Naval Institute Press, 1991), 470. There is a discussion of the battle, its problems, and implications in Craven and Cate, vol. 1, 457–62; Arnold's quotes are from Arnold, *Global Mission*, 378–79; and Marshall's recollections appear in Pogue, 325. The issue was raised again as Arnold returned to the United States on 1 October. See diary entry for that date and note 208.

123. Vice Adm William F. "Bull" Halsey Jr., USN, commander, Carrier Forces, US Pacific Fleet; Rear Adm Raymond A. Spruance, USN, served at this time both as deputy commander, US Pacific Fleet as well as Nimitz' Chief of Staff.

124. Port Moresby, capital of Papua, New Guinea, had been under attack by the Japanese forces now attempting an unsuccessful assault from the north side of the island. Port Moresby would not become completely secure for the Allies until mid-October.

125. Although fighting for its control remained fierce for the next 10 weeks, Henderson Field on Guadalcanal had received its first American aircraft on 20 August. Several times during September, Japanese naval fire forced temporary discontinuation of its operations. However, its use remained limited for some time for aircraft larger than fighters. Even the use of steel mats failed to solve the mud problems satisfactorily in this period. The supply problem there remained critical for aircraft until at least mid-November. Admiral Nimitz, who disliked to fly anyway, must have been enlightened to say the least by the somewhat primitive conditions he found at Henderson Field at this time. Departing after a visit there on 1 October to return to Espiritu Santo en route to his Hawaii headquarters with its white, starched-uniform naval staff, sideboys, Marine sentinels in dress blue, and a retinue of mess attendants, he was greeted by the pilot of the B-17 that was to lift him from Henderson Field. The AAF major sported a black beard, was in bare feet, and clad only in a flight suit. No doubt the pilot provided the four-star admiral with an unforgettable ride as the B-17 first aborted a takeoff in the rain unable to gain sufficient speed before ground looping in the mud. After lunch he was more successful in straining the B-17 to lift from the 2,000-foot steel Marston mat then serving as a runway. See Potter, 193–94 and the account of conditions there in Craven and Cate, vol. 4, 42–43.

126. Ellice Islands are part of the Gilbert and Ellice Islands, in the South Pacific, due east of the Solomons.

127. Arnold's reference is to the Japanese loss of the aircraft carriers *Ryuho* and *Chitose* at the battle of the Eastern Solomons, 24 August.

128. Kiska is the westernmost of the Rat Islands in the Aleutian chain off the west coast of Alaska where the Japanese had landed without opposition on 6 June 1942 and still remained.

129. Sumatra is an island, then part of the Dutch East Indies, now Indonesia in the Indian Ocean, south and west of the Malay peninsula; Borneo is an island, Dutch East Indies, part Dutch, part British, largest of the Malay archipelago.

130. USS *Saratoga*, aircraft carrier, *Lexington* class, commissioned in 1927, was damaged by a Japanese torpedo off Guadalcanal, August 1942; USS *North Carolina*, battleship, *North Carolina* class, commissioned in 1941, was torpedoed 14 September 1942 in the battle of the Eastern Solomons; USS *Chicago*, heavy cruiser, *Northampton* class, was damaged by torpedoes in the Battle of Savo Island, 9 August 1942.

131. Rear Adm John S. McCain, USN, COMAIRSOUPAC.

132. Although Gen MacArthur may have felt that he had "brought up" Marshall, the latter did not progress in any spectacular manner under MacArthur as chief of staff. Col Marshall's assignment to the Illinois National Guard in 1933 would not have been a coveted one. On the other hand, a biographer dismisses the story that Marshall's promotion to Brig Gen was held up by MacArthur as chief of staff in 1935 because of differences between the two officers dating back to World War I. See Forrest C. Pogue, *George C. Marshall: Education of a General* (New York: Viking Press, 1963), 254.

133. The reference is to the loss of American aircraft, particularly the B-17s destroyed on the ground at Clark Field on Luzon in the Philippines in the hours following the Pearl Harbor attack. Maj Gen Lewis E. Brereton was CG of the Far East Air Forces and Lt Col Eugene L. Eubank Jr., commanded USAAF Fifth Bomber Command. Arnold wrote in *Global Mission* (272) that he never did get "the real story of what happened in the Philippines." Brereton was one of the few senior AAF officers in World War II whose seeming failure did not seriously inhibit his future with Arnold.

134. Truk, the so-called Gibraltar of the Pacific is one of the 55 or so coral islands in the East Carolines in the western Pacific, lying approximately 900 miles due north of the Solomons. The Japanese maintained a major naval base at Truk until February 1944.

135. US forces first conducted reconnaissance of Christmas Island 18 October–2 November 1941. Construction of an airbase was underway by 26 November with plans to have it operational by 15 December. By 7 February 1942, runways were 29 percent completed with an estimated completion date of 1 June. Details are in AP.

136. These incidents are not otherwise identified. The C-53 was a modification of the Douglas C-47.

137. When crossing the International Date Line westward, a day is lost; crossing eastward, a day is gained. See below for Arnold repeating the day of 30 September eastbound.

138. Nandi is a town on the west coast of Viti Levu, largest of the Fiji Islands. Its airport was located at 177° 20' E, 17° 40' S, about 130 miles

west-northwest by road from the town of Suva. The 70th Fighter Squadron, equipped with P-39s, began operations from nearby Narewa airport in May 1942. This was Arnold's first experience with the World War II steel matted runways; Arnold, *Global Mission*, 340.

139. Arnold's reference to the Western Air Force here is not clear.

140. The Hudson was the Lockheed-built twin-engine attack/light bombardment aircraft designated A-29 by the AAF; the Vincent was Vickers Ltd.'s general purpose, single-engine biplane.

141. Tongatabu is an island group in the Tonga Archipelago of the Friendly Islands, approximately 400 miles east of Fiji, where the 44th Fighter Squadron operated P-40 aircraft. Maj Gen Robert S. Beightler, USA, CG, 37th Infantry Division.

142. Col Edgar T. "Bromo" Selzer, was the commanding officer at Nandi in Fiji. His future appeared behind him as early as 25 July 1942 when Maj Gen George Kenney, passing through en route to become MacArthur's air commander, recorded on his arrival at Nandi: "Col. 'Bromo' Selzer, local commander, too busy taking a sun bath to see me. I don't believe from General Harmon's looks when he got the news, that 'Bromo' will last long." Cook is not otherwise identified. Kenney Diary, 25 July 1942, AFHRA.

143. From 1874, when the islands were proclaimed a possession and dependency of the British Crown until the practice was discontinued in 1916, indentured laborers from India migrated to the Fijis.

144. The officers are not otherwise identified. The unit was the 44th Fighter Squadron, operating P-40 aircraft.

145. Plaines de Gaicacs was the site of an AAF airfield on northern New Caledonia, operational after 1 May 1942.

146. Brig Gen Nathan F. Twining was chief of staff, US Army Forces, South Pacific area.

147. The airport and the city are not otherwise identified.

148. Maj Gen Alexander M. Patch, USA, was CG, US Americal Division; the city is not otherwise identified.

149. Ghormley's headquarters were on the USS *Argonne*, auxiliary vessel completed in 1920.

150. Rear Adm Daniel Callaghan, commander, Cruiser Forces, US Pacific Fleet, killed during the battle for Guadalcanal, November 1942. Arnold clearly sensed this unfriendly reception by the naval officers of whom two (Ghormley and McCain) were known as "King men." No doubt they had been informed from Washington of Arnold's arrival, his mission and his strong opposition to more airplanes to the theater in lieu of those for Europe. Colonel Cabell recalled that he found at Noumea "much confusion and a great amount of back-biting." Charles P. Cabell, *A Man of Intelligence: Memoirs of War, Peace, and the CIA*, ed. Charles P. Cabell Jr. (Colorado Springs, Colo.: Impavide Publications, 1997), 52.

151. Arnold's assessment of the 80 ships seemingly immobilized in Noumea harbor at a time when shipping around the world was in critically short supply, inhibiting AAF as well as other operations, is confirmed by others. Nimitz' biographer, favorably disposed towards the Navy, has written

that the ships "could not be sent to the forward area because at their points of origin . . . they had not been combat-loaded; items used together . . . in many cases were in separate vessels . . . The only recourse was to turn the ships around . . . and send them to New Zealand for unloading and reloading." He continued that the blame was not Ghormley's but "lay chiefly in Washington." Potter, 190-91. Marshall was also impressed with Arnold's account of this waste of assets, remembering "long after the war" of the "ships . . . tied up at the docks at Noumea" that were "desperately needed . . . elsewhere." Pogue, *Education of a General*, 388-89.

152. Espiritu Santo is the largest and westernmost of the New Hebrides, extensively developed after May 1942 as a US air, naval, and supply base; Canton Island is a coral atoll, largest of the Phoenix Islands, central Pacific, 1,700 miles northeast of the New Hebrides.

153. Rear Adm Leigh Noyes, USN, commander Air Support Force, had been on board the USS *Wasp* (aircraft carrier, *Hornet* class, commissioned 1940) which had been damaged by a Japanese submarine off Guadalcanal, 15 September 1942 and finally sunk. Lt Cmdr Ernest M. "Ernie" Snowden, Arnold's son-in-law, had been serving on the ship and was among its survivors.

154. Arnold meant Adm D'Argenlieu, French military commander of New Caledonia, who was leaving the area. See Arnold's brief comment and proper identification in Arnold, *Global Mission*, 342.

155. McCain would become the chief, Navy Bureau of Aeronautics, before becoming assistant chief of naval operations for Air. His relief was Rear Adm Aubrey W. Fitch, whom Arnold and the AAF much preferred.

156. Port Moresby, New Guinea, although threatened to within 30 miles over the Kokoda trail from the north, appeared to be safe from ground attack in view of the success of Australian attacks that began on 27 September. The conference was held on 28 September.

157. Approximately 30 miles northwest of Noumea, Tontouta was the main American base in New Caledonia, having been taken over by American units in early April 1942.

158. Air Marshal Sir John Baldwin, RAF, commander Tactical Forces, Eastern Air Command; or possibly Hanson Baldwin of the *New York Times*; Melvin Maas, longtime Minnesota congressman then serving as a colonel in the US Marine Corps Reserve (USMCR) on Guadalcanal.

159. McClain of the Army is not otherwise identified.

160. The Northwest Airways manager is not otherwise identified.

161. Brisbane is a city on Australia's east coast, capital of Queensland, and site of MacArthur's headquarters. Maj Gen George Kenney had assumed command of Allied Air Forces in the Southwest Pacific, 4 August 1942. He was not at all pleased by the way advance arrangements had been handled for General Arnold. According to Kenney, Arnold's schedule had been "sent in by punch card code which can be broken in half an hour. . . . His staff didn't use their heads very well unless they want the Nips to pull an interception on the old man." To prevent the disaster, Kenney rearranged Arnold's entire schedule and route, changing his flights while in the theater

to be flown primarily at night rather than the daylight as originally planned. Occasional daylight flights were provided with fighter escort. Kenney Diary, 24 September 1942. Seven months later, in April 1943, American aviators prepared and carried out a successful attack against Japanese Admiral Yamamoto.

162. Either the military version of the twin-engine low-wing cantilever monoplane built by Lockheed called the Lodestar and designated the C-60 by the AAF or a smaller twin-engine monoplane designated the C-40. The airport is not otherwise identified but its runways were not long enough to accommodate Arnold's C-87. Cabell recalled that the operational Lockheed to Brisbane was "bare of any seats" with Hap sitting on an ammunition box while Kenney squatted beside him discussing problems. Cabell, 54. Maj Gen Richard K. Sutherland, USA, was chief of staff to General MacArthur.

163. The two American divisions were the 32d and 41st.

164. Until 4 August 1942, when succeeded by Kenney, Lt Gen George H. Brett had served as deputy supreme commander, Allied Forces Southwest Pacific and as MacArthur's air commander. MacArthur much preferred Kenney. Brig Gen Kenneth N. Walker, CG, Fifth Bomber Command; Brig Gen Ennis C. Whitehead, deputy CG, Fifth Air Force.

165. The lunch was at Lennon's hotel. Brig Gen Donald Wilson was Chief of Staff to General Kenney. The latter was well prepared for his meeting with Arnold. Kenney's diary entry for 25 September gives an extensive account of their conversation. His five-page memo of the same date entitled "Notes to Discuss with General Arnold" covered such subjects as aircraft and personnel requirements, organization and personnel changes, analyses of the operational capabilities of AAF aircraft in the theater, promotion policies and radio command and control problems. Since the two were old friends, Kenney was not inhibited in any way in these conversations with his chief from Washington. Modern commanders will have a sense of déjà vu when reading of Kenney's complaints that the Air Staff was trying to run the war from Washington. As he wrote, Arnold "has a few 'career' boys who like to dip their fingers into everything. I'll probably keep on having trouble and insulting someone if they try to interfere with me. One thing that helps is that one Douglas MacArthur believes in me and will not let me down—because among other things he knows I'll not let him down." Kenney Diary, 25 September 1942.

166. Lae is a town in Papua, northeast New Guinea.

167. Buna is a town at the eastern terminus of the Kokoda trail over the Stanley Mountains, New Guinea. The significant operation is covered in Craven and Cate, vol. 4, 98.

168. Maj Gen Robert L. Eichelberger, USA, CG, I Corps.

169. Cabell contrasted the "gloom and foreboding" he—and presumably Hap—found in the leadership at Noumea with the confidence and determination among Kenney and his staff in Australia; Cabell, 54. No requests to go home are recorded in the unit histories although the reference is probably to the 19th Bomb Group, whose members had been in active combat in the theater since Pearl Harbor.

170. Townsville is a city and port, Queensland, northeast coast of Australia.

171. Their contact in the period between the two wars is not completely documented. Certainly their paths had crossed in the decade 1925-1935 when both were in and out of Washington, Arnold as chief of Information for the Air Service during the Mitchell court-martial trial where MacArthur was a member and later when MacArthur was Chief of Staff (1930-1935). In the latter period Arnold, although stationed in California, testified several times before congressional committees and they had contact when Arnold departed from and returned to Washington on his historic B-10 flight to Alaska in 1934. As the biographical sketch above indicates, Arnold had met with MacArthur in 1934 to ascertain why he had not been promoted to the rank of general. Arnold's impression of MacArthur's appearance and manner during this trip was shared by Kenney who, in his first meeting with MacArthur a month earlier, had found him "drawn, nervous, tired and harassed." Kenney Diary, 30 July 1942. Cabell, traveling with Arnold, found MacArthur, whom he greatly admired, "an old man" with a "generally emaciated appearance." Cabell, 55.

172. Capt William G. Stoddard Jr., had graduated in 1940 from West Point along with Arnold's son, H. H. Jr., "Hank."

173. Darwin is a port, Northern Territory, northern Australia, that had been raided by Japanese carrier-based aircraft as early as 19 February, killing more than 240 people. Kenney indicated that the raid of 25 September was the 37th thus far by the Japanese. Kenney Diary, 16 September 1942.

174. Gen Sir Thomas A. Blamey, Australian Army, commander, Allied Land Forces; Lt Gen S. F. Roswell, Australian Army Corps commander.

175. Although the physical conditions he found at Port Moresby were ignored by Arnold, Cabell described the "appalling unpleasant" ones marked by clouds of dust and ubiquitous black flies; Cabell, 57. The 19th Bombardment Group had been in the Philippines since late October 1941 and had suffered considerable strain and losses after the Japanese destroyed most of their B-17s on Clark Field just hours after Pearl Harbor. The unit then participated in the defense of the Philippines and took part in the battle of Coral Sea. They were returned to Pocatello, Idaho, by December 1942, having left Mareeba, Australia, late in October, no doubt as a result of Arnold's and Kenney's agreement on their war-weary nature. The 90th Bomb Group, then in Hawaii and equipped with B-24s, replaced them in the theater, arriving in Australia in early November. Kenney had concluded almost immediately upon his arrival in the Pacific that the 19th needed to be sent home, feeling at the time of his meeting with Arnold that, psychologically, "they are not worth fooling with." The group served after its return to the United States as a replacement training unit until reconstituted in April 1944 as a Very Heavy Bombardment Group equipped with B-29 aircraft and moved to Guam in December 1944. By the time it entered combat against the Japanese home islands in February 1945, the unit had undergone a complete change of combat personnel and equipment. Kenney Diary,

1, 5, 10, 13, 15, 21 August, 25 September 1942; and Arnold to Kenney, 19 October 1942, AP.

176. Salamaua was a Japanese supply base on Huon Gulf, northeast New Guinea. By early October, Port Moresby appeared safe from ground attack.

177. "Feathering" is the shutting down of an engine and changing the blade angle of a controllable pitch propeller so that the blades are parallel to the line of flight, thereby offering less resistance than if the blades remained in their normal position. The result is less drag and reduced probability of destructive vibration.

178. Not unexpectedly, there is no record of their rowdy arrival into Port Moresby in their unit histories.

179. Col LaVerne G. "Blondy" Saunders, CO, B-17-equipped 11th Bomb Group, New Hebrides; probably Brig Gen William C. Rose, USA, who had been sent out to Espirtu Santo in late May and had completed a survey for an airfield there.

180. Rear Adm Aubrey W. "Jake" Fitch, USN, had succeeded Rear Admiral McCain as COMAIRSOPAC on 20 September 1942. Arnold did not regret the change.

181. Col Roger W. Ramey, Director of Operations, Seventh Air Force. As a result of Arnold's visit, he became CO of the B-17 equipped 43d Bombardment Group at Port Moresby on 21 October 1942.

182. This was the twin-engine, low-wing, cantilever monoplane built by Cessna Aircraft Company, designated AT-17 when used as an advanced trainer, as UC-78 when in service as a light personnel transport, which was their use in this theater at the time.

183. Lt Col James T. Connally, who commanded the 19th Bombardment Group from 15 April 1942 to 10 July 1942 and was succeeded by Lt Col Richard N. Carmichael who led the unit until 1 January 1943; Lt Col Eugene H. Beebe, now operations officer, Fifth Air Force; Col John H. "Skippy" Davies, who had commanded the B-24 equipped 3d Bombardment Group from its base at Charters Towers, Australia, since 2 April 1942 and was relieved by Lt Col Robert F. Strickland on 26 October 1942, no doubt as a result of a decision made during Arnold's visit. Davies returned to the Pacific theater in December 1944 at Tinian Island as a brigadier general, CG of the 313th Bombardment Wing of B-29s. The 43d Bombardment Group, equipped with B-17s, had been in Australia since late March 1942. They got a new commanding officer, Col Rogert W. Ramey, on 21 October as a result of Arnold's visit. See note 175.

184. Maj Gen George S. Stratemeyer, chief of the Air Staff, Headquarters AAF.

185. USS *Hornet*, aircraft carrier, *Yorktown* class, commissioned in 1941, took part in the Battle of Midway, later lost in October 1942 at the Battle of Santa Cruz.

186. Rear Adm Richmond Kelley Turner, USN, now commanded Amphibious Forces, US Pacific Fleet; Col William M. Ritchie, Operations Division, War Department General Staff, accompanied Arnold on this trip.

His oral report on his findings to Stimson was made to the Secretary on 13 October 1942; Stimson Diary, 13 October 1942.

187. See Postscript to this chapter for Arnold's candid but discouraging remarks at this meeting.

188. From Arnold's viewpoint, this succinct sentence characterized the differences of opinion regarding the two theaters.

189. In his diary entry for this date, Kenney assessed this meeting as a "combined courtesy call and discussion in general terms between SWPA and SOUPAC." He commented that Ghormley "looked tired and about due to go home. Perhaps this is why we were not invited to stay for dinner" although the meeting lasted until after 8 P.M. Ghormley was relieved on 18 October. Arnold was probably not in disagreement with Kenney's summary of the major Army-Navy differences at the conference: "Navy thinks they have all the troubles and believe that we should forget everything but helping them out at Guadalcanal." Kenney Diary, 28 September 1942.

190. Maj Robert A. Ping, who continued as Arnold's pilot on this trip, in 1944 was a colonel in command of the 505th Bombardment Group of B-29s at North Field, Tinian.

191. Dated the previous day, Arnold wrote Kenney: "The entire nation is watching your efforts and applauding your success." Recommendation for promotion of Kenney to Lt Gen was made two days later, clearly as a result of Arnold's pleasure at what he had seen, even though Kenney had been in the theater less than two months. Letter to Harmon not located; by comparison he was not promoted until February 1943. See Sutherland memo, 30 September 1942, Kenney Diary; copy of Arnold's letter to Kenney is in AP.

192. La Foa is a town, south central New Caledonia; Brig Gen Edmond B. Sebree, USA, assistant CG, US Americal Division.

193. The hotel and its proprietress are not otherwise identified.

194. Although both the handwritten diary and the typescript read "Fuller," Arnold meant Col. Lewis B. "Chesty" Puller, USMC. Later that month, Puller led the reinforcement of the First Marine Division on Guadalcanal while earning his fourth Navy Cross.

195. Maj Ashwell is not otherwise identified.

196. Button was the code name for location of base on Espirtu Santo, New Hebrides, from which the 11th Bombardment Group was then operating; Roses was the code name for Efate, an island, central New Hebrides, from which B-17s and B-26s raided the Japanese in the Solomons. It had been a US base since March 1942.

197. It would be another six weeks, until 11-12 November, before 6,000 troops were sent as reinforcements to Guadalcanal. By 9 December General Patch had assumed command there with troops of the Second Marine Division and the Army's 25th Division, replacing Marine Maj Gen A. A. Vandergrift and the First Marine Division who were evacuated to Australia.

198. Cactus was the code name for the Guadalcanal operation. Arnold, fearing loss of his diary, occasionally used code names.

199. Upon his return to Washington, Arnold immediately sent for the headquarters personnel responsible for the design and procurement of life

rafts. After requiring them to spend some time in the Potomac River in similar rafts, changes were made in their number and design, and in the fishing gear provided as emergency equipment. See Arnold's efforts to resolve the problems in Arnold, *Global Mission*, 348, 354–55.

200. Col Truman H. Landon would become in January, as a brigadier general, CG, Seventh Bomber Command. His stay in the United States was brief and the reason for his return to the United States is unknown. Maj Gen Robert Olds, CG, Second Air Force, Fort George Wright, Washington. The letter to Emmons was not sent; see AP.

201. Reference is to the geographical division of responsibility between the areas under control of the two services; the memo is not located.

202. Col Arthur W. Meehan did not go to Australia but assumed command on 21 October 1942, for less than a month, of the B-24 equipped 90th Bombardment Group stationed at Hickam Field, Hawaii. In view of the problems at Guadalcanal, the unit was dispatched to Iron Range, Australia, prior to November 1942. The group had then moved to Port Moresby by early February 1943. Ramey did go to Australia, later becoming commander of the 43d Bombardment Group at Port Moresby on 21 October 1942.

203. Maj Gen Harold L. George, CG, ATC; see discussion in the Postscript to this chapter of this memo written during Hap's stay in Hawaii.

204. Brig Gen William E. Farthing, CO, Seventh Air Force Command; Maj Gen Henry J. F. Miller would become CG, Eighth Air Force Service Command in Britain in November 1942; the reference to Fort Worth, Texas, is not clear but at this time it was headquarters for the AAF Training Command. A flight surgeon is a medical officer of the AAF specifically trained to diagnose and treat aviators and illnesses associated with flying.

205. Arnold functioned as an airborne King Neptune in initiating all first-time crossers of the equator.

206. Col Emil C. Kiel, chief of staff, Fourth Air Force.

207. This was the San Francisco waterfront restaurant named for the New York Yankee baseball player.

208. Although his assignment at the time is not known, Thach as a US naval officer had commanded VF-3 on board the USS *Yorktown* at the Battle of Midway. He was known as the developer of the "Thach weave," a maneuver wherein two aircraft flying a parallel course moved from side to side in trail to protect each other. He recently had stated to the press, covered in the *New York Times* of 1 October 1942 for example, in lauding carrier-based aircraft, that no major ship in the war had been sunk by horizontal bombing. Realizing that Hap could be interviewed by the press on his arrival on the West Coast, and knowing Arnold's impetuosity as well as his views on the Navy, General Marshall wired Arnold on his arrival in California that War Department policy was "to make no comment publicly [sic] and not to mention the matter [Thach's comments] . . . on the grounds that the indiscretion is so gross that the initial moves for correction should come from the Navy." He also wanted to "warn" Arnold against comments and to have him "suppress possible comments by your people." Hap apparently heeded Marshall's request and made no public statement on the issue. For the next

several months, however, Arnold sent memos to the White House, to General Marshall, (6 October) and to Admiral Leahy (7 October) on the efficacy of horizontal bombing by land-based aircraft. The communications are in AP. Unfortunately, the results of AAF high-altitude bombing of naval vessels were not outstanding. See the discussion in Craven and Cate, vol. 4, 63-68. Secretary Stimson's account of his heated discussion with Secretary of the Navy Frank Knox over the issue of AAF high-altitude bombing is in Stimson Diary, 20 October 1942.

209. A supercharger is a pump or compressor for forcing more air or fuel-air mixture into an engine than it would normally take in at prevailing atmospheric pressure, thus enhancing its performance especially at high altitude.

210. Brig Gen James A. Ulio was the assistant Adjutant General of the Army.

211. The others on the aircraft were awarded the Air Medal; Cabell, 59. Interestingly enough, Arnold's modesty ignores completely the awarding of his medal in his memoirs. Arnold, *Global Mission*, 350.

212. Kenney to Arnold, 3 October 1942, AP.

213. Cabell, 57-58.

214. Ibid., 55-56. Arnold made no mention in his autobiography of a JCS request that MacArthur be assessed by Hap in terms of possessing the stamina required to continue the war "on the long road to Tokyo." One possible reason for any omission, assuming he had been so commissioned, was that at the time of writing *Global Mission* in 1948, all of the 1942 members of the JCS were still alive and MacArthur was very forcefully and successfully presiding over the postwar occupation of Japan, still going strong six years after Arnold's 1942 assessment and visit. Arnold, *Global Mission*, 343-46.

215. Arnold, *Global Mission*, 330; and Stimson Diary, 3, 16 October 1942.

216. Potter, 192; and Samuel Eliot Morison, *History of United States Naval Operations in World War II*, vol. 5, *The Struggle for Guadalcanal, August 1942 to February 1943* (Boston: Little Brown & Co., 1948), 117.

217. Arnold to Kenney, 8, 24 October 1942, AP.

218. Arnold to Eaker, 2 November 1942, AP.

219. Pogue, *Ordeal and Hope*, 388.

220. Stimson's accounts of Arnold's oral reports to him on his trip are in Stimson Diary, 3, 16 October 1942. McCain's remarks are in Adlai E. Stevenson, *The Papers of Adlai E. Stevenson*, vol. 2, *Washington to Springfield, 1941-1948*, ed. Walter Johnson (Boston: Little Brown & Co., 1973), 104, 29 January 1943.

221. Arnold to Eisenhower, 23 October 1942, AP.

222. King to Marshall and Leahy, 3 October 1942, MPMS.

223. Pogue, *Ordeal and Hope*, 393.

224. FDR to Leahy, King, Marshall and Arnold, 24 October 1942, AP.

225. Marshall to FDR, 26 October 1942, MPMS.

226. Marshall to King, 24 October 1942, MPMS.

227. Marshall to FDR, 26 October 1942, MPMS.

228. Pogue, *Ordeal and Hope*, 390-91.
229. Arnold to Hopkins, 21 August, 3, 13 September, 7 October 1942, AP.
230. Arnold to Harmon, 1 November 1942, AP.
231. Craven and Cate, vol. 4, 69-72.
232. Harmon to Stratemeyer, 6 December 1942, AP.
233. See the discussion in Craven and Cate, vol. 4, 61-72.
234. Arnold to CG, AFATC, 1 October 1942; and Preliminary Report on Future Air Transport Possibilities by the Special Committee of the AAF, 30 November 1942, AP.
235. See Arnold's diary entries of 11, 15, 16 September 1944, chap. 9.
236. Arnold to Kenney, 8 October 1942, AP.

Chapter 5

North Africa, Middle East, India, China 9 January–17 February 1943

Introduction

This 40-day odyssey was the most extensive of Arnold's World War II travels in terms of time away from Washington, distance traveled, and demands on his stamina and negotiating skills. The journey was important to the AAF since it resulted in the continuation of US strategic daylight bombing without the opposition Churchill had planned. During the 12 days in Casablanca, Hap participated in the first major overseas diplomacy/strategy meeting with Roosevelt and the British since US entry into the war. The remaining 25 days were spent in visiting AAF combat units in North Africa and then flying east to Iraq, India, and China. On his return, the itinerary included Oman, the Anglo-Egyptian Sudan, Gold Coast, Ascension Island, and two days in Brazil before arriving back on American territory.

The topical scope of the trip was almost as broad as the geographical span. The tasks presented cast Arnold in the role of strategist, airman, diplomat, logistician, peacemaker, allocator of aircraft, and even morale officer. He appeared to move easily from the strategy deliberations of the CCS with Churchill and Roosevelt to eating from mess kits in desert tent meetings with his aircrews. There, Hap listened to the airmen's combat experiences and tried to assess their morale. In stark contrast, he next spent five days in India, amidst what he considered luxury and a British lack of interest in pursuing planned combat operations in Burma. These British officers seemed to be enjoying their posh Indian offices and their distance from the fighting. The India stopover was followed by six days in bleak wartime China. En route over the famed "Hump," Arnold experienced a flight as potentially life threatening as any he had taken since his crash at Fort Riley 30 years earlier. Navigational errors, unexpected weather phenomena, and the overconfidence of some flight crew members combined to produce some tense hours in the air. During his busy days in China, Arnold spent more time in negotiations with Chiang Kai-shek than had any other member of the JCS during the war. These negotiations with the Chinese leader, his officials, and the two feuding senior American officers serving there dealt with seemingly unsolvable problems, including those of command, logistics, personnel, and strategy.

No matter what else his 27,842 miles of travel brought, he retained his sense of humor and continued to record the details of his surroundings. His brief and hence superficial exposure to many new and different cultures often revealed a naive curiosity as well as an occasional failure to understand and appreciate the differences between these cultures and his own. In spite of his earlier travels, this three-star general's reaction was little different from those of millions of other American service personnel who found themselves thrust into locations and cultures they had never studied in geography books.

As he left Washington on this journey, Arnold and the JCS had to have been encouraged by the marked improvement in Allied fortunes since Hap's return from the Pacific the previous October. Although important decisions and intensive fighting still lay ahead, the previous three months had produced some Allied successes. The precarious position of the US Marines on Guadalcanal, in part prompting Arnold's September 1942 visit to the Pacific theater, had been eased. The Japanese had been unable to effectively reinforce and resupply their troops there since early November. By December 1942, US troops outnumbered Japanese troops on the island. Ten days before Arnold departed from Washington on this journey, the Japanese had decided to evacuate Guadalcanal; the last of their forces had departed the island before Hap's February return to the United States. Other Allied triumphs in the Pacific had thwarted the Japanese threat to Port Moresby by the time of the Casablanca meeting. In that same theater, the US Navy had been successful in sea battles at Cape Esperance and Santa Cruz after having experienced earlier losses. Elsewhere, American troops had landed in the Aleutians in early January 1943, presaging Japanese expulsion from these islands.

The invasion of North Africa that had begun on 8 November was proceeding well. Setbacks such as that at Kasserine Pass still lay ahead. In the fighting there, a tactical air-ground partnership was being forged between American air and ground units that would prove eminently successful. This was a phase of air operations that had not been stressed or visualized by Arnold in the prewar period. It would prove to be successful not only there but later in northern Europe as well. In a harbinger of future air attacks against the Third Reich capital, the RAF raided Berlin for the first time while Roosevelt, Churchill, Arnold, and their staffs deliberated in Casablanca. The US Eighth Air Force, Arnold's projected instrument to validate daylight strategic bombing, ventured on its first raid over Germany proper on 27 January while Arnold was still on his travels. The news was equally encouraging in Russia as much of the German Sixth Army's leadership surrendered before Stalingrad along with the remnants of the now defeated army. The battle of the Atlantic against German U-boats was far from being won, but new British airborne radar offered some encouraging prospects for Coastal Command. Shipping losses continued to mount, however, as the dreaded submarines increased their toll of Allied shipping sunk from 200,000 tons in January to 360,000 tons in February and 627,000 tons in March, the worst monthly loss of the year. This menace would be reflected in the agreement, reached at Casablanca, that attacks on the submarine pens and yards were to have the highest priority for Allied bombers.

Although there was little exhilaration expressed among the conferees at Casablanca (and Hap recorded no emotion over the limited Allied victories), Churchill's injunction to the combined chiefs of staff during the meeting, "we must not relinquish the initiative now that we have it," was a continuation of the prime minister's prediction two months earlier that these late 1942 victories were the "end of the beginning."[1]

In many ways, this trip was a major milestone among Arnold's World War II experiences. Probably unknown to him at the time, only 20 months earlier he had been on the verge of forced retirement by the president, who had lost confidence in his chief Army aviator. Now Hap traveled to Casablanca as a full-fledged member of the Combined Chiefs of Staff and, reflecting FDR's increasing faith in his abilities, the president sent him from this conference to India and China via Egypt and Iraq on missions that were as much diplomatic as they were military. Before Arnold left the Casablanca meeting, decisions reached there appeared to ensure that the concept of daylight strategic bombardment would be given the chance to succeed that he had planned and hoped for.

Although Arnold had gained stature during the last two years, his campaign of paralyzing Germany through strategic daylight bombing was in serious jeopardy as the conferees sailed for Casablanca. It is not clear to what extent Arnold was aware of Prime Minister Churchill's increasing concern over the US Eighth Air Force's lack of progress in England. Even though daylight attacks by the American bombers were an article of faith for Arnold and much of the US leadership, including the White House, results since the first raid on 17 August 1942 against targets in France were disappointing. In the two weeks of August remaining after the first attack, the Eighth had dispatched bombers on only six days. The record in the remaining four months of 1942 was even less encouraging. American heavies were launched against the enemy on only four days in September, three in October, eight in November, and four in December.[2] From Arnold's point of view, as well as that of the commander of the Eighth Air Force, there were logical explanations for this limited showing, the most serious being the weather over both Britain and the continent. Other inhibiting factors included the growing pains associated with Eighth Air Force's development of operating methods and the drain of airplanes and crews to support Torch as well as the diversion of air assets to the Pacific. Churchill however, struck by the contrast between the feeble US efforts and the increasing number of raids flown by the RAF, began to question the nature, viability, cost, and impact of the American effort. This concern was a reversal of his support for the US program expressed as recently as Arnold's trip to the Pacific. In his 16 September telegram to FDR, the

British leader had called for the addition of "a few hundred fortresses . . . while German Air Forces are still in Russia." He then had urged that we "concentrate every available fortress . . . as quickly as possible."[3] Only a month later, however, Churchill wrote his helpful White House conduit Harry Hopkins, urging that the United States shift its emphasis away from the heavy bombers in the 1943 aircraft production schedule then in final stages of preparation. The prime minister insisted that the few missions flown into France thus far by the AAF "do not give our experts the same confidence as yours in the power of the day bomber."[4]

A week later, in a 22 October meeting with his military chiefs, Churchill raised a host of questions about US air operations. Beginning with the suggestion that we "should urge them to take up night bombing on a large scale," he went on to recommend the manufacture of Lancaster heavy bombers in American plants and the development of the P-51 Mustang fighter "with the right [Rolls-Royce] engines." He felt that the British should attempt to convince the Americans to tailor production of aircraft in 1943 to "70,000 of the right kind" of planes rather than "100,000 of those we are now projecting." He was realistic, however, in appreciating that the British would have "to accommodate themselves" to the United States.[5] His disparagement of the limited American efforts thus far, his strong desire that the US airmen abandon daylight bombing and join the RAF in their night operations, and his concern about the proposed production schedule for 1943 were among the issues that the prime minister intended to raise at the forthcoming Casablanca meeting.

Not surprisingly, the prime minister's query of 22 October prompted a reply the next day from Archie Sinclair, the secretary of state for air. In his response, the British official conceded that Churchill's recommendations might prove "decisive" in influencing the American schedule for 1943 before it reached final form. Sinclair stressed, however, that if the US program continued to emphasize heavy bomber production (which Churchill, Portal, and the entire British leadership had urged on Arnold and Roosevelt during Hap's first trip to England in the spring of 1941 and on many occasions since), a combined RAF-USAAF force of some 4,000–6,000 bombers along with ground troops might "bring the harvest of victory" in 1944. In acknowledging the division of US opinion over Pacific versus European strategy and the debate over tactical as opposed to strategic air employment, Sinclair counseled that any gratuitous suggestions by Churchill about the types, functions, and numbers of US aircraft to be produced in 1943 might well "crystallize American opinion." However, this solidification might well throw the advocates of strategic daylight bombing "into impotency and confusion if you pit yourself against their cherished policy of daylight penetration." He went on to caution against rushing the Americans into "impatience" and speculated optimistically that by early 1943 there could be raids of 1,000 RAF bombers hitting a target at night complemented the next day by 500–600 US heavies in pinpoint daylight attacks against the same target. If successful, Sinclair felt, these combined raids would "go a long way towards winning the war." Overgenerously praising the "astonishing accuracy of American bombing thus far," Sinclair suggested that it would be "a tragedy if we were to frustrate them on the eve of this great experiment." Recommending against any effort of the British to divert the AAF into the U-boat struggle which he labeled "disastrous," the secretary warned that the United States might, in the face of criticism of their limited European success thus far, allocate the assets planned for use in Britain to the war in the Pacific.[6] Aware of Admiral King's as well as others' strong interest in the Pacific becoming the main theater of American operations, the possibility that the United States would shift emphasis to that theater remained a significant factor in tempering British opposition to American daylight bombing plans.

In his response, Churchill remained "not at all convinced" by either Sinclair's memo of 23 October or the secretary's estimate of the "merits of daylight penetration."[7] In his 2 November memo to RAF Chief Portal, he complained that although 18,000 AAF personnel had arrived in England in July and their numbers had since expanded more than threefold to 55,000, "results thus far have been pitifully small." He pointed out that US bombers had not penetrated beyond Lille,

France, while requiring "very strong British fighter escort" with losses to the protecting fighters exceeding those of the bombers. In all of this, he lamented, "not a bomb has been dropped on Germany." The prime minister acknowledged the "high reputations" involved in the daylight strategy, clearly meaning Roosevelt, Stimson, Marshall, and Arnold among others, and regretted that in this testing period "a large number" of US flyers would be in Britain "playing a very little part in the war." He continued to feel that the current production program with its emphasis on producing heavy daylight bombers was "in an unprofitable groove." In contrast to his disappointment with the limited American showing thus far, the prime minister was encouraged by the new technical developments in night operating equipment and procedures now being used or adopted by the RAF. Churchill's memo to Portal ended with the question, hardly intended to be rhetorical, "What are we to do?"[8]

Portal, joined by Air Vice Marshal Slessor from Washington, disagreed with the prime minister and concurred with Sinclair. They cautioned Churchill against premature opposition to the American daylight operations. They argued for more time to assess the daylight results and Portal conceded he was "keen to give the Americans every possible chance" to achieve success.[9] Realizing Churchill's growing concern, Portal cabled the RAF delegation in the United States to push Arnold for an attack on Germany proper "at the earliest possible moment."[10] Unfortunately, the first raid over German soil was not to be mounted until 27 January, four days after the Casablanca conference adjourned. It was in this atmosphere of serious concern over the continuation of the American daylight bombing effort that Arnold and the JCS departed for the Casablanca conference.

Diplomatic/strategic issues were among the major concerns that had prompted the calling of this gathering. As Allied progress was being achieved in North Africa, decisions to be made included where the next major Allied attacks were to be mounted. In simplest terms, the British would insist that further Mediterranean operations rather than the cross-Channel attack desired by the Americans should be the next major steps. Although the US military leaders were unanimous in their position, they were not to be successful at Casablanca.

The first day's flight from Washington en route to the meeting terminated overnight in warm Puerto Rico, which provided a welcome change from the frigid temperatures left behind. The next three days involved overnight stops in Belem, Brazil; Dakar, French West Africa; and Marrakesh, French Morocco. Arnold arrived in Casablanca before noon on the fourth day of this trip. Opening on the following day, the conference proceeded with varying degrees of intensity over the next 10 days.

It is not certain when Arnold learned of Churchill's doubts over the continuation of American daylight bombing, but as soon as Hap reached Casablanca he sent word to Eisenhower requesting that the Eighth Air Force commander, Maj Gen Ira Eaker, be detailed to join the conferees as soon as possible.[11] It seems logical that Arnold would have had Eaker present at the opening of the meetings if he had known of Churchill's opposition. Arnold's other commanders in the theater were also quickly assembled, including Maj Gen Tooey Spaatz and Lt Gen Frank Andrews. In view of this gathering of his senior commanders and the success they achieved in gaining Churchill's willingness to allow continuation of daylight bombing by the AAF, it seems curious that Arnold devoted so little coverage in the diary to this aspect of the conference. A partial explanation may be that a designated Allied secretariat was present and responsible for maintaining a record of the deliberations at these formal meetings of the CCS. There is no doubt that Arnold saw, approved, and was given a copy of the Top Secret Combined Bomber Offensive pronouncement agreed on at Casablanca, making the inclusion of its details redundant in a diary that was expanding rapidly and was to be continued for another several weeks while traveling. Also, having achieved validation of continued American daylight bombing, Hap may have seen little reason for including it in a diary that might well be exposed to unauthorized reading while he was on the long journey that still lay ahead. Another reason may have been Arnold's preoccupation with preparing for his forthcoming visits to other locations, including India and China, and the delicate but important problems that

Roosevelt and Marshall expected him to help illuminate if not attempt to resolve.

Given Churchill's intention of influencing Roosevelt to switch the relatively modest daylight Eighth effort to join the RAF in night bombing, Arnold and his supporting generals' efforts have to be evaluated as successful on this issue at Casablanca. The result was the agreement on the Combined Bomber Offensive (CBO), which marked the abandonment, at least for the moment, of Churchill's objections to the continuation of the American daylight effort. This major accomplishment makes it difficult, except for security considerations, to explain Arnold's limited coverage of the efforts that went into its achievement. Hap's laconic entry of 15 January, that he "Met Prime Minister on walk and asked for a chance to get him straight on US bombing; he agreed," hardly appears to give proper emphasis to the importance of the issue and the final decision reached.[12] As was his wont, Arnold was content, as reflected in the diary, not to claim credit for Churchill's change of heart. However, although not spelled out in the diary, the bulk of the plaudits belonged to General Eaker, the Eighth commander who appeared to have persuaded Churchill during their noon meeting of 20 January. The British prime minister has written that Eaker's succinct, well-reasoned arguments, particularly about the potential for round-the-clock operations with daylight AAF combined with RAF night bombing, convinced him not to oppose continuation of the American effort. As the prime minister later wrote, "I decided to back Eaker and his theme, and I turned around completely and withdrew all my opposition to the daylight bombing."[13]

Arnold's first stop after leaving Casablanca was in Algiers, where his main purpose appears to have been discussions with American airmen in combat units. He met with 10 combat groups in the 10 hours he was in the country. In informal meetings in small groups, which he appeared to enjoy, he ate their rations and asked about their problems with particular emphasis on morale and airplanes. These meetings involved more than pleasantries with the general from the Pentagon. The discussions involved every aspect of their operations, ranging from armor plate on the aircraft to the "red-lining" of their instruments that recorded air speed, inches of manifold pressure, and revolutions per minute (rpm). Other topics included turret operations, radio sets, maintenance procedures, parts shortages, and even the incidence of head colds from sleeping on the ground. A recurring discussion was the desirability of replacing crews individually in combat-experienced units versus bringing over entirely new inexperienced Groups. As evidence of the value he placed on this dialogue, Arnold dispatched to his chief of staff in the Pentagon by air courier a careful nine-page analysis of the problems encountered, instructing that they be "carefully studied" and, when possible, to "take corrective action."[14] For whatever reason, he does not record in the diary the honors bestowed on him and Colonel Smart. At a French Army outpost manned by Spahi native cavalrymen who were colorfully attired in their long red cloaks, Arnold, a three-star American general, was awarded the rank of staff sergeant and Colonel Smart the rank of private first class as honorary members of the unit.[15]

Hap's next flight took him to Cairo for three days, where he discussed the ramifications of the Casablanca decisions with senior AAF officers. He then flew to Tobruk in Libya to visit more American units. When he returned to Cairo, he had a long conversation with Churchill concerning what kind and how many American airplanes could be furnished to Turkey in the event Churchill was successful in inducing President Inonu of Turkey to enter the war. Although he was unsuccessful in getting Turkey to enter the fray, the fact that the prime minister discussed disposition of the planes was recognition of Arnold's now dominant role in the allocation of American aircraft.[16] Following his stay in Cairo, which allowed some time for sightseeing, Arnold next flew to Iraq where, according to his memoirs, "One of the missions given me by the President was to see what could be done to expedite the movement of U.S. planes . . . to the Russians." As his diary reflected, he met with both American and Russian officials but he has left no assessment of his success.[17] He next flew to Karachi and then on to New Delhi where for five nights he saw the reluctance of Wavell and his staff, in spite of the verbal commitment by Churchill at Casablanca, to plan seriously for the Anakim operation to retake Burma. Aided by Sir John Dill, Hap felt they had been somewhat successful in stirring the British staff in New Delhi to commence serious planning, which they anticipated assessing on their return from China.[18]

Continuing his practice, dictated by time and space constraints, of committing brief impressions to the diary rather than detailed assessments of the problems he anticipated, Arnold has left little written insight into what he expected as he flew on into China, probably his most difficult assignment. During the Casablanca meetings, Hopkins reported discussing the India-China mission and its prospects with Hap.

Discounting the prospects of getting the Burma Road reopened, which had been among the topics discussed at the conference, Arnold, according to Hopkins, indicated that the only intelligent move immediately is to "strengthen Chennault's air force and get at the bombing of Japan as soon as possible." Unable to appreciate how this could be done until he visited China, he was well aware of the problems between Bissell and Chennault but was "very confident . . . that the whole business can be worked out." Except for capturing Arnold's normal optimism, the sentiments reported were probably closer to Hopkins' thinking than to Hap's.[19]

Although Arnold's trip to China was planned before he left Washington, his mission seemed to gain urgency as a result of Casablanca. When discussing the final report on the last day of the CCS meetings, FDR indicated that he was disturbed to discover "no reference to operations in or from China" in the section dealing with the Pacific and the Far East theaters. Discounting operations in Burma that he felt "would not have a direct effect upon the Chinese" and stating that an "island-to-island advance across the Pacific would take too long," he stressed the "opportunity" to attack Japanese shipping, which could be done by "aircraft operating from China" where 200 planes were planned to be in use by April. Taking his cue from Roosevelt, Arnold added that he was aware of the need for more planes in China and that a bombardment Group (308th) was just about to depart the United States for that theater. He said he would assess "the best method of operating the aircraft" when he arrived in India. He cautioned, however, that demands for transport planes in other theaters "could not be neglected" but hoped that 135–150 transport planes would be providing service between India and China by late fall.[20]

The Allied conduct of the war in the China, Burma, India (CBI) theater appeared in many ways more difficult than others. The seemingly unstoppable Japanese advances southward, which included the losses of prewar bases in the Philippines and Singapore during the early months after Pearl Harbor, suggested Chinese territory as one of the few locations from which the Allies could attack enemy holdings in the Far East. The Japanese lines of communication between the home islands and their newly won southern conquests appeared vulnerable only to air interdiction. Operations from mainland China were limited, however, by several important factors.

Significant among them was that the Japanese occupied all of coastal China and had forced the Chiang Kai-shek government inland to Chungking, 700 miles from Hong Kong and 1,500 miles from the major shipping routes in the East China Sea. This put the enemy's communications lines, except those to Burma, well beyond the range of any Allied aircraft that could be supported logistically from existing Chinese bases. With the fall of Lashio in northern Burma in late April 1942, which was followed quickly by Japanese control of the entire country, the Burma Road was effectively closed, leaving air as the sole avenue available for getting supplies into China.

Among other major considerations in dealing with China were wide philosophical differences between FDR's and Churchill's concepts of the role and importance of that nation in wartime as well as the postwar world. Roosevelt's view that China had to be kept in the war at all costs led him to treat Chiang Kai-shek as a viable fellow leader in control of his country. As a result, Chiang was able to gain considerable leverage over Lend-Lease aid, planned Allied Asian operations, and the American command structure in China. Whereas Britain and the United States were strong national states having modern industrial bases, China lacked not only national unity but manufacturing capability and technical skills as well. Her most usable asset was her vast unskilled and untrained manpower pool. Chinese territorial claims, some ages old, against Tibet, Burma, parts of India, and Hong Kong, did not encourage the British Prime Minister to enthusiastically support the creation of a strong China. The postwar British aim for Asia was a return to the status quo ante, which clearly conflicted with the idealistic Roosevelt's hope of China emerging as a stable power, strong enough to occupy the vacuum anticipated by the defeat of Japan.

Additional pressure came from a Chinese campaign to lobby the White House and Congress for increased aid. One of their techniques was to portray nonexistent military campaigns as Chinese victories to the seemingly gullible media.[21] Many of these, relayed through a naive Harry Hopkins, found their way into the sympathetic Oval Office. As the official US Army History has concluded, "An ardent, articulate and adroit Sinophile faction claimed that the Chinese were courageously and competently resisting the Japanese and needed only arms to drive them into the sea." Joseph Alsop, a distant relative of FDR and later a uniformed member of Chennault's staff, regularly wrote to Hopkins about conditions in China. An example of his alarmist prose, written before he ever reached China, was hardly dispassionate but probably not untypical as he informed Hopkins, who furnished the assessment to FDR, that the AAF in China "was a national tragedy . . . a national scandal . . . greatly dishonoring to the President, Army and country." He joined others in insisting that the solution was to recall Stilwell and elevate Chennault.[22] Material flattering to Chiang and his government appeared in the press, aided and embellished by the lobbying efforts in Washington of Foreign Minister T. V. Soong and his attractive sister Madame Chiang. These lobbying tactics made a realistic appraisal of China by the White House and the Congress exceedingly difficult. As Barbara Tuchman has written, "in the [US] public mind China was the favorite ally." Additionally, pro-Chiang forces did not hesitate to play on Roosevelt's fears of China signing a separate peace with Japan.[23] Shortly after Pearl Harbor, Roosevelt and Churchill at their Arcadia meetings in Washington agreed that China was to be a major theater of operations. Chiang Kai-shek was named supreme commander, China Theater, on 29 December 1941. Soon thereafter, Chiang requested that an even more senior American officer than the on-site Brig Gen John Magruder should be sent to Chungking.[24] In Secretary of War Stimson's view, the newly dispatched officer was to develop "an effective ultimate counteroffensive by or from China proper against Japan."[25] The officer selected was Joseph W. Stilwell, a career infantry officer recently promoted to lieutenant general, who had been three years ahead of Arnold at West Point, knew China as a result of two tours there, and spoke the language. The anomalous nature of his position was reflected in his titles as chief of staff to Chiang Kai-shek and commander of US Forces in the CBI theater. Additionally, he was responsible for allocating Lend-Lease material to China.[26]

While Stilwell was en route to this assignment, Allied fortunes in the Far East worsened. Singapore was surrendered with the loss of 138,000 British men, MacArthur was ordered to abandon the Philippines, and Japanese successes threatened the Burma Road. This route was further jeopardized after Stilwell's arrival when Rangoon fell on 8 March. Loss of this last major Burmese port resulted seven weeks later in complete closure of the road. As the situation there grew worse for the Allies, FDR enjoined Arnold, in the week following the fall of Lashio, to confer with the Chinese "on alternative air routes." Arnold was directed to "explore every possibility, both as to airplanes and routes. It is essential that our route be kept open, no matter how difficult." For the most part, these instructions were to dictate American air policy in China for the next two years.[27] These orders were issued while Arnold was struggling with the aircraft allocation issue that led to his trip abroad in May 1942. At the same time, Hap was scrambling for sufficient planes to support the expanding AAF programs and completely fill the Russian allocation, as directed by FDR.

Even before the Japanese attack on China in July 1937, Chiang had sought outside assistance in strengthening his military. In addition to negotiations with advisors from other nations, negotiations with a US Air Corps officer, Claire L. Chennault, had begun as early as July 1936. As a result, Chennault sailed for China within 10 days after his 1937 retirement from the US Air Corps. Chennault had joined the

US Army in World War I but was not awarded his wings until after the armistice. He spent the bulk of the twenties in pursuit assignments and by 1935 had become the leading defender of the pursuit plane on the faculty of the Air Corps Tactical School where his advocacy has been described as "rabid."[28] The Japanese began their attack on China six weeks after his arrival, commencing the war that was to last until 1945. In the four years between Chennault's arrival in China and the Japanese attack on Pearl Harbor, his efforts to test his combat theories were hampered by factors that would continue to limit China's fighting effectiveness throughout the war. Among these was Chiang's insecure position among his generals, which gave rise to his inability to commit to a consistent military policy. Additionally, China's airplanes, maintenance personnel, and logistical support remained primitive by US standards. Chennault instituted a crude but effective human-based early warning system for approaching Japanese aircraft, but the limited education and skill levels of Chinese trainees and pilots, the lack of a technological support base, a shortage of modern aircraft, and airfields built by hand—almost rock by rock—reduced its effectiveness. Massive corruption, which appeared endemic to the Chinese military and many other facets of Chinese society, was only one of many manifestations of the vast cultural differences he and numerous other Americans encountered.

As World War II engulfed Europe after 1939 and US public opinion appeared more sympathetic to support for China, short of entering the war, Chennault began to acquire modern aircraft and to attract a group of American civilian fliers and mechanics, most with military aviation experience. Recruitment of these Americans, formally labeled the American Volunteer Group (AVG), began in earnest in the summer of 1941. They commenced combat operations against the Japanese two weeks after Pearl Harbor. Publicity about their aerial exploits and newsreel pictures of their aircraft, P-40s with menacing large jaws and teeth painted on the noses, quickly endeared the group to the American public, which named them "Flying Tigers." The skill of the pilots, Chennault's fighter tactics, and his early warning system enabled them in their short six months' existence to claim the enviable record of 297 Japanese aircraft destroyed for the loss of only 14 AVG planes in combat.[29]

In order to regularize their operations as part of the US military, AVG personnel who were willing and qualified were integrated into the AAF as the China Air Task Force (CATF) on 4 July 1942. Brigadier General Chennault, who had opposed the arrangement, was named commanding general of the new organization. This unit was made subordinate to the Tenth Air Force, which was based in India and commanded by Brig Gen Clayton Bissell, who purposely was given a date of rank one day senior to that of Chennault. Chiang was reported to have said this action was a "direct kick in the teeth," reflecting that China "would not be given the air strength" he wanted. According to one source, however, "it reflected General Arnold's distaste for Chennault."[30] Arnold offers only a glimpse into this, writing in his memoirs that he was "responsible for General Bissell's being in command over Chennault."[31] Chennault himself explained that although he had been senior to Bissell in the "Regular Army," the dating of the promotions was such that Bissell "became senior to me. It was an old and effective Army routine."[32] Whether this action was due to Arnold's and Marshall's desire to ensure that the CATF was properly organized, run, and supported according to AAF and War Department guidelines cannot be established. The resulting system of command, operations, and accountability, however, bore little resemblance to the haphazard but effective way Chennault had operated the Flying Tigers. Given the delicate nature of the change of status with its ramifications beyond the Pentagon, there seems little doubt that Marshall was informed and that he approved of the new structure.

Sorting out the Bissell-Chennault-Arnold-Stilwell-Generalissimo problems from half a century later is a daunting task. There is little doubt that the perception of Chennault in Washington military circles was different from the way he was perceived in Chungking. In China, he was assessed as a "can do" heroic fighter whose only concern was success in the air over the Japanese. His disdain for protocol, bureaucracies, regulations, and formal logistics systems, combined with his earlier advocacy of the supremacy of the fighter, had earned him the reputation while in the Air Corps as a maverick. This perception and his reputation were factors in facilitating his 1937 retirement, officially for a hearing deficiency. While in the service of Chiang, he had proven his fighter tactics, been innovative while improvising his own supply system, and earned worldwide publicity for his record against the Japanese Air Force. On the other hand, he was probably remembered in the military for his criticism of bomber doctrine and his unorthodox ways, both of which probably influenced his wartime relationships.

The differences between Bissell and Chennault were striking, even though both had been fighter pilots for most of their careers. Bissell had earned his wings during World War I and was credited with shooting down five German planes over the Western Front. He had been one of the pilots who bombed the *Ostfriesland* during the Mitchell attacks on Navy ships in the Chesapeake and later had served in AAF headquarters. In all probability, he was specifically chosen for command of Tenth Air Force and the CATF for the very reasons that Chennault disliked him. As Chennault characterized him, he was "a fanatic for meticulous staff work and detailed reports."[33] In addition, he was familiar with current Army procedures and regulations, understood the AAF logistics system, and had the ability to get along with the British theater commander in India to whom he was subordinate. He was labeled an "old man" and "cold . . . with a filing cabinet mind" by Chennault and the personnel of the CATF as well as the Generalissimo. More important, he was viewed as an impediment to progress because of the control he exercised through Stilwell over getting supplies into China.[34] In contrast, Chennault had become the favorite foreigner fighting for China. He was endeared to Chiang Kai-shek and his wife, not only because of his successes against the Japanese but because Chennault and his Flying Tigers, now the CATF, posed no threat to Chiang's regime. A common shortcoming of all three American generals serving in the CBI—Stilwell, Bissell, and Chennault—was their lack of tact.

Reverses in the field and demands for resources and plans during the spring of 1942 appeared to divert Washington's attention away from the Chinese theater. In any event, no viable Allied program to relieve China's isolation in the Burma-India-China area was developed immediately. By May 1942, with China cut off completely except by air, many questioned whether Chiang Kai-shek's will to resist would survive China's isolation.

After the loss of Burma, Stilwell visualized the major operation from China against the Japanese as a ground invasion there, where success would open a usable surface supply route to China and allow further offensives. His background in troop training, experience in infantry tactics, knowledge of the language, and respect for the valor of the Chinese soldier led him to remain optimistic that sufficient numbers of Chinese troops could be trained by a minimum of US ground troops to dislodge the Japanese. Stilwell did not endear himself to Chiang, who was accustomed to almost slavish agreement with his policies by his subordinates.[35]

In contrast, Chennault never abandoned his belief that airpower could deliver a devastating if not fatal blow to the Japanese air force, interdict Japanese shipping, and eventually lead to victory without commitment of any large numbers of ground troops, which Marshall opposed. As Marshall's biographer has written, the US chief of staff "had never been willing to commit large combat forces" to the CBI theater.[36] Chennault, as an employee of the Chinese from 1937 to 1942, was much more willing than Stilwell to agree with Chiang and present undesirable facts to Chiang in as favorable a light as possible. Chennault's facile prescriptions for victory would become even more appealing to Chiang, Roosevelt, and others as the tenacity and ferocious resistance of the Japanese in defending their newly won empire was demonstrated in the Guadalcanal campaign and would be repeated in battles for Tarawa, Okinawa, and Iwo Jima. Not unexpectedly, the opposing views of the two senior American officers in China produced considerable friction throughout most of the war. The limited logistical support for any course of action had to come over the Hump. Stilwell, the overall American theater commander, controlled allocation of the supplies coming over the Hump, as more immediately determined by Bissell and the Tenth Air Force operating from India. Additionally, the departure bases in Assam province, northeastern India, for aircraft flying into China were built, defended, and controlled in the first two years of the war by the British, who were less than ardent supporters of enhancing Chinese military strength.

Whatever means were chosen to attack the Japanese from Chinese bases, the Achilles heel of any action remained logistics support into China. The supply pipeline from the United States was 12,000 miles long in its easiest segment, by sea from the United States to west coast Indian ports. Then a 1,500-mile rail journey to Calcutta was followed by travel over 1,100 miles on less than reliable narrow-gauge railways to Dinjan and other airfields in Assam province. There still remained more than 550 miles to be flown to the nearest Chinese bases at Kunming and then an additional 450 miles to the Chinese capital at Chungking. This Dinjan-Kunming portion of the journey required traversing the Himalayas with peaks rising above 16,000 feet. In the May–June 1942 period, scarcely 25 aircraft operated over the Hump with the result that less than 100 tons a month were being delivered into China. The impact on operations is obvious, since it took an estimated 18 tons of supplies flown into China to allow one ton of munitions to be dropped on the enemy.[37] To the Chinese, the criterion for success and the measurement of support from the United States after the closing of the Burma Road in April 1942 until the opening of the Ledo Road in January 1945 became the monthly tonnage flown into China. As a student of the period has observed, "The endless, torturing problem of tonnage over the Hump had become the fulcrum of the theater."[38] The result, however, was the retention of China as only a secondary theater.

There were other ways in which the Chinese government felt unequal as an ally. It had no representation on the Combined Chiefs of Staff, the Generalissimo had not been invited to the high-level post-Pearl Harbor strategy conference and felt correctly that his materiel needs were given lower priority than the other two major Allies. The situation was exacerbated in the summer of 1942 by the exigencies of war. The fall of Tobruk on 21 June threatened the British position in the Middle East and resulted in the Tenth Air Force being ordered to furnish crews and aircraft from India to stem further Rommel advances. Additionally, the B-24 HALPRO Group that had been en route to China to operate against Japan was halted at Khartoum. It never arrived in the CBI theater.

The loss of assets Chiang wanted and expected came on the heels of the Chinese expulsion from Burma and Stilwell's defeat there. The Chinese leader transmitted to Stilwell on 28 June his "three minimum requirements essential for the maintenance of the China Theater of War." The demands included three American divisions in India in the late summer and early fall to "cooperate with the Chinese Forces in restoring the line of communication through Burma." The other two specified that, as of August, the China theater of war would require 500 planes "continuously fighting at the front" and, finally, that the tonnage by air into China beginning in August 1942 would be 5,000 tons per month or 50 times current deliveries.[39] Stilwell was informed that failure to meet this ultimatum would result in the "liquidation" of the theater and "other arrangements," a less than subtle threat to make a separate peace with Japan.[40] Stilwell, the American ambassador to China, and others discounted the possibility of a separate peace with Japan. The White House, however, put more faith in this and similar threats that followed throughout the conflict.[41]

While FDR awaited the report of a special emissary who had been dispatched to China, and while other pressing concerns including Guadalcanal and Torch preparations occupied the American leadership, little was done by Chiang Kai-shek to carry out his threat. Consequently, it was not until 13 October that a definitive answer was given to the Generalissimo from the White House. In his response, FDR promised "almost 500 aircraft for the Chinese theater" in addition to the 100 transports that were scheduled to fly the Hump in 1943. He "regretted" that the requested three American divisions could not be furnished, emphasizing the necessity for the Allies, using Chinese as well as other troops, to reopen a surface supply line into China. He reported that the JCS was developing plans for the retaking of Burma as recommended by Stilwell and necessitated by the inability of air traffic over the Hump to provide sufficient logistical support for continuing Chinese and Allied needs.[42]

Seemingly mollified by Roosevelt's response, which in effect was a vote of confidence in Stilwell, in whom Chiang was losing faith, the Chinese leader tasked Stilwell to begin planning for retaking Burma in the operation discussed at Casablanca bearing the code name Anakim. This would necessitate the training of Chinese troops by the American Army in China as well as India. From Chiang's point of view, it also required a sine qua non naval superiority in the China and Java seas along with Allied domination of the Bay of Bengal. This included an amphibious operation against the Andaman Islands to protect Rangoon and prevent Japanese reinforcements through that port.[43] This three-nation operation would not be easy, particularly given the "long second thoughts about operations in Burma" by both the British and the Chinese.[44] The role of air in all of this would be the responsibility of the China Air Task Force in China and the Tenth Air Force in India.

Matters were not helped by the October arrival in China of defeated 1940 Republican presidential candidate Wendell Willkie, who was to report to Roosevelt as a result of his world travels. In his discussions with Willkie, Chennault made "another convert" to his air theories and registered complaints about Stilwell, Bissell, and the lack of logistical support. His most extravagant statements about what air could accomplish if properly supported had important repercussions. In retrospect, it is difficult to believe that his assessment was taken seriously.

Chennault's program was set forth in his 8 October 1942 letter to Willkie, which was furnished to the White House. Stilwell's biographer has assessed Chennault's message accurately as "one of the extraordinary documents of the world." A careful student of Chennault has described it as having "overweening arrogance and a deceptive simplicity." The aviator reported: "I can accomplish the overthrow of Japan" with "105 fighter aircraft of modern design, 30 medium bombers, and in the last phase . . . 12 heavy bombers . . . constantly maintained." He was confident that these planes "can destroy the effectiveness of the Japanese Air Force, probably within six months, within one year at the outside." After that, he said, "I will guarantee to destroy the principal industrial centers of Japan" and cut the sea routes to her new empire which "is a simple matter." Other requirements for success included "an aerial supply line" that, in disparagement of Bissell, needs only "good command–good management." Chennault continued, claiming, "in a few short months the enemy will lose so many aircraft that the aerial defense of Japan will be negligible." No need to worry about the security of the ferry route across the Hump, for Chennault would "maintain full ground installations in China." As to command, it was essential for Chennault to have "full authority as the American military commander in China" so that he will be able to "deal directly" with Chiang and his forces. Dusting off the Open Door arguments, Chennault was confident that not only could he bring about the "downfall of Japan," but "I am confident that I can create such good will that China will be a great and friendly trade market for generations." In a conclusion addressing overall strategy, Chennault said his plan "will enable the Chinese ground forces to operate successfully, and most assuredly will permit MacArthur to successfully advance and will decisively aid the Navy's operations in the Pacific. Moreover, it will make China our lasting friend for years after the war."[45]

Although no immediate assessment by Arnold of this proposal has been located, it contrasted sharply with Hap's emphasis on building up the Eighth Air Force to defeat Germany with heavy bombers through strategic rather than tactical air operations while allocating a minimum of air assets to Asian operations. Arnold may well have agreed with Marshall's assessment of Chennault's letter as "just nonsense; not bad strategy, just nonsense," and Secretary Stimson's evaluation of it as "a jackass proposition."[46] Its danger, aside from its impracticality, was that it offered a panacea and viable alternative by an American general who had earned considerable credibility with the Chinese leader, who embraced the unrealistic claim. If followed, it would lessen the dependence of Chiang on his unreliable armies, their generals, and the Chinese population at large. Instead, it promised victory with modern American aircraft, leadership, personnel, and support equipment, which would depart China after the war and pose no threat to the stability or continuation of Chiang's regime. As the US Army official history has concluded, Chiang's "correspondence of 1943 suggests Chennault's claims had decisive effect on the Generalissimo's policies." He could now use American airpower rather than reform his army.[47] There appears little doubt that Willkie relayed his impressions to FDR, confirming the recommendations in Chennault's letter. In the volume written on his return, Willkie confirmed his belief in Chennault's proposals, writing that Chennault speaks "with great conviction of what could be done to harass the Japanese in China, to cut their supply lines through the China Sea." All he needed was supplies transported across the Himalayas, but Chennault had "a sense of bafflement at the failure of officials back home to see what to him is so clear." Unfortunately, Roosevelt began to "see."[48]

Encouraged by FDR's response to his three demands, Chiang offered to support Stilwell's planned spring offensive to reopen a land route to China through Burma. The Chinese leader promised on 3 November to commit 15 Chinese divisions from the Yunnan area and two from those training in India to the campaign. An important caveat, as the US Army history has explained, was that the "Generalissimo attached but one condition—Allied sea and air forces must be present in strength to dominate the Bay of Bengal and prevent the Japanese from reinforcing through Rangoon."[49] As preparations continued, however, British interest in the enterprise, as expressed by General Wavell in India, appeared to proceed from lukewarm to decidedly cool.[50]

As he learned of the British lack of enthusiasm, Chiang, in a message to FDR in the last week of December, withdrew from the planned Allied 1943 operation. Insisting that, while the Chinese forces in training would be ready by March, the

Generalissimo indicated they could not attack unless the British controlled the Bay of Bengal and furnished the supporting manpower they had earlier promised.[51] FDR responded on the second day of the new year. Without specifically mentioning the upcoming Casablanca conference, which was scheduled to convene in the next two weeks, Roosevelt promised to take up with the "highest Allied authorities" the reopening of the Burma Road, reaffirming its importance.[52] This did not mollify Chiang, who replied firmly on 8 January to the White House that he was withdrawing from the proposed operation. His main problem was the navy's inability "to control the Burma seas." Even more important, his rationale showed that he had drunk deeply from Chennault's 8 October elixir of "victory through air power." As Chiang explained to FDR, "remarkable potentialities" had already been shown by a "small and ill-supported [air] force." If an "early air offensive" was undertaken, seeming to read from Chennault's script, "the return . . . will be out of all proportion to the investment," allowing attacks on Japanese sea traffic and preparations "for the ultimate general offensive."[53] These were the circumstances governing the CBI theater and the relations between Chiang, Stilwell, Chennault, Bissell, and Wavell as the Allies prepared to meet at Casablanca.

As Arnold's diary and the explanatory notes indicate, the discussions and negotiations at Casablanca concentrated on the next movement in Europe that would follow the North African successes. However, Roosevelt and the US chiefs injected the Anakim proposal and the problems of China into the meetings. Arnold's and Dill's six-day stop in India en route to China was made in order to inform the reluctant British leadership there of the planned Anakim operation and encourage them to support it.

Following other stops along the way, Arnold undertook his difficult and potentially dangerous flight over the Hump to Kunming on 4–5 February. This needs little elaboration beyond that recorded in his diary. Once he arrived there, he spent three days in that country, two of them in extended discussions with Chiang. If Hap had any doubts about Roosevelt's having been influenced by Chennault's air plans, the president's letter that Arnold delivered to Chiang dispelled them. Dated 25 January from Casablanca, the first paragraph told the Chinese leader that FDR was sending Arnold to meet with him "because I am determined to increase General Chennault's Air Force in order that you may carry the offensive to the Japanese at once. General Arnold will work out the ways and means with you and General Chennault." He added that Hap would "talk . . . over . . . in greatest detail" the strategy agreed upon at Casablanca for 1943 against both Japan and Germany.[54]

It is difficult to speculate on Hap's thinking about the problems in this theater and their implications as he contemplated his meeting with the Chinese leader. Aware of the contents of Roosevelt's letter, he had extensive discussions with Chennault and Stilwell, the latter having flown to Delhi to meet with Dill, Arnold, and Wavell, before he met with the Generalissimo. Foremost among Arnold's tasks was obtaining Chiang's participation in Anakim, particularly in view of the Generalissimo's 8 January withdrawal from the project. Arnold had been informed that Roosevelt's expressed desire was to retain China as a participating ally and that the president gave greater credence than most other observers to Chiang's threats to sign a separate peace. Arnold supported Marshall's position that the key to any operations in China was solving the logistics problem, which could only be done by ground action to open the Burma Road. However, the AAF would be involved in any action, and Hap appreciated the problems involved in running a freight line to support military action over a supply chain thousands of miles long. In addition, there was a three-hour flight, in unpressurized twin-engine aircraft, most of them at their maximum operating service ceiling, over rugged enemy terrain marked by 16,000-foot mountains. He was well aware of the competition between Stilwell, supported by Marshall and Stimson, and Chennault, supported by Chiang, Hopkins, and FDR. Each wanted the bulk of tonnage that was flown into China. Arnold was cognizant of Stilwell's unsuccessful efforts to get Washington to require specific action, and even reforms, by the Chinese in return for open-ended Lend-Lease largesse. Any quid pro quo, however, was opposed by the White House. Hap agreed with Marshall's thinking that ground forces were necessary to be ready to defend air bases in China and that, for the most part, Chinese troops could not be relied on for those duties. He had to have been skeptical of Chennault's claims of a quick and easy defeat of Japan by air if only the former senior Flying Tiger had the necessary resources and command authority. Making Hap's mission yet more difficult was the fact that he knew this "jackass proposition" was embraced wholeheartedly by Chiang and support for it was increasing in the White House.

On the other hand, strategic airpower, which the Combined Bomber Offensive agreement at Casablanca now recognized, was where he felt the emphasis of multiengine aircraft should be placed. Conversely, Hap was aware that airpower in China would be limited to tactical operations until the question of logistical support could be resolved. He appreciated his less than warm relations with Chennault, the Flying Tiger's difficulty in handling the administrative and command responsibilities of large organizations, and Chennault's less than admiring opinion of him. He knew that he had enjoyed strong support and general agreement with the White House over most air matters since his trip to England in April 1941, but his current inclinations were to support Stilwell, Stimson, and Marshall over what the president desired. This knowledge, as well as his knowledge of the personalities of the American leaders involved, was part of Arnold's thinking as he prepared to meet with the Chinese leader. Arnold's and Dill's success in securing Chiang's promise to support Anakim was a major accomplishment, coming as it did in spite of their long, serious, and sometime acrimonious discussions. One source has labeled Arnold's answers in his meetings with Chiang a "blend of tact and firmness."[55] Soon after the second day's meeting with Chiang, Hap flew to Kunming. After spending the night there, he flew to Calcutta and the British headquarters, which Arnold had termed an "old man's" home. The meetings with Wavell, his staff, and the Chinese appeared much more successful in promising British cooperation for Anakim than had been the case in their conferences five days earlier.[56]

Arnold's route back to Washington, which he no doubt planned, called for stops dictated not only by weather, fuel, and crew rest considerations but which allowed visits to airfields in countries somewhat off the beaten path. The Air Transport Command had established a number of detachments he wanted to visit, many manned by only a handful of US airmen. He continued an awareness of potential British postwar competing transport activity along these routes and directed the CG ATC, as he had from Casablanca, to be alert to potential problems. He concluded that ATC "has acquired considerable experience in unsatisfactory relationships with the British throughout the world."[57] With the difficult negotiations in India and China now behind him, he continued to include extensive, perceptive comments in the diary about the places and people visited. When he landed at airfields, he provided encouragement while assessing the morale of the AAF personnel he met. Stops in Oman, the Sudan, Nigeria, and Gold Coast were followed by a brief refueling stop on Ascension Island before continuing across the South Atlantic. Two full days in Brazil permitted some time relaxing on the beach before flying to Puerto Rico. He returned to US territory almost six weeks and 27,000 miles after having departed. As tired as he must have been, he probably would not have relished his distinction as the most traveled member of the wartime JCS.

The Diary

<u>TRIP TO NORTH AFRICA</u>
January 9, 1943–February 17, 1943
<u>LIEUTENANT GENERAL H. H. ARNOLD</u>

<u>Saturday, January 9, 1943</u> [Washington, D.C. to Borinquen Field, Puerto Rico]

At Gravelly Point 7:45 A.M.: King, Cooke, Somervell, Leahy, Dill, Dykes, Deane, McCarthy, Wedemeyer (King's male stenographer),[58] all waiting. Bradley, Handy, Peterson, Foster and others as kibitzers.[59] Two C-54s all set with tugs ready to go.⁶⁰ Found lockbox to put papers; deposited same with detonators.⁶¹ Put bags aboard.

Everything ready, weather overcast for first part of trip; Marshall arrived. First plane: Marshall, Dill, Arnold, Dykes, Deane, McCarthy; Otis Bryan, captain of our plane.⁶² King, Somervell, Wedemeyer, Libby,⁶³ Cooke and stenographer on second plane.

Took off 8:30 A.M., climbed through overcast, reached top of lower layer about 5,000 [feet], climbed to about 8,000. Flew along, in and out of cloud banks, picking up some ice but not much, on top at 10:00 A.M., upper layer about 500 feet above. No dearth of reading material as everyone seems to have brought ample. Broke out into clear weather with usual tropical broken clouds at 10:30, our position right opposite Vero Beach [Florida]. Prepared to land at 4:30 P.M., actual landing 4:55. We landed first followed by King's plane. He had to wait forty minutes for us; was not in very good humor.⁶⁴

Met by General Collins and Colonel Sartain;⁶⁵ went to [Officer's] Club. Lots of vacant houses on Post. It looks like an entirely different base from my last visit: runways, houses, hospital, barracks, storehouses all finished. Four thousand men, 18 planes, 100 transients a month; we must use it as Navigation school, bomber [Bombadier] school or OTU.⁶⁶ Trip over Post with Wedemeyer and Cooke; dinner at 7:00. Marshall, Somervell and I in one house. As I must be up at 4:30 A.M., adios.

Sunday, January 10, 1943 [Borinquen Field, Puerto Rico to Belem, Brazil]

Grand, cool breeze all night. Awakened at 4:30, shaved and dressed, breakfast at Club, 5:00. All our party present and General Collins and Colonel Sartain.

Aboard plane at 5:55, ready for take-off but held by tower at 6:00. At 6:15 I told tower to clear us; he had instructions to hold us for other [Admiral King's] plane. Took off 6:15 with a faint glow in east.

Usual tropical broken clouds and patches of overcast, occasional showers. Took over pilot's job at 7:00, did same thing yesterday for 2 hours. Our altitude 7,500, had to go over, around, and under in order to keep out of bumps. Passed San Vincente[67] right on course at 8:45. Bryan took over for me at 11:15 A.M. when we were about 100 miles SE of Trinidad.

First land, Dutch Guiana; Paramaribo[68] at 12:48; coastline covered with broken clouds. One engine kicked up for about 500 miles and then settled down and ran smoothly for last 100. Mile after mile of level pasture land with thousands of cattle, wide Amazon River mouth. Flew over Devil's Island; three small islands, none look large enough to handle prisoners who we all were led to believe were there. Several large buildings on two islands, only a few small ones on third.[69]

Only boats we have seen were in Amazon, near Belem. Belem spread over a large area, about 15,000 [square miles]. Post looks excellent, many new buildings.[70] Landed at 4:20 P.M., met by Bob Walsh and Jonas Ingram.[71] Second plane ten minutes in back of us. Trip around Post, visit to Mess Hall, talked to enlisted men, food good and plentiful, enlisted men's morale very high, buildings going up nicely. BOQ [bachelor officers quarters] one of the finest I have seen. Many kinds of fruits: bananas, excellent; papayas, wonderful; pineapple, delicious; sapodilla,[72] lime juice, very refreshing; orange juice, fine, etc. Weather comfortable, individual rooms for big brass hats. Told Jonas Ingram I would stop at Ascension[73] on my return.

Monday, January 11, 1943 [Belem to Natal, Brazil, en route to Dakar, French West Africa, now Senegal]

Began to get warm in night. Up at 6:45, breakfast at 7:15; all kinds of fruit, eggs, toast. Bob Walsh going to Natal with us. Took off at 8:00 A.M. Took my three hour turn at controls. Entire aspect of terrain changes as we proceed toward Natal, more like southern California, sand and brown vegetation.

Discussed use of C-54s to carry AF troops to Europe: 50 to 75 men per plane, 100 [trips] per month and they go entire route; 300 per month if we use St. John's [Newfoundland] or if 2-engine planes carry the men to Natal; 25 planes could take care of 2,500 to 7,500 per month. That should take care of all groups we send.

Fontenjaleos, small town of 5,000 with 2 airports; one sod field, no runways for Brazil; other, 1 long runway with black top, one short runway, constructed by PAA for USAAF.[74]

Plane running very smoothly. Natal to all appearances a spot on the coast of southern California, brown sage brush, [similar to] Carmel Bay (California), sand dunes, blue ocean, tile roofs. The airport with no trees or green vegetation, long, low buildings. Airplanes of all types dispersed. Long blacktop runways, miles of open brown country.

Landed at 1:45, other plane came in at 2:00. Lunch at Club, Colonels Burt and Dallam (ex PNG [Pennsylvania National Guard]) met us.[75] Good lunch, plenty of fruit, especially fine pineapple, better than Hawaii, good mangoes. Inspected Post, found no plan for expansion; need barracks, Mess Halls, BOQ badly. Wired to Strat [Stratemeyer].

Back to plane and took off at 4:55 P.M. Pat J. Hurley and Adler coming on plane from east; we will pass them en route.[76] Took my turn at wheel from 7 to 10 crossed equator at 8:05. Subs in South Atlantic hear planes and send up rockets, then subs try to shoot planes down when the planes investigate rockets.

<u>Tuesday, January 12, 1943</u> [Dakar, French West Africa, now Senegal, to Marrakesh, French Morocco, now Morocco]

At 12:05 G.M.T. this date, while at 3° N and 28° W we saw the rockets. A sub hoping to lure us down? A raider waiting until we got within range of their AA? (One of our planes was hit by AA and came to US with 6 holes—3" x 6" in her tail surface.) A raider with advance notice of our trip picking us up on her radar and waiting to catapult planes off to shoot us down? A torpedoed ship asking for help? Who knows? In any event we asked no questions; we went into the clouds, changed our course, made a detour.[77]

Called at 2:00 A.M., dressed, landed 2:20 Natal time, 4:20 Dakar time. Still dark and cold. Met by C. R. Smith and Tom Hardin, Creighton of PAA.[78] One runway covered with metal planking, spoiled. Breakfast at Mess.

Heard that whole trip and purpose is known. Three reporters came down and told C. R. Smith that they were going to go aboard the *Memphis* and see the President: leaks, leaks, leaks. Bob Walsh told me that all Cairo knew of Marshall's trip;[79] C. R. Smith told me all about mine, including the hop into China.

Delightful breakfast, [day]light at 6:00 A.M., took off at 7:00 after sending wires about flares and necessity for more men. Made arrangements with Somervell to have spoiled metal planking taken up and straightened. British have more of it stacked away. It doesn't cost them anything so why should they worry; no it doesn't cost them a cent. We took the planking off the dock and are laying it at Dakar. Dakar field will be ready in 30 days.[80]

Marrakesh is apparently the best bet for our conference (local idea only).[81] Saw fine navel oranges, just like the best California has, that come from Marrakesh, very sweet as are tangerines.

Native blacks with spades, shovel and picks march to work in column of threes with swinging arms. Wages, one cupful of rice a day; prefer cup of rice to 5 dollars. Yellow-brown sand dunes, dry water holes, miles without a single tree, brown hills, salt sinks. Four camel caravans crossing a dry river; no other signs of life for hundreds of miles; the town of Adrar out in the middle of nowhere.[82] A 35 mile wind right on our nose. Barren soil for thousands of miles, sand dunes without end. Out of the north comes a view of high, snow-covered mountains, high mountains, 14,000 feet.[83] The territory covered would be quite similar to our Southwest were all roads, railroads, trails, habitation removed between El Paso [Texas] and the San Jacinto Mountains.[84] Five hundred miles of country with no sign of human habitation and then a wonderfully fertile valley. Such is the valley in which Marrakesh is located; a city of 50,000 perhaps 100,000.[85] Orange orchards, irrigation ditches come down from the snow-capped mountains. A typical sub-tropical town with its adobe and varicolored houses. The airport with 4 hangars ruined by Navy bombers because the French did not surrender further north.[86] All kinds of American and French planes around the airport.

We landed at 4:00 P.M., met by General Hyde and American Vice Consul.[87] We jumped into cars and drove to Mrs. Moses Taylor's house: it looks very much like the more magnificent Santa Barbara [California] houses; wonderful garden, beautifully kept with palms, dates, olives, navel oranges and tangerines, etc., etc.; large Moorish type house with mosaic walls everywhere and above, a tower that permits a view all over the city.[88]

The Pasha's luxurious mansion where he has his 6 wives who no one sees; he has 6 sons he admits, many daughters and dozens of other sons one never speaks about; he has a big palace up in the mountains and a large park with all the fixings.[89] Arabs everywhere, hundreds of them all in dirty nightgowns, women with faces covered. Market place with all kinds of fakirs[90] and merchants, runs from morning to morning, with about 5,000 there constantly. The turnover amounts to 200,000, all trading something: leather, vegetables, personal charm, singing, dancing, for what? The things they want most are green tea, sugar and cotton cloth. French troops all over town. A high wall surrounds the city proper, 20 feet of adobe with emplacements and embrasures, built many hundreds of years ago, now falling to pieces.[91] The Mosque built in 1200 and one of the best.[92]

Wednesday, January 13, 1943 [Marrakesh to Casablanca, French Morocco, now Morocco]

Up at 6:45, took off at 8:30. Low overcast on last part of trip, ceiling 300 feet. Went out to sea and came in under, landed at 9:30. Met at airport by Generals Clark and Gruenther.[93] Drive in to Anfa Hotel taken over for British and US CCS [Combined Chiefs of Staff].[94] President and Prime Minister have villas all enclosed by wire fence. Hank (my son) on duty at hotel.[95] Fixed up details re Bryan['s] return to Bathurst to bring up special party.[96]

British landed at 10:00: Portal, Brooke, Ismay, Pound, Prime Minister, Mountbatten, Slessor, etc. Had lunch with Somervell and Mountbatten; meeting after lunch with King and Marshall. Sent word to Eisenhower asking that Eaker come down.[97] Dinner at night: Marshall, Clark, Portal, Brooke and Arnold. Had my things all unpacked and then moved. Gave Hank his share of the loot which had arrived.[98]

Thursday, January 14, 1943 [Casablanca, Morocco]

Casablanca has been stripped of practically everything by the Germans. Two airports, one close in, the other 19 miles out. Hotel and villas are quite modern and up-to-date but Hank says they were stripped and the advance party here had to find hardware to fix them up.

[An account of the] Rommel campaign from Portal and Brooke: Rommel information received from his deputy who was captured.[99] Rommel in breakthrough tried old tactics of getting British armor into range of anti-tank guns. British did not fall for it, Rommel withdrew. From then on, neither Rommel nor his deputy used air properly. British built up great strength in reserves and ammunition, artillery prepared for 24 hours. Break-through on right near road along coast instead of on south flank. Several times things looked awfully bad. Finally armor unit broke through and started shooting up rear areas. Then came tanks, finally rout and disorder, gasoline supply was attacked by British planes and Germans were forced to abandon trucks and tanks. Germany has now run out of Rumanian and Hungarian Divisions. Further must cut down on own force by 4 to 6 divisions these next few months, very short on manpower and gasoline. German Air Force steadily decreasing in strength. Goering reported by deputy for Rommel [General Ritter von Thoma, now a prisoner of the British] as saying that if Germany cannot win this winter, she is licked.

Up at 7:30, breakfast at 7:50; meeting JCS, 8:30. Discussed presentation of problems to British. Meeting of CCS started at 10:00 and adjourned for lunch at 12:45, opened again at 2:30 and adjourned again at 5:00 P.M. Discussed war in all theaters and then decided to have planners work up: "Assuming that Germany is principal enemy, what dispositions and troops are necessary for Pacific to maintain pressure against Japan?"[100]

Lunch with all British: Brooke, Dill, Portal, Pound, Ismay and me. President and party took off Bathurst at 9:00 GCT,

10:00 A.M. local; should arrive at 7:00 or 8:00 depending on whether he is C-54 or C-73.[101] No military will be at field to meet him on account of security and secrecy. Meeting today not bad, everything seems to be smoothing out, I hope. British and US have not as yet put all cards on table, perhaps things will get worse then.

Took trip with Hank downtown and to the docks. Beautiful villas along coast, land very fertile, city has clean, wide streets, see very few natives in foreign section. Large, freshly painted buildings. At the docks, *Jean Bart* with holes in bow and stern large enough to take a small bungalow, made by 1,000 lb bombs as it fired at our fleet.[102] Harbor full of wrecks, one steamer on side at dock. French sailors on ships, American soldiers unloading ships.

Arrived at hotel to find that President had invited me to dinner at his villa, all within barbed wire compound. [At] 8:15 dinner: President, Prime Minister, Pound, Brooke, Portal, Marshall, Arnold, King, Mountbatten, Harriman, Hopkins, and Elliott Roosevelt. Many things discussed.[103] Everyone tried to keep President and Prime Minister from making plans to get too near front, both seemed determined, could see no real danger. Finally President said: "Portal, Arnold, Bunny (Elliott), you make up the plan but Bunny you have no say in fixing the places, you are merely secretary." He doesn't know it but the plan is already made.[104]

Other subject: "Who will govern France?" Anyone but Lebrun will be only nominal head, de facto until end of war. DeGaulle, Giraud both possibilities but only temporary. Must be brought together and made to see reason for one chief. Where is Lebrun?[105] We have come many miles and must stay long enough to solve very important problems. Churchill: "This is the most important meeting so far. We must not relinquish initiative now that we have it. You men are the ones who have the facts and who will make plans for the future."

Friday, January 15, 1943 [Casablanca, Morocco]

Up at 8:00; JCS 9:15; conference with President 10:00: [attending] Marshall, King, Arnold, Hopkins and Harriman;[106]

lunch with Eisenhower, Marshall and King. CCS at 2:30; Eisenhower with CCS until 4:00;[107] CCS conference with President and Prime Minister at 5:00, back to hotel at 7:30.[108] Ira Eaker came in at noon; Peterson, Shelmire, Parker, Smart, etc., arrived at 4:00.[109] Received rest of my goods and chattels. Dinner with Ira and Averell Harriman; talked over brief of bombing as expressed by Prime Minister. Met Prime Minister on walk and asked for a chance to get him straight on US bombing; he agreed.[110] Alexander and Tedder arrived here and were at President's mansion at 5:00.[111] Bed.

Saturday, January 16, 1943 [Casablanca, Morocco]

Conference JCS, 9:15; conference CCS, 10:30; lunch, 1:00; conference, Portal, Tedder, Slessor, Eaker and Smart at 2:00; conference, CCS 3:30;[112] conference, President and JCS at 5:00;[113] dinner, 7:00; conference, Portal, Tedder, Slessor, Eaker and Smart at 9:00, adjourned with most everything finished at 11:00; bed, 11:30. At 8:00 A.M. it is still dark. Introduced Hank, whom I see occasionally, to General Ismay. Conference proceeding and we are getting things done but awfully slow. Air command over Mediterranean and overall concept of our war strategy the points under discussion now. Eaker here and a big help.[114]

Sunday, January 17, 1943 [Casablanca, Morocco]

No different than any other day. I got up from bed, had breakfast, looked over my homework, met with JCS, we discussed many things. Then at 10:00 the CCS.[115] Some people did not have their homework completed so we had to adjourn until next day.[116]

Hull arrived after quite a thrilling trip. They took off from Tobruk, headed for Algiers, expecting a six hour trip; they ran into a storm, turned back and with only about 3/4 hours gas in tanks, landed on their belly. Very fortunately they landed 40 miles west of an Italian outpost, west instead of east, what a break. They were taken 160 miles across the desert to Biskra.[117] Thumbed a ride to Algiers and then came in here.

Admiral Cunningham here,[118] lunch, got sick in my tummy, lost my lunch. In P.M. we telephoned down to Villa 13 and made arrangements for a working force. Added Parker and Peterson to the staff.[119] Saw Shelmire, who was tickled pink just to be here.

Generals Giraud and Mast arrived.[120] Talked with 3 pilots who just arrived in group from England in P-39s, 10 out of one group of 28 did not complete flight and landed in Portugal.[121] That is far too many. We cannot afford to lose planes at such a rate: 4 B-17s one day, 10 P-38s next; B-17s trying to fly from Marrakesh to Biskra.

Went to town and looked at two very excellent rugs, bought both. Owe Mrs. H. A. Bartron, $166.66, will send check when I get back; done.[122] Had dinner with Beam, Bartron, Parker, Peterson, Wildman and Elliott Roosevelt at hotel in town, excellent. Gave talk to staff officers. Back to Anfa in time to meet with Eaker, Smart, Parker, Wildman and clean up a few things. Thank God the sick stomach did not last long, only a short few minutes, must have been something I ate.

Monday, January 18, 1943 [Casablanca, Morocco]

Meeting with JCS, not much agreed on. Meeting CCS started out with no accord and adjourned at noon with agreement as to general war policy. Meeting CCS after lunch. Adjourned to meet at Villa: President, Marshall, King, Arnold, Hopkins, Dill, Prime Minister, Brooke, Pound, Portal, Mountbatten. Received outline of general war policies.[123] After dinner went out and saw Brown demonstrate ground A.S.V. and meeting of two Beaufighters coming from many directions. Talks the fighter to target the same way our men in tower used to talk down a plane through overcast. Tries to get fighter to turn right on to target. A.S.V. in plane can pick up target for certain at 6 miles but surely at 2 miles.[124]

Tuesday, January 19, 1943 [Casablanca, Morocco]

Breakfast with Harry Hopkins; JCS, 9:00; CCS, 10:00; pictures and more pictures, then to business.[125] [Generals]

Andrews, Spaatz came in, Eaker also. Lunch with Prime Minister, discussed operations in England.[126] Appointment with President at 4:00, CCS at 4:00 [sic]. General Giraud gave quite a talk.[127] Walk with Eaker, Spaatz and Andrews from 5:45 to 7:10. Talked with Bryan re trip home for President. Dinner with Marshall, Andrews. Conference re air command in North Africa and in England with Marshall, Andrews, Eaker, Spaatz, and later with Portal.[128] Looks as if we may get away on Sunday.

Wednesday, January 20, 1943 [Casablanca, Morocco]

Not so much doing today. Spaatz in at 8:30; JCS at 9:00; CCS at 10:00;[129] picture JCS with President at 11:30; conference with Bryan, Andrews, Spaatz, Eaker and Elliott Roosevelt;[130] CCS at 2:30; adjourned at 4:30.[131] Ride down beach with Jack Crosthwaite and Bud Tinker, first real vacation I have had.[132] The surf is certainly rough; that explains why so many boats upset in [8 November 1942 Torch] landing; three cargo ships were torpedoed; one ship loaded with transportation is now on rocks.[133] Lighthouse was fitted with a range finder. Bomb craters here and there.[134] Admiral Hall said that *Jean Bart* was hit by three 1,000 lb. bombs, sank in shallow water and shifted to a berth alongside the dock where she now lies.[135] Soldiers in dog [pup] tents. Tents raised on scrap lumber until man can stand, all raised above ground to keep out of wet, swampy ground.[136]

Thursday, January 21, 1943 [Casablanca, Morocco]

For a while it looked as if we might get away from here on Saturday, now I don't know when we will leave. The agenda grows by leaps and bounds, just when we thought we had it cleaned up.[137]

Breakfast, 7:45; JCS, 9:00; CCS, 10:00; adjourned 12:00. Made plans for departure; talked to Lewis Parker, Peterson, Bryan. CCS, 3:00;[138] adjourned at 4:30.

Went aboard Mountbatten's command ship, complete communications set-up for Army-Navy-Air; radio sets galore.[139] Seems to be a very necessary arrangement for such commands as MacArthur's, Halsey's and others where a beachhead must be established.

The Bride (de Gaulle) has not arrived so perhaps that will cause us a delay.[140] It looks now as if we may have to return to Marrakesh. Dinner with Bill Somervell; talk with Dill, Brooke, Portal; bed early, and on to tomorrow.

Friday, January 22, 1943 [Casablanca, Morocco]

And on that day when the world was created, God had just finished making man out of clay and putting life into him. Man came to life and God continued his work with clay, making animals. Man said: "Let me have a try at it." God gave him the clay. Man was clumsy and with no idea as to the fitness of things, made an ugly, ungainly, misshapen thing out of the clay. Man said: "I have been a failure; I will destroy this terrible thing I have made." "Not so," said God, "you have made it and it will be with you always." And so it has been and there are none of these animals running wild on the earth. They all stay within the close environs of man. So came the camel into the world. Thus sayeth the Arab.

Not much excitement. Breakfast with McCarthy. He is trying to get the biggest brass hats to accept a program of departure but no luck. Everyone seems to like it here, to be satisfied with life. Secret Service, Army and Navy would all like to see the super brass hats started for security reasons but no luck so far.

JCS, 9:00; CCS, 10:00; much to everyone's surprise we agreed on a lot of things.[141] Pictures with President and Prime Minister at 12:00 noon. Hank officiated with the photographers, 15 of them. They seem to have sprung up from everywhere.[142]

Lunch with Portal; talked over organization, operations, supply, training. He is shooting for 537 squadrons and 9,870 airplanes by December 1944. That with about 1,200,000 men means 130 men per plane. I don't know what ours is but I'll bet it is a lot more. CCS at 2:30, once again we seem to agree and adjourned at 5:00 P.M.[143]

Went down to Patton's house, a wonderful big one on a hill. Owned by the fellow who runs the local paper, very modernistic. Was occupied by the Germans who seem to have stripped it of everything that they wanted including the hardware and furniture. When we came they were surprised and left without collecting their goods and chattels; over 100 German uniforms in the basement, also German equipment. German titles still on the various doors.[144]

Marshall came in and we went out for a walk, about two miles. Saw the lighthouse [El Hanke] with the range finder that made it possible for the artillery to do so much damage to our ships; the wall wrecked by one of our bombs. Dirty Arabs; good-looking horses, Arabian, pulling all kinds of vehicles.

Dinner with Hank and Burgess, introduced Hank to King, McIntire and Libby.[145] DeGaulle would not see the President after coming all the way down here, has another date for tomorrow; what a bunch these Frenchmen are. We hope to finish tomorrow and start for Algiers on Sunday. The President and Prime Minister expect to leave on Sunday by auto for Marrakesh and to start for home the next day.

Saturday, January 23, 1943 [Casablanca, Morocco]

Breakfast with Marshall, Deane, McCarthy and Libby. JCS 9:00; CCS 10:00; adjourned at 11:30.[146] Began to get things arranged for a get-away.

Marshall suggested an auto trip to Fedala, north of town, La Fedala. Hurried through lunch. Marshall, Patton and I went to Fedala and inspected several camps. Heard full description of [Torch] landing, saw battle-scarred buildings, French forts, Moroccan troops.[147] Back in time to learn that meeting with President and Prime Minister postponed until 5:30.[148]

Trip with Marshall in auto, driver got lost and we arrived at meeting just in time to sit down; President and Prime Minister and all the CCS. Corrections made it necessary for CCS to meet again at 9:30. Have a letter to get from President to

Chiang Kai-shek.[149] (See attached)' Dinner at Patton's with Keyes, Gay, Patton.[150] CCS in final meeting at 9:30 to 10:30, packing at 11:00.[151]

---

*THE WHITE HOUSE   CASABLANCA
Washington   January 23, 1943
My dear Generalissimo:

This note will be given to you by Lieutenant General Henry H. Arnold, U. S. Army, the commander of our Air Force. I am sending him to you bcause I am determined to increase General Chennault's air force in order that you may carry the offensive to the Japanese at once. General Arnold will work out the ways and means with you and General Chennault.

General Arnold will also tell you about the plans to intensify our efforts to drive the Japanese out of the Southwest Pacific. As I wired you, I have been meeting with the Prime Minister and our respective Chiefs of Staff to plan our offensive strategy against Japan and Germany during 1943. I want Arnold to talk all this over with you in the greatest detail bcause I think it would be best that I not put it on the cables.

Mrs. Roosevelt has seen Madame Chiang Kai-Shek several times and we are all hoping that she can come to see us very soon. Her health is improving rapidly.

I have great hopes for the war in 1943, and like you, I want to press it home on the Japanese with great vigor. I want to convey not only my warm regards for you personally, but my everlasting appreciation of the service which your armies are giving to our common cause.

         Cordially yours
         (Signed) Franklin D. Roosevelt
Generalissimo Chiang Kai-shek, Chungking

NORTH AFRICA, MIDDLE EAST, INDIA, CHINA

Sunday, January 24, 1943 [Casablanca, Morocco to Algiers, Algeria]

Up at 6:45; breakfast at 7:00. Hank, Pete, Parker and I took off for the aviation field. Prime Minister and President worked all night on their press notices; Hank said last change came over at 4:00 A.M.[152] We took off at 8:20, in Algiers at 12:20, clouds of all kinds along the route. On two occasions we saw planes, little black specks in distance. We manned guns for the Stratoliner. With all of the brass hats had no other protection. In both cases they turned out to be our own planes, B-25s.[153] Weather cleared as we approached Algiers. Countryside very much like Los Angeles to Riverside, orange orchards, trees along road, irrigated land, mountains and sea.

Was met at airport by Tooey and Jimmy Doolittle. Rode out to Tooey's mansion, and it is a mansion, it must have 25 bedrooms.[154] Most of his staff and all of the senior "visiting air firemen" stop or live there. For lunch: Portal, Tedder, Doolittle, Tooey, Arnold, Allard, Ted Curtis,[155] Slessor and about 15 others. The place has a big garden: lemon, orange, tangerine, banana, all kinds of trees, dates and dates.

Worked in office with Portal, Tedder, etc., Tooey, Jimmy. Called on Eisenhower, Cunningham. Back to dinner. Conference with General Mendigal, Chief of French Aviation. Made no promises other than those already made.[156] Bed at 11:30.

Monday, January 25, 1943 [Algiers, Telergma, Berteaux, Ain M'lila, Biskra, Algeria, en route to Cairo, Egypt]

Breakfast at 8:00, Doolittle arrived at 8:30. [Went to] Tooey's office and dictated memo to President to be taken by Otis Bryan. I wonder if he will get it. It was one excellent story anyhow; 2 US airmen taken from rubber boat by Italian submarine. Submarine bombed and broken in half, two airmen among few rescued. Picked up by destroyer and landed at Malta. What a story for circulation in US.[157]

[Will visit units at]

Telergma	319th, 17th, 82nd, 52nd
Berteaux	310th, 14th
Ain M'lila	301st
Biskra	97th, 1st, 52nd

Left Algiers, 10:00; arrived Telergma 11:15; left Telergma, 3:00; arrived Biskra, 4:17; left Biskra, 10:00 P.M.; arrived Cairo 6:30 A.M. (January 26,1943). Visited airdromes of the 319th (Spitfires), 17th (B-26s), 32nd (P-38s), and 52nd (B-25s) Groups at Telergma; of the 310th (B-25s), and 14th (P-38s) at Berteaux; and of the 97th (B-17s), 1st (P-38s) and 52nd (Spitfires) at Biskra. Talked to Group CO, Squadron CO and pilots.[158]

Weather from Algiers to Telergma was lousy; the Atlas Mountains are high.[159] Marshall was supposed to visit same stations but couldn't make it, probably he was directed otherwise by the staff. A good idea as no need of his taking risks. Told him last night when I talked over my visit with Stilwell and Chiang Kai-shek that I would see him again in Washington.

Two planes arrived at Algiers airport while we were waiting for Wedemeyer: 1 The C-87 from Moscow; Kelly, pilot; to be used by Somervell. 2 The B-17 to take King back to Casablanca.[160] The field at Algiers is large with two runways, one black top, the other steel mat. It has been bombed several times and shows the scars. Mud is awful after a rain. Personnel all seem very cheerful.

Algiers is quite a city spread all over the sides of the hills along the bay; villas everywhere. Beadle Smith has a palace,[161] Tooey's #2 palace. French soldiers, French Moroccans, French Sudanese, Arabians all moving around, mixed up with American troops.

I gave instructions here that as the air war for control of the Mediterranean is now at its height and will continue for some time and as there is always the possibility of an offensive coming in Tunis, we must build up the 12th Air Force; 3 groups with P-38 planes now have 90 instead of 240 [authorized]. Hence:

    a. One more load of P-40s to come on [USS] *Ranger*; King agrees.
    b. P-38s to come as deck load.[162]
    c. 90 P-38s now in England to be flown down at once.
    d. Sufficient more P-38s to make up a total of about 330 to be flown across by Ascension.

e. 1 squadron of P-47s to be sent to build up Spitfire Group.
f. P-39s to complete these groups.

All to start at once with crews. This is to take place even though the new Groups do not get their planes or pilots. The first question all Group COs and Squadron COs ask is when will we get our planes. All are firm in recommendations that it is far more important to fill up existing units than send over new ones. The airdrome area at Telergma very much like Riverside Valley [California], flat with mountains on both sides. Airdromes can be placed almost anywhere. Men have pup tents mounted on anything that will raise them off the ground; make use of empty gas cans, packing crates or stones, dirt piled up. Then a hole dug underneath and the home is complete.

B-26 men like the plane very much. Technical changes and criticisms taken down by Smart. B-25 pilots like their planes. P-38 pilots think they have the best plane in the world. It is a grand feeling to know that the pilots are now so busy fighting the war that each is satisfied with his plane and has full confidence in it. The P-38s are used for everything in all theaters.

Had to cancel a mission today on account of weather. The roads out of Gabes were filled with retreating Germans.[163] The P-38 pilots hit autos, tanks, motorcycles, railroad engines with equal facility and consider such missions a field day. They hand the [Me] 109s nothing but cannot maneuver with the [Focke-Wulf] 190s above 20,000 feet. The firepower of the P-38s is tops.[164]

The stories of the pilots are interesting beyond telling, thrilling. While we were sitting in a long dugout covered with canvas, 2 bunks, one in each end, mud just like Texas gumbo for walls, chilly, almost cold, a small table, improvised oil stove made out of gas drum, talking about operations, planes and training, shooting Huns, technique for shooting down Huns, the telephone rang. Colonel Olds, the Group CO answered. It was one of his pilots, shot down a week before, behind the German lines. He ran, he walked, he hid in deserted adobe huts, he was sheltered by Arabs, he rode a donkey through the German lines at night and he was reporting in. His Squadron CO, Walsh, said: "I knew that he would make it. I knew that he was still alive and would come back." This Group, the 14th, has had about 100 combat hours and believe that they can continue for another 50 or 100.[165]

Our equipment is standing up quite well in spite of: shortgage of spares, hard usage, enemy cannon and machine-gun fire.[166] Shot full of holes and parts torn asunder but somehow they get back; rudder almost all shot away, elevator looking like a sieve, hole in the wing as large as a wastebasket, control wires cut, with only one of two strands left, but our planes get back.

Lunch with the 309th:[167] corned beef, canned spinach, boiled spuds, coffee, cake and sauce. British rations not as good as ours but the best they can get that close to the front.

Took off in overcast, flew under, through and over top, almost over German airdromes. It was question to take a chance with the Atlas Mountains or with a badly battered German Air Force; we chose the latter. Turned south and then west around the mountains, came out into the Sahara. Saw a green spot in the midst of the brown, sandy, stretches. It was Biskra, an oasis in the desert. Airplanes dispersed everywhere. Hit a sandstorm that completely obliterated the airport, circled to get our bearings, looked down into the sand, and finally landed on an almost completed runway some distance from the airport.

Biskra, the Garden of Allah, where the sheiks and Arabian chieftains assembled to meet, to confer, to arrange for fighting and defense. A metropolis in the desert where Europeans came to get the hot desert sun and dry air, where there is a good hotel and an enticing casino, where artists came.[168] Arabs, dirty; goats, pigs, donkeys, and their Arabian horses all living under one roof. It is no wonder that the Arabian night shirt looks dirty, not clean as in the movies. He sleeps in it on the ground with his head propped up against an adobe wall. He never seems to change or wash it. I hate to think what kind of clothes if any there are underneath; rags, dirty clothing, who knows? Perhaps the Arab has not had a look at them for so long he does not know.

Hamp Atkinson commanding the 97th (B-17) Group. It has had a lot of missions over Italy, over Tunis, over Bizerte.[169] Their losses are very few, their victories many.

We had dinner at the hotel which our aviators have taken over.[170] We have also taken over the Garden of Allah, where

Marlene Dietrich played the important role in the movie. As a matter of fact that seems to be far more important in the minds of the Arabs than the historic setting of a place which started long before most of our American History.[171] Dates, plenty of them. The Garden of Allah, one path after another, green trees, palms, rubber trees, all arranged so that it is possible to walk for hours and get lost within an area of but 50 acres. A thoroughly delightful spot in the middle of the desert.

Back to the airport after talking to pilots, bombers, squadron COs for an hour and giving a talk to the assembled officers.[172] Blackout, for the Germans have bombed this place also, several times. At each of these places I inspect the messes; here I did the same. The Mess Sergeant, he looked familiar; after talking to him for some time I asked where I had seen him. He said: "I was in the 9th Squadron at Mather Field [Sacramento, California]." Mather Field in 1921, Biskra in 1942, at opposite sides of the world.

Doolittle was cussed out by a sentinel for having big headlights on. Jimmy was only trying to fix the dummies, but "Captain PM" [Provost Marshal] wanted his orders so the sentry took Doolittle's name to report him to, well whom? Doolittle, perhaps?[173]

The field was dark, two small lights, smoke pots at the far end of the runway. We headed for them [on taking off], knowing that there were many dispersed planes all over the field. We missed them and were in the air at 10:00 P.M. One small front after another; the moon in sight then it disappears as we fly blind through clouds or we see a small glow where the moon is. I took over the 10:00 to 2:00 shift with Parker; Peterson and Smart go to bed. For 4 hours we flew through one cloud formation after another, nothing violent but we did get a thrill at seeing lightning down below us. Our course to the southeast. At 2:00 A.M., Pete and Smart relieve us.

Tuesday, January 26, 1943 [Cairo, Egypt]

Went to bed in a sleeping bag with a strong draft blowing on my head from the opening around the ball turret. Awoke with the sun shining on my face, climbed out to see Cairo underneath. The airport: tanks being tested, Egyptian troops being drilled. Landed before anyone knew we were here. Cars arrived and we started for town. Saw Andrews and Crawford on street, stopped and walked to headquarters with them, scads of photographers.[174] Finally went to Andy's house to get cleaned up.

Cairo: haven't been here since 1909, 33 years, but there are many things unchanged.[175] Strickland and Brereton came to see me.[176] Made plans for this P.M., tomorrow, and for leaving at 6:00 A.M. Thursday.

Lunch with Andrews, Douglas, Tedder, Drummond and Brereton at Cairo Club.[177] With Brereton's staff after lunch, talked over general matters. Went to Andrews' office for conference with Tedder, Drummond, Dawson, Kauch, Ent, Andrews and Brereton re supply and maintenance. Gave approval to general system but put responsibility of actual approval on Andrews and Brereton.[178]

Brereton wanted definite information re his movements as 9th Air Force went into action; could give him none.[179] Dinner at Andrews' house with Minister and his wife, Minister from Iran and his wife, Casey and Mrs. Casey, Crawford, Andrews and Ent.[180]

Wednesday, January 27, 1943 [Cairo to Tobruk, Libya to Cairo, Egypt]

Up at 6:45, breakfast with Andy and Bob Crawford; Brereton arrived at 7:40, airport and take off in C-47 at 8:00; 380 miles to Tobruk and inspection of 3 fields and the 93rd, B-24 Group from England sent down there for 10 days with no ground crews and still here after two months. Then the two other fields where there were B-24s and B-25s. All very well pleased with their equipment. All looking for and asking when replacements would arrive.[181]

Back to Cairo, over the Pyramids at 4:15. Met Tooey, Andy and Crawford in Andy's office. Dinner at Kirk's, American Minister; Somervell, Dill and about twenty others. Prime Minister [Churchill] in town trying to see me; I will see him tomorrow. Somervell leaves tomorrow; Dill not ready until

Friday, we leave Friday at 7:30. Wedemeyer and Wildman leave tomorrow with Somervell; they will meet us in Delhi. On trip saw wrecks of airplanes, tanks and trucks over wide area where battle of Saluum took place.[182]

Thursday, January 28, 1943 [Cairo, Egypt to Basra, Iraq to Abadan, Iran]

We think of Egypt, Cairo, as hot. On the contrary it is cold, chilly during the winter months. There are fireplaces in the rooms but I have yet to find an American who will admit that he has been warm any time during the winter.

The battle area of Saluum was very much like our western desert. The sand was hard enough for tanks and trucks to go almost anywhere. Tracks lead across the desert in all directions; airdromes are made by simply smoothing out the sand and clumps of vegetation. A German airdrome with its defensive parapets and 50 destroyed planes, destroyed by our light bombers and fighters. Small groups and individual disabled and abandoned tanks, trucks, planes and cars. German and Italian supply dumps now changed into salvage areas, tents dispersed at occupied points, water cars on the railroad and water tank trucks for the troops. Convoys running along the high-speed roadway at very high speeds. Small Bedouin villages that look almost like rows of deserted trucks, no green, no signs of life. One wonders what they live on.

The Pyramids and Sphinx in the afternoon sun as we came in for a landing, look very small, almost insignificant from our 2,000 feet. Cairo spread all over the map with tents, marching soldiers, Arabians, truck columns, and tank-testing yards on all sides. It is by far the most warlike area we have seen yet. The green delta contrasting vividly with the brown sand of the desert, fanning out to the north.

Nothing to do this A.M., so Shelmire, Smart, Parker and I went out to the Caves, the Caves from which the (sandstone-limestone) for Cairo's masonry, perhaps the Pyramids came from. But why build them on the other side of the Nile? How did they get all their large pieces of rocks across? The Caves now used by the RAF to repair, rebuild, salvage engines, props, instruments and radio sets; 1,800 men turning out Allison engines, Cyclones, Packard-Merlins, British Merlins, Bristol, Pegasus and Hercules; props straightened out, cut down, smoothed out, balanced and sent back to service. Props with cannon shot holes, smoothed down, rebalanced and sent back with the holes still there. Mile after mile of caves, 7 engines a day, 14 engines a day coming up; one RAF man for every two to three Egyptians.[183]

On the road to Heliopolis, the virgin tree, the tree where the Virgin Mary and the Holy Child rested on their trip to Egypt; old, gnarled, half-dead, lying on its side, supported by cross beams, but still a living balsam. The well, dirty and nasty when they arrived, now a pure drinkable water well. They were supposed to have performed a miracle on the well. Anyway it cost 2½ piasters to see it.[184]

The obelisk at Heliopolis looks like all others with hieroglyphics on its sides.[185] The Egyptians almost like Arabs: dirty, slow, no apparent means of livelihood, but still here after 7,000 years. Past the King's palace with its mud walls, 10 feet high. Shepherd's Hotel looking quite shabby, not the gorgeous, enticing place it was 33 years ago.[186]

Back to Andy's house for lunch; conference with Tooey, Brereton and Andrews; cables to Strat [Stratemeyer]; letter to Lovett; letter to Bee; conference with Tedder, Drummond, Pirie and Spaatz. Home to pack for the dinner tonight with the Prime Minister [Churchill]. Will be a long one if it is in accordance with past ones.

Dinner at the British Embassy with Prime Minister, [British] Ambassador and his wife, American Minister, Sir Alan Brooke, Andrews, Spaatz, McCreery (Alexander's Chief of Staff), Randolph Churchill and two or three lesser lights.[187] Talked for a long time with Prime Minister.[188]

Friday, January 29, 1943 (Cairo, Egypt to Abadan, Iran)

Home fairly early. Prime Minister talked at length of Turkey's entrance in war and its value and effect upon final victory. I stressed importance of timing; no promises should be made that would affect other operations. He stressed point that with 82,000 planes produced [by the US], there could be no interference [with American output]. I indicated that 82,000 planes by December was far different than 28 squadrons in Turkey by June. He assured me that his actions would be such as would not interfere with planned operations.[189]

Prime Minister outlined data I should give to Wavell re army headquarters, corps headquarters, aviation, escort and landing craft. Also outlined necessity for concerted action between Chiang Kai-shek and Wavell in any operations in future;[190] necessity for 8 more C-87s for fifth column work in Yugoslavia;[191] desirability of Dill and I returning to United States via England. He tried to make me promise, but I didn't.[192]

Breakfast at 6:30, goodbye to Andy and Ent, at plane 7:20, took off 7:30, arrived Basra 12:45. Landed at wrong field due to poor briefing and then landed at Abadan, right one.[193] Lunch at 2:30, Persian time. Inspected field, facilities and work in erecting planes for Russians; very favorably impressed by Colonel Porter's work.[194] Russians hard taskmasters; demand everything be done 100% perfect and plane be ready for combat when accepted. Score to date: [of aircraft here en route to Russia under Lend-Lease]

P-39s

Total received to 1-19-43	86
Delivered to USSR	33
Erected but not delivered	36
Being erected	17
Erected per day	4

P-40s

Received to date	31
To USSR	10
Being erected	21
Erected per day	4

A-20s

Received	689
Delivered to USSR	634
Delivered to RAF	40
Awaiting delivery	9
Being erected	6

Sir John Dill very favorably impressed by work. Conference with Colonel Petrov, Russian representative. It was like pulling teeth to get him to admit that the work was satisfactory but eventually I made him admit that the planes were in excellent shape when delivered and that unsatisfactory conditions were always fixed up prior to delivery.[195]

The trip today was interesting only insofar as first part over Suez Canal and along Mediterranean Sea and second part down the Euphrates River to Basra were concerned. Suez was very impressive; desert for 800 miles not so interesting. Euphrates, Tigris and mouth of Persian Gulf very interesting and educational. Dinner with Colonel Shingler and Colonel Porter.[196] Dill and I both gave a talk to 1,500 Douglas employees and to the enlisted men.[197] Bed early. I gave an extra talk to the enlisted men.

Saturday, January 30, 1943 [Abadan, Iran to Karachi, India now Pakistan to Delhi, India]

Abadan, an oil town, large refinery run by British; good houses, fine technical buildings, barrage balloons around as they are around both RAF airdromes.

Heard last night that RAF Spitfire had shot down one of our C-47s; 2 were flying along coast of Palestine. No one asked any questions, the Spitfire pilots just closed in and shot down one. Just why is hard to answer; for the life of me I can't find any German plane that looks like a DC-3. The result is that we have lost a good plane, 2 good pilots, 1 good mechanic and a cargo of engines.[198]

Russians will not talk even in their cups; neither will they fight. When they get drunk they want to dance. They dance our boys crazy and when all are exhausted they just as likely as not will kiss our boys on both cheeks and that does start a fight. These Russians are peculiar people; they have women interpreters with them, but the women can't speak English. Our boys don't seem to be able to cut in on the fun at all.

Up at 6:00, breakfast at 6:15, took off for Karachi, 7:05; arrived Karachi, 1:45.[199] Country desolate, looks like Death

Valley [California] even though it is along the shores of the Persian Gulf.

Somervell tried to get from Habaniyah to Teheran but the mountains were too high.[200] He returned to Habaniyah. He will be one day late when he arrives at Delhi. Almost froze last night; I had but one blanket. As a last resort, I had no extra clothing with me, I got up and put on my fur-lined slippers; that helped but not enough to keep me warm.

I don't believe that Abadan received any Christmas. The boys were quite guarded in their remarks but my questions brought out facts that indicated they never received anything from Washington.

While endeavoring to master the top rear gun 50 miles out of Karachi the roof blew out of my hands and mighty near took me with it.[201] The result was a windy, drafty ride into Karachi. Fortunately they had a spare roof and Sir John [Dill], Meade and I can travel onward without being blown to pieces. Met at Karachi by Brady, Wheeler, Mason and several others.[202] Had delicious lunch, talked over operations into China. Took off with new roof at 3:40, Karachi time, should reach Delhi at 7:20, Karachi time.

On through night without a sign of anything much; stars overhead, our exhaust flames. Hundreds of small bright dots pass underneath us but seldom more than one at a time, not enough in one place to even form a village. Then after some 600 miles the glare of a city, the bright lights of the airdrome beacons, the individual lights of the city and the smoke pots of the landing strips. We land and roll up to the hangar: [met by] General Wavell, General Bissell,[203] and many staff officers. It is 10:00 P.M. India time, one time for all India.

Oliver is in hospital so I take his suite in the hotel.[204] After cleaning up, dinner, then Charlie Caldwell and Levi Beery came in; Beery who I saw last time in New Caledonia.[205] There is less sign of a war here than any place I have been for some time. A big dance for men and women alike, officers from all branches of the British service in all kinds of uniforms; I am afraid the war is not being taken very seriously. It reminds me of the Shoreham about three years ago.[206] Dill stays with Wavell; all our officers are here.

Sunday, January 31, 1943 [Delhi, India]

Tired, slept late. Have a man Friday. He draws my bath, puts out my clothes, tells me by so doing when I put on clean ones, lays out my uniforms and does everything he can to keep me from thinking. I don't like it; I want to decide something and not have everything decided for me. His name is Sam. I would like nothing better than to tell him to go sell his papers and come back after I am gone but I haven't the nerve or heart, I don't know which.

Talked over problems with Bissell. Met Wavell and Dill at 10:00. Agreed to a series of conferences and the following of an agenda with Secretariats: USA members, Arnold, Stilwell, Somervell, Bissell; British, Dill, Wavell and others.

Stilwell due in tonight. Wired for Wedemeyer and Somervell to help out.[207] Notified Marshall of plans. Lunch with Wavell and family, a beautiful place, as large as a hotel with many acres of grounds. The British War offices put us to shame; they have buildings that look like palaces.

Called on Mr. Phillips, American Minister.[208] Talked to group of officers at 5:00. Trip to Old Red Fort, built in 1200 by a maharaja. Palace: virgin or wife department, bath department, beautiful gardens, has own mosque, inlaid ornaments, gold, silver, precious stones, hot water system, stream through buildings. Despoiled and plundered many times, now a museum. The carved marble wonderful: screens, windows, railings, all carved from marble.[209]

Monday, February 1, 1943 [Delhi, India]

Met prior to my tea by Bissell, Smart and Parker. We discussed the problem confronting us; decided that something must be done to keep British from dragging their feet any longer. Office at 9:00.

Called Sir John Dill, met him at 9:45. He agreed that paper submitted by BP [British Plans] was not a plan but merely a lot of alibis telling why the project could not be done. Meeting at 11:00 at which I said my piece and quoted CCS report to President and Prime Minister to prove my point. Wavell agreed that the paper was not final and said that he would give additional instructions to BP. General discussion until 1:15.[210]

Lunch with Ferris, Bissell, Smart, Merrill, O'Donnell, and talked over what to do next.[211] Sent cable to [Admiral] King after lunch and fixed cables re replacements for planes for Tenth Air Force. Inspected barracks.

Took Box, Parker and Shelmire and visited old Hindu tower, 220 feet high, 354 steps, faced with carved sandstone. Five different levels, each with columns of special shapes, all different. Built in 1350 and still in good repair.[212] It looks as if the British have made India an old man's home, veteran of many fights and battles, but slowing up. During the years that passed, the place was looted and destroyed, torn to pieces, all to build up new temples and palaces, but the one tower still stands as it was. Its twin has been torn down, destroyed many years since and has stub of piled rocks as a reminder. The Mohammedans were the last to take a fling at it and they built up a Mohammedan temple. It is in ruins now. In the center of the court is an iron column, 40 feet high, once hit with a cannon shot when the emperor of bygone days wanted to prove his marksmanship. Just a dent, that's all. The column was built in 900 AD in commemoration of an old king who sacrificed his life for his Army by grasping a bunch of spears to his bosom and now his name is forgotten. Such is fame.[213]

Back at 7. Looked at emeralds, diamonds, rubies, star sapphires, beautiful beyond description. I didn't buy any.[214] Somervell in at 9:00, Stilwell not due until 10:30. Dinner? I don't know when.

Tuesday, February 2, 1943 [Delhi, India]

With Stilwell not getting into the airport until 10:30 P.M. and waiting dinner until he arrived, we did not get up from the dinner table until 11:30. As a result I was too tired to get up. But in comes Sam: "Your tea is here, Master. Your bath is drawn. Which clothes will you wear? Here is your orange juice. Your handkerchief, Master." What's the use, try as you will, the results the same: he wins. Born in Habaniyah, a valet to an Englishman for 25 years; he admits he is 35 years old. What chance have I?

Met with Stilwell and Somervell; talked over events to date. Met with Wavell and company at 10:30. Things are going along better; it looks as if we will come to an understanding; I hope so. Had lunch and talked things over with the American members.[215]

This P.M. the whole atmosphere changed. Things look so good now that we have made the following program: adjourn February 3rd, on to Dinjan February 5th, on to Chungking February 6th, return to Calcutta for final session, February 9th.[216] Dinner at Wavells: lots of Lords, Sirs, Ladies, Dutchesses, etc., etc., Admirals, Marshals, Generals; a mere Lieutenant General was low ranking. Auckenlecht was there with his wife from Tacoma, home at 11:00, bed.[217]

Wednesday, February 3, 1943 [Delhi, India]

Jehu was at the dinner; Jehu who was the mysterious personage on the Clipper, San Francisco to Honolulu. Name only Jehu; had everyone guessing, then he would tell us nothing of his business or occupation. It now appears he is a Major in British Army; regular business a newspaper man whose real name is Jehu.[218]

Breakfast: hot cakes, so-called maple syrup, with Wheeler, Stilwell, Somervell, Bissell, Wedemeyer (I just can't say "Wedemeyer," I always say "Weedemeyer" when pronouncing his name), Holcomb, Ferris, Smart and I.[219] We all had to sign our names on the tablecloth.

A meeting of USA [personnel] to go over British paper, an agreement as to action taken. Meeting with British at 10:30, everything cleaned up except questions of command. Agreed to have a final meeting to approve proceedings at 7:00 P.M.[220]

Had our photos taken in all kinds of angles and positions. Went to call on Pierse at hospital, seemed to be in fine shape.[221] Lunch with Stilwell and Ferris. Meeting with Stilwell and Somervell after lunch on command; agreed to send cable to Marshall outlining plan.[222] Went to office and cleaned up; back to room and packed. Paid Sam: he has lost all interest in me since I paid him; no fire, no clothes, no cashew nuts, no attention.

Evening meeting with British at 7:00, dinner with Viceroy at 9:00. His palace is as big as the Pentagon, more formality than any place I have been. Talk three minutes with one person and then on to another.[223] He does not seem to have as much of what it takes as most Englishmen in high places. Wavell seems brilliant, but worn out, his staff mostly old men mentally. Escaped from Viceroy and back home for bed at 11:15, completed packing by 11:30.

Thursday, February 4, 1943 [En route from Delhi, India to Kunming, China]

Sam did come back, awoke me at 6:30. I think that he did it for spite, didn't offer to help pack, just awoke me and brought tea. Parker and Pete in at 6:45 and took my luggage. At airport at 7:25, Bissell finally arrived and we took off at 7:30. The tomb of some high mogul with its dome and towers all illuminated with red lights, glow from indirect lighting is very effective.[224] Left Delhi 7:35; arrived Agra, 8:30; left Agra, 9:30; arrived Dinjan, 3:10.

Trip to Agra not very impressive until we saw the Taj Mahal. It is most impressive, even more from the air the beauty is striking. Surrounded by a brick wall, marble doors, marble dome, double set of towers on both sides, separated from the gate by a large garden and reflection pool. And all the old fellow got for building it in memory of his wife was a sentence to serve in the nearby prison from which he might have been able to look out of the window and see his memorial.[225]

More men with diapers. Agra, a repair and supply depot; well-started and will probably soon produce quantities of engines and planes; worthwhile.[226] We are a sanitary race, we recognize athlete's foot and cholera but we can't change the Indian way of life. We need water; we hire someone to dig a well; water is reached 100 feet down. A platform is erected with a pulley, a leather or skin bag attached to a rope provides the means to haul up the water. Can we go ahead with that? Not yet. We must make a track, an inclined plane from the pulley dome at an angle of 30°. Then we get two sacred bulls and a driver. The two sacred bulls are attached to the rope; now we are ready to get water. The leather bag is down in the water well. The oxen start pulling the rope. To make it easier the driver climbs aboard the rope, the leather bag reaches the platform. Now here's the secret to the whole system. An old man in diapers catches the bag and empties the water over his feet into a cement enclosure and it runs into the water system for our men to drink. I must admit in fairness that the water is chlorinated before they drink it.

Passed Himalayas, saw [Mount] Everest in all its glory standing in the blue sky with its snow peak well above the haze. There are so many high peaks that it is difficult to say which is the highest.

Well sir, what a night this was. All the emotions that come with an occurrence in which anything can happen. In the first place we all take our flying too much as a matter of course but let's get back to our story. We reached Dinjan on time, landed about 3:20, taxied to a dispersal point and announced that we would spend the night. I was informed that I would stay with a tea grower. There is tea growing everywhere, it is the one industry of this area.

We inspected the anti-aircraft units, their gun positions, fighter squadrons, their dispersal positions under bamboo dumps, where one rides within 20 yards of a plane prior to seeing it; the operations office, where we talked to the youngsters and saw their pet trained pigeon. They live in small nipa shacks around the airdrome. Then on to the Group Headquarters with Alexander; here we met Major Siefler, an undercover man who has just returned from inner Burma. How an American can run loose in and around Mandalay, I don't know, but he did.[227] In the meantime, learning that Sir John [Dill] and Stilwell had gone on to Kunming,[228] I said: "We would start right after dinner, everyone get ready." We had dinner, a very good one, completed about 6:15. At 6:10 I told Pete and Louis [Parker] to go and get their briefing completed; they departed. We said our good-byes and went to the plane. Soon Pete and Parker came. I asked about the briefing and was given a sketchy reply; that was my mistake.

The route to Kunming goes over a ridge about 14,000 feet; at irregular intervals the ground is held by the Japs. Kunming and the country for 100 miles to the west is held by the Chinese. I learned incidentally that there was a 50 mile an hour wind blowing from the west right on our tail. We climbed to 19,000 feet and all became more or less goofy from the altitude until we took oxygen. After 2 hours flying we saw little or nothing; the distance we had to go [to Kunming], 525 miles. I saw a red glare off to the south and asked what time we would land. The answer came: 20 minutes. We flew for another hour and then some more and still had not reached our destination. Then I learned that there was considerable apprehension among our combat crew as to our locality.

Thursday and Friday night, February 4th and 5th, 1943 [En route to Kunming and Chungking, China]

Well, the Japs occupy country extending well into China from the coast. There is always the possibility of Jap planes being abroad. They probably have radar and plot the course of all visiting aircraft such as ours. If we turn back into the wind do we run out of gas in the mountains? Do we jump? If so, when? Will we be captured over by Mandalay? What should we take with us if we have to jump? What will the people back home think if they hear that the Commanding General, US Army Air Forces and the Commanding General, 10th Air Force and others with us have been taken prisoners? What are the best shoes to wear in hiking through the jungle? Can we take emergency rations with us if we jump?

Well to make a long story short I told the pilots to cut out the plotting and turn back on the reverse of the course taken going out. Then asked the navigator to get a position at once, the radio operator to start working on any station. He replied that he could get Chinese and Japanese stations but no American stations. Where were we and why?

It was some time before the navigator gave us two fixes about (*sic*): the first 300 miles east of Kunming and the second about 50 miles to the west of the first. In the meantime, having been at 19,000 feet for over five hours we were all getting somewhat goofy. Soon our radio operator picked up a station, then another after getting a new frequency, then the navigator got another fix that clinched our position. We landed at 1:45 A.M. at Kunming. Everyone on the station was alarmed and concerned. But not more than we for there are a lot of things I would rather do than have coffee with the Japs at Hanoi.[229]

We drove through the town to the old AVG [American Volunteer Group] barracks and were in bed by 2:30.[230] At 6:00 A.M. Chinese started celebrating their New Year with firecrackers and loud talking. At 6:00 one came in and started a fire in an earthen oven. At 8:00 I got up and hinted for a bath. Hot water, dirty, yellow for shaving, but no bath. Breakfast with Sir John, Stilwell and the crowd, and we were all taken for a ride [teased] on account of our midnight jaunt.

Had a long talk with Chennault,[231] Stilwell, Wedemeyer, Bissell and Sir John present. Agreed on policy for operations in East China:

 a. Heavy [bomber] Group to operate.
 b. New airdrome for logistical purposes—US money.
 c. Extensions to airfields—Chinese money.
 d. An additional fighter group.
 e. A plan of operations against Japs.[232]

Tour of Post, saw members of the 73rd Squadron, 23rd Group, old Flying Tigers, AVG.[233] Had many pictures taken with them; they gave me a squadron scarf.

Lunch with Chennault. Took off in CNAC [Chinese National Air Company) airplane for Chungking. Buffet supper with Stilwell; all brass hats from Chinese Army there, also American Ambassador.[234] Upon landing Chungking, [Chinese] Secretary of War, Chief of Staff, Chief of Aviation, etc., etc., awaiting us.[235] Sir John and I inspected troops. Then were taken to place where bearers had chairs. Accompanied by all Chinese brass hats, Sir John and I were carried across the [Yangtze] river, up flights of 347 stairs. Knowing my weight, I was sure that I would soon be dropped and the stairs were steep and made of stone. Pictures were taken in all kinds of unusual positions by a dozen photographers. The angle at which I was carried was conducive to my slipping backward off the chair over the heads of the bearers in rear and down the stairs. We finally landed on top side. Now it is arranged, different from first program that would have us meet with the

Chief of Staff, that I see the Generalissimo by myself tomorrow at 10:00. Now to bed at 10:30.

Saturday, February 6, 1943 [Chungking, China]

Yesterday as we drove through the city we came upon the New Year's parade, men carrying banners and long dragons 30 feet or more in length. I was driven to General Stilwell's house by the Chinese Minister of War. The Assistant Secretary of War was present too.[236] He spoke English. Chungking is situated within the V formed by two rivers.[237] The airport is on an island down in the valley. The city is on the top of a rocky plateau 600 feet above the river. It has been bombed and rebombed by the Japs; on the worst day they killed 20,000 Chinese. Now they have literally thousands of caves in the rocks but the Japs haven't been back for a year and probably will not return again. There are still many marks of the bombings, ruins of buildings, open spaces where buildings used to be, etc. The city itself is like many other Chinese towns; the same type of houses crowded together and the thousands of Chinese that one wonders where they live.

Breakfast with the crowd. During breakfast received an invitation in Chinese for dinner tonight at the Generalissimo's house; it had already been accepted for me.

At 10:00 Stilwell, Parker and I appeared at T. V. Soong's house, an exceptionally fine place.[238] There started the tea drinking which continued during the next many hours. Stilwell departed and Parker, Soong and I started out in his car through the city, down many slippery hills to the ferry. It has been snowing and still is. It is cold and there is very little heat in any of the houses. Everyone, even the Chinese, are shivering. We drove up many steep, slippery hills for about 15 miles and came to a waiting station. Here we again took chairs; that is, Soong and I, Louis walked. Up we went, stone steps galore, but the #3 boy on my chair has the heaves and I am afraid that he can't make it. As we proceed, the stairs get steeper and the heaves get stronger. He made it. We step out of the chairs at the top of the hill. The trees are covered with snow. After a few minutes wait, the Generalissimo enters and I deliver the President's [January 25, 1942] letter.[239]

The conference that followed lasted for 2 and 3/4 hours. It covered many things:

- a. World military situation, 30 minutes.
- b. Casablanca Conference, five minutes.
- c. Burma campaign, about 45 minutes.
- d. Independent command for Chennault, 45 minutes.
- e. China's Air Force, 20 minutes.
- f. Miscellaneous, 15 minutes.

Luncheon was served in between times. The house was far too cold, I was shivering; hot tea was served every five minutes. Lunch: excellent beef broth, fish and potatoes, roast duck and carrots, Chinese spinach, hot biscuits, lemon meringue pie, hot tea. We took our hair down at lunch on the independent [air force for Chennault] command idea. Chiang Kai-shek's ideas about the independent command centralized around:

- a. Lack of confidence of Chinese in present organization.
- b. Additional planes put in China will be ineffective without a new organization.
- c. Chennault is the only one who can handle operations on account of the many complications.
- d. Chennault is the only one who has the confidence of the Chinese.
- e. There must be a complete understanding and accord between the Chinese and the United States Air Forces.
- f. Chennault is the only one who can handle the Chinese Air Force.
- g. Chiang Kai-shek has reorganized the Chinese Air Force and wants to place it under American control. Chennault is the only one who he will consent to handle it.
- h. The Chinese have had no cooperation since AVG was terminated.
- i. Chennault was the one outstanding tactician and strategist in the Far East today.
- j. It would be very easy to get someone to handle the administrative end of things for Chennault.

I told Chiang Kai-shek that I would give a full report on this matter to the President on my return. Chiang Kai-shek said that he had told me things that he was saving for the President and was being entirely frank. I assured him that I appreciated the frankness and would not divulge what he said except to the President. A summary of the conversation leaves me with the following impression:

  a. He was not particularly interested in the Casablanca Conference or CCS except where it concerned Burma or China.
  b. He wanted a firm commitment for 500 planes at a given time.
  c. He would not listen to logic or reason when it came to realities as to logistics.
  d. He wanted to build up the Chinese Air Force.

As a matter of fact the area around Sadiya, Dinjan and Ledo is being used for:

  a. Center of road construction.
  b. Base for air transport operations.
  c. Base for moving 1 Chinese corps.[240]

The logistical system depends upon:

  a. The river now used to capacity.
  b. The railroad now used to capacity but expected to get additional rolling stock.
  c. Air cargo - difficult to increase due to gasoline situation.

Eighty octane in limited quantities comes from Big Boy, all 100 octane must be freighted [over the Hump].[241] Lack of airdromes in China; need additions to two and one new one.

Col. Vincent, Col. Holloway re Jap Zeros, both flew them and in test flight against P-40s.[242] "It is a nice Sunday afternoon plane; I feel sorry for the Jap aviators who have to fly them; it is so flimsily constructed that I could have bent the rudder bar with the pressure of my feet; I understand now why they fly to pieces when hit by our 50s." [.50 caliber machine guns]

[At] Kunming [I was told that]: Bissell is an "old woman" but a very efficient one; he is a detail man who is getting results.

His supervision over Chennault's operations irritates and irks the Chinese. However it is his detail work that has made the Chinese air operations effective so far. Example: Chennault's request for medium bombers when there was no possibility of gasoline for them.

At 4:00 P.M. we mounted the stairs and assembled at the Generalissimo's house, present: Chinese Chief of Staff, his Air Chief, and most of the chiefs of the Generalissimo's Division. Sir John gave a dissertation on the Burma situation, many questions were asked. The Chinese Chief of Operations gave his estimate of Japanese strength: 77 combat divisions, 3,000 combat planes.[243] Chiang Kai-shek became nervous, he had to go [to the bathroom]. The meeting adjourned, opened up again. Stilwell told of the part to be played by the Chinese Army. Chiang Kai-shek agreed to sending a letter to the President and to the Prime Minister stating that he would join in operations.[244] We adjourned till dinner.

American food at dinner for about 24, American Ambassador present. After dinner Chiang Kai-shek, Stilwell, Chennault, Chinese Chief of Staff, Chief of Aviation, new Chief of Aviation, Soong and I assembled to talk over aviation. Transport [over the Hump] bogged us down, we never got any further. Every effort was made to stretch 4,000 tons into 5,000 but no go.[245] Back to my room, still cold, bed at 11:00.

Sunday, February 7, 1943 [Chungking, China]

Breakfast in a cold room; four inches of snow on the ground, trees all covered, still snowing lightly. House so cold that water pipes in the bathroom frozen; water brought in wooden buckets. At breakfast T. V. Soong announced that the Generalissimo wanted to see me after breakfast.

It was still cold as hell when I started up the long flight of stone steps alone—no one must accompany me. The Generalissimo met me and T. V. Soong and I sat down. The Generalissimo:

"I am going to be very frank with you, more so than I usually am. The conference so far has been a failure and I want you to tell the President so for me. It has accomplished nothing."

"Our Army has been carrying on at war now for six years. We have gotten no supplies from anyone. Our movements have been made by our own legs; we have had no trucks, we have carried our artillery on our backs, our men have starved. If as the CCS say this is an important theater for operations against Japan, why are we not treated fairly? Why do we not receive supplies?"

"Russia has been fighting and fighting hard. She has killed many Germans but so have we killed Japs. Russia gets convoys even though they get sunk. You give them battleships and cruisers to protect them. I want you to tell the President that we are entitled to at least a regular flow of supplies, 10% maybe of what Russians get."

"This conference has been a failure. I have asked for things and the only answer I get from Bissell is why we can't get more tonnage, cannot operate more planes. He cites the railroad up to Assam, the river traffic, and states that the airports will not be able to handle more planes; excuses, more excuses."

"Tell your President that unless I can get these three things I cannot fight this war and he cannot count on me to have our Army participate in the campaigns."

"1. Independent Air Force in China who will be directly under me. Without this we have no Air Force. Bissell has prevented our planes from operating. Without this independent Air Force I cannot go on. I want to put my Air Force under Chennault, the orders are out. My men, soldiers, officers, have confidence in Chennault but they will not serve under Bissell.

2. 10,000 tons a month over the air transport route into China. That must be done not now but at a stated time; excuses do not go. I must have the tonnage. When you suggested the four-engine cargo planes, Bissell gave many reasons why it could not be; he cannot handle this matter.

3. 500 airplanes to China operated by USA or China by November. It is all right to say that there is no gasoline—($9.00 a gallon) but there are ways and means of doing things and they must be accomplished."

"I am speaking to you frankly because I want you to tell your President nothing has come so far out of this conference and I want him to know it. I am sorry that you are leaving. I had hoped that you might be my guest for several days more but as you must go I hope you will tell your President what I have said."

My reply: "I am duly appreciative of your frankness for without it we could not determine just how you feel in these matters. I want you to know they in the United States, from the President down through the War Department, the Secretary of War, the Chief of Staff through the ranks, we must express nothing but the highest praise for the splended courage and heroism of the Chinese soldiers; their bravery and endurance of hardships are outstanding. I must tell you that I am sincerely disappointed in your message to the President for it is not in any way in accordance with my understanding of what has occurred."

"Upon my arrival here, I found that there were but 62 transport planes on the India-China run. Within 24 hours orders were issued to raise that number to 137. The tonnage carried in December was 1,700; I have arranged to bring it up to 4,000 by the month of April."

"I was told by the officer in whom you have the greatest confidence, General Chennault, that heavy bombers could not be operated out of China; he wanted medium bombers. Upon investigation it was proven that the medium bomber could not operate, while the heavy bomber could and 35 have already been ordered to China for operations against Jap bases, coastwise shipping, and other vital targets. I have outlined to you a plan for creating a Chinese fighter Squadron then another and if conditions warrant building it up to a Group. All that is needed is your approval."

"I also outlined plans for creating 4 bomber Squadrons in the same manner. With your approval we can start that at once. These plans may bring 500 planes to China by November but as yet I have not received your OK. 500 planes in themselves mean nothing but when they have gasoline, bombs, fields from which to operate and American and Chinese combat crews, that is something else. So you must see that we have accomplished quite a lot if you will give us your aid."

"You told me that you would give us the aid and assistance in building new airfields, extending runways and moving freight. For that we are grateful for such action will be necessary to enable us to carry out the plans I have outlined. You must see now why when I take your message to the President I must also give him my plans to you which you have not accepted."

"As to the independent air force for Chennault, I am not in a position to approve such an organization but I assure you that I will give your remarks completely to the President. As a matter of fact we are not far apart. I have agreed to build up a tonnage to 4,000 a month as soon as it can be done. I have given instructions to build it up beyond that as soon as facilities are available, build it up as rapidly as we find ways and means to do so but I cannot say it will reach 10,000 tons by November. As I have said we are practically in accord insofar as the 500 planes are concerned. It may not be 500, it may be 600, it all depends upon the facilities available. So we are not far apart. You have great confidence in Chennault. I suggest that you bring Chennault, Sir John Dill, your two aviation heads, your Minister of War, General Stilwell and any others you desire and permit me to tell them of my proposals and ask for their comments, particularly those of Chennault." All of the above through T. V. Soong as interpreter and I don't know just what he said to the Generalissimo and what the Generalissimo said in reply. I had no representation.[246]

The crowd collected. Chiang Kai-shek asked Sir John a few questions about Burma. Sir John smoked him out as to China's participation.[247] He allowed me to ask a few questions of Chennault as to air transport. That did not get very far as Chennault professed profound ignorance. The Minister of War had his say; then Chiang Kai-shek gave his summary of the conference. (See attached notes)[248] We adjourned to the porch, had our pictures taken, said good-bye. He kept Sir John after school.[249]

Took off in the snow from Chungking at 3:15, over overcast to Kunming, came down through and landed at 6:10 P.M., back to the hospital [to visit Col Smart?].

China prices in American money:

1 airdrome	$190,000,000.00 less equipment
1 package cigarettes	120.00
1 day['s wages]	1,050.00
1 suit	6,000.00
3 mules, 6 days	5,000.00
1 tangerine	20.00
1 cup coffee	14.00
Breakfast for 4	————
Lunch for 4	————
1 night	————
Gasoline	180.00 gallon

Monday, February 8, 1943 [Kunming, China to Calcutta, India]

The Generalissimo does not impress me as a big man; he casts aside logic and factual matters as so much trash. Apparently he believes his power can force from his subjects the impossible. He never gave any indication of thoughts of the outside world, except insofar as it gave aid to China. He gave evidence of quick thinking at times but only at times. He did have an orderly mind, one capable of arranging details and asking very pertinent questions. However, the effort died after the first question.

Apparently he has had the power of life and death so long that he expects and his subjects give him the answer he wants. Accordingly, he does not have to think things through. It makes no difference as long as he has his way. Perhaps the absence of his wife has had an effect; perhaps she has the brains.[250] In any event he did not impress me as being in the same class as the President or Prime Minister.

Last night our Chinese experts, professional as well as correspondence school, were airing their knowledge of the Chinese language. One called a Chinese waiter and carefully with signs and with great details asked for what he thought would secure a cup of tea. After a long wait, the boy returned with a plate of dinner: meat, potatoes, corn and gravy. Everyone laughed but the expert linguist. Stilwell then asked the boy in Chinese to bring a cup of tea, that was what was wanted. The boy brought the tea to the linguist and said in perfectly good English: "Here is your cup of tea, sir." He knew it all the time but tried to do not what was wanted but what he was told.

At airfield found B-17 still without a tire. It is on the way somewhere. No arrangements for assignment to the two C-87s. No seats in planes and no one in authority to straighten matter out, worst I have seen yet.

Took off forty-five minutes late, 8:45; over Dinjan 12:20, arrive Calcutta 2:00 P.M., Indian Standard Time (thirty minutes ahead of China time). Through overcast on take-off at 8,000 feet. Over the Hump, beautiful snow-capped mountains at 16,000 feet; deep ravines, long spur ridges with steep sides dropping off in all directions. Soon came out over Brahmaputra River, clear skies, no overcast. River very much like the lower reaches of the Mississippi.

Smart may or may not catch up with us.[251] Peterson and Parker back with B-17. The tire should get to Kunming today. The plane with Stilwell and all of the Chinese turned back and will catch up with us at Calcutta. Stilwell returned with one engine having blown off a cylinder head, one supercharger out of action. The Chinese all were sick, it must have been one hell of a trip. We arrived on schedule and were met by Haynes and many local men. Came to the Hotel Great Eastern, had lunch.[252] Met Alexander and told him of plans for future for the transport line into China. Also told him of rotten service at Kunming. Went out and inspected Haynes' headquarters, went over his operations and troubles. He lives in a wonderful house on the river; has tame deer, flamingoes on the grounds; red and carmine Bougainvillaea over the trees, native boats going up and down the river continuously. Dinner at 8:15 at Governor of Province Government House, a delightful affair with all brass hats present.[253] Left early to read notes and minutes before meeting at Governor House of conference at 9:30 A.M.

Tuesday, February 9, 1943 [Calcutta, India]

Conference with all present, including Chinese. Wavell asked Chinese War Minister Ho to tell of their war plans, which Ho did. Then Wavell further expanded on Allied war plans for same theater.²⁵⁴ The Air problem cropped up again when the Chinese said that 500 planes might be assembled in theater. I said: "Couldn't see it." Chinese had agreed that total air strength of Japs was between 2,500 and 3,000 combat [located as follows]

Solomons, New Guinea	500
China	300
North China, Mongolia	1,000
Philippine Islands, Sumatra Java and Malay	500
Total	2,300

That leaves a total of 700 for Formosa, Japan, Naval Air, and Burma.

Chinese indicated all-out effort to tie in with ours. It looks as if either our fears were groundless or our work in Chungking did some good after all. The question of air strength in China, 500 planes and 10,000 tons for the Transport Command, came up again. All agreed to do everything possible to improve facilities to make increase in tonnage possible. Adjourned when everyone was talked out.

Lunch very nice buffet at Government House. Said good-bye and thanks. Must write letters of thanks to this Governor and to others. P.M. meeting at General Irwin's headquarters. Approved all preceding meetings' minutes and Chinese conferences. If Chinese approve that, they are committed and they did.²⁵⁵ Made a little speech of appreciation, etc., for the American officers. Forgot my homework, it was not too bad.

Returned to Government House for pictures at 6:00, arrived 6:20, many pictures. Last meeting with Chinese, all accepted minutes of meeting. Gave General Ho 2 bucks to bet on horses this P.M. He at first could not understand then he got quite a kick out of it when I asked that he make sure it had four legs before he bet on it. He did not win for me.

Back to hotel. Signed several letters re China's Air Force, Air Transport and 308th Group.²⁵⁶ Out to Haynes' for dinner, 15 miles through town and the suburbs. There the air is heavy with smoke from burned sacred bull dung. They use it here for cooking their dinner. They use it in place of wood which is hard to get and coal that is almost never seen. They catch it in their hands and make round flat patties out of it and then stick it against the wall to dry in the sunlight.

Haynes had Bissell, Shelmire, Box and me out to dinner with Combs and Bailey.[257] Combs went through the Philippine Islands, retreat to Australia and on to India. They gave me the story of Stanley Robinson's death and also that of Strudler, very different from the one that we received in Washington.[258] Haynes gave me a Ghurka (medium-sized) khuckri (a 3-handled murderous knife that has a special notch for blood to drip). Bailey gave me a man-sized one.[259] Haynes told of the Japanese broadcast that told Japanese they should not fear Haynes as he was a worn-out, old transport pilot. The Chinese made him some paper slips that had printed: "Presented by your 'old, worn-out transport flier, Haynes'" (see attached)* in English, Japanese, and Chinese. When Haynes' outfit goes on a raid they usually drop several thousands of these with their bombs.[260]

Very fine dinner, home to pack at 11:30. Shelmire slept all the way back through the pungent smoke to town. Packed my bags and in bed by 12:00.

Wednesday, February 10, 1943 [Calcutta, Panda, India to Karachi, India, now Pakistan]

Up at 6:45. Peterson there to take my bags before I was dressed, but I gave him the bags. Incidentally, I bought a new shoe horn to replace the broken one I bought in Calcutta 34 years ago. It looks all right. I owe Pete $13.00, he paid my hotel bill. I owe Smart $____?, he got some rupees for me.[261] Smart is still quite sick; he tries not to show it but can't quite make the grade. The hotel is full of Indians, RAF, British Army and a few USA. The city is full of mendicants, sacred bulls, natives wearing diapers and others very nondescript. Here and there are scars and ruins from the bombing Calcutta received a year ago.[262] We visited the Viceroy's mansion, the old fort and other points of interest. There are Hurricanes everywhere, defending the city. It won't be long now until they must move farther to the east. Calcutta need fear nothing now but a nuisance raid.

---

* No attachment of these papers accompanies the diary.

Said good luck to Wedemeyer, Parker and Wildman. They return via Australia. Adios to Stilwell; he gave me a note to Marshall. Soong gave me a letter to the President yesterday, no change in demands;[263] Wedemeyer, one for his wife; Bissell, one for his wife. Out to airport for an 8:30 take-off.

Now here is where things are all tied up again. As we approached our plane, no Britisher being with us, I saw an escort of honor and said: "Drive on, that is for Dill." I heard cries of "Stop, wait." We stopped and were informed it was for me; I took it. A fine, military group of men, smart in appearance and in movements. Uniform excellent as to cleanliness but it explains great malaria rate: no sleeves, no covering for legs, open necks.

Thanked the CO and went to the ARGONAUT (B-17).[264] Soon Dill, Wavell and Irwin arrived and I found out that I was to have taken the review with them. How was I to know? Off at 8:45, landed at Panda, 9:45.[265] Dill and I took the salute of about 2,000 man escort. Shelmire, acting as Adjutant, read off the list to be decorated with citations. Haynes #1, 56 others, including Combs; I pinned medals on all; Dill congratulated them. Afterwards they were formed in hollow square and Dill and I both gave them a talk. Met former sergeant, now Captain Suggs and Sergeant Dennis, son of the old sergeant.[266]

Left Panda 10:45, arrived Karachi 6:30. Took my turn; 4 hours and 30 minutes at controls. I leave India with a feeling that our trip, Dill's and mine, was a distinct help. At first it was the British in India who were dragging their feet. We managed to step up their thoughts and create a will to do, this was necessary before we went to China. We had to have a definite line of action prior to going to see the Generalissimo. Looking backward, it did not take long to get Wavell headed right; it took longer for his staff.

Chiang Kai-shek started the conference with the "China first" principle—get what he could for China and then work with the Allies, but when he put on the heat and couldn't win his point 100%, he did agree to play the game. It was long, a tedious operation.

Brady met us, went to look at [Japanese] Zero. Told Brady to send the pilot and one mechanic back to states with Zero.

The other mechanic being very much German-born, thought it would avoid complications if he were to tell the whole story in a cable before sending the German back. The German claims to be American by joining the Army; joined the AVG in China.

Thursday, February 11, 1943 [Karachi, India, now Pakistan to Salala, Oman to Khartoum, Sudan]

Last night Brady gave me a letter to give to Johnny Andrews, mustn't forget.[267] Movies until 11:30, in bed at 12:00, up at 5:00, took off 6:15, [arrived] Salala 12:15.[268] Took my turn at controls 7:30 to 10:30, reached Arabian coast at 10:25, very barren. No signs of life except fishing boats along shore, probably pearl fishers. Many trails leading across desert to points where it is possible to climb down cliffs to sea but where the trails lead to in desert is another story. There is not a tree, a bud, a living creature of any kind in sight as far as the eye can see.

Camels are very prevalent in India [Arabia?]; they are the normal means of transportation. They travel in long columns along the road at night, with no tail lights, and the Arabs fast asleep. The auto must watch for the camels, not the camels for the auto. Little donkeys, they probably weigh 175 pounds; upon them will be a load balanced, hanging on both sides, weighing 200 pounds and an Arab or two sitting atop the donkey.

At Salala, Lieutenant Pike is in command; an airport in the midst of the desert, reminded me of Muroc [California];[269] tents, improvised mess halls, serving facilities, Arabs on guard, pouring gasoline, working in kitchen. Everywhere Arabs but they are black. Either someone made a mistake, they have been out in the sun too long or there is an Ethiopian in the background.

The crew here, Lieutenant Pike, 3 sergeants, and 2 privates, have high morale, very high. Pike used to be with PAA. Nothing seems to daunt him: sand, heat, dust, 3 planes a day for service, no permanent buildings, he takes them all in his stride. Came from Boston. I promised that I would get them a radio, a phonograph and some records. Pike should be made a

Captain.²⁷⁰ RAF have 2 officers, non-flying, 3 non-commissioned officer pilots and 6 mechanics. An Imperial Airways official was there; they are not overlooking a single bet. Left Salala 1:30 (Salala time 11:30), due in Khartoum 9:30²⁷¹ (Khartoum time 5:30).

Arabs live in caves, on what? Who knows? They have their camels and their goats but what do the camels and goats eat? From Salala our course was west. The map gave the terrain a forbidding description—(unexplored). That wasn't the half of it. It was not even marked by man, bird or beast for 500 miles, nothing but barren hills, sand dunes, sandstorms, desert, dry stream courses and very infrequently a well-marked trail that seemed to start nowhere and go to the same place.

As we approached the Red Sea we came to mountains. We were flying at 9,500 feet and the mountains about 4,000 feet below us. Solid stone, weather-beaten, with deep valleys that turned into canyons all through them. All of a sudden in a broad valley, green fields appeared and strange creations of man, high buildings nestled close together forming villages and in some cases cities. All made of stone and giving the appearance of lower New York and its skyscrapers. Some were round, others square, windows at irregular intervals. As we flew along, the mountains became much higher until some 50 miles to the north they were 1,000 feet above us.²⁷²

The mountains flattened out and formed many plateaus. Here also was cultivated ground, dikes and the same kind of villages. In some cases they were built right up on top of the highest peaks. Trails led from one village to another. Who are they? How long have they lived there? Do they ever go out into the other world? There were no trails leading out that we could see. Then came a sudden drop, the plains bordering on the Red Sea and the sea itself. On those plains the houses were flat and in appearance just like all other Arab houses.

Great consternation when we landed at Khartoum. We landed at an airport 22 miles out, while the Governor was waiting for us at another airport within three miles of town. Our CO, Colonel Kerr and the British did not get together for we radioed in for instructions.²⁷³ Dill, Shelmire, Pete and I went to Government House, others to Grand Hotel. Big garden party for Egyptians; we did not participate. Dinner with the Kaid and his daughter and General B. O. Hutchinson [Huddleston].[274] In bed then at 11 P.M. Read Chinese Gordon at Khartoum to get picture of what happened.[275] Big conference here soon, apparently Somervell has called it: Brereton on way, Crawford, Fitzgerald, Somervell, Wheeler. When? Where? I know not.[276] Brereton and Crawford here now.

Friday, February 12, 1943 [Khartoum, Sudan]

The palace here is a wonderful building; large U-shaped with very beautiful garden. Largest yellow and mauve (?) Cannas I have ever seen, marble stairways. Gordon killed here at end of siege. Palace rebuilt by a sapper Captain right on banks of Blue Nile.[277] Khartoum at junction of White and Blue Niles, rivers clean and clear. Villages cleanest tropical towns I have seen anywhere. Natives black, and how black; houses adobe. Native nightgowns, they all wear them, cleaner than any so far on any natives, snow white nightgowns. What an ad for somebody's soap: white nighties on black bodies.

Forgot to say while I was in Calcutta I bought a new shoe horn. Thirty-four years ago I bought one, nice figure of woman with long shoe horn. In the intervening years the dame lost her head, one arm was broken 20 years ago and shoe horn has been dropped and pieces broken off. It became too rough to use on silk hose. It had to be cut and smoothed. It looked sort of sad, so 34 years later I bought another one in Calcutta, a nice, bright, smooth shoe horn. Governor Huddleston, Lady Huddleston.[278]

Up late, breakfast 9:00. Took car with Dill, met Brereton at Grand Hotel, went out to Omdurman. There Kitchener completely and for all time destroyed the power of the Arabs. The ruins of the old Arab Mahdi (who was a religious fanatic) house still stands, made into a museum. He only lived for six months after Gordon's death. Had a fine, majestic tomb created as a shrine. Kitchener opened his artillery on it and after blowing the top off, opened the grave and to revenge Gordon's death cut the head off the body and dumped both into the Nile.[279]

In the town are markets that go the ones in Panama and the Philippine Islands one better. The natives can buy anything or any part of an animal. The silver shops are very attractive and they do excellent work. The ivory work is not as finished as that done in India. The natives have home-made lathes. They hold the tension on the lathe center with their feet. They hold the cutting tool with their feet and they rotate the work with a bow and string the same as the boy scouts make fire.

The animal market was most interesting: camels, goats, cattle, all brought in from sections as far as 500 miles away. All look to be in good condition. A camel, skinny, long-legged, small chest and no barrel, mean, grumbling and growling. It looked as if it would cave in after a few miles of hard riding, was the best riding animal in the corral. The owner wanted 20 pounds for it. Others bigger, stronger, heavier and in much better condition that could be bought for 15 pounds.

The natives are obviously an inherently cleaner race than any others that we have seen. Their houses are made of adobe and will stand up for about two rainy seasons. They have about 6 inches of rain a year. At 12:00 noon a black Mohammedan from his perch high up on the tower of the mosque starts singing for all faithful to come in and start praying. They come in and stream in the gates from all directions. I wonder how many Methodists or Baptists a fellow could get using the same tactics.

A letter from Kitchener written in clear, bold handwriting. Evidently the War Office sent him a letter stating that they did not have his letter as forwarded by his superior, positively swearing to his fitness. Kitchener came back:

> I have been my own CO for ten years. During that period you have sent me three such letters. I call your attention to the fact that I have had three letters of commendation from the War Office and one from the Queen which should attest [to] the fact that I am officially fit. Those letters should speak for themselves.

Lunch at the Palace. Somervell gets in about 3:00. We go out on the government boat in the Nile and have tea this P.M. Right now for the first time in I don't know how many months I have nothing to do for four hours. Saw Crawford and Connelly at the hotel with Brereton.

Saturday, February 13, 1943 [Khartoum, Sudan to Maidguiri, Nigeria to Accra, Gold Coast, now Ghana]

Khartoum. Very formal dinner last night at the Palace. Shelmire went in his shirt, all of the British had on dinner coats, except Army and Air who wore blouses.

Shades of Cleopatra, a boat ride up the Blue Nile at sunset. Excused myself at 10:00, packed and in bed; was awakened at 12:00, left Palace at 12:30 A.M., took off for Maiduguri 12:55, arrive Maiduguri, 8:20. Could not see much of the ground on account of dust and darkness. First point recognized Fort Lamy.[280]

Maiduguri, Nigeria; Central Africa, blacks even more blacker. Long and tall, work for 30 cents a day, more money than they have ever seen. When they save up enough they buy themselves more wives. They revel in uniforms, some are in the British Nigerian Corps. They strut around in their uniform with canteens, knives, belts, ammunition and hats, no shoes, but they walk on sharp stones and thorns that would go through our light shoes. Rags and more rags. Apparently there is no policy with regard to covering up nakedness but caste means a lot and clothes mean caste.

In the midst of this is our airfield, operated jointly with the RAF. Very well built, administered by a First Lieutenant commanding. However it is so close to the diseased natives in the village I fear for the future without a constant inspection by experienced inspectors. Most of the officers served once with PAA and know little about Army administration and standards. They have put the native village off limits but after a while these fellows who have been away from home a long time find the native women getting lighter day by day.

Took off at 11:10 A.M., arrived Accra 4:30 P.M.; at controls 5:30 to 8:30. More about the black natives who go stark naked and revere things only in the order named: their cattle, their children and their wives. They have nothing but these things. Everything they live on comes from the cattle. They must have enough so that as is their custom when they sink a spear into the neck of a bull and drink its blood it has time to recover and there are many others so that they do not have to repeat on one animal and so do the women and the children. What a countryside we have our airports in and fly over. Sorted out baggage and then inspected Post. Sir John [Dill], Somervell, Smart and I go ahead on C-54; B-17 and C-87 follow leisurely.

Dinner with Governor and his Lady, beautiful palace on waterfront, breakers right below house.[281] Post in excellent shape, very good messes.

Sunday, February 14, 1943 [Accra, Ghana to Ascension Island to Natal and Recife, Brazil]

Took off at 12:30 P.M., arrived Ascension [Island] 7:25 A.M., left Ascension 9:45, arrived Natal 4:20. Ran through thunderstorm area as we crossed Equator, otherwise excellent trip. Plane jumped and kicked, lightning flashed but when we broke out into the clear there was the Southern Cross[282] just over our port bow. Arrived at Ascension at daybreak: a small volcanic island with no foliage at lower levels, hills composed of volcanic ashes. Runway dug out between two hills, 6,900 feet long. Two thousand planes went through last year; lost only 2 B-26s, 2 B-24s, 2 A-20s (crew saved), 2 P-39s (crew saved). Clouds stand on top of large mountain all the time. Condensation causes rain, green grass and almost jungle vegetation, but it only drops down the mountain to about the 1,000 ft. level. Cattle, sheep and wild donkeys thrive at the upper levels. Water obtained for troops by distilling sea water; for cable station employees by collecting rain water from cement-covered side of mountain. Island held by various nations almost continuously since 1600, British held it since 1700. Ships unload in roadstead and goods brought in on lighters.[283] A C-87 and Boeing Stratoliner took off before we did last night. The C-87 beat us in, we beat the Boeing Stratoliner in.[284] The Governor of the Gold Coast, Sir Allan Burns, Christianborg Castle, Accra, Gold Coast—letter of thanks for a very excellent dinner at a very relaxing Government House.

Upon arrival at Natal the heat was intense. We had to be de-insected. Walsh was waiting, suggested that we go to Recife for the night. The Minister for Air and General Gomez were awaiting me there.[285] We climbed into a DC-3 and took off, arrived at Recife within an hour to find an escort of honor, band. The Minister of Air and Gomez insisted that I take it which I did. Then out to the beach house where Bob [Walsh] sends his worn-out pilots, it is nice and cool. All of us were dog-tired so we soon fell asleep.

Conference with the Minister and Gomez at the hotel in town. They [Brazilians] want:

(1) More training for mechanics. That I fixed up by having Walsh agree do it here.
(2) Train more pilots, 300 during this year - that I could not agree to but said I would look into it and have as many as possible.
(3) Materials for their aircraft factory. Walsh is going to send me a list and I will see what can be done, if anything.

The only thing I promised was the mechanic's training and Bob Walsh can do that. Then the Minister decorated me with the Order of the Southern Cross, a magnificent looking medal.[286] Home to bed and slept like a log until 6:30.

Monday, February 15, 1943 [Natal, Recife, Belem, Brazil]

Minister for Air (Aeronautics), J. Salgado Filho, Rio de Janeiro; he gave a very excellent dinner. Left Natal 2:30, arrived Recife 3:45, left Recife 10:00 arrived Natal 11:15.

Recife appears to be a very modern city, streets clean, buildings look new and well-built. However there is an air of laziness all around the city, men lying around, looking out of windows. They do not seem to have enough pep to ever really put the place on the map.

Saw Jonas Ingram who gave me some messages for Admiral King; will deliver same when I get there. Searchlight development for airplanes, Jonas Ingram wants same.[287] Tell [Admiral] King Ingram wants amphibians, one squadron for Ascension, one squadron B-24s, B-25s.[288]

What makes flying so tiring? Is it the unrecognized wear and tear on the nerves? Is there a physical strain that we don't recognize? Is it the long hours, the curtailed sleep?

Karachi - we arrived and did not turn our watches back. Up at 6:00 and off at 7:00. However we were up next morning at 5:00 and off at 6:00. We arrived at Khartoum and set our watches back 2 hours, the day was then 26 hours long. Up at 12:00, off at 1:00 A.M. Upon arrival at Accra we set our watches back 2½ hours and thus had another long day. Accra, took off at 12:00 midnight and upon landing at Natal set our watches back 2 hours. All were dead tired and slept a full eight hours last night. We all had naps and are all still tired. Is it the altitude and lack of oxygen?

Recife is a nice place to rest. Bob Walsh's Casa Verde is a good rest camp, right on the beach, good bathing.[289] The B-17 came in last night. Pete is in the hospital today. Told Shelmire to hold him there until he gets well, told the medico the same thing. Provided for a pilot from the C-87 to help out on the B-17. Took off Natal 12:00 noon, arrived Belem 5:00 P.M. Weather rotten for first 100 miles, rain, thick clouds, then broken clouds and sunshine.

Went to Para (Belem) and found a very interesting city. French type of architecture predominating, but just where did the ultra high, narrow, very narrow doors come from? They must be at least 12 to 15 feet high and but three feet wide, split down the middle.

The old rubber millionaire's houses are not the same any more, they look sort of out of place, down at the heels. The town has seen better days. The one exception is the Catholic cathedral, wonderful mosaics, statues, marble columns. The mosaics actually have depth and expression on their faces.[290]

Tuesday, February 16, 1943 [Belem, Brazil to Borinquen Field, Puerto Rico]

Left Belem 7:30, arrive Borinquen 4:45. No matter where one goes, there are signs of people not following through, not diagnosing results to obtain causes, of accepting things and not trying to change for better; what's to be is to be [for example]. Accidents, too many accidents by far between Miami and Accra. Causes: weather, inexperienced pilots and crews, improper briefings. We can't change the weather but we can change our operations to conform to the weather. We can't change the inexperienced pilots, that's all we have so we must protect them. Our briefing must be carried out to get the best results, taking into consideration weather, inexperienced pilots and communications. Have we ever on any part of this bad section said: "Heavy bombers can proceed from X to Y, medium bombers only from X to Z, light bombers and pursuits stay on ground or proceed from A to Y or Y to A, all based on weather?" No. Who briefed the P-40 pilots proceeding from Dallas to Natal? What did that guy know about it? Why didn't they go via Miami instead of the usual route? We lost four out of five, that speaks for itself. Why haven't we gotten the proper crystals down there?[291] They have been requested time and time again. One would think sometime that we go out of our way to make things hard for the young pilot.

Belem was cool last night. Planes by the dozen taking off at 3:00 A.M., they are clearing now at the rate of 360 a month, or 4,300 a year. The accident rate is not too bad but it is too high, there are too many ships that disappear very mysteriously over the water. Too many people do not have confidence in their instruments and will not believe them. There is a great necessity for securing closer coordination in shipping of: a. organizational equipment; b. backlog of supplies at Miami, Trinidad, Natal, San Francisco; c. passengers awaiting air transportation.

Memo to Frank [Walsh] telling him to confer with Somervell re above. [Need for a] School for briefing officers.

Fine weather this trip ever since we went through very narrow front just north of Belem. No action yet on future of Borinquen: 2,500 men, good men being wasted. Why so long a time to reach a decision; a staff study on the obvious?

Beebe's Group on the ground when we arrived; planes looked good with names individually selected by crews. One is typical—a naked gal sitting on a cake of ice and the name "Miss Carriage." Gave Beebe the information re his mission, conference with his Executive, G-1, 2, 3, 4. Gave talk to all of his officers and men and wished them luck.[292] Dinner with Collins, he wants a plane, needs it badly. Agrees as to the use of Borinquen, turning it over to Transport Command. Collins flew back to San Juan after dinner. Bed at 8:30; it must be the lack of oxygen as a result of continuous flying above 18,000 feet for several hours.

Wednesday, February 17, 1943 [Borinquen Field, Puerto Rico to Washington, D. C.]

Dropped my watch on the concrete floor and it bounced; it also stopped. Took off Borinquen 8:00 A.M., arrived Washington 4:06 P.M.

Postscript

In evaluating the journey that took Arnold to all but two of the world's continents, he could have tallied the results by using won/loss metaphors from athletic contests he enjoyed watching and on which he occasionally placed a bet. In the second week after leaving Washington, Arnold and the assembled AAF generals scored a major victory in convincing Churchill to drop his planned opposition to AAF daylight strategic bombing. This meant a continuation of the strategy to which Hap and the AAF had already committed considerable human and materiel resources and for which Arnold had high hopes in terms of not only winning the war but of establishing a raison d'être for a separate AF in the postwar structure.

The resulting agreement at Casablanca termed the Combined Bomber Offensive (CBO) was a validation of both the area night bombing of the RAF aimed at the enemy's morale and the AAF daylight effort attacking their industrial resources. By the document, the "appropriate British and U. S. Air Force Commanders . . . in the United Kingdom" were instructed that their "primary object will be the progressive destruction and dislocation of the German military, industrial and economic system and the undermining of the morale of the German people to a point where their armed resistance is fatally weakened." Further delineating the daylight mission of the Eighth, Eaker was directed that he should "take every opportunity to attack Germany by day, to destroy objectives that are unsuitable for night attack." In so doing, he was enjoined to "impose heavy losses on the German fighter day force and to contain German fighter strength away from the Russian and Mediterranean theaters." Becoming more specific, the CBO set forth a system of priorities to govern their operations. Before any success could be obtained against significant German targets, the first attacks were to be made on their outer defense limits. The first two priorities were assigned to the "German submarine construction yards" and the "German aircraft industry." The next three items in priority order were transportation, oil plants, and "other targets in enemy war industry."[293] Marshall's comment at the 21 January CCS morning session, that the "control of bomber operations" of the AAF was to be "in the hands of the British" and "would be a matter of command rather than of agreement with US Commanders," resulted in "responsibility" for the operations being lodged with Portal, who directed the CBO as the agent of the CCS.[294] Targets and tactics within the five categories were left to the respective commanders. Although security considerations precluded any comment in his diary, he left no doubt of his feelings in his memoirs when he wrote: "We had won a major victory, for we would bomb in accordance with American principles, using methods for which our planes were designed." As a further indication of the CCS advocacy of US daylight bombing, their decision in their 19 January session, which Hap omitted from his diary because of security concerns, was important. It provided that "bombing attacks on . . . the Rumanian oilfields [Ploesti] be undertaken as soon as other commitments allow." This would lead to the significant raid of 1 August 1943.[295]

Hap joined Marshall and King in their disappointment that the final conference agreement on European strategy identified the next Allied operation as an attack on Sicily, codenamed Husky, instead of the cross-Channel assault in 1943.[296] This meant further diversion of air assets from Britain such as happened for Torch, compounded by the fact that most of the aircraft sent to support the North Africa invasion had not yet returned to England—and some never would. Yet Arnold realized that any successful invasion of France required air superiority, which had not been and could not be obtained until German aircraft production facilities and the

Luftwaffe were successfully attacked. Such success could only be achieved by a program such as that provided under the CBO. Although Arnold does not document his thinking about the impact, the CCS in its final report indicated an appreciation that airborne troops would be required in Husky, thus placing additional demands on American transport aircraft, which were the umbilical cord connecting China logistically to the outside world. However, Arnold was becoming increasingly skeptical, as were the other JCS members, of British intentions regarding a cross-Channel attack. Three months after Casablanca, Arnold conceded in a memo, "It is becoming more and more apparent that the British have no intention of invading France and continental Europe."[297]

Upon departing Casablanca and reaching India, Hap discussed the planning of the agreed-upon Anakim operation for the fall of 1943. Arnold expressed in his memoirs as well as his diary that he and Sir John Dill had been successful in getting Wavell and his British staff in India to make more realistic plans for the Burma invasion. They reassessed the progress on their return from China.[298]

The results of his days in China are hard to categorize in any win/loss column. Although Arnold discussed the problems of the theater with Stilwell, Chennault, and others, he could not claim success in his meetings with Chiang even though two scholars have evaluated Hap's conversations with the Generalissimo as a "blend of tact and firmness."[299] The three conditions necessary for China to participate in the Anakim operation as explained to Hap differed little from the demands that Chiang had made previously. These called for an independent air force under Chennault, 10,000 tons per month over the Hump, and 500 aircraft operating in China by November 1943. Arnold is quoted as telling Stilwell, "I'll be — damned if I take any such message back to the President."[300] Even before meeting with Chiang, Arnold cabled Marshall that in his opinion logistical problems made a "separate air force in China impractical" and that Chennault's "administrative and executive control" of his CATF did not "warrant its independence" as Chiang demanded.[301] This coincided with Marshall's sentiments that had been expressed a month earlier to the president, prompted by Chennault's letter to Willkie that had been furnished to the White House. In his memo for FDR, after praising Chennault's operational "genius," Marshall touched on what Arnold, Stimson, and most of the War Department felt was the crux of the issue in China. The Army chief of staff wrote that Chennault "appears to disregard the actualities of the logistical problem which our responsible commander, Lt. General Stilwell, is struggling to master by the spring operation in Northern Burma."[302]

Nevertheless, a possible win could be accorded for Arnold as he, Stilwell, and Sir John Dill got Chiang to agree during their 6 February meeting to participate, however conditionally, in the planned Burma invasion. On his departure, Arnold's beliefs probably had not changed as a result of the visit. He expressed considerable empathy for Stilwell's difficult position, telling him, "You ought to get a laurel wreath." On arriving back in Washington, he wrote to Stilwell: "You have one S. O. B. of a job. If at any time you think I can help, just yell."[303] As usual, given security and other considerations, Hap was careful in what he committed to the diary regarding others. However, the entry for 8 February, probably written either in his plane flying from China to India or penned that night on arrival in Calcutta, reflected his estimate of Chiang. He commented that the Chinese leader was not "a big man" but one who "casts aside logic . . . as so much trash" and "does not have to think things through" since he expected his subjects to "give him the answer he wants."[304]

Another win might be recorded for Dill and Arnold as they returned to India for three nights and found reaffirmation with the Chinese Minister of War and General Wavell to participate in the Anakim operation. The Chinese assent was facilitated by the British, who planned their support with a greater sense of urgency than had been the case when Arnold and Dill passed through Calcutta the week earlier.[305]

From India, the itinerary of Arnold's weeklong trip back to Washington, which he probably planned himself based on the limitations of the airplane and the crew, appeared to provide for stops in relatively isolated locations. He took the opportunity to observe the roles and problems of the sites, which were part of the expanding AAF Air Transport Command network of stations around much of the world. These stops included Oman, the Sudan, Nigeria, the Gold Coast, Ascension Island, and two days in Brazil, with some leisure there before a brief stop in Puerto Rico en route to Washington. At these locations, he recorded perceptive comments on the living and working conditions of the service personnel while attempting to assess their morale. The diary also reflected his practice of noting local customs and culture.

Arnold is careful in his memoirs about recording the results of the trip, particularly the difficult and politically sensitive problems in China. He showed awareness in his memoirs of the many ramifications of that situation when he wrote that the "personal clashes among the key leaders in China made it rather difficult for me to give the President a clean-cut report."[306] He did not need to add that by now the lines were drawn between Marshall, Arnold, Stimson, and the War Department on one side in support of Stilwell and an appreciation of the dominance of logistics in determining any military action in China. The opposing viewpoint was dominated by Roosevelt, Chiang Kai-shek, Chennault, and the intense Sinophile propaganda campaign directed through Hopkins, which advocated increased aid for China, the recall of Stilwell, and sovereignty for Chennault. It is disappointing that Arnold did not record what he reported to the White House. As he wrote in *Global Mission*, "Logistics, air and general military progress were one thing. Matters like Chiang's attitude toward Bissell, his unlimited confidence in Chennault, Chennault's oversimplification, along Chinese lines, of various problems, and above all the personal position of Stilwell . . . these were complications a bit beyond the Book."[307] Arnold also was the courier for Chiang's 7 February letter to Roosevelt. In it, Chiang praised Chennault as a genius who should have an air force of his own and said he needed the 500 promised aircraft. The Generalissimo added that, in order for fall participation by the Chinese in Anakim, 10,000 tons over the Hump by November was required. Arnold conceded that he brought Stilwell's memo, outlining in detail the gloomy conditions in China, back to FDR, Stimson, and Marshall: "Finally, I made my report to my superiors as I saw the problem, supporting my conclusions and inferences with specific details."[308]

Presumably ignoring or discounting any data or recommendations Arnold brought back, as well as the known opposition of Stimson, Marshall, and Arnold, FDR acceded, only two days after Hap's return, to everything Chiang wanted in behalf of Chennault. As the details emerged over the next month, little light was shed on the reasons for Roosevelt's actions. Obviously influenced by the pro-Chiang forces operating in Washington through Hopkins, Roosevelt had been impressed by Chennault's earlier unrealistic claims forwarded by Willkie.[309] The president had indicated as early as December his inclination to give Chennault his own air force but held off in view of Marshall's opposition, the Casablanca meeting, and Arnold's trip.[310] As the official Army history has concluded, Roosevelt was disturbed by Stilwell's letter to Marshall of 9 February, extracts of which were furnished to the White House on 18 February. In it, Stilwell reiterated his position that Lend-Lease should be used to extract a quid pro quo of performance from the Chinese and that stern tones were needed in dealing with Chiang. FDR took strong exception to what he considered Stilwell's lese majesty.[311] Other influences included a recent *Time* magazine that was critical of Stilwell and laudatory of Chennault. *Time*'s editor, Henry Luce, was the son of American missionaries to China, and he had been consistently using his influential publications to lionize Chiang.[312] Possibly most illuminating was FDR's admission to Marshall on 2 May that politically he "must support Chiang Kai-shek" and that, given the state of Chinese morale, the air program was "of great importance."[313] Roosevelt's actions could not be labeled as a victory for Arnold and the War Department.

In spite of Stilwell's assessment that Arnold's and Somervell's visit had been "very helpful" and that Hap saw the "personalities we have to deal with," Roosevelt's actions in creating the Fourteenth Air Force (in the estimate of a friendly biographer of Chennault, the "only air force created during the war for political rather than military reasons") was only part of Chiang's success.[314] This action was followed immediately by promotions for both Chennault and Bissell to major general, with Bissell given the rank one day senior to Chennault. Additionally, Chiang was promised that 500 planes would constitute the new Fourteenth Air Force and that airlift over the Hump would eventually be increased to 10,000 tons per month. Chennault would be given control of the 308th Bombardment Group, which was headed for the theater, and would be independent of Bissell but not of Stilwell. Three months later, Chiang would be successful in securing Bissell's ouster.

Marshall and Stimson held out for another year against FDR's strong suggestions, short of a direct order, that Stilwell himself be recalled.[315] Arnold has left no direct comment on the president's many concessions to Chiang, Chennault, and Hopkins. He continued his practice of not making comments about his commander in chief. However, considering his diary coverage of Chennault and Chiang and what he deduced from his visit, there is little reason to believe that he was not disappointed by what had been ordered. Nevertheless, he continued to implement Roosevelt's instructions concerning an increase in the number of transports assigned to the Hump. In spite of what he believed was the Flying Tigers' current standing in the White House, Arnold's 3 March letter to Chennault is revealing. He wrote, rather sternly, "Recently you have been accorded the status of independent commander of an air force. With this status comes, as you know, certain responsibilities that you must meet."[316]

Regardless of how a win/loss accounting might interpret the presidential resolution of the China problem, the AAF and Hap experienced a serious loss when Hap suffered a heart attack within 10 days after his return. The demands of the 39-day trip covering almost 28,000 miles in an unpressurized combat B-17 not configured for passenger comfort, together with irregular hours, varying diets, and no exercise took their toll on this 57-year-old aviator. It was to be the first of four attacks that he experienced during the war.

The exact date of its onset is not certain, but on 27 February, 10 days after Hap's return, his chief of staff, General Stratemeyer, informed Hopkins that, as you know, "General Arnold has been a bit under the weather and confined to his quarters the last two or three days. He expects to be back for duty, March 1st."[317] The AAF chief surgeon thought otherwise and "made all arrangements" for Hap to be flown to Miami Beach, Florida, on 5 March. There, isolated in a hotel operated by the AAF with cook, attendants, and an automobile but no publicity, he was to take "golf clubs, bathing suit and a fishing reel."[318] He returned to Washington sometime before 24 March, having remained optimistic as well as impatient to "get back to work" while in Miami. As Hap described the circumstances, he was "sort of worn out" and was there for a "rest" with "nothing to do and nobody can get at me to bother me so it is really a grand setup."[319]

While Arnold convalesced in Florida, General Marshall recommended to Roosevelt that Hap be promoted to four-star rank. The inferences that might be drawn from this recommendation are several. Albeit in a wartime environment, it would be the highest rank ever achieved by an Army aviator, acknowledging the importance of this branch, now 1,300,000 strong. Although the recommendation was based on past performance, the military ideally promotes in anticipation of further service at the higher rank. It is therefore not illogical to assume that Marshall and Stimson saw Arnold's medical problems as not sufficiently serious to prevent his further service.

It had to have been encouraging to Arnold that his leadership was so recognized, and he knew the Army well enough to appreciate that he was not being recommended for promotion to go on the retired list.

Although no specific documentation exists to support this thought, could the recommendation have been Marshall's and Stimson's polite rebuke of the White House? FDR's actions in satisfying Chiang's demands, against the recommendations of the War Department supported by Arnold's findings from his trip, took place just after Arnold's return and were being announced while Hap was in Florida. If the War Department's position and Arnold's recommendations were being overridden, was Marshall's recommendation for Hap's promotion (which was made by the White House three days after Marshall's recommendation) a not too subtle but nevertheless polite way of informing the commander in chief of the War Department's displeasure?[320]

There is little doubt that Arnold returned with considerable vigor to the Pentagon in spite of efforts to slow his activities. Unfortunately for him and the AAF, he would be stricken with a second attack in May, just over six weeks after his return from the hospital. This seizure prevented him from participating in the Trident Washington meeting of Churchill, Roosevelt, and the CCS.[321] The casualties of war are not restricted to aerial dogfights and trench mortars.

Notes

1. Warren F. Kimball, ed., *Churchill & Roosevelt: The Complete Correspondence*, vol. 1, *Alliance Emerging October 1933-November 1942* (Princeton, N.J.: Princeton University Press, 1984), 669-70; Diary of Gen Henry H. Arnold (hereinafter cited as Arnold Diary), 14 January 1943, in Henry Harley Arnold Papers, Library of Congress, Manuscript Division, Washington, D.C., hereinafter cited as AP.

2. Roger A. Freeman, Alan Crouchman, and Vic Maslen, *Mighty Eighth War Diary* (London: Jane's, 1981), 14-32.

3. Churchill to Roosevelt, 16 September 1942, in Kimball, 597-99.

4. Public Record Office London (PRO), Air Ministry Records (Air) 8/711, Churchill to Hopkins, 16 October 1942.

5. PRO, Air 8/711, Churchill, Minute on Air Policy, 22 October 1942.

6. PRO, Air 8/711, Sinclair to Churchill, 23 October 1942.

7. PRO, Air 8/711, Churchill to Sinclair, 26 October 1942.

8. PRO, Air 8/711, Churchill to Chief of the Air Staff (Portal), 2 November 1942.

9. PRO, Air 8/711, Portal to Churchill, 7 November 1942.

10. PRO, Air 8/711, Air Ministry (Portal) to RAF Delegation, Washington (RAFDEL), 21 November 1942.

11. Arnold to Eisenhower, 13 January 1943, AP.

12. Arnold Diary, 15 January 1943.

13. Department of State, *Foreign Relations of the United States, Diplomatic Papers, 1938*, 2 vols. (Washington, D.C.: Government Printing Office, [GPO]1970), 666-67, hereinafter cited as FRUS; quotes from Winston S. Churchill, *The Hinge of Fate* (Boston: Houghton Mifflin, 1950), 678-79; Diary of Gen Ira C. Eaker, 20 January 1943, Ira C. Eaker Papers, Manuscript Division, Library of Congress, Washington, D.C., hereinafter cited as EP; H. H. Arnold, General of the Air Force, *Global Mission* (New York: Harper & Brothers, 1949), 393, 395-97; and James Parton, *"Air Force Spoken Here," General Ira Eaker and the Command of the Air* (Bethesda, Md.: Adler & Adler, 1986), 219-22. Although space, time, and security considerations may have deterred Hap from any detailed explanation in the diary of getting Churchill to change his thinking, Arnold was not as modest in his memoirs. Hap does not give Eaker the same credit Churchill and others

accorded him. See Hap's account in *Global Mission*, 396-97, where he explained "Again I outlined to him [Churchill]" and "I told him" and "I also told him" and "I talked long and hard!" He does write, "after Spaatz, Eaker and Andrews had talked" with him, Churchill "told me he was willing for us to give it a trial." See the other accounts that make a strong case for Eaker's having carried the day, such as Churchill's own account cited above, Eaker's Diary of 20 January and Spaatz's biographer, who concluded: "Eaker proved by far the most convincing," Richard G. Davis, *Carl A. Spaatz and the Air War in Europe* (Washington, D.C.: Center for Air Force History, 1993), 162.

14. Arnold to Stratemeyer, letter, by air courier, 27 January 1943; also Arnold to Lovett, two letters, 28 January 1943, AP.

15. Col Jacob E. Smart, a member of Arnold's Advisory Council who accompanied him on this trip, has kindly annotated Hap's diary for this trip. It is hereinafter cited as SC, with the date, and is in the possession of the editor. SC, 25 January 1943.

16. Martin Gilbert, *Winston S. Churchill*, vol. 7, *Road to Victory, 1941-1945* (Boston: Houghton Mifflin, 1986), 319-25; and Arnold, *Global Mission*, 403.

17. Arnold, *Global Mission*, 404; and Thomas H. Vail Motter, *The United States Army in World War II: The Mediterranean Theater of Operations: The Persian Corridor and Aid to Russia* (Washington, D.C.: GPO, Department of the Army, 1952), makes no mention of Arnold's effectiveness.

18. Arnold, *Global Mission*, 408-09; Barbara W. Tuchman, *Stillwell and the American Experience in China, 1911-1945* (New York: Macmillan, 1970), 341, 345, 356.

19. Hopkins memo is quoted in Robert E. Sherwood, *Roosevelt and Hopkins: An Intimate History* (New York: Harpers & Brothers, 1948), 681-82.

20. *Foreign Relations of the United States, Diplomatic Papers, The Conferences at Washington, 1941-1942 and Casablanca, 1943* (Washington, D.C.: GPO, 1968), 718-19, cited hereinafter as FRUS, Casablanca.

21. Tuchman, 280, 300, provides examples.

22. Charles F. Romanus and Riley Sunderland, *United States Army in World War II: The China-Burma-India Theater: Stilwell's Mission to China* (Washington, D.C: GPO, 1953), 23; "National tragedy," etc., is from Alsop to Hopkins, 19 December 1943, quoted in Tuchman, 358.

23. Tuchman, 250, 311-14, 357. Sherwood probably accurately expressed Hopkins and Roosevelt's thinking in saying there was "always the possibility that the Kuomintang might make a separate peace," 740. The CCS in August 1942 had discussed the possibility of China making peace with Japan and suggested aiding China by retaking Burma and reopening the Burma Road, CCS 104, 25 August 1942, quoted in Romanus and Sunderland, 223.

24. Romanus and Sunderland, 62, 66.

25. Quoted in Tuchman, 242.

26. Tuchman, 246.

27. Roosevelt to Arnold, 5 May 1942, copy in AP.

28. Quoted in Martha Byrd, *Chennault: Giving Wings to the Tiger* (Tuscaloosa, Ala.: University of Alabama Press, 1987), 40. This is a balanced account of the aviator and a necessary antidote to Chennault's bitter autobiography, Claire Lee Chennault, *Way of a Fighter: The Memoirs of Claire Lee Chennault, Major General, U. S. Army (Ret.)* ed. Robert Hotz (New York: G. P. Putnam's Sons, 1949).

29. Byrd, 152.

30. Tuchman, 309; Chennault, 170, for opposition to integration into the AAF.

31. Arnold, *Global Mission*, 419.

32. Chennault, 171.

33. Ibid., 180.

34. Ibid., 201, "Filing cabinet mind." The bitterness is shown in Chennault's followers (and probably Chennault) teaching the Chinese coolies that a proper greeting in English for Bissell, instead of "hello" was the phrase using the profane four-letter word for urine, making the salutation "P - - - on Bissell"; Byrd, 149. Chennault cleans up the language in his memoirs on page 201, but the meaning remains clear.

35. Even though the American forces in the theater were commanded by a US Army ground officer, it never changed from a predominantly air one. Three months after Stilwell arrived there in 1942, the air personnel in the CBI numbered 3,000 as opposed to only 94 "ground" personnel. Two and one-half years later, the proportion was changed but the dominance of AAF continued as there were now more than 78,000 airmen as contrasted with only 25,000 ground personnel. Wesley Frank Craven and James Lea Cate, eds., *The Army Air Forces in World War II*, vol. 4, *The Pacific: Guadalcanal to Saipan, August 1942 to July 1944* (1950; new imprint, Washington, D.C.: Office of Air Force History, 1983), 406; Tuchman, 305; and Arnold Diary, 8 February 1943.

36. Forrest C. Pogue, *George C. Marshall, Organizer of Victory, 1943–1945* (New York: Viking Press, 1973), 479.

37. Tuchman, 309.

38. Ibid., 308.

39. Three demands quoted in Romanus and Sunderland, 172; and Tuchman, 311–14.

40. Tuchman, 312.

41. Ibid., 313.

42. FDR radio to Chiang Kai-shek, 10 October 1942; and Romanus and Sunderland, 224–25.

43. Romanus and Sunderland, 226.

44. Ibid., 247–50, for British objections.

45. Chennault, 216–20, reproduces his letter. Tuchman, 337, uses the term *extraordinary*. Byrd is the source of "overweening," and so forth, 173.

46. Quoted in Byrd, 176.

47. The quote is from Romanus and Sunderland, 251; see their chapter 9, 313–54, "Air Power Rather than Army Reform."

48. See also Wendell Willkie, *One World* (New York: Simon & Schuster, 1943), 143–44.
49. Romanus and Sunderland, 231.
50. Ibid., 244ff.
51. Ibid., 258.
52. Roosevelt to Stilwell for Chiang, 2 January 1943, quoted in Romanus and Sunderland, 258.
53. Chiang Kai-shek to Roosevelt, 8 January 1943, quoted in Romanus and Sunderland, 260.
54. FDR's letter to Chiang was included by Arnold in the Diary and is printed in Arnold, *Global Mission*, 415.
55. Romanus and Sunderland, 273.
56. Arnold Diary, 1 February 1943.
57. Arnold to Gen Hal George, letters, 28 January and 4 March 1943, AP.
58. Rear Adm Charles M. "Savvy" Cooke Jr., USN, assistant chief of staff (plans), Staff of the Commander, US Fleet; Brig Gen John R. Deane, USA, secretary, JCS; Lt Col Frank McCarthy, USA, assistant to the US Army Chief of Staff; Brig Gen Albert C. Wedemeyer, USA, chief, Strategy and Policy Group, OPD; King's male stenographer is not otherwise identified. Although Admiral Leahy may well have been present at their departure, he did not accompany them. He flew en route to the conference two days later with Roosevelt but was taken ill in Trinidad and did not attend the meeting.
59. Maj Gen Follett Bradley, AAF Headquarters; Maj Gen Thomas T. Handy, USA, assistant chief of staff, War Department; Air Vice Marshal W. F. MacN. Foster, RAF Liaison Officer, Headquarters AAF. The kibitzers did not make the trip and were there to wish the travelers bon voyage.
60. The tugs were small, powerful, wheeled vehicles used to position aircraft.
61. Classified material was locked in steel containers that had explosive charges or detonators to provide quick, emergency destruction of the contents.
62. Bryan is the same Trans World Airways pilot who flew Arnold to Britain in 1942. On return from the current trip, during which he flew President Roosevelt, he became vice president for Operations for the airline in February 1943 and later was commissioned a major in the AAF. See Arnold Diary entries for 13 and 19 January 1943.
63. Cmdr Lutheven E. Libby, USN, assistant to Admiral King for JCS matters.
64. Protocol dictated that Sir John Dill as senior fly in the first aircraft. The ever-petty Admiral King exhibited his normal behavior here.
65. The landing was at Borinquen Army Airfield, later called Ramey Air Force Base (AFB), in northwest Puerto Rico. Maj Gen James L. Collins, USA, CG, Puerto Rican Department, had been a classmate of Arnold's at West Point. He and Arnold discussed the numerous aircraft accidents occurring between Miami and Accra, British Gold Coast, now Ghana, involving AAF planes and crews. Upon his return to Washington, Arnold indicated that he had "put the heat on" to have as many of these incidents as possible eliminated. See Arnold to Collins, 26 February 1943 in AP, and diary entry for 16

February. Marshall was unimpressed with Collins feeling his "habit of decided opinions is a detriment to higher command where more poise is required" and had Collins transferred. See Marshall, "Personal and Most Confidential Memorandum for General McNair," 7 February 1943, in Larry I Bland, ed., and Sharon Ritenour Stevens, assoc. ed., *The Papers of George Catlett Marshall*, vol. 3, T*he Right Man for the Job, December 7, 1941–May 31, 1943* (Baltimore: Johns Hopkins University Press, 1991), 536–37. Hereinafter cited as MP. Col Clarence M. Sartain commanded Borinquen Field.

66. Arnold probably visited this airfield in connection with his visit to Panama in 1939. It did not become a major training base during World War II and remained essentially a stopover point for aircraft headed to Europe via the Caribbean. In the words of the official history, it became "the most important ferrying and transport base in the Caribbean and a key defense outpost." See Wesley Frank Craven and James Lea Cate, *The Army Air Forces in World War II*, vol. 7, *Services Around the World* (1958; new imprint, Washington, D.C.: Office of Air Force History, 1983), 49.

67. Arnold meant St. Vincent, British island possession, Windward Islands.

68. Paramaribo is the capital of Dutch Guiana, now Surinam.

69. Devil's Island is the smallest and southernmost of Isles du Salut in the Caribbean off French Guiana where the French maintained their ill-famed penal colony, which they had begun to phase out in 1938.

70. The base at Belem where Arnold and his colleagues landed was the northernmost one in Brazil capable of accommodating heavy air traffic. It had been developed by Panair do Brasil, a Pan American Airways subsidiary operating under the US Airport Development Program of 1940. It provided for construction and improvement of US-controlled airfields on foreign territory. Arnold had stopped in Belem on his return from Europe in April 1941.

71. Brig Gen Robert LeG. Walsh, CG, South Atlantic Wing, ATC; Vice Adm Jonas H. Ingram, USN, Commander, South Atlantic Forces, US Lant Flt, with headquarters in Recife, Brazil.

72. Sapodilla trees produce, in addition to chicle, a yellow-brown translucent plum-sized fruit.

73. Ascension is a British island possession in the South Atlantic. An air base had been completed there in July 1942. Arnold stopped there for an hour and 20 minutes on his return. See diary entry for 14 February above.

74. Arnold meant Fortaleza, northeast Brazil, where the United States had established an air base.

75. Probably Byron T. Burt Jr., assignment unknown; Dallam is not otherwise identified.

76. Brig Gen Patrick J. Hurley, USA, although ostensibly US Minister to New Zealand, was returning from a "fact-finding" mission to Russia for FDR where he had been since 3 November. His travels had brought him home via Iran, Iraq, and Egypt. Brig Gen Elmer E. Adler, CG, Air Service Command, US Middle East Air Forces.

NORTH AFRICA, MIDDLE EAST, INDIA, CHINA

77. Col Jacob E. Smart, a member of Arnold's Advisory Council in Washington and who assisted Arnold on this trip, recalls traveling the same route several days later in a B-17 and seeing similar flares. Although "sorely tempted" as Arnold had been, Smart's crew did not respond to the "SOS." They reported the location and time of sighting and were informed upon landing in Africa that the flares were a nightly occurrence. See SC.

78. Brig Gen Cyrus R. Smith, chief of staff, ATC; Brig Gen Thomas O. Hardin, operations officer, Africa-Middle East Wing, ATC. Arnold does not identify Creighton further, although he mentions him in *Global Mission*, 391.

79. Although Roosevelt flew across the Atlantic using the same route Arnold had taken, he landed at Bathurst, British protectorate, now Banjul, Gambia, on Wednesday evening, 13 January. For security reasons, he spent the night on board the cruiser USS *Memphis*. As the diary reflects, Arnold remained concerned about the seeming lack of security for the conference. Marshall returned from the conference via Algiers, Dakar, and Trinidad.

80. The AAF base in Dakar was called Eknes Field or Station # 2, North African Wing, ATC. A 6,000-foot steel-mat runway was completed prior to 22 February 1943.

81. Marrakesh is a city in west central French Morocco. Arnold's comment about a location for the conference is not clear in this context.

82. Adrar is a town, west central Algeria, 550 miles southeast of Marrakesh.

83. These were the Grand Atlas Mountains south of Marrakesh in central Morocco.

84. The San Jacinto Mountains are located in southern California.

85. Actual population of Marrakesh at the time was 190,000.

86. This reference is not clear.

87. Hyde was either Frederick W. or James F. C., both USA, ranks and assignments not otherwise identified; American Vice Consul was Kenneth Pendar.

88. Mrs. Moses Taylor had loaned her six-bedroom villa to the United States for use by American personnel. Roosevelt and Churchill (who painted his only work during World War II from the tower of the house) stayed there for two days, 24 and 25 January, following this conference. His staff remained an additional two days after the American president's departure. Arnold stopped at the house twice more during his travels. Arthur Bryant, *Turn of the Tide: A History of the War Years Based on the Diaries of Field-Marshal Lord Alanbrooke, Chief of the Imperial General Staff* (Garden City, N.Y.: Doubleday & Co., 1957), 459. Diary of Gen Richard C. Lindsay, Arents Library, Syracuse University, Syracuse, N.Y., copy in Air Force Historical Research Agency (AFHRA), Maxwell AFB, Ala. For Churchill's account of his visit there with FDR on 24–25 January following the Casablanca conference, see Churchill, 694–95; and Gilbert, 310–13.

89. Arnold meant Sidi Mohammed Ben Youssef, the Sultan of Morocco.

90. Arnold's meaning, although not clear, was probably not intended to be complimentary.

91. The wall with 10 gates was built during the twelfth century, probably around 1120–1132 under the Almoravides dynasty that ruled Morocco from 1062 until overthrown in 1149. The wall had been built and rebuilt many times.

92. The Koutoubya Mosque with its 220-foot high minaret was completed in 1195 and still dominated the skyline of Marrakesh in 1943.

93. Lt Gen Mark W. Clark, USA, CG, Fifth Army; Brig Gen Alfred H. Gruenther, USA, deputy chief of staff, Allied Forces Headquarters.

94. Anfa is a suburb approximately five miles south of Casablanca. The modern three-story Anfa Hotel there, and a number of adjoining villas, housed the conferees. The location had apparently been chosen after reconnaissance by Eisenhower's staff and correspondence with Marshall. See Robert E. Sherwood, *Roosevelt and Hopkins: An Intimate History* (New York: Harper & Brothers), 663–65. Descriptions of the site are in Bryant, 444; Churchill, 675; Pogue, 17; and the papers of James Parton, Harvard University Library, Cambridge, Mass.

95. Arnold's oldest son "Hank," then serving as a captain on Eisenhower's staff, was temporarily assigned to the Casablanca conference as a courtesy to Arnold. The Roosevelt villa was named Dar es Saada; Churchill's was Mirador.

96. Piloted by Bryan, Arnold's aircraft was dispatched to Bathurst where it picked up President Roosevelt and his party and flew them to Casablanca on the following day, Thursday, 14 January. Even after his arrival at the conference site, Arnold remained cognizant of the need for security and hence does not specifically mention the president in this diary entry.

97. Aware that the limited success and utilization of the Eighth Air Force heavy bombers now operating from England under General Eaker were to be challenged by Churchill, Arnold requested Eaker to join him at this conference. Eisenhower's message of the same date ordering Eaker to "proceed at earliest practicable time for Casablanca conference . . . [that] involves method of air operations from United Kingdom" is in EP.

98. There were items from home Arnold had brought for his son, including delayed Christmas presents.

99. Gen Ritter von Thoma, commander of the Afrika Corps and Rommel's deputy, had been captured by the British during the second battle for El Alamein, October–November 1942.

100. The opening session began with Admiral King suggesting that there should be an increase in the 15 percent of total Allied assets now committed to the Pacific. Brooke, in what he termed an address of about an hour, summarized the "world situation and our [British] proposed policy." He was followed by Pound and Portal, both of whom discussed the status of the enemy and assessed the problems faced by the Allies on sea and in the air. There was little comment by the US Chiefs. The speakers concentrated on the European theater, although there was mention of other areas. The 2:30 session began with Admiral King assessing the difficulties in the Pacific. Marshall and Arnold followed King, discussing other facets of the war. There

was more interaction between the chiefs in the latter session. FRUS, Casablanca, 536–56.

101. Although Arnold's diary identified the plane as a C-73, he meant the C-74, which was a larger and improved version of the C-54. The C-74 was equipped with Pratt and Whitney R 3350 engines, which provided greater speed than the C-54. This would account for the difference in projected elapsed flying time.

102. The *Jean Bart* was the newest French battleship that, although uncompleted and temporarily immobilized, made use of her operational turrets of four 15-inch guns and 90 millimeter batteries against the American landing forces on 8–10 November 1942. She was temporarily silenced by salvos from the USS *Massachusetts* on 8 November. Her turrets were quickly repaired and she continued to oppose the landings until finally put out of operation by gunfire and aircraft from the USS *Ranger* on 10 November. See diary entry for 20 January 1943 above.

103. The discussions were lengthy, resulting in FDR, who normally retired early, not doing so until 3 A.M. Among items considered were dealings with the French in North Africa, the submarine menace as well as a general discussion of the conduct of the war. "Towards the end of the evening," Brooke recorded, Admiral King "became nicely lit up." Bryant, 446.

104. No copy of a "plan" dealing with FDR and Churchill visiting the front lines is extant in AP. FRUS, Casablanca, 529–30. Arnold's account in *Global Mission*, 394–95, covered the visit of FDR to the front lines. Churchill does not mention the discussion.

105. The question that was discussed but not resolved at this conference was the postwar government of France. After some difficulty, as Arnold's diary indicated, General de Gaulle and Gen Henri Giraud were reluctantly brought together. Giraud was then High Commissioner of North and West Africa. FRUS, Casablanca, 652–55. Albert Lebrun was the last president of the Third French Republic, which ended with France's surrender in June 1940. In 1944, Lebrun recognized General de Gaulle as the provisional president of France. Sherwood, 675–94 provides an account of Hopkins' views on the French situation at Casablanca.

106. The 10 A.M. meeting took place with the president in his bedroom and lasted until 12:30. Discussion covered the overall British strategic concept of the war and the British favoring Sicily over Sardinia as the next Allied target. Other topics included the perceived British reluctance to a northern Europe invasion, the possibility of Turkish entrance in the war, antisubmarine warfare, and British reluctance to undertake operations in Burma. From Arnold's viewpoint, the most important item discussed was Marshall's statement that the "Prime Minister was concerned over the effectiveness of our bombing operations in Europe." FRUS, Casablanca, 558–62.

107. Extensive discussion of the problems of enemy submarines opened this meeting, resulting in the combined planners being tasked to "report the minimum requirement of escorts (including aircraft carriers) and aircraft" necessary for the remainder of 1943. Eisenhower briefed on the North African situation. Considerable discussion covered future operations in the

Mediterranean, the cross-channel invasion, and the future roles of Turkey and Spain. See FRUS, Casablanca, 563-73; Bryant, 447; and Pogue, 21.

108. Both Eisenhower and Alexander explained the ongoing North African operations to the leaders at this session where Brooke felt "we did little." FRUS, Casablanca, 573-78; and Bryant, 447.

109. Col Horace W. Shelmire, an old friend who was present at Arnold's wedding, was serving as special assistant to Arnold for congressional relations; Col Lewis R. Parker was an aide to Arnold; Col Jacob E. Smart, was a member of Arnold's Advisory Council. Smart accompanied Hap on the remainder of the trip.

110. Presumably at this meeting, Churchill agreed to discuss the American daylight strategic bombing effort with Andrews, Spaatz, and Eaker. According to Colonel Smart, the Americans were interested in learning what differences separated the views of the British and American airmen regarding employment of strategic bombers from Britain and in countering Harris's efforts to get the Eighth Air Force to join the RAF in night operations. Smart further remembered that Slessor "wanted more help for his Coastal Command and Portal was rather noncommittal except that he wanted more [US-manufactured] aircraft for the RAF." SC.

111. Air Marshal Sir Arthur W. Tedder, RAF, AOC Middle East, became, after this conference, Air Commander in Chief, Mediterranean Air Command. Gen Sir Harold R. L. G. Alexander, British Army, Commander in Chief, Middle East Command, became Eisenhower's deputy in Allied headquarters.

112. These long CCS discussions centered on the British-proposed action against Sicily, to be code-named Husky, about which the American chiefs continued to be very dubious. General Marshall asked if the invasion of Sicily was a means to an end or was an end in itself. Arnold asked, "what relation would such an attack have to the whole strategic conception?" The result was instructions to the planners to "reexamine" the British plan for invading Sicily and provide the earliest date for that operation. Brooke, no admirer of Americans, found the morning session "slow and tedious business." He recorded, condescendingly, that the US Chiefs "can't be pushed and hurried and must be made gradually to assimilate our proposed policy." He was more optimistic about the afternoon meeting. Bryant, 448; and FRUS, Casablanca, 580-94.

113. At this meeting, the US chiefs reviewed their previous discussions with the British. The Americans' skepticism was clear in Admiral King's statement to the president that they were attempting to "obtain" from the British chiefs their "concept" as to how the war should be won. King continued that, although the British had "definite ideas" on the next operation, they seemed to lack "an overall plan for the conduct of the war." He lamented that the British "make no mention of where or when a second front on the continent should be established." Further discussion covered many areas, concentrating on the European theater. However, FDR and Arnold discussed an increased number of aircraft to China. Hap offered, in reference to his

upcoming trip, that he "wished to see for himself" if a larger air force in China could be logistically supported. FRUS, Casablanca, 594-600.

114. The conferees would decide that Tedder would become Air Commander in Chief, Mediterranean. Spaatz would be one of his two deputies as commander, Northwest African Air Forces. Although the new assignment was not welcomed by Spaatz, who preferred a return to the strategic effort in England, it represented an advance towards Arnold's desire for a supreme air commander in all of Europe. This was only partially achieved with creation of the United States Strategic Air Force (USSTAF) in December 1943. Hap was still working towards a single air commander as the goal for an American airman as late as the second Quebec conference in September 1944.

115. This relatively short session concerned three topics. The first was the Pacific, where the US chiefs insisted on the Anakim operation proposed for late 1943. It called for an attack in Burma to open the Burma road and enhance the flow of supplies to China through the port of Rangoon. The second dealt with the size of the force to occupy Iceland. The third was the need for Russian assistance in attacking German bases in Norway, from which the Luftwaffe attacked Murmansk-bound convoys. Brooke labeled it "a desperate day." Bryant, 449; and FRUS, Casablanca, 601-5.

116. Colonel Smart, the only AAF planner on this trip, indicated that he was the "culprit" behind in his work, being a "participant in informal meetings and present at JCS and CCS meetings leaving little time for homework," SC. Although Brig Gen Wedemeyer (OPD) provided considerable assistance, the problem was essentially that the American planning staff, which had been kept to a minimum, did little actual pre-conference planning. They found themselves responding to detailed British proposals that had been worked out and extensively staffed in London far in advance by their large delegation of planners. In addition, the British had a fully staffed communications ship in the harbor—HMS *Bulolo*—that permitted a speedy exchange of information between the conferees and the various staffs in London. The arrival of Brig Gen John E. Hull, USA, OPD, mentioned in the following sentence in the diary, increased the capabilities of the American planning staff. Given Roosevelt's normal method of operation, this problem was faced by American military leaders and staff during other wartime meetings, although the Americans learned some lessons about planning for future conferences. See General Albert C. Wedemeyer, *Wedemeyer Reports* (New York: Henry Holt & Co., 1958), 174-82, for the demands on the US planners who were there.

117. Had Hull and his companions landed east of the Italian outpost, they would have been in enemy territory. The northeastern Libyan port city of Tobruk, scene of much recent North African fighting, had been in British hands only since 30 November 1942. Biskra is a city in northeastern Algeria that Arnold would visit eight days later. It had been built on the site of the Roman military base of Vescera. See diary entry for 25 January.

118. Admiral of the Fleet Sir Andrew B. Cunningham, Royal Navy, naval commander in chief, Allied Expeditionary Force.

119. This was the nearby villa occupied by Colonel Smart and Maj Frederick S. Wildman, staff officer, A-2, AAF Headquarters, and other staff members. Arnold was concerned about the few AAF officers available on the scene as planners.

120. Following Admiral Darlan's assassination in December 1942, Gen Henri Giraud became High Commissioner of French North and West Africa; Gen Charles E. Mast was chief of staff, French XIX Corps, Algeria.

121. International law and the practice of the day provided that the aircraft and crews were to be interned by the neutral Portuguese.

122. She was the wife of Col Harold A. Bartron, commander, Northwest African Air Service Command, to whom Arnold sent a check for the amount due on 18 February 1943, AP.

123. Arnold does not seem to have offered much during what Brooke labeled as a "very heated" morning session. After a discussion of the proposed Burma operations, some basic differences remained. Marshall (and presumably King and Arnold) emphasized that they opposed "interminable" Mediterranean operations, insisting that northern France was considered as the "main effort against Germany." Portal indicated a terminal Mediterranean date was impossible to establish since knocking Italy out of the war was their main aim. Further discussion touched on escort vessels, the potential of Polish forces, RAF raids on Berlin, and naval operations in the western Mediterranean. The general outline agreed upon at the 5 P.M. meeting dealt with the submarine menace and concentrating on defeating Germany by aiding the Russians by continuing Allied Mediterranean operations attacking Sicily. In the Pacific, they agreed on operations against Rabaul and eastern New Guinea, and on proceeding with Anakim. Efforts were to be made to induce Turkey to enter the war on the Allied side. Bryant, 449–53; FRUS, Casablanca, 627–37. Pogue, 27–31, provides a glimpse of the intensity of the feelings involved.

124. Could have been Col Roger J. Browne, European Theater Group OPD or, more probably, a British officer not otherwise identified. A.S.V., or airborne search radar, as the name implies, was an airborne to surface radar that was designed for and was achieving success against submarines and surface ships in the Atlantic while mounted in RAF Coastal Command Liberators. Further refinements allowed bombing through overcasts and eventually blind bombing of land targets from the air. The A.S.V., although termed by different names, allowed the attacking aircraft to steer to the target even through clouds.

125. This relatively short meeting essentially approved the outline of the previous day on strategy to be pursued in 1943. FRUS, Casablanca, 637–41; and Bryant, 453.

126. Lt Gen Frank M. Andrews, now CG, US Forces Middle East, was named CG, US Forces in the European Theater in February. He was killed in an airplane crash in Iceland on 3 May 1943. As indicated in the introduction to this chapter, the arrival of Andrews, Spaatz, and Eaker reflected Arnold's assembling his major commanders in the theater to assist in countering Churchill's objections to continuation of US daylight bombing of

Germany. Hap continued to discuss the need to continue AAF daylight operations with Churchill.

127. No record appears to exist of Arnold's meeting with FDR. At the CCS meeting, the importance of the synthetic oil refineries in Ploesti, Rumania, to the Axis was stressed with the CCS. Clearly acknowledging their approval of US daylight bombing, the chiefs recommended that bombing attacks "be undertaken as soon as other commitments allow." This undoubtedly contributed to the decision for the AAF raid on them 1 August 1943, planned by Colonel Smart. Relations with Turkey were covered and, before they adjourned, General Giraud addressed the CCS. Citing recent French fighting in support of Allied forces in North Africa, he indicated in a discussion, in which Arnold participated, that the French could form 13 divisions and man 1,000 aircraft in 80 squadrons if the Allies could furnish the equipment. The CCS pointed out that the impediment to arming the French was shipping. FRUS, Casablanca, 647–55. According to an observer, Giraud not only requested equipment from the Allies but related his experiences as a German prisoner of war from May 1940 when he was captured while commanding the Ninth French Army until his escape from the German fortress at Koenigstein, Saxony, in April 1941. SC.

128. The topics included the implications of Spaatz's new assignment as CG of the Northwest African Air Forces as well as Arnold's frustration at the seeming lack of progress by the Eighth Air Force.

129. Aid to Russia, British responsibility for Turkey, the bomber offensive from North Africa, and command responsibilities in the Middle East were discussed at this CCS; FRUS, Casablanca, 655–58.

130. Given the participants, the discussion probably touched on arrangements for the return trip, particularly as it concerned the president.

131. These discussions centered on the invasion of Sicily, Operation Husky, resulting in the CCS instructing the planning staff to arrive at a date and structure for the operation. Although Hap might not have known of the results of the meeting, Eaker had met at noon with Churchill concerning the Prime Minister's potential opposition to the US daylight operations. Also Gilbert, 303–4; Parton, 220–22; and Arnold, *Global Mission*, 395–97.

132. Col John C. Crosthwaite, commanded the 47th Bombardment Wing at Casablanca. Bud Tinker is not otherwise identified and is not to be confused with the only Tinker listed in the *Army Register* of the period, Maj Gen Clarence L. Tinker for whom Tinker AFB, Oklahoma, was named. General Tinker had been lost leading a flight of B-24s in an attack on Japanese ships in the aftermath of the Battle of Wake Island, 7 June 1942.

133. Photos of the landing craft negotiating the high seas en route to the beach and abandoned vessels on the beach appear in Samuel Eliot Morison, *History of United States Naval Operations in World War II*, vol. 2, *Operations in North African Waters, October 1942–June 1943* (Boston: Little Brown, 1947), 82.

134. The lighthouse at El Hanke, mentioned by Arnold in the diary entry for 22 January, contained a coastal artillery battery and was located four

miles due west of the city of Casablanca. Morison, 96. Although Morison makes no mention of a range finder, such equipment would have been normal.

135. Rear Adm J. L. Hall, USN, commander, Western Task Force, Sea Frontier.

136. Dog tents were larger than pup tents and they had a more square shape.

137. The difficulties between Giraud and De Gaulle were among the major items causing delay in adjournment.

138. This session began with a discussion of protecting sea lanes with increased air support. Admiral Pound reminded them that defeat of the U-boat "must remain the first charge on their resources." Other topics included the approval of the Combined Bomber Offensive. Arnold mentioned that the previous removal of half the bombers in England to support Torch would be remedied with a total of 900 AAF airplanes now to be available in Britain. Modification was made of a draft telegram to Stalin, and approval was given to the proposed Anakim operation to be undertaken in October 1943. Considerable discussion followed, concerning the Bolero buildup in England prior to the invasion of northern France. The planning staff was tasked with submitting the next day, "recommendations . . . relative to the command, organization, planning and training necessary for entry of Continental Europe" in 1943 and 1944. FRUS, Casablanca, 667-79, shows only one CCS meeting on this date but Bryant, 455, confirms Arnold's diary that two CCS sessions were held.

139. This was HMS *Bulolo* that had been used all during the conference to provide rapid communication between the British delegation and London.

140. Who spoke and acted for France continued as a vexatious problem for Roosevelt and Churchill and their difficulties in getting the "groom" (as Giraud was termed by the conferees) together with the haughty "bride," de Gaulle, were problems for the participants. De Gaulle at first refused to travel to the meeting but finally arrived at Casablanca the next day (22 January), two days after Giraud, delaying the adjournment of the meeting until the morning of 24 January. The Allied conferees felt that getting the two reluctant French leaders to pose shaking hands for the press was a major accomplishment. See Gilbert, 305-6.

141. As Arnold noted, their considerable agreement is reflected in the record in FRUS, Casablanca, 680-86. They approved the modified telegram to Stalin and discussed the invasion of either Sicily or Sardinia, finally directing the invasion of Sicily as operation Husky with July as the target date. They agreed that Eisenhower would be supreme commander, Alexander his deputy, Cunningham and Tedder the naval and air commanders respectively. Bryant, 456-57.

142. Colonel Smart recalled that when he was being interrogated as a prisoner of war by the Germans after his capture in May 1944, his captors showed him pictures of himself among the conferees and staff at Casablanca. These had been published in an American magazine and were used by his German interrogators as evidence of Smart's background and knowledge of high-level planning. See SC.

143. This afternoon CCS session briefly discussed the war in the Pacific, with Arnold citing the theoretical radius of action of the B-29 and B-32 aircraft and stressing that the best bases for their immediate operation were the Russian Maritime provinces. After brief mention of the press communiqué to be issued following the conclusion of the conference, the remainder of the session was devoted to the cross-Channel invasion of northern Europe. Deferring for the time being the appointment of a supreme commander for this operation, they approved a US-British staff for the invasion, the group later to be called Chief of Staff to the Supreme Allied Commander (COSSAC) (Designate). FRUS, Casablanca, 687-92; and Bryant, 456.

144. Maj Gen George S. Patton, USA, commander, Western Task Force in the North African campaign. The house, its specific location, or its former owner are not otherwise identified.

145. Burgess is not otherwise identified. Rear Adm Ross E McIntire, USN, continued as Roosevelt's physician.

146. This session concerned the Bolero build-up, airborne troops in Husky and elsewhere, approval of the CCS report to the president and prime minister and their directive to Eisenhower, followed by a brief mention of problems with engines for landing craft. FRUS, Casablanca, 697-700.

147. Fedala is a coastal town, 15 miles northeast of Casablanca, where the northern segment of the North African landings had begun on 8 November 1942.

148. This meeting saw the CCS, Roosevelt, and Churchill covering the major conclusions of the conference, sometimes in detail. After some platitudes congratulating the military chiefs on their labors, discussion proceeded on the issue of continuing to convoy to Russia and establishing a timetable for the invasion of Sicily which Churchill wanted moved from July to June. July was retained with every effort to be made to advance it to June. Discussion followed concerning the Bolero buildup with Roosevelt concluding the meeting by expressing his concern that there was "no reference to operations in or from China." Discussion followed, with FDR urging the need for increased aircraft operating against Japanese shipping from Chinese bases. Arnold, conceding the need for "reinforcing" the AAF in China and the demands for transports worldwide, responded that he would examine "the best method of operating the aircraft," hoping to have 135-150 transports operating between India and China by fall. FRUS, Casablanca, 707-19; and Bryant, 457-58.

149. Arnold departed the next day, en route to China for a meeting with the Chinese leader. The letter is included by Arnold as part of the diary as well as being printed in Arnold, *Global Mission*, 465, and FRUS, Casablanca, 807. At the conclusion of the conference, FDR sent a telegram on 24 January from Marrakesh to Chiang, printed in FRUS, Casablanca, 807.

150. Maj Gen Geoffrey Keyes, USA, deputy CG, I Armor Corps; Col Hobart R. Gay, USA, chief of Staff, US Seventh Army.

151. This brief meeting was concerned primarily with final approval of changes authorized in the previous session along with some final platitudes. FRUS, Casablanca, 719-22.

152. Churchill has offered an extensive account of the final report entitled "The Conduct of the War in 1943" in *The Hinge of Fate*; also FRUS, Casablanca, 791-98.

153. Arnold and his party flew in an AAF B-17 that, with its normal complement of .50 caliber machine guns, was the protection for the unarmed Stratoliner.

154. Maj Gen Carl A. Spaatz was now commanding general (CG) Allied Air Forces Mediterranean; Maj Gen James H. Doolittle was now CG, Twelfth Air Force. The location of Spaatz's villa in Algiers is not known but was referred to as Villa #2. See AP.

155. Brig Gen Edward P. "Ted" Curtis, chief of staff, Allied Air Forces, Mediterranean.

156. Gen Jean M. Mendigal, commander of French Air Forces, North Africa. At this meeting, Mendigal pleaded for materiel with which to equip squadrons of the Free French Air Force, asserting that he could provide pilots, mechanics, and all other necessary personnel but needed the Allies to furnish aircraft, fuel, and other logistical support. See SC.

157. The details of the incident are in Arnold, *Global Mission*, 400.

158. The four airfields visited by Arnold that day were located in Telergma, in the Rhumel valley of northern Algeria between the Maritime and Saharan Atlas mountains; Berteaux, near the city of Constantine, approximately 200 miles east of Algiers; Ain M'lila, approximately 30 miles south of Constantine; and Biskra, approximately 100 miles south, southeast of Constantine. All the units mentioned were AAF Groups. The information noted by Arnold was correct, with three exceptions: (1) the aircraft of the 319th Bombardment Group were B-26s vice his identification as Spitfires; (2) he located the 52d Fighter Group at both Telergma and Biskra when it was located at the former site and flew Spitfires rather than B-25s; and (3) the 301st Group flew B-17 aircraft.

159. The Atlas Mountains reach 13,600 feet in Morocco and would have been visible during Arnold's flight from Casablanca but are not near that height in Algeria.

160. Lt Gen Brehon B. Somervell, USA, chief of services and supply, headed to India and China to join Arnold; the B-17 took Admiral King to Dakar on 25 January.

161. Brig Gen W. Bedell Smith, USA, now chief of staff, Allied Forces in North Africa.

162. In view of the need to transfer the maximum number of aircraft quickly and their lack of long-range capability, the planes were tied to the deck of the ship for transport.

163. Gabes is a city and gulf, east central Tunisia.

164. The P-38 armament consisted four .50 caliber machine guns and one 20 mm cannon.

165. Col Thayer S. Olds commanded the14th Fighter Group, P-38 equipped unit stationed at the time at Berteaux, Algeria. Walsh is not otherwise identified. Later this month the group was withdrawn from combat

and reassigned to Mediouna, French Morocco, for temporary rest and relaxation before returning to combat at Telergma on 5 May 1943.

166. Normally the term spares as used by Army aviators referred most often to additional aircraft but also, less frequently, to spare parts.

167. Arnold meant the 319th Bombardment Group equipped with B-26 aircraft and commanded by Lt Col Wilbur W. Aring, who was stationed at Telergma.

168. The Garden of Allah in Biskra was actually that of Count Landon, a young Frenchman who had settled there. It was so named in Robert Hitchen's 1905 novel about a woman whose husband was an escaped Trappist monk. The garden gained additional fame in the 1936 movie *Garden of Allah* with Marlene Dietrich, Charles Boyer, and Basil Rathbone, which Arnold undoubtedly had seen. Biskra's mosque is reputed to be the oldest Moslem structure in Africa.

169. The B-17 equipped 97th Bombardment Group now stationed at Biskra and recently commanded by Brig Gen Joseph H. Atkinson had been transferred from Polebrook, England, in November 1942 to support Operation Torch. It remained in the Mediterranean theater throughout the remainder of the war and was an example of a bombardment group Arnold feared lost to the North African invasion from the strategic effort in England. Bizerte is a northern Tunisian port strategically located near the narrowest part of the Mediterranean. It was a stronghold heavily attacked by Allied bombers, among them those from the 97th.

170. The hotel is not otherwise identified.

171. Hap's reference is to Biskra's origins when it was known as Vescera and was used as a base by Roman legions.

172. Col Smart accompanied General Arnold to these meetings. According to his recollection, Arnold "thoroughly enjoyed these visits, especially when the men would tell him how things were. Most were surprised and reticent. Some would bitch, others would talk straight: their wants, mail from home, more airplanes, more spare parts, faster action to get the war over. He admired those who told it as it was but I sensed that he secretly sympathized with those who were baffled and unprepared and otherwise unsuited for the roles they were required to play. If this sympathy actually existed it did not show. He exuded competence, confidence, a 'gung ho' attitude. Without question he raised the spirits of all those to whom he spoke." See SC.

173. The Provost Marshal in the US Army was responsible for most of the duties performed by police in the civilian sector.

174. Maj Gen Robert W. Crawford, USA, CG, Services of Supply, US Army Forces in the Middle East.

175. As indicated in the biographical sketch, Arnold returned to the United States in 1909 from his first duty assignment in the Philippines, making his way via Hong Kong, Singapore, Alexandria, and Cairo before traveling in Switzerland, France, and England.

176. Brig Gen Auby C. Strickland, CG, IX Fighter Command; Maj Gen Lewis H. Brereton, now CG, Middle East Air Forces.

177. Air Marshal A. M. Drummond, RAF, deputy commander in chief, RAF, Middle East. The club is not otherwise identified.

178. Air Vice Marshal Graham G. Dawson, RAF, was serving as maintenance and supply officer, RAF Middle East, Cairo, but would become director of Maintenance and Supply in Tedder's Mediterranean Air Command on 17 February; Col Robert Kauch, commander, IX Air Service Command; Col Uzal G. Ent, chief of staff, US Middle East Forces. The general system discussed is not otherwise identified nor is there any mention of the meeting or the problem in the Brereton diary.

179. Brereton's Ninth AF had arrived in Egypt from the continental United States on 12 November 1942 where it played a major role in supporting the Allied operations in Egypt and Libya. It would later move to bases in England in October 1943 and become the AAF Tactical Air Force for the June 1944 cross-channel invasion, although these later roles were not able to be discerned at the time.

180. No doubt Arnold meant Alexander G. Kirk, US Envoy Extraordinaire and Minister Plenipotentiary to Egypt and Saudi Arabia; US Minister to Iran was Louis G. Dreyfus Jr.; Richard Gardiner Casey was British Minister of State for the Middle East.

181. The airfields are not otherwise identified except as being in the vicinity of Gambut, Libya. Normally based at Hardwick, Norfolk, England, a detachment of the B-24 equipped 93d Bombardment Group commanded by Col Edward J. Timberlake Jr., served in North Africa from December 1942 through February 1943. Arnold would meet with Timberlake and his Group in England in September. Their return to England was probably hastened by the interest of Arnold. The B-25 group is not otherwise identified; the other B-24 group was probably the 98th operating from Fayid, Egypt, and commanded by Col John R. "Killer" Kane.

182. Saluum is a Mediterranean port and gulf in extreme northwestern Egypt, scene of extensive fighting in 1941–1942.

183. Southeast of Cairo, these caves had been important in the building of the pyramids. They were then in use by the RAF overhauling the various makes of aircraft engines Arnold cited. See "Notes Made in Middle Eastern Theater," prepared by Col Smart, 31 January 1943, AP.

184. Heliopolis is a Greco-Roman town about seven miles north northeast of Cairo. An old sycamore tree, planted here sometime after 1674, is said to have marked the spot where the Holy family rested on its flight into Egypt. There is mention of their journey in Matthew 2: 13-15, 19-21. The water is potable as contrasted with that of other springs in the area, which is brackish. The pure quality is said to exist because the spring was called into being by the child Jesus. At 23 piasters to the American dollar, admission was slightly over four cents, "nonetheless this simple, ancient place was impressive." See SC.

185. This was the 60-foot-high obelisk erected by Sesostris I, who died about 1926 B.C. Its hieroglyphics set forth the details and reasons for its erection. There is reference in Jeremiah 43:13 to the Lord's threat to "smash the obelisks of the temple of the sun in the land of Egypt."

186. The King's palace was the Abadin. Shepherd's was a famed hostelry in central Cairo. Colonel Smart recalls sitting there with General Arnold in large rocking chairs on the porch of the hotel, drinking a gin concoction and swishing flies with a horsetail swatter. Arnold reminisced that he had sat, drank, and swished in the same place in 1909. According to Smart's recollection, the current story he and Hap heard at Shepherd's, probably apocryphal, "related to an RAF officer who allegedly had been charged with unbecoming conduct and being out of uniform, i.e., chasing a nude woman while he himself was nude through the halls of the hotel at 2 A.M. He pled innocent on the grounds that he was properly attired for the sport he was engaged in as required by service regulations." See SC.

187. The British Ambassador was Sir W. M. Lampson; Gen Richard L. McCreery, British Army, chief of staff to General Alexander; Capt Randolph Churchill, the prime minister's son, was then serving with British commando forces in the Middle East.

188. Gilbert provides no insight into the conversations of the evening other than what Arnold covers in the next diary entry.

189. This discussion became academic in view of Turkey's continued neutrality. This topic was foremost in the Prime Minister's mind as he was planning to fly to Turkey the next day in what became an unsuccessful effort to convince President Inonu to enter the war on the side of the Allies. See Gilbert, 320–25. The number of aircraft produced in the United States in 1943 was 85,898. The fact that Churchill was discussing numbers of AAF aircraft, their production and deployment with Arnold, is revealing of Hap's increased role in this area.

190. Field Marshal Sir Archibald P. Wavell, British Army, Commander of Allied Forces in India and Burma, with headquarters in New Delhi, with whom Arnold would visit three days later. Wavell, like his British colleagues in London, had consistently shown little enthusiasm for Anakim, the proposed invasion of Burma agreed upon at Casablanca. Tuchman, 341–42, 345–46, describes the reluctance of Wavell and the British.

191. These were B-24 aircraft modified to provide air drops to Tito and his Yugoslav partisans operating against German occupation forces.

192. As is clear from the remainder of the diary, Arnold and Dill did not return via England.

193. Basra is a port, southeast Iraq, at the head of the Persian Gulf. It was the major equipment and transportation terminal for materiel destined for Russia under Lend-Lease. Abadan is a city, Khuzestan province, southwest Iran. Although the two airfields are only about 30 miles apart, Colonel Smart recalls it as having been an "unpleasant and embarrassing experience"; not only did they land at the wrong airport but in the wrong country. SC.

194. Col Charles Porter, USA, was in charge of the Air section of the Iran-Iraq Service Command of the United States Army Forces in the Middle East, responsible for delivery of US Lend-Lease aircraft through Iran and Iraq to Russia.

195. Commander of the Russian detachment at Basra, where US planes were delivered to the Soviets, Colonel Petrov was very conscious of his

responsibilities and accountability to higher headquarters. It seemed clear to some of General Arnold's party that much of the fault found with American Lend-Lease supplies was for the self-protection of Colonel Petrov against criticism by Moscow officials. See SC. The US Army study of this activity cites Russian "fastidiousness in inspection" marked by "unnecessary objections" regarding the 4,874 aircraft delivered during the war to the USSR via this route. See Motter, 125-38.

196. Col Donald G. Shingler, USA, was commander, Persian Gulf Service Command.

197. Douglas Aircraft Corporation had held a contract since November 1941 with the US government for servicing in Iran the Lend-Lease aircraft destined for the Soviet Union.

198. No US unit history or RAF archives referencing this incident were located.

199. Karachi is an Indian port on the Arabian Sea near the Indus river delta, now Pakistan.

200. The city of Habaniyah is approximately 60 miles west of Baghdad in central Iraq; Tehran is the capital of Iran. Traveling in a straight line between the two cities, the highest peaks, which would be encountered in the Zagros Mountains, were about 11,600 feet. According to Arnold, weather was also a problem. Arnold, *Global Mission*, 406.

201. According to Sir John Dill, who was beside him, Arnold's feet actually lifted off the floor before he turned loose of the turret door. Colonel Smart felt Hap could easily have been pulled out of the aircraft by the force. SC.

202. Meade was the British officer, not otherwise unidentified, who was the aide to Dill. Brig Gen Francis M. Brady, CG, Karachi American Air Base Command; Maj Gen Raymond A. Wheeler, USA, CG, Services of Supply, CBI Theater. Arnold may have meant Col George H. McNair, who commanded the 51st Service Group and Karachi Air Base. No officer named Mason of senior rank appears assigned to the area at the time.

203. Brig Gen Clayton L. Bissell was CG, Tenth Air Force.

204. Brig Gen Robert C. Oliver was CG, CBI Service Command.

205. Col Charles H. Caldwell, assistant Chief of Staff, Personnel, Tenth Air Force; Col Levi L. Beery, assignment at this time unknown. Arnold had visited New Caledonia during his Pacific trip in September 1942.

206. The Shoreham was a noted Washington, D.C. hotel overlooking Rock Creek Park. Arnold no doubt found the gaiety and entertainment of officers visiting there inconsistent with the realities of the war overseas. This was further confirmation of Arnold's thinking that the British in India were less than enthusiastic about any active operations in this theater.

207. Arnold was looking for further American arguments and support to convince the British of the importance of implementing Anakim. Wedemeyer would represent OPD in Washington and Somervell, as CG of Services of Supply, could furnish insight into the logistics of the operation.

208. William Phillips was a career diplomat who had been named US Ambassador to India in December 1942.

209. Arnold visited the Radput, the citadel containing Lal Kot (red fort), which was built in 1052.

210. The paper outlined planning for the recapture of Burma. Colonel Smart's recollections confirm Arnold's and Dill's displeasure at the proposal, which seemed to set out rather unrealistic requirements for the operation and then provided a litany of reasons why the action could not be undertaken. This was consistent with Stilwell's experience thus far with Wavell and his staff in India. See Arnold, 407-8; and SC.

211. Brig Gen Benjamin G. Ferris, USA, commander of Stilwell's rear echelon at New Delhi; Brig Gen Frank D. Merrill, USA, CG, "Merrill's Marauders"; Col Emmett O'Donnell, assistant chief of staff, Operations, Tenth Air Force, later a member of Arnold's Advisory Council in Washington.

212. Lt Col Clyde Box, deputy chief of staff, Tenth Air Force. The reference is to Kutb Minar, thought by some to be the most perfect tower in the world. It stands 238 feet high and is considered one of the seven architectural wonders of India. Construction was begun around 1200 AD. Box, as a retired major general, recalled Arnold's impatience with the Indian guide "who tried to steer him [Arnold] another way. After the guide made several attempts, Gen. Arnold turned to him and said: 'Ever since my arrival in India, people have told me what to wear, when to go to bed, when to get up, what to eat, but I'll be damned if you are going to tell me where to look.'" Box letter to editor, 24 June 1984.

213. The facts are slightly different from those recorded by Arnold. Standing in the inner courtyard of the mosque built by Kutb-ud-din shortly after the capture of Delhi in 1193, the column is solid wrought iron and stands 23 feet high. It is thought to have been brought from Muttra (now Mathura, approximately 90 miles south of Delhi) by Anang Pal, a Radput chief, and was erected by him in 1052.

214. One of Arnold's officer associates did not possess Arnold's sales resistance and bought some of the "jewels" offered. He sent the treasures to his wife in the United States and received in return the candid cable: "They're glass, you ass!" SC. For one officer's personal papers that confirm his predilection for purchasing local items for his family in the United States, see papers of Gen Emmett O'Donnell Jr., United States Air Force Academy Library, Special Collections, Colorado Springs, Colo.

215. Arnold's optimism seems justified in view of what he found and recorded in his diary on his return to India, 8-10 February.

216. Dinjan is an Indian town, eastern Assam province at 27° 33' N, 95° 17' E, where the 51st Fighter Group operated. Commanded by Col Homer L. Sanders, the 51st was equipped with P-40 aircraft. Chungking is a city in western China at the junction of the Yangtze and Chia-ling rivers. It became the capital of wartime China following the fall of Nanking to Japanese forces in November 1937. Calcutta is the capital of West Bengal state, east India.

217. Gen Sir Claude John Eyre Auchinleck, British Army, commander in chief, India, had married Jessie Stewart of Perthshire, Scotland, in 1920. The Tacoma reference is not clear.

218. Arnold meant Irw S. Jehu, postwar editor of the *Times of India*. At this time, he was a brigadier in the Indian Defense Department serving as head of the InterService Relations Directorate. The reference to the Pan American Clipper is to Arnold's trip from San Francisco to Honolulu in 1939.

219. Col Leslie P. Holcomb, assignment unknown.

220. Arnold continued to be pessimistic about getting the British moving on Anakim. As he commented in his memoirs: "I could not get the impression out of my head that the British had been using India as a place to which to send officers who had more or less outlived their usefulness." Arnold, *Global Mission*, 409.

221. Air Chief Marshal Sir Richard Pierse, RAF, was now AOC RAF, India.

222. Although Arnold has some confusion of dates in his memoirs, he was beginning to see some progress, which he probably relayed to Marshall. Arnold, *Global Mission*, 408-9.

223. Victor Alexander John Hope, 8th Earl and 2d Marquis of Linlithgow, was Viceroy of India. There is a description of his palace in Tuchman, 331. One of Arnold's party was informed by an aide that the Viceroy, who possessed a knowledge of farming, would like to discuss American pig farming with him. Although a farm boy, the American officer had reservations about his ability to converse on this subject. They met and the Viceroy did speak on this topic, but the officer involved "need not have worried about my knowledge of pigs. His Excellency did all the talking." SC.

224. The tomb not otherwise identified.

225. Agra is a city, north central India. Shan Jahan built the Taj Mahal in honor of his favorite wife, Muntz Mahal. The mausoleum was begun in 1630 and completed in 1648.

226. The 3d Air Depot Group was stationed at Agra, as was the CBI Air Service Command depot, performing maintenance for Allied aircraft in the theater.

227. Col Edward H. Alexander, CO, India-China Wing, ATC; Major Siefler is not otherwise identified. Mandalay is a city in central Burma on the Irrawaddy river.

228. Kunming, city, capital of Yennan province, south China, Arnold's next destination.

229. Col Smart remembers that Gen Bissell's aide/pilot went to the navigator's compartment and announced to General Arnold's navigator (who was junior in rank but had served in that capacity for Arnold since the airplane left Washington) that he (the aide) was to assist in the navigation since he knew the route over the hump "like the back of his hand." In spite of this self-proclaimed and unsolicited expertise, Arnold's navigator attempted unsuccessfully to utilize celestial navigation but the severe turbulence encountered precluded accurate fixes, some of which had triangular legs 200 miles long. Only by relying on dead reckoning did the navigator finally get proper bearings and determine that the winds aloft had been 100 rather than the 50 knots forecast. This was probably Hap's and the crew's first experience with what is accepted today as the "jet stream." The result was

their overflying Kunming and having to turn back to land there. Hanoi was a French Indo-China port that had been occupied by the Japanese since September 1940. See SC. Arnold's account of the flight is in Arnold, *Global Mission*, 410–12.

230. The American Volunteer Group, or Flying Tigers, had begun arriving in China under Claire Chennault to fight the Japanese in the summer of 1941. Some of its pilots accepted commissions in the AAF in July of 1942.

231. Claire L. Chennault had served as a special advisor to the Chinese Air Force since 1937 and was at the time of Arnold's visit an AAF brigadier general serving as CG, China Air Task Force. He was promoted to major general in March 1943 on orders from FDR as a result of pressure if not the insistence of the Generalissimo. Arnold is very circumspect in this segment of the diary, not commenting on his attitude towards Chennault. Hap's correspondence with Chennault before and during World War II, which is extant in AP, with its consistent emphasis on winning the war rather than rehashing personal relations, reflects a professional but less than warm relationship. See for example, Chennault's ten-page comment of 7 March 1935 on Arnold's 26 November 1934 letter, in AP.

232. There appears little doubt that Arnold had discussed the increased numbers of aircraft, command relationships, and other logistical aid to China with FDR and Marshall during the Casablanca meetings.

233. Arnold erred here. The 73d Squadron did not serve with the 23d Fighter Group but instead was serving with the 18th Fighter Group in Hawaii. The 16th, 74th, 75th and 76th squadrons flew P-40 aircraft from Kunming and were the component parts of the 23d, then commanded by Lt Col Bruce K. Holloway. This Group, activated in China on 4 July 1942, consisted of some former AVG Flying Tiger pilots.

234. Clarence Gauss was the American Ambassador.

235. General Ho Ying-chin was serving as chief of staff as well as minister of war. This is probably Arnold's way of indicating that he had several titles.

236. The Chinese Assistant Secretary of War is not otherwise identified.

237. These are the Yangtze and Chia-ling rivers.

238. T. V. Soong was the American-educated Chinese Minister of Foreign Affairs and the brother of Madame Chiang Kai-shek. His house is not otherwise identified.

239. As indicated elsewhere, the letter is made part of the diary following 23 January 1943, above.

240. Sadiya is a city in northeastern India in Assam province; Ledo is just south of Sadiya and was the originating point of a supply road into China begun in December 1942 but not completed until 1945.

241. The reference is to the Brahmaputra river in India which, along with the narrow gauge railroads that were originally built to transport the tea crop, were now used to transport supplies to Assam province in northeast India for air transport over the Hump. Big Boy was the pipeline from Calcutta to Kunming that brought fuel to China. This difficult problem would be discussed at the Quebec Conference of August 1943. By late 1944, it had been completed from Calcutta to Myitkyina in North Burma. Due to

its difficulty of construction and the increased capacity flown over the Hump, it was never completed. Different aircraft engines required fuel with different octane ratings. These are numbers designating the relative anti-knock value of the fuel in a reciprocating engine with the higher octane number reflecting the more compression a fuel can withstand without deterioration.

242. Lt Col Clinton D. Vincent, executive officer, China Air Task Force, Kunming. Lt Col Bruce K. Holloway had assumed command of the 23d Fighter Group only three weeks earlier. Based at Liuchow, China, the 23d flew P-40 aircraft.

243. The Air Chief, officials of the Generalissimo's division, and the Chief of Operations are unidentified.

244. Dated the next day, 7 February 1943, Chiang's letter to FDR said, "the Chinese Army will be in readiness . . . without fail" to participate in the proposed operation to retake Burma. Quoted in Romanus and Sunderland, 276.

245. Neither the Chinese Chief of Aviation nor his successor is otherwise identified. The banquet of the evening was apparently in celebration of Chiang's agreement to support Anakim; Romanus and Sunderland, 274. The tonnage problem would continue to vex Arnold and his air commanders in this area during most of the remainder of the war. To the Chinese leader, 10,000 tons per month over this route at this time was the desideratum. In view of the many obstacles posed by weather, communications, operations, aircraft shortages, aircraft and crew limitations together with the relatively low priority for this theater as contrasted with combat operations elsewhere, the goal seemed insurmountable—particularly in view of the fact that only 1,227 tons had been hauled to China in the month of December 1942. However, new and additional numbers of aircraft, (C-46, C-87, and C-54), more crews, better training, higher priority for aircraft and crews, improved command and control procedures, and strong pressure from the president and Arnold contributed to the ATC's meeting its goal of 7,000 tons in July 1943. The 10,000 tons per month goal was reached by December 1943. By July of 1944, the monthly net tonnage had been increased to 18,975; by November of 1944, it was 34,914; in July 1945, it totaled 71,042 tons. For the increased priority and attention this received from Arnold upon his return, as well as the ambitious timetable established for aircraft replacement, see Arnold to Col E. H. Alexander and Maj Gen Harold George, 4 March 1943, AP. Arnold ended these letters with: "Weekly progress reports will be sent to me concerning this subject," an admonition that left little doubt as to his strong interest in the subject, which reflected the pressure of FDR. See the discussion in Craven and Cate, vol. 5, 114–51, 220; and vol. 6, 405–34.

246. Probably as a result of discussions with Stilwell, Arnold had good reason to be wary of Soong's translations. As one student of the situation has observed, Soong "interpreted his chief to the Americans and vice versa as he saw fit in the interest of smoothness." Stilwell described Soong as "devious and slippery." His dissembling extended to correspondence when he wrote to Roosevelt in January 1942 proposing that the AAF begin opera-

tions over the Hump, the route described by Soong as "flying over comparatively level stretches" hardly an accurate description of the 16,000-foot Himalayas. He became infamous in US circles for transmitting correspondence to Chiang, providing whatever interpretation to the altered message he thought would be most acceptable to the Chinese leader. This led to problems since copies of the original messages were usually transmitted to Stilwell, who was tasked to deal with Chiang—who had altered interpretations of the messages from Roosevelt. The problem was solved by sending messages directly to Stilwell for Chiang, but this did not stop Soong from providing his own "interpretation" of what the message meant. See Tuchman, 244, 314; Soong to Roosevelt, 31 January 1942, is quoted in Tuchman, 246–47.

247. Participation in Anakim.

248. General Arnold's notes not located.

249. Given Chiang's knowledge of the reluctance of the British officials in India to support Anakim, he probably sought assurances from Dill of British and Wavell's support.

250. The Generalissimo's wife, Madame Chiang Kai-shek, was a sister of T. V. Soong. American-educated, attractive, she spoke fluent English and was well known for her frequent appearances in the United States in behalf of aid to China. At this time, she was en route to the United States for medical treatment. Reflecting her stature in the administration, Hopkins met her on her arrival in New York. She lived for a time in the White House and received a warm welcome when she addressed a joint session of Congress in March before returning to China in early July.

251. Col Smart was hospitalized with malaria, which he surmised he had contracted in North Africa earlier. SC.

252. Brig Gen Caleb V. Haynes, CG, Bomber Command, China Air Task Force; the Great Eastern was a well-known luxury hotel in Calcutta.

253. The governor, not otherwise identified, ruled West Bengal state.

254. Chinese War Minister Ho Ying-chin no doubt discussed Chinese contributions to Anakim, welcome news to Arnold and Dill.

255. Lt Gen N. M. S. Irwin, British Army, CG, Eastern Army with headquarters in Calcutta. The reference is to the Chinese agreement to proceed with Anakim.

256. The letters were not located. The 308th Bombardment Group equipped with B-24s joined the newly formed Fourteenth Air Force in Kunming, China, in March 1943, commanded by Arnold's former aide, Col Eugene H. Beebe. Arnold's meeting with Beebe and elements of the Group a week later in Puerto Rico en route to China is mentioned in the diary entry for 16 February.

257. Col Joseph P. Bailey, assignment at this time unknown.

258. Maj Stanley K. Robinson, an aviator since 1928 and friend of Arnold, was killed on 29 January 1942. CO of 7th Bombardment Group, he was leading a squadron against Japanese ships in the Macassar Straits area. The reference to Strudler's death is not clear; no one of that name appears in the *Army Register*. The officer cited in Hap's handwritten account

seems to mean Maj A. A. Straubel, a pilot since 1929 whom Hap would also have known. Robinson's successor as CO of the 7th, Straubel was shot down six days later over Surabaya, Java. Walter D. Edmonds, *They Fought With What They Had* (Boston: Little Brown, 1951).

259. The Ghurkas are the warlike people of the Rajput race who settled in the province of that name in Nepal in the latter half of the eighteenth century and quickly dominated the area. Most sources spell the name of the curved short sword with a broad blade, which was made in a variety of sizes, as kurki or kukeri.

260. Although the broadcast is not otherwise identified, copies of the dropped papers are in AP. No attachment of these papers accompanies the diary.

261. The rupee, the standard currency of India, was worth 62 cents in American money at this time.

262. *Times* (London), 28 February 1942, quotes *Star of India* regarding the declaration of Calcutta as an open city.

263. No copy of the letter from Soong to FDR is in AP.

264. *Argonaut* was the name of Arnold's B-17 aircraft on this and subsequent travels. By the time of the June 1945 trip to the Pacific, covered in chapter 11, Hap called it *Argonaut IV*.

265. Panda is an Indian city 100 miles southwest of Allahabad.

266. Neither Captain Suggs nor Sergeant Dennis is otherwise identified.

267. She was the wife of Lt Gen Frank M. Andrews.

268. Salala, or Salalah, is a city, in southwest Oman.

269. Muroc Lake is the location of the Air Corps base north of Los Angeles, California, activated in 1933 when Arnold, as commander at March Field, took efforts to acquire it as a bombing range. It later became a test center and is currently called Edwards AFB.

270. First Lieutenant William M. Pike, a former Pan American Airways employee, apparently made a very favorable impression on Arnold and his party. He was promoted to captain as a result of the general's interest within a week after Arnold's return to Washington. He also received considerable recreational equipment from the United States as a result of Hap's "interest." See telephone logs, AP; also Arnold to Lt McFawn, letter, 7 July 1943, AP.

271. Khartoum is the capital of Anglo-Egyptian Sudan, now Sudan. Arnold continued to remain alert to postwar US civilian aviation possibilities and constantly took notice of potential British competition.

272. Arnold's route of flight would have taken him across Yemen where the Mahrat Mountains in and around the capital of Sana, located at 7,700 feet, rose to as high as 12,300 feet outside the city. From his flight altitude of 9,500 feet, he clearly could have seen the stone buildings that elicited his comment.

273. Lt Col Adolph P. Kerr commanded the 13th Ferrying Group, Wadi Siedna, Sudan. The base was also known as Station No. 20, Central African Section, Africa-Middle East Wing, Air Transport Command; British Governor General Hubert Huddleston of the Anglo-Egyptian Sudan, now Sudan.

274. The kaid, or head, of a tribe or chief of a village is not otherwise identified.

275. Charles George "Chinese" Gordon attempted to evacuate Egyptian garrisons from the Sudan, but the Mahdists laid seige to the garrisons for 10 months. Gordon was killed two days before a relief expedition from Great Britain reached Khartoum in 1885. Arnold may have read *Chinese Gordon*, which was written by Hugh E. Worthman in 1933.

276. Brig Gen Shepler W. Fitzgerald, CG, Africa-Middle East Wing, ATC. Maj Gen Brereton, recently named CG, US Army Forces, Middle East, replacing Lt Gen Frank Andrews, made no mention in his published diary of a meeting planned or having taken place at this time.

277. This is the palace of the Governor General that was built on the site of the previous structure, which the dervishes seized and destroyed in 1885. It had been designed by Colonel Gorringe of the British Royal Engineers at the turn of the century.

278. Arnold had dinner this evening with British Governor General Huddleston and his wife. No doubt the entry was a reminder to send a note thanking them for their hospitality.

279. The hotel is not otherwise identified. At Omdurman, the city on the White Nile opposite Khartoum, the Anglo-Egyptian army of Lord Kitchener defeated Khalifa Abdallahi in 1898 at the battle of Karari, marking the end of the Mahidst state in the Sudan. Although most of the city was destroyed after the battle, the house of the Khalifa (the Mahdi's successor) was made into a museum. Maj W. S. Gordon, General Gordon's nephew, accomplished the grisly task of disposing of the Mahdi's remains. Only the body was dumped into the Nile. The press of the day criticized Kitchener for failing to dispose quickly of the skull, which was eventually buried in Wadi Halfa, 400 miles north of Khartoum, on the border of Egypt.

280. Maidriguri is a city in northeast Nigeria. Fort Lamy is a city in French Equitorial Africa, now Ndjamena, capital of Chad.

281. Arnold identified the Governor, Sir Allan Burns, and his lady in the next day's diary entry.

282. Also called Crux after the Latin word for cross because its four most prominent stars resemble that shape, it was the brightest constellation visible to Arnold at this latitude.

283. Ascension Island remained unoccupied until the British stationed Marines there after 1815 to keep watch over the exiled Napoleon on St. Helena. The US-built installation there was named Wideawake airfield. The ditty among AAF aviators transiting the island was: "If I don't hit Ascension, my wife will get a pension."

284. The Stratoliner was the Boeing Aircraft Company's four-engine, all-metal, low-wing monoplane designated the C-54 by the AAF.

285. Minister for Air was J. Salgado Filho; Maj Gen Eduarado Gomez commanded #2 Air Zone, Brazilian Air Force.

286. This Brazilian decoration was established in 1822. The badge contains the five stars of the Southern Cross constellation, which resembles a Latin cross.

287. The reference to searchlight development is not clear.

288. With the shortage of aircraft in some theaters, it is not clear whether these planes were furnished to Admiral Ingram.

289. This was the name of General Walsh's quarters in Recife.

290. This reference is to the great cruciform cathedral on the Prada Caetano Brandao, which dates from the mid-eighteenth century.

291. Neither the official AAF history nor the history of units that might have been involved reveals this specific incident. Figures for the year 1943 show 5,922 aircraft ferried on this route with an attrition rate of 1.3 percent. Craven and Cate, vol. 7, 66–69, provides an account of the difficulties involved with inexperienced pilots flying over this route at this time. Crystals are interchangeable quartz particles used for frequency control of radio communications.

292. Col Eugene H. Beebe, Arnold's previous pilot and close friend, was en route as the commander of the B-24-equipped 308th Bombardment Group to their new duty station in Kunming, China. Arnold's remarks to them remain unknown, but in view of Arnold's recent return from China and conversations there with Chiang Kai-shek and others, there seems little doubt that Arnold would have attempted to impress on the Group their important role in the buildup of airpower in China. Beebe provided Arnold an optimistic report on their progress once the Group reached their destinations, writing that the 308th pilots "have taken the hump in their stride"; Beebe quoted in Arnold to Chief of Staff, letter, 9 May 1943, AP. Presumably, the 308th was successful; Beebe returned to Washington as a brigadier general.

293. FRUS, Casablanca, 781–82.

294. Ibid., 671–72; Wesley Frank Craven and James Lea Cate, *The Army Air Forces in World War II*, vol. 2, *Europe: Torch to Pointblank* (1949; new imprint, Washington, D.C.: Office of Air Force History, 1983), 308.

295. Arnold, 397; and FRUS, Casablanca, 648.

296. A bitter assessment was made by Brig Gen Albert C. Wedemeyer, a Casablanca participant. His distrust of the British had emanated in part from his 1936–1938 tour at the German Staff College. He evaluated Casablanca as the "watershed" meeting of the war, where "World War II became politicized [sic] in an utterly irretrievable manner," Wedemeyer, 169.

297. FRUS, Casablanca, 698; and Arnold, Memo, 1 May 1943, AP.

298. Arnold, *Global Mission*, 408–9; Arnold Diary, 1, 2, 9 February 1943.

299. Romanus and Sunderland, 275.

300. Joseph W. Stilwell, *The Stilwell Papers*, arranged and edited by Theodore H. White (New York: William Sloane Associates, 1948), 196.

301. Romanus and Sunderland, 273; and Arnold to Marshall, 5 February 1943, AP.

302. Marshall to Leahy, 4 January 1943, MPMS, vol. 3, 502–3.

303. Quoted in Tuchman, 358.

304. Arnold Diary, 8 February 1943.

305. Romanus and Sunderland, 277.

306. Arnold, *Global Mission*, 433.

307. Ibid.

308. Chiang Kai-shek to Roosevelt, letter, 7 February 1943; and Arnold, *Global Mission*, 433-34. Unfortunately, the reader is left without any understanding by Hap's general statement of what, if anything, Arnold reported to FDR. The implication can be drawn that he did not present his findings in writing since they would not have represented what the president was inclined to accept or believe. If so, this was a serious omission since he could offer the most recent assessment of the situation based on the difficult personalities he had met and observed, his professional aviation expertise, and his knowledge of the current supply and transport problems over the Hump. However, he did orally brief the commander in chief.

309. With both of his subjects dead, and writing *Roosevelt and Hopkins* when much of the corruption and inadequacies of the Chiang Kai-shek regime were newsworthy, Robert Sherwood chose to downplay Hopkins' role as advocate for Chiang and Chennault. See Sherwood, 739-40, where he limits Hopkins' role to one sentence in a long paragraph discussing the problem. See also the contrasting view in the AAF official history, "Hopkins has been credited by some with having been largely influential in persuading the President to activate the Fourteenth Air Force," Craven and Cate, vol. 4, 439.

310. Marshall for Secretary of War, Memo, 14 December 1942, MPMS, vol 3, 481-82; and Marshall for Admiral Leahy, Memo, 4 January 1943, MPMS, vol. 3.

311. See the account in Romanus and Sunderland, 279-80, particularly the printed excerpts from FDR to Marshall, 8 March 1943.

312. *Time*, 15 February 1943, 64-66.

313. Marshall memo for General Stilwell, 3 May 1943, MPMS, vol 3, 675-76.

314. Stilwell to Marshall, letter, 9 February 1943, quoted in MPMS, vol 3, 585; and Byrd, 187.

315. Craven and Cate, vol. 4, 439-40. It was agreed in the White House in July, only three days after Chiang requested it, that Bissell would be removed; Craven and Cate, vol. 4, 451; and Romanus and Sunderland, 346. Marshall's retention of Stilwell for another 15 months against extremely strong White House and Chiang Kai-shek pressures until October 1944, when Roosevelt gave "direct and positive" orders for Stilwell's recall, was a reflection of the chief of staff's stature. Tuchman, 501, uses direct and positive; Byrd, 262-63; and Pogue, 478-79. Hayes, 645-52, provides a synopsis of the problems. Wesley Frank Craven and James Lea Cate, eds., *The Army Air Forces in World War II*, vol. 5, *The Pacific: Matterhorn to Nagasaki* (1953; new imprint, Washington, D.C.: Office of Air Force History, 1983), 225-32, emphasizes the last months of the problem.

316. Arnold to Chennault, 3 March 1943, AP.

317. Maj Gen Stratemeyer for Mr. Hopkins, memo, 27 February 1943, AP.

318. Telephone memo, no author, 3 March 1943, AP.

319. Stimson Diary, 24 March 1943; Hap to Lois Arnold Snowden, 15 March 1943, AP.

320. Marshall's 16 March 1943 Memorandum for the President in re Arnold's promotion is in MPMS, vol. 3, 589-90.

321. Stimson Diary, 10, 12 May 1943; Arnold to Marshall, 10 May 1943; and Marshall to Arnold, letter, 14 May 1943, MPMS.

Bibliography

Manuscript Collections

Arents Library, Syracuse University, Syracuse, N.Y.
    Richard C. Lindsay Diary
Franklin D. Roosevelt Library, Hyde Park, N.Y.
    Harry L. Hopkins
    Henry Morgenthau Jr., Diary
George C. Marshall Research Library, Lexington, Va.
    George C. Marshall
    Paul McD. Robinett
Harvard University Library, Cambridge, Mass.
    James Parton
Library of Congress, Manuscript Division, Washington, D.C.
    Frank M. Andrews
    Henry H. Arnold
    Ira C. Eaker
    Benjamin D. Foulois
    Curtis E. LeMay
    William Mitchell
    John C. O'Loughlin
    Carl A. Spaatz
Royal Air Force Historical Branch, London, England
    John C. Slessor
United States Air Force Academy (USAFA), Colorado Springs, Colo.
    Henry H. Arnold Papers in Murray Green Collection
    Laurence S. Kuter
    George C. McDonald
    Emmett O'Donnell Jr.
United States Air Force Historical Research Agency, Maxwell Air Force Base, Ala.
    George C. Kenney
University of Virginia, Charlottesville, Va.
    Edwin M. "Pa" Watson
Yale University, New Haven, Conn.
    Henry L. Stimson Diary
In private hands:

Arnold Ranch, Sonoma, Calif., papers loaned to editor by the late Col William B. Arnold.

Public Records and Documents

Unpublished
> US National Archives and Records Administration, Washington, D.C.

> Records Group 18, Records of the Army Air Corps

The Public Records Office (PRO), Air Ministry Records (Air) Kew, England
> Air 8/48, 8/140, 8/294, 8/378, 8/487, 8/634, 8/637, 8/647, 8/648, 8/711, 8/847, 8/891, 8/1011, 8/1050, 8/1108, 8/1360

Published Records and Documents

US Official Histories

Craven, Wesley Frank, and James Lea Cate, eds. *The Army Air Forces in World War II.* 7 vols. 1948–1958. New imprint, Washington, D.C.: Office of Air Force History, 1983.
> Vol. 1: *Plans and Early Operations, January 1939 to August 1942.*
> Vol. 2: *Europe: Torch to Pointblank, August 1942 to December 1943.*
> Vol. 3: *Europe: Argument to V-E Day, January 1944 to May 1945.*
> Vol. 4: *The Pacific: Guadalcanal to Saipan, August 1942 to July 1944.*
> Vol. 5: *The Pacific: Matterhorn to Nagasaki, June 1944 to August 1945.*
> Vol. 6: *Men and Planes.*
> Vol. 7: *Services Around the World.*

Carter, Kit C., and Robert Mueller, comps. *The Army Air Forces in World War II: Combat Chronology, 1941–1945.* Washington, D.C.: Office of Air Force History, 1973.

The United States Army in World War II (known familiarly as the Army "Green" series).

Subseries: The War Department

Cline, Ray S. *Washington Command Post: The Operations Division.* Washington, D.C.: Office of Chief of Military History (OCMH), Government Printing Office (GPO), 1951.

Matloff, Maurice, and Edwin M. Snell. *Strategic Planning for Coalition Warfare, 1941-1942.* Washington, D.C., OCMH, GPO, 1953.

Watson, Mark S. *Chief of Staff: Pre-War Plans and Preparations.* Washington, D.C.: OCMH, GPO, 1950.

Subseries: The European Theater of Operations

MacDonald, Charles B. *The Last Offensive.* Washington, D.C.: OCMH, GPO, 1973.

Subseries: The Mediterranean Theater of Operations

Motter, T. H. Vail. *The Persian Corridor and Aid to Russia.* Washington, D.C.: OCMH, GPO, 1952.

Subseries: Miscellaneous

Holley, Irving Brinton, Jr. *Buying Aircraft: Materiel Procurement for the Army Air Forces.* Washington, D.C.: OCMH, GPO, 1964.

Subseries: The China-Burma-India Theater

Romanus, Charles F., and Riley Sunderland. *Stilwell's Mission to China.* Washington, D.C.: GPO, 1953.

United States Government and Air Force Publications

Arnold, Henry H. *Report of the Commanding General of the Army Air Forces.* Washington, D.C.: GPO, 1944.

Baker, Newton D. *Final Report of the War Department Special Committee on Army Air Corps, 18 July 1934.* Washington, D.C.: GPO, 1934.

Cameron, Rebecca Hancock, *Training to Fly: Military Flight Training, 1907-1945.* Washington, D.C.: Air Force History and Museum Program, 1999.

———. "AAF Training in World War II." Unpublished Manuscript. Washington, D.C.: Office of Air Force History, n.d.

Daso, Dik, Maj, USAF. *Architects of American Air Supremacy: General Hap Arnold and Dr. Theodore von Kármán.* Maxwell AFB, Ala: Air University Press, 1997.

Davis, Richard G. *Carl A. Spaatz and the Air War in Europe.* Washington, D.C.: Center for Air Force History, 1993.

Foreign Relations of the United States, Diplomatic Papers: The Ambassador in Great Britain to the Secretary of State, 20 September 1938, 2 vols. Washington, D.C.: GPO, 1970.

———. *The Conference at Berlin (The Potsdam Conference), 1945,* 2 vols. Washington, D.C.: GPO, 1960.

———. *The Conferences at Washington and Quebec, 1943.* Washington, D.C.: GPO, 1970.

———. *The Conferences at Cairo and Tehran, 1943.* Washington, D.C.: GPO, 1961.

———. *The Conference at Quebec, 1944.* Washington, D. C.: GPO, 1972.

———. *The Conferences at Washington, 1941-1942 and Casablanca, 1943.* Washington, D.C.: GPO, 1968.

Frisbee, John L., ed. *Makers of the United States Air Force.* Washington, D.C.: Office of Air Force History, 1987.

Greer, Thomas H. *The Development of Air Doctrine in the Army Air Arm, 1917-1941.* USAF Historical Study 89. Maxwell AFB, Ala.: USAF Historical Division, Research Studies Institute, Air University, 1955.

History of Santa Ana Army Air Base, Installment 1, 1942. Maxwell AFB, Ala., Air Force Historical Research Agency (AFHRA).

Maurer, Maurer. *Aviation in the U. S. Army 1919-1939.* Washington, D.C.: Office of Air Force History, 1987.

———. *Air Force Combat Units of World War II.* Washington, D.C.: GPO, 1961.

Murray, Williamson. *Strategy for Defeat: The Luftwaffe, 1933-1945.* Maxwell AFB, Ala.: Air University Press, 1983.

Neufeld, Jacob. *The Development of Ballistic Missiles In the United States Air Force, 1945-1960.* Washington, D.C.: Office of Air Force History, 1990.

Shiner, John F. *Foulois and the U.S. Army Air Corps, 1931-1935.* Washington, D.C.: Office of Air Force History, 1983.

Wolk, Herman S. *Planning and Organizing the Postwar Air Force, 1943-1947*. Washington, D.C.: Office of Air Force History, 1984.

British Official Histories

Hall, H. Duncan. *North American Supply*. London: Her Majesty's Stationery Office (HMSO), 1955.

Webster, Sir Charles, and Noble Frankland. *The Strategic Air Offensive Against Germany, 1939-1945*, 4 vols. London: HMSO, 1961.

Books

Alperovitz, Gar. *The Decision to Use the Atomic Bomb and the Architecture of an American Myth*. New York: Alfred A. Knopf, 1995.

Anders, Wladyslaw. *An Army in Exile: The Story of the Second Polish Corps*. London: Macmillan Co., 1949.

Andrews, Allen. *Air Marshals: The Air War in Western Europe*. New York: Morrow, 1970.

Arbon, Lee. *They Also Flew: The Enlisted Pilot Legacy, 1912-1942*. Washington, D.C.: Smithsonian Institution Press, 1992.

Arnold, Henry H. General of the Air Force. *Global Mission*. New York: Harper & Brothers, 1949.

Arnold, Henry H., and Ira C. Eaker. *Winged Warfare*. New York, London: Harper & Brothers, 1941.

Berle, Adolph A. *Navigating the Rapids, 1918-1971: From the Papers of Adolph A. Berle*. Edited by Beatrice Bishop Berle and Travis Beal Jacobs. New York: Harcourt, Brace, Jovanovich, Inc., 1973.

Bland, Larry L., and Sharon R. Ritenour, eds. *The Papers of George Catlett Marshall*, vol. 2, *"We Cannot Delay", July 1, 1939-December 6, 1941*. Baltimore and London: Johns Hopkins University Press, 1986.

———. *The Papers of George Catlett Marshall*, vol. 3, *"The Right Man for the Job," December 7, 1941-May 31, 1943*. Baltimore and London: Johns Hopkins University Press, 1991.

———. *The Papers of George Catlett Marshall*, vol. 4, *"Aggressive and Determined Leadership," June 1, 1943-December 31, 1944*. Baltimore and London: Johns Hopkins University Press, 1996.

Blum, John Morton. *From the Morgenthau Diaries*, vol. 2, *Years of Urgency, 1938-1941*. Boston: Houghton Mifflin, 1959.

Brereton, Lewis H. *The Brereton Diaries: The War in the Pacific, Middle East and Europe*. New York: William Morrow & Co., 1946.

Brown, Jerold E. *Where Eagles Land: Planning and Development of U.S. Army Airfields, 1940-1941*. Westport, Conn.: Greenwood Press, 1990.

Bryant, Arthur. *Triumph in the West: A History of the War Years Based on the Diaries of Field-Marshal Lord Alanbrooke, Chief of the Imperial Staff*. Garden City, N.Y.: Doubleday & Co., 1959.

———. *Turn of the Tide: A History of the War Years Based on the Diaries of Field-Marshal Lord Alanbrooke, Chief of the Imperial General Staff*. Garden City, N.Y.: Doubleday & Co., 1957.

Buell, Thomas B. *Master of Sea Power: A Biography of Fleet Admiral Ernest J. King*. Boston: Little Brown & Co., 1980.

———. *The Quiet Warrior: A Biography of Admiral Raymond H. Spruance*. Boston: Little Brown & Co., 1974.

Bullitt, William C. Edited by Orville H. Bullitt. *For the President, Personal and Secret Correspondence Between Franklin D. Roosevelt and William C. Bullitt*. Boston: Houghton Mifflin, 1972.

Byrd, Martha. *Chennault: Giving Wings to the Tiger*. Tuscaloosa, Ala.: University of Alabama Press, 1987.

Cabell, Charles P. *A Man of Intelligence: Memoirs of War, Peace, and the CIA*. Edited by Charles P. Cabell Jr., Brig Gen, USAF, Retired. Colorado Springs, Colo.: Impavide Publications, 1997.

Caine, Philip D. *Eagles of the RAF: The World War II Eagle Squadrons*. Washington, D.C.: Brasseys, 1993.

Chennault, Claire Lee. *Way of a Fighter: The Memoirs of Claire Lee Chennault, Major General, U.S. Army (Ret.)*. Edited by Robert Hotz. New York: G. P. Putnam's Sons, 1949.

Churchill, Winston S. *The Second World War*, vol. 2, *Their Finest Hour*. Boston: Houghton Mifflin, 1948.

———. *The Second World War*, vol. 3, *The Grand Alliance*. Boston: Houghton Mifflin, 1950.

———. *The Second World War*, vol. 4, *The Hinge of Fate*. Boston: Houghton Mifflin, 1950.

———. *The Second World War*, vol. 5, *Triumph and Tragedy*. Boston: Houghton Mifflin, 1953.

Christie, Carl A., and Fred Hatch. *Ocean Bridge: The History of the RAF Ferry Command*. Toronto: University of Toronto Press, 1995.

Ciardi, John. *Siapan: The War Diary of John Ciardi*. Fayetteville, Ark.: University of Arkansas Press, 1988.

Coffey, Thomas M. *Hap: The Story of the U.S. Air Force and the Man Who Built It General Henry H. "Hap" Arnold*. New York: Viking Press, 1982.

———. *Iron Eagle: The Turbulent Life of General Curtis E. LeMay*. New York: Crown Publishers, Inc., 1986.

Coit, Margaret. *Mister Baruch*. Boston: Houghton Mifflin, 1957.

Colville, Sir John Rupert. *The Fringes of Power: 10 Downing Street, 1939-1955*. New York: W. W. Norton Co., 1985.

Copp, DeWitt S. *A Few Great Captains: The Men and Events That Shaped the Development of U.S. Air Power*. Garden City, N.Y.: Doubleday & Co., 1980.

———. *Forged in Fire: Strategy and Decisions in the Air War over Europe, 1940-1945*. Garden City, N.Y.: Doubleday & Co., 1982.

Cox, Sebastian, ed. *The Strategic Air War Against Germany 1935-1945: Report of the British Bombing Survey*. London: Frank Cass, 1998.

Cozzens, James Gould. *A Time of War: Air Force Diaries and Pentagon Memos, 1943-1945*. Edited by Matthew J. Bruccoli. Columbia, S.C.: Bruccoli Clark, 1984.

Crane, Conrad. *Bombs, Cities and Civilians: American Airpower Strategy in World War II*. Lawrence, Kans.: University of Kansas Press, 1993.

Doolittle, James H. *I Could Never Be So Lucky Again: An Autobiography of General James H. "Jimmy" Doolittle with Carroll V. Glines.* New York: Bantam Books, 1991.

Douglas, Sholto, Baron Douglas of Kirtleside. *Combat and Command: The Story of an Airman in Two World Wars by Lord Douglas of Kirtleside with Robert Wright.* New York: Simon & Schuster, 1966.

DuPre, Flint O. *U. S. Air Force Biographical Dictionary.* New York: Franklin Watts, 1965.

Edmonds, Walter D. *They Fought With What They Had.* Boston: Little Brown, 1951.

Eisenhower, Dwight D. *The Eisenhower Diaires.* Edited by Robert H. Ferrell. New York: W. W. Norton & Co., 1981.

Frank, Richard B. *Guadalcanal.* New York: Random House, 1990.

Freeman, Roger A. *Airfields of the Eighth: Then and Now.* London: After the Battle Magazine, 1978.

———. *B-17: Fortress at War.* New York: Charles Scribner's Sons, 1977.

Freeman, Roger A., Alan Crouchman, and Vic Maslen. *Mighty Eighth War Diary.* London: Jane's, 1981.

Galland, Adolph. *The First and the Last: The German Fighter Force in World War II.* Mesa, Ariz.: Champlin Museum Press, 1986.

Gilbert, Martin. *Winston S. Churchill,* vol. 7, *Road to Victory, 1941–1945.* Boston: Houghton Mifflin, 1986.

Griffith, Thomas E., Jr. *MacArthur's Airman: General George C. Kenney and the War in the Southwest Pacific.* Lawrence, Kans.: University Press of Kansas, 1998.

Grumelli, Michael L. *Trial of Faith: The Dissent and Court-Martial of Billy Mitchell.* Ann Arbor, Mich.: University Microfilms, 1991.

Haight, John McVickar, Jr. *American Aid to France, 1938–1940.* New York: Atheneum, 1970.

Halder, Franz. *The Private War Journal of Generaloberst Franz Halder, Chief of the General Staff of the German Army, 14 August 1939 to 24 September 1942.* Arlington, Va.: University Publications of America, 1975.

Hansell, Haywood S., Jr. *The Air Plan that Defeated Hitler.* Atlanta: Higgins-McArthur, Longino & Porter, 1972.

Harriman, W. Averell, and Elie Abel. *Special Envoy to Churchill and Stalin, 1941–1946.* New York: Random House, 1975.

Harris, Marshal of the R. A. F. Sir Arthur, G.C.B., O.B.E., A.F.C. *Bomber Offensive.* New York: Macmillan, 1947.

Hayes, Grace Person. *The History of the Joint Chiefs of Staff in World War II: The War Against Japan.* Annapolis: Naval Institute Press, 1982.

Hinton, Harold B. *Air Victory: The Men and the Machines.* New York: Harper & Brothers, 1948.

Howitzer 1907, vol. 8, *Being a Record of the Year at the United States Military Academy.* New York: Hoskins Press, 1907.

Howitzer, 1908, vol. 9, *Being a Record of the Year at the United States Military Academy.* New York: Hoskins Press, 1908.

Hughes, Thomas Alexander. *OVERLORD: General Pete Quesada and the Triumph of Tactical Air Power in World War II.* New York: Free Press, 1995.

Hurley, Alfred F. *Billy Mitchell: Crusader for Air Power.* Bloomington, Ind.: University of Indiana Press, 1964.

Ickes, Harold L. *The Secret Diary of Harold L. Ickes*, vol. 2, *The Inside Struggle, 1938–1939.* New York: Simon & Schuster, 1953–54.

Ismay, Baron Hastings Lionel. *Memoirs.* New York: Viking Press, 1960.

James, D. Clayton. *The Years of MacArthur*, vol. 1, *1880–1941.* Boston: Houghton Mifflin, 1970.

Jane's. *All the World's Aircraft.* London: Bridgman, 1940.

Kimball, Warren F., ed. *Churchill & Roosevelt: The Complete Correspondence*, vol. 1, *Alliance Emerging October 1933–November 1942.* Princeton, N.J.: Princeton University Press, 1984.

———. *Churchill & Roosevelt: The Complete Correspondence*, vol. 2, *Alliance Forged, November 1942–February 1944.* Princeton, N.J.: Princeton University Press, 1984.

———. *Churchill & Roosevelt: The Complete Correspondence*, vol. 3, *Alliance Declining, February 1944–April 1945.* Princeton, N.J.: Princeton University Press, 1984.

King, Ernest J., and Walter Muir Whitehill. *Fleet Admiral King: A Naval Record*. New York: W. W. Norton, 1952.

Lee, Gen Raymond E. *The London Journal of General Raymond E. Lee*, ed. James Leutze. Boston: Little Brown & Co., 1971.

LeMay, Curtis E., with MacKinlay Kantor. *Mission with LeMay: My Story*. Garden City, N.Y.: Doubleday & Co., 1965.

LeMay, Curtis E., and Bill Yenne. *Superfortress: The Story of the B-29 and American Air Power*. New York: McGraw Hill, 1988.

Lindbergh, Charles A. *The Wartime Journals of Charles A. Lindbergh*. New York: Harcourt Brace Jovanovich, 1970.

Lisiewicz, M., ed. *Destiny Can Wait: The Polish Air Force in the Second World War; Foreword by Viscount Portal of Hungerford*. London: Heinemann, 1949.

MacIsaac, David. *Strategic Bombing in World War Two: The Story of the United States Strategic Bombing Survey*. New York: Garland Press, 1976.

McFarland, Keith D. *Harry H. Woodring: A Political Biography of FDR's Controversial Secretary of War*. Lawrence, Kans.: University Press of Kansas, 1975.

McFarland, Stephen L. *America's Pursuit of Precision Bombing, 1910-1945*. Washington, D.C.: Smithsonian Institution Press, 1995.

Morison, Samuel Eliot. *History of the United States Naval Operations in World War II*, vol. 2, *Operations in the North African Waters, October 1942-June 1943*. Boston: Little Brown, 1947.

Morton, H. V. *Atlantic Meeting*. London: Metheun, 1943.

Morrow, John H. *The Great War in the Air: Military Aviation from 1909 to 1921*. Washington, D.C.: Smithsonian Institution Press, 1983.

Parton, James. *"Air Force Spoken Here," General Ira Eaker and the Command of the Air*. Bethesda, Md.: Adler & Adler, 1986.

Patrick, Mason M. *The United States in the Air*. Garden City, N.Y.: Doubleday, Doran & Co., 1928.

Perera, Guido. *Leaves from My Book of Life*, vol. 2, Washington and the War Years. Boston: privately printed, 1975.

Pickford, Mary. *Sunshine and Shadow*. Garden City, N.Y.: Doubleday, 1955.

Pogue, Forest C. *George C. Marshall: Education of a General, 1890-1939*. New York: Viking Press, 1963.

———. *George C. Marshall: Ordeal and Hope, 1939-1942*. New York: Viking Press, 1965.

———. *George C. Marshall: Organizer of Victory, 1943-1945*. New York: Viking Press, 1973.

Potter, E. B. *Nimitz*. Annapolis: Naval Institute Press, 1976.

Potter, E. B., and Chester W. Nimitz, Fleet Admiral, USN. *Sea Power: A Naval History*. Englewood Cliffs, N.J.: Prentice Hall Inc., 1960.

Reynolds, Clark G. *Admiral John H. Towers: The Struggle for Naval Air Supremacy*. Annapolis: Naval Institute Press, 1991.

Richards, Denis. *The Hardest Victory: RAF Bomber Command in the Second World War*. New York: W. W. Norton Co., 1994.

Roosevelt, Franklin D. *The Public Papers and Addresses of Franklin D. Roosevelt*, vol. 7, *The Continuing Struggle for Liberalism*. New York: MacMillan, 1941.

Samson, Jack. *Chennault*. New York: Doubleday, 1987.

Schaffer, Ronald. *Wings of Judgment: American Bombing in World War II*. New York: Oxford University Press, 1985.

Sherry, Michael S. *The Rise of American Air Power: The Creation of Armageddon*. New Haven, Conn.: Yale University Press, 1987.

Sherwood, Robert E. *Roosevelt and Hopkins: An Intimate History*. New York: Harpers & Brothers, 1948.

Slessor, Sir John, G.C.B., D.S.O., M.C. *The Central Blue: The Autobiography of Sir John Slessor, Marshal of the Royal Air Force*. New York: Frederick A. Praeger, 1957.

Stevenson, Adlai E. *The Papers of Adlai E. Stevenson*, vol. 2, *Washington to Springfield, 1941-1948*. Edited by Walter Johnson. Boston: Little Brown & Co., 1973.

Stilwell, Joseph W. *The Stilwell Papers*. Arranged and edited by Theodore H. White. New York: William Sloane Associates, 1948.

Stimson, Henry L., and McGeorge Bundy. *On Active Service in Peace and War*. New York: Harper & Brothers, 1947.

Taylor, A. J. P. *Beaverbrook*. New York: Simon & Schuster, 1972.

Tedder, Lord. *With Prejudice: The War Memoirs of Marshal of the Royal Air Force, Lord Tedder, G.C.B.* London: Cassell & Co., 1966.

Thetford, Owen G. *Aircraft of the RAF Since 1918*. 6th ed. London: Putnam, 1976.

Thomas, Lowell, and Edward Jablonski. *Doolittle: A Biography*. Garden City, N.Y.: Doubleday & Co., 1972.

Tillett, Paul. *The Army Flies the Mail*. Tuscaloosa, Ala.: University of Alabama Press, 1955.

Truman, Harry S. *Memoirs*, vol. 1, *Year of Decision*. Garden City, N.Y.: Doubleday & Co., 1955.

Tuchman, Barbara W. *Stilwell and the American Experience in China, 1911-1945*. New York: Macmillian, 1970.

Wedemeyer, Gen Albert C. *Wedemeyer Reports*. New York: Henry Holt & Co., 1958.

Weigley, Russell F. *The American Way of War: A History of United States Strategy and Policy*. New York: Macmillan, 1973.

Wells, Mark K. *Courage and Warfare: The Allied Aircrew Experience in the Second World War*. London: Frank Cass, 1995.

Willkie, Wendell. *One World*. New York: Simon & Schuster, 1943.

Wilson, Theodore A. *The First Summit: Roosevelt and Churchill at Placentia Bay, 1941*. Ed. Rev. Lawrence, Kans: University of Kansas Press, 1991.

Wolfe, Robert, ed. *Captured German Documents and Related Records, A National Archives Conference: Papers and Proceedings of the Conference on Captured German and Related Records, November 12-13, 1968, National Archives*

Building, Washington, D.C. Athens, Ohio: National Archives Building; Ohio University Press, 1975.

Zuckerman, Solly. *From Apes to Warlords*. New York: Harper & Row, 1978.

Periodicals and Articles

Agoratus, Steven. "Clark Gable in the Eighth Air Force." *Air Power History* 46, 1999: 4–17.

Air Corps Newsletter 21, no. 19 (October 1938).

Ford, Daniel. "Gentlemen, I Give You the Whittle Engine." *Air and Space*, no. 2 (October/November 1992): 88–98.

Kuter, Laurence S. "The General vs. the Establishment: General H. H. Arnold and the Air Staff." *Aerospace Historian* 22, winter (December 1974): 185–89.

New York Times, 3 December 1925; 8 February 1926; 30 August 1931; 4 November 1931; 18 February 1934; 25 February 1934; 15, 16 October 1938; 1–12 November 1938; 13, 24 July 1945; 27 January 1939; 2, 7, 13, 24 May 1941; 25 June 1941; 6, 14, 16 August 1941; 8, 11 August 1942; 1 October 1942; 15 February 1943; 8 January 1995.

Reader's Digest, July 1942.

Times (London), 2 May 1941; 16, 23 August 1942; 13 April 1945.

Sunday Times, 16, 23 August 1942.

Oral History Interviews

Arnold, Mrs. H. H. Maxwell AFB, Ala.: AFHRA, n.d.

Beebe, Eugene. Special Collections, USAFA, Colorado Springs, Colo., n.d.

Douglas, Donald. Columbia University, N.Y., n.d.

Eaker, Ira C. Maxwell AFB, Ala.: AFHRA, 1959–60.

Giles, Barney M. Maxwell AFB, Ala.: AFHRA, 12–13 May 1970.

Masefield, Peter G. Special Collections, US Air Force Academy, Colorado Springs, Colo., 10 July 1971.

Pogue, Forrest C. George C. Marshall Research Library, Lexington, Va., 15 January 1957.

Quesada, Elwood R. Columbia University, N.Y., n.d.

Index

11th
  Bomb Group: 409
  Bombardment Group: 367
16th Observation Squadron: 20
1935 Air Corps Baker Board: 77
1938 Munich settlement: 66
19th
  Bombardment Group: 367
  Group: 394, 397
23d Fighter Group: 539
29th
  Division: 4
  Regiment in Manila: 3
3d Infantry Regiment: 8
43d
  Bomb Group: 364
  Bombardment Group: 367
7 December: 265
73d Squadron: 539
7th Aero Squadron: 8
8:15 dinner: President, Prime Minister, Pound, Brooke, Portal, Marshall, Arnold, King, Mountbatten, Harriman, Hopkins, Elliott Roosevelt: 464
90 P-38s now in England to be flown down at once: 472

A-37A Northrop: 47
ABC-1: 126, 237–38, 245, 251, 267
ABC-2: 126
advances,
  Axis: 238
  Japanese: 362, 407, 442
  Rommel: 451
Africa,
  AAF combat units in North: 431
  air-ground cooperation in North: 377
  decision to invade North: 345
  invasion of North: 347, 357, 411, 433
  Prime Minister Jan Christian Smuts of South: 308
Air Corps Act of 1926: 73
Air Corps Tactical School: 58, 245, 445
Air War Plans Division (AWPD)-1: 127
aircraft,
  disagreements about the deployment of AAF: 366

Grumman Wildcat carrier-based: 278
  pleading for additional: 368
  successful offensive use of: 42
Air Mail crisis: 30
Aleutians, Japanese invasion of the: 292
Alexander, First Lord of the Admiralty: 154
Allied program to relieve China's isolation: 448
Alsop, Joseph: 443
Anakim: 441, 454–56, 512–14
Andrews,
  Frank M.: 37, 48, 247
  Lt Gen Frank: 438
  Maj Gen Frank M.: 48
  as the Army G-3: 92
Anglophobia: 11
Archie Sinclair, the secretary of state for air: 435
Arizona, University of: 41
Arkansas: 232–33
Army/AAF
  position: 368
  Field Manual 31-35: 377
  General Order No., 20: 20
  Regulation 95-5: 285
  turned down the Navy's request: 366
Arnold,
  2d Lt "Hap": 3
  Brig Gen: 42
  Captain: 8–9, 226
  Colonel: 11
  family: 8, 13, 22, 24, 26, 41
  Hap suffered a heart attack: 516
  Hap's feelings: 6
  Hap's fitness report: 10
  Hap's strong belief in unity of command of air units: 282
  Herbert: 1
  Lois, daughter: 24, 41, 51–52, 59
  President had invited me to dinner: 464
  urgent communications from: 351
  and the AAF's perspective: 348
  -Portal: 271
Attlee [Clement]: 233

561

AVG personnel: 446
AWPD-1: 244, 246-49, 375
AWPD-2: 246
AWPD-42: 375-77

B-17 Flying Fortress: 48
B-17s and P-38s: 389
B-18: 45, 67, 97, 265
B-24 HALPRO Group: 450
B-29 Superfortress: 46
Baker, Newton D.: 32
Baldwin, Hanson: 26, 46
Balkans, losses in the: 208
Baltic, USS: 12
Baruch, Bernard: 71
Battles of Coral Sea and Midway: 366
Beaverbrook,
　Lord: 134
　Minister of Aircraft Production Lord: 134
Beck, Consul: 136
Beebe, Col Eugene H.: 315
Beery, Wallace: 27
Bell, Larry of Bell Aircraft: 179
Berle, Adolph A., Jr.: 1
Birdie Wrights, the: 135
Bissell-Chennault-Arnold-Stilwell-Generalissimo: 446
Bissell, Brig Gen Clayton: 446
Blackout,
　even in the country: 153
　streets all dark: 142
Blériot, Louis: 3
Board,
　Baker: 33, 36, 77
　Drum: 32
　Morrow: 18-19
Booth, Brig Gen Ewing E.: 21
Borglum, Gutzon: 63
Bracken, Brendan: 149, 161
Brett, Maj Gen George H.: 251
Britain, Battle of: 63, 208, 248
British,
　Defeat: 311
　Lack of enthusiasm: 454
　unsatisfactory relationships with the: 457
Bristol Engine Works: 164
Buell, Thomas B.: 62
Bullitt, US Ambassador William C.: 69
Burma,
　Chinese expulsion from: 450

Burma Road,
　closing of the: 276, 449
　Ground action to open: 455
　Japanese successes threatened the: 444
　was effectively closed: 442
Burns, Maj Gen James H.: 244
Bush, Dr. Vannevar: 180

C-41: 217
C-53: 387
C-54s: 457, 459
C-87 (B-24 made into cargo plane): 382
Cabell, Colonel: 379
California: 8-9, 12-13, 25, 27-29, 35, 38, 41, 44-45, 64, 88, 126, 138, 300, 374, 378, 382-83, 388, 402, 459-62, 473, 475, 480-81, 501
Canal, Panama: 7
Canton, Conditions at: 400
career, biggest gamble of his: 46
Carter, Amon G.: 287
Casablanca: 162, 353, 431-35, 437-41, 451, 454-57, 462-71, 490-91, 510, 512, 515
CATF, Tenth Air Force and the: 447
Caum, Maj Military Attaché: 137
Chaney,
　Eaker may have outmaneuvered: 283
　Maj Gen James: 250
Channel, English: 167
Charles de Gaulle's unwarranted pretensions: 63
Chemidlin, French Air Force capt Paul: 88
Chennault,
　Bissell and: 441, 447, 454, 515
　Brigadier General: 446
　Claire L.: 58, 444
　and his Flying Tigers, now the CATF: 447
　air force: 441, 455, 470
　claims: 453, 456
　letter as: 452
　program: 451
　staff: 443
Chequers: 291, 305
Chiang,
　Kai-shek: 79, 432, 442-44, 447-48, 450, 453, 470, 472, 479, 490-92, 495, 500, 514-15

Madame: 470
Stilwell did not endear himself to: 448
Kai-shek's will to resist: 448
point of view: 451
promise to support Anakim: 456
China,
American command structure in: 442
getting supplies into: 442, 447
Japanese occupied all of coastal: 442
logistics support into: 449
operations in or from: 441
Chungking: 442, 470, 484, 487–89, 492, 495, 498
Churchill,
first meeting of Roosevelt and: 216
Prime Minister: 129, 434, 476, 478
Winston: 61, 71, 224, 232
ability to influence Roosevelt: 275
increasing concern: 434
Civilian Conservation Corps (CCC): 29
Clark, Brig Gen Mark: 288
College,
Amherst: 18
Army Industrial: 13–14
Park, Maryland: 4–5
Collins, Capt Harry E: 85, 98
Command,
Air Corps Ferrying: 178
Air Force Combat: 285
Air Transport: 178, 410, 457, 514
Coast Defense: 295
RAF Bomber: 176, 283, 298
Committee,
House Military Affairs: 6
Liaison: 98–100
McSwain: 38
Senate Foreign Relations: 129
Connor, Maj Gen Fox: 16
Consolidated Aircraft Company: 11
Coolidge,
Administration: 14, 16
President: 17–18, 22
Coral Sea: 366, 397
Corps,
Ninth Army: 38
Signal: 4, 6–7, 10
Corregidor, last-ditch resistance on Bataan and: 268

corruption, massive: 445
Cozzens,
James Gould: 1, 60
Maj James Gould: 60
Craig,
Army Chief of Staff General Malin: 50, 68, 79
Gen Malin: 29, 38, 45, 58, 68, 93
Maj Gen Malin: 29
Curtiss P-40: 87
Curtiss-Wright P-36s: 66
Daladier, French Premier: 70
Daniels, Bebe: 27
Dargue, Maj Herbert: 19
daylight, bombing: 376
Dayton, Ohio: 4, 34, 38, 179
Dern, Secretary of War George: 32, 56
Devers, Maj Gen Jacob L.: 377
Dill,
General CG of Army: 146
Sir John: 441, 480–82, 486, 495, 506, 512–13
Division,
Morgenthau and his Procurement: 312
Panzer: 146
War Plans: 126–27, 130, 241, 244, 286
Dolphin: 222, 232–33
Donovan, William: 128
Doolittle, James H.: 288, 357
Douglas DB-7: 87
Durston, A. W.: 295
Eagle Squadron: 143
Eaker,
Brig Gen Ira: 280
Col Ira C.: 247
Maj Gen Ira: 438
succinct, well-reasoned arguments: 439
Earhart, Amelia: 27, 35
early army aviators: 6
Early,
Press Secretary Steve: 49
Steve: 49, 175
Eden, Anthony: 134, 162
Edmonton: 34
Edwards Air Force Base: 29
Eighth Air Force's lack of progress in England: 434
Eisenhower,

563

General: 348
Maj Gen Dwight D.: 288
Marshall nominated: 312
Spaatz, Eaker, and Doolittle worked in harmony: 357
El Alamein, Egypt: 347
Embick, Maj Gen Stanley: 67
Europe,
 invasion plans for: 366
 Supreme Commander of the Allied Forces in: 312
Evatt, Herbert L.: 309
Everest, Col Frank: 409
Evill, Air Chief Marshal: 270

F4 (P-38): 395
Fairbanks on 24 July: 35
Fairfield Air Depot: 25
Faymonville, Col Philip R.: 212
FDR's opposition to dispatching another AEF: 239
Fechet, Maj Gen James E.: 24
Field,
 Langley: 37, 56, 126
 March: 25-30, 35, 37-38, 41, 126
 Patterson: 34
 Rockwell: 8, 12, 359
 Wright: 25, 106
Finest Hour: 243
Fitch, Aubrey: 409
Fleet,
 Maj Reuben: 11
 Reuben: 11, 93
flight,
 Alaska: 35, 47
 Douglas World Cruiser: 13
 Pan American Goodwill: 20
Flyer, Wright: 4
Flying Tigers, AVG: 447, 488, 516
Folly of the 'numbers racket': 74
Force,
 China Air Task: 446, 451
 Eighth Air: 280-83, 288, 312-14, 346, 351, 355, 405, 433-34, 438, 452
 Fourteenth Air: 515-16
 General Headquarters Air: 32, 247
 Japanese Air: 448, 452
 Royal Air: 13, 127, 132
 Tenth Air: 446-47, 449-51
 Thirteenth Air: 409
 Twelfth Air: 356

US Eighth Air: 346, 433-34
Western Air: 387
Forces,
 American Expeditionary: 15
 Axis air: 375
 Pro-Chiang: 443, 515
Fort
 Leavenworth, Kansas: 24
 Riley, Kansas: 5-6, 20-23, 431
Foulois,
 Maj Gen Benjamin: 30
 Major General: 35
France: 7, 10-13, 15, 49, 53, 66, 68-73, 83, 85, 89, 96, 99-103, 105, 126, 141, 156, 357, 367, 434-35, 437, 464, 511-12
Freeman,
 Air Marshal Sir Wilfrid: 69
 AVM Assistant to Portal: 140
 Vice Chief of Air Staff: 284
Gable, Clark: 27, 35
George,
 Gen Harold: 410
 Lt Col Harold L.: 245
Germany: 358
 beginning of the offensive against: 374
 industrial base: 375
Gerow, Brig Gen Leonard T.: 245
Ghormley,
 Adm: 360, 370
 despair and indecisiveness of: 403
 Vice Adm Robert: 368
 hostility: 360
GHQAF came into existence: 37
Gladwyn, Pennsylvania: 1
Governor's Island, New York: 4
Great Depression: 42
Greece, British evacuation of: 208
Group, American Volunteer: 445, 488
Guadalcanal,
 Conditions in: 411
 Marines
  at: 398
  on: 432
 Naval Battle of: 370
 Navy is hard-pressed at: 381
Halsey, Vice Adm William F., Jr.: 408
Handley Page 99: 139
Hangchou: 79
Hank, oldest son: 41

564

Hansell, Brig Gen Haywood S.: 375
Harmon, Maj Gen Millard F. "Miff": 367
Harriman, Averell: 128, 130, 132, 218, 223, 246, 465
Harris, Air Marshal: 283
Hay, Rep. James: 6
Hazlett, Elmer: 136
Heatter, Gabriel: 219
Hibbard, Mr. of [American] Embassy: 137
HMS *Prince of Wales*: 214, 223-32, 235-36, 244
Ho, Chinese War Minister: 497
Hopkins,
  Harriman and: 134, 182, 215, 230, 235, 464
  Harry L.: 128
  naive Harry : 443
  very bitter: 230
Hornet: 397
Howze, Lt Col Robert L.: 2
Howitzer yearbook: 1
Hull, Cordell: 174
human-based early warning system: 445
Hump, tonnage over the: 449
Hurley, Brigadier General Pat J.: 522

Ickes, Secretary of the Interior Harold: 71
improper use of assets: 407
Ingram, Jonas: 459, 507
Ismay, Gen C of S (Chief of Staff) for Churchill: 146

Japan, public outcry for action against: 358
Johnson,
  Assistant Secretary Louis A.: 47, 56
  Louis A.: 68
  Philip, the president of Boeing: 177
Journal, Army Navy: 50

Kelly, Jack, of Pan Am: 137
Kenly, Maj Gen William L.: 10
Kennedy, Joseph P.: 69, 128
Kilner, Walter G. "Mike": 53
King,
  Admiral: 35, 62, 222, 287, 311, 348, 359, 365, 367, 369-71, 373, 376, 380, 405, 407-9, 436, 458, 483, 507
  Brig Gen Edward: 24
  George VI: 134, 160, 176, 181, 228

Knudsen, William S.: 246
Kraus, Sydney M.: 85
Kristallnacht: 79
Kuter,
  Brig Gen Laurence S.: 277
  Gen Laurence S.: 55, 277

Laval, Pierre: 71
leadership, deficiencies in: 407
Leahy, Chief of Staff Adm William D.: 356
Lee, Maj Gen John C. H.: 313
Lend-Lease,
  Act: 207
  aid: 442
  congressional approval of: 131
  transports acquired under: 276
Levée, Charles: 3
Lindbergh,
  Charles: 27, 68
  transatlantic flight: 27
London,
  battle-scarred: 154
  German blitz against: 247
  shortage of fruit or food in: 139
  Spaatz in: 346
  Sunday *Times* of: 352
  of 1942 is far different from London of 1941: 304
Lovett, Robert A.: 127, 246
Luftwaffe: 373

MacArthur,
  Chief of Staff Douglas: 25, 32, 36
  forced to evacuate Luzon: 268
  Fort: 29
  Gen Douglas: 25, 32
  gloom and doom assessment from: 374
  pessimism of: 403
Magruder, Brig Gen John: 444
Marshall,
  Brig Gen George: 75, 92
  Gen George C.: 56
  General: 62, 130, 174, 179, 211, 225, 229-30, 236, 242, 246, 270, 348, 367, 369, 378, 517
  Lt George C.: 7
Martin,
  Glenn: 93
  167: 87
  B-10 bombers: 34
Masefield,

565

Peter: 177, 352
  critical article in the Times: 355
McChord, Col William: 47
McCloy, John J.: 132
McNarney,
  Col Joseph: 126
  Joseph: 286
McSwain, Rep. John: 32
Miami Navigation School to train RAF navigators: 179
Midway,
  Battle of: 292
  success at the Battle of: 518
Millikan, Dr. Robert: 28
Minneapolis: 34
Mission, Anglo-French Purchasing: 98
Mitchell,
  Arnold and: 13, 15-16, 36, 40, 44, 285
  Billy: 2, 7-8, 14, 16-17, 39, 47, 57, 175, 285
  brashness: 16
  Capt William D. "Billy": 7
  martial-court: 13, 19, 104
Mobile Air Force,
  Central Pacific: 367
  Southwest Pacific: 367
Molotov,
  Vyacheslav Mikhailovich: 347
  Winant gave me information re: 296
Monnet, Jean: 72-73, 83, 86
Morgenthau, Secretary of the Treasury Henry: 67, 73, 128
Morrow, Dwight: 18
Mount Shasta: 26
Navy,
  US: 45, 79, 85, 87, 107, 173, 221, 227, 233, 267, 269, 291, 297, 300, 363, 366, 432
  Undersecretary James R. Forrestal: 374
Neutrality Act: 72, 88, 97
New Deal: 29, 56
New Guinea,
  Impression of situation: 395
  Japanese gains in: 361
New York *Times*' front-page story: 26, 46, 174, 351-52
Newsletter, Air Corps: 53
Nimitz,
  Adm Chester: 374
  very optimistic as compared to Emmons: 385
Nye, General: 146
O'Loughlin, Col John: 50
Offensive,
  Combined Bomber: 353, 438-39, 456, 510
  strategic bombardment: 292, 349, 374
  Top Secret Combined Bomber: 438
Old AVG [American Volunteer Group] barracks: 488
Olds, Col Robert: 178
Omaha, Nebraska: 22, 35, 177
operation,
  Anakim: 441, 454, 512
  Torch: 371
operations,
  Allied Asian: 442
  American daylight: 437
  Chinese Chief of: 492
  from mainland China were limited: 442
  Navy,
    does not understand ground or air: 401
    is departing from true role of: 380
  US air: 435
  Division (OPD): 288
P-38: 296, 373, 380, 395, 472-73
P-39: 66, 250, 266, 296, 309, 379-80, 387-89, 473
P-40 airplanes to the Soviet Union: 212
P-400 pursuits: 372
P-40s to come to USS *Ranger*: 472
P-47s to be sent to build up Spitfire Group: 473
P-51 Mustang fighter: 435
Pan American Airways: 234
Patrick,
  Gen Mason: 12-14
  Maj Gen Mason: 13-14
Pearl Harbor: 59-60, 62, 64, 96, 214, 250, 252, 265, 268, 286-87, 345, 358, 363, 378, 385, 401, 442-43, 445
Peoples, Rear Adm Christian: 85
Pershing, John J.: 15, 50
Piccard, Auguste: 28
Pickford, Mary: 27
Platte River: 22

Pool,
   Anti-Axis: 246
   Eleanor: 3, 6-7
Port Moresby: 242, 367, 369, 390, 394-95, 432
Portal,
   Air Chief Marshal Peter: 284
   Charles F. A.: 63
   RAF Chief: 308, 436
   Sir Charles: 127
Potomac: 218
Pratt, Adm William V.: 25
Quesada, Maj Elwood R.: 135
RAF raided Berlin: 433
Rainbow 5: 127, 245, 251
Rangoon fell: 444
Reader's Digest: 353
Representatives, US House of: 32, 244
Rickenbacker, Capt Eddie: 27, 354
Rockwell Field, North Island, San Diego: 8
Rogers,
   Cong. Edith Nourse: 31
   Will: 27
Rolph, James: 27
Rommel's
   continuing eastern push: 365
   successes in the desert: 346
Roosevelt,
   Churchill, and their staffs: 207, 433
   Elliott: 222
   President: 31, 35, 55, 65, 127, 132, 174, 221
Russian resistance: 362
San Antonio: 17, 25, 217, 220
San Diego: 8, 12, 382-83, 389
San Francisco: 12, 400, 402, 484, 509
Schoultz, Dr. R. of General Electric: 179
Schrieber, Wing CO Jack: 137
Scott, Riley: 7
Selective Service Act, extension of: 244
Sevastopol, fall of: 347
Seversky, de Alexander: 353
Shenandoah: 18
Sinclair, Secretary of State for Air: 144, 149, 160
Singapore was surrendered: 444
Sledgehammer, decision to abandon: 349
Slessor,
   Air Vice Marshal John C.: 126

Squadron Leader John: 69
Snowden, Lt Ernie: 51
S.O.B. of a job: 513
Solomons, Navy to invade the: 367
Soong, Foreign Minister T. V.: 443
Spaatz,
   Carl A.: 282
   Lt Col Carl A. "Tooey": 82
   Maj Gen Tooey: 438
Squier, Maj Gen George O.: 10
Stalin, Josef: 40-41, 48, 54, 61, 67, 69, 90, 96, 103, 211, 220, 222, 241, 267, 280, 352, 371, 381, 390, 436, 444, 488, 505
Stalingrad: 362, 433
Standley, Adm William: 25
Stark, Adm Harold R.: 174
Stilwell,
   Joseph W.: 444
   defeat: 450
Stimson,
   Henry L.: 55, 103, 129
   Secretary of War: 55, 132, 212, 242, 269, 444
   view: 444
Stratemeyer, Maj Gen George E.: 357
Street, Sir Arthur: 157
Symmonds, Brig Gen Charles J.: 23
Tarawa, Okinawa, and Iwo Jima: 448
Thomas, Lowell: 63
Tobruk, fall of: 347, 450
Tokyo, Doolittle raid on: 287
Torch, assets for: 371
Towers,
   John H.: 85
   Prime Minister called on: 297
   Rear Adm John: 270, 288
Treaty, Nine Power: 79
Treasury Department: 76, 79, 83-84, 86, 89-91, 96, 100, 102, 105, 107, 128
Trident Washington meeting: 518
Trophy, Mackay: 5, 35
Tuchman, Barbara: 443
Turkey, President Inonu of: 440
Turner, Burns, Bundy, and I called on Admiral King: 218
U-boats,
   German: 433
   struggle: 436
US Marines' assault on Guadalcanal: 345

USS *Augusta*: 210, 217, 226
USS *Memphis*: 523
USS *Olympic*: 11
USS *Tuscaloosa*: 215, 217-19, 221-23, 225, 228-29, 231-33, 235

Vaughan, Guy: 135
Venning, General: 146
victory through Air Power: 249, 353
von Kármán, Theodore: 28, 63

Wake Island: 268
Walsh, Bob: 459, 461, 507-8
Warner,
    Dr. Ed: 163
    Jack: 63
Wasp: 389
Watson, Brig Gen Edwin M. "Pa": 49, 117
Wavell, General: 453, 481, 513
Weaver, Col Walter: 49

Wehrmacht: 104, 211, 363
Welsh, Al: 5
Westover, Brig Gen Oscar M.: 33
White, Harry Dexter: 128
Willkie, Wendell L.: 128
Wilson, Hugh R.: 70
Winant, Ambassador: 296
Winged,
    Defense: 18
    Warfare: 247
Winnipeg: 34
Wolfe, Maj K. B.: 47, 88
Woodring, Secretary of War Harry H.: 47, 56, 67
Woodring-Johnson feuding: 64
Wright,
    Brothers 1, 4, 40, 48
    Burdette: 93
    Wilbur and Orville: 2

XB-299 bomber: 38

AMERICAN AIRPOWER COMES OF AGE
General Henry H. "Hap" Arnold's
World War II Diaries

Volume 1

Air University Press Team

Chief Editor
Preston Bryant

Copy Editor
Peggy S. Smith

Cover Art and Book Design
Steven C. Garst

Illustrations
L. Susan Fair

*Composition and
Prepress Production*
Vivian D. O'Neal

www.maxwell.af.mil/au/aul/aupress

Made in the USA
Coppell, TX
10 February 2020